The Making
of Social Movements
in Latin America

Series in Political Economy and Economic Development in Latin America

Series Editor

Andrew Zimbalist

Smith College

† *The Making of Social Movements in Latin America: Identity, Strategy, and Democracy,* edited by Arturo Escobar and Sonia E. Alvarez

Industrialization in Sandinista Nicaragua: Policy and Practice in a Mixed Economy, Geske Dijkstra

Peasants in Distress: Poverty and Unemployment in the Dominican Republic, Rosemary Vargas-Lundius

The Latin American Development Debate: Neostructuralism, Neomonetarism, and Adjustment Processes, edited by Patricio Meller

Distorted Development: Mexico in the World Economy, David Barkin

State and Capital in Mexico: Development Policy Since 1940, James M. Cypher

Central America: The Future of Economic Integration, edited by George Irvin and Stuart Holland

Struggle Against Dependence: Nontraditional Export Growth in Central America and the Caribbean, edited by Eva Paus

The Peruvian Mining Industry: Growth, Stagnation, and Crisis, Elizabeth Dore

Cuban Political Economy: Controversies in Cubanology, edited by Andrew Zimbalist

† *Rural Women and State Policy: Feminist Perspectives in Latin American Agricultural Development,* edited by Carmen Diana Deere and Magdalena León

†Available in hardcover and paperback.

The Making of Social Movements in Latin America

Identity, Strategy, and Democracy

edited by

Arturo Escobar
Smith College

Sonia E. Alvarez
University of California–Santa Cruz

Westview Press
Boulder • San Francisco • Oxford

Series in Political Economy and Economic Development in Latin America

Copyright © 1992 by Westview Press, Inc.

Published in 1992 in the United States of America by Westview Press, Inc., 5500 Central Avenue, Boulder, Colorado 80301-2847, and in the United Kingdom by Westview Press, 36 Lonsdale Road, Summertown, Oxford OX2 7EW

Library of Congress Cataloging-in-Publication Data
The making of social movements in Latin America : identity, strategy, and democracy / edited by Arturo Escobar, Sonia E. Alvarez.
    p.   cm. — (Series in political economy and economic development in Latin America)
    Includes bibliographical references and index.
    ISBN 0-8133-1206-X. — ISBN 0-8133-1207-8 (pbk.)
    1. Social movements—Latin America.   I. Escobar, Arturo.
II. Alvarez, Sonia E., 1956-   .   III. Series.
HN110.5.A8M325   1992
303.48'4'098—dc20   92-9068
                                                                            CIP

Printed and bound in the United States of America

The paper used in this publication meets the requirements
of the American National Standard for Permanence of Paper
for Printed Library Materials Z39.48-1984.

10   9   8   7   6   5   4   3   2   1

The making of social movements
in L.A.

Contents

Preface and Acknowledgments   ix
About the Editors and Contributors   xiii

1   Introduction: Theory and Protest in Latin America Today,
Arturo Escobar and Sonia E. Alvarez   1

PART 1
CONCEPTUALIZING SOCIAL MOVEMENTS
IN CONTEMPORARY LATIN AMERICA

2   Social Movements: Actors, Theories, Expectations,
Fernando Calderón, Alejandro Piscitelli,
and José Luis Reyna   19

3   Marxism, Feminism, and the Struggle for Democracy in
Latin America, *Norma Stoltz Chinchilla*   37

4   The Study of New Social Movements in Latin America
and the Question of Autonomy, *Judith Adler Hellman*   52

5   Culture, Economics, and Politics in Latin American
Social Movements Theory and Research,
Arturo Escobar   62

PART 2
THE MAKING OF COLLECTIVE IDENTITIES

6   "I Dreamed of Foxes and Hawks": Reflections on Peasant
Protest, New Social Movements, and the *Rondas*
Campesinas of Northern Peru, *Orin Starn*   89

7   From Resistance to Social Movement: The Indigenous
Authorities Movement in Colombia,
María Teresa Findji   112

v

8   Power, Gender, and Development: Popular Women's
     Organizations and the Politics of Needs in Ecuador,
     Amy Conger Lind   134

9   The Venezuelan Ecology Movement: Symbolic Effectiveness,
     Social Practices, and Political Strategies,
     María Pilar García   150

10   Rethinking the Study of Social Movements: The Case
     of Christian Base Communities in Urban Brazil,
     John Burdick   171

11   Homosexual Identities in Transitional Brazilian Politics,
     Edward MacRae   185

PART 3
ARTICULATING STRATEGIES AND
DEMOCRATIZING DEMOCRACY

12   Feminisms in Latin America: From Bogotá to San Bernardo,
     Nancy Saporta Sternbach, Marysa Navarro-Aranguren,
     Patricia Chuchryk, and Sonia E. Alvarez   207

13   The Evolution of Urban Popular Movements in Mexico
     Between 1968 and 1988, *Vivienne Bennett*   240

14   Radical Opposition Parties and Squatters Movements
     in Pinochet's Chile, *Cathy Schneider*   260

15   Democratization and the Decline of Urban Social Movements
     in Uruguay: A Political-Institutional Account,
     Eduardo Canel   276

16   Popular Movements in the Context of the Consolidation
     of Democracy in Brazil, *Ruth Corrêa Leite Cardoso*   291

17   Social Movements and Political Power in Latin America,
     Orlando Fals Borda   303

18   Conclusion: Theoretical and Political Horizons of Change
       in Contemporary Latin American Social Movements,
       Sonia E. Alvarez and Arturo Escobar   317

List of Acronyms   331
Bibliography   334
About the Book   365
About the Series   366
Index   367

Preface and Acknowledgments

This book grew out of our shared and growing interest in contemporary social movements and the vast theoretical literature on these movements produced during the 1980s, particularly in Latin America and Western Europe. The fact that this literature was very little known in the United States was one of the motivating forces behind our effort. This anthology, however, was also a logical extension of our respective previous projects. Sonia Alvarez's study of the rise and development of the Brazilian women's movement pointed toward the broader problem of understanding the nature and impact of social movements under conditions of "transition to democracy." Arturo Escobar's dissertation on the "invention" of development and the crucial role played by this discourse in the production of post-World War II Latin America equally called for an investigation of the actual and potential role of collective action in transforming entrenched notions and strategies of local, regional, and national development.

We first conceived this project in 1988, when we both were teaching at the University of California at Santa Cruz. We wanted to convey to our students the excitement that we sensed in the writings of our Latin American colleagues about the forms of protest observed in the region during the 1980s, perhaps as an antidote to the otherwise gloomy picture offered by what has been called Latin America's "lost decade." Although the Nicaraguan revolution and the struggle in El Salvador had fueled the hopes of many—and rightly so—we nevertheless wished to provide a view of the multiple forms of organized resistance that many people had been able to maintain during the 1980s, though perhaps less glamorously and against all odds. We both had the opportunity to teach undergraduate courses on social movements, with partially different but complementary orientations. We also started to meet regularly with a small group of Bay Area people interested in social movements issues, which included Vivienne Bennett, Cathy Schneider, and Teresa Carrillo. The momentum provided by these activities crystallized in the organization of panels on the topic for both the 1989 and 1991 Latin American Studies Association (LASA) congresses, to which we were able to invite some of the authors represented in this anthology—Orlando Fals Borda, María Pilar García, Vivienne Bennett, Judith Hellman, Amy Lind, and Cathy Schneider.

The LASA panels were but one of the strategies we used in working closely with our contributors to develop a coherent framework for this anthology and encourage fruitful debates and collaboration among contributing authors. What we have assembled is an interdisciplinary collection that examines comparatively the three dimensions of change most commonly attributed to social movements in contemporary Latin America: their role in forming or reconstituting collective identities; their innovative social practices and political strategies in pursuit of socioeconomic, cultural, and political change; and their actual or potential contributions to alternative visions of development and to the democratization of political institutions and social relations. In this way, the anthology represents a collective theoretical reflection on the nature and present status of the study of social movements in the region—a subject in which all of our contributors, who include some of the foremost scholars in the field, have been significantly engaged.

In selecting the essays, we were careful to strike a balance on several levels. In terms of disciplines, anthropologists, sociologists, and political scientists are equally represented, with some authors from other disciplines. We wished, moreover, to transgress the disciplinary boundaries and conventions that so often inhibit our understanding of multidimensional phenomena like social movements. The inclusion of anthropologists has been particularly fruitful because, until now, they have been largely absent from these debates, even when the debates lent themselves in clear ways to anthropological inquiry. The second type of balance we wanted to preserve was between authors working in Latin America and in the United States. By including prominent Latin American scholars, we accomplished two critical goals. We ensured that this collection represented Latin American perspectives in ways that are not overly mediated by the concerns of the U.S. academy, and we brought the import of such perspectives to bear on analyses of movements whose limited focus on Western cases has compromised the critical assessment and generalizability of European and North American theories.

The final and crucial balance we insisted on was between the various approaches to social movements theory and research—particularly between Latin American and European orientations, which give primacy to questions of identity, and North American approaches, which privilege aspects of strategy. By challenging our contributors to explore simultaneously the dynamics of identity, strategy, and democracy, our anthology provides readers with a more integrative, complex, interdisciplinary, and multilevel understanding of the contributions of social movements to contemporary socioeconomic and political transformations in the Latin American region.

The selection of case studies was further informed by an effort to cover a wide range of movements in many countries. We were, of course, unable to do full justice to this rich variety. In particular, our treatment of the Central American and Caribbean regions is scant at best. We also regret that, despite our efforts, we were unable to include a chapter on Afro–Latin American movements. Racial and ethnic dimensions are crucial to contemporary collective action, and many of our chapters reflect this reality. Outside the Caribbean region, growing black movements can be found, for instance, in Brazil, Colombia, and Peru.

We are grateful to all of our contributors for their sustained commitment to the project. This anthology is the result of their work of several (sometimes many) years in a variety of Latin American countries. Some of our senior colleagues, particularly Orlando Fals Borda, Judith Hellman, and Fernando Calderón, have been very supportive since the early stages of the project. Norma Chinchilla and Andy Zimbalist took on the task of revising and commenting on the entire manuscript, and we greatly appreciate their efforts in this regard. The support of Barbara Ellington, our editor at Westview Press, has also been very important to the success of the project.

Financial support has been provided by the University of California at Santa Cruz and by Smith College (through the Jean Picker Fellowship for faculty research). This support enabled us to hire our assistants—Ann Scott at Smith College and William Veiga, Brian Wampler, and Vince Chhabria at Santa Cruz. Patricia Sanders, Lisa Morgan, and Rebekah Levy provided invaluable word-processing and clerical assistance at Santa Cruz. Translations from the Spanish were artfully prepared by Celso Alvarez C. and Cathryn Teasley, who worked on the chapter by María Pilar García and María Teresa Findji, and by Ann Scott and Arturo Escobar, who translated the chapter by Fernando Calderón, Alejandro Piscitelli, and José Luis Reyna. Edward MacRae's contribution was fluently translated by Maria Morris and Sonia Alvarez. We are thankful to each of them for this essential task. Computer assistance by Celso Alvarez C. and partial editing by Tracey Tsugawa were also timely contributions. Joan W. Sherman of Westview Press did an outstanding job of copyediting the final manuscript.

Between March and November of 1990, the fathers of this volume's editors and of two of our contributors (María Pilar García and Amy Lind) passed away. We want to acknowledge their importance in our lives as well as that of our mothers and other members of our families. We are also grateful for the encouragement we received from our extended family of friends over the course of this project. We thank Judit Moschkovich, Tracey Tsugawa, Alvaro Pedrosa, José F. Escobar, Ana Cannober, Jacqueline Urla, and Jennifer Terry.

Arturo Escobar
Sonia E. Alvarez

About the Editors
and Contributors

Arturo Escobar is assistant professor of anthropology at Smith College. He has an interdisciplinary Ph.D. from the University of California–Berkeley. His book *Anthropology and the Development Encounter: The Making and Unmaking of the Third World* will be published in 1993. His current interests include the application of critical cultural theory in development studies.

Sonia E. Alvarez is associate professor of politics at the University of California–Santa Cruz. She holds a Ph.D. in political science from Yale University. She is the author of *Engendering Democracy in Brazil: Women's Movements in Transition Politics* (1990), and her writings on Latin American gender politics, social movements, and democratization have appeared in *Signs*, *Feminist Studies*, and several edited collections. She is presently working on a monograph on social movement networks, radical urban regimes, and progressive democratic alternatives in South America.

Vivienne Bennett has a Ph.D. in Latin American studies from the University of Texas at Austin. She has taught Latin American studies at the University of California–Santa Cruz and at San Diego State University. She is currently a research fellow at the Center for Mexican Studies, University of California–San Diego, where she is preparing a monograph on urban popular movements in Mexico after 1968. She is also completing a book on the politics of water in Monterrey, Mexico.

John Burdick received his doctorate from the City University of New York in 1990 and currently teaches anthropology at Syracuse University. He has written in both English and Portuguese on issues of politics, gender, race, and religion in Brazil. Since recently completing the manuscript for a book, *Looking for God in Brazil: The Progressive Catholic Church in Brazil's Urban Arena*, he has begun working on mythical narratives of racial identity in the New World.

Fernando Calderón is executive secretary of the Latin American Social Science Council (CLACSO). He has a Ph.D. in sociology from the Ecole Practique des Hautes Etudes in Paris and is currently working on social movements and the changing relationships between state, society, and economy. He has been visiting lecturer at the University of Texas at Austin, the University of Buenos Aires, Argentina, and the University of Barcelona, Spain. His major books are *La*

Política en las Calles (1983), *Urbanización y Etnicidad: El Caso de La Paz* (1984), *La Mina Urbana* (1985), and *Búsquedas y Bloqueos* (1987).

Eduardo Canel is a Ph.D. candidate in sociology at York University, Toronto, Canada. He is currently lecturer in Latin American studies and research associate with the Center for Research on Latin America and the Caribbean (CERLAC) at York University.

Ruth Corrêa Leite Cardoso is an anthropologist and professor in the Department of Political Sciences of the University of São Paulo and member of CEBRAP, the Centro Brasileiro de Análise e Planejamento. She has written extensively on social movements and politics in Brazil.

Norma Stoltz Chinchilla is professor of sociology and director of the Program in Women's Studies at California State University–Long Beach. She has written articles on political economy, social movements, and gender in Central America and is currently working on a book about the role of women in social movements in Guatemala.

Patricia Chuchryk is associate professor and chair of the Department of Sociology at the University of Lethbridge in Alberta, Canada. She has published several articles on feminism and the women's movement in Latin America. Her research interests include career paths of academic women, feminist pedagogy, and Latin American women and women's movements. She has recently finished a project on First Nations women of Canada and is currently working on a book about the Chilean women's movement and the transition to democracy.

Orlando Fals Borda is professor emeritus of the National University of Colombia; deputy to the National Constituent Assembly; former dean of sociology, vice minister of agriculture, and director of research at United Nations Research Institute for Social Development (UNRISD); winner of the Hoffman and Kreisky prizes; and author of books on peasant life, participatory research, and cultural history.

María Teresa Findji holds a Ph.D. in sociology from the University of Paris and is professor of contemporary Colombian history at the Universidad Nacional and the Universidad del Valle. She is presently director of the Masters' Program in Andean History at the latter institution. She is coauthor of *Territorio, Economía y Sociedad Páez* (1985). For many years she has been working on nonformal education and the recuperation of the history of indigenous communities in Colombia.

María Pilar García is a Venezuelan sociologist, environmentalist, and urban planner. She holds an M.A. in demography and human ecology and a Ph.D. in urban sociology from the University of Chicago. She is presently professor at the Universidad Simón Bolívar, Caracas, Venezuela. She has also been a visiting professor at the University of La Sorbonne, Paris (1983–1984); Fulbright professor at the College of Charleston, South Carolina (1984–1985); and British Council postdoctoral honorary research fellow at the Institute of Latin American Studies, University of London (1990–1991). She has written extensively on environmental issues and movements in Latin America and is editor of *Estado, Ambiente y Sociedad: Crisis y Conflictos Ambientales en América Latina y Venezuela*. She is currently preparing a book, tentatively entitled *Development, Democracy and the Environmental Social Movements in Latin America and Europe: Theory and Praxis*, which will be published as a special issue of the *International Journal of Sociology and Social Policy*.

Judith Adler Hellman is professor of political and social science and director of the Graduate Diploma Program in Latin American and Caribbean Studies at York University, Toronto, Canada. She is author of *Mexico in Crisis* (1978, 1983, 1988) and *Journeys Among Women: Feminism in Five Italian Cities* (1987) as well as articles on peasant movements, rural development, Latin American politics, feminism, ideology, and social movements in Europe and Latin America. Currently, she is writing a book on popular, middle-class, and elite responses to the economic crisis in Mexico.

Amy Conger Lind is a Ph.D. candidate in city and regional planning at Cornell University. Her research focuses on grass-roots women's movements and household survival strategies in Ecuador.

Edward MacRae received his Ph.D. in anthropology from the Universidade de São Paulo and is presently a senior researcher at the Escola Paulista de Medicina. He is author of *O Que é Homossexualidade?* (with Peter Fry, 1983), *A Construçao da Igualdade* (1990), and numerous articles on lesbian and gay movements and sexual politics in Brazil.

Marysa Navarro-Aranguren teaches Latin American history at Dartmouth College and is presently visiting professor at the University of California–Santa Cruz. Her specialties are Argentine history and Latin American women's history. She is the author of *Evita* (1981), *Eva Perón* (with Nicholas Fraser, 1980), *Los Nacionalistas* (1969), and numerous articles on historical and contemporary women's movements in Latin America. She is currently working on a book on the Mothers of the Plaza de Mayo and Argentine gender ideology during the *Proceso de Reorganización Nacional*.

Alejandro Piscitelli is deputy secretary of the Latin American Social Science Council (CLACSO). He has an M.S. degree in systems science from the University of Louisville and a master of social sciences degree from the Latin American Social Sciences Faculty (FLACSO–Buenos Aires). He is involved in the sociology of innovation and the linguistic behavior of organizations. Among his main papers are contributions to constructivist epistemology, the sociology of sociology, and paradigmatic analyses of substantive social theories. He is actively involved in building up computer networking for the social sciences throughout Latin America.

José Luis Reyna is former director of the Sociological Studies Center of the Colegio de México and current vice chancellor of the Colegio de México. He has an M.A. in sociology from the Latin American Social Sciences Faculty (FLACSO–Chile) and a Ph.D. in sociology from Cornell University. His major books are *An*

Empirical Analysis of Political Mobilization: The Case of Mexico (1971) and *El Movimiento Obrero en el Ruizcortinismo: La Redefinición del Sistema Económico y la Consolidación Política* (1981).

Cathy Schneider is visiting assistant professor of political science at Brown University. Her book on squatter movements, *Shantytown Protest in Pinochet's Chile,* is forthcoming (1993).

Orin Starn is assistant professor of cultural anthropology at Duke University. He carried out his doctoral research on the *rondas campesinas* in Peru's northernmost department of Piura in 1986–1987 and returned to Peru in 1990–1991 to research the origins of the *rondas* in the department of Cajamarca. He is currently coediting *The Peru Reader* with Carlos Iván Degregori and Robin Kirk and at work on a book called *"Rondas Campesinas": The Making of a Peasant Movement in Northern Peru, 1976–1990.*

Nancy Saporta Sternbach is assistant professor of Spanish at Smith College. She is the coeditor of *Breaking Boundaries: Latina Writing and Critical Readings* (1989) and the author of many articles on Latina and Latin American women's discourse. Her research focuses on a re-reading of the Latin American literary canon, including a feminist critique of *modernismo.* Currently she is working on a book of Latin American women's essays with Lourdes Rojas.

corollary of soc. mvmt's
Westview 1992

1

Introduction: Theory and Protest in Latin America Today

Arturo Escobar
Sonia E. Alvarez

Since the early 1980s, Latin America has seen, in the minds of many, its worst crisis of the century. In 1982, Mexico's announcement that it could not meet its debt payment obligations unleashed the infamous "debt crisis." What followed is well known by now: repeated attempts at economic stabilization and adjustment; "austerity" measures that quickly translated into rapidly declining living standards for popular and middle classes; industrial decline in the wake of the adoption of strong neoliberal and free market economic policies, even negative growth rates in some countries—in sum, a "reversal of development." And the social and political implications of these changes were no less onerous and menacing. Social exclusion and violence of all kinds significantly increased. "Transitions to democracy" begun during the first half of the decade became more and more difficult to achieve and increasingly limited in scope as the decade progressed. Even nature seemed to have taken issue with the region, as tornados, volcanos, earthquakes, and, more recently, the resurgence of cholera brought on the region more than its usual share of nature-related but socially aggravated hardships.

In the midst of all this, one might be surprised to find any significant degree of struggle and organizing on the people's part. On the contrary, one might expect the population to be so overwhelmed by the tasks of daily survival and so fragmented and downtrodden by the intensified exclusion, exploitation, and, in many cases, repression that it would be practically impossible for people to find the time or energy to mobilize and fight for a better life. At best, one would expect to find spontaneous manifestations of popular rage and frustration, such as the so-called International Monetary Fund (IMF) riots witnessed in Santo Domingo or Caracas, among other places. But even this would seem to corroborate the fact that people were more or less quiescent in their daily lives, exploding only when they could not take it anymore. After all, the 1960s, the decade when both development and revolution had reached their height, had been left well behind. The 1980s was another story altogether, clearly inimical to people's efforts at organizing for change. Yet despite all this, what one found in practically every country of the region was an impassioned experience of resistance and collective struggle on many fronts, even if less visible than in former decades and, at times, submerged.

It was the richness, novelty, and variety of this experience that motivated us to write this book. Popular mobilization by no means disappeared during the 1980s, and it is unlikely that it will in the 1990s. Indeed, the mosaic of forms of collective action is so diverse that one even doubts whether a single label can encompass them all. From squatters to ecologists, from popular kitchens in poor urban neighborhoods to Socialist feminist groups, from human rights and defense of life mobilizations to gay and lesbian coalitions, the spectrum of Latin American collective action covers a broad range. It includes, as well, the movements of black and indigenous peoples; new modalities of workers' cooperatives and peasant struggles; middle- and lower-middle-class civic movements; the defense of the rain forest; and even cultural manifestations embodied, for instance, in Afro-Caribbean musical forms (such as salsa and reggae) and incipient antinuclear protest in some countries. This rich mosaic of identities is at the heart of our project. Clearly, it represents a changed social, cultural, economic, and political reality in the continent.

Generally speaking, this book is concerned with the nature of resistance and social change in contemporary Latin America. This is an old question, some might say. But the 1980s witnessed the appearance of new forms of understanding and discussion on resistance and social change that marked a significant discontinuity with past forms of analysis. These new forms of theoretical awareness have been fostered by equally significant changes in historical conditions and, more specifically, by changes in the popular practices of resistance and collective action themselves. Critical reflection in the region has recognized the questionable and limited character of the approaches widely accepted until the 1960s and 1970s—namely, functionalism and Marxism. But, more importantly, it has embarked on a systematic effort at renewing our understanding of the complex processes that account for the evolution of Latin American societies today.

This process of theoretical renewal has centered around the nature of social movements to such an extent that a veritable explosion of writings on this topic has occurred, particularly since the early 1980s. And the character of these writings has been continuously changing. During the first years of the past decade, many collective forms of protest, especially in urban areas, were characterized in an undifferentiated manner as "new social movements" (NSMs). NSMs were believed to give expression to "new popular interests," to practice "new ways of doing politics," and even to embody the possibility of creating a "new hegemony by the masses."[1] Highly optimistic assessments of these movements and their actual or potential contributions to radical social change appeared in increasing numbers in social science journals and alternative newspapers throughout much of the region. In most analyses, the catchall concept of NSMs lumped ecclesiastical base communities and urban protest of various kinds together with ethnic movements and primarily middle-class ecology, feminist, and gay liberation movements. All of these movements, some theorists insisted, challenged the state's economic and political models and called into question authoritarian and hierarchical ways of doing politics.

This optimism was tempered in the second half of the decade as some of the movements declined, even in the context of democratic consolidation, as in Southern Cone countries (Mainwaring 1987; Cardoso 1987; Canel, Chapter 15). Some studies in these countries painted a sobering picture, suggesting that NSMs were unable to move from the confrontational tactics of the transition period to the strategies of negotiation and compromise necessitated by the new democratic status quo. A certain pessimism thus set in. More recent studies, however, have systematically investigated what has happened to social movements beyond the transition period or, more generally, how they have fared in relation to the economic, social, and political crisis of the 1980s. These studies have opened up new questions, many of which we pursue in this anthology.

Also in the second half of the 1980s, continuities between old and new practices and structural determinants began to be recognized (Mires 1987) as a step toward reassessing the "newness" of the movements. At the same time, the use of European theories was more thoroughly examined (Calderón 1986), and empirical studies were more systematically conducted and evaluated.[2] Although these developments did not result in a clearly defined "paradigm" or research program, they did advance and transform significantly the state of the field, making it possible to launch a new wave of research and theorizing for the 1990s.

The most recent literature on social movements takes for granted the fact that a significant transformation has occurred in both reality and its forms of analysis. The "old" is characterized by analysis couched in terms of modernization and dependency; by definitions of politics anchored in traditional actors who struggled for the control of the state, particularly the working class and revolutionary vanguards; and by a view of society as an entity composed of more or less immutable structures and class relations that only great changes (large-scale development schemes or revolutionary upheavals) could significantly alter. In contrast, the new theories see contemporary social movements as bringing about a fundamental transformation in the nature of political practice and theorizing itself. According to these theorists, an era that was characterized by the division of the political space into two clearly demarcated camps (the bourgeoisie and the proletariat) is being left behind. In the new situation, a multiplicity of social actors establish their presence and spheres of autonomy in a fragmented social and political space. Society itself is largely shaped by the plurality of these struggles and the vision of those involved in the new social movements.

Whatever one might think of these claims, the clearest indication of the need for continued research on social movements is the persistence of multiple forms of collective mobilization in the continent. These manifestations indicate great complexity not only at the level of the actors but, as the following chapters will amply demonstrate, also in terms of modes of organization and action, causes and goals of the struggle, magnitude and composition of the forces, relation to political parties and the state, and so forth. As Calderón, Piscitelli, and Reyna argue in Chapter 2, a significant change has taken place in the structure of collective action. What is important to emphasize at present is that these collective manifestations are found in all countries of the region—in varying political regimes, "levels of development," cultural contexts, and traditions of protest.

If a point of origin for the current wave of protest forms and styles were to be assigned, we would have to say that they emerged out of the historical conjuncture that started to coalesce in the late 1960s and has since branched out in a number of directions. The two factors most commonly cited in this regard are (1) the crisis of development in most of the region, particularly that in the developmentalist/populist state in Mexico and South America and the oligarchic state in Central America (with a related strengthening of the national security state in South America and of counterinsurgency regimes in Central America) and (2) the crisis of political parties and mechanisms of representation on all sides of the spectrum, from traditional parties in most countries to leftist parties and 1960s-style guerrilla groups.

The 1980s saw the deepening of some of these features and the appearance of others. The debt crisis is best seen as the reflection of the debacle of the post-World War II development model, based on rapid industrialization, the technological transformation of agriculture, and cultural modernization (in the sense of adopting a rational, scientific, and secular approach to social life). As the 1990s advance, it is becoming increasingly clear that a restructuring of economic conditions is taking place across the world, based on high technology in electronics and information and on the selective incorporation of countries and even regions within countries to the exclusion of others.[3] Amid these ominous changes, the presence and the struggles of social movements continue to be important factors. Moreover, they embody a transformative potential in at least two dimensions: first, the widening of "sociopolitical citizenship," linked to peoples' struggles for social recognition of their existence and for political spaces of expression, and second, the transformation or appropriation by the actors of the cultural field through their search for a collective identity and the affirmation of their difference and specificity (Jelin 1990). Both of these dimensions will be documented and discussed in this anthology.

To refer to social movements in terms of "collective identities" represents a new trend and a new way of thinking. Social action is understood as the product of complex social processes in which structure and agency interact in manifold ways and in which actors produce meanings, negotiate, and make decisions. Generally speaking, social movements are seen to be engaged in a significant "political struggle in terms of access to the mechanisms of power but also [a] cultural [struggle] in the search for different identities" (Jelin 1990: 206). Our anthology is an attempt to capture and explore the significance of this regionwide trend along three main axes, broadly defined in terms of identity, strategy, and democracy. For this last criterion, what must be assessed is the impact of social movements on the democratization of cultural, social, economic, and political life; this is especially important with regard to the terrain of "daily life" because it is at this level, our authors contend, that many of today's forms of protest emerge and exert their action and influence.

In terms of strategy, it is important to convey the range of tactics, strategic initiatives, and forms of political organization developed by collective actors in their struggles, especially those that deviate from conventional ways of doing politics. The range of these forms, once again, is vast, from those practiced by small women's organizations to those adopted by movement-inspired political party coalitions such as the Partido dos Trabalhadores (Brazilian Workers' Party, PT) or the M–19/Democratic Alliance in Colombia. In some cases, strategies have shifted from resistance to protest and from protest to proposal, without implying any linear movement from one to another of these forms but rather suggesting their coexistence and mutual feedback (Fals Borda, Chapter 17). The question of strategy, of course, is intimately linked to how social actors construct a collective identity for themselves, often out of conflictual roles and positions. This is our final axis of analysis.

Trends in Latin American Social Movements Theory and Research

Research and theorizing on social movements have become central issues in the Latin American social sciences landscape. How existing European and North American theories have influenced work in Latin America and, conversely, how Latin American intellectual production parallels or deviates from them, modifies them, or develops its own autonomous frameworks and concepts are questions that are discussed in some of the chapters that follow.

Jean Cohen's (1985) distinction regarding social movements theories—differentiating those concerned with strategy and those centered on the notion of identity—is already well established. Resource mobilization theories, which make up the first group, dominate in the Anglo-Saxon world and highlight questions of strategy, participation, organization, rationality, expectations, interests, and the like.[4] The identity-centered theories, dominant in continental Europe and Latin America, emphasize the processes by which social actors constitute collective identities as a means to create democratic spaces for more autonomous action. Referred to by some as the "new social movements approach," this school can be situated generally within poststructuralist and post-Marxist trends of growing importance since the 1970s. Some are also influenced by theories of postmodernism.[5]

Analyses of Latin American social movements by North American scholars have been relatively neglectful of Latin American contributions along the lines of the "new social movements approach."[6] The paucity of literature in English in this area is striking. Two important exceptions are the collections by David Slater (1985a) and Elizabeth Jelin (1990). Although Slater's book was very important for those making their first forays into the field in the English-speaking world, its contributions were constrained by the incipient stage of theorizing and, as we mentioned, by the somewhat uncritical optimism of the period. Like much of her work, Jelin's book is a welcome addition to the literature, even if focused only on women's forms of collective action and primarily conceived within the identity-centered conceptual framework. The significance of this last qualification derives from the more recent observation that the Latin American researchers' neglect of the concerns addressed by resource mobilization approaches has been costly in terms of understanding the concrete practices, constraints, and possibilities of the movements. Not only have "new identities" been celebrated prematurely, the presence of old features within them has also been overlooked. A sort of "cross-pollination" of research—between identity-centered and resource mobilization approaches, quantitive and qualitative methods, endogenous and external theories—is deemed necessary (Alvarez 1989b; Starn, Chapter 6).

A recent and valuable collection of essays entitled *Popular Movements and Political Change in Mexico*, edited by Joe Foweraker and Ann L. Craig (1990), moved in this direction. The collection was explicitly concerned with "the interaction of popular movements and the political system" (Foweraker 1990: 3), paying special attention to the political organization and strategic initiatives of the movements and to the movements' impact on state institutions, laws, and practices. Questions of identity, political culture, and consciousness were given less attention, perhaps, as the concluding chapter (Craig 1990) suggested, because of the political rather than ethnographic orientation of the majority of the authors. Craig's open question of "how are we to describe these collective identities and track processes by which they are formed" (1990: 283) is given central importance in our anthology. And though the contributors to the Mexican collection highlighted processes of interaction with the state as one of the most immediate and important sources of popular identities, our contributors cover a broad range of identity-defining factors. One important reason for this difference is that the Mexican collection focused on more strictly defined popular actors (peasants, workers, and low-income urban residents), which are covered in an unusually rich and insightful manner; it left aside other movements in which the questions of identity formation can also be fruitfully investigated, such as ecology, feminist, gay, and indigenous peoples' movements, all of which are represented in the present anthology.

One final issue that should be addressed before we provide brief introductions to the following chapters is that of determining what constitutes a "social movement." This is by no means a simple question. Alain Touraine, whose work has been among the most influential in Latin America, showed the complexity at hand when he asserted that "most of all, the empiricist illusion must be clearly rejected: It is impossible to define an object of study called 'social movements' without first selecting a general mode of analysis of social life on the basis of which a category of facts called social movements can be constituted" (1988a: 63). Similarly, Ruth Cardoso warned that often "movements form a unity only when we look at them from the outside searching for similarities. If we prioritize their differences, they cease to form a uniform object, showing their fragmentation" (1987: 32). Elizabeth Jelin pointed in the same direction when she stated that

> it is the researcher who proposes the reading of a set of practices as a social movement. . . . Social movements are objects constructed by the researcher, which do not necessarily coincide with the empirical form of collective action. Seen from the outside, they may present a certain degree of unity, but internally they are always heterogeneous, diverse (1986: 22).

What all this means is that the definition of what counts as a "social movement" involves a complex epistemological process. It is therefore not surprising that few scholars have actually ventured a definition; some even believe that the whole idea of a "social movement" as a description of collective action should be abandoned because it traps our language in conceptual traditions that have to be discarded (Melucci 1985). Touraine's system of classification of forms of collective action (1988a: 63–70) is well known and has been applied by some in Latin America.[7] Others, such as Ernesto Laclau and Chantal Mouffe (1985), have provided not so much a definition of "social movements" but a complex theoretical system in which collective practices can be analyzed in terms of a process of "formation of identities." Some of our contributors maintain the tension between mode of analysis and qualification of protest modes.

It would be tempting, of course, to propose yet another definition of social movements. This is a temptation we have sought to avoid in our efforts to provide a more disaggregated and nuanced view of contemporary collective action in Latin America. Moreover, social movements cannot be defined solely in terms of economic and social categories; they must also be placed in political and cultural domains. Today's social movements—even those that take place solely in the public arena—do not restrict themselves to traditional political activities, such as those linked to parties and state institutions. Rather, they challenge our most entrenched ways of understanding political practice and its relation to culture, economy, society, and nature. As our authors contend, we need to be open to rethinking the nature of these relations.

It is also important to differentiate among various forms of collective action and yet to avoid reified and reductionistic uses of the concept of social movement. Not all forms of collective action have the same social, cultural, or political significance. But at the same time, it is also important not to dismiss some forms of collective action because of their limited reach in observable social terms. "Minor" forms of resistance, many authors today believe, should not be despised merely because they do not lead to the fulfillment of sizable demands or important structural transformations. Part of the problem in this regard is a certain empirical simplification and political reductionism that lead researchers to focus their attention on the measurable aspects of protest, such as confrontation with the political system and the impact on state policies; consequently, they disregard the less visible effects at the levels of culture and everyday life. Our authors grapple with these issues in their assessments of the struggles they study.

Related to the question of what constitutes a social movement is the issue of their newness; in other words, what is *new* about new social movements? This question is usually raised as a criticism of NSMs theorists. As some put it, the "new" is really in the theorists' minds. "Out there," some would say, the practices have always been the same, multiple and heterogeneous; it is only that theorists, burdened by paradigms, were unable to see them. In dismantling this "epistemological misunderstanding," Alberto Melucci made the important observation that both critics and adherents of the "newness" paradigm share "the same epistemological limitation: Both sides regard the contemporary phenomena as a unitary empirical object. Starting from this unity, the supporters seek to qualify its novelty, the critics deny or question it" (1988a: 336). Underlying this limitation is a conception of social movements as "personages" moving on the historical stage like characters of an epic drama endowed with an unchanging essence. In other words, researchers assume the existence of unitary, coherent collective social agents moving along the historical flow. This assumption, Melucci insisted, hides the changing character of collective action at the level of orientations, meanings, levels and historical systems. If one takes into consideration these aspects, many of the debates around this question, he concluded, would vanish.[8]

To deny, on the other hand, that there is anything new in today's collective action—in relation, say, to the earlier part of the century—is to negate the changing character of the world and its history. Of course, some things remain the same, and it is important to acknowledge the continuity of forms and practices. But as historical contexts change, so do peoples' ways of seeing and acting in the world, as well as the theories that seek to explain both actions and their contexts. Despite important continuities, Latin America in the 1980s is certainly very different from Latin America in the 1920s, 1930s, and even 1950s. Women, for instance, do not organize in the same way today as they did in the 1920s, nor do women's struggles have the same ideological and symbolic content that they had then. Social conflict has moved to previously untouched terrains, and at least some new practices have been developed. Even "classical" social actors such as workers and peasants have models of action that are very different from those of earlier movements. Similarly, not all the actors of today were present fifty years earlier, nor were people subjected to the same economic, social, and political forces. For example, there was not much of a gay or an ecology movement in previous decades, nor did the cities see so many varied forms of protest.

An Overview of the Book

Theoretical reflection on social movements has been rich during the 1980s, and we start our anthology with a series of chapters that address a variety of theoretical questions. For the case studies, we asked our contributors to pay attention to the three axes of identity, strategy, and democracy. Because some of the following chapters emphasize one aspect rather than all three, we have divided them into two parts, one in which questions of identity are highlighted and a second one that more closely follows the concerns of strategy and democracy. In those chapters belonging to the first group, however, issues of strategy and democracy are by no means neglected. The converse is also true, although more explicitly in some cases than in others: The strategies of the movements under consideration and their contribution to democratization processes entail an underlying collective identity that the strategies themselves help to construct.

The overall goal of the anthology is to help advance our understanding of the nature and extent of social movements in Latin America, building particularly on Latin American theory and research produced during the 1980s but also on advances and applications achieved in other parts of the world. More specifically, we explore the following aspects of contemporary social movements:

The Process of Continuity and Change in Latin American Social, Cultural, and Political Struggles. Our contributors seek to identify the new in the old and the old in the new; perhaps more importantly, they examine the potentially innovative aspects of the historical meeting of old and new forms.

The Construction and Reconstitution of Identities and Their Impact on Social and Cultural Innovations. What new identities have emerged in Latin America in the past two decades, particularly the 1980s? How are these identities being formed? What is their relation to social, cultural, and economic fields?

The Existence of New and Old Forms of "Doing Politics" and the Changing Character of Political Practice. In what ways is daily life being politicized? What new domains of social conflict give rise to political forms of expression? What are the relations between the personal, the cultural, and the political?

The Relation Between Social Movements and the Nature of the Development Process. If it is true that social movements tend to challenge and demystify established definitions and strategies of development, are organized groups making demands in response to difficult social and economic conditions in ways that nevertheless do not amount merely to the meeting of "survival" needs nor the desire for conventional "development" goals?

The Extent to Which Social Movements Foster Reconceptualizations of Democracy, Reform, and Revolution. More generally, we explore the implications of contemporary collective action in terms of possible strategies for change in the 1990s, including the achievements and the potential of social movements for bringing about democratization processes of importance.

Our authors represent many different backgrounds and perspectives; some of them have been active for a long time in both the movements themselves and the research conducted on them. For this reason, readers should not expect a unified logic among the chapters, despite the authors' unity of orientation. Even when the degree of analytical convergence is more significant, a certain amount of heterogeneity and disagreement will be found. This variety of perspectives, we think, enriches the collection.

We open the first part of the book, "Conceptualizing Social Movements in Contemporary Latin America," with an overview piece by Fernando Calderón, Alejandro Piscitelli, and José Luis Reyna. These authors make the strong claim that a fundamental change in the structure of collective action is occurring in the continent, a change that is reflected in the great increase in new faces and practices observed in the social and political arenas. This increase, they argue, is an expression of the deep changes occurring in the nature of Latin American societies, such as the growing tension between society and state and the increased urbanization. Their assessment of the future of the movements is cautiously optimistic. They see today's movements as "dwarf stars" that might bring about more meaningful political participation and representation.

These authors also contend that social movements research is prompting a renewal in social science activities in Latin America. A similar conclusion is reached by Norma Chinchilla in her essay reviewing changes within Marxism and feminism. Contrary to the opinion of many that Marxism has become obsolete in explaining Latin American reality, Chinchilla shows that a "new Marxism" is not only alive but also experiencing a significant convergence with feminism, particularly in the social movements context. Chinchilla's review of Latin America's feminist "second wave" and of Marxism's internal critique in recent times is meant to demonstrate the rapprochement between these two tendencies in the context of the more pluralistic and democratic political practices of the 1980s.

One of the key features associated with new social movements, in the minds of many of their proponents, is the emphasis on their autonomy vis-à-vis more conventional political arenas, such as political parties and the state. In some cases, Judith Hellman argues in Chapter 4, this insistence on autonomy has not been sufficiently critical but stems, instead, from the analysts' desires, particularly in Latin America where the analysts are often external to the movement and tend to romanticize the movement's spontaneity and autonomy. As the experiences of countries such as Italy, Mexico, and Brazil show, the relationship between social movements and political parties is a dialectical one in which both movements and parties potentially stand to win a good deal.

Another important feature of contemporary social movements is the role of cultural factors in their constitution and actions. Yet, especially in the Latin American case, these aspects have received little theoretical attention and are not well understood, partly because of the dominance of economic and political forms of analysis. As Arturo Escobar shows in Chapter 5, social movements in Latin America must be seen as economic, political, and cultural struggles. This view has important consequences in terms of how researchers are to approach the movements. A prerequisite for this task is a critical reinterpretation of the nature of development and modernity in ways that stress their fundamental cultural nature.

The value of a close analysis of meanings and cultural practices for understanding contemporary social movements is made patently clear in the set of articles on South American movements in Part 2, "The Making of Collective Identities." Orin Starn's study of a peasant movement that started in northern Peru in the late 1970s with the establishment of vigilante patrols and has since spread to a large number of communities is an excellent example of the type of work that embraces both identity- and strategy-oriented approaches. Starn demonstrates how people fashion their worlds and their struggles out of cultural elements that originate in multiple spaces, from long-standing traditions to modern and even transnational forces, according to a creative process that includes a unique innovation and recombination of elements. The *rondas campesinas,* he argues, is probably the most sustained and important peasant movement in Latin America today.

For several indigenous groups in southwest Colombia, the right to live according to their cultural and political identity is at the basis of their struggle. In Chapter 7, María Teresa Findji documents the "public" emergence of these groups in the early 1970s and their transformation into a social movement of national proportions in the 1980s. The recuperation of their territories, histories, and forms of organization, as well as the repressive and co-optative responses to their actions by landowners, police, and the state, forms the backbone of the struggle of a movement that does not want to be "integrated" into development and the national society but seeks the establishment of a pluralistic society in which the right to difference is fully respected. Anchored in their own culture, ideas, and traditions, Guambianos and Paeces are articulating an alternative to the national social model based on individualistic values and impersonal bureaucratic institutions.

The links between gender and identity are explored in Chapter 8 by Amy Conger Lind. Her work on popular women's organizations in Ecuador examines the interrelation between gender identity formation, organized political activity, and the search for alternative forms of satisfying basic needs. As Lind shows, poor women do not only fight for "survival"; in their struggle over needs, they also shift prevailing understandings of gender and development as they collectively resist the forms of power that are present in patriarchy and the development establishment.

If it is perhaps difficult to see that when poor women are struggling to put food in their mouths they are actually doing much more than that—that is, that they are actively constructing a way of life, resisting forms of oppression, and dreaming of a better world—it is impossible to overlook the symbolic aspects of contemporary manifestations such as the ecology movement, as María Pilar García shows in her analysis of the Venezuelan environmental movement. Restricted in terms of their numbers and actions, these movements nevertheless have a significant impact given the magnitude of the symbolic challenge they pose for society. From the purely scientific-conservationist perspectives of the 1960s to the more politically and symbolically oriented positions of the 1980s, the ability of this movement to articulate challenges and alternative proposals to official development policies has grown steadily.

Throughout the book, we emphasize the fact that collective identities are not given but constructed and that this process often involves negotiation and conflict. One of the conflictual aspects that is usually overlooked is that of how people can be brought together in a group when there are competing arenas for their allegiances. Why do people decide to participate in a movement? Why join one particular group and not another? John Burdick explores these questions in his chapter by comparing popular participation in two competing arenas of progressive Christian base communities and Pentecostals. He finds that there are a host of factors, both external and internal to the groups, that shape peoples' decisions to join one group versus another. More generally, he stresses the need to study the competing and overlapping discourses and practices in which social movements exist if we want to understand more fully the motivations and dynamics of individual participation.

Gay movements the world over are considered to be among the most clear cases of "identity politics," and the one in Brazil is no exception. In Chapter 11, Edward MacRae discusses the evolution of the Brazilian gay movement since the late 1970s. Born in the context of changes in the national and progressive political climate of the 1970s—which made possible the articulation of questions of values and life-style as political issues—the homosexual movement was faced with manifold tasks throughout the 1980s: forming solidarity links with other movements, particularly those of women and black people; creating an autonomous space and means of expression; projecting into national society through media and public actions; establishing a "gay identity" and a set of values, while allowing for diversity of practices and opinions; and claiming legal and institutional rights. Some of these issues were played out in the context of the spread of AIDS in the country.

The final set of chapters in Part 3 highlights questions of strategy and democracy, although, as we mentioned before, this does not mean that identity considerations are completely disregarded. Some of the chapters, like "Feminisms in Latin America: From Bogotá to San Bernardo," approach their subject from both perspectives. This chapter by Nancy Saporta Sternbach, Marysa Navarro-Aranguren, Patricia Chuchryk, and Sonia E. Alvarez follows the development of Latin American "feminisms" by focusing on five continent-wide *encuentros* ("encounters or meetings") held in various countries between 1981 and 1991. This retrospective look at the encuentros reveals that a transition has been achieved, with the movement growing from small groups of dedicated feminists to a large, broad-based, politically heterogeneous, multiclass and multiracial movement. As the encuentros show, this achievement has necessitated working out many ideological and political differences among the women attending the meetings. And as the authors suggest, the ongoing nature of the debates gives Latin American feminism a unique character and makes it a source of insights for women's movements elsewhere.

No observer of contemporary social movements in Latin America can overlook the salience of urban popular movements, as Vivienne Bennett and Cathy Schneider amply demonstrate in their discussions of urban movements in Mexico and Chile, respectively. Mexico provides a clear example of the growth and articulation of urban movements. Bennett's analysis identifies three major phases in the development of urban movements from the late 1960s to 1988. Originally fueled by student activists and the increasingly exclusionary character of the Mexican development model, urban movements proliferated in cities throughout Mexico, articulating their demands not only within the neighborhoods but also at the regional and national levels. As a result, several nationwide networks of urban popular movements have been in existence since the early 1980s. The action of these networks and their impact, Bennett argues, raise important questions about the nature of the process of social change.

The cycle of protest that started with the storm of popular uprisings in Santiago's streets in 1983 and reached its peak in 1986 with that year's nationwide strike is the subject of Schneider's contribution. This wave of protest cannot be seen solely as the result of increased popular discontent in the wake of economic crisis, nor can it be reduced to an account of the construction of autonomous organizations. Such interpretations, Schneider shows, cannot explain why protest reemerged in some neighborhoods but not in others characterized by analogous conditions. Based on on-site interviews with residents and activists in various poor neighborhoods in Santiago, Schneider's chapter brings to the forefront the importance of continued left-wing activism in Chile for the survival and resurgence of protest.

In Chile, the renewed prominence of political parties with the opening created by the 1988 plebiscite entailed an ebbing of grass-roots activism. Something similar occurred in Uruguay after the return to democratic rule at the end of 1984. The restoration of "politics as usual," Eduardo Canel shows with concern in Chapter 15, meant that many hoped for changes went unrealized; democracy also brought with it, by a curious twist, the disappearance of many grass-roots movements that had been active during the years of dictatorship. To understand the decline of urban social movements in his country, Canel turns to changes in the relationship between the movements and the political actors, such as the state, political parties, and municipal governments. His analysis shows that the process of constructing collective identities by the movements was intimately mediated by existing political institutions in ways that made their survival difficult under the particular conditions of transition to democracy in Uruguay.

If social movements and popular organizations are significantly affected by the state and political institutions, the converse is also true. This aspect of social movements research is particularly relevant in terms of the movements' contribution to the consolidation of democracy. In the Brazilian case, examined by Ruth Corrêa Leite Cardoso in Chapter 16, the state apparatus gradually became more receptive to popular participation, and local organized groups became significant interlocutors. At the same time, links were established between party militants and grass-roots organizations. These processes, however, have not been easy but have involved continuous negotiation within and among the movements, the parties, and the state. It is through dialogue with all these social actors, Cardoso argues, that grass-roots groups increasingly construct their self-image.

Chapter 17, by Orlando Fals Borda, gathers together many of the issues dealt with in previous chapters. For Fals Borda, the redefinition of political action brought about by popular movements during the past two decades raises a crucial question—namely, how to conceptualize the expansion and duration of the movements. As a result of their own dynamics over the past years, Fals Borda believes, social movements in various parts of Latin America have begun to move from the micro level to the macro level and "from protest to proposal." This process of growth and articulation has resulted in an expanded domain of action, noticeable networks and coalitions, and the formulation of significant political alternatives. Movement networks, such as the M-19/Democratic Alliance in Colombia, Fals Borda concludes, are not only contributing to the redefinition of styles of politics, political parties, and democratic participation but are also providing alternative solutions to problems of violence and development.

Taken as a whole, the ensuing chapters reflect the uniqueness of Latin American social life, its cultural reality, and its economic and political situation. As readers will realize, the differences between these countries and North America and Europe are vast. Even if there are some similarities (for instance, to the extent that there are women's, ecology, gay, and indigenous peoples' movements in Latin America as well as Europe and North America), the nature of these movements, their needs, their cultural makeup, and their significance are dramatically different. This does not mean, however, that there are unbridgeable gaps between movements across cultures. Indeed, the task of comparative research and dialogue cross-culturally and internationally is becoming ever more urgent. Capital knows no barriers, and it is, to an extent, culturally malleable. While respecting differences (and precisely as a way to strengthen them and learn from them), the time has come for greater communication and coalition-building transnationally and transculturally, as a necessary strategy to oppose the consolidation of a "new world order" according to the dictates of capital and of the global cultural, economic, and military powers. Only peoples' *collective* resistance and creativity can fulfill this role. In the essays of this book, we hope that readers will find some clues for this essential task—a task in which some of the movements themselves are already engaged.

Notes

1. Examples of this early literature include the special issue of *Nueva Sociedad* on "Nuevas Formas de Hacer Política," or "New Forms of Doing Politics" (1983); Mainwaring and Viola 1984; Slater 1985a; Fals Borda 1986.

2. The most complete and systematic study of social movements in Latin America to date is the project sponsored by the Latin American Social Science Council (Consejo Latinoamericano de Ciencias Sociales, CLACSO) and the United Nations University. Fifty-four researchers participated in the project under the direction of a national coordinator in each of ten South American countries. Studies were carried out on the five or six most prominent movements in each country, and national summaries for each country were published in book form, as was a summary of the entire project (Calderón 1986). Readers are encouraged to become acquainted with this work if they wish to develop a more comprehensive view of social movements in specific countries. For a useful recent anthology in Spanish, with national summaries, see Camacho and Menjívar, eds., 1989.

3. Some authors refer to this restructuring in terms of the emergence of "post-Fordism" as a new regime of accumulation with profound cultural and economic consequences. See, for instance, Harvey 1989; Hall 1991; Mayer 1991; Escobar, Chapter 5. The role of high technology in the new international division of labor was discussed in Castells 1986. The "reversal" of development was documented in Portes and Kincaid 1989; Dietz and James, eds., 1990; and Amin 1990.

4. The resource mobilization and political process paradigm privileges systemic and middle-level variables—such as political opportunity space, ideological and organizational resources, mobilizational networks, leadership, and so on—in explaining movement emergence and development while paying limited attention to the discursive practices and political identities forged by social movements. For reviews of the political process and resource mobilization perspectives as applied to the study of social movements in the United States, see Morris and Herring 1987; Tarrow 1988. For one of the most compelling formulations of the political process model, see McAdam 1982. A few students of Latin American movements have incorporated elements of this approach. See, for example, Boschi 1987; Boschi and Valladares 1983; Foweraker and Craig, eds., 1990.

5. The names of Alain Touraine, Alberto Melucci, Ernesto Laclau, and Chantal Mouffe are undoubtedly the most well known within this loosely defined camp, which primarily includes authors from Italy, France, and Germany. More recently, some scholars on both sides of the Atlantic have begun to integrate European and North American approaches, even if there has not yet been a sufficiently significant effort on the part of these scholars to include work being done in other parts of the world, such as Latin America, Eastern Europe, and India. A useful summary of these efforts is found in Klandermans and Tarrow 1988. For Eastern Europe, see Misztal 1985, 1988, 1991.

6. This was the case, for instance, in the collection edited by Susan Eckstein (1989). With very few exceptions and despite its value, this collection neglected questions of collective identity and focused instead on questions of strategy and structural causality; its contributions did not reflect the large body of work on Latin American social movements that is at the basis of the present anthology.

7. Touraine defined a social movement as "the action, both culturally oriented and socially conflictual, of a social class defined by its position of domination or dependency in the mode of appropriation of historicity, of the cultural models of investment, knowledge and morality, toward which the social movement itself is oriented" (1988a: 68). (For an explanation of the terms of this definition, see Escobar, Chapter 5.) Touraine introduced two additional distinctions: the first concerns the types of conflict and distinguishes, in order of complexity, between collective behavior, struggles, and social movements; the second distinction concerns types of movements, differentiating between sociocultural movements, sociohistorical movements, and social movements proper (1988a: 63–73). For Touraine (1987), most of what people referred to as "social movements" in Latin America would only be struggles or sociohistorical movements. For Jelin, the notion of social movement refers to "forms of collective action with high degree of popular participation, which use non-institutional channels, and which formulate their demands while simultaneously finding forms of action to express them, thus establishing themselves as collective subjects, that is, as a group or social category" (1986: 18). Readers can take these definitions as starting points for approaching the chapters.

8. A fuller analysis of the spurious nature of the question "What's new about NSMs?" would take us into deeper epistemological waters. Suffice it to say that within the poststructuralist currents that inform much of theory today, including some of the NSMs theorists, it is impossible to appeal to empirical reality as the ultimate arbiter about the truth of a statement. This is because representations of reality are always open to debate and reinterpretation. What has to be examined is the constructed character of past and new understandings and their dependence on historical situations. Those who argue that nothing or little has changed, on the contrary, still function within a positivist epistemology, within which "truth" about social reality can be given once and for all. They also treat the statement "There is nothing new in NSMs" as an empirically testable proposition. This is their "new" reality; in other words, what is new for them is the realization that the world was always different than we believed, say, ten years ago. Paradoxically, this very realization is made possible by the insistence of NSMs theorists that there *is* something new!

As an aside, it should be pointed out that Melucci (1988a) called for abandoning the whole idea of an NSMs "paradigm" (if it is true that a paradigm ever existed), even as a way of finding out what is new in today's collective action. This is a welcome suggestion. The NSMs notion should be treated as a temporary analytical construct that should give way to a clearer and more rigorous definition of contemporary collective phenomena. As such, we have not imposed a unified usage of the notion on our authors.

Part 1
Conceptualizing Social Movements in Contemporary Latin America

2

Social Movements:
Actors, Theories, Expectations

Fernando Calderón
Alejandro Piscitelli
José Luis Reyna

If we had proposed, a quarter century ago, to undertake a study of social movements, we would have analyzed national liberation movements; populist or national popular movements; labor union, peasant, and agrarian reform movements; and student revolutionary movements. A common denominator of all these was their search for political power or, rather, for its redefinition. Many of these movements were centered around their relationship with the state and oriented toward models of more autonomous industrialization. Possibly, issues related to political parties, particularly those surrounding the question of the so-called revolutionary vanguards, would have merited special attention.

Today, something different is unfolding. But the new does not just appear suddenly. Rather, the old transforms into the new for not all things that finish actually come to an end. Is this not, perhaps, what happened with Zapata, as well as with the miners of the Siglo Veinte, Catavi, and Llallagua mines? What has changed and what continues to change are the patterns of social organization within the context of the industrialist state and its modernizing imagery. Who can deny today the centrality of the marginals in the political citizenry of the future? Moreover, what is important is that society is capable of thinking consciously about itself. The rest is speculation.

When we review the enormous number of social movements throughout Latin America and the Caribbean today, the multiplicity of actors, themes, conflicts, and orientations is overwhelming; beyond that, we are overwhelmed because the questions they raise have little to do with those we observed a quarter century ago. In this chapter, we will attempt to represent the new—that is, the multiplicity and complexity of the new sociocultural actors who today produce our societies. In the first section below, we present the current landscape of social movements in Latin America and outline the main reasons for their appearance, without delving into the study of any single movement in particular. In the second section, we attempt to make sense of the relationship between the new manifestations of collective action and the social science models through which they are studied.

In the first section, we detect significant changes in the nature and scope of collective action, but in the second, we outline the necessary parallel changes that must take place (and are now occurring) at the level of Latin American social sciences if we are to provide appropriate interpretations of the new movements.

The Hidden Eruption

New Faces, Old Masks

The collective forms of sociocultural production in Latin America today include an impressive variety of manifestations (Lampe Romero 1987; Marley 1980; Molina n.d.). Among these forms are cultural movements in the Caribbean, such as the Rastafarians who are characterized by their radical ideological ambiguity, their communal search for primeval origins in Ethiopia, and their fantastic political critique and cultural affirmation expressed primarily through dance and music. Such movements can become untapped mechanisms for finding new forms of identification in places where culture and politics meet face to face, apprehensively, with their boundaries somewhat unclear.

Current sociocultural production also includes movements of an ethical orientation, such as the *Madres de Plaza de Mayo* (Mothers of the Plaza de Mayo) in Buenos Aires (González Bombal 1987). The plaza symbolizes the encounter of popular power and political power in Argentina. Every Thursday afternoon at 3:30, the madres parade around the plaza's central pyramid, calling for *aparición con vida y castigo a los culpables* ("the return to life of the missing and punishment of the guilty"), making countless claims relating to the thirty thousand "disappeared" in the "dirty war." They derive their power not so much from opposing the state as by the fact that the state has systematically opposed them.

Like Antigone confronting the corpse of her unburied brother, the Madres de Plaza de Mayo demand peace for their dead by way of legal punishment or the return of their dead to life. And thus, like Antigone, they sentence themselves to fight forever. But the actions of the madres contradict the reason of the state. They would bring an end to the armed forces; they would have their dead returned. They are condemned to repeat their claims endlessly, and their demands constitute the ethical force of the madres as they confront the whole of society— a society that remains frustrated, like Antigone, and ever conscious of its own impotence. Whatever may happen, the madres' task is eternal for they embody a situation that has no solution: that of tragedy.

In addition, movements have appeared that are based on gender opposition and the demand for political participation, such as the movement led by Chilean women (Molina n.d.; Ovalles 1987). Building on relations at the individual, emotional, and sexual levels and generally basing their actions on everyday domestic life, these women gained the recognition of civil society through their opposition to the authoritarian regime. Although for the most part the participants were not militant members of any political party, they waged strong political opposition and were admirable advocates of democracy. They exemplify the kind of social movement that operates over and above—and in spite of—institutions.

Another powerful movement—striking, absolute, cruel, and disconcerting—is *Sendero Luminoso* ("Shining Path"), a movement that has transformed Peru. In addition to combining millenarian orientations with authoritarian communism (a combination expressed in the phantasmagoric leadership of *Puka Inti*, the "fifth sword of Marxism," or "President Gonzalo," all titles attributed to Abimael Guzmán, leader of Sendero), the movement reflects the complex processes of exclusion and disintegration occurring in Peruvian society. Sendero appears to be a movement of people in despair, who derive their raison d'être from the implacable breakdown of relations in Peruvian society (Degregori 1986, 1990).[1]

Sendero Luminoso is strong because the Peruvian working class is weak; the movement parallels the tragedy of Peru and the creative search of this society, still overshadowed by its own past. No doubt the new Peruvian theatrical genre, in which the actors perform in masks, is an invitation for the reappearance of Peru's hidden face. This search for a primeval identity in the Andean world is also reflected in the work of the Bolivian filmmaker Jorge Sanjines. In his film *La Nación Clandestina* ("The Clandestine Nation"), he suggested that it is only through dancing with our own masks that we can die and thus be reborn.

One also must consider the region's peasant movements of an indigenous nature, characterized by a tension-ridden but nevertheless hopeful trio of orientations—the demands for ethnic autonomy, class transformation, and affirmation of citizenship (Chiriboga Vega et al., 1986; Foguel 1986; Rivera 1985). Two such examples are the *Katarista* movement in the Bolivian altiplano and the *Unión de los Comuneros "Emiliano Zapata"* in Michoacán, Mexico.[2] Both groups employ vernacular practices, often rooted in the distant past, to articulate their complex demands: communal autonomy, changes in the agricultural power structure, and increased political participation. It is curious to discover that places as distant and apparently dissimilar as the Andean region and the Caribbean have generated, almost simultaneously, social movements that problematize matters of national autonomy, class transformation, and ethnic self-affirmation; one must recognize that perhaps this has more to do with the constitutive process of the identities of these societies than with the theoretical parameters of orthodox and alien forms of sociohistorical analysis.[3]

In this way, the responses given by the Katarista movement to certain vital issues through the exaltation of their ancestral identity and lineage probably have a universal configuration. One can likewise interpret the proliferation of indigenous music performed with modern instruments, for instance by the *Grupo Wara*, or the jumping and screaming of young people who come to sing and dance in La Paz during the *Fiesta del Gran Poder*. In addition to movements such as these, characterized by symbolic practices that reflect social exclusion, other cases more directly related to new forms of capitalist integration are also present. These types of collective action are formed in direct response to the postindustrial (or, if one wishes, postmodern) capitalist transformation.

One example of this sort of movement is that of the São Paulo metalworkers, which has already begun to respond to diverse challenges: the multiple problems posed by technocratic state policies and their impact on salaries; the effects of industrial automation and its consequences for workers' jobs and culture; and the global process of transnationalization of the economy. Although these processes limit the traditional strategies of the workers vis-à-vis capital, the workers have not abandoned their claims for more autonomous, institutionalized political participation. The movement of the Paulista auto workers appears to be the kind of movement that implicitly calls for an important institutional transformation—more substantive and pluralist, rather than "formal" or instrumental.

Still another case is the ecology movement in Brazil, of interest not only for what it says about the global environmental crisis but in terms of its own history and evolution (Viola 1987). Today, this movement includes many ecological tendencies, and it has expanded its interests beyond the primary issues of environmental destruction to a search for social alternatives in a transnational world that is increasingly menaced by ecological imbalances. It is clear that ecological issues have become inextricably intertwined with politics, making them even more complex than before (see García, Chapter 9).

Equally novel are those movements that refer to the decentralization and democratization of microlocal urban territories, such as those in the southern colonies of the Federal District in Mexico (Arau Chavarría 1987a, 1987b; Bennett, Chapter 13) or in Villa El Salvador in Lima (Tobar 1986), which, for the most part, attempt to construct local governments based on reciprocal relations and comanagement of neighborhood organizations (Giraldo and Camargo 1986). At the same time, these groups often oppose the state by re-creating an internal social life for themselves, one that is both intimate and intense, based on face-to-face relations, even in the midst of cities that only seem to offer implacable and devasting social and cultural conditions (Jelin and Vila 1987; Ovalles 1987).

How can such movements be interpreted—that is, are they regression or progress? How, for example, does one interpret the social critique that has appeared in Mexico in the shape of the anonymous masked figure *Superbarrio*, who demands democratization, justice, and the resolution of numerous concrete problems? Does this figure not embody a ferocious critique directed at the power of the Mexican state, which has proved itself incapable of responding to the city's most pressing problems, such as those experienced during the 1985 earthquake?

Another movement to be included is that of national liberation in Central America, where the issues of social transformation and national autonomy are increasingly problematized in relation to the democratization of politics and society. Here, the pluralism of identities in the process of change is acknowledged. A study of the Miskitos' role in the Nicaraguan revolution would illustrate this new attitude (Boege and López Rivas 1985).

Finally, our intention in reviewing these movements—which also include youth (Vila 1985; Valenzuela 1986), rock (Vila 1985), salsa (Colón 1986; Quintero Rivera 1985), student (Valenzuela 1986), and ethnocultural movements; those of ruling classes (Castillo 1986); and those by region (Flores 1985)—is to show the mosaic of Latin American diversity and the new complexity our region is experiencing and perhaps to convey the strength entailed by the fragmentation of collective action. There is, then, a wide spectrum of social movements. Many of them center on specific actors, others are self-referential or monadic; some are synchronic and latent, others of long duration; some are the product of the intensification of capitalism, others of exclusion; some are unprecedented, perhaps ambiguous, constantly changing, with polivalent meanings. All of the movements, based on identities that are often changing, are internally complex and produced themselves within novel historical processes. In short, they represent new historical movements in the making.

Is it possible that we are facing a new diaspora of collective action? What happened to the analysts in this quarter century? Why have we become aware only recently of the new diversity of action? Are we dealing with new actors and new social practices or, rather, with old actors utilizing new practices? Perhaps these questions are too limiting to permit an answer, except in the most ambivalent terms. But we cannot overlook the fact that the social movements of twenty-five years ago had strong state/political orientations and that, in contrast, many of today's actors are searching for their own cultural identities and spaces for social expression, political or otherwise. Perhaps these collective practices are so unprecedented and uncertain if looked at through known forms of analysis that we can detect in them, prima facie, something we can refer to as AVM strategies, in that these practices are characterized in their everydayness by: A(nomie) because they come unexpectedly and cannot be situated within existing sociological conventions (who could have predicted, for instance, the popular explosions in Caracas and Rosario?); V(olitional-emotional), given the fact that actors are motivated by subjective elements and primary relations of the "cheek-to-cheek" type; and M(utating), always changing as much at the level of historical relations as in terms of identities and the knowledge of collective action (Calderón, in press).

We should not forget that past analyses were intensely ideological and opaquely structuralist, and, thus, many of us are perplexed today because that very ideology and opaque structuralism functioned as our great paradigms. No doubt, yesterday as well as today, important phenomena, the manifestations of which so often have passed beneath our noses without our being able to grasp or understand them, have been best perceived by our artists. Perhaps, however, we learned the best possible lesson that there is to learn for those in the pursuit of knowledge: that reality is always richer than theory, that Caribbean and Latin American societies are rich in sociocultural expression, and that this expression, though often ignored by analysts, can be historically contradictory, of short or long duration, metamorphic, interconnected or hybrid, creative as well as self-destructive, and either challenging to the status quo or stubbornly conservative.

But is this proliferation of new social movements, centered in the constitution of identities, sufficient to re-create a system of social actors? Is the problem that is inherent in this explosion of dreams and projects, limited in themselves, tied to the fact that they are condemned to perish if they do not find ways to connect with each other? We will attempt to address these questions in the next section, starting with a consideration of recent important changes in sociopolitical factors in the region and their effect on the tensions experienced by social movements and their perspectives for the future. Our aim is to map out the great stage setting within which, if only metaphorically, the actors we have summoned can make themselves present.

What Happened?

Since the end of World War II, Latin America has experienced profound transformations. We would like to refer briefly to those processes that lend meaning to the thorny issues into which we are venturing. To begin, we can say that one of the greatest changes that occurred in the last four decades has been the increasing complexity of Latin American societies. For now, let us consider this society as a monolithic entity, in order to highlight our argument: that its complexity resulted in a multiplicity of social demands, most of which were neither heard nor processed and which usually had a common end point, the state. It is from this central fact that one of the most important social tensions in recent Latin American history arises. The emerging demands—regardless of which actor, sector, or segment of society voiced them—could not find accommodation within the prevailing institutional scheme, thus demonstrating the inability of today's Latin American states to respond to these demands. We propose as a hypothesis that it is from this tension that social movements arise and multiply independently of whether they involve old or new actors, old or new demands.

This is not to say that all unsatisfied social demands necessarily evolve into a social movement. Nor do we deduce that a given demand, should it become established as a social movement, will become an oppositional force within the political realm. Not all the party histories that were conceived as revolution-bound ended up as such. This party history was believed, but at the same time it became progressively diluted, exhausting itself. Nor do we wish to imply that every emerging movement opposes the state. On the contrary, to a great extent the state is no longer the "object of attraction"; instead, the Latin American sociopolitical process is undergoing a process of inflexion. This fact would explain those movements of ethical or ethnic orientation, as well as ecology movements or rock movements, that we referred to earlier in this chapter.

We also credit the proposition that social demands have exceeded in significant ways the institutional infrastructure of the state. Those demands that eventually resulted in movements had to initiate the search for a different space of expression. When society is suffocated by the state, it seeks a mechanism of defense and different ways of coming together; in the process, it makes actors of those who try to affirm themselves, to define their identities apart from and in spite of the state. Do we face an obsolete Latin American state? Do we want to reconstruct it? Or will it, instead, be necessary to replace it? But why would we want another state?[4]

What we are dealing with is a search for autonomy in a context in which autonomy is undoubtedly limited and relative. We are dealing with a reaccommodation of society, its actors, and its sectors regarding the sorts of changes that the state itself propitiated through projects of modernization, industrialization, education, and so on. The state, more successfully in some cases than in others, implemented all these projects, some of which turned against the state itself. The state "trained" society in new forms of social life only to show its inability to assimilate new groups when they became effective. This clearly implies that the great thematic of today (though extremely fragmented) is the tension between an aging state and a society that wants to grow. Essentially, there is a terrible tension between society and the state, which necessarily entails the germination of a new power structure that, for now, is more latent than manifest.

This tension between society and the state affects existing political systems, whether or not they contain real elements of representation. In fact, there is no Latin American or Caribbean country without a party system—parties appeared even in Augusto Pinochet's Chile. On the other hand, social movements also challenge the monopoly of representation, indicating, as much as the obsolescence of parties does, the need for new forms of representation. State and known systems of authority, parties and representation—are they all at a crossroads? Indeed, there is a crisis of political representation in Latin America, and a desperate, though often fruitless, search for new forms of representation is occurring, while existing forms are being rejected. For now, social movements allow us a glimpse of this process; in their newly created spaces, they attempt to nurture the seeds of their own forms of representation.

We must emphasize that the relationship between state and society is never static; rather, it is being redefined and re-created continuously. Populism, for example, has been replaced by the hope and expectation, increasingly generalized, of installing or reestablishing democracy. If we were to speak in general terms about democracy, without entering into its multiple components and dimensions, we would have to say that democracy today, as a process, must be defined as that form of government capable of generating an institutional infrastructure that can provide society with the conditions for its desired restructuring. Some of the serious challenges accompanying this process include the problems of institutional transition, the creation of new institutions and the suppression of others, and the linkage between new and continuing institutions. Ideally, a new institutional scheme would be one in which conflicts and demands are recognized and processed. What remains to be created, in short, is the institutional and political basis for a new society.

It is true that the state is a referent for almost all social movements. Whether it is being approached, opposed, or kept at a distance, in the end the state acts as a fundamental referent. Thus, in periods of authoritarian populism, the social actor was associated with the state or, rather, needed to be close to the state, while the state relied on the mechanism of co-optation. Today, however, the generalized crisis experienced in the region makes co-optation difficult on the part of the state, thereby complicating and redefining the state's relation with society. Moreover, there are segments of society today that instead of getting close to the state attempt to keep a distance from it in order to reaffirm their identity and find their "small" representativity within their own space. Thus, the state is faced with a significant breakdown and fragmentation of society, and one can hypothesize that these phenomena might spawn a new society that will eventually reconstruct its own state. It is within this tense relationship that we can find an explanation for the diversity and plurality of the social movements that flourish today in every area of our region. They are new in essence because the tension has finally crystallized. The state's response to the social demand for integration was exclusion. Is this not our form of modernity?

Yet another important process associated with today's social movements in Latin America is urbanization, a process that has made society more complex but also has activated it. This is not to say that social movements are nonexistent in rural areas; rather, it is to propose the hypothesis that urbanization has accelerated the search for spaces of expression. We know well that a close statistical relation exists between urbanization and education and that education is more actively promoted in urban areas. We also know that the urbanization process exposes society to more heterogeneous ways of living, to multiple components of political participation, and to demands of all kinds; in short, it politicizes people. Nevertheless, the tensions between political citizenship and urbanization are grave, and they continue to increase. Latin America became urbanized very rapidly in the last decades, thus constituting a propitious terrain for the "social emergence" that we are witnessing today.

In sum, although they are charaterized by "small" social actors (that is, blacks, rockers, mothers, and so forth) compared to the protagonists in earlier movements who were "grand" and more clearly visible (workers and peasants), the social movements of today nevertheless exhibit a marked political propensity. It is not impossible to imagine that these numerous small actors might communicate with each other and thereby connect their spaces, not in a simple aggregate manner, but organically. And this might provide one of the necessary conditions for reconstituting the institutional fabric of a type of democracy that is yet to come.

The Dwarf Stars

What is it that these new practices and the new values of collective action really express? Can we say that society, uncertain of its goals, is dispersing itself across an incomprehensible field of signification? Or is it, perhaps, that this same society, unequaled in its versatility of expression, is finding answers to questions that we, the analysts, have yet to formulate? We know for certain that the analytical instruments at our disposal, as well as the rationality that drives them, yield an insufficient understanding of the multiple and versatile manifestations and orientations of today's collective actors and the multiplicity of meanings of the internal worlds of these protagonists. It is obsolete to think that what we are witnessing are new, spontaneous forms or "embryos of consciousness" that at any moment might converge because of the agitation of a single party in pursuit of revolutionary change. Nor is it sufficient to view the new orientations as mere secularizations of social action, a process that could carry us from particularism to universalism.

In Latin America and the Caribbean today, after many semisuccessful or semifrustrated attempts at modernization and after terrible political defeats or long periods of reverie, societies and their social movements claim the right to their specific differences and to self-determination in making their decisions. Perhaps, because of this, the issues of cultural identity and social autonomy constitute the two greatest problems raised by society as it attempts to change and to rethink development.

When the Miskitos demand recognition, they also are affirming their desire for self-determination. When the Kataristas propose a pluriethnic state of Aymaras, Quechuas, and Tupi-Guaranís, they also are telling us that they are and want to be different. For their part, are not the ecologists, obsessed with environmental destruction and the search for a "green" life, speaking to us about a new relationship with nature? And when the Bolivian miners enter La Paz, are they not demanding a new social ethic, such as the one they exhibit through their own class solidarity?

Practically speaking, almost all social movements, in different ways and at different levels of intensity, express a critical position in respect to their dependence on political parties, state institutions, or national caudillos. If this were not true, how would we interpret the demand for autonomy and participation made by civic movements in Colombia, the tremendous absenteeism of that country's voters in national elections, the insistence on direct participation in the process of constitutional reform by workers and urban movements in São Paulo, or the Michoacán peasants' genuine distrust of party and state manipulation?

Certainly, these new movements also harbor contradictory orientations, including certain tendencies toward self-destruction. But even if one considers these negative aspects, the search for new paths of social action and representation seems to prevail. Thus, the multiplicity of practices by the new social actors in the region—stimulating, colorful, and polyvalent—teaches us that "small" does not amount to "insignificant," that small can be beautiful, terrible, and extremely complex. We must understand that this plurality of identities and the demand for autonomy that these identities present to us are essential for the development of any theory, utopia, or project for change. The question remains, however, whether these identity-centered actions are sufficient by themselves. Can they oppose present national and global power relations in order to create a new space of struggle and debate over the historicity of societies?

It would seem that the answer to this question is no, especially if we look at the international economy. The forces of international domination are generating important transformations regarding relations between capital and technology, in which capital's productivity becomes increasingly decisive. These forces are also bringing about changes at many levels, including, among others, the cultural homogenization of the market, due to the increased pervasiveness of mass media; the political victories of conservative forces in various developed countries; the loss of development visions and the destruction of the welfare state; and, of course, the external debt and the central role of finance capital in the economy. These transformations are perhaps most clearly reflected in the increasingly crucial role played by information technologies in organizing relations of domination and of daily life; in other words, they are manifested in the growing concentration and centralization of decisions in the hands of phantasmagorical elites.

Given this situation, the position of the Latin American and Caribbean states and societies tends to lose relative importance within the international market and global power relations. Paradoxically, however, these societies must necessarily become integrated into the world system because complete autonomy in the context of societal globalization seems no longer possible. The main question, it would seem, has to do with the form that this integration will assume and with its possible effect on the systems of collective action. In addition, we might hypothesize that, should this tendency toward global integration continue, the social cost might be the acceleration of social exclusion and a growing deactivation of incipient social movements. Thus, we find ourselves facing a paradigmatic situation, one that we might refer to as a "historical out-of-phase" between a diversity of social movements—fractioned, autonomous, monadic, and merely reacting to exclusion and crisis—and new patterns of domination sustained by the current technological revolution, market culture, and meaningless social relations.

Certain schools of thought, reflecting on these important sociohistorical processes, are proposing new interpretations and even some answers. We will expand on this assertion in the next section of the chapter. For some, exclusion is so strong and brutally intense that it becomes necessary to think about alternative societies—self-governed and communitarian. Theories of peasant and/ or ethnic communitarianism are especially relevant in this regard, although communitarian interpretations also offer rich theoretical lessons at the level of urban or ecological movements. Nevertheless, such formulations seem to be insufficient, and they may end by imprisoning what they attempt to liberate.

One also finds catastrophic analysts (and/or postmodernists) who consider that the current social fragmentation is so intense that it is already intrinsic to society, thus making impossible the visualization of new systems of uniting and totalizing historical action. Gino Germani, for example, believes that the transformation we have been discussing will bring about the destruction of the nation-state and the emergence of societies that are intensely fragmented and sustained by the concentration of a type of power based on a new kind of highly rational authoritarianism. Other analysts, conversely, welcome the coming of the new phenomena of collective action, believing this marks the death of the totalizing thinking of progress and modernity and the emergence of new forms of freedom.

Still other analysts insist on interpretations based on classic evolutionist models (Camacho and Menjívar, eds., 1985); for these authors, what we are witnessing is a new phase of the crisis and restructuring of global capitalism. Accordingly, social movements, always potentially led by revolutionary vanguards, would be at the threshold of a new way of articulating their systems of action, and national liberation processes would be entering into a new phase. In such schema, however (and unlike the orthodox Marxism of the past), there is a rich tendency to reevaluate social and cultural diversity, a reevaluation in which the Gramscian concepts of hegemony, historic bloc, and the nature of the national and the popular found in Antonio Gramsci's work function as a renewing matrix. In addition, more rationalist thinkers maintain that the state-social movements pattern, which organized the system of historical action in Latin America during the previous decades, has become exhausted. Now, they claim, Latin America is undergoing a process of secularization of collective action that is differentiating, at last, social action from political action and the state from society. These analysts clearly recognize the reemergence of new collective actors, but at the same time, they insist warily on the absence of new historical subjects capable of confronting the challenges of so-called postmodern society (Touraine 1987; Campero 1986; Zermeño 1990).

Regardless of which perspective is adopted, it is impossible to deny that an important change in the structure of collective action has begun to take place. The fact is there, defining a new space for theory and social action, the form of which we are beginning to visualize even if we cannot yet fully explain it. Our critical and balanced analysis of these and other analytical positions leads us to conclude that the central question before us today is the following: How can social actors reconstruct a system that enables them to relate to each other, project themselves into the political arena, and participate actively in discussions about development alternatives?

Within this new space are strife and conflicts, cultural and political affirmations, expectations and frustrations, hope and despair—all of which appear to be rooted, as a common denominator, in the struggle for a new system of political institutions conducive to new expressions and forms of representation. Although we may be unable to foresee, at this point, the content and structure of this new system, we can hear the clamor for it reverberating throughout present-day Latin America. This new institutional framework would be particularly important in the present conjuncture, not only because of the demands for democratization implicitly or explicitly made by the collective actors but also because this system could provide a propitious space for the strengthening of social movements as historical subjects. In fact, what we are witnessing is a new type of conflict that originates in peoples' efforts to bring about a new institutional order. This order may result in either an expansive democratic system that would integrate political and social democracy or, on the contrary, in yet another regime characterized by the restricted exercise of democracy (Calderón and dos Santos 1987).

Social movements might be pointing the way for the redefinition of the institutionalized political system; what they seek, for the most part, is precisely the reconstitution of the regime of rights through the transformation of the mechanism of social representation. Thus, social movements would be aspiring not only to actualize the rights of social and political citizenship (that is, participation in decisionmaking mechanisms) but also to create a space of institutional conflict in which to express their demands. We believe that this restructuring of the institutional order may well be a basic condition for constituting a new system of historical action, in which attention is drawn to the various orientations, identities, and conflicts of the social actors and the manifold character of the drama of social relations and relations of domination. How these phenomena will occur and how they will operate will depend on the specific national and international situations. For the moment, we are only asking ourselves about this crucial problem, which we believe is common to all Latin American and Caribbean historical processes.

Even in the process of disintegration and social anomie experienced in the region, Latin American societies have managed to maintain their capacity for invention and cultural creation. It is the richness and multiplicity of this experience that we have tried to capture in the first part of this chapter, albeit in a very general and provisional manner.

Shortcomings of Conventional Approaches:
Toward a Latin American Social Movements Theory

Facing Current Theoretical
and Methodological Challenges

Latin American researchers wishing to understand the nature of contemporary social movements confront a number of conflicting demands in two respects: at the level of theory and methodology and in relation to the current situation. In terms of theory and methodology, the conflict stems from the fact that, although researchers must make use of the best available theoretical and methodological tools (some of which originate outside the continent), they must also account for the specific processes proper to the region. These include the generalized defeat of popular movements and leftist parties, the weakening of the labor movement (with the exception of Brazil), deindustrialization and endemic crises, and the often aborted processes of democratization that are under way. With respect to the present situation, analysts must take as a starting point, on the one hand, the fact that (in ways rarely experienced in the countries of the center) Latin America is witnessing a reappraisal of civil society as an ordinary lebensraum, reflected in the growing importance of the micropolitics of everyday life and the pluralism of people's behavior; on the other hand, however, they cannot overlook the persistent presence in the continent of the counterparts of these highly acclaimed civil virtues, such as factionalism, violence, insecurity, and terrorism (Calderón and Piscitelli 1990).

These contradictory demands are difficult to meet by relying on existing paradigms. From the 1970s onward, however, these challenges have brought about a renewal in the agenda of Latin American social sciences. This renewal started with the realization that the dominant frameworks of the past—especially functionalism and Marxism—that for so long provided theoretical legitimacy to the social science enterprise are now relatively exhausted. Additional insights are derived from the more general questioning of the epistemology of classical physics and the reassessment of theoretical transdisciplinary models, particularly second-order cybernetics and self-reproduction and self-organizing theories (Morin 1980; Gargani 1983).

An assertion that a radical shift in theoretical approaches is well under way would be far from true. Nonetheless, it is clear that the limitations of functionalist and structuralist theories have triggered types of analysis that focus on the complexities of social life, incorporating in their explanations political, social, cultural, spatial, and temporal dimensions that are not reducible to structural determinations, economic or otherwise. The renewal we have been discussing points away from reductionist and deterministic thinking, emphasizing instead nontotalizing models and, in general, the partial nature of truth and understanding and the historical processes in which these are embedded. It was the need to fill in the gaps left by structuralist and functionalist approaches that paved the way for the theoretical innovations that permit us to visualize the new actors and processes that are becoming so salient throughout the continent.

Understanding the New Actors

It is thus our conviction that, because of their limitations, theories widely espoused in previous decades cannot account for the acceleration and deepening of the social processes triggered by the economic and political crisis of the 1980s. The prognosis of the historical processes of the region offered by these paradigms proved most inadequate, and, more importantly, so did the characterization of the social actors affected by those processes. Today, a new understanding of the factors motivating the crisis is needed.

One crucial element in this regard is the ongoing sociotechnological transformations experienced by developed societies. During the past twenty years, these societies have been undergoing a complex process of capitalist restructuring, initiated during the oil crisis of the 1970s and aggravated by the fiscal crisis of the state. The weaknesses at the level of the state, however, were more than compensated for by the dynamism of international markets in the hands of a new breed of transnational entrepreneurs. At the heart of these processes, the "new technologies"—particularly electronics and information technologies—made possible a massive increase in the productivity of capital, which swept across every domain of science and technology and changed not only the landscape of technological possibilities but also the entire set of international power relations. Needless to say, the new technologies have also greatly affected social and cultural life. How did this new scenario affect Latin America? And to what extent did this new set of forces contribute to the emergence of the new social actors described in the first part of this chapter?

Among the most salient political events of the last two decades has been the implementation of the harshest economic adjustment policies under pressure by the International Monetary Fund, not infrequently associated with populist forces now allied with neoliberal and neoconservative elites. Adjustment policies, in turn, have led to new forms of insertion in international markets, usually under the imperative of the new technologies. What is important to point out in this regard is that social actors of all types are now forced to pursue their actions within the context of this internationalization, even if from the platform of the national economy and society. It is precisely the technological capacity of the national and regional economies that determines the viability and stability of national systems or, on the contrary, their instability and marginalization (Castells 1986). Some key actors have begun to appear, such as the entrepreneurial class and the private and public research institutes linked to new technologies. But other types of actors, oppositional in character, also have become visible worldwide in the wake of these transformations, such as the Italian workers' unions at FIAT, the German Green party, and women's movements in many countries. In Latin America, the Brazilian labor movement in the automotive industry and certain movements of symbolic power, such as ethnic and human rights movements, also reflect these trends, although these latter movements have arisen more as a defensive rather than an interactive response to the internationalization process.

From a Latin American perspective, the key question becomes: Given that the essential feature of postindustrial (or "programmed") society (Touraine 1981; Castells and Laserna 1989) is the link between knowledge, information, and symbolic systems with the logic of institutionalized power, how will Latin America insert itself in the world order? What kind of new syncretism will take place between new and existing social forces, in the context of societies characterized by dependent industrialization and strong premodern (or partially and perhaps perversely modern) features? Another important characteristic of the emerging programmed society is the deepening of the management of power by the state, even if in more subtle and indirect fashion. Thus, while the state becomes more decentralized, it also reconcentrates information at the level of services, transportation, social programs, and the like. Given this trend and considering the irrational processes of privatization under way in Latin America, what is the future of the Latin American state, and what will be its shape and modes of operation?

The new technologies, it must be stressed, are more than the support of the global economy. They also determine the competitiveness of firms in international markets because the incorporation of new technologies increases the levels of capital accumulation, thus propitiating a "virtuous circle," as Castells (1986) aptly called it, among the various components of the development process: The greater the technological level, the greater the competitiveness in global markets. This, in turn, creates higher levels of economic development, thus making possible further investments in human capital and technological innovation and a more stable economy, which tends to foster greater sociopolitical stability. This stability, finally, permits more increases in technological innovation and a higher technological level. Latin America would either be marginalized from this process or participate in it in a very limited manner; what is clear is that the region will be completely integrated into its effects and modes of operation. Thus, a new situation is being created by the coexistence not of a center that exports industrial products and a periphery that exports raw materials but of regions characterized by products and processes of different technological levels (Calderón and dos Santos 1991).

Given these conditions, what is the state of the art in poststructuralist actor-oriented research in the region? A survey of recent studies in the area of social movements research clearly shows that, although certain research trends seen elsewhere are not found in Latin America, a multiplicity of approaches—sometimes in competition with one another, sometimes with a significant degree of convergence—is emerging. At least four major types of analyses and approaches can be identified:

Theories of Social Movements, Particularly Based on Those Developed by Alain Touraine. These theories have had a significant impact, although more at the level of theory and critical thinking than in terms of actual methodologies and empirical studies. Some fieldwork has been done in the region in an effort to adapt (or, rather, syncretize) the approach of sociological intervention developed by Touraine (1981, 1988a) to Latin American conditions. A good example of this kind of research is that being carried out by Eugenio Tironi and others in Santiago, Chile (Tironi 1983). It must be mentioned, nevertheless, that Touraine himself (1987, 1988b) has cautioned against this type of application; he has, in fact, emphatically stated that the categories developed by him to analyze European social movements can hardly be applicable to Latin American social actors, given their decisively political character. As he has also noted, in most if not all of the transitions from tyranny to democracy, social movements have rarely been able to overthrow the authoritarian regimes by themselves. In Touraine's view, although Latin American social movements have played a broader role than interest groups, their strength has depended more on their capacity to negotiate with the state than in their ability to foster direct action leading to regime changes.

New Forms of Class Analysis. New types of class analysis, more nuanced and disaggregated than those of the past, have been particularly relevant in Central America. It is not surprising that the value of class as an analytical tool has increased in Central America and decreased in the Southern Cone countries and the Andean region, where a certain level of political stability (even if it is precarious and highly conditioned) has emerged in the wake of democratization processes (Torres Rivas 1986; Calderón and dos Santos 1991).

Analysis of Communal Practices. At the community level, new practices have appeared that have caught the attention of social scientists. Ideas of reciprocity, cooperation, and solidarity, for instance, have been strengthened and amplified in various countries. Communal kitchens in poor urban neighborhoods, mothers' committees, consumer cooperatives, other kinds of communitarian traditions, and peasant movements in rural areas are only a few examples of the proliferation and reinvigoration of social relations forms at the community level (Fals Borda 1988b; Hardy and Raseto 1984).

The transformation of the Catholic church, after Puebla,[5] represents another important research area, and a noticeable return to a popular church is reflected in the importance of Christian base communities in social science writings (Codina 1986; Gutierrez 1973; Brischka and Mainwaring 1986). This type of communitarianism has had an impact on researchers interested in analyses based on participant observation and participatory action research—that is, those in which the researcher actually becomes involved in the actor's transformative actions and goals. Here, theory and practice, observation and action are blended in the research process; a significant component of research in these cases is a reassessment of local and practical knowledge and of community traditions, sometimes leading to the formulation of new approaches to development, such as "grass-roots" or "small-scale" development (Fals Borda 1988a, 1988b).

A More Recent Research Trend. This trend refers to the plurality of social actors and their behavior, particularly their opposition to totalizing social processes. This trend highlights the importance of new social movements proper (for example, those initiated by women, ecologists, and homosexuals), based on the search for autonomous identity, pluralism, and the right to difference. Studies by writers such as Guillermo Campero, Sergio Zermeño, Elizabeth Jelin, Joel dos Santos, and their colleagues are examples of this type of research (Calderón 1986; Evers 1985; Cardoso 1987).

A barely visible but emerging trend includes those studies couched in terms of "postdevelopment" and "postmodernism" that are conceived, broadly speaking, within poststructuralist tenets (Calderón, ed., 1988; Calderón and Piscitelli 1990; Escobar, in press a). Although ackowledging the risk of falling back into forms of global theorizing, these studies arise out of the need to link sociopolitical, economic, and technological concerns with cultural preoccupations and domains. These studies are made increasingly necessary and relevant not only by the growing danger of a nuclear holocaust but (and perhaps more pressingly for the Third World) by that of its symbolic and material annihilation, given the Third World's ever more intense subjection to forms of cultural and economic control originating in the north, such as "development" discourses and the mass media.

Irreducibility of the Latin American Social Actors to Eurocentric Standards

One critical question in the analysis of civil society is the extent to which the new social subjects observed in Latin America today exist because categories that do not derive from dominant European and North American paradigms are used—categories that are unfamiliar to the main currents of thought in those parts of the world—or if, on the contrary, the categories used to visualize the new actors have already been swallowed by the labeling clichés of these societies. Is conventional social science viable for understanding contemporary collective action? This is a highly complex question. We already referred to the limitations of Marxism and functionalism, and, more generally, the representational and positivist biases still present in standard social science must be eradicated. It is easy to forget, for instance, that social class is an analytical tool that makes possible the description of social structures in terms of a theoretical model. But more often than not, "social classes" cannot be observed in the empirical realities with which the research is concerned. Thus, whenever we address social reality, looking for the social agents of change, we do not see ready-made groups of classes acting organically as such. What we face, on the contrary, is the behavior of a multiplicity of social actors around a multiplicity of "social movements" that differ in their capacity to cope with existing social conditions.

One question that has to be addressed—loaded with methodological consequences—is whether there is not something present in the social movements of the region that is impervious to the analytical categories provided by European analysts, despite their richness. In spite of their caution, most of these analysts still fall prey to teleological and rationalistic biases, according to which certain inevitable fates await the movements; consequently, they easily overlook the will and direction of the changes prescribed by Latin American societies themselves. In fact, it is all too easy to construct a pyramid of social movements at the top of which would be placed those that directly address control over the means of production and other macro forms of power, such as the state; on such a pyramid, those social movements whose agendas refer to changes in cultural institutions, the distribution of services, or new ways of building social and interpersonal relationships would be relegated to the bottom.

But there are other notions that must also be reassessed. There is no such thing as a "Latin American historical system of action" (Touraine 1987), nor can the changes we are witnessing today be reduced to the emergence of a new system as a result of a simple and progressive rationalization of the main traits of collective social action. In a moment of worldwide paradigmatic crisis, methodology and theory are being revised daily in ways that sometimes are not so visible in the countries of the center as they are in those of the "periphery." To face this crisis, new styles of thought and research must be developed. In this respect, both the peculiarities of Latin American social formations and the traditional and historical capability of Latin American social science to elaborate syncretic thought systems place the region in a privileged position as an extraordinary social laboratory for sustained theoretical and methodological innovation. The emerging research program on social movements is one of several prominent arenas in which these innovations are currently being tested.

The time is not yet ripe to provide a final assessment as to the soundness of the theories and methodologies being produced. Nonetheless, there are already indications that Latin American researchers are leading the way—as they did earlier when they coined the local versions of dependency and modernization theories—in the production of theories of social movements that are capable of accounting for the changing realities the region is facing and will continue to face in the coming years. In fact, questions posed by social movements researchers— such as how to deal with causality, syncretism, temporality, data, and so forth— are still wide open.

Syncretism, Technology, and Social Change

Syncretism has been an important feature of Latin American social science. Syncretism is defined here as the always adaptive and transforming use of sociological approaches and concepts generated outside the region where the research is actually being carried out. Dependency and modernization theories are well-known examples. In the same way that it is incorrect to see the theory of dependency as a mere translation of theories of imperialism, it is unwise to read the diffusion of functionalism in Latin America as mere acritical intellectual borrowing. Germani did not copy Talcott Parsons—he transformed him. The same was done by Fernando Henrique Cardoso and Enzo Faletto with Karl Marx and Max Weber.[6]

In Latin America, there has always been a highly creative transformation of the categories and theories generated in the center. By syncretism, we point exactly to this process: the creative metamorphosis of old forms into new ones, the transposition of universal theories and concepts into locally relevant forms of understanding, and the rendering of ahistorical frameworks into concrete forms of explanation. Someday, perhaps, the role and importance of this type of syncretism, which characterizes the production of local theories in Latin America, will be recognized as part of a broader ecology of ideas (Bateson 1974; Geertz 1983).

Current research shows that social scientists are more likely to provide appropriate answers to today's situations by pursuing further the paths recently opened by social movements theorists (as far as the behavior of new social actors is concerned) than by treading in the paths of other approaches that, despite their relative success, were unable to change with the rhythm of the times. We live in an uncertain transition between a labor-based society and societies organized in terms of technological and informational relations; what is at stake are not only our production and consumption modes but our very ways of thought, knowledge, pleasure, and experience. Social movements theorizing may enable us to have greater control over this transition by enriching our ways of studying and practicing politics and by nurturing and carrying to new heights the value of our own traditions and ways of life.

Notes

1. Whenever we face military violence in protest movements, we witness the severance of relationships with the original social movement and its transformation into an antisocial movement. Terrorist actions are an extreme form of social movement breakup. Within antisocial movements, the references are not to social relationships but, instead, to moving subjects that become enemies. Antisocial movements are neither homogeneous nor theological entelechy. Some may become so radical as to get entangled in terrorist violence or develop into sects. An antisocial movement is the locus of terrorist production, but not every antisocial movement is synonymous with terrorism. A thorough account of this phenomenon may be found in Wiwiorka (1988).

2. *Katarismo* refers to a Bolivian peasant movement started in the 1960s by Aymara immigrants to the city of La Paz. Taking their name from Tupaj Katari, leader of the 1781 indigenous rebellion against colonial rule, the Kataristas have become an ethnic/nationalist force independent from Bolivian populists and the traditional Left. [Editors' note]

3. See Albo, in press. For ethnic problems and movements in Brazil, see dos Santos 1985; Abramo 1987.

4. The present and possible future of the state in Latin America is the subject of a large research project coordinated by CLACSO. (See the volumes published by the Projecto PNUD-UNESCO-CLACSO RLA 86/001, "Hacia un Nuevo Orden Estatal en América Latina?")

5. The emergence of liberation theology and a progressive wing of the Catholic church was marked by the Latin American Bishops Conference (CELAM) in Medellín in 1968. The 1979 CELAM conference, held in Puebla, Mexico, and inaugurated by Pope John Paul II, restricted many of the radical elements of the 1970s but without dismantling the progressive church completely. [Editors' note]

6. Gino Germani is the most well-known exponent of modernization theory; Fernando Henrique Cardoso and Enzo Faletto are the leading advocates of dependency theory. See Germani 1962; Cardoso and Faletto 1979 (originally published in Spanish in 1969). [Editors' note]

3

Marxism, Feminism, and the Struggle for Democracy in Latin America

Norma Stoltz Chinchilla

One of the liveliest debates in Western European and North American feminism during the 1970s was over the past, present, and future relationship of Marxism to feminism. In a paper first circulated among U.S. feminists in 1975, Heidi Hartmann and Ann B. Bridges argued that "the 'marriage' of marxism and feminism has been like the marriage of husband and wife depicted in English common law: marxism and feminism are one and that one is marxism. . . . Either we need a healthier marriage or we need a divorce" (Hartmann 1981: 21).

Marxist-feminists such as Mary Bailey acknowledged that, all too often, women who identified with the hyphenated theoretical perspective and political strategy had been seen as "Marxists to our feminist sisters and feminists to our Marxist brothers" and urged that work be intensified to dissolve the hyphen rather than accepting it "comfortably as a self-explanation, a cipher, instead of a project" (cited in Petchesky 1979: 375).

During the 1980s, however, work on dissolving the hyphen and transforming Marxist-feminism into a political project languished on the back burner in the United States and Western Europe as a result of a call to "join ranks" against the right-wing attack on feminism and women's rights. Toward the end of the decade, efforts to revive a Marxist-feminist dialogue were further hampered by confusion over the content of socialism and the meaning of Marxism in light of developments in the Soviet Union and Eastern Europe and the lure of a postmodern critique of the notions of "truth" and "progress." Ironically, however, it has been in the effort to build a common denominator defense of women's rights and the corresponding critique of racism in the women's movement by women of color that the need to understand differences among women and interrelationships between gender, class, and race/ethnicity and between class politics and feminist politics is finally beginning to be understood.

Reprinted by permission from *Gender & Society* 5, no. 3 (September 1991): 291–310.

In contrast, by the end of the 1980s, the synthesis of ideas from contemporary Marxist and feminist traditions and their transformation into a concrete political strategy for social change has become a high priority for a growing number of Marxists and feminists in Latin America, especially in Mexico, Nicaragua, Peru, Brazil, Chile, and the Dominican Republic.[1] While the views of activists and groups who enthusiastically embrace Marxism *and* feminism still represent a minority perspective within the organized Marxist and non-Marxist Latin American Left, they are growing in popularity as a result of their potential to link opposition movements together. This difference in emphasis in the Latin American and North American feminist movements is directly related to the different political and economic contexts within which social movements in the two areas have developed over the last decade. Conservative governments in the United States and Britain have reduced or dismantled social programs that benefit the poor and increased investment and tax incentives to the rich while maintaining the illusion that capitalism will continue to provide for all who are deserving. Events in the Soviet Union and Eastern Europe are generally interpreted by the press in those countries as definitive proof that socialism is terminally ill while capitalism is eternally young.

Meanwhile, the basically capitalist Latin American economies are undergoing one of their worst crises in history with devastating effects on the living standards of the majority of people. Widespread opposition to the human rights abuses of authoritarian military governments in some countries has resulted in chronically unstable elected civilian governments unable to retain legitimacy because of their inability to overcome a massive foreign debt, stagnant or negative economic growth, and antipopulist austerity programs imposed by the International Monetary Fund. In other countries, such as Mexico, civilian, ostensibly democratic governments have become increasingly identified with human rights abuses at the same time that their traditionally populist internal economic policies are increasingly dismantled by economic policies demanded by foreign banks.

In response to these crises, a myriad of social and political groups have mobilized with new demands, tactics, utopian visions, and definitions of what it means to "be political" or "do politics" (*hacer política*) or, in the case of Central America, "make revolution" (*hacer revolucíon*) (see Kirkwood 1987; Nun 1989). The range of issues represented in such groups and organizations is great—daily survival, independent labor organizing, human rights, democracy, antiracism, autonomy for indigenous peoples, feminism, and the environment. Their degree of autonomy from the state, political parties, or armed revolutionary organizations in the case of Nicaragua, El Salvador, and Guatemala varies—but all are experimenting with new ways of facilitating direct political participation by the diversity of groups that arise from capitalism's multiple and complex contradictions. In the process, the unilateral "either/or" choices that dominated Latin American Marxist discussions in the 1970s (reform *or* revolution, class *or* ethnicity, rural *or* urban, armed *or* electoral struggle, etc.) are giving way to a more complex view of how individuals and social groups influence the course of history.[2] The issues raised by these contemporary social movements in their search for a more democratic and egalitarian society have profoundly affected the thinking of key feminist activist-theorists and adherents to what might be called, for lack of a better term, *the New Marxism* in Latin America.[3] The ideas that have emerged from these experiences are important for anyone interested in forging a class- (and racial/ethnic-) conscious feminism and feminist Marxism and for those interested in assessing the significance of such efforts.

This chapter presents a discussion of the relationship of feminism and Marxism to ideas about democracy and socialism and about the relationship of Marxist and feminist perspectives to each other in the context of contemporary social movements in Latin America. The basic argument is that there is a growing convergence of thinking on issues that once divided or were the source of serious tension: the importance of pluralism and democracy and its relationship to the idea of plural (potentially revolutionary) social subjects or actors (such as women) and the relationship of democracy to the principle of autonomy for popular organizations (such as those composed of women) in their relationship to the state and to political parties (including vanguard or cadre organizations). Related to each of these debates are new conceptions of the relationship of class to gender and of daily life to the struggle for democracy and socialism. Before discussing the content of these converging ideas, the evolution of contemporary feminist and New Marxist movements in Latin America will be reviewed to provide a context for discussion.

Latin American Feminism's "Second Wave"

The appearance of a second wave of Latin American feminism is often attributed to an external international event: the United Nations Conference on Women held in Mexico City in 1975. The conference was undeniably an important catalyst in many Latin American countries for discussions about women's situation. Preparations for and follow-up from the conference stimulated the formation of many official and unofficial groups and conferences, conferring on them a degree of legitimacy, protection from political persecution, and, in some cases, access to external funding. Although government-sanctioned activities were often short-lived and heavily biased toward the involvement of elite professional women, official party female office holders, and spouses of high government officials, individuals and groups with other agendas (particularly journalists, students, academics, trade union activists, and opposition party activists) were able to take advantage of the political and intellectual opening created by this international event to hold their own discussions of women's condition and proposals for improving it (see Alvarez's [1990a] description of this process in Brazil).[4]

But to link Latin American second-wave feminism so intimately to the conference is to underestimate the importance of feminist activities prior to the conference, in countries such as Mexico, Brazil, and Argentina, and the hostile environment that kept the ranks of feminism small and relatively isolated from other social and political sectors until the end of the decade (see accounts by Alvarez 1990a; Chester 1986; Lau 1987; Lozano and Gonzalez 1986; Kirkwood 1987, 1986).

During official and unofficial proceedings of the conference and in a wide variety of public arenas afterward, religious and political groups representing a range of political inclinations argued that feminism was alien to and/or inappropriate for the Latin American context. The Catholic church argued that women were destined, by nature and divine plan, to be self-sacrificing and self-abnegating vessels of virtue and guardians of family and public morality. Feminism, they argued, pointed women in the direction of materialism, individualism, and egotism and, thus, was inherently opposed to church doctrine.

Liberal and nationalist politicians, on the other hand, declared that males and females were already "different but equal" in Latin American culture and argued that feminism demotes women from their elevated special status. Left groups, influenced by Stalinism's hostility to feminism and its mechanical, economistic stageist conceptions of social change ("first the socialization of the means of production and the incorporation of women into wage labor, then automatic equality for women in the family and society" [see Molyneux 1982]), warned women that feminism was a bourgeois deviation from the primary focus of the class struggle. This sequencing of demands was justified by some Marxists on the grounds that sexism could not be eliminated *without* the overthrow of capitalism. Other Marxists argued, however, that capitalism was gender neutral and could theoretically *concede* gender equality as a result of its pursuit of cheap labor and profits while still leaving exploitation on the basis of class intact.[5]

Reinforcing traditional religious and left thinking, the Latin American mass media stigmatized feminism as a "radical and crazy" movement of relatively privileged, but unhappy, women from economically developed countries (Chinchilla 1985–1986, 1977, 1990; Cordero 1986; Molina 1986; Murguialday 1989; Portugal 1986). The low level of class, ethnic, and international political consciousness among U.S. women constituted a serious obstacle to fruitful exchange of ideas and experiences with Latin American women during the international conferences held during this early period.[6] Latin American women who had attempted to organize feminist groups after having lived or traveled abroad tended to be viewed as having lost their cultural and national perspective.

The birth of second-wave feminism in Latin America was made more difficult by the loss of a collective memory of the earlier period of Latin American feminism, particularly the ideas and organizing experiences of radical, Socialist, and anarchist women. Historical accounts of earlier feminist efforts available during the late 1970s emphasized reformist tendencies in nineteenth- and twentieth-century Latin American feminism and the upper- and middle-class origins of radical as well as reformist feminist leaders.[7] It took a while to rediscover and disseminate examples of Socialist and working-class women's efforts to make women's equality a priority in early twentieth-century social movements, such as the Socialist women in the autonomous Movement for the Liberation of Chilean Women (MEMCH) in the 1930s and the more than 50,000 Mexican women representing some 800 organizations and a variety of social sectors and classes organized in the autonomous coalition *Frente Unico Pro Derecho de la Mujer* (Molina 1986: 19; Rascón 1975: 160–161). It is not surprising that the growing influence of feminism in many Latin American countries (most notably Mexico and Chile) coincides with the recovery of a progressive women's history that had been hidden for many years.

Despite the ideological containment of previous decades, by the mid-1980s, conditions for and attitudes toward women's involvement in politics had begun to change in dramatic ways throughout the hemisphere. First, women were involved in politics to a degree and in a variety of forms without precedent in Latin American history (Alvarez 1989a, 1990a; de Barbieri and de Oliveira 1986; Jaquette, ed., 1989; Jelin, ed., 1990). Secondly, women's organizations were beginning to carve out a space for themselves in local and national political life, and feminism was slowly making inroads into political and academic institutions as reflected in a growing number of consciousness-raising and political action groups, service and popular education centers, research institutes, and university-based women's studies programs (Deutsch 1989). Finally, a conscious Marxist-feminist tendency had begun to appear, in theory and in practice, in Latin American Marxism, and the diffusion of a feminist perspective and agenda within popular movements had been adopted as a priority by a number of feminist groups (Flora 1984; Gonzalez, Loria, and Lozano 1988; Lozano and Gonzales 1986).[8]

The most dramatic early examples of women's contributions to a redefinition of what constitutes political activity or "doing politics" in Latin America come from the protests of Argentine and Chilean women against military dictatorships in their countries even when other groups were still reluctant to confront the regimes openly and directly. Women in Argentina used their "moral force" as mothers, grandmothers, and sisters of the disappeared to demand an accounting of relatives who had been victims of political repression, while in Chile women converted homes and neighborhoods into centers of collective resistance and survival after the emergence of the Pinochet dictatorship (Agosín 1987; Feijoó 1989). In both cases, these struggles by women contributed significantly to the demise of the respective military regimes. In the last two years before the Somoza dictatorship in Nicaragua was overthrown in 1979 (and throughout the hemisphere during the decade of the 1980s), women acquired unprecedented importance in opposition movements, often through new organizational forms and with new tactics that they themselves helped to invent. In rural areas, women became active in peasant organizations and in ethnic/racial movements; in urban areas, they formed the backbone of neighborhood-based grass-roots protest movements. In both rural and urban areas, they formed the foundation of the Christian base community and human rights movements (Alvarez 1988; Chinchilla 1990; Jaquette, ed., 1989; Jelin, ed., 1990; Randall 1981).

Women's growing participation in these protest and social change movements during the 1980s was often derived from an attempt to fulfill, rather than subvert, the traditional gender division of labor (mothers entering the public sphere to save the lives of their children, housewives turning to collective action to provide for the survival of their families, etc.). But the experiences women gained in the process often created fertile ground for links between a gender-specific consciousness (what Molyneux [1986] calls "women's practical interests"), feminist consciousness ("women's strategic interests"), and social consciousness (consciousness of class, social sector, nation, etc.).

Parallel to women's growing visibility in nontraditional forms of civilian politics was the unprecedented incorporation of women into cadre revolutionary organizations and political parties in countries with broad-based revolutionary movements, such as Nicaragua, El Salvador, and Guatemala (Chinchilla 1990; Gargallo 1987; Murguialday 1990). The ties of these women with women in neighborhood and other organizations nurtured their appreciation of women's potential for courageous and creative protest and encouraged them to analyze the concrete conditions of women's lives in greater depth (Randall 1981; my interviews with Guatemalan women participants in politico-military organizations). Women's visibility in human rights organizations and groups for the defense of basic survival, in turn, encouraged women in traditionally male-dominated class organizations (such as trade unions) to form women's caucuses and commissions and create mechanisms for greater representation of women in leadership (for example, the Nicaraguan Agricultural Workers Union) (Chinchilla 1990; Criquillón and Espinoza 1987; Murguialday 1990). Increased contact with feminist ideas within and without the movement, at international conferences, and as a result of international solidarity efforts and the ability to test ideas in practice served as incubators for a new-born revolutionary Marxist-feminist current within socialism and the feminist movement.

Latin American Marxism's Internal Critique

As early as the 1950s, decades before the changes in Eastern Europe and the dramatic increase of women's involvement in Latin American politics, Latin American Marxists critical of traditional Communist parties' intellectual and strategic dependence on the Soviet Union embarked on a search for an indigenous version of Marxism capable of guiding movements for social change. The search led to experiments with various revolutionary strategies and theoretical perspectives and the eventual rediscoveries of works of earlier Latin American Socialist and nationalist revolutionary thinkers, such as Jose Carlos Mariátegui (Peruvian), Agusto Cesar Sandino (Nicaraguan), and Carlos Fonseca Amador (Nicaraguan). During the 1970s and 1980s, these discussions drew on the writings of Italian Marxist Antonio Gramsci and "liberal Socialist" Norberto Bobbio (1989), the experiences and ideas of 1960s social movements from around the world, and theoretical debates among Western European and U.S. Marxists (see Barros 1986; Burbach and Nuñez 1987; Cueva 1987; Hodges 1974; R. Munck 1990; Moulián 1982; Portantiero 1982; Vasconi 1990; Winn 1989).

Democracy and feminism were not, however, topics of serious discussion in the search for an indigenous Latin American Marxism until the 1980s. During the 1960s, the Latin American (non-Communist party) New Left revolutionary groups' assessment of the alternatives for the region "left very little room for seriously integrating democracy" into their theory and practice (Barros 1986: 53). Reformist democratic governments were seen as incapable of breaking the cycle of economic stagnation; economic development was seen as the key missing element for Latin America with little attention paid to political institutions. No form of development was seen as possible unless it challenged the dominance of (capitalist) imperialism; socialism and fascism were seen as the only alternatives, and the only road to socialism was a revolution (like that of Cuba). Democracy was seen as a facade used by anti-Communist reformist governments posing as alternatives to the Left. The New Left and the Old Left (the Soviet-aligned Communist parties) disagreed on the need for development of the productive forces in stages and the potentially progressive character of a "national bourgeoisie." Both shared, however, "the objectivistic Marxism of the Third International":

> The Communist parties, ideologically subordinate to the international line of Moscow, despite their electoral activities, never produced any democratic theory. In the term "bourgeois-democratic" the weight has always been on the side of the "bourgeois" with the "democratic" side of the conjunction left dangling. For the revolutionary Left, on the other hand, democracy could have no value as a mode of will formation: ends were known, the real problem was one of the proper combination of tactics and strategy (Barros 1986: 53–54).

The underlying view of politics was instrumental, even for groups that emerged in countries with formal democratic political structures (periodic elections, etc.). "At best," Barros concludes, "democracy presented the possibility of 'an additional form of struggle.' But just as often, it was rhetorically cast off as a bourgeois trap" (1986: 54).

By the mid-1970s, the economic expansion of the 1960s had been replaced by significant economic stagnation and a decline in living standards of the majority of people. Right-wing military dictatorships had replaced civilian governments in a majority of countries in the hemisphere (e.g., Brazil, Argentina, Uruguay, Chile, Peru, Guatemala, El Salvador); officially sanctioned repression and torture became commonplace. These trends, together with changes in the demand for women's labor (as the result of the internal capitalist expansion and increased penetration of foreign multinational corporations), heightened women's importance as economic producers, sustainers of household units, and spokespersons for human rights, social justice, and peace (Chinchilla 1990; Murguialday 1989). They also created a broad spectrum of individuals and organized groups that stood to benefit from an end to dictatorship.

In response to the systematic violence and intolerance of differences imposed by authoritarian governments, Marxists joined others in the denunciation of authoritarianism in the name of human rights. The defense of life replaced the defense of a political agenda. All statist perspectives (including Socialist ones) were reconsidered with a critical eye; formal and "real" democracy came to be seen as compatible by some and necessarily interconnected by others. Brazilian Marxist Michel Lowy's argument that democracy is the essence of socialism reflects the latter view:

> Democracy is not a problem of "political form" or institutional "superstructure": it is the *very content* of socialism as a social formation in which workers and peasants, young people, women, that is, the people, effectively exercise power and democrati-

cally determine the purpose of production, the distribution of the means of production, and the allocation of the product (1986: 264).

Just as important, because of its link to contemporary feminism, was the discovery by some male leftists of the importance of the invisible activities that make up daily life (*lo cotidiano*). This discovery, made because survival itself was threatened by the harsh conditions of military dictatorship, was interjected by some into theoretical discussions of the relationship between democracy and socialism. Norbert Lechner, for example, linked successful democratization to changes in daily life and political culture: "[Democracy's] possibilities and tendencies are conditioned by the standards of normalcy and naturalness that common people develop in their daily life. It is the concrete experiences of violence and fear, misery and solidarity, that give democracy and socialism their meaning" (1990: 4).

Critics have argued that Marxist advocates of a greater emphasis on democracy have not clearly articulated its relationship to socialism, particularly under the precarious material conditions of Third World societies, and that some position statements seem to imply that democracy can automatically evolve into socialism. Nevertheless, the attempt to elaborate a Marxist understanding of democracy and daily life is an important step forward and, in my opinion, an essential precondition for a convergence with contemporary feminism and with contemporary social movements in general. The discussions of feminist and Marxist views on the notion of a plurality of potential revolutionary actors (as opposed to simply the industrial working class) and the application of the principle of autonomy to popular and vanguard or cadre organizations, to which I now turn, are meant to underscore this point.

Democracy and the "Pluralism of Social Subjects"

The tendency of orthodox Marxists to rank social sectors and classes according to their revolutionary potential, with industrial wage workers at the top, has always been a problem for feminists who, as housewives and nonindustrial workers, have frequently been seen only as auxiliaries to the "central actors" in the class struggle. Feminist arguments about the interrelatedness of production and reproduction have helped to clarify the centrality of women to the struggles of the classes and social sectors to which they belong.

But, in addition to the new awareness of women's roles in reproduction, another important conceptual revolution within Latin American Marxism has begun to take place, influenced by the social movements of the 1960s and 1970s, the writings of Italian Marxist Antonio Gramsci, and the experience of the Nicaraguan revolution: the acceptance of the view that the contradictions of contemporary capitalism may create a plurality of potential social subjects (i.e., people who act politically on their own behalf) that any broad social or revolutionary movement must learn to articulate (i.e., coordinate or interrelate) for long-term revolutionary change. Although this is true for contemporary capitalism generally, it is particularly true where capitalism has developed extremely unevenly as a result of conquest, colonialism, intervention, the appropiation of precapitalist structures, and a continuing pattern of external economic and political dependence. Class struggles, in and of themselves, are necessarily complex and multidimensional.

Within the working class alone in Latin America, there are often large differences in age (an age structure highly skewed toward those under 25 years), ethnicity, employed and unemployed status, concentration in services versus manufacturing, formal and informal sectors, rural versus urban areas, and so on (Chinchilla and Dietz 1982; Petras 1981; Portes 1985: 16, 22–23; Vilas 1986). Beyond that, class struggles can combine with cross-class aspects of gender, ethnic, generational, and other struggles in important and potentially powerful ways.

The extent to which these various social groups, fractions of classes, or classes jell as a coherent political force depends not only on the political character of the opposed regime (e.g., the internal divisions in its base of support or factors such as the indiscriminate character of its repression) but also on the capacity and political will of the vanguard organization, if such an organization exists. The character and coherence of the opposition force is also determined by the past history of resistance and protest and the way in which real alliances have been forged in struggle (Vilas 1986: 21).

Roger Burbach, a U.S. Marxist theorist/activist, and Orlando Nuñez, a Nicaraguan Sandinista theorist/activist, referred to this pivotal group who can spark revolutionary movements and help lead them as a "third force" that, unlike propertyless wage laborers, is "not a new class or even a single consolidated class" but a category made up of "diverse social groups and social movements that are more defined by their social and political attributes than by their relationship to the work-place" (1987: 64). The radical potential of this force comes from the "discrimination and oppression they experience in the general social structure . . . in the evolution of capitalist society as a whole, i.e., in the totality of social and class structure" (1987: 64). Although the composition of the third force will "vary from country to country, and particularly between the developed and underdeveloped countries" (1987: 65), examples of social groups in Central America that make up this category, some of which have a multiclass composition themselves, include women, ethnic minorities, and young people.

Burbach and Nuñez did not point out any particular contribution that women's organizing or feminism can make toward the class struggle and the building of socialism. Latin American Marxist-feminists do, however, explicitly discuss these contributions and interconnections in their writings and documents. Activists in mixed groups such as shantytown and trade union organizations in Chile, for example, turn the traditional argument that feminism is divisive on its head and argue instead that men and women will remain divided unless they engage in a common political project that acknowledges women's subordination and directly confronts machismo. A feminist perspective thus can make the class struggle "more efficient."

This argument, embedded in a broader argument that the revolution should be a popular one in which the majority of people participate and contribute, made it easier for Nicaraguan feminists to convince some key male leaders that revolutionary feminism was "a necessity and an imperative for the survival and development of the Revolution and not just an ethical principle or, much less, a secondary task" (Criquillón 1987: 193).

Having said this, the exact relationship between class and gender has yet to be clarified among those who would sympathize with the above position. Burbach and Nuñez, on the one hand, do not appear to agree with some European theorists who appear to abandon altogether the notion of a "privileged articulating principle" (that is, primary contradiction), in either the alliances needed to overthrow capitalism or in the construction of socialism (see, for example, Mouffe 1988). They argue that "the working class will always be at the core of any revolutionary process [and] because of its central position in society, it alone can be the central social force in building a socialist society" (Burbach and Nuñez 1987: 64–65). Many Latin American feminists, on the other hand, adamantly refuse to establish a hierarchical relationship between class and gender oppression. Instead they emphasize the ways in which class struggle and gender issues intersect. (Chuchryk 1989: 171). The views of Chilean sociologist Julieta Kirkwood, a pioneer feminist theorist/activist whose talks and writings had a major impact on Latin American feminists, are typical in this respect:

> It is not part of the [feminist] project to deny the reality and validity of the analysis of class domination. On the contrary, a feminist analysis, which exposes the economistic bias of class analysis enriches it. . . . In fact, feminism truly constitutes a social movement for liberation in Chile because it successfully links the struggle against class and sex oppression simultaneously (Kirkwood 1983: 8–9).

Although this formulation leaves questions about the interrelationship between class and gender unanswered, it is not a dismissal or underestimation of the importance of class. On the contrary, second-wave Latin American feminism has generally been distinguished by a high level of class consciousness since its emergence, and this class consciousness is central to its theoretical and practical discussions.

There is a growing recognition, for example, that women of different classes and sectors are likely to come to feminism in different ways: some through general social consciousness (class, nation, ethnicity), some through struggle around practical gender interests (which tend to be highly differentiated by class and ethnicity), and some through an analysis of gender subordination (strategic gender interests). These diverse starting points inevitably imply diverse forms of action through which women may contribute to the construction of an individual and collective gender identity (Murguialday 1990).

The central knot of feminist practice, particularly for those who aspire to create a feminist current within popular movements, is how to link practical (women's) interests derived from the existing gender division of labor and strategic (feminist) gender interests derived from a critique of the existing gender hierarchy. Chilean feminists have attempted to do so when they link authoritarianism in the family to authoritarianism (dictatorship) in society, and Nicaraguan feminists do when they link women's demands to the overall success of the revolution. Neither aspect of women's interests, Peruvian feminist Virginia Vargas points out, is complete without the other: "The challenge is to achieve the articulation of both. This means politicizing practical gender interests in such a way that they advance towards a modification in the situation of the subordination of women" (1989: 82–83).

Democracy, Autonomy, and Vanguard Organizations

Closely related to the notion of a plurality of social subjects is the argument that popular organizations have the right to autonomy in relation to the state and political parties, that is, the right to carve out a political space within which they can choose their own leaders, criteria for membership, and political agenda. In the case of women's organizations, Gonzalez, Loria, and Lozano suggest that it also means "the creation of a correlation of forces favorable to the raising of women's demands, one which does not imply their subordination" (1988: 22). At the same time, it means the existence of safe spaces where women can discover their identities, give mutual support, build trust, explore previously forbidden topics (such as women's bodies and sexuality), and invent new forms of political struggle or definitions of what it means to "do politics." In Latin America, these safe spaces are usually linked to political activity in such a way that autonomy, for the majority of groups, is not simply a defensive concept and does not signify isolation or ghettoization in "a world of women" (Vargas 1989: 97). Murguialday pointed out that, in fact, the spaces that women have created in different Latin American countries over the last decade have facilitated coordination with other struggles and social groups such as Christian base communities, urban social movements, human rights groups, ethnic movements, and youth groups. Meetings conducted in these spaces have been the catalyst for theoretical and ideological discussions about the ways in which different contradictions intersect and different demands and struggles interconnect (e.g., domestic violence and political violence, male dominance over women and children in the domestic sphere, capitalist dominance in society, the interaction of inequalities based on class, gender, and ethnicity, etc.) (Vargas 1989: 9). This emphasis on understanding interconnections represents an important break from the past when debates centered around the ranking of different oppressions. Autonomy thus defined "entails a recognition of the diversity of social interests, the refusal of class reductionism, and, above all, of economism" (R. Munck 1990: 117–118).

An important aspect of the autonomy of popular organizations involves their relationship to a vanguard or cadre political organization (where it exists). Some Latin American feminists have argued that the concept of a revolutionary "vanguard" is *inherently* inconsistent with the kind of democratic, popular movement of which the women's movement is, or aspires to be, a part (see, for example, Costa Rican feminist Ana Sojo 1985: 90). Vargas, a founding member of the feminist movement in Peru, is critical of cadre organizations' tendencies toward "homogenizing opinions, of liberating subjects from their responsibility for vital decisions, of repressing their freedom and creativity" (1989: 37). She believes that she and other activists were guilty, in the early stages of the Peruvian women's movement, of reproducing some of the negative characteristics they had learned in cadre organizations:

> We conceived of ourselves as a group of people who were holders of the truth. We considered that only those who were faced with double exploitation, of class and gender, were justified in demanding their rights. . . . We accepted the principle of the vanguard as the superior bearer of knowledge, which was characterized by messianism and "machismo." In this view, people—in our case women—were regarded as virgin lands where the seeds of wisdom could be sown (1988a: 137).

Others argue, however, that the *concept* of a vanguard is not inherently problematic, but certain definitions and practices that have characterized it in the past are (for example, a sense of elitism, a "top-down" internal and external leadership style, intolerance of minority views, suppression of gender, and racial/ethnic conflict within the vanguard organization). Burbach and Nuñez, for example, believe that "there is a need for direction and guidance in any revolutionary process but this direction should help nurture and organize the democratic tendencies rather than repress them" (1987: 49), and some feminists use the term to describe the role feminists should play within the broader (nonfeminist or prefeminist) women's movement (i.e., as teacher and student, repository, organizer, and interpreter of past and present experiences and as link between the different parts of a global cause or struggle) (Gonzalez, Loria, and Lozano 1988: 22; EMAS et al. 1987: 293, 332–333). This latter view seems to be consistent with other attempts to redefine the role of vanguard groups or parties in Latin American political struggles (see Lowy 1986: 272; Brown 1990).

Although Latin American feminists, including Marxist-feminists, vary in the degree to which they believe a vanguard political organization is necessary for revolution, there is considerable consensus about the reasons why organizational autonomy for popular organizations is essential for democracy and the building of socialism. The strong arguments of independent feminists (many of whom are ex-party militants) in favor of autonomy frequently put them in conflict with women from left political parties who come from a tradition of party control over mass organizations. This also creates tensions between independent feminists and female political party militants when they work together in the same coalitions and attend the same conferences; it adds to the pressure on those who try to be activists in both types of groups at once, the condition Latin American feminists refer to as "double militancy." Female militants of political parties frequently feel that independent feminists regard them as impure in their feminism and inherently subordinate to men in their political party activities. Feminists, on the other hand, often feel that their credentials as revolutionaries and commitment to class as a fundamental axis for understanding Latin American society are constantly being challenged (Chuchryk 1989a; Bonder 1989; Kirkwood 1986; Sternbach et al., Chapter 12).

In the best of circumstances, however, the interaction between women militants of political parties and independent feminists in a multiplicity of forms (in consciousness-raising groups, battered women's shelters, and soup kitchens as well as multiorganizational bodies coordinating political protest) has a positive effect on both groups of women, reinforcing the goal of a class-conscious current among feminists and making left political parties more open to feminism (Molina 1986).

Conclusion

It is common for Marxists critical of feminism and feminists critical of Marxism to see their own intellectual tradition and the social movements based on it as dynamic, evolving, and self-correcting while regarding the other as unable to transcend earlier weakness. Thus, Marxism is often seen by feminist critics as inherently economistic, reductionist, and gender-blind, whereas Marxist critics of feminism often regard it as inherently white, middle class, "First World," and reformist.

The reality is, of course, that both Marxist and feminist thinking have changed in important ways over the last two decades. For Latin America Marxists, for example, the hope of overthrowing corrupt, unpopular, and elite-based authoritarian regimes as a result of the efforts of a small but dedicated clandestine guerrilla band has been exchanged for the growing consensus that the power of entrenched privileged elites and their external allies can only be overcome by the broadest, most democratic grass-roots movement possible. Feminism is seen by a growing number of Latin American Marxists as not only compatible with this effort but essential to it. The very existence of new social movements in Latin American societies (i.e., the multiplicity of class, sectorial, and other opposition groups that challenge some aspect of authoritarian relationships, exploitation, or alienation) challenges left political parties to develop more tolerant, democratic, and pluralistic political practices in spite of a weak democratic tradition.

The mainstream of Latin American feminism takes Marxist contributions to the understanding of class and the mode of production seriously, while contributing to an understanding of the interconnectedness of production and reproduction, practical and strategic gender interests, and an evolving understanding of the relationship between class and other forms of oppression. In addition, feminist demands for equality in the social relations of daily life, control over reproduction, and greater freedom in sexual expression draw attention to the need for a holistic view of change and offer a vision of the future in a context decidedly lacking in alternative utopias (Arizpe 1990; Lozano and Gonzales 1986; Vargas 1988a).

Thus, while many feminists in developed capitalist countries choose to ignore or consciously reject Marxism as outmoded, irrelevant, or, worse yet, an obstacle to the emancipation of women, feminist activists in Latin America are adding to and converging with new Marxist thinking in important ways. Their debates and discussions are not simple reflections of changes in intellectual trends in the developed countries (although they are inevitably influenced by them) but are also reflections of changed social, economic, and political structures within such societies as well as conclusions drawn by activists from their own and others' successful and unsuccessful organizing experiences. The evolving understanding of the interrelationship between women's movements, the class struggle, and the struggle for socialism is not only grounded in the particular realities of Latin American societies (the complexity of the class structure, for example, and the extent to which it has been conditioned by external forces, i.e., imperialism) but in a new appreciation of the role of culture, ideology, democratic practice, and daily life in the struggle against capitalism and the construction of socialism. These are insights that have potentially universal importance for anyone who seeks to understand the link between class, race/ethnicity/nationality, and gender and between Marxism and feminism.

Notes

1. See, for example, *Debate Feminista* (Lamas, ed., 1990); FEM magazine; the publications of ISIS International; and reports (*memorias*) from hemisphere-wide conferences, such as the Fourth and Fifth Feminist Encuentros. Ironically absent from the list of countries is Argentina, which had one of the hemisphere's strongest first-wave feminist movements (see Carlson 1988). Since the 1970s, a variety of feminist groups and research centers have existed in Argentina, with a resurgence of feminist activity in the 1980s, but they appear to be smaller in size and influence than those in the other countries listed and reflect a separation between activists and professionals (Chester 1986). However, some 5,000 women attended the national feminist conference in preparation for Argentina's hosting of the Fifth Latin American and Caribbean Feminist Encounter in November 1990, and the encounter itself was more than twice as large as the previous one in Taxco, Mexico.

2. This is not to imply that economically and politically conservative "New Right" and "neoliberal" (free market) ideas do not have a growing number of followers among intellectuals and politicians in Latin America as elsewhere in the world, but it is to argue that these intellectual and political trends offer little hope for improvement in the situation of the vast majority of Latin Americans who are poor, peasant, and working class and are thus likely to continue to encounter relatively strong organized opposition. Postmodernism has also begun to be discussed among Latin American intellectuals, but it would be logical to anticipate that it will undergo significant adaptation to the Latin American reality before gaining many adherents.

3. The term *New Marxism* is problematic in that it is not necessarily used by the adherents themselves; nor is it particularly accurate because some of the ideas it encompasses have roots in early twentieth-century Marxist writings and social movements. Nevertheless, I have chosen to use the term because a more satisfactory term does not appear to be available.

4. For more detailed descriptions of the origins of recent feminist movements in Latin America, see articles in EMAS et al. (1987), Jaquette, ed. (1989), and FEM (numerous issues), as well as works by Alvarez (1990a), Chuchryk (1984), Murguialday (1990, 1989), Vargas (1989), and Chinchilla (1990).

5. For a succinct composite of other objections to feminism advanced by Chilean Marxists as recounted by past and present women militants, see Chuchryk (1984).

6. See, for example, Bolivian Indian Domitila's account of her encounter with U.S. feminist Betty Friedan (Barrios de Chungara 1978).

7. The educated middle-class origins of earlier feminists were seized on by male-dominated left groups in the 1970s as evidence that feminism in Latin America had been an *inherently* middle-class concept. In fact, the social origins of core Latin American feminist activists, past and present, had not been that different from those of the leadership of many male-dominated left groups, especially in their early stages of formation. Though bourgeois historians are partly to blame for overlooking this earlier history, the close ties between Latin American Marxism and the international line of the Soviet Union are also at fault. The Soviet-inspired anti-Fascist popular front policy of the late 1930s and early 1940s led to the dissolution of the Mexican

women's front (in favor of undifferentiated support for Cárdenas) and a lack of support for the principle of organizational autonomy for popular organizations, thus contributing to the prolonged period of feminist silence.

8. In the Fourth Latin American Feminist Encounter held in Taxco, Mexico, in October 1987, this "popular feminist" perspective appeared to have the sympathy of the majority of the 1,500 women in attendance, many of whom were grass-roots activists in unions; neighborhood, housewife, and peasant organizations; and in religious groups, who publicly declared their receptivity to feminism for the first time. (Monroy Limón 1987; "Compañeras, Solidarity, Movement" 1988; Sternbach et al., Chapter 12; Zimmerman 1987).

4

The Study of New Social Movements in Latin America and the Question of Autonomy

Judith Adler Hellman

The study of social movements in Latin America has come of age, with the program of the fifteenth meeting of the Latin American Studies Association in 1989 featuring no fewer that fifteen panels on the subject. The fact that women's, peace, ecological, neighborhood self-help, and similar social movements have emerged in Latin America, Western Europe, and North America has tempted some theorists to draw broad cross-national generalizations about the social movements phenomenon. However, as stimulating as it is to compare movements on three continents, it is important to identify both the differences and the similarities between the movements that have developed in advanced industrialized countries and those that have grown in Latin America.

Important Distinctions

Some who come to their interest in these movements through experience in Latin America have been quick to assert that social movements arise where the Left has been suppressed, precisely *because* it has been suppressed (see, for example, Evers 1985). The development of grass-roots movements in places like Chile, Brazil, or Mexico is often taken as evidence that such movements result from the stifling effect of authoritarian rule. From these cases, it would seem that movements spring up in settings marked by very imperfect democratic institutionalization or limited opportunities for open political expression. New movements are thought to appear in order to fill the vacuum created by the repression of other legitimate forms of popular organization and representation.

Although this assertion may hold for most Latin American cases, a quick look at the development of new social movements in Western Europe indicates that movements there (in Italy, France, and Germany) expanded most rapidly during a period when the formal organized parties and unions of the Left were growing in strength, electoral support, and political influence. The new movements represented a development that paralleled but did not substitute for traditional political participation. What the movements did was *extend* the "political space" available to citizens, bringing into the public realm the concerns of "everyday life" and of the "personal" (J. Hellman 1988).

Apart from the analytical problem of accounting for the emergence of social movements in starkly contrasting political systems, yet another key distinction makes it difficult to draw generalizations that cover new social movements around the world. In all cases, new movements may be distinguished from traditional political parties and unions in that they focus on the realm of consumption rather than production. But new social movements in Europe mainly represent a response to postindustrial contradictions, and those in Latin America primarily arise in response to clearly material demands. In advanced industrial societies, movement participants struggle to overcome feelings of personal powerlessness generated by the satisfaction of material needs without a corresponding sense of full self-realization. In contrast, Latin American participants may well come to enjoy some greater sense of personal fulfillment as a consequence of their involvement in new social movements. But their struggles are principally organized around the satisfaction of basic needs.

To these fundamental differences we might add those identified by David Slater in his comparative treatment of European and Latin American social movements. Slater's analysis focused on the contrasting roles of the state in Latin America and Western Europe. In particular, he cited the degree of state penetration of civil society, differences in the welfare functions of the state, the degree of centralization of state power, and the erosion of state legitimacy as the critical differences between the contexts in which social movements grow in Latin America and in Europe (Slater 1988: 8–9).

A Key Similarity

Notwithstanding all the contextual distinctions we may draw, it is clear that new social movements in both Latin America and Western Europe do share at least one defining characteristic. This is their fundamental distrust of the traditional parties and formations of the Left. Movement participants often see parties and unions as interested in the success of the new social movements only insofar as they can manipulate these movements for their own partisan ends. Movement activists accuse the parties and unions of feeding off their popular support, sapping the movements' strength in an effort to reinforce the traditional leftist forces' faltering positions.

For example, in his study of the *coordinadora* movement in Mexico, Barry Carr quoted an angry outburst to the press made by a leader of the National *Plan de Ayala* Coordinating Committee (CNPA). Referring to the Unified Socialist Party of Mexico (PSUM), the Revolutionary Workers' Party (PRT), and the Mexican Workers' Party (PMT), this leader said: "What we reject are attempts by parties to manipulate the CNPA. They see us as 'booty' and want to take advantage of our strength, something we will never allow . . . the vanguard of the left is among the masses, not in the parties or in the Chamber of Deputies."[1]

What is noteworthy about this statement is that the language of hostility toward the parties of what is, after all, a tiny, fragmented, and desperately weak Mexican Left could have been that of any new social movement activist in Italy speaking about the Italian Communist Party (PCI) at the peak of its strength in the mid-1970s when it enjoyed the support of almost 2 million members and received the votes of 34.4 percent of the Italian electorate. That Italian feminists, environmentalists, or peace movement activists should have feared loss of identity through absorption by a highly organized, mass party of the Left like the PCI, with its deep historical roots and broad-based support, is easy enough to understand.[2] But that the terms of angry complaint should be so similar for Mexican social movements with respect to the PSUM, PMT, and PRT is indeed striking and indicates that the question of autonomy is fundamental to new social movements *wherever* they arise.

Social Scientists and the Fetishism of Autonomy

The development of new social movements in Western Europe in the late 1960s has been carefully analyzed and documented (see, for example, Touraine 1975; Melucci 1977; Tarrow 1985), often by former participants in those same movements (for example, Bobbio 1979; Viale 1978). The literature on new social movements in Latin America, however, has been more the product of observation (much of it participatory and highly sympathetic) by analysts external to the movements and, indeed, often foreign to the settings in which they unfold (see Evers 1985; Slater 1988; Laclau 1985). In their writings, Andre Gunder Frank and Marta Fuentes distinguished between what they referred to as movements of the North and South in terms of their class base: middle class in North American and European movements, lower class in Latin America. If Gunder Frank and Fuentes were correct, it is not surprising that participants in northern movements have written about themselves and that Third World activists and their activities more often have been described, analyzed, and interpreted by others.[3]

Various features of the new movements account for their great appeal to European and North American social scientists as research subjects. For some analysts, it is the excitement of witnessing the emergence of new identities and novel practices. What others find compelling is the activists' efforts to conduct themselves in a genuinely democratic fashion within a broader context marked by authoritarian social customs. For some researchers, the study of Latin American movements is a page out of their own political autobiography; it permits them to relive a satisfying experience or rework an unsatisfying one from their own youthful days of militance in antiauthoritarian movements in Europe. In addition, the search for autonomy, "the defence and affirmation of solidarity, the struggle against hierarchy and alienation" (Slater 1988: 6) are all characteristics of new social movements that have deeply moved those who study them.

Perhaps the most compelling attraction that new social movements hold for many researchers is the heavy representation of women in both the ranks and the leadership of these groups.[4] It is difficult to establish whether the new movements are more democratic because they include more women or if they attract more women because they are less hierarchical. In either case, the participation of that half of the population that is conspicuously absent from traditional political organizations is a common characteristic of the new movements and a large part of what marks them as "new" (Jaquette, ed., 1989).

A more questionable basis for scholars' attraction to new social movements as a subject of study is the belief that these groups are nonpolitical and have nothing to do with the development of class consciousness or class conflict. The presence of participants of various social class origins linked by issues cutting across class lines is sometimes cited as evidence of the fundamentally nonpolitical nature of the movement, as if only the distribution of potable water or public transport, rather than power and influence, were at stake.[5] In the parlance of some analysts, peoples' "energies" get "channeled"; their "potential" gets "harnessed"; they *feel* "empowered." But none of this is posed as political in the commonly held sense of the word. The emphasis is on the "social" in new social movements.[6] Such analyses are characterized by what appears to be either a willful innocence or a disingenuous desire to portray as "nice" (folks in a community getting together to work out their common problems) what the researcher may privately consider rather "nasty" (political actors engaged in a struggle for power, if only over their own lives and immediate environment).

Whichever the particular characteristic that first attracts scholars to the study of new social movements in Latin America, it may be the researchers' externality that accounts for the intensely protective attitude toward the movements manifested by nonactors engaged in documentation and analysis of this phenomenon in Latin America. As any student of methodology knows, researchers' close identification with their subjects carries both positive and negative consequences. But, beyond the emotional price paid by those who come to identify with the actors in the movements they study, many analysts of contemporary movements in Latin America compound the pitfalls of overidentification with yet another problem. Even when movements they study are not repressed outright, these scholars nonetheless find the assessment of the results of struggle a difficult and depressing exercise. This occurs because, in their evaluations of success, they fail to distinguish among three possible outcomes.

The first outcome is the partial or total fulfillment of the demands of the movement by some agency of the state. Such a result often has the effect of demobilizing the movement, and it is generally labeled by analysts as a clear example of co-optation and understood as the death of the movement as such.

A second possibility is the incorporation of an urban or rural movement into the personal following of a populist figure (such as Janio Quadros or Leonel Brizola in Brazil) who, in the event of his or her election, promises to deliver the sewers, potable water, bus line, land, agricultural credit, or other specific goods or services sought by the group.[7]

A third outcome is the incorporation of a geographically or thematically isolated movement that is highly specific in its demands into a broader-based, political struggle led by a party or coalition of parties (such as the Workers' Party in Brazil or the PSUM in Mexico) that formulates a program that goes well beyond the narrow, specific demands of the social movement.

Unfortunately, no meaningful distinction is made among these three outcomes in the writings of some scholars. Given their preference for wholly autonomous movements, these analysts see the incorporation of an independent neighborhood group into a broad Socialist workers' movement as a result every bit as disappointing as co-optation by the state or absorption into a personal network. In either or any case, something pure and wonderful (a popularly based, grass-roots movement) disappears and is replaced by something less desirable. These writers do not recognize any fundamental difference between demobilization through co-optation, adherence to a charismatic, populist figure based on personal loyalty, and the kind of political learning and growth of consciousness that may occur when a neighborhood group articulating narrow, limited goals is drawn into a broader struggle (Evers 1985; Vink 1985).

Without entering the shadowy area of speculation about the psychological predispositions of scholars, we may find it difficult to understand the manifest preference of some analysts for the small, weak, isolated, and powerless community movement over the very same group of people once their demands have been satisfied. What is clear, however, is the antiorganizational bias of the work of those who are pleased and excited by the spontaneity of isolated grass-roots movements and dismayed when these autonomous movements link up with others in a stronger, far better organized and coordinated political coalition. This bias may simply reflect deep suspicions about the inevitability of bureaucratization in centralized organizations—even those that do not correspond to a Leninist model. Certainly, concern about bureaucratization has been a common theme for the European Left since the beginning of the century when Roberto Michels first formalized the problem as the "iron law of oligarchy."[8] Thus, it is not surprising to find analysts preoccupied with the fate of autonomous movements "swallowed up" by parties.

Alternatively, the concern that grass-roots groups may be absorbed by parties like the PSUM or the Brazilian PT may reflect the anti-Socialist, antiworker slant of scholars who have "skipped a stage," moving directly from pre-Marxist to post-Marxist positions without having actually passed through a period in which workers' struggle, worker-peasant coalitions, or Socialist revolution at least *seemed* a good idea. Stimulated by Chantal Mouffe and Ernesto Laclau's unabashed post-Marxism (Laclau and Mouffe 1985, 1987), writers like Tilman Evers similarly assert that there are now new and multiple forms of subordination that are not reducible to class antagonisms and that class and class struggle are no longer central to the transformation of contemporary capitalist society. If this is the case, as Evers clearly believes, then traditional workers' or Socialist parties are not suitable instruments to bring about the kind of transformations required to overcome the forms of alienation that oppress Latin Americans today. Because Evers sees social movements as designed not to challenge structures of power but to bypass them altogether through the creation of "countercultures," he views the incorporation of such movements into broader struggles led by parties of the Left as an entirely negative outcome (Evers 1985).

In contrast to the post-Marxist view, the Marxist position on new social movements is relatively straightforward. Scholars like Lucio Kowarick posit a direct and logical link between the struggles of workers in the realm of production and those of neighborhood groups concerned with consumption issues. Kowarick argues that the Brazilian "miracle" rested on a strategy of exploitation of labor in the factories *and* the limitation of collective consumption goods and services available to the urban poor. Thus, when Brazilian unions mobilize to fight the superexploitation of workers and the *bairro* associations struggle to protest the underprovision of social services, their activities "fuse" in a way that is more than conjunctural. Collective action that brings together both forms of protest becomes, by definition, a common struggle on two fronts of the same battle against capitalist exploitation and the "pauperization" it requires (Kowarick 1985: 86–89).

The Cardenista Movement
and the Question of Grass-roots Autonomy

The examination of the 1988 candidacy of Cuauhtémoc Cárdenas highlights a number of the analytical problems and the debates outlined earlier. In the case of Mexico, there is no doubt that the previous development of local neighborhood associations, student movements, coordinadoras, and democratic tendencies within the unions provided crucial support and impetus to the break of Cárdenas and reformist members of the Institutional Revolutionary Party (PRI) (S. Escobar 1988: 4–5). The grass-roots organizational activity of the last decade created a context of popular mobilization in which a progressive/reformist breakaway from the official party became a thinkable and, ultimately, workable alternative. That the Cardenista Front, the *Frente Democrático Nacional* (FDN), could only stand on the foundation of these earlier organizational efforts is clear. But what was the meaning of *cardenismo* for the new social movements themselves? Did their support for the Cárdenas ticket represent a loss of autonomy by formerly independent grass-roots movements? Did the entry of so many groups into an electoral coalition spell the end for these movements as authentic popular expressions from the base?

The first analytical problem in responding to these questions is to determine how to categorize the link between Mexican social movements and the Cardenista Front. Is it best described as an example of the way in which urban and rural movements may be drawn into the clientelistic following of a populist leader? Or should it be seen as an instance of the incorporation of geographically or thematically isolated movements into a broader political mobilization around a program for comprehensive and even radical change?

Had the FDN come to power, not only would tens of millions of Mexicans be delighted but much of our analytical dilemma would be resolved. As it is, we are obliged to approach these questions in a speculative way. If the Cardenista Front had been merely a populist movement, a personalistic following of a charismatic leader, its nature would have been revealed once Cárdenas assumed the presidency and acted to meet his supporters' most superficial demands with piecemeal handouts. If, on the other hand, Cárdenas had taken office and moved forward with radical structural changes, we would be able, in retrospect, to say that the new social movements that had given him their support had been incorporated into a broad political movement with goals more comprehensive and radical than the positions originally held by each group.[9]

It would seem that the platform on which Cárdenas ran was not a comprehensive program for change but, at best, a formula for reform within the Mexican tradition of economic nationalism and development with social justice. Yet, the very dynamic of the incorporation of new social movements into electoral coalitions is a radicalizing one. Often, social movement activists who cast their lot with a progressive electoral coalition may influence their new allies by stimulating new concepts, providing different ways of understanding social problems, and posing novel solutions to those problems. Some analysts, as I have noted, insist that the incorporation of autonomous social movements into broader political movements represents the loss of an authentic popular voice. But those who hold this view fail to grasp that the encounter between movement and party is a dialectical one in which the movement is altered but so, too, is the party— whether the party in question is a small, precariously situated leftist coalition or the Italian Communist Party with 1.8 million members.[10]

We need to bear in mind the dialectical character of the relationship between movements and parties when we ask if neocardenism put an end to the creative identities of the new social movements it incorporated. Here, the example of Brazilian social movements in the 1986 election is instructive. Ilse Scherer-Warren described the grass-roots movements of São Paulo as a "transition" to expanded forms of popular expression or the "conquest of political space" (1987: 48). For Scherer-Warren, the autonomy of new social movements from parties is a temporary situation. In the long run, she argued, grass-roots movements in Brazil prepare their activists for political participation in direct elections. But if the new parties of the Left that have emerged in Brazil since the *abertura* (or political opening) are to retain the support of the grass-roots groups they have won as electoral allies, they have to incorporate the movements' demands into a radical program for transformation. Scherer-Warren saw this process as the creation of a new political culture, a process through which the old pattern of authoritarianism could be broken (1987: 48).

Likewise, Sonia Alvarez raised the possibility that grass-roots movements might "foster a political culture that is supportive of democracy," pushing or extending "the parameters of democratic politics" and opening the way to the development of effective nonclientelistic links between movement activists and political parties. Alvarez's work on women's movements in Brazil suggested that parties and policymakers could adapt their political practices to become more responsive to popular interests as articulated by social movements (1989b: 17–18).

What is most significant about the Mexican popular mobilization of 1988 is not simply that the Cardenista FDN was able to mount a serious challenge to one-party rule or that it won what was probably a plurality of votes in the country and unquestionably a majority in key areas of the republic. Rather, it is the fact that the FDN did all this by building on the foundation of contemporary social movements that remain active and distinct at the local level (Tamayo 1990; Perez Acre 1990). Observers of abertura in Brazil see the critical support given by new social movements to leftist parties as a crucial step in the development of a new political culture. So, too, in the Mexican case do the links between grass-roots movements and a broad progressive/populist electoral front provide the opportunity for new social actors to contribute fresh and radical perspectives on the program for transformation required in Mexican society. As Jorge Tamayo noted: "The sudden politicization of these emergent social movements and their inclusion in *cardenismo's* national project, has not so far affected their independence. Quite the contrary, it has allowed them to expand their intersectoral alliances without diminishing their autonomy" (Tamayo 1990: 134). Tamayo's judgment of the situation was confirmed by the assessment of Francisco Saucedo, a leader of the Asamblea de Barrios in Mexico City:

> Together with other organizations in the popular movement we have been discussing the relationship between the movement and parties. There is an idea, widespread among movements, that participation in electoral politics represents a loss of consistency for the movement; that the party uses the movement. But this has not happened to us. Our participation in the cardenist front gained for us great credibility and growth. For people who are principally interested in the struggle for democracy rather than for housing, the adhesion of these other people is a very positive thing.
>
> The movement is very important to the party and it is the movement that molds the party which, in turn, serves as the political instrument that the people require. We have to play an active role in the party so that it will be permeated by the movement and so that it will be the people that shape its program.[11]

Conclusions

As we have seen, distrust of traditional parties is a characteristic shared by grass-roots movements in both Latin America and Western Europe. The presumption that the goals of movements and those of political parties are fundamentally *contradictory* (rather than merely tension-ridden) is a view expressed not only by social movement activists but also by their scholarly observers.

The concern of analysts of social movements for the survival and continued independence of the movements they study is an understandable outgrowth of their observation that grass-roots movements may—and often do—disappear from the scene as autonomous actors once they give their support to, formally ally themselves with, or in some other fashion cast their lot with political parties. But this position overlooks the possibility that movements can influence parties or contribute to the rise of new political formation, radicalizing and transforming political programs and dictating an agenda of new issues—a phenomenon that actually occurred in Mexico and Brazil, as in France, Italy, and West Germany.

In this sense, the experience of the Italian social movement sector provides some important clues for Latin Americanists. The responsiveness of the Italian Communist Party to pressures exerted by women's, Green, peace, and gay rights activists illustrates the way in which a party may be altered by contact with social movements. To be sure, the changes presently under way in Italian communism also reflect the political isolation the PCI suffered in the 1980s and the recent collapse of communism in Eastern Europe. But the refoundation of the Italian Communist Party as the *Partito Democratico della Sinistra* (PDS) is also a clear indicator of the influence and impact of the social movements active in Italy since the late 1960s. A process of transformation that began with the imposition of a 50-percent-female quota in the party's leadership, the selection of gay activists to head some of the party's electoral lists, and the formulation of a position opposing nuclear energy eventually called into question the party's very symbol, name, and identity.[12]

Thus, what we witness today is a traditional leftist party attempting to remake itself in a form that will appeal to the "new social subjects" whose support it desperately needs. In this respect, the Italian case may point to possible realignments in the relationship between movements and parties in other regions of the world. The capacity of new social movements to mobilize dynamic and growing sectors of the population that had either been ignored by political parties or proved resistant to the parties' traditional modes of organization has contributed to the crisis of party politics in Europe as in Latin America. And it is precisely this crisis that has forced parties to open up to new movements in the hope of reaching those sectors of the population—the new subjects in Europe or the new urban masses in Latin America—whose political relevance can no longer be ignored.

Notes

A previous version of this chapter appeared in LASA Forum 21, no. 2 (1990): 7-12.

1. Guillermo Correa, "La Marcha Rechazó Oportunismos," Proceso 389 (April 16, 1984): 29–31, quoted in Carr and Montoya 1986: 16.

2. For the "movementist" critique of the Italian Communist Party, see J. Hellman 1987: 40–46.

3. Gunder Frank and Fuentes 1987. However, in a paper prepared for the fifteenth meeting of LASA in 1989, entitled "The Role of Social Movements in the Analysis of Sociopolitical Change," Susan Street noted a growing tendency for the leaders of Mexican movements to study and record the development of their own movements. See Hernandez 1981 and 1986; Moctezuma 1988.

4. For example, both Carr and Montoya (1986) and Gunder Frank and Fuentes (1987) underscored the participation of women as one of the most positive aspects of the new movements.

5. The concept of new social movements as nonpolitical is currently very diffuse among Canadian scholars. This, I believe, reflects the influence of Canadian research-funding bodies.

6. This kind of confusion is most understandable where the movement under examination is a church-sponsored, ecclesiastical community of the base. It is harder to accept these formulations when used to describe nonreligious grass-roots movements.

7. Castells outlined the process by which the state takes control of neighborhood associations in exchange for delivery and management of urban services. See Castells 1982: 251.

8. Michels 1959. For example, Karner extended Marx's theory of alienation to participation in political parties. Because parties are centralized, inhibit social creativity and the construction of "concrete utopias," and are "an impediment to the development of alternative forms of production and new forms of social life," he argued that alienation cannot be overcome and a free human society cannot be built by means of a revolutionary organization that is centralized, authoritarian, and hierarchical. Karner 1983: 30–31.

9. On the distinction between personalistic and ideologically based movements, see J. Hellman 1983b.

10. For a discussion of the way in which the feminist movement altered the Italian Communist Party, see S. Hellman 1987. On the impact of Brazilian feminists on the PT, see Alvarez 1989a.

11. Interview with Paco Saucedo of the Asamblea de Barrios, Mexico D.F., June 1991.

12. For feminist analyses of this process of transformation, see Cattaneo and D'Amato 1990; Tatafiore, ed., 1990: 26–29; Mancina et al., 1990.

5

Culture, Economics, and Politics in Latin American Social Movements Theory and Research

Arturo Escobar

Why should we theorize, and how should we do it? The neutral, "positive" character of theory can no longer be taken for granted. The questions of who speaks and from what institutional sites are only the starting points of the inquiry. The assertion that all knowledge, particularly in the human and social sciences, is "socially constructed" is intended to point to the historically and socially determined nature of knowledge, to the ways in which power and knowledge are intertwined, to how both become entangled in the fight over what counts as knowledge, and, finally, to how this process is related to struggles over real, concrete worlds. Some argue that "reality" itself is partly created in the process of knowing it and naming it or at least that this naming has profound and systematic effects on the real. Representations of the world, such as the representation of the Third World in terms of "development," are social facts—that is, effects and instruments of power—not pristine descriptions of an external reality to which the theorist can appeal as the ultimate arbiter of truth. To represent the Third World as "underdeveloped" is less a statement about "facts" than the setting up of a regime of truth through which the Third World is inevitably known, intervened on, and managed.

This means that theory is, in itself, a practice linked to power. It is always related to changing historical conditions and, more often than not, to situations that have become conflictual and "problematized." Theory purports to tell us what is going on in the world by discovering the more or less stable regularities produced by human action. This knowledge may strengthen, challenge, or overthrow the (largely implicit) self-understanding of the agents whose actions theory tries to explain. In fact, one role of theory is to feed back into a practice so that this practice can be continued, reformed, or rejected altogether. Increasingly, it would seem, modern society makes the demand that we subject our practices to the "correcting" or "enlightening" effect of rigorous theory. Our bodies, our minds, and our social forms are increasingly placed under the gaze of theory.[1] People turn to theory "because they feel the need to get clearer what society's practices involve" (Taylor 1985: 106). Conversely, we can say that "what makes a theory right is that it brings practice out in the clear; that its adoption makes possible what is in some sense a more effective practice" (Taylor 1985: 104). In sum, theory not only attempts to explain, it may also affect how people live their lives and orient themselves in the social field.

Theory thus must start with people's self-understanding, with giving an account of people as agents whose practices are shaped by their self-understanding. It is only by getting as clear a picture as possible of this self-understanding that we can hope to identify what should be relevant for theory in the first place. This requires a close engagement with the agents—a mutual exchange between the "subjects" that are written about and the critics who write about them. Conventional social science is, of course, inimical to this approach. By emulating the model of the natural sciences, social theory almost inevitably bypasses the domain of people's self-description. Does it not assume beforehand a model of reality? Even when surveys are conducted, the data are used to corroborate the model, not to detect the range of self-understandings of the people so that an appropriate model can then be constructed. An interpretive approach grounded on how people understand themselves as creators and practitioners of their world is increasingly recognized as necessary.[2]

The arena of social movements research and theory offers a great opportunity to explore some of the predicaments of contemporary theory just sketched. Poststructuralist and postmodernist insights of various kinds inform social movements theory in different parts of the world, especially in Western Europe and Latin America. More clearly in Latin America than elsewhere, the move toward a grand "theory of social movements" is actively resisted. While Latin American researchers continue to work with European theories (although with a growing degree of autonomy), European scholars in this field have also often followed the routes of Latin American social movements and theorists. Both theories and theorists travel between the two continents, between uneven spaces, at times sharing the space and at times contesting it. There is no linear path between the two (multiple) places, no epistemological center and periphery (even if European and North American theorists not infrequently continue to act as if this were the case); rather, there are multiple and mutual creations, appropriations, and resistances—and, as Calderón, Piscitelli, and Reyna remind us in Chapter 2, syncretisms—that create an overlapping and decentered network within which both theories and theorists travel.[3]

This chapter looks at some of the most salient aspects of contemporary social movements theory and research. Rather than pretending to survey the landscape of theories, it focuses on the epistemological and political context within which theory is being produced, especially in Latin America. One essential aspect of this context is the crisis of development and its models for it is largely in response to the failure of development that social movements emerge. Here, it is crucial that development not be seen solely as an economic and political project but as an overarching cultural discourse that has had a profound impact on the fabric of the Third World. Moreover, the crisis of development must be assessed in terms of the broader crisis of the civilizational project of modernity. Once we situate social movements within a reinterpreted context of the crisis of development and modernity, it becomes impossible to see them only in economic or political terms. Indeed, their fundamental cultural character has to be recognized and subjected to theoretical analysis. Most of this chapter is devoted to this endeavor, that is, to developing a framework for understanding Latin American social movements as economic, political, *and* cultural struggles.

The first part of the chapter presents, in a succinct manner, a critical view of development and modernity that highlights their fundamental role in shaping the context within which contemporary social movements emerge and exert their action. The second part is an attempt to develop a framework and methodology that may allow researchers to understand and examine the cultural aspects of contemporary collective action in the context of changing global economic and political conditions. This attempt relies on a critical and selective use of existing theories of social movements and popular culture in various parts of the world. Current notions and theories of everyday life, historicity, and the practice of cultural innovation by social actors, as well as the "ethnosemiotic" approach to the study of popular culture developed recently by some scholars, provide some of the building blocks for this endeavor. The interface of cultural and political aspects is explored in terms of the concept of "articulatory politics" developed by Laclau and Mouffe. The chapter concludes with a reinterpretation of the "epistemo-politics" of theory production in the area of social movements research worldwide.

The Crisis of Development and Modernity in Latin America

It is no secret that Latin America is going through its worst crisis in history. For some, the 1980s amounted to a "reversal of development" (Portes and Kincaid 1989; Dietz and James, eds., 1990), particularly through the transfer of capital from Latin America to Center countries through debt service "obligations." Persistent violence, growing political instability, falling standards of living, and aggravated social and economic conditions are the most dramatic manifestations of the crisis. Given the current restructuring of capital at the global level (Castells 1986; Harvey 1989; Amin 1990), most authors predict not an improvement but a worsening of conditions.

Much talk about the crisis, however, is imprecise at best, and it tends to focus exclusively on economic conditions, the need for the right "adjusment" packages, and the renewal of development. This is quite understandable, given the precariousness of living conditions and the magnitude of macroeconomic dislocations. But if forty years of "development"—always interspersed with adjustment and stabilization periods, at least since the early 1950s—have not produced stability and sustained economic improvements, it would seem unlikely that "more of the same" will yield different results. To the extent that Latin America continues to be seen in terms of the need for "development" based on capital, technology, insertion into the international division of labor, and so forth, the crisis will only continue to deepen, new forms of colonialism and dependence will be introduced, and social fragmentation and violence will become more virulent. Perhaps because it is becoming more and more evident that "development" has dug its own grave, a significant rethinking of the whole strategy has become a real possibility and is, indeed, in order.

To understand development in a radically new manner, we must first distance ourselves from prevalent forms of understanding it. Since its inception in the early post–World War II period, it has become customary to see development either as a series of strategies intended to bring about "progress" or, in the opposing view, as a form of neocolonialism and dependency, that is, an instrument of control over the Third World. What advocates and foes alike share is the assumption that some form of "development" must take place, even if they dispute the character and rationality of the necessary interventions. That the development process implies the destruction of traditions, the normalization of living conditions along Western criteria, and the restructuring of entire societies does not seem to concern those who advocate "progress" and the modernization of national societies.

The history of development is relatively recent and even precarious. It dates back to the early post–World War II period when the scientific gaze of the West focused on Asia, Africa, and Latin America in a new manner. It was during this period (roughly from 1945 to 1960) that the institutional apparatus for producing knowledge and forms of intervention in and about the Third World (the World Bank, the United Nations, bilateral development agencies, planning offices in the Third World, development organizations on the local level) was actually created. The terms *Third World*, *underdeveloped areas*, *development*, and the like were inventions of this period, integral components in a new system for producing truth about those parts of the world. During those years, Third World countries witnessed a steady influx of experts in all fields—economics, industrialization, agriculture, nutrition, family planning, education, health, the military—each of them measuring and observing a small part of their reality, each of them addressing a "problem" to be corrected by the appropriate development intervention. Like the orientalist discourses addressed by Edward Said (1979), development discourses have functioned as powerful instruments for shaping and managing the Third World.[4]

The discourse of development portrayed Third World societies as imperfect, abnormal, or diseased entities in relation to the "developed" societies; the cure for this condition would be, of course, the development prescriptions handed down by Western experts and very often willingly adopted by Third World elites. The development discourse undoubtedly brought about a new hegemonic formation that has since significantly defined what can be thought and done—or even imagined—when dealing with the economies and societies of Asia, Africa, and Latin America. This hegemonic discourse transformed the system through which identities were defined. What we now have is a vast landscape of identities—the "illiterate," the "landless peasants," "women bypassed by development," the "hungry and malnourished," "those belonging to the informal sector," "urban marginals," and so forth—all of them created by the development discourse and cataloged among the many abnormalities that development would treat and reform through appropriate "interventions" (for instance, literacy campaigns, the Green revolution, birth control, basic needs programs, and integrated rural development projects). As I will show, this fragmentation of identities is essential for understanding contemporary movements. After all, is this not the cast of characters that are now becoming social actors in their own right?

Two factors have been central to the effective functioning of development: the systematic production of knowledge about all aspects—economic, cultural, and social—and the establishment of vast institutional networks at all levels—from the global to the very local. Once Third World communities became the target of new and increasingly detailed interventions, their economies, societies, and cultures were appropriated as objects of knowledge by modern development disciplines and subdisciplines that, in turn, made them into new targets of power and intervention. The productivity of development thus must be seen in terms of this efficient apparatus that systematically links knowledge and power as it deploys each one of its strategies and interventions (Foucault 1977, 1980; A. Escobar 1988; Ferguson 1990). The depiction of the Third World as "underdeveloped" has been an essential and constitutive element of the globalization of capital in the post–World War II period; perhaps more importantly, a cultural discourse began that not only placed the Third World in a position of inferiority but that, more clearly and efficiently than ever, subjected it to the "scientific," normalizing action of Western cultural-political technologies—in even more devastating ways than its colonial predecessor.

In other words, perhaps we have not yet fully realized the utmost significance and impact of "development" as both economic *and* cultural discourse—the incredibly profound and long-lasting consequences for the Third World of having been invented as "underdeveloped" by First World and Third World rulers alike. From a critical perspective, one may say that this discourse has been, for forty years, the most efficient mechanism for producing the Third World economically, socially, and culturally—as some have articulately and insightfully proposed in recent years (Sachs, ed., 1992; Dubois 1991; Apffel Marglin and Marglin, eds., 1990; Ferguson 1990; Mueller 1986; A. Escobar 1984, 1988). This critique, however, does not do justice to the full range of consequences implied by this process. Although one may also visualize the increasing opposition to development interventions[5] or, more encouragingly, the potential of grass-roots groups to posit alternatives to development,[6] the means to neutralize or at least partially dismantle the discourse are far from clear. This would require changes in social relations and institutional practices, openness to other forms of knowledge and cultural manifestations—not so mediated by the language of development—and greater autonomy for communities over the creation of their own ways of thinking and doing things. Within the actions of contemporary social movements may lie important clues for reformulating these questions.

To analyze development as a cultural and economic discourse is also to locate it in the soil and space of modernity. Some authors identify the origins of modernity with Christopher Columbus's travel across the Atlantic; "it is in fact the conquest of America that heralds and establishes our present identity" (Todorov 1984: 5). This is because, with the conquest, Europe completed its picture of the world, placing itself at the apex of history and inaugurating an unprecedented process of expanding and transforming the globe to fit the European image. More specifically, however, modernity is taken to be that period in European life that took off fully at the end of the eighteenth century when "Man" [sic] developed forms of knowledge about himself and the world that required a distancing, objectifying posture. Epistemologically, therefore, the boundaries of modernity are marked by the birth of modern reason and forms of rationality. Socially, modernity entailed the separation of life into distinct domains, such as the "economy," "religion," "politics," "culture," and the like, without much functional connection among them and with each sector having a science devoted to revealing its secrets. Economically, modernity built on the consolidation of capitalism. And politically, "the fundamental characteristic of modernity is the advent of the democratic revolution" (Mouffe 1988b: 33).

In this way, modernity can be seen as an attempt to provide a foundation for society that is grounded in reason, the economy, and a project of global emancipation. Usually overlooked are the manifold techniques of power necessary to create modern classes, modern rationalities, and, especially, the modern subject. "Modern man" became not only the subject of liberty and equality, of objectivity and efficiency (Homo oeconomicus), but also the disciplined and normalized subject, the policed subject. The consequences of this transformation were enormous (for instance, in terms of the marginalization of other types of knowledge and the control of women, nature, and subaltern classes). The modern practices of reason, knowledge, and even democracy, although already naturalized because of the spread of European self-understanding, must be looked at anthropologically: as peculiar, even exotic, and always historically locatable practices. This "anthropology of modernity" shows the culturally specific character of many of our practices that are most taken for granted and "rational."[7]

What is at stake with "development" is precisely the completion of the modern project, the transformation of Third World subjectivities that are allegedly not yet rational enough into fully modern modes. But even without questioning the success of modernity for the European world, it must be recognized that the crisis of development is a striking sign of modernity's failure in the Third World. In the Latin American case, it is undeniable that modernity has left an indelible mark on the continent, yet it is also true that the Latin American "modern" is quite different from the European and North American one. In Latin America, the differentiation of economic and cultural modes of production and the segmentation and transnationalization of cultural and economic systems presuppose and produce a mixture of pre- or nonmodern, modern, postmodern, and even antimodern forms.

Latin American modernity is therefore plural, contradictory, and uneven. Even today, there are cultural matrices that are not of modern origin (indigenous and African) and large groups of people who are to a greater or lesser extent marginalized from the dominant circuits of material and symbolic production. In Latin America, unlike Europe, cultural and economic forms of different temporal origins coexist, forming layers rather than stages, constituting at the same time simultaneity and sequence. This simultaneity of time and cultural forms is undoubtedly best captured by writers and artists, through aesthetic-mythic modes such as magical realism. And magical realism represents another rationality and the uniqueness of the Latin American universe, quite different from the instrumental rationality of Western modernity (Quijano 1988). Is this not also relevant to our understanding of social movements?

Social polarization, heterogeneity, and exclusion have reached unprecedented proportions in the development era. The erosion of modernity is evident in everyday life, in the concrete behavior of people, in the economic crisis, and in the disenchantment with the modern projects of nation-building, politics, and development. What is hanging in the balance is not only politics, progress, and democracy but also a whole civilizational design based on modern reason. Moreover, the crisis of modernity has been intensified in Latin America, as perhaps in no other place, by the global restructuring of capital. To this extent, the crisis is not conjunctural but organic. The response of the elite has been to advocate the further transnationalization of the economy and the dismantling of the state in the name of (market) neoliberalism and individual (economic) freedom. But the challenge of social fragmentation and fracture is also being met by the new social actors, to the extent that they question—as the contributors to this volume testify—the existing mechanisms for the production of meanings, identities, and social relations.

Often working at the margins and in the fissures of peripheral capitalism, social actors of various kinds take space away from capitalism and modernity, and they hint at different ways of seeing the relationships between capital, the state, culture, and the economy. They may well offer important insights for the redefinition of democracy and development. As these groups come together in networks or national arenas, they also foster the formation of public domains that are quite different from the social domain associated with the state. This alternative to the private and public domains of capital and the state is "a Latin American proposal which originates in the fact that Latin America, perhaps like no other place, is the most ancient source of an historical rationality made up by the confluence of many conquests and many rationalities and cultures" (Quijano 1988: 34).

The task ahead is the construction of collective imaginaries capable of orienting social and political action. Epistemologically, this requires nonreductionist and nonteleological notions of politics and development; politically, the task is to foster the democratizing potential of the new subjects. Postmodern critiques of certain types of rationalism, theorizing, and political practice can be helpful in this regard, as a number of Latin American scholars cautiously argue; these critiques can also be helpful in the reappropriation of some of modernity's principles, such as social change, the commitment to justice, and the emancipation from poverty and oppression. The valorization of popular culture and of the importance of marginality for the Latin American future and the reworking of the concept of class to take account of the salience of cultural production and social heterogeneity are two of the most important elements of the rethinking that is still to be done in the wake of the crisis of modernity and development. They are also aspects of the advent of the cultural configuration referred to in the

Center as postmodernity and tentatively and warily accepted as a label by Latin American researchers as they continue their quest for more autonomous ways to characterize the emerging Latin American reality.[8]

Aníbal Quijano perhaps best summarized the utopia of the Latin American "postmodern":

> What I propose is that today in Latin America the dominated masses are generating new social practices founded on reciprocity, equality and collective solidarity as well as on individual liberties and the democracy of collectively agreed upon decisions against external impositions. . . . Latin America, because of its peculiar history, because of its place in the trajectory of modernity, is the most apt historical terrain to achieve the articulation of what until now has been separated: the happiness of collective solidarity and that of a full individual realization. We do not have to give up either of them, because both are our genuine history (1988: 68).

The Nature of Culture in Social Movements Research

It is essential to recognize the importance of economic factors and their structural determinants. But just as crucial as the reconstruction of economies—and indelibly linked to it—is the reconstitution of meanings at all levels, from everyday life to national development. Social movements must be seen equally and inseparably as struggles over meanings as well as material conditions, that is, as cultural struggles. Are economies not cultural forms, anyway? Do they not entail profound cultural choices, as the anthropology of modernity demonstrates? Certainly, Homo oeconomicus is not a culturally neutral subject. "Material needs" and "technologies" are permeated by cultural contents. Every new technology inaugurates a ritual—a way of doing things, of seeing the world, and of organizing the social field. How, then, could we brush aside the consideration of the cultural content of "economies"?

Thus, there is a cultural politics that must be brought to light in examining the politics of social movements. This cultural politics is rarely visible through conventional forms of analysis, although we already have some clues to help us in this task. The first is found in the importance granted by some authors to the terrain of everyday life—which, as anthropologists would have it, is fundamentally shaped by culture. Another guiding source originates in a number of concepts generated from within social movements theory itself, particularly Alain Touraine's notion of historicity, Alberto Melucci's proposition that social movements find their reason for being in submerged frameworks of meaning and in the daily practice of cultural innovation, and Ernesto Laclau and Chantal Mouffe's complex argument of politics as a discursive articulatory process. Contemporary theories of popular culture, especially those that highlight the role of the subalterns themselves in shaping the world in which they live, contribute an additional set of insights. These guideposts are briefly described in the rest of this chapter in an attempt to develop a coherent, albeit rudimentary and provisional, account of the cultural politics of social movements in Latin America and a cultural theory of social movements.

Social Movements and the Practice of Everyday Life

Not until recently has the domain of everyday life been given critical attention by scholars.[9] Yet, an adequate theorization of *the practice* of everyday life (especially collective practice) has proven elusive. Social movements research involves situations in which the interrelations between daily life, political practice, and social relations can be fruitfully investigated. This possibility has been best expressed by Elizabeth Jelin:

> If we study the meaning of political practice in daily life, the construction of identities and discourses, we do not do it assuming that these are determinant—or necessary—of practices at the institutional level. Neither do we assume the autonomy of democracy in relation to people's quotidian practices. The relationship between one and the other level are complex, mediated. Our intention is to point to *a field of construction of democracy* that, in the first place, is important in itself, that of the social relations of daily life. . . . We believe that *daily life and social movements are privileged spaces in which to study these processes of mediation*, since social movements are situated, at least in theory, in the intermediate space between individualized, familiar, habitual, micro-climactic daily life, and socio-political processes writ large, of the State and the institutions, solemn and superior (1987b: 11, emphases added).[10]

This is perhaps demonstrated most clearly when we look at women's movements, as Jelin concluded in her study of Latin American women's mobilizations. The fact that these movements seem to arise "naturally" out of daily life does not imply that their action is less important or restricted. What it means, actually, is that "the type of action in which women engage does not restrict itself to the traditional rules of politics but attempts to give a new meaning to politics" (Jelin, ed., 1990: 204). This conception is a far cry from older models of political practice that focused on the visible, macro aspects of protest and on empirically observable results (such as, in the classical model, the capture of the state). Said succinctly, the personal is political and cultural. To live differently, to assert one's difference, is to practice cultural innovation and to engage in some sort of political practice (even if not necessarily progressive, as the 1980s have shown in many parts of the world).

The centrality of daily life for social movements is difficult to perceive; like the self-understanding of the people, daily life has been rendered invisible or secondary by conventional social sciences, especially the positivist ones. The prevailing static understanding of culture as something embedded in a set of canonical texts, beliefs, and artifacts and characterized by a certain abstract universality for those who share it has contributed to this state of affairs. Culture is not something that exists in the abstract; it is embedded in practices, in the everyday life of people. Culture *is* (made of) people's practices. Encounters with others who are different from us intensify the awareness of our own culture and make us realize how we think and feel in some ways rather than others, that is, that we have "a culture."

When people "practice" their everyday lives, they are thus reproducing or creating culture. "We are all cultural producers in some way and of some kind in our everyday life," insisted a contemporary theorist of popular culture (Willis

1990: 128). Symbolic creativity in everyday life is vibrant, if somewhat invisible; it involves language, the body, performative rituals, work, and both individual and collective identities. It is essential for social movements research to tap into this level of popular practice. Everyday life involves a collective act of creation, a collective signification, a culture. It is out of this reservoir of meanings (that is, a "tradition") that people actually give shape to their struggle. Put in a more abstract and general manner, daily life is located at the intersection of processes of articulating meaning through practices, on the one hand, and macro processes of domination, on the other. Struggles over meanings at the level of daily life—as feminists and others do not cease to remind us—are the basis of contemporary social movements. The implications of this realization for theory and methodology are enormous, as we are just beginning to appreciate.

Historicity and the Symbolic Challenge of Social Movements

There is, then, the need to rethink the relationships between everyday life, culture, and politics. A series of notions produced by some prominent social movements theorists are helpful to our efforts to do this in the context of social movements. Let us start with Alain Touraine's notion of historicity. Touraine's central insight is that, for the first time, (postindustrial) society is the result of a complex set of actions that society performs on itself (1977, 1981, 1988a). No longer can social action be seen as the result of some metasocial principle—such as Tradition, God, Reason, the Economy, or the State; society itself is the result of a set of systems of action involving actors who may have conflictual interests but who share certain cultural orientations. Social movements, therefore, are not "dramatic events" but rather "the work that society performs upon itself" (Touraine 1981: 29). The goal of this action is the control of *historicity*, which is defined as "the set of cultural models that rule social practices" (Touraine 1988a: 8) and is embodied in knowledge, economic, and ethical models. What then is a social movement? "A social movement is the action, both culturally oriented and socially conflictual, of a class defined by its position of domination or dependency in the mode of appropriation of historicity, of the cultural models of investment, knowledge and morality towards which the social movement itself is oriented" (Touraine 1988a: 68).

The essential feature of this definition is that actors recognize the stakes in terms of a cultural project; in other words, what is at stake for social movements is historicity itself, not merely organizational forms, services, means of production, and the like. Moreover, only societies that have reached "the highest level of historicity" (that of self-production)—namely, postindustrial or "programmed" societies—can be said to be characterized by social movements of this kind.[11] By the same token, Touraine concluded that most forms of collective mobilization in Latin America are not social movements proper but rather struggles for the control of the process of historical change and development. Given the reality of dependency, modernization, and the state, together with the state's intervention in all aspects of life, the stake for social actors is not historicity but greater participation in the political system. Latin America would be in the process of acceding to a higher level of historicity—that is, becoming a truly modern society—through industrialization and development (Touraine 1987).

Touraine's insistence on the cultural stakes of collective action is of utmost importance, even if many questions remain to be answered. For instance, what are the processes through which historicity is produced and contested, including the dynamic interaction of tradition and modernity, domination and resistance? How are long-standing, implicit cultural contents increasingly undermined and appropriated by "modern" scientific discourses, and to what extent is this process contested by social actors? What is the relation between political action and cultural forms? By highlighting action, Touraine's sociology affords many important elements for reinterpreting the nature of social movements. Yet, as Melucci (1988a), for instance, has pointed out, Touraine and others do not explain the process by which actors build a collective identity through interactions, negotiations, and relationships with the environment. For these authors, identity appears as an already accomplished fact, the essence of the movement. But, Melucci insisted, rather than assuming the existence of a relatively unified collective actor, the researcher must precisely explain how collective action is formed and maintained. This demands that the researcher provide a view of how actors construct common actions, explain how different elements are brought together, and describe the concrete processes through which individuals become involved in action.

The social construction of collective action and identity, according to Melucci, involves complex interactions along three axes: ends, means, and relationships with the environment. For the researchers, this entails making sense of the plurality of meanings and analytical levels and processes that define those axes—if they hope to account for the apparently unified empirical behavior of collective actors, which is actually the result of a process of construction. Melucci's "constructivist" view, in contrast to structural models or those based on individual motivations, focuses on collective action and identity as a process, not as a fact or an event. As he pointed out, concepts proposed by resource mobilization theory (such as "structure of opportunities," "discretional resources," and the like) are not really "objective" realities; they "imply the capacity of the actors to perceive, evaluate and determine the possibilities and limits afforded by the environment" (Melucci 1988a: 342). These prior operations are what have to be brought to light in the research process; they are what constructing an action system is all about, which Melucci referred to as "collective identity":

Collective identity is an interactive and shared definition produced by several individuals and concerned with the orientations of action and the fields of opportunities and constraints in which the action takes place: by "interactive and shared" I mean a definition that must be conceived as a process, because it is constructed and negotiated through a repeated activation of the relationships that link individuals. The process of identity construction, adaptation and maintenance always has two aspects: the internal complexity of an actor (the plurality of orientations which characterizes him), and the actor's relationship with the environment (other actors, opportunities and constraints) (Melucci 1988a: 342).

The question of identity construction is crucial even in terms of thinking about strategy, as other theorists contend. Gerardo Munck's statement that "only on the basis of a constructed identity does it make sense to talk of strategies" (1990: 25) left no doubt in this regard. "Only by drawing upon the . . . 'new social movements' approach," he continued, "can we hope to explain how strategic calculations are made" (G. Munck 1990: 25). Melucci pointed to yet another level of analysis that most theorists of social movements overlook. Because these theorists concentrate on collective action as a fact, not a process, they make analytically invisible a crucial network of relationships that underlie collective action before, during, and after the events. The exclusion of this level from the field of analysis is of paramount importance because it is at this level that the creation of cultural models and symbolic challenges by the movements actually occurs. Melucci referred to this level as a "submerged reality" that constitutes both the condition of possibility and the very stuff of social action. Contemporary collective action, in his words,

> assumes the form of networks submerged in everyday life. Within these networks there is an experimentation with and direct practice of alternative frameworks of meaning, as a result of a personal commitment which is submerged and almost invisible. . . . The "movements" emerge only in limited areas, for limited phases and by means of moments of mobilization which are the other, complementary phase of the submerged networks. . . . What nourishes [collective action] is the daily production of alternative frameworks of meaning, on which the networks themselves are founded and live from day to day. . . . This is because conflict takes place principally on symbolic grounds, by challenging and upsetting the dominant codes upon which social relationships are founded in high density informational systems. The mere existence of a symbolic challenge is in itself a method of unmasking the dominant codes, a different way of perceiving and naming the world (Melucci 1988b: 248).[12]

Social movements, in this way, cannot be understood independently from the "submerged" social and cultural background from which they emerge. This might be described as the latent aspect of the movements, no less real because it is less readily observed empirically. A corollary of this notion is that it is more appropriate to speak of "movement networks" or "movement areas," rather than "movements"; the network would include both the movements and the "users" of the cultural products produced by the movements (that is, both latent and visible components). "The normal situation of today's 'movements,'" Melucci concluded (1985: 800), "is a network of small groups submerged in everyday life which requires a personal involvement in experiencing and practicing cultural innovation." Social movements thus bring about social practices that operate, in part, through the creation of spaces for the production of meanings. But how does this "daily production of alternative frameworks of meaning," this "practice of cultural innovation," actually take place? Recent studies of popular culture and resistance, of growing importance in Latin America as well, shed some additional light on these questions.

Social Movements and Popular Culture and Resistance

As mentioned before, the relationships between the practice of everyday life, collective action, and politics is not yet well understood. Does cultural resistance in daily life, for instance, amount to anything politically? Can it foster more "visible" forms of protest? How are researchers to study "oppositional" or "alternative" meanings produced at the micro level of daily life by subaltern groups, as well as their relation to politics? Moreover, is it possible to study social movements without relying on existing models of political practice, such as those couched in terms of parties, organizations, resources, and so forth? In other words, can we place popular practice and culture at the center of social movements inquiry? And if we can, how do we do this?

It is true that most models of social production and action have largely focused on the macro aspects of these processes, especially on the structures and mechanisms of domination. In recent years, however, investigators have begun to give attention to the other side of the coin—namely, the subordinate—and not as a massive datum ("the masses") but as something characterized by complex, fluid, and heterogeneous elements and processes. A type of microsociology and ethnography of popular resistance is emerging. The work of Michel de Certeau has been quite important in this regard. If domination proceeds through *strategies* (economic, political, technological, institutional) that organize the world in ways that lead to the colonization of physical, social, and cultural environments, de Certeau argued, the "marginal majority" (that is, all those who have to exist within structures of domination) are nevertheless not merely passive receivers of these conditions. As "users" of them, people effect multiple and infinitesimal transformations of the dominant forms under which they inevitably have to live and operate in order to adapt them to their own interests and, to the extent possible, to subject them to their own rules. Users "reappropriate the space organized by socio-cultural production" (de Certeau 1984: xiv), thus effecting a veritable cultural production in their own right.

Unlike the strategies of domination, which structure the world into "readable spaces" (de Certeau 1984: 36) that dominant institutions can understand and control, popular production operates through *tactics*, small procedures and ruses in the realm of everyday life. Strategies and tactics are two different ways of knowing, of practicing life and organizing the social space. Strategies seek to discipline and manage people and institutions, whereas tactics constitute a sort of "antidiscipline," an "art of making" that proceeds by manipulating imposed knowledge and symbols at propitious moments. Tactics are "weapons of the weak," to use James Scott's catchy label (1985); they introduce a certain play into the system of power. Given the expansion of technocratic rationality in postindustrial societies, neither strategies nor tactics are any longer regulated by local communities. Strategies are produced by largely impersonal mechanisms (science, media, transnational economic forces, anonymous institutions); but tactics, too, are increasingly "cut loose from the traditional mechanisms that circumscribed their functioning" (de Certeau 1984: xx, 40). The universalization of the commodity form and the increased autonomy of the culture industries entail that "there is a loss of the fundament of culture in the local enactments of the speaking subjects," which undermines "the core activity that produces meaning" (Angus 1989: 345)—specifically, the link to community.

In Latin America, the breakdown of the local systems for the production of meaning is not as extended as it is in the postindustrial world. But the fact that the Latin American population is already 70 percent urban and very exposed to modern informational systems cannot be underestimated. Nevertheless, this fact must be considered together with the recognition that there still exist *socially significant* groups that represent alternative cultural possibilities. For instance, as Starn and Findji amply demonstrate in Chapters 6 and 7, local tactics—some bound to community, some not—allowed peasants and indigenous groups to main-tain an important degree of control over their environment and worldview. In sum, even if it is increasingly reinscribed into the market system, the production of meaning in Latin America retains a certain "hybrid" character, partly linked to the market and the transnational cultural system but also partly arising out of embodied communal systems and "the local enactments of the speaking subjects."

This conceptualization of popular resistance, although helpful, does not yet enable us to construct a direct link with social movements research. With this goal in mind, what else can we say about the nature of "popular cultural production"? In postindustrial societies, it is said, "people make popular culture at the interface between everyday life and the consumption of the products of the culture industry" (Fiske 1989b: 6). The aim of this productivity is to create meanings that are relevant to everyday experience. Part of this process takes the form of a sort of "semiotic resistance," which originates in "the desire of the subordinate to exert control over the meanings of their lives, a control that is typically denied them in the material social conditions" (Fiske 1989b: 10). Those who focus merely on the "escapism" of the popular classes as they consume the products of the culture industries (TV, music videos and video games, school, shopping centers, romance novels, fashion, and so on) overlook the vibrant symbolic creativity that goes on in the daily encounter with those products.

This form of "semiotic power" is a type of social power, and hence it is actually or potentially political:

> Those who dominate social relations also dominate the production of the meanings that underpin them: Social power and semiotic power are different sides of the same coin. Challenging meanings and the social group with the right to make them is thus no act of escape. . . . Semiotic power is not a mere symbol of, or licensed substitute for, "real" power. Its uses are not confined to the construction of resistant subjectivities but extend also to the construction of relevances, of ways of negotiating this interface between the products of the culture industries and the experience of everyday life (Fiske 1989b: 132).

Beyond that, "resistances at the micro-level are necessary to produce social conditions for political action at the macro-level" (Fiske 1989a: 172). I will come back to this point when I discuss the concept of articulation. For now, it is important to emphasize that it is in the terrain of everyday life that the interests of the dominant culture are negotiated and contested: "speaking our meanings with their language," as Fiske (1989a: 36) summarized this dynamic. Popular culture involves the recognition of social difference and the affirmation of the culture's rights and identity. Difference is a social need and a social practice. This is true in the Third World as well, although the dynamics of cultural production are somewhat different. Cultural politics in Latin America cannot be reduced to the "uses" of dominant products or texts; this is doubly so given the state's acute limitations in providing services for large segments of the population, so that not infrequently people have to provide for their own. In Latin America, the production and circulation of meanings are not so overdetermined by the commercial forms of Western capitalism. There still exist practices, "residual" and "emerging" (Williams 1980), that have a decisive collective character, and these provide a different basis for resistance and collective action.

Finally, how are people's production and negotiation of meanings going to be studied? If this production is at the basis of cultural politics, whether in the form of social movements or in "minor" forms of resistance, how is it going to be made visible? Generally speaking, one needs to understand how meanings are made (for example, through "development," mass media, or seemingly trivial daily acts of creation and resistance) and how they relate to social experience (that is, how they allow people to create elements or engage in practices that are relevant to them, particularly in terms of their struggles against specific forms of power). Theorists of popular culture advocate a type of ethnographic approach that moves from dominant "text" (cultural form or product) to its concrete appropriations by the people (its "users"). This "ethnosemiotic approach" highlights the role of the people as "agent[s] of culture in process" and as "structured instances of culture in practice" (Fiske 1990: 86). Here, we are speaking of a type of cultural analysis that requires a close reading and interpretation of popular experiences, including, but not restricted to, class, gender, ethnic, and politico-economic aspects. "Ethnography," Fiske summarized (1990: 98), "is concerned to trace the specifics of the uses of a system, the ways that the various formations of the people have evolved of making do with the resources it provides. Ethnosemiotics is concerned with interpreting these uses and their politics and in tracing in them instances of the larger system through which culture (meanings) and politics (action) intersect."

This approach has important methodological consequences for social movements research. It requires a close relationship between investigator and people and a significant engagement in concrete situations. Ethnographic techniques, critical inquiry, and textual analysis are all involved. One possible and provisional way of imagining the research process from an ethnosemiotic perspective is in terms of the following processes. First, the popular practice/"text" (produced either through more or less autonomous creation or through the consumption of a dominant product/text) and its context have to be generated for analysis, always in terms of "peoples' own practices, meanings and usages of them, as gathered through our direct fieldwork methods" (Willis 1990: 7). Second, this "re-generated" text, along with the processes by which it was produced, must be interpreted; this interpretation has to start with the self-understanding of the agents and move beyond it, toward an explanation couched in terms that make the practice in question clearer to both agents and researchers (and, hopefully, permit a more effective or clairvoyant practice by the agents, as Taylor (1985) would have it). Third, the practice/text's relation to a politics, that is, to the redistribution of social power, has to be ascertained. Finally—and of particular importance in the case of social movements research—the extent to which this cultural politics fosters alternative political cultures must also be examined.

All of these steps involve complex theoretical and methodological questions that I will not attempt to analyze here. The end result of the process should be a more intimate and complex account of the movement and of those who make it, not merely an overview of its organizational structure, its relation to parties, and the like. As in the case of the life history of individuals, this research approach requires that we see the social actor "as engaged in the meaningful creation of a life world":

> Rather than looking at social and cultural systems solely as they impinge on a life, and turn it into an object, a life history should allow one to see how an actor makes culturally meaningful history, how history is produced in action and on the actor's retrospective reflections on that action. A life history narrative should allow one to see the subjective mapping of experience, the working out of a culture and a social system that is often obscured in a typified account (Behar 1990: 225).

Behar's complex life history of a poor Mexican woman suggests that there are possibilities for seeing Latin American women in terms different from those already fixed in much academic and political discourse (mothers, wives, activists, "beasts of burden," and so forth). "It suggests that, if looked at from a cultural perspective, Latin American women can emerge as thinkers, cosmologists, creators of worlds" (Behar 1990: 230). So it would be with contemporary movements and those enagaged in them. They would appear as engaged in the self-production of their reality in multifaceted and complex ways, including their responses to harsh social and economic conditions.

Social Movements and Articulatory Politics

That the "subjective mapping of experience" is an integral part of history should be clear after this discussion of the role of popular culture in social life. This mapping always takes place in a broader socioeconomic and cultural context. And this context is also experiencing significant transformations; a new phase seems to have started with changes in the nature of the production process in the 1970s, which scholars summarized by the decade's end under the rubric of the new international division of labor (Froebel 1980). Throughout the 1980s, scholars emphasized the role of high technology in the new division of labor (Castells 1986), as well as a number of related issues, such as the feminization of the labor force (Fuentes and Ehrenreich 1983; Mies 1986; Benería and Roldán 1987; Ong 1987) and the growth of the "informal" sector of the economy (Portes, Castells, and Benton, eds., 1989). More recently, the present global restructuring is defined in terms of a "post-Fordist" regime that, as theorists suggest, implies a fundamental restructuring of political, economic, *and* cultural life.[13]

The important question raised by this new situation, in terms of the interests of this chapter, is how the new context will affect social movements. Will it accelerate the fragmentation of collective action, making it more difficult for people to come together? Will it open up new possibilities, create new rules of the game? Most observers seem to be pessimistic in this regard. Yet, as Calderón, Piscitelli, and Reyna argue in Chapter 2, it is by no means clear that the new actors will be swept away by the deepening of surplus extraction mechanisms or by the vagaries of capital's circulation. If it is true that the new structures of accumulation can render entire regions and even countries superfluous to capital (Castells 1986), it is also true, as Mayer (1991) convincingly hypothesized, that even in terms of competing in international labor and capital markets, local communities will have to be more inventive and autonomous and that this may open up possibilities for renegotiating class, gender, and ethnic inequalities at the local and regional levels. When the grip of power tightens (perhaps by a curious twist unintended by those in power but quickly apprehended by those under it), unexpected spaces may be created or freed up (Tsugawa 1991).

One fruitful—and possibly the most general—way of thinking about this set of questions is to understand post-Fordist restructuring as an attempt at bringing about a new "hegemonic formation." As any such formation does, post-Fordism inevitably introduces a series of antagonisms that motivate collective action. Here, we can draw on the work of Laclau and Mouffe regarding what they called "the hegemonic form of politics" (Laclau and Mouffe 1985; Laclau 1985, 1988; Mouffe 1984, 1988a, 1988b). A purposeful and extremely brief presentation of some of the tenets of their work will allow us to approach the questions posed above and extend our understanding of other aspects already mentioned, especially Melucci's notion of the constructed character of collective action and popular culture theorists' idea that "minor" forms of resistance can lead to larger forms of mobilization.

Clearly situated within the poststructuralist and post-Marxist theorizing of the past two decades, the work of Laclau and Mouffe represents a significant departure from earlier political theories, especially regarding the agent of social change and the nature of political spaces and historical transformations. For these authors, such processes, as well as all social practice, are fundamentally discursive. An intuitive way of understanding what they mean by the discursive nature of social life is to consider that social life is always endowed with and apprehended through meaning (for instance, again, as in the case of "development") and that meaning can never be permanently fixed because it is always situated and open to contestation and reinterpretation. This has consequences for understanding the making of collective identities. Melucci argued that the "we" that actors construct is produced by "interaction, negotiation, and the opposition of different orientations" (1988a: 332), and that this depends on how they define the situation as susceptible to common action. The construction of collective identities "has two aspects: the internal complexity of the actor (the plurality of orientations that characterizes him), and the actor's relationship with the environment (other actors, opportunities and constraints)" (Melucci 1988a: 342).

Because all of these aspects are laden with meaning, actors are left with the only possibility of building collective identities through the *articulation* of meaning. This was one of Laclau and Mouffe's strongest conclusions. They referred to "the plurality of orientations" of the actors as "subject positions."[14] The articulation of elements in terms of subject positions makes the construction of a collective identity possible. Of course, this construction also depends on the perception of common interests, but these, too, are discursive. The consequences of the need for this articulatory logic are significant. First, identities are never just given; there is no privileged political subject, and all actors have to struggle within their own spheres in a plural political space (as, say, women, workers, students, and so forth). What is crucial is how all actors articulate positions for themselves and with other movements or their environment.

Politically, the main problem thus becomes that of exploring the kinds of articulations that may result in the formation of identities and collective mobilization. Like Touraine, Laclau and Mouffe believe that this process takes place in different forms at the center and the periphery of the capitalist world economy:

> In the [advanced] countries, the proliferation of points of antagonism permits the multiplication of democratic struggles, but these struggles, given their diversity, do not tend to constitute a "people," that is . . . to divide the political space into two antagonistic fields. On the contrary, in the countries of the Third World, imperialist exploitation and the predominance of brutal and centralized forms of domination tend from the beginning to endow the popular struggle with a center, with a single and clearly defined element. Here the division of the political space into two fields is present from the outset, but the diversity of democratic struggles is more reduced. . . . We will therefore speak of *democratic* struggles where these imply a plurality of political spaces [that is, the center], and of *popular* struggles where certain discourses *tendentially* construct the division of a single political space into two opposing fields [that is, the Third World] (Laclau and Mouffe 1985: 131, 137; emphases in the original).

More clearly stated, Laclau and Mouffe believe that the type of articulatory or "hegemonic form of politics" that results in democratic struggles is only observed "in societies in which the democratic revolution has crossed a certain threshold" (1985: 166), in other words, in "developed" or Center countries. The notion of threshold, let it be noted, implies some sort of evolution, and this teleology and rationalism almost inevitably is accompanied by a certain degree of Eurocentrism. Here again, the Third World is represented as having a different type of historical agency, somewhat reduced in relation to that of European society. But is this so? The authors in this volume make it clear that, even if capital and the division of social labor underlie many of the identities of the new social agents, the potential *unity* of these identities cannot be taken for granted but must be constructed through articulation. True, there are some demands that can be universalized, such as the demand to democratize the state, family, local community, and so on; these demands originate in large part in the capitalist mode of production and the unity of social labor (O'Connor 1988). Yet, even these demands are understood and experienced in very different ways by the various social actors. The "center" of the popular struggles that Laclau and Mouffe refer to is by no means self-evident.

One may wish, of course, that these struggles coalesced into more unified forms of opposition, and, indeed, sometimes this happens. Fals Borda's notion of movements shifting from "the micro to the macro" and from "protest to proposal" (presented in Chapter 17) is an example of articulatory politics at work. So are the continent-wide networks of groups of women and indigenous peoples.[15] According to Laclau and Mouffe, whether this type of articulation actually takes place depends on the nature of the "antagonisms" introduced by the hegemonic formation. In postindustrial society, this formation is characterized by pervasive processes of commodification, bureaucratization, and massification of life, and it is as a response to these conditions that the new movements emerge. In the Third World, the hegemonic formation took the form of development. Development resulted in a multiplicity of antagonisms and identities (differentiated peasants, urban marginals, "traditional" groups, women, and the like) who, in many instances, are becoming the subjects of struggles in their respective domains. It would then seem more appropriate to say that Latin America oscillates between two forms of politics: a logic of popular struggles in a relatively ("tendentially") unified political space (against oligarchies, imperialism, and the developmentalist state) and a logic of "democratic" struggles in a plural space (as in the case of many of the movements discussed in this volume). Both are the result of articulations.

Can we glean the importance of historicity, articulation, and cultural innova-tion in today's Latin American social movements? The women's, gay, and ecology movements (that is, those that some refer to as the "new" movements proper) are rightly seen as challenging models of historicity, to the extent that they seek to redefine gender identities, styles of relation to nature, and ethnocentric concep-tions (Calderón 1986; Slater, ed., 1985; Evers 1985). Jelin asserted that the analytical interest in social movements stems from the "search for evidence of a profound transformation of the social logic. What is at stake is a new form of doing politics and a new way of sociability" (1986: 21); Mires (1987) spoke of a veritable "social reconfiguration" fueled in part by the new movements. One aspect discussed by some authors is the appropriation of the city by the urban poor not only as an economic but also as a cultural space (Verdesoto 1986; Díaz-Barriga 1990). In analyzing the impact of social movements in Peru, Eduardo Ballón (1986) highlighted the movements' role in the consolidation of collective memories and symbols through a variety of cultural demands. And Colombia's civic and regional movements were seen as fostering new values and cultural practices, despite their seemingly limited awareness of broad structural problems (Santana 1989; Fals Borda, Chapter 17; Findji, Chapter 7).

In analyzing Venezuelan social movements, Gabriela Uribe and Edgardo Lander (1988) found that some of the movements elicit changes in symbolic-cultural frameworks that result in new modes of constructing political facts (see also García, Chapter 9). Social and political problematics are thus seen as linked within an overarching cultural field, to the extent that the social practice of the movements relies on the creation of new spaces for the production of meanings that can be projected onto wider social and political domains. Luis Verdesoto's assessment of Ecuadorian social movements, reminiscent of Aníbal Quijano's notion of the emergence of a new public domain in the Andean world, gave a good indication of the politics of articulation at work:

Rather than a massive proletarianization, the main feature of social life in Ecuador is the multiplication of identities of social groups. *Pobladores*, women, the young, indigenous groups, regions, etc., construct themselves under other types of political parameters and other forms of addressing the instances of power. What is at stake is precisely their right to a space in social life. . . . These identities propitiate an open order, at the same time that networks of solidarity are established among them. Perhaps their most important goal is the creation of a *popular collective* capable of constantly redefining its objectives through action. This feature effectively fractures the restrictive face of institutionalized politics. The identities in gestation begin to develop new forms of understanding and questioning the state, not from the vantage point of the power of the state, but, on the contrary, from that of the *construction of a different social power*. To this extent, their goal is not to replace the state but to construct an alternative society (1986: 186, 187; emphases added).

The logic of articulation is seen at play in many instances—for example, in the formation of networks of urban popular movements and in the role of the "neighbor" (*vecino*) as a powerful new identity category (see Bennett, Chapter 13). Municipalities, neighborhoods, and regions are seen as new sites of articulation, no less important than the state because of their different or reduced institutionality. One may detect in these conceptions a certain dose of normativism and even utopianism. Needless to say, those who proclaimed the end of poverty and the advent of a kingdom of abundance in the 1940s and 1950s, to be brought about by development, or those who today preach ad nauseam yet another "stabilization package" as a way out of the crisis were and are at least as romantic as some of the social movements researchers. Who knows? Perhaps those who stick to conventional paradigms, known by now to be fruitless and futile, are truly more romantic than those who dare to dream and imagine what has not yet been thought. In any case, today's Latin American researchers—either engaged with or independent of European and North American theories—are in the process of developing a powerful program for social movements research and theorizing, as Calderón, Piscitelli, and Reyna adamantly argue.

This brings my argument full circle. I opened this chapter with some general comments regarding the nature of theorizing today, and it might be fitting to close it in the same tone. It is feasible to raise the question (particularly, perhaps, from a certain North American perspective) of why Latin American researchers still make use of European theories. Does this not reinforce their "intellectual dependency" on Europe and North America? Such thought arises from a relatively conventional reading of the nature of the social movements research area. Why not admit, on the contrary, that for authors like Touraine, Castells, Laclau, Mouffe, Evers, and Slater—all of whom have had very significant experience in Latin America, usually spanning many years—Latin America has become a "center" of theories and insights? True, in the travel of theories and theorists that characterizes the postcolonial context, the West is partly reproduced as a site of discourse production, but it is also transformed, displaced, and resisted. It is also true that Latin American intellectuals, while trying to extricate themselves from uncritical dependency on the theoretical traditions of the West, do remain bound to them in important and complex ways (this chapter clearly included).[16]

But, as I already mentioned, theory production today cannot be seen in simple terms, as being produced in one part and applied in another. Rather, it must be seen as a process of multiple conversations in a discontinuous terrain (Mani 1989; Clifford 1989). Today, as in the past, for Latin American researchers to create an authentic epistemological system that represents Latin American sociocultural practices, that system must engage with prevailing systems (Western and others). Researchers must seek what is enabling in the prevailing systems, being wary of the risks of doing so—to avoid replicating those features deemed ethnocentric or normalizing, especially the positioning of the West as a center of discourse concerning Latin America and the Third World. And, finally, they must reach out toward new regimes of truth that recenter the Latin American experience.

Conclusion

A point stressed throughout the chapter is that contemporary social movements in Latin America have a multiple character, as economic, social, political, and cultural struggles. The boundaries and dependencies among these domains are blurred, in some cases indistinguishable. In particular, it is important to be open to the deeply cultural character of these struggles. This realization is crucial even in terms of the economy; as Stuart Hall pointedly stated (1991: 64), "Everybody, including people in poor societies whom we in the West frequently speak about as if they inhabit a world *outside* of culture, know that today's 'goods' double up as social signs and produce meanings as well as energy." Social movements are about the transformation of many of the practices of development and modernity, about the envisioning and reconstruction of social orders, perhaps alternative modernities or different modes of historicity.

To understand these processes, I have argued, one must look at the micro level of everyday practices and their imbrication with larger processes of development, patriarchy, capital, and the state. How these forces find their way into people's lives, their effects on people's identity and social relations, and people's responses and "uses" of them have to be examined through a close engagement and reading of popular actions. It is also true that the system that accounted for and stabilized identities has changed dramatically. Even up to the 1960s, identities were, in a sense, clearly defined and unproblematic. One knew who was who, so to speak, and how he or she was defined as a member of a group. One also knew what to do and how to do it (Development or Revolution, depending on one's perspective). But this is no longer true. Theorists refer to this change as the proliferation of identities and cite the fact that identities are constructed and that this construction takes place through processes of articulation. In the interface of identity and articulation one finds the manifold political strategies and tactics that more clearly account for a "movement." It is at this level that the various "paradigms" of social movements research cohere. Questions of strategy and questions of identity are inextricably linked, and the links can be most fruitfully investigated at the level of the cultural politics of the movements.

This also means that the nature and impact of social movements is not restricted to their most visible manifestations. Even when the state, becoming conscious of a new challenge in the form of a movement, tries to co-opt it or repress it, it is possible that the movement has already spread thin throughout a vast social domain. In other words, social movements are somewhat exterior to the state, and if it is true that the state is a key interlocutor for the movements, these latter cannot be reduced to the logic of the state.[17] The state, to be sure, is too powerful a social force to be left to the politicians and economic elites; it is still particularly important in relation to the provision of basic needs. Yet, at least in part, the social reconfiguration that social movements are bringing about has to be found in a different space, in whatever way we may be able to think of it (for instance, social relations of daily life, transformed cultural understandings, new political cultures, new public domains, and the like). Beyond the borders of the region, Latin American social movements are nourishing a crop of meanings that in some ways are freer of modern forms of rationality and control and that could foster a renewal not only of the awareness of suffering but also of the awareness of forms of freedom and of life as a collective process. And this might have unique importance in today's world.

In her study of "the alchemy of race and rights" in the system of North American law, Patricia Williams spoke thus of the reality of "unowned" or emancipated slaves after the Civil War:

> After the Civil War, when slaves were unowned—I hesitate to use the word emancipated even yet—they were also disowned: They were thrust out of the market and into a nowhere land that was not quite the mainstream labor market, and very much outside the marketplace of rights. They were placed beyond the bounds of valuation, in much the same way that the homeless are or that nomads and gypsies are, or tribal people who refuse to ascribe to the notion of private space and who refuse or are refused traditional jobs or stationary employment; they became like all those who cannot express themselves in the language of power and assertion and staked claims—all those who are nevertheless deserving of the dignity of social valuation, yet those who are so often denied survival itself (1991: 21).

One is tempted to think similarly of many people in the Third World today, the vast numbers of people placed under conditions of marginality or in the space of the informal economy, "not quite the mainstream labor market"—which, as we know, shrank significantly in the 1980s—"and very much outside the marketplace of rights" because the language of rights and the language of justice also seemed to fade away from public discourse in the wake of the worst-ever IMF-imposed "austerity" and "stabilization" programs. But perhaps the same people are learning how to negotiate more explicitly their participation in the transnational markets of commodities and meanings that characterize Latin America today; perhaps they are coming to reject more efficiently the "bounds of valuation" within which they can only be seen as second-class, "underdeveloped" subjects; perhaps they are coming to assert themselves in a language of power that they have crafted through forms of collective action such as those discussed by many of the authors in this volume.

Notes

1. This is clear in so many domains, from childrearing and nutrition practices to political and economic behavior. More and more, our daily lives are permeated and mediated by theory, so the self-understandings that we take for granted are replaced by theoretical considerations. In the Third World, this "theorization" of daily life is not as pervasive as in the more economically advanced countries. On the nature of social theory as practice, see the excellent essay by Charles Taylor (1985).

2. On this trend toward "interpretive social science," see Taylor 1985 and Rabinow and Sullivan 1987.

3. The notion of "traveling theories and theorists" (the fact that, in the late twentieth century, the producers and audiences of theory can no longer be situated in stable geographical areas such as "first" and "third" worlds) originated in a special 1989 issue of the Santa Cruz journal *Inscriptions*. See especially the contributions by Mani (1989) and Clifford (1989). See also Said 1983.

4. For a more exhaustive discussion of the origins and modes of operation of the discourse of development, see A. Escobar 1984, 1988.

5. Here, what I have in mind is the 1980s literature on resistance, particularly in anthropology. See Taussig 1980; Fals Borda 1984; Scott 1985; and Ong 1987. Opposition to specific development programs is periodically featured in journals such as *The IFDA Dossier* (Nyon, Switzerland) and *Cultural Survival* (Cambridge, Massachusetts).

6. A group of Third World intellectuals and activists are voicing a radical antidevelopment message that they see emerging from the grass roots. Rather than speaking about "development alternatives," they prefer to talk about "alternatives to development," that is, a rejection of the entire paradigm. See especially Nandy 1989; Rahnema 1988a; Sheth 1987; Esteva 1987; Shiva 1989.

7. On the anthropology of modernity, see Rabinow 1986, 1988; Urla 1990; A. Escobar, in press b; Rofel n.d.

8. Discussions about modernity and postmodernity are relatively recent in Latin America, yet they are increasingly visible and important. See especially the excellent collection on the subject edited by Calderón (1988). See also Quijano 1988; Lechner 1988; García Canclini 1990; Sarlo 1991; and A. Escobar, in press b. For valuable reviews of these works, see Montaldo 1991. These authors accept postmodernism as a fruitful horizon for theorizing, to the extent that it poses again the question of the nature of social life as a central issue, even if they adamantly insist that postmodern insights have to be reworked according to the interests of Latin American peoples.

9. The work of the Annales School, Norbert Elias (1978), and Foucault, as well as feminist theory and ecology, are among the most important factors behind the increasing interest in everyday life.

10. This and all other translations from the Spanish are my own.

11. The notion of "levels of historicity" is problematic and Eurocentric. For Touraine, only postindustrial societies have achieved the distancing that historicity requires (from God, tradition, the world as object). As anthropologists have shown, however, this type of objectifying distancing is only one possibility among many for the development of historical consciousness. From recent studies, one learns, for instance, about the sophisticated historical consciousness of the Saramakas of Surinam (Price 1983, 1990), eighteenth-century Hawaiians (Sahlins 1985), the Ilongot of the Philippines (Rosaldo 1980), or today's Colombian peasants (Fals Borda 1984, 1986; Gudeman and Rivera 1990).

12. This English translation from the Italian original was slightly modified by me based on the Spanish translation in Calderón, ed., 1988.

13. Post-Fordism is believed to entail changes in the realms of production, exchange, consumption, and politics, such as: the replacement of mass production with flexible "just-in-time" techniques; the growth of the financial sector and speculative activities; uneven and selective incorporation of regions worldwide; growing commoditization and a new informational culture of advertising and consumption; and forms of politics characterized by authoritarian populism, fragmentation, and the possibility for a progressive renewal in the form of new social movements. Women, ethnic minorities, and part of the proletariat are among those most affected by these changes. See, for instance, Harvey 1989; see also the special 1991 issue of *Socialist Review* on the topic, especially the contributions by Stuart Hall, David Harvey, and Margit Mayer.

14. For instance, a *poblador* is characterized by many partial and potentially conflictual subject positions: as poor, employed or unemployed, woman or man, member of a Christian base community or a Protestant group, "white" or "preto" (black), and so forth. All of these positions have different susceptibilities of being attached to a "collective identity." The chapters by Burdick and Starn in this volume give some idea of what could be done with an analysis in terms of articulatory practices.

15. There is a crucial question underlying the "growth" of movements through articulation: How is this growth going to be assessed? Assessment of social movements today usually takes place in relation to some known model of growth and effectiveness, such as their evolution into political parties or broader organizations. But this should be avoided because what is at stake for the new movements is precisely the challenge to these criteria. As Munck (1990) demonstrated, most authors approach this question with a dichotomous mind-set: It is thought that movements are either accepted by the state (but also made dependent on it or co-opted) or that they maintain their autonomy but necessarily remain isolated and limited. "In both scenarios, we see failed social movements" (G. Munck 1990: 37). A more fluid way to "assess" the movements would be to think in terms of power: What forms of power (state/economic/gender, and so on) are upset or undermined by the movement? What types of "freedoms" does the movement obtain from a relation with the state, parties, and so on? Conversely, what is being "extracted" from the movement in such a relation? Who decides politically the nature and importance of this relation? What forms of popular power are fostered by the movement?

Or one can think, for instance, of the following questions: How do "we" perceive "effects," and who *are* we? According to what criteria? Based on whose political culture? If the risk of recolonization by the state is present at the same time that the movement breaks into light, is this not a sign that the movement is already having some effect? Is it not necessarily exposing the dominating character of the state? What real practices are transformed by the movement, and what is the relation of these practices to the state, the economy, and so forth? Is the movement creating new openings that nourish the popular experience? Criteria for assessment, in other words, should not derive solely from existing understandings of political culture.

16. This digression on the politics of theory is motivated by the fact that, when I presented a "theories of social movements" paper at U.S. universities, almost inevitably somebody objected to the use of "complicated European theories." I appreciate whatever good intentions exist in this attempt by North American audiences at helping us (Latin Americans) see that by doing this we are still "intellectual colonies" of Europe. But I would say that believing that European or Euro-American theories—because of their systematicity, elegance, abstractedness, and completeness (for example, the theories of Touraine and Laclau and Mouffe)—are necessarily better is more *their* problem (and usually the Europeans' as well). The fact that these theories shine higher in the intellectual firmament is a reflection of the power with which these constructions are still endowed in the academy, not of any intrinsic "lower" quality of theories produced under different rules of discourse. We might even entertain the thought that less comprehensive, more fluid, and even "nomad" forms of theory, such as those that tend to be produced in the Third World, are more conducive today to improved understanding and action.

17. The hypothesis of the exteriority of social movements in relation to the state originated in the work of Deleuze and Guattari (1987). See also A. Escobar, in press a.

Part 2
The Making of
Collective Identities

6

"I Dreamed of Foxes and Hawks": Reflections on Peasant Protest, New Social Movements, and the Rondas Campesinas of Northern Peru

Orin Starn

I dreamed of foxes and hawks. This was a sign that the cattle rustlers would come that night. Ay, compañeros! To be ronderos we must be brave, very brave: persist and lose our fear of the rustlers; not be afraid of the evil night hours, the mud, and the cold.
—Anonymous voice on Radio San Antonio
Bambamarca, Peru, 1985

On April 27, 1990, 2,000 peasants flooded down from the green mountains around the northern Andean town of Chota to protest a sudden hike in the interest rates of the government-run Agrarian Bank. As the big-bellied bank functionaries retreated behind a row of nervous young riot police, the peasants stormed around the old main square and then assembled to listen to their leaders denounce the government's agrarian policy. Most of the marchers were men. Some wore ponchos and tire-tread sandals. Others sported polyester pullovers and Ecuadoran-made rubber boots. Straw hats and a sprinkling of tractor caps shaded tough, weather-beaten faces. Many of the men also carried stout canes or rawhide whips.

Suddenly, another 200 *campesinos* ("peasants") burst out from a narrow side street. They paraded two heavily bound young cattle rustlers around the square. Just in back of the unfortunate thieves ambled the black cow they had tried to steal, led on a rope by its grizzled owner. The new marchers melded with the others to surge once more around the square and then down another side street to the provincial prosecutor's shabby cement office. The prosecutor was defended only by a second small police squad. He acceded to the peasant demand for immediate charges against the thieves. "Thousands of campesinos marching in from the countryside stoned on *coca* and cane liquor," the lanky, moustachioed lawyer would complain to me several days later. "It's dangerous to the city, and to us duly constituted authorities."

The events of April 27 were directed by new rural justice groups called *rondas campesinas* ("peasants who make the rounds"). The first *ronda* ("round") began in the hamlet of Cuyumalca—just an hour walk uphill from Chota—on December 29, 1976, as a community-run vigilante patrol against thieves. Hundreds of other hamlets in Chota and the rugged neighboring provinces of Hualgayoc and Cutervo formed their own night patrols over the next three years. During the 1980s, the movement spread hundreds of miles across the rest of the department of Cajamarca and into the adjoining departments of Amazonas, La Libertad, Labayeque, and Piura. At the same time, rondas dramatically expanded their functions. They evolved into an entire alternative justice system with open community assemblies to resolve problems ranging from wife-beating to land disputes. The movement became a point of pride for peasants, who were tired of inefficient and often corrupt town bureaucrats. Today, the organizations have virtually eliminated the once serious problem of stock-rustling; they arbitrate thousands of disputes and direct small public works projects; and a formerly unorganized peasantry has developed the political strength to stage protests like the one in Chota against the interest rates. Rondas now operate in more than 3,400 hamlets across Peru's northern Andes.

The rondas represent one of the largest and most sustained rural movements in late twentieth-century Latin America. But they have attracted little serious attention from journalists and scholars,[1] and the organizations remain almost unknown outside Peru. Within the country, most Peruvians confuse them with the very different rural vigilante patrols, also known as rondas campesinas, that are organized by Peru's army in the southern mountains to fight Shining Path guerrillas. In this chapter, without making any redemptive claim to speak for northern peasants, I seek to provide a measure of understanding regarding the limits and accomplishments of their efforts to organize.

At the same time, I link the literatures on new social movements and peasant protest. Most scholarship on new social movements ignores peasants and thus misses some of the most vital new politics on the planet. And most work on agrarian protest sorely lacks the sensitivity of the new social movements literature, especially that of its so-called identity-focused wing, to the power-laden processes of syncretism and invention that go into the making of all political protest. I hope to show how a dialogue between the two literatures can be of mutual benefit.

My analysis does not drive toward a new grand theory of peasant organizing. Indeed, I am convinced of the need for close hermeneutic readings that convey the unique cadences of every rural movement. Nor does my interest in the semiotics of rural protest imply a slight to fundamental questions of causality and strategy. Quite the contrary is true: A firm grasp on problems of meaning and identity can assist greatly in answering questions about why rural protest occurs and how it unfolds.

In the end, this chapter advances a framework in which rural protest is seen as more than a dry matter of determining forces or the bland calculation of economic interests. I also want to show how peasant activism represents the active creation of alternative modes of political vision and identity. The urban world, as the rondas will demonstrate, has no monopoly on innovation. In the peripheries of the periphery, people are also articulating fragile new orders of difference and possibility.

*   *   *

The rise of the rondas must be situated in the context of a continuing record of frequent and hard-fought political engagement by rural people in Latin America. Backing from peasants now fuels insurrections—if in very different contexts—in Colombia, Guatemala, and Peru. Across the region, local protests spring up around causes as diverse as access to land, loan subsidies, and crop prices.

Despite the strong evidence for the continuing willingness of many rural people to engage in frank and unabashed protest, peasant mobilization has received little attention in the literature on new social movements. One obvious reason for the oversight rests with the greater visibility of urban politics, which unfold in the backyards of the leading scholars in debates on contemporary social activism (Touraine 1981, 1988a; Laclau and Mouffe 1985; Gilroy 1987). More deeply, it is easy to ignore or dismiss peasant organizing as outdated class politics. Movements like those for human rights, racial and sexual liberation, and the environment appear to mesh with a postmodern condition of shifting, plural, and nonessential subjectivities. Peasant protest, by contrast, brings to mind modernist images of class struggle and Socialist revolution. The word *peasant* sounds not even modern but medieval.

The question of rural political mobilization has also slipped down the agenda within peasant studies. Although the 1970s brought a proliferation of works on agrarian protest, the 1980s generated a fresh caution toward the politics of the rural poor. Several scholars contended that the intense interest in well-publicized cases like the Vietnamese and Chinese revolutions left the distorted picture that major upheaval was the norm in the countryside of the Third World. Geographer Michael Watts (1988: 118), for example, wrote of an "obsession with the high visibility areas" and a failure to recognize "that in many instances and for significant periods of time there was indeed little *explicit* politics in the country-side."

Rather than abandoning a view of peasants as political actors, many scholars turned to the study of what James Scott (1985) called "everyday resistance." Their work stressed that the political struggles of poor farmers do not just unfold in the high drama of rebellion, revolt, and revolution but also occur through the more undercover mediums of gossip, foot-dragging, false deference, evasion, and petty thievery. Peasants resort to these covert strategies, argued Scott in his influential and intelligent *Weapons of the Weak*, because they recognize the high costs of open protest: lost patronage by local elites and bloody repression by the authorities. The tactics of everyday resistance partly represent what poet Czeslaw Milosz once called the "glory of slaves"—actions that do little to change overarching structures of inequality and domination. At the same time, though, the existence of small-scale strategies of opposition signals that peasants are never passive, even in periods of apparent calm.

Although Scott may have painted the private views of peasants as too neatly untouched by the claims of the powerful, the everyday resistance literature represents a welcome broadening of academic appreciation for rural political agency. But there is a danger that we may lose sight of the frequency and force of *open* peasant movements. A picture of rural people as mostly quiescent, if never passive, neither jibes with the situation in much of Latin America nor does justice to the hundreds of thousands of campesinos who give their time and often risk their lives to press for change. Peru's great Socialist José Carlos Mariátegui (1968: 40) wrote that the "tragic secret" of suppressed rebellions was guarded by "the silence of the *puna* ['high moors']." Half a century later, rural struggles again threaten to become hidden histories.

How can we go about producing the sort of engaging and sharp-sighted accounts that might help to keep rural protest from dropping out of view? Perhaps a good way to start is by returning to the classic peasant revolt literature of the late 1960s and 1970s. This scholarship was governed by what historian Lynn Hunt (1984) called "metaphors of structure." Protest was treated as the expression of "underlying" forces, events that could be deduced or even predicted from structural causes. How to conceptualize these forces became the key point of dispute. Explanations ranged from Scott's (1976) "moral economy" model to Jeffrey Paige's (1975) "class-relational" view.

In retrospect, two related problems existed in the debate. One was the presupposition that a single answer could be developed to the question of why peasants rebel. In advancing their contending models, scholars tended to overlook the fact that every protest emerges from a unique and historically specific set of circumstances. Certainly, it would be a mistake to retreat into a particularism that denies the value of comparative study. But the attempt to discover a common denominator had the effect of downplaying the fundamental fact that the reasons for protest vary tremendously from case to case.

A second problem arose in the unspoken premise that the analysis of peasant movements was exclusively a matter of establishing causality. Unrest, as historian Steve Stern (1987: 6) astutely observed, tended to be portrayed as a "reaction to changes determined by all-powerful external forces or 'systems.'" What the literature largely ignored was that peasant activism also involves construction and creation. Concentrating on questions of determining forces, most scholars did not recognize that protest additionally rests on the ability of rural people to fashion a vision, symbols, and procedures for their organizing.

Here, I think, the new social movements literature can be of use, with its emphasis on the "constructedness" of political identity.[2] Much conventional social science has presupposed "preconstituted categories" of political actors—whether women, workers, peasants, or racial minorities. By contrast, much recent thinking about new social movements explores what Michel Foucault (1972) called the "constitution of subjectivity." Their attention turns to how politics represents the fashioning of original kinds of self-identification through innovation and recombination. Identity becomes something to be built, articulated, and invented rather than explained exclusively by reference to social structure. From this perspective, politics does not reduce to a limited number of "privileged subjects." Instead, it becomes crucial to recognize that people forge a rainbow of fresh political options in response to a variety of social ills. To paraphrase Alain

Touraine (1988a), society itself becomes a self-creating process, rather than a finished edifice or structure.

"Peasant protest" may sound like a cut-and-dried affair of class mobilization. On close inspection, though, the heterogeneous movements that go under that label come into being through the same power-charged processes of collective self-imagination as any other contemporary political activity. Rural protests do not embody prefabricated categories. They are also about the molding of fresh forms of political vision and practice.

Like their urban cousins, all rural people move within the densely interlinked world of high mobility, mixed-up intercultural traffic, and a fast-changing transnational political economy at the brink of the twenty-first century (Harvey 1989). Peasant protest emerges through choices—albeit never separate from the dance of power—from within the belly of the advanced capitalist beast. To draw from cultural critic James Clifford (1988), rural movements represent "impure products." These products, in turn, derive from local spirits of synthesis and invention. Thus, homesteaders in the Peruvian Amazon galvanized elements of Socialist, nationalist, and liberation theology discourse in a mass protest for higher corn prices during Holy Week of 1983. And Ecuadoran farmers meld an ethnic sense of Quechua identity with a class-based understanding of themselves as small farmers in the National Federation of Peasant and Indigenous Peoples (FENOC). The creative definition of peasant political identity can occur even in the heartlands of the industrialized West. In downtown Stockton in California's Central Valley, for example, a fresh-painted sign hung on the door to a small office reads: *Unión Campesina "Lázaro Cárdenas."* A group of migrant Mexican farmworkers has defined itself as peasant, formed a new labor association, and attached the campesino label to the name of Mexico's great agrarian reform president to form their own group's name.

To be sure, enthusiastic talk about "autopoiesis" and the "construction of collective identity" can gloss over basic questions of origins and causes. Indeed, much writing in the continental wing of the new social movements literature partakes in the "negation of teleology" that Dick Hebdige (1986: 84) found characteristic of postmodern social theory. The questioning of easy functionalisms is welcome, but, in my view, one should not go too far. It seems to me possible to share postmodern skepticism about model-building and master narratives without jettisoning modernist concerns for how and why. Likewise, one should be able to explore the politics of rural identity without losing sight of the often quite elemental matters of scarcity and survival that drive people to act.

Nor should issues of strategy be overlooked. Several years ago, Jean Cohen (1985) pointed out a split in the new social movements literature between work concerned with strategy and with identity. The former focuses on goals, resources, and organizational structure; the latter explores the formulation of political subjectivities. The stolid empiricism of mainstream Anglo-American social science led to a prime concern with strategy. High-flying poststructuralism on the Continent, by contrast, lent itself to a concentration on identity. However, there is no intrinsic reason for this academic division of labor to exist. As many scholars now stress, the investigation of strategy and identity should go hand-in-hand (Escobar and Alvarez, Chapter 1).

Clearly, peasant studies need to be more sensitive to the contours of meaning. But this should accompany, not replace, the study of tactics, interests, and organization.

A view of rural activism as the product of recombination and invention has a pair of important corollaries. One is the need to make a decisive break from all understandings of peasants as the bearers of pure pastoral values. Apart from Samuel Popkin's (1979) criticism that it overplays rural collectivism, Scott's concept of rural "moral economy" must be located within a time-honored representational tradition where peasant culture appears as a transhistorical phenomenon beyond the bustle of urban modernity. In Latin America, the national variants of *indigenismo* represent the most obvious incarnations of this thinking. Thus, the Peruvian Socialist lawyer Hildebrando Castro Pozo (1979) wrote in the 1930s about modern Andean communities as perpetuating Incan values. And anthropologists like Robert Redfield (1956) and many others could depict Mexican villages as embodying age-old "little traditions." These views have always underplayed the location of small farmers in larger networks of ideas, exchange, and authority under precolonial and colonial rule. Intensifying world interconnections during the twentieth century have fortified and multiplied these ties. Peasant values and protest need to be understood not as the consequence of distance or separation from the rest of the world but as being formulated from particular positions *within* the global village.

A second and related corollary is the need for great caution in speaking of a "subaltern domain." One of the leading figures in the Subaltern Studies Group, historian Ranajit Guha (1988: 40), reexaminined British-ruled India to argue for an "autonomous domain" of peasant consciousness that "put it in a category apart from elite politics." To support his claim, Guha documented a long series of radical uprisings in the countryside. This at once careful and passionate scholarship did much to write the rural poor back into Indian history. In part, though, the language of "autonomous domain" and "category apart" recycles old stereotypes about peasants as people living in a separate world. Guha recognized, of course, that relations of economic domination bind the wealthy and impoverished. Indeed, he saw the radical consciousness of peasants as a response to exploitation. But Guha did not explore the full impact on rural values of accompanying forces like evangelization and state-run education. As I have argued, peasants may rework these kinds of influences into their own special idioms (de Certeau 1984). Yet, the multiple interconnections between city and countryside also create partial continuities between rural outlooks and those of other social strata. Peasant politics may be distinctive, but it is never autonomous.

If peasant movements can benefit from insights in the new social movements literature, then it also behooves students of rural activism to listen to what recent scholarship has to say about the limits of contemporary politics. One key admonition from many thinkers warns against the perception that contemporary social movements represent a step in the inevitable rumble of history toward human emancipation. Especially in the Marxist-influenced scholarship, much classic writing of the late 1960s and 1970s tended to treat rural revolts as part of a growing critical understanding of world capitalism and the momentum toward its overthrow (for example, Wolf 1969; Feder 1971). Of course, the events of the last few years have tarnished the dream of Socialist transformation within which these representations of peasants were wrapped. In Latin America, moreover, the past two decades have offered no examples of triumphant peasant revolutions. Even cases of sustained regional strength, like the rondas, represent relative rarities. Perhaps the majority of rural protests follow a pattern of "erupt and fizzle": Angry action explodes in a land invasion, highway blockade, protest march, or burning of a government office. But any combination of factors at least temporarily ends up defusing the fiercest militance—demands may be satisfied, divisions may arise among the protesters, or state repression may be effective. Perceiving this fragility ought not to detract from the recognition of the frequency of rural protests or the courage of their protagonists. It does, however, suggest that peasant movements should not be squeezed into the progressive linear designs of most conventional brands of Western historical vision.

A second important qualification revolves around the ideological purity of social movements. Clearly, one needs a sense of the status of new political activism in relation to structures of domination. Some movements, too, obviously have more radical and transformative potential than others. At the same time, though, most initiatives defy neat categorization as "hegemonic" or "counterhegemonic." They interweave resistance and accommodation, innovation and continuity, perpetuation and subversion of orthodox ways of thinking. Good analysis, as Donna Haraway (1985: 91) insisted, "requires not sorting consciousness into categories of 'clear-sighted critique grounding a solid political epistemology' versus 'manipulated false consciousness,' but subtle understanding of emerging pleasures, experiences, and powers with serious potential for changing the rules of the game." Rather than premising that a movement will be either purely oppositional or power-serving, it is more fruitful to approach each new movement as unique and dynamic, with multivalent implications for relations of power and inequality.

On close scrutiny, peasant protests in Latin America tend to combine both a challenge of and an acceptance of authority. On the one hand, most movements coalesce in opposition to the powers that be—most often big landowners and/or the state. On the other, they accept and reproduce many of the prevailing arrangements of representation and command. Thus, admiration for high office-holders can mix with disdain for local bureaucrats. Recourse to illegal measures like roadblocks and squatter invasions joins with respect for the law, and patriotic desires for national unity can mix with revolutionary fervor. Making sense of rural politics requires a fine-tuned ethnographic sensitivity to the interlocking nuances of resistance and accommodation.

A third caution centers around the issues of partialness. One of the most basic contributions of poststructuralist theory is to question the concept of the unified subject. As thinkers from Foucault to Haraway have admonished, people cannot be defined through a single set of essential attributes. Rather, personal identity comprises multiple layers of subjectivity. In the context of peasant politics, this means realizing that identification as a *rondero* ("a participant in the ronda"), corn producer, squatter, or cane cutter consists only of a partial marker, more or less prominent depending on the circumstances. It also demands awareness that the overeasy application of terms like *ejidatario* ("a member of an ejido," which is a collective landholding system in Mexico) and *comunero* ("a member of a peasant community")—or, for that matter, *campesino*—can mask very differing interests and values along lines of gender, age, sexual orientation, religion, income, and ethnicity.

A final point strikes into the very production of subjectivity. If one should investigate the social construction of politics in the countryside, then the same should apply for other dimensions of rural identity. This becomes especially important in connection with that most elementary sounding of markers: *peasant*. Although scholars have devoted much energy to the question of defining the term (Foster 1967), they have almost uniformly overlooked the fact that, in the countryside, determining who qualifies as a "peasant" does not just boil down to assessing "objective" criteria. It also depends on a shifting and politically charged process of negotiation, choice, and imposition. Many Latin Americans who would seem to fit the strictest requisites do not regard themselves as campesinos (for example, many corn-farming Mayans in southern Mexico and Guatemala). The reverse applies to many who derive their principal income from nonagricultural sources (such as village traders in Ecuador who also work a bit of land). From above, development agencies, political parties, and government institutions can be pivotal in these identity politics. In Bolivia, for instance, the abrupt official replacement of the term *indio* with *campesino* under the revolutionary regime of the Movimiento Nacional Revolucionario (MNR) had an important influence in leading many rural people to adopt the new term. From below, the rural poor may latch onto campesino identity as a rallying point. Peru's "military Socialist" government under Juan Velasco Alvarado brought the term *campesino* into wide circulation and associated it with a sense of injustice and exploitation. By the time of Velasco's ouster, the term and its charged meaning had stuck with many rural Peruvians. Campesino organizing became a thorn in the side of Peru's succeeding governments.

Sometimes, too, use of the term *campesino* becomes a strategy for village elites to attempt what Pierre Bourdieu (1979) would call the "euphemization" of their real economic position. In the Andean foothill community called Canal where I worked from 1986 to 1987, no one was more assiduous in use of the word in first-person contexts than a small farmer-turned-storeowner/denture-maker. In short, who will count as a peasant at a given time and place—and what this will mean—can never be predetermined. Instead, it rests on a vortex of forces that range from local interests to national political discourse.

In sum, the literature of the late 1960s and 1970s for the most part bypassed the cultural dynamics of peasant revolt. It did not explore how the rise of rural movements involves the making of alternative political cultures. Developing this line of analysis meant turning to parts of the new social movements literature that pay close attention to the semiotics of protest. But as I stressed, unpacking questions of political identity should not entail abandoning inquiry into basic issues of origins and tactics. Solid analysis demands a simultaneous sensitivity to the play of meaning and to questions of causes, strategies, and limits.

*   *   *

Let me now turn to the steep green mountains of northern Peru and the striking case of the rondas campesinas. In the modernist spirit of the peasant protest scholarship, I want to begin by specifying the forces that spurred campesinos to establish their alternative justice system. Why do they patrol through the cold mountain nights? Why do they have spirited assemblies to hammer out solutions to disputes? And how have the rondas taken root in so many far-flung communities across the northern Andes?

The most immediate factor leading to the formation of the rondas was robbery. Thievery is a long-standing problem in the Andes (Stein 1962; Orlove 1980). By all accounts, though, the theft of animals both between villagers and by organized bands shot up with the onset of economic crisis in the mid-1970s. Necessity impelled many of the thieves—peasants who could not make a living from their own steep mountain plots and few animals. Others made rustling into a profession. They developed elaborate networks for trucking the stolen stock to the coast, where fast-growing cities like Piura, Trujillo, and Chiclayo offered an expanding market for meat.

The rise in theft was devastating. More than 80 percent of farm families in the northern sierra own less than five hectares, and few earn more than $2,000 a year (a hectare equals 2.2 acres, roughly equivalent to a mid-sized parking lot). For these families, the abrupt loss of a pig, mule, horse, sheep, or cow was a serious blow. Some families therefore began to herd their animals into their bedrooms for the night. Others locked their cattle into iron hobbles and then slept near them in their fields. According to most campesinos, though, the thieves seemed only to grow bolder. Some moved from rustling into housebreaking, mugging, and sometimes rape.

Peasants were also completely disenchanted with the official justice system. This discontent has long historical roots, dating at least to the arrival of the Spanish and the abuses of the colonial regime. In the 1570s, the mountain-born chronicler Guamán Poma de Ayala (1978: 133–135) railed against the corruption of the Spanish authorities. The eighteenth-century neo-Inca rebel Tupác Amaru denounced government officials "who sell justice by auction to whoever bids the highest or gives the most."[3] So did a mid-twentieth-century northern balladeer: "They free the guilty / And punish the innocent, / Jail the petty thief / And adore the rich who steal millions."[4] Today, adjectives like "sticky-fingered" and "bribe-hungry" continue to spice the speech of contemporary campesinos discussing the police. They share the perception that judges, police, and prosecutors serve only the rich and powerful.

Dissatisfaction sharpened in the economic crunch. Rural people became even more resentful of bogus "fees" and "fines." Bribery has always been the standard way for police and judges in Peru to augment their modest salaries, and as wild inflation cut further into their purchasing power, many government authorities turned even more frequently to illicit means. Corruption gained a strong momentum of its own. Headlines rocked with news of bribery, kickbacks, and extortion: "Band of Republican Guards Carried Out Six Kidnappings" (El Popular, May 15, 1983); "Drug Godfather Chose Judges" (La República, May 12, 1985); "Police Chief Charged with Theft of Checks" (Correo, June 9, 1983).

In the countryside, the police were understaffed as well as corrupt. Due to payoffs and bad prosecution, moreover, acquittal rates were very high for the few thieves who were arrested. Only 10 percent of the criminal cases brought before the Chota provincial court between 1970 and 1976 resulted in conviction. Many peasants believed that the authorities were in league with the thieves.[5]

The rondas, then, grew from a context of worsening crime and complete distrust of the official justice system. There was also a certain political space for local organizing. Velasco had dealt the death blow to the *haciendas* ("large estates"), which in most of Cajamarca were broken up even before the reform. Most northern villages, moreover, lacked the institutions of self-government still common in Quechua-speaking southern Peru. For its part, the central government had only a loose hold in mountain hamlets through the local peasant who was appointed lieutenant governor. In short, a partial vacuum of authority existed, making it a propitious time for the development of new community organizations.

The specific concept of vigilante patrols also meshed with the cultural premium in the northern countryside on being tough, ornery, and unafraid of violence. This is a region, as John Gitlitz and Telmo Rojas (1983: 177) put it, where strong men or women, ready to grab rifles to defend themselves, earn "the respect of all." In Chota, peasants still speak with enthusiasm of famous outlaws of the 1920s, like Daniel "The Beast" Vasquez, the Villacorta brothers, and the *hacendado* ("estate owner")-turned-rebel caudillo Eleodoro Benel (Taylor 1985). Popular legends farther to the north tell of tough social bandits like "The Black Man" (*El Negro*) Froilán Alama and "The Macho Woman" (*La Machona*) Rosa Palma. They roamed Piura's scrub brush deserts during the 1930s to rob from the rich and defend the poor (Espinoza n.d.). Northern campesinos retain a reputation as being outgoing, heavy on the *aguardiente* ("cane liquor"), and quick with the blade. This aggressive energy helped to nourish the rondas, which at the same time rechanneled it into the service of order and discipline.

There were also special local reasons for the emergence of the rondas. In the original ronda province of Chota, a handful of activists from the Maoist Red Homeland (*Patria Roja*) party took an early and active role in promoting the new organizations. Four were teachers and lawyers, and one was a recent dropout from a coastal university. Red Homeland's political wing, the National Union of the Revolutionary Left (UNIR), would join the United Left (IU) coalition in 1980. The Maoists hoped through their involvement with the rondas to win electoral support and backing for their Socialist agenda. In the first years, they printed pamphlets, organized regional meetings, and spread the news about the rondas.

The church played an important part in the neighboring province of Hualgayoc. Since the early 1960s, activist priests in the parish had trained peasant catechists in the tradition that was to be termed liberation theology (Gitlitz 1985). Many of these catechists became early ronda leaders, and a succession of priests and nuns in Bambamarca, Hualgayoc's capital, became defenders of the new organizations. Cajamarca's crusty progressive bishop José Dammert Bellido, who supported the activist church in Bambamarca as well as the rondas, even arranged a summit meeting in 1980 between ronda leaders and military authorities in an attempt to smooth conflicts between the peasants and the government.

In Peru's far northern mountains of Piura, the legacy of the agrarian reform was vital. Unlike most of Cajamarca, more than half of Piura's sierra remained in the hands of hacendados into the 1960s. Many peasants in Piura talk about the era of the estates as "the time of slavery" and recall Velasco, son of a humble Piura family, as a great emancipator. According to many, however, the abrupt abolition of the often authoritarian estates also exacerbated rustling, as thieves no longer had to fear the haciendas' punishment of whipping or the stocks. The sudden demise of the seigneurial system also made the need for alternative communal organization all the more urgent.

The terrible flooding caused by El Niño in 1983 catalyzed the formation of rondas in Piura. Torrential rains washed out roads and bridges, paralyzing commerce. Crops rotted. The government's response was plodding and riddled by corruption. As hunger became widespread in the countryside, stealing surged. In response, peasants at last formed rondas across Piura's sierra provinces of Ayabaca, Huancabamba, and Morropón, seven years after the founding of the first patrol two hundred miles to the south in Chota.

During the 1980s, rondas across the entire north made the crucial jump from vigilantism into dispute resolution. Discontent with the official system was again a pivotal factor. Pursuing charges through the Peruvian judiciary was an expensive, long, and usually fruitless process. Many cases passed through more than a dozen offices between the prefecture and the prosecutor. The average resolution took more than three years, and there was only a one-in-four chance of conviction. Keeping a case going demanded lawyer's fees, as well as bribes to the judge, prosecutor, and/or police. On top of all this, dealing with the system required a humiliating deference. Campesinos were expected to remove their hats on entering government offices, to avoid direct eye contact, and to use titles of respect like "doctor," "boss" (*jefe*), and "little master" (*taitito*).

The ronda provided an efficient alternative. Instead of expensive and drawn-out judicial proceedings, peasants could bring their cases before the community for debate. There were no fees, and the close knowledge of the ronderos about local affairs gave them a big edge over city-based magistrates in making effective decisions. Depending on the circumstances, those found at fault received a warning, a fine of a day of community labor, or a whipping.

Rondas in some Chota hamlets had dealt with scattered cases of land battles and family fights from as early as late 1978. Not until the mid-1980s, though, did they begin to arbitrate a big flow of disputes. This partly resulted from the success of the rondas against rustling. The virtual elimination of thievery freed campesinos to turn their organizations to conflict resolution; it also gave the rondas an aura of prestige and efficiency that made them attractive places to bring one's problems. By the late 1980s, many rondas were adjudicating a tremendous volume of cases. The committee in Piura's Canal addressed 138 conflicts in 14 different village assemblies between July 1986 and August 1987. Back in Chota, there was at least a ronda meeting a week during 1990 in the founding village of Cuyumalca, and peasants presented more than 100 cases a month for arbitration. Everywhere in the north, campesinos expressed far greater faith in the rondas than in the official system. In 1989, respondents in the district of Frías in Piura's Ayabaca said they trusted the rondas more than the authorities to deal with village feuds by a margin of more than eight to one (Huber and Apel 1990: 4).

Campesinos came to associate the rondas with a new spirit of local cooperation and autonomy. In some communities, rondas began not only to patrol and resolve disputes but also to take charge of small community public works projects like the construction of community halls, medical posts, irrigation channels, and the repair of paths. The ronda made sure that each family contributed its share of labor, fining those who did not fulfill their obligations. Patrols continued in many villages, though more sporadically than in the early days. But the organization of works and especially the resolution of disputes had become the real heart of the rondas. No longer, as many peasants put it, were the rondas just *cuidavacas* ("cow protectors"). Instead, they were making a strong bid for greater campesino power over the working of their communities.

To this point, I have provided a capsule introduction to the rondas and the reasons for their rise. But as I earlier stressed, it does not suffice to identify the historical conditions that produce a peasant movement. Rural organizing must also be understood as involving the elaboration of new modes of political identity and culture.

In the case of the rondas, this process of construction has been very rich. New *huayno* ballads detail the exploits of the organizations: "Animals and farm fields / were saved by the ronda. / In the time of the thieves, / they left us with nothing."[6] "Give me your heart," goes the soft romanticism of another, "let me carry it away. / If I should happen to lose it / then with the ronda / I'll set out to find it."[7] Schoolchildren recite long poems to the rondas on Independence Day and other holiday celebrations. Peasant señoras weave saddlebags and wall-hangings depicting scenes of confrontations with thieves and the police. Many hamlets celebrate the date of the founding of their ronda with a raucous fiesta of skits, parades, speeches, food, drink, and music. Tens of thousands of rural people have come to think of themselves not just as campesinos and Peruvians but also as ronderos.

What are these new politics of the ronda, and how have they developed? Here, one must first appreciate the long engagement of peasants in northern Peru in far-ranging patterns of power and meaning. Roads, radios, universal education, political campaigns, commerce, evangelization, military conscriptions, and migration have tightened the links between the Peruvian sierra and the rest of the world during this century. Rural people do not occupy a separate "Andean world." Rather, they live at one point on a busy circuit that connects city and country, Lima and the provinces, and urbanized coast, coca-growing jungle, and precipitous mountains through a constant flow of goods, ideas, and people (Starn 1991).

Campesinos turned to both local experience and their knowledge of the larger world to forge the rondas. In fact, the idea of antithievery patrols came from the haciendas. In the turbulent 1920s, the estate owners and their majordomos in Chota and Hualgayoc had bands of thugs to protect their property. After President Augusto Leguía's government reasserted control, many hacendados instituted obligatory patrols by estate serfs that became known as *"rondas de hacienda"* ("rounds of the estate"). These rondas operated in both the mountains and on the coast.

A well-respected peasant named Régulo Oblitas, the lieutenant governor of the hilly green hamlet of Cuyumalca in 1976, had participated in patrols on the great coastal estate of Tumán in the early 1950s. Memories of this experience led Oblitas, a farmer of modest means, to think that patrols might be the solution to the growing problem of robbery in Cuyumalca. Oblitas proposed the idea in a Cuyumalca assembly on December 3, 1976. But many peasants were scared of reprisals, and the assembly decided against patrols. But after a series of thefts from the village school, Cuyumalcans were finally persuaded to act. A meeting was held on the afternoon of December 29, and more than 500 citizens signed an agreement "to organize 'Night rondas' to defend the interests of the school and of the whole community."[8]

Peasants also drew on their understanding of military procedure. More than a quarter of the adult men in the countryside are veterans, often having been caught in levies and forced to serve against their will. This martial experience led many communities to dub their ronderos as "soldiers" (*soldados*) and their rounds as "patrols" (*patrullas*). At the suggestion of the veterans, some rondas also adopted the formal army language of "Halt, who goes there?" (*Alto, qué gente?*). Many ronderos also carried rifles and put to use the knowledge of firearms gained during their army days.

The rondas, though, did not reproduce the structures of the hacienda and the army. Instead, they integrated practices of these two oppressive institutions into an original and more democratic system. In contrast to the army and estates, the ronda patrols operated from the start under the collective authority of the community. Coordinating committees were elected at well-attended assemblies and usually rotated every couple of years. Signaling the campesino flavor of their new organizations, most ronderos stuck to the two items of dress most identified with peasants in the north—the poncho and the straw hat. To patrol for the hacienda or army was a resented obligation; to do so with the ronda was a matter of pride. "You go back to bed," goes the bravado of one ballad, "I'm going out to rondar."[9]

The same appropriation and remolding occurred in the ronda's move to arbitration. Here, campesinos borrow heavily from the protocol of state bureaucracy. A rough table at the head of the typically dirt-floored meeting hall becomes the *mesa*—an imitation of the judge's bench. Grimy legal statutes, scattered papers, and a Bible often lie on the table for an additional flavor of official authority. Most rondas also purchase a bound book of minutes and have it notarized by a justice of the peace. A designated secretary then painstakingly records the proceedings of each meeting in a style that follows the Byzantine format of official documents, including fingerprints from key witnesses. The testimonies of suspects become "affidavits" (*declaraciones*); trips to other villages, "commissions" (*comisiones*); letters, "memorandums" (*memoriales*). Copying town officials, ronda leaders seal all documents with small rubber stamps.

It should be stressed, though, that the rondas do not borrow only stilted notions of hierarchy and bureaucracy from the state. They also draw on concepts of participatory democracy that are at least formally enshrined in the Peruvian political system. The ronda's expansion into dispute resolution coincided with

Peru's return to elected government in 1980 after a decade of military dictatorship, and many parliamentary procedures have found their way into the new campesino justice. The most obvious borrowing is in the structure of the steering committees—the elected president, vice president, secretary, and delegates. Some committees—most notably in Cutervo and Huancabamba—even use secret ballots to choose their leaders. Within the assemblies themselves, the principle of majority rule has great importance. After a long period of debate, it has become customary in many rondas for the president to ask, "What does the assembly say? What does the majority say?" The final decision then depends on the president's evaluation of the response or sometimes on a show of hands. Leaders who are perceived as not respecting the majority opinion can quickly find themselves out of office.

Again, however, campesinos do not mimic. Instead, they reconfigure official practices into their own distinctive brand of justice. To be sure, the steering committee presides. But a ronda assembly follows a rhythm different from that of any court or parliament. To begin with, assemblies are often held in the open air on what peasants call "the place of the deeds" (el lugar de los hechos). This may be the farm plot where ownership is in question or the site of an assault or murder to be investigated. Campesino slang, moreover, spices the debate. Elaborate local knowledge of family relations, geography, and gossip come repeatedly into play. Everyone can—and often does—jump into the barrage of charges, countercharges, and efforts at moderation. The very shape of the gathering, a wide circle, helps to give the meeting a communal and egalitarian feel. In a country without a jury system, ronda assemblies have grown into a spirited, homegrown version of trial by one's peers.

In conjunction with patrols and assemblies, an entire way of thinking and talking about the ronda has developed. To be a rondero is to be associated with efficiency and honesty. Farmers speak of an atmosphere of reform where rustlers could become ronda leaders. Putting a new spin on the nationalism drummed into every Peruvian's head through the schools, mass media, and civic calendar, campesinos present the rondas as the real patriotic champions of national sovereignty in the face of spiraling crime and government corruption. "Ronderos of great virtue," goes the lyric to a high yaraví (a sad Andean ballad), "we're fighting for the fatherland, for our beloved Peru."

On the surface, at least, the rondas seem a textbook example of the "new way of doing politics" heralded in the scholarship of the 1970s and early 1980s. Communities seize partial power over their affairs. Direct democracy prevails. And the original "subject-position" of the rondero flowers.

As I have underlined, however, the analysis of contemporary peasant mobilizations demands a healthy caution. Indeed, one has only to skim the other chapters in this volume to realize that most scholars have arrived at a guarded view of the entire concept of new social movements. In addition to the kind of limits discussed in the previous section, one refrain in recent thinking addresses the existence of continuities between the "new" politics and the "old." Many studies document how present-day movements may still be haunted by evil ghosts like clientelism, sexism, and hierarchy that they were thought, at first, to have exorcised. Too often, as Arturo Escobar writes in Chapter 5, scholars picture the "new" and "old" political spaces as "totally sundered from each other, instead of elucidating the manifold connections that exist among them."

This basic point is vital for the rondas. Despite its striking originality, the campesino justice system remains enmeshed in old problems. The most obvious entanglement is with traditional political parties. Red Homeland, for example, jumped in from the start. Led by a charismatic, baby-faced former law student of peasant origins named Daniel Idrogo, party militants hoped the rondas might become the agents of revolution, part of a popular front that would circle the cities from the country in good Maoist fashion. The Socialist realism of Red Homeland pamphlets in the late 1979s depicted the rondas as a people's militia with sticks and fists raised in presumed opposition to the capitalist order. While playing an important part in encouraging peasants to take a more aggressive view of ronda independence, the Maoists also had a clearly partisan agenda, seeking to place local rondas under an overarching federation controlled by Red Homeland.

Partisans of the populist American Popular Revolutionary Alliance (APRA)— long the most powerful party in the Peruvian north—did not like Red Homeland's involvement. In 1979, the APRA began to sponsor "pacific" rondas under the leadership of Chota merchant and longtime *aprista* (member of the APRA party) Pedro Risco. These were also village-based patrols. In theory, though, they renounced physical punishment. Instead, peasants were to turn thieves over to the police. By contrast to Red Homeland, the more conservative APRA envisioned the rondas as dealing mainly with stock-rustling and collaborating, as a statute written by Risco proclaimed, "with a mutual cordiality with Political, Police, Judicial, and Municipal officials."[10]

The rivalry over the rondas between Risco and Red Homeland militants was bitter. Risco played especially dirty. He railed against Red Homeland as "Communist terrorists" and "miserable slanderers" who "disorient the peasantry or psychologically terrorize them to impede them from joining our pacific rondas." Ignoring the role of Régulo Oblitas, the self-proclaimed "president of the presidents" of pacific rondas also began to advance the specious claim that he had founded the movement during his tenure as acting subprefect in late 1976.

The election of the APRA's Alan García to the presidency of Peru gave Risco and his fellow apristas new clout in Chota. They used a carrot of handouts and sinecures and a stick of threats and intimidation to persuade many peasants to distance themselves from the Red Homeland–controlled Federation of Rondas Campesinas of Cajamarca. By the end of García's disastrous five years in office, however, the APRA had lost much of its influence. Many campesinos returned to the Red Homeland Federation.

These political squabbles have weakened the ronda movement. At the village level, little difference exists between the APRA's pacific rondas and the Left's so-called independent rondas. Pacific rondas tend to be less narrow and conservative than APRA honchos would like to imagine. By the same token, few independent rondas adhere to the radical tenets promoted in the piles of ronda manifestos churned out by Red Homeland and federations allied with the Partido Unificado Mariateguista (PUM). This wide common ground at the grass roots contrasts with the extreme and often ludicrous fragmentation that plagues the ronda movement at regional and national levels. Rival APRA and Left-allied ronda unions trade insults in most northern towns. In the extreme case of the city of Cajamarca, four different federations claim to represent the region's ronderos—two connected with APRA and two with different factions of the Left, all in backbiting antagonism. "Unity" may not always be a necessary ingredient in productive progressive politics (compare with Alvarez 1989b). But less political division would surely give the ronda movement more power to advance demands of broad interest to peasants—more campesino representation in government, more state investment in the countryside, better prices for rural products.

In the context of the discontent with traditional parties that resulted in the election of political novice Alberto Fujimori to Peru's presidency in 1990, some signs exist of a decrease in partisan division within the rondas. A number of committees have dropped the suffix of "pacific" or "independent" to call themselves simply "rondas campesinas." In the notable case of Hualgayoc, a group of PUM, Red Homeland, and APRA-allied committees merged in a united front. But fierce divisions still persist in many zones. Even in Bambamarca, the March 1990 kidnapping and torture of the Left-leaning president of the new united front by a disgruntled pacific ronda pointed to the difficulties of real unification. There is no doubt that the rondas will remain entwined in party politics for the foreseeable future.

The relation between the state and the rondas forms a second partial nexus with "conventional" political arrangements. The movement has a vigorous anti-state component, challenging the government's monopoly on the administration of justice. But the radicalism of the rondas, like that of so many other peasant movements, is mixed with feelings of respect for the law and state. The vast majority of ronderos see themselves as seeking the ouster of corrupt officials, not the overthrow of the government. In a November 1988 interview, the president of the central ronda committee in the Piura village of Tunnel Six told me, "The laws are good, but the problem is those who administer them." Ronderos like the Tunnel Six president consider their organizations not as illegal but as the genuine upholders of the law and constitution. Historically, many ronda leaders were or would become the lieutenant governors or justices of the peace in their hamlets. And even as they began to make their own justice, most rondas stayed in close coordination with sympathetic government officials, inviting them to meetings and keeping in constant communication about important cases.

The government's position on the rondas has shifted. Official authorization from Chota's subprefect helped to get the movement off the ground in 1977. The secretary of conservative military president Francisco Morales even sent a telegram congratulating peasants on their initiative. By early 1979, though, the military regime watched the increasing independence of the movement with growing dismay. Troops were sent to Chota after the rondas led the sacking of a warehouse where sugar was hoarded by a town merchant, and ronda leaders were arrested. On May 18, 1979, the minister of the interior sent a secret radiogram to the prefect of Cajamarca, ordering him to abolish the rondas:

We consider that the existence of the so-called night rondas in the provinces of Chota, Hualgayoc, Cutervo, and Jaen, particularly in the first, has generated an

alarming situation. . . . Taking into consideration that these groups assume responsibilities that in our juridical order are assigned to the Police Forces, the Ministry of
Interior cannot allow them to continue to function.[11]

The conservative civilian administration of Fernando Belaúnde continued to
maintain that the rondas should be disbanded. Petitions for legal recognition of
the organizations were refused. Government officials looked the other way when
ronderos were harassed, tortured, and, in several cases, murdered by the police,
who angrily viewed the organizations as an infringement on their turf.

But Alan García reversed government policy. In November 1986, he issued an
executive decree that legalized the rondas. Many Lima leftists worried that the
mention of "pacific" in the one-paragraph statute was meant to legitimate only
APRA rondas. And the law's requirement that peasants obtain permission for
patrols from local civil authorities prompted fears that the rondas might be made
into extensions of official police and courts.

But the opposite occurred. The law has, in fact, strengthened the ronda
movement. It gives ronda leaders legal standing to defend themselves from the
attacks of police and judges, many of whom remain hostile to the rondas. The
statute also adds legitimacy that makes it easier for peasants to enforce decisions
within their communities. All this has occurred without making the organizations
any more beholden to the APRA or formal justice system. Most rondas have
simply ignored the registration requirement, as well as those of a second decree
issued in March 1988.

It should be noted that much of the new social movements literature tends to
present anything less than antagonism toward the state as "dirty," a falling off
from the purity of uncompromised opposition. Popular movements, as Manuel
Castells (1983: 41) therefore asserted, "lose their identity when they become
institutionalized, the inevitable outcome of bargaining for social reform within
the political system." However, this position, I believe, unwittingly propagates
Marxist orthodoxy, wherein only total rejection of the system counts as good
politics. Hundreds of popular initiatives in Latin America have been corrupted
and co-opted; no case is more poignant than that of the revolution in Castells's
own research site of Mexico. But state manipulation does not always produce the
intended results. As the case of the ronda law suggests, the protagonists of popular
movements may navigate within the system and turn attempts at control into
material to use in fortifying their autonomy. The present attitude of most ronderos
toward the state remains much the same as it was at the beginning of the
movement: respect intertwined with resentment, willingness to cooperate with
the authorities coupled with a desire for autonomy.

A third overlap with traditional politics consists of the partial conservation of
top-down leadership. Many ronda presidents serve as wonderfully democratic
facilitators. The constant rotation in many communities also discourages the
enshrinement of permanent chiefs. In some local rondas, however, leaders stay
on for many years and hoard power. The president's opinion comes to count for
more, and favoritism to friends and family begins. The problem is most acute at
the regional level, especially in the city of Cajamarca. Here, the leaders of three
of the competing federations have installed themselves as virtual leaders for life.

Many townspeople refer to the organizations not by their names but by their chiefs' names—"Eriberto's," "Seferino's," "Quiroz's." Although it is an extreme case, Cajamarca does indicate how the familiar specter of *caudillismo* ("bossism") can reappear within an ostensibly new and more democratic mode of organization.

Interwoven with vestiges of caudillismo, the problem of patriarchy represents a fourth point of intersection between the rondas and old-style politics. Despite several vocal feminist centers in Lima, the international women's movement as yet has less impact in Peru's cities than in those of countries like Argentina, Brazil, and Chile; in the countryside, its impact is imperceptible. Men may go out alone at night, travel as they wish, or get drunk in public. They control finances and represent the family in community affairs. Women, by contrast, are chained to cooking, cleaning, herding, and childrearing. The young woman who goes to a dance without her father soon finds herself the target of biting talk. The married woman who ventures alone to a fiesta risks a beating from her husband. In the prevailing gender ideology, accepted by many women as well as men, the husband is the boss. The rest of the family serves at his command.

Some changes in women's lives have come about through the ronda. Seizing the chance to participate, many campesinas marched at the forefront of early ronda protests in Chota. They took the brunt of police tear gas and billy clubs. Women also made sure men fulfilled their turn on patrol. They formed women's committees within some rondas to take charge of discipline. Stout señoras roused recalcitrants—dubbed "yellows" (*amarillos*)—from bed with whips and sticks. The rondas also gave women a place to denounce wife-beating, a major problem in the countryside and one regarded with indifference by the police and courts. A husband can still escape punishment by showing that his wife "deserved" a beating. Yet, a number of offenders have received a stern warning or whipping. Many señoras across the north believe that the ronda has decreased the incidence of battering.

But the rondas also perpetuate the oppression of women. Only men patrol, stemming from the notion that a woman belongs in the house. Furthermore, female participation in assemblies is limited. Many husbands do not like their wives to go to meetings, and attendance tends to be about two-thirds male. Unless they are parties to disputes, few women take an active role in the assemblies. Some are afraid of ridicule. Others know that a woman who speaks too much can be the subject of censuring gossip; her husband may also become angry, not wishing to be labeled a "dress-wearer" (*saco largo*). In addition, no woman is ever elected the president or vice president in a local ronda or regional federation. A campesina can, at most, aspire to the presidency of the women's discipline committee or the largely token women's affairs section created within some of the Left-allied federations. Much about the rondas, in sum, recycles the all-too-familiar concept in Latin American politics of the male right to rule public affairs. Once again, appreciation for the "newness" of the movement needs to be tempered with an awareness of the recurrence of the old.

Finally, the topic of violence must be addressed. Fear and force are enduring features of politics in much of Latin America, and they reappear in the rondas. The measures that some committees use to extract testimony can include night baths in icy mountain lakes, hours on the ronda with no shoes, or even burns with a Coleman lamp or whipping with barbed wire. Here, ironically, methods also derive from syncretism and invention. Torture is standard practice in provincial police stations across Peru. The rondas, in turn, draw from this example. Thus, many ronderos use the same euphemism as the security forces do to gloss their own practices—"investigation" (*investigación*). They also borrow methods from the security forces. Hanging accused rustlers by their arms with a rope still occurs in Huancabamba and Ayabaca, and campesinos relate that they got the idea for the so-called little bird (*periquito*) from their knowledge of the investigative police (Policía de Investigación del Peru, or PIP).

Even in interrogation, though, peasants do not simply imitate. The most noticeable change lies in the ronda's restraint. Torture by the security forces often leads to death or permanent disability. Former prisoners say that the army's periquito often involves steel handcuffs used for many hours, opening raw wounds that an interrogator may then bathe in salt water or crushed hot peppers to sharpen the pain. Rondas have almost never acted so severely. Part of this restraint results from a concern with avoiding legal charges—which is not a worry for the state forces, given their virtual impunity to allegations of human rights abuses. But a real sense of limits also prevails in the rondas and there is an absence of the gratuitous sadism of many Latin American police and military men. Ronderos, for example, seldom administer the little bird for more than fifteen minutes, and they always wrap the suspect's arms in a poncho to prevent lasting injury.

But, in addition to their sometimes harsh interrogations, rondas have also killed. In late 1979, a mass of ronderos captured and murdered five rustlers near windy Samangay Pass between Chota and Bambamarca. The authorities could not gather enough evidence to prosecute, despite heavy pressure for action from the families of the thieves. Six years later, peasants from Rejopampa, Tandayoc, Coclopanza, and La Colpa in Cajamarca province, outraged at the theft of a bull, beat two rustlers to death and dumped their bodies into the icy Milpo Lake. In this case, seventeen ronderos went to prison until their provisional release on appeal (compare with Zarzar 1991). Suspected rustlers also perished in ronda custody in three separate incidents—all tried in 1991—between November 1989 and June 1990. One in Cutervo was probably pushed off a cliff; another in a hamlet near Chota was thrown into a stony well; a third was beaten to death in the district of Miraflores in Santa Cruz province.

Although it would be wrong to minimize the seriousness of these incidents, some important qualifications should be made. For a peasantry fed up with being victimized by rustlers and corrupt authorities, violence was a means to secure a measure of peace and order. Cases of harsh physical treatment, moreover, have noticeably diminished as the rondas have brought rustling under control. Many ronda leaders—mostly calm and thoughtful men—are well aware of the dangers of abuse and have worked within their communities to prevent excessive force. Without doubt, the flavor of vigilantism and sharp fury against thieves, sometimes fueled by drink and local feuds, can turn explosive. But the normal atmosphere in the rondas is not one of vindictive violence; rather, it is characterized by ready forgiveness for the repentant offender. In sum, the strong-arm tactics of the rondas should neither be overlooked nor overplayed. What should be clear, however, is that the problem of violence in Latin American politics does not disappear from campesino justice. From yet another angle, the break between new and old proves only partial.

How, in the end, should the rondas be evaluated? After all, pessimism now reigns regarding the potential of new social movements in Latin America. Technocrats in tailored suits walk the halls of power. Much popular protest flounders in apathy, division, and repression. In Peru, the early and middle 1980s brought great enthusiasm about shantytown committees, women's clubs, mine-workers' unions, religious base communities, and peasant and indigenous federa-tions. By 1990, many of these groups were swamped by economic crisis and the terror of the army and Shining Path. The United Left was supposed to galvanize these movements into a winning electoral coalition to lead a government of the oppressed. Instead, it self-destructed in stupid bickering.

Part of the answer about the rondas depends on the criteria used to evaluate success. By the grand standards of modernization theory or orthodox Marxism, the rondas have little to show. Peasants remain poor, infant mortality stays high, and only a few campesinos have broken into elected office. But the fading hopes for total transformation force a new appreciation for the politics of the possible. The rondas do not amount to sweeping change. Yet, they have brought major benefits. The most obvious dividend is the sharp decrease in theft. To gauge the significance of the reduction, one must consider the tremendous scale of the loss. In the not unusual case of Canal, thieves took 762 animals between 1980 and 1983: more than 40 cattle, 282 goats, and 190 chickens. Losses totaled more than 6 animals per family in a place where campesinos struggle to scratch a living from dry plots.

The ronda brought a remarkable change. In 1986–1987, just 8 animals were lost to robbery.[12] Today, peasants no longer must face the gnawing fear of rustling raids, and there is a bit more meat in the starchy peasant diet. At the same time, income has increased from the sale of animals. As in so many other northern villages, a new sense of security prevails.

The resolution of disputes represents a second important benefit. Campesino justice has become so brisk that a sharp drop-off has occurred in official business. The offices of Chota's land court are half abandoned. The secretary estimates that the number of cases has declined over the last ten years by 90 percent, and a scribe in the criminal court says the caseload has fallen by half. Campesinos not only avoid small bribes and fees but save both time and money that otherwise would be spent in traveling to city courtrooms and police stations. "We solve in a night," says one ronda president, "problems that lasted for years with the authorities."

The rondas have also helped to block the northern expansion of the Shining Path. Over the 1980s, the Gang of Four Maoists combined cold-blooded violence and appeals to the desire for social change among Peru's vast underclasses to become a powerful force in the south central Andes and coca-growing Upper Huallaga Valley (Degregori 1990; Gorriti 1990). The government answered by placing half the country under the administration of the equally merciless Peruvian military. Peasants became the targets of both sides. More than 50,000 fled the terror in the countryside for the shantytowns of Ayacucho, Huancayo, Ica, and Lima.

Relations between the rondas and the guerrillas are not always clear-cut. Some young men in the north come back from labor in the Upper Huallaga with a favorable view of the Shining Path, the self-styled champion of small coca producers. Attempting to exploit potential sympathies, the Maoists have tried in scattered instances to take over rondas in Cutervo and Santa Cruz. They have controlled and eventually deactivated many weak and recently formed rondas in Cajamarca's southern provinces of Cajabamba and San Marcos, which marked the far northern front of serious Shining Path activity in mid-1990.

In general, though, the Shining Path has made few inroads where rondas operate. Most ronderos understand that the army follows the guerrillas and that peasants become the first victims. The influence of the APRA and Red Homeland also encourages anti–Shining Path sentiment. In addition to having a history of anticommunism, the APRA has viewed the Maoists with special hatred since their assassination of party leaders under President García. In addition, Red Homeland has a feud with the Shining Path that dates to a 1968 schism. And a 1982 declaration by the Chota ronda federation that is allied with Red Homeland scorned the Shining Path as "anarcho-infantilist-terrorists."[13]

As a result, most Shining Path organizers who have arrived in Chota, Cutervo, and Hualgayoc have received a firm warning to leave. Many especially remember a meeting in 1982, held in Morán Lirio in Hualgayoc province, where peasants, encouraged by Red Homeland activists, rejected the overtures of campesino-born Shining Path leader Felix Calderón. Calderón had to leave the district. Just months later, he was arrested by the police on the highway out of Cutervo.

Rondas, in short, have played an important part in preventing the northern countryside from being drawn into the murderous conflict that has devastated the south. It was partly out of frustration with the stubborn obstacle of the rondas that a Shining Path column brutally slaughtered seven ronderos, including the former president of the departmental federation, in the hamlet of Choras in the department of Huanuco in early July 1990. "Death to the rondas campesinas and all traitors," read the red-paint graffiti left by the Maoists on the peeling adobe walls of the village.

In conjunction with the more measurable benefits, the rondas renew a powerful sense of independent identity among campesinos. As a Chota leader explained simply, "We feel more valued with the rondas." Thus, ronda anniversaries celebrate not only the organizations but also campesino culture. The look in fashion is a characteristic northern peasant amalgam of ponchos, wool skirts, straw hats, and Rambo or Surf California t-shirts. Bands with wood drums and flutes made from plastic tubing blast old huaynos and their own versions of the latest *cumbias* (Colombia-inspired dance rhythms) from the coast. Speakers make proclamations of peasant pride into scratchy microphone systems powered by car batteries.

In the wide view, the rondas can be understood in terms of forging what anthropologist Arjun Appadurai has called "alternative modernities." At one time, it was supposed that all indigenous and peasant cultures would be erased by the forward march of free markets and Western values, and many traditions are, indeed, lost or destroyed. But the world is also witnessing the persistence and even multiplication of new orders of difference and identity (Clifford 1988). People carve these different paths through modernity in the kind of synthesis and innovation I have tried to describe in the particular context of the rondas.

Indeed, a striking sense of alternative modernity flows through the jagged hinterlands of the Peruvian north. It slips into modest details like the campesinas' tight black braids secured with aluminum barrettes from Hong Kong and the rich smell of guinea pig fried in Friol-brand vegetable oil. And it infuses through such elemental institutions as *mingas* ("collective work parties"), *landas* ("ritual first haircuttings for toddlers"), and *pararaicos* ("housewarming celebrations") where *chicha* ("maize beer"), aguardiente, and Pilsen bottled beer flow freely and sturdy farm couples dance deep into the night. Nowhere, though, does the feeling of alternative vision come through any stronger than in the rondas. There, as the faint light of a kerosene lamp flickers across the big circle of campesinos and voices blend into the steady murmur of debate, peasants carve a space of their own.

*   *   *

By late afternoon on the day of the ronda protest against the interest rates, campesinos melted back into the mountains around Chota as suddenly as they had arrived. Night left the town to its regular residents. The gringo anthropologist stretched out in bed with a trashy mystery novel. Policemen on a street corner talked about the upcoming World Cup. Four young blades just back from the coast swaggered around the plaza in fashionably baggy bermuda shorts, rap music blaring from a boombox.

Up in the hills, people moved to other rhythms. A small boy in tennis shoes shifted cows to a new patch of pasture under the starry light of the Southern Cross. A señora crouched over her stone hearth to boil new corn and Nescafé over a smoky fire of green eucalyptus. Five ronderos set off onto the muddy trails, laughing and joking about local gossip and the upcoming runoff in the presidential election. One tuned in his battered portable radio. The strong vibrato of a huayno ballad wafted across the dark mountains, sounds of difference and renewal.

Notes

Research for this paper was generously supported by grants from the Inter-American Foundation and the Wenner-Gren Foundation for Anthropological Research.

1. John Gitlitz and Telmo Rojas (1983) wrote an excellent article that detailed the early history of the movement. Other useful sources include Huber and Apel 1989, Rojas 1989, and Starn 1989.

2. I am sidestepping the tricky question of whether what are now labeled "new social movements" should really be thought of as new. My general feeling, with Jelin (1986), is that the birth of the new social movements literature reflects—perhaps more than anything else—a

refocusing of interpretive lenses, an increased sensitivity from academics on the Left to the plural lines of political activity that always exist in any society.

3. From an unpublished translation by Jan Mannel of "Proclamation Túpac Amaru" (1791), Department of Spanish and Portuguese, Stanford University, Stanford, California.

4. From a recording by Ernesto Sanchez, known as *El Jilguerode Huascarán,* a now deceased balladeer from the central highland department of Ancash.

5. This information is based on a sample of more than 100 cases from the First Circuit Appeals Court in Chota.

6. By Valentín Mejía of San Antonio in Hualgayoc province, 1979.

7. By Los Obreritos de Santa Rosa, Hualgayoc province, 1987.

8. From the official minutes of the meeting, now in the possession of Régulo Oblitas.

9. By Filiberto Estela of San Antonio, Chota, 1985.

10. Quote from "La Historia de los Orígenes de las Rondas Campesinas Pacíficas en Chota," an unpublished manuscript by Pedro Risco.

11. Memorandum on file in the office of the subprefect of Chota province.

12. The figures come from my research in Tunnel Six (Starn 1989).

13. Mimeoed announcement from the files of the *Federación Departamental de Rondas Campesinas de Cajamarca in Chota.*

7

From Resistance to
Social Movement:
The Indigenous Authorities
Movement in Colombia

María Teresa Findji

The Colombian National Constituent Assembly, convened during the first semester of 1991 and entrusted with the reform of the constitution, included two indigenous delegates among its seventy popularly elected delegates: a young attorney of Embera descent, a native of the Chocó rivers and rain forest area, and a middle-aged Andean campesino, formerly a *terrajero* and governor of the Guambiano people.[1] The first delegate was supported by the National Indigenous Organization of Colombia (*Organización Nacional Indígena de Colombia*, ONIC); the second, by the Indigenous Authorities of the Southwest, at that point transformed into the Indigenous Authorities of Colombia (*Autoridades Indígenas de Colombia*) thanks to the support of other indigenous peoples and to an important vote from nonindigenous sectors. Public opinion registered the election of these delegates as one of the big surprises of the electoral confrontation. The Indigenous Authorities situated it in a double temporal framework: within the context of the twenty-year revival of the indigenous movement in Colombia and at the threshold of the five hundred years after the Spanish conquest. Many indigenous communities deeply felt that this was the beginning of a new era for American societies.

This chapter analyzes the thoughts and practices of the protagonists of this movement and their interrelation with various contemporary, social, and political forces. We will draw on Touraine's definition of a social movement to address the following questions:[2] To what extent have the indigenous struggles that made their appearance on the national scene in the early 1970s succeeded in constituting a social movement? How are political and social struggles articulated? And what is the role of cultural and symbolic elements in the making of the movement? Although our observations focus on the case of the Colombian southwest, we situate this case, in its specificity, within the Latin American context as a whole.

Indigenous Identity and Historicity in Colombian Society: The Protagonists of the New Movement

Three Indigenous Demonstrations "in the Public Scenario"

In July 1973, the national press registered with great profusion the sudden appearance "in the public eye" of the indigenous people of the Andean ranges of southern Colombia. At that time, the third assembly of the Indigenous Council of the Cauca Region (Consejo Regional Indígena del Cauca, CRIC), a group established in 1971, was being held. Those who identified themselves as "indigenous campesinos," as well as those who joined them—mostly peasant and mestizo settlers and intellectuals—were surprised to see so many "Indians" speaking publicly in languages other than Spanish and asserting their right as the "legitimate owners of America."

To understand this event fully, we must start by recalling that Colombia's contemporary national consciousness was shaped, during the period of "conservative hegemony,"[3] around the glorification of a prototypical figure—namely, the Colombian mestizo, corresponding to the Roman Catholic Spanish-speaker that the concordat between the church and the state (constitutionally established as central in 1886) helped to shape. What mattered most at this initial stage in the construction of national identity was to break with the colonial situation: "We are not Indians" (see Findji 1983). Nineteenth-century liberal ideology—still in force in the late years of the twentieth century—continually legitimated this goal, under the premise that "we are all equal,"[4] with the concomitant implementation of republican policies to eliminate all Indians or to "civilize" them.

Thus, when the Indigenous Assembly took place at the beginning of the 1970s, the country was surprised. In the national imagination, the Indians—living evidence of the colonial situation—existed only as those who had disappeared, those who were about to disappear, or those who were ultimately doomed to disappear. In no way could they be part of contemporary Colombia, nor could they show up in the public plaza and speak on their own behalf. For many years, the national discourse about the public demonstration of the indigenous people was to be directed by this Western linear view of progress, which equated "Indian" with the past and thereby relegated indigenous people to be always behind the times.[5] We would like to underscore the implications that the appearance of communities claiming to be "legitimate Americans," which predated the dominant national society, had for Colombia's growing national consciousness. With this in mind, one may more easily interpret the social movement we are examining.

When 4,000 Indians marched in Silvia, Cauca, in July 1973, the streets appeared otherwise deserted. The village mestizos and "whites" had withdrawn to their houses and securely bolted doors and windows. The mayor had attempted in vain to stop the march. Those who had "humiliated" the Indians daily were now fearful.

Three months later, in the entrepreneurial "industrial capital" of Colombia—Medellín—delegations from the same indigenous groups participated in a "week of solidarity with the indigenous struggles," an event organized by intellectuals, with support from the peasants' association and the labor unions of Antioquia. This joint action was held simultaneously with the first national congress prepared by Catholic missionaries, organized in the Indigenist Association (*Asociación Colombiana Indigenista*, ASCOIN) and backed by prominent national political figures, both liberal and conservative, with the intention of pushing forward the reform of the existing legislation on indigenous communities. Massive rallies took place in trade union locales, neighborhoods, and universities in order to air the indigenous peoples' views. "We belong to the Earth," said the Arhuacos with great authority. "We demand our rights," said the Caucanos. "We are legitimate Americans," they all said in their own voices.

The echo of these meetings was to reach many other communities, as if saying, "There are some indigenous groups, independent from the government and the church, who are speaking out on their own behalf." Finally, in August 1974, on the occasion of the third congress of the National Association of Peasant Producers (*Asociación Nacional de Usuarios Campesinos*, ANUC),[6] four hundred indigenous delegates from twenty-two different communities gathered in Bogotá in what would prove to be a highly instrumental public presence on the national scene (see ANUC 1974).

The Social Juncture at the End of the National Front Period

The indigenous presence in the national scenario corresponds to a political moment dominated by the interests of "Colombian society," when indigenous people are relegated to a marginal position. Nevertheless, both the official statistics (DNP 1989) and the latest elections show that not a single area of the "national territory" is without the presence of indigenous people, whose territorial occupation is not proportional to the mere demographic volume, either due to their social organization or their symbolic value.[7]

As we mentioned earlier, the first urban appearance of the indigenous movement took place in the streets of Medellín. The action was launched in opposition to the Catholic missionaries who were seeking to reform the legislation governing indigenous affairs. We must first situate this event and its protagonists in the context of the times, an era when broad sectors of Colombian society, identified with the Liberal party, were fighting for the reform of the concordat and the Agreement on Missions (*Convenio de Misiones*). The 1968 publication of *Siervos de Dios y Amos de Indios* (Bonilla 1968),[8] which discussed the relationship between the state and the missions in Putumayo, had stirred national and international controversy. At this juncture, the protagonists were not the indigenous people; they were the "nationals" (nonindigenous Colombians) seeking changes in the relationship in their society between church and state.

On another front, the country had been committed to carrying out a land reform approved by congress in 1961 ever since the agreements of Punta del Este were signed. The class conflict molded in the existing land tenure system found a propitious juncture for maximum expression in the issue of land reform. And many of the country's restless youth turned to the countryside to join the land reform movement, leftist groups, or newly created guerrilla groups, such as the Revolutionary Armed Forces of Colombia (*Fuerzas Armadas Revolucionarias de Colombia*, FARC, linked to the orthodox Communist Party) and the pro-Cuban National Liberation Army (*Ejército de Liberación Nacional*, ELN). The importance of the peasantry as a social and political force grew greatly, even if the 1964 census revealed that Colombia's population was by then predominantly "urban." The legal framework of the Land Reform Law provided justifications for the actions and organizations that were to develop primarily around ANUC, whose period of maximum influence on the national level coincided with the indigenous "revival" we are examining. Landowners, closely connected to the two traditional parties exercising power under the National Front Pact, were the main adversaries that indigenous peasants or settlers had to face in their fight for land.

In more general terms, the National Front period corresponds to the strengthening of the centralized state apparatus and the spread of its intervention in many regions and sectors of the country. One of the hypotheses of our work has been the existence of a close connection between the revival of the indigenous movement and the junctures of reaffirmation of the national state.[9] During these junctures, political parties penetrated further into the various social sectors, under the clientelist model, which was renewed after the installation of universal male suffrage in 1936.

Why from the Cauca Region?

The indigenous groups present in the public events discussed thus far came from several regions. But the main indigenous force to rise up—serving as the center for the others—was that of the Cauca region. Why was this so? What does it represent for the national society? And who are those "indigenous people" of the Cauca?

The present province (*departamento*) of Cauca was established from part of the old Sovereign State of Cauca, formerly the Government (*Gobernación*) of Popayán, which, in colonial times, was under the jurisdiction of the Quito High Court (*Audiencia*). As a sovereign state, Cauca participated in all the civil wars that marked the process of unification of national classes in the nineteenth century; until 1905, the state comprised half of today's Colombian land (Velez 1986, Findji and Rojas 1985). The Indians who inhabit the Cauca are not "primitive" and "marginal" tribes but the very product of the colonial system established in the Andes—they are populations related to the "centers" of power dating back five hundred years.

In the 1960s, the modern metropolis of Cali, capital of the departamento of Valle del Cauca, had already become consolidated, thanks to significant agroindustrial transformations that made possible its insertion into "national" society, leaving the diminished departamento of Cauca to its "backwardness." But in reality, it is not this "backwardness" that we want to emphasize but the permanent relationships of these "indigenous communities of Cauca" with the process of conformation of contemporary Colombian society. These communities have a way of life distinct from that of the other Colombian sectors, and they keep alive the memory of their past, while the "national" society, on the contrary, condemns this same past to oblivion.

By the late 1960s, the policy of national integration carried out by the republic (Jimeno and Triana, eds., 1985) had resulted in the following situation in the Cauca mountain region: Large ranches (haciendas) coexisted with resguardo lands in mutual segregation, and terrajeros who paid their obligations communally to the landowner coexisted with comuneros, governed by a council (cabildo) that was often loyal to the local priest and the local political powers. Likewise, two institutions of local power coexisted, both relatively weak in comparison to the power of the hacienda: the indigenous council (cabildo de indígenas), governed by a special law (Law 89 of 1890), and the municipality, the local link with the central government.[10] In most cases, both institutions exerted their jurisdiction over the same territory and the same population, namely, resguardo lands belonging to indigenous communities. The struggle became more evident regarding the "areas of settlement"—that is, resguardo plots that by law can be set apart by the municipalities for resettlement by non-Indians—by definition, the repositories of "progress and civilization." In spite of the penetration by both traditional political parties, the indigenous cabildos always opposed the separation of part of the territory of their resguardos, and they continued to defend themselves against the municipality.

The collective memory of the elders, who felt "humiliated," bred resistance and strengthened their determination to defend their "rights."[11] In the minds of the young people, who had been acculturated by Catholic, evangelical, or public schools, the "shame" associated with being Indians grew. Meanwhile, efforts to reproduce the culture of the community failed. Moreover, harsh living conditions forced many to migrate temporarily or permanently, finding work as laborers, domestic servants, or, in the most favorable of cases, as settlers of new lands.[12]

It is in this Cauca region—where the hacienda system was not simply a unit of production but a territorial unit of domination as well, where the appropriation of territory by national settlers implied overlapping jurisdictions, and where resistance entailed barely human living conditions for many—that indigenous people were to "come out" and demonstrate "in the public eye." They were "demanding the rights," but the national society interpreted such acts solely as a "fight for the land."

Segregation and Integration: The Communities as Protagonists

In the late 1960s, fighters (luchadores) appeared in the haciendas. They were the communities of terrajeros who started to exercise their rights over their ancestral lands in the Páez way: by putting the land to good use through their work in times of rocería.[13] Hacienda owners labeled these actions as "invasions," but the indigenous people, identified with "the community," spoke instead in terms of "rights."

Often, these communities fought alone, with no previous mutual coordination. They had, indeed, been isolated, "enclosed" by the terraje system.[14] What these actions revealed, however, was the communities' autonomy, their capacity for initiative, and their potential for action. The indigenous movement was born out of these communities. We must stress the existence of this collective actor—the community—which is the protagonist of the movement that has taken shape historically in the haciendas. The hacienda itself reinforced and reproduced the communal structure of "the Indians," both because of the hacienda's internal structure and because of the resistance that this structure generated among the people.[15]

The community is the product of contradictory social forces that have simultaneously segregated and integrated "the Indians" into the colonial-republican system. The community existed in the haciendas prior to the emergence of the indigenous movement we are examining—it was the referent for the social and political identity of these descendants of pre-Columbian, colonial, and postcolonial people who are called "Indians."

Indigenous people also have an institutional referent, the cabildo, in charge—according to Law 89 of 1890, which is still in effect—of managing the communal lands of the resguardo, even though in practice these lands had been greatly reduced by landowner occupations and by demographic growth. It is interesting to note that the leaders that appeared and/or were recognized in the indigenous organization emerging in the Cauca region around those years were the most Hispanicized members of the community and the most integrated into national circuits. In contrast, the communities that actually organized and led their struggles in each area were invisible to the national society, which ignored their existence. The history of the movement in the last twenty years shows how the leaders have had to either walk the long distance of reunification with the communities or else follow the path of permanent integration and remain as links in the chain to "outside" interests and powers.

In this regard, we may recall another initiative from the early 1960s. Some young, modern, acculturated Guambianos created the Farmers' Union of Eastern Cauca, through which they established links with the Paeces of Jambaló. When they had to confront the land problem, these young farmers found out that the union was impotent—the cabildos continued to hold the power over land matters, and farmers were obliged to deal with them to solve their problems. Out of this experience emerged an entire group of activists who were to be among the founders of a new organization that would have been inconceivable in the context of integrationist thought—a genuinely indigenous organization formed in 1971, calling itself the Regional Indigenous Council of the Cauca (*Consejo Regional Indígena del Cauca*, CRIC).

It is worthwhile to analyze the redundance of this first self-identification. The name of the organization is charged with all the weight of the domination concretely suffered and identified. This social domination, inscribed territorially in today's Cauca, produces the "indigenous" condition. At the local and regional level, the domination is felt in terms of "humiliation"; at the national level, it is experienced as denial and total ignorance.

Being indigenous is a concrete condition and a social relationship inscribed in historical time and space. But many analysts and activists of the times lacked historical vision of the Colombian society in formation. Rather, an anti-indigenist discourse, which viewed class as the organizing principle, prevailed. Nevertheless, the nascent movement came into the public light precisely as a concrete, historically "Caucan" force: No "ethnic" vision served as a frame of reference for its creation. The organization was born out of terrajero struggles, even if the Indians (the terrajero community) maintained links with other sectors of the rural society, thus amplifying their potential for mass mobilization. Since then, resguardo members, union delegates, and the organized peasants have all converged in the indigenous movement (CRIC 1973). It is clear that their current ability to mobilize goes beyond the community boundaries to reach broader social sectors.

Specific Modalities of Action and Initial Results

It has not been easy to understand the specificity of the new movement's modes of action in the Colombian context. We pointed out earlier that the movement's protagonists are rendered invisible in the dominant representations of the national present. In the process of struggle, when, in fact, actors confronted each other, they were identified and they identified themselves in different manners. Part of the struggle itself has revolved around such forms of identification, although a detailed analysis of this aspect is beyond the scope of this chapter. It is crucial to understand that the indigenous movement entails not only a conflict of sectoral interests between landowners and campesinos, as it has most often been interpreted to be, but also a confrontation in the sociocultural order of the entire society.

The debate has been hard, and it is not over yet. But we can already establish its initial periodization. During the 1970s, indigenous struggles were most commonly read as a "struggle for land." In the 1980s, they started to be read as a "struggle for territory." We will now examine some of the concrete indigenous actions and their outcomes.

The Fight for the Land Puts an End
to the Terraje System

The fight for land took the form of communal work on lands previously usurped by landowners or settlers, and many haciendas were effectively recovered. The community that considered itself the legitimate owner claimed possession in the Páez way: working the land. Although many people could not see it then, the protagonists of land recoveries were the communities.[16] Once the movement broadened and communities secured each other's support for a recovery, the protagonist community was, whenever repression struck, the one to assume by itself the confrontation with police. The right and the obligation to defend it belonged specifically to that community.

The communities knew they were exercising a right. They even recognized that other existing rights should be respected, and they did, indeed, respect them. During the recovery of a hacienda in Jambaló, for example, where the landowner had hired paid assassins to stop the community's actions, the occupants' removal was carefully organized. Community members came and dismantled the house, roof tile by roof tile, window by window, door by door. They piled everything up outside, and nothing was destroyed. Finally, the occupants were told, "Take with you what you brought in, but the land is ours." The same was done with the landowner's cattle, removed from the hacienda so that its occupants would leave.

The recovered lands were reincorporated into the resguardo territories and placed under cabildo jurisdiction. To the extent that the cabildos supported the struggle, it became evident that the fight for land strengthened both the communities and the cabildos themselves. This was an important achievement for the movement: to reconnect community and cabildo. Moreover, the movement transformed the very function of the cabildo. The cabildo's legitimacy rests in an external juridical source, Law 89 of 1890. Thus, with the cabildos' backing of community struggles, the right to the land that the elders had traditionally claimed "from the inside" was ratified "from the outside" and "for the outside." Through this reencounter with the right to the land demanded by the community, cabildos started to distance themselves from the local "legitimate" bosses, and what came to be called "combative cabildos" (*cabildos luchadores*) began to emerge.

Now, instead of functioning as "conveyor belts" for the central power, the cabildos began to coordinate land recoveries and communal work. An essential traditional feature of indigenous communities has been the work they had to perform by virtue of their tributary status. Community work was done to pay the tax to the king, the tithe to the church, the terraje to the hacienda owner, and subsidiary work to the municipality.[17] The fact that the cabildos have actually been the ones to organize the community for this work also earned them authority in the community. In the fights for land, this order was, of course, subverted; instead of linking community interests with the demands of outside powers, the cabildos began to facilitate intercommunity relationships. Under these circumstances, members of the communities participated in great numbers, at times traveling substantial distances to do so. When they were not part of the community to which the land to be tilled belonged, their main motivation was not to obtain land but simply (and crucially) to secure a kind of delayed retribution that is at the basis of reciprocal relationships: the support of other communities when needed.

Confabulated landowners and local caciques used private justice and public security forces against the communities.[18] These struggles over land were carried out amid the most vicious and bloody repression: police who imprisoned and landowners who assassinated, either by their own hands or by means of hired assassins. The communities defended themselves by demonstrating massively in villages and municipalities, appealing to the "modern" national government against the "colonial" regional powers. Occasionally, the repression stopped as a result of these protests, and new social spaces were conquered.[19]

Solidarity forces denounced this state of affairs.[20] The most representative traditional politician—also the most widely opposed—was Víctor Mosquera Chaux, the author of a 1944 bill to put an end to resguardos in Tierradentro. Haciendas for terraje did not exist there; instead, the church was in command. Since the creation of the apostolic prefecture early in the century, the church had unsuccessfully tried to convince the communities that their lands were not resguardos but unused public lands (*baldíos*) (Jimeno 1985). For this reason, they unambiguously supported the movement in the defense of their resguardos.

It is interesting to point out how the indigenous movement did not present claims to the state as services or "aid," as the contemporary Colombian clientelist tradition would suppose, but instead claimed the recognition of its "rights."

Once the strength of the communities' movement made land recovery a reality, the state's only option was to find a way to resituate land recovery within the legal framework that had been subverted. The task was entrusted to the Land Reform Institute (*Instituto Colombiano de Reforma Agraria*, INCORA), which played a special role in the Cauca.

Originally, the land reform's model of "family units" implied a reenactment of the republic's long-standing policy of parceling out resguardos. The indigenous struggle, however, halted the implementation of the parceling plan, which was replaced by the modern concept of "community enterprise" based on the model of producers' cooperatives. For many in the Cauca, cooperativism appeared to be a solution to the demands generated by the indigenous movement, intrinsically communitarian in the nation's eyes. Soon, however, it became evident that INCORA's sense of the communal did not coincide with the community's own sense of it. What INCORA would do was select a number of families to become "associates" of the enterprise and grant them joint private ownership of the land that had been recovered by the community as a whole. In other words, these lands were taken out of the community resguardo system, while the associate families were effectively left out of the community, and the jurisdiction of the cabildos was eliminated. Besides the juridical implications, the policy of awarding loans to these enterprises further weakened the position of the cabildos, always short of resources; it also had a considerable impact on those who had to repay the loans.[21]

An ample sector of the indigenous movement refused to accept INCORA's enterprises, defending instead the value of the community's own effort and organizing community enterprises under cabildo jurisdiction. However, though this opposition was an important factor in the gestation of the movement we are analyzing, this is not the place to detail the political struggles that took place within the indigenous movement itself over INCORA's policies (see, for example, CRIC 1980). What is noteworthy is that the state continued to ignore the specific nature of indigenous communities and to view their members merely as peasants or those who were doomed to be peasants. Whenever INCORA's community enterprises failed, went bankrupt, and dissolved, the national policy of resguardo land division would triumph, along with its denial of the communities as social subjects. For indigenous communities in those regions where resguardos never existed, INCORA implemented the system of "reserves" (*reservas*). The reserves were demarcated territories provisionally allocated to a given community, but, unlike resguardos, they belonged to the nation and not to the community. In other words, the state did not recognize any indigenous territoriality.[22]

Recovering the History of Juan Tama and Redefining Indigenous Identity

In the face of landowners, police, and the army, the communities legitimized their land possessions on the basis of the title deeds of the resguardos that persisted in

the elders' memories, if not in colonial documents. Resorting to memory—
"remembering the rights"—played a major role in the communities' mobilization
and in their decision to undertake land recoveries. At times, the solidarity services
of accredited researchers were employed to dig into archives for relevant documents. This task provided new knowledge: For example, several Páez resguardos,
forming chiefdoms (*cacicazgos*), were mentioned in the same colonial document
from the eighteenth century. And a central figure, the cacique Juan Tama,
previously believed to be a mythical figure, took on historical reality. It was then
possible to further the analysis of Páez political history (Bonilla 1977) and to fuel,
with this "recovery of history," the ongoing debate over the identity of the
protagonists of the indigenous movement and over the direction of its struggles
(Bonilla 1976).

Historical records did more than document the existence of eighteenth-century
Páez chiefdoms and their boundaries, until then unknown to Colombian historiography. They also provided elements helpful in the reconstruction of the
process of political unification through which the Páez people took shape, in the
late colonial period and not in pre-Hispanic times, as a socially differentiated
conglomerate that has survived until the present. Records helped to understand
the hidden behavioral dynamic of the land-recovering communities: They showed
that the communities' prolonged memory of the landmarks of the chiefdoms was
a sort of substratum or unconscious force behind the perceived duty to defend
the lands assumed by the struggling communities. The fights for land were not
only fights for a plot as a unit of agrarian production, they were also fights for a
"territory." It was in this sense that the struggles started to be understood by
critical minority sectors within CRIC, while the leadership rejected such a reading
and even refused to discuss it with the communities during the fifth congress,
held in Coconuco in 1978.

Although the land reform was part of the context in which the indigenous
movement unfolded, the modalities of the communities' actions allow us to see
that community policies differed from those of INCORA and ANUC, intended
to pressure the state to broaden peasant private property at the expense of large,
contested land-holdings. CRIC leadership's refusal to consider such differences
of views and its support for both INCORA and ANUC prompted the emergence
of what is known today as the Indigenous Authorities Movement of Colombia
(*Movimiento de Autoridades Indígenas de Colombia*, MAIC). This movement,
which is the focal point of this chapter, developed a different approach and
organization and encompassed communities from outside the Cauca region,
particularly that of the Pastos from the Nariño area.

Today, "territory" is part of the vocabulary of the indigenous movement in all
of its tendencies, and it is even found in some official texts.[23] This, however, does
not mean that the concept has been appropriated by all or equally assumed in the
political arena.

In the late 1970s, confrontations within CRIC, ANUC, and their respective
allies over the political leadership of the indigenous struggles were expressed
within the Left in terms of the opposition between the class and indigenist
perspectives. The struggling communities, in turn, perceived the opposition in

terms of campesinos and Indians. A negative self-identification, understandable only in this context, emerged. The indigenous people maintained that they were not campesinos in an effort to express the different focus of their struggles more forcefully. By doing so, they were, in fact, redefining their social and political identity.[24]

Land Recovery as Conscious Recovery of Territory: Guambía and Munchique-Tigres

The public became aware of the positive side of the nonpeasant identity through the Guambianos' actions, although its origin must be traced to the terrajero struggles of the Páez and their relationships with the Arhuacos, an important indigenous group of the Sierra Nevada de Santa Marta in northern Colombia.

Guambiano practices became evident in their first assembly. After they failed to recover Chimán, the Guambianos had not participated in the struggles. In 1978, however, the old fighters gathered for one week to evaluate fifteen years of experiences concerning the Las Delicias cooperative.[25] They concluded that their actions should not remain focused on this institution, which symbolized the "progressive-integrationist" policies imposed on the community from the outside. Instead, the Guambianos set out to rejoin the community at large in order to recover a combative cabildo. This decision by the most acculturated sectors to reunite with the most traditional sectors, as well as the success of its implementation, lies at the core of the subsequent development of the Indigenous Authorities Movement.

Numerous meetings and internal discussions marked this process, which first resulted in the election of cabildos and in the establishment of linkages with other Páez combative cabildos in the region. During the celebration of the recovery of Guayupe, in the Jambaló resguardo, a cry was heard: "Long live the indigenous authority!" A few months later, during the First Assembly of the Guambiano People,[26] the Guambianos presented themselves not as "non-peasants" nor even generically as "indigenous" but as "Guambiano" authorities. That same day, in a section of their manifesto, they proclaimed: "We don't want to be 'humiliated' indígenas—we want to defend, for our children's sake, our right to be Guambianos." This public identification as "the Guambiano people" had a major impact, all the more so because of the militarized situation of the Cauca region due to M-19's guerrilla actions. Before this point, the militarization had involved CRIC and caused the communities to seclude themselves for defensive purposes; against this background, the Guambianos' massive "coming out" was even more significant.

Also present at the assembly, in solidarity with the indigenous movement, were six hundred delegates among nonindigenous intellectuals and representatives of popular organizations. A few weeks later, these individuals were to publicize the indigenous actions and views when the Guambianos effectively recovered the Las Mercedes hacienda. And the "peaceful and hard-working" image that Guambianos enjoyed in the region predisposed the public to pay attention to them. Their image contrasted with that of the "dangerous, lazy, and subversive" Páez people, with whom the Guambianos have, nevertheless, had a long relationship that is frequently ignored by students of the region.

That day, the Guambianos proclaimed before the entire world the tenets of the "Principal Right" (*el Derecho Mayor*): *Ibe Namayguen y Ñimmereay Gucha* ("this belongs to us, but it's for you, too"). The proclamation of the manifesto took place after the cabildos of Guambía solemnly entered, carrying their authority symbols, and after a Guambía flag, especially created for the occasion, had been hoisted. The impact of this symbolic differentiation also had a verbal expression: *No somos una raza: Somos un pueblo* ("We are not a race, we are a people"). In Old Spanish, *raza* ("race") was simply a synonym of *gente* ("people"). It was in this sense that the term was understood among the indigenous people. Today, the word connotes the racism that justifies domination and subordination.

Another look at the Spanish spoken in various Colombian sectors will help to clarify some of the implications in using the word *pueblo*. Among members of the Left, *pueblos* meant *los de abajo*, the subordinate ones. In their opinion, there was no room for the notion of law (*derecho*)—which was viewed as "bourgeois"—or for the representatives of the state that they were striving to seize. The Left was therefore surprised when the Guambianos—the public voice of the indigenous movement—introduced the term *pueblo* and linked it to the defense of their right to exist as Guambianos, on the basis of a long memory materially inscribed in a territory. We will return to this point in the last section; here, let us simply point out that this term would be used in communiqués to the public entitled "From the Guambiano People to the Colombian People," thus expressing a new position in the representation of their mutual relationships.[27]

It is important to analyze some modalities and practices of land recovery. When the Guambianos came to Las Mercedes, a hacienda dedicated to raising purebred cattle and owned by a senator of the republic, they started by removing the pasture grass, cutting it into squares that they would then roll up and easily carry away. They did this as communities, organized by locality and supported by Paeces on several occasions. When the army showed up to remove them, the cabildo confronted the troops; with the massive strength of the community behind it, the cabildo then imposed a two-month deadline for the national government to consider not only a senator's right to private property but the "principal right" of a people who predated the Colombians in their territory, not merely brandishing the colonial resguardo title. The solidarity movement aided in the legitimation of this struggle. It assumed the need to recognize the rights of the Guambiano people, and it expressed this publicly by handing to the cabildo of Guambía in Popayán a document signed in several cities of the country.

The rejoicing came one year later, when the landowner sold or relocated his cattle and the community effectively gained permanent possession of Las Mercedes. Throughout the long night of celebration that followed, traditional dances were performed "so that the land can realize that it is us who are stepping on it again." The hacienda was then christened Vereda Santiago, in memory of an early-twentieth-century fighter. The godfathers were the governors of Jambaló (Páez) and Cumbal (Nariño). From then on, people continued to work the land using various methods, and the hacienda house became the gathering center for the "encounters of authorities" that were now held periodically. The third encounter was nationally renowned, as newly elected President Belisario Betancur was invited to its closing session in November 1982.

Several recoveries of Páez lands also took place during those years, always with reference to the territoriality of colonial chiefdoms. One of them occurred within the boundaries of Juan Tama's chiefdom, resulting in the restoration of the cabildo and resguardo of Munchique-Tigres, which had been abolished forty years earlier during the period of "la violencia" (see CGM 1985a).

Even though the Guambiano community started to use the recovered lands in 1981, only in 1985 was the property legally handed over to them, under circumstances worth detailing here. The fact that the community had carried out a land recovery implied that it saw these lands as a restitution and was therefore not willing to pay for them. However, INCORA had previously bought the lands from the owner. What appeared to be an administrative problem arose, which brought to the surface a juridical problem: The INCORA auditorship could not agree to freely transfer to private individuals lands that had been purchased by the state.

The highest levels of government had to be consulted to break this impasse. Finally, the Council of State (*Consejo de Estado*) ruled that

> Law 89 [of 1890] . . . recognizes the existence of Indigenous Cabildos as autonomous forms of government in the resguardos . . . a special function of indigenous resguardos . . . is to protect and recover the vernacular indigenous properties . . . therefore, the Cabildos are Public Law entities of a special nature . . . according to the precepts of Law 89" (Decision of 11/16/1983).

Once the dispute over the transfer of possessions and lands between the state, the cabildo, and INCORA was resolved on September 14, 1985, the old hacienda was "transferred/restituted" directly to the cabildo of Guambía by the governor of Cauca and the official of INCORA. From that moment on, INCORA's policy of land transfer to indigenous communities changed. Now, lands would be handed over to the cabildo, not to individual families, and that group would decide how members of the community would make use of them. Once again, the state recognized this form of autonomy.

> Throughout the country, between 1982 and 1989, the national Government, in full recognition of the dominion it has exerted upon the country's indigenous communities from time immemorial, handed over to them lands comprising 18,949,405 hectares, and forming a total of 157 new resguardo units. . . . During the same period, in order to attend to the demands of small farming, indigenous populations in the Andean region, the national Government purchased a total of 57,336 hectares of private property (Roldán, ed., 1990: vi–vii).

These small farming communities were the same ones that are fighting today, side by side, with the Taita Lorenzo Muelas,[28] their representative to the National Constituent Assembly. They struggle for the recognition of their rights and authority over their territories, not only for lands for agricultural production. At the twilight of the twentieth century, the state has created 157 resguardos in Amazon and coastal lands where none had existed during colonial times.

Strategies of the Indigenous Movement and Democratization of Political Life in Colombia

The strategy of recovering land to guarantee the reconquest of indigenous rights, which had been made explicit to the Colombian people, initially emerged among struggling terrajero communities, particularly Páez, throughout the 1970s. Both the public and the government establishment perceived the matter as exclusively an indigenous issue because they heeded only the first part of the title of the movement's manifesto—"This belongs to us" (Ibe namuyguen)—and disregarded the second part—"but it's for you, too" (y ñimmereay gucha). However, the closest solidarios (people in solidarity with the indigenous movement) did understand the Guambiano message, and they worked to advance a movement for the recognition of the indigenous rights. Although now visible under the current context of constitutional reform, this movement encountered major obstacles in the Colombian political arena of the 1980s. And the debate about politics within and around the indigenous movement, which we will now address, leads us to another issue: the redefinition of the political in Colombian life.

The Fight for Rights and the Redefinition of the Political

Two distinct positions on Law 89 were present within CRIC from the group's inception: either to nullify the law or to make it widely known.[29] The indigenous people believed that a key source of the humiliation they experienced was contained within that document for it declared them "minors" and described them as "savages" to be "broken into civilization." However, the law's recognition of resguardo lands as inalienable, permanent community property emerged as an important element to support the people's struggle. The Seven Points of the indigenous program that was ultimately developed proposed to make the indigenous laws known and to demand their fair application.

In the cultural order that has surrounded the shaping of Colombian society, rights for most people have been precarious, and public discourse about them has been quite limited. To listen to the indigenous people demanding their rights immediately suggests another cultural order—a long, collective memory with which most Colombians, a relatively new people of colonizers of unused public lands, were unfamiliar. In that political milieu, permeated by the Marxism of the 1960s, rights were perceived as inherently "bourgeois," and to "fight for one's rights" consequently made no sense. The eruption of the struggle was, as a matter of fact, an atypical inconvenience; it had no place in the system of representation that generally prevailed.

However, it was this "fight for rights," not only for land, that from that moment on—and more visibly than ever during the 1980s—developed into one of the axes for the redefinition of the political in Colombia. The communities built an identity along this axis, and they started to act as the Indigenous Authorities Movement of the Southwest. In contrast, CRIC and ONIC pursued a different strategy. The differentiation among these organizations can be observed in the context of two different issues: the reform of indigenous legislation and the recognition by the central government of the indigenous authorities.

We have already summarized how the missionary church was planning to promote a legislative reform on the subject of the indigenous people. This project was stopped without the existence of a consensus in the CRIC on its strategic implications. A new project for the reform of existing indigenous legislation emerged in 1979. This time, the president of the republic himself asked congress to prepare an "indigenous statute." The Julio César Turbay Ayala administration (1978–1982), in line with the national security doctrine imposed on Latin American governments at the time, had already implemented its "statute of security." The indigenous statute project was unanimously rejected because it was believed that it did not consult with the indigenous communities.

This multiple opposition responded by adopting various political strategies. Supporters of one position, which entailed backing the current laws, merely rejected the project, utilizing the existing law to the extent possible on behalf of indigenous clients (for instance, to get them out of jail or begin lawsuits on their behalf) but leaving unquestioned the institutional framework. The second position's proponents found in this issue an opportunity to defend the rights of indigenous peoples before the national powers and to make them known to popular sectors. To this end, Guambiano, Páez, and Nariño cabildos resolved to organize a "governors' march" from the Ecuadorian border to Bogotá, gathering support along the way in order to face the challenge.[30] The march took place in November 1980 and lasted for three weeks. Demanding "authority, community, and future," as march flyers read, the cabildos disseminated their alternative thought, based on the principal right that had been proclaimed in June.[31] Links were established in villages and towns, neighborhoods, trade unions, and universities with all those who could recognize and support such rights. In retrospect, many now view these actions as the founding practice of the Indigenous Authorities Movement (CGM 1981).

In Bogotá, the cabildos did not receive much attention from the government or the congress commission that received them, although they did establish their position. After they returned to their respective communities, their march was evaluated and participants formed a group named the "Marching Governors" (Gobernadores en Marcha), which would continue to meet whenever coordinated action was required, without mediation from any "center."

March, path, movement—these terms were often used in counterdistinction to the notions of a centralized, vertical type of organization. Furthermore, the new group's name incorporated an important plural: "Authorities Movement." It also included a geographic delimitation: It was a movement "of the Colombian Southwest," thereby crossing over administrative boundaries. There was no executive committee nor any coordinating body to guarantee unity. And there were several leaderships: After all, the Guambianos were not the Paeces or the Pastos of Nariño (see CGM 1985b).

Two years later, the Indigenous Authorities invited President Betancur to close their third encounter in "Santiago, Guambiano territory." The president's helicopter landed directly on the recovered hacienda, a gesture that was quickly and unanimously interpreted as the legitimation of the recovery.[32] The president was received by the indigenous governors, and local and regional power representatives of the national system were excluded. A private meeting was held between indigenous authorities and national officials, during which the president announced his decision to withdraw his predecessor's indigenous statute project. This was followed by a massive public event, where Betancur recognized the indigenous communities as legitimate interlocutors.[33] The communities themselves, who had been "searching for their own idea,"[34] understood this as Colombia's recognition of its need to contribute to their project for "economic and social reconstruction of the indigenous peoples." Such was the public formulation of the movement's strategy, which then and there demanded to be treated "from authority to authority"—as if between one authority and another.

Government institutions continued to view the situation in terms of indigenous "integration into development," as conceived by the 1958 legislation, although public officials did begin to appear before the cabildos to present their greetings prior to the introduction of any of their new community programs.[35]

We have already pointed out, with regard to the adjudication of land, that the movement was able to modify state policy on the basis of a decision of the Council of State that recognized the legitimate character of the public rights of the indigenous cabildos. In this manner, the Authorities Movement had modified state-Indian relations in a way that was qualitatively different from those commonly employed by popular Colombian organizations. The latter—including CRIC and ONIC—tended to demand the state's intervention in the form of social services and benefits. But the Indigenous Authorities Movement took as a point of departure the recognition of their difference, while simultaneously emphasizing their understanding of social relations in terms of reciprocity. As mentioned earlier, the Guambiano title of the manifesto translates literally as "this belongs to us, but it is for you, too." And in the introduction to a slide show produced in 1981 by a Medellín solidarity group, the idea was more explicitly stated in the following terms: "We are certain that the recognition of our rights will help the Colombian people to understand better, and fight for, their own rights; this realization will bring with it their support for our struggle" (Medellín Solidarity Group 1981). This concept was also present in the posters of the campaign for the National Constituent Assembly: "Because we defend our rights, we support the rights of everyone. Vote for the Indigenous Authorities candidate."

This reciprocity as a cultural model, present in today's indigenous movement, was perhaps not contemplated in Touraine's notion of historicity. But in the limited framework of this text, we cannot properly address this question.[36] Instead, we will proceed with the analysis of the case at hand.

New Conflicts over Territoriality

When the Indigenous Authorities decided to invite President Betancur, the Guambía cabildo and the communities were again suffering persecution on the part of the civil, political, and military authorities. The reaffirmation of indigenous territoriality questioned not only the hacienda boundaries but the entire political-administrative order of the republic. Conflicts, consequently, continued to surface. At about that time, the decision by the M-19 to move from Caquetá to the Cauca and turn it into their own "Sierra Maestra" radically altered the region's social and political situation. For many years, the FARC (*Fuerzas Armadas Revolucionarias de Colombia*, or Revolutionary Armed Forces of Colombia)—the country's oldest guerrilla group—had been operating in the region and had coexisted with indigenous and peasant communities, although with a very different agenda. But "the dangers" that FARC associated with the Indigenous Authorities Movement's territorial, organizational, and political-ideological demands, coupled with CRIC's centralizing claim to be *the* indigenous organization in the Cauca (thus denying the existence of the communities organized in the Marching Governors movement), inevitably became elements of conflict. The result was "a quiet war between CRIC and FARC, followed from the distance by the M-19 and the Communist Party. Indigenous people from one band and the other began to fall" (GSI 1986; see also GSPC 1984).

The M-19's project was thus welcomed by the CRIC leadership as a possible barrier against FARC (CRIC 1984) because they considered that, more than the unions or other political organizations, it was the guerrilla groups that had the greatest presence in the indigenous territories.[37] Indeed, the various armed organizations, both old and new, concentrated up to six "armies" in the Cauca, thereby turning the indigenous territories into the theater of guerrilla actions and also in order to obtain men and resources for their maintenance. The national army had opted to stay on the periphery, intensifying intelligence actions and instigating conflicts among the various guerrilla organizations to the detriment of the communities (CGM 1985c), who nevertheless expressed themselves in various ways.

The confrontation with the indigenous project and with the authority of the consolidating cabildos was very intense. Several indigenous leaders were assassinated.[38] The Indigenous Authorities insisted that all political organizations, including the armed groups, demonstrate a respect for life. In April 1984, that group held a massive rally in Cali, as a result of which M-19 publicly gave its support to the formation of the Quintín Lame armed group.[39] The creation of this group was justified on the basis of the belief that political action in Colombia at that point in time could only be accomplished through armed struggle. Simultaneously, CRIC was working in Tolima (as it had been since 1980) to organize, with support from government officials and other organizations, a Colombian national indigenous organization. This organization—ONIC—was the sole interlocutor with the national government until the CRIC congress of November 1988, when the MAIC started to be recognized as an interlocutor at the request of organizations linked to the presidency of the republic.[40] Although CRIC was obliged to grant such recognition to the MAIC at the congress, its opposition to the group continued at the community level; this included intimidation and threats made during the electoral campaign for the National Constituent Assembly.

Nevertheless, despite the fact that the central power recognized the indigenous communities as interlocutors with the state in its discourse, locally and regionally everything remained the same. Mayors and municipal councils continued to use the police and other available "legal" means to prevent or suppress community actions (for example, in the Chimán neighborhood). Traditional political organizations (such as the Liberal and Conservative parties) still enjoyed exclusive access to governmental assistance or financial aid through the community organizations (*juntas de acción comunal*), bypassing cabildo authority and jurisdiction.

Such was the state of affairs when, in 1987, the Indigenous Authorities took notice of the municipal reform that had been undertaken by the national government. It was, indeed, "decentralizing" and potentially democratizing for Colombian political life, but it again ignored the existence of the indigenous cabildos and their territorial jurisdiction over the resguardos (Findji and Rojas 1985). In effect, in the Cauca departamento, for example, there are thirteen or fourteen contiguous municipalities in which the resguardos occupy the major part of the *municipio* ("rural zone"); this superposition of territorialities has been characteristic of the colonial-republican process of conformation of national territories in those regions. In late 1987, the Indigenous Authorities Movement organized a second march to Bogotá to discuss the problem.[41] It also decided to participate in the first local elections that took place in 1988 (a period in which popular candidates were assassinated) to advance the recognition of the Indigenous Authorities. The movement also presented a former Guambiano governor, the Taita Lorenzo Muelas, as a candidate for the 1990 elections to the national congress. This experience constituted the immediate precedent for his election as a delegate to the National Constituent Assembly at the end of the same year (see Findji 1990b).[42]

The ancestors of the Guambianos had inhabited the city of Popayán when the Spaniards arrived, and the Guambianos clearly described their actions as a recovery of their territory, establishing their own authority and conceptions. This, of course, was threatening to the established order, and attacks by landowners and the multinational Smurfit Cartón Colombia escalated. The landowners sought support from rural sectors and mestizo peasants, in addition to the intervention of security forces under the direction of local and regional politicians. Such actions were shared by some of the indigenous leaders who were more integrated and politicized in the clientelistic national way and who also defended traditional municipal boundaries (for instance, in Caloto). These more integrated leaders, backed by state officials, also promoted the creation of cabildos and resguardos, aimed at halting the process of internal indigenous unification in places where the cabildos already existed (for example, in Jambaló) or in settlements and haciendas that could have been reintegrated into a larger territory, as happened in 1983 in Ambaló.

Conclusion

The questions posed by and within the indigenous movement are: What does the "democratization" of political life in Colombia mean? Is the objective to secure the "participation" of the marginalized and neglected citizens, Indians and non-Indians alike? Is it the participation in a single political project of "integration into development"? Or is it perhaps a participation to rejuvenate the practice of "popular representation," individually delegated to an elected official?

But, on the contrary, what is at stake is the rethinking of society on the basis of the diversity of projects and actors involved. We have seen how a multiple and pluralist relationship has been practiced in the Colombian southwest among various types of indigenous communities—communities that simultaneously question their internal reunification, the form of reconstructing their "own destiny," and the redefinition of their relationship with the powers that have long dominated them. There is a clear political meaning in the defense of their own authorities on the part of the struggling communities that are becoming unified under the Indigenous Authorities Movement.

If land is essential to the communities' existence, so, too, is leadership. The Spanish Conquest entailed not only the pillage of gold but also the beheading of peoples. By remembering this, by administering historicity through their refusal to cease to exist as peoples (as Guambianos, as Paeces, or as the Sierra Nevada "three tribes"), the indigenous leaders of today are striving to orient and lead the action, not merely submit to it.

At the same time, the authorities themselves are undergoing a transformation, as we pointed out regarding the cabildos at several moments of their struggle: in their reencounter with the communities; when they draw on the elders' history as retrieved by the younger generations; when they organize councils of cabildos with former governors to ensure the continuity of a given policy; or when they build relationships "from authority to authority," beyond the limits of each individual resguardo and beyond the haciendas, municipalities, or provinces.

It is evident that the individuals who are protagonists of this social movement are neither fossilized people nor witnesses from bygone times. They belong to the present, and they are animated by the spirit of the century to take their destiny into their own hands. This is why they question and awaken the interest of nonindigenous sectors of Colombia, for whom the redefinition of their own identity as subjects requires questioning the cultural model that has thus far governed the reputedly "civilized" or progressive modes of collective action.

They are not "citizens"—they are communities, even if they have undergone profound socioeconomic changes, which they acknowledge. Social differentiation (not all Indians are destined to become campesinos, and there are hierarchies among members) demands the defense of autonomy, a drive that the Indigenous Authorities Movement is heading. They are not delegating their power in this search for autonomy. So it is not a movement of "masses" but of "authorities." This goes against the advocacy of some for an "indigenous-peasant" or "ethnic" movement,[43] where it is unclear whether the indigenous rests on the cultural or on the ethnic; both concepts are confusing as guidelines for action and serve to mask various interests, particularly the continued adherence to unidirectional and reductionistic models of integration.

At the core of the Indigenous Authorities Movement's struggle is the defense of the concept of the community as a guiding cultural model and an alternative to the citizen—the plain, dispossessed individual of the large, crowded cities who is invited to "participate" in a power actually held by others. For the movement protagonists, the challenge consists in finding analytical tools to orient action while taking into account the multiplicity of conflicts in which the communities are involved. The Authorities Movement does not fight for its identity. On the contrary, its very action in the current context of constitutional reform has proven that the movement already possesses a political identity and that it is fighting for its right to exist as such. These last twenty years of struggles, which now find their concrete expression in proposals for general political rearrangement, suggest that the indigenous struggle has generated a social movement whose outcomes will affect and depend not only on the indigenous communities but "Colombian" society at large. What remains to be seen is which nonindigenous sectors will accept and incorporate into their own actions the enormous and crucial challenges posed by the movement.[44]

Notes

1. The terrajeros (or *terrazgueros*) are those indigenous people who must pay the landowner with their work (two to eight days a month) for the right to set up their homes and have subsistence plots in the hacienda—often located in resguardo lands, in the case of the Cauca. A resguardo is a portion of territory that is recognized as the inalienable, permanent common property of an indigenous community. In economic terms, resguardos are lands segregated from the market. In sociopolitical terms, they are managed by a small council according to specific legislation.

2. "A social movement is the conflictual action by which cultural orientations—a field of historicity—are transformed into forms of social organization which are simultaneously defined by general cultural norms, and by relationships of social domination" (Touraine 1984; editors' translation).

3. Colombian historiographical tradition refers in this way to the 1880–1930 period, during which the Second Colombian Republic was constituted and the Conservative party assumed state power alone, by excluding the opposition.

4. The Indians say, "We all have rights, but not everything is equal." See the interview with the Páez governor of Jambaló in Bonilla 1978; see also Bonilla 1989.

5. This word association is impossible in Guambiano, Páez, Quechua, or Aymara languages because in their conception of time the past is ahead.

6. The ANUC was originally created by the government of Carlos Lleras Restrepo as a support for the land reform program. In its second congress, held in 1972, ANUC decided to become independent from the government.

7. The National Front (*Frente Nacional*) was a pact reached by the two main political parties, the Liberals and the Conservatives, at the conclusion of what is known as the period of *La Violencia*. Under the terms of this pact, the two parties would hold power alternately and distribute public offices between them. It excluded the participation of any third party and lasted from 1958 to 1974.

8. Editions exist in English (*Servants of God or Masters of Men*, Penguin Books, 1972), in French (*Serfs de Dieu, Maitres d'indiens*, Fayard, 1972), and Japanese (*Gendaikikakushitsu*, Tokyo, 1987). Furthermore, at the beginning of the National Front period, the Colombian government had signed an agreement with the Summer Institute of Linguistics as part of its liberal strategy to limit the monopoly of the Catholic church.

9. See Findji 1983, where this relationship is also discussed in reference to the Quintín Lame Movement at the beginning of the century.

10. Before the 1986 reform, mayors were appointed by the governor of the province, who was, in turn, designated by the president of the republic. The governors of the indigenous councils are elected annually by the community.

11. On the collective memory of the resistance, see Findji 1990a.

12. Indigenous migrants have thus contributed, as they have since colonial times, to constructing the Colombian mestizo society. Indigenous centers of resistance to integration have also persisted until the present.

13. In the Páez system, the period of rocería is the beginning of the agricultural cycle, when the bush is burned and the land is prepared for the sowing of corn and beans.

14. In the vocabulary of the Cauca, the "enclosure" is the piece of land granted by the landowner for the terrajero to build his home and work a subsistence plot.

15. See the detailed study in Findji and Rojas 1985.

16. Those who could not see the community's protagonism were the landowners, the traditional politicians, the police, and the army, all of whom were always searching for "professional agitators," "Communists," and "subversive elements." Activists and militant leftists themselves could not see it; they used to brand indigenous peoples as "nonpoliticized" and "indigenist" activists as apolitical or even as CIA agents.

17. Subsidiary work is unpaid community work required by the municipal government, particularly for road repairs. It is mandatory, as is any other form of tax.

18. The original passage includes two Colombianisms. *Amangualado* is the word for "confabulated." The word for "local boss" is *gamonal* or *cacique*, as used in other parts of Latin America and Spain, by extension of its original meaning as "local indigenous chief, headman"). [Translator's note]

19. It is impossible to review here all the struggles and violations of indigenous rights; see LNR 1980. For the Cauca region, we could mention the actions related to the recovery of Cobalo in Coconuco (with the involvement of the archbishop of Popayán). Names like Puracé (a multinational mining company), Caldono, Caloto, and Corinto are among those most prominent in public opinion.

20. See, in particular, the weekly publication *Alternativa* for the years 1974 and 1975. Starting in 1978, groups of solidarity with the indigenous struggles were created outside of the existing political organizations in Pasto, Medellín, Yumbo, Cali, Bogotá, and Popayán.

21. On the distinction between "communal community" and "community of associates," see Findji 1987.

22. Indigenous communities (for instance, the Arhuacos) fought against the reserve system. During the 1980s, the movement succeeded in putting an end to the system and in forcing the state to pursue a policy of transforming reserves into resguardos and creating new resguardos. This is discussed later in this chapter.

23. See Presidencia de la República: Fuero Indígena Colombiano. However, the term *territory* is absent from the project for constitutional reform put forward by the presidency of the republic in early 1991.

24. See "Mensaje del Cabildo-Gobernador de la Sierra Nevada," Carta al CRIC #2, 1976, where the Arhuacos questioned the notion of peasanthood and offered to help the "Caucanos" in their search for their "own idea." The proposal was rejected by the CRIC leadership.

25. See the pamphlet "Las Delicias: 15 Años de Experiencia," Despertar Guambiano, no. 1, 1978.

26. See the pamphlet "Para Proclamar Nuestro Derecho," Despertar Guambiano, no. 2, June 1980.

27. See, for instance, a communiqué dated September 10, 1983. See also GSPI 1982.

28. *Taita* is the title given to the senior leaders of the Guambiano people once they cease to hold an official position. [Editors' note]

29. Two were also the general assemblies where the CRIC program was defined. See CRIC 1974.

30. In Nariño, there are some twenty resguardos, with their respective comuneros and cabildos. These lands are, for the most part, occupied by haciendas. The process of affirmation and differentiation from the "campesino" took place there in the late 1970s, parallel to the process in the Cauca. Land recoveries, however, are still being carried out today, through direct confrontation with the landowners.

31. On derecho mayor, see the *Manifiesto Guambiano*. The Arhuacos, Koguis, and Arsarios of Sierra Nevada de Santa Marta think of themselves as the *hermanos mayores* or "older siblings," while "Colombians" are the "younger siblings," each group having different rights and duties.

32. See, for instance, the editorial in *El Liberal*, a Popayán newspaper, on the following day, November 24, 1982.

33. See Findji 1990b; Roldán, ed., 1990, particularly pp. V-XVIII; at the time of the publication of the first edition (1983), Roldán was head of the Indigenous Affairs Division of the Ministry of Government. See also GSP 1982.

34. The expression "[our] own idea," *la idea propia*, in the Spanish of the Arhuacos, Paeces, and Guambianos, was used by them to denote their own policy, in contrast to both official and leftist policies.

35. This entailed a further change in the cabildos; the final outcome is still unforeseeable.

36. Others have posed similar questions. See, for example, Platt 1982.

37. CRIC document published in response to *Violencia Hegemónica*, which questioned the assassination of indigenous leaders by armed groups close to CRIC.

38. Among them were: Bautista Guejía, former governor of Jambaló (see GSPI 1984); Luciano Labio, Paila leader (see GSI 1986); and Juan Tunubala, former governor of Guambía, assassinated in July 1988 (see MAI-CAJ 1988).

39. See the interview with Commander Iván Marino in the Popayán daily *El Liberal*, on April 13, 1984. Contrary to what is suggested in a discourse that presents Quintín Lame as a community self-defense group organized against landowners—actually an earlier stage of the movement—the November 1984 assassination of the only Páez priest (parish priest of Toribío Father Alvaro Ulcué) by confabulated establishment forces was not one of the causes for the creation of the Quintín Lame group.

40. Specifically, these are the Council for Peace and the National Rehabilitation Plan, a government program for areas affected by the war.

41. See the pamphlet published on that occasion: *Pueblos Indígenas y Reforma Municipal*.

42. A more remote precedent would be the letter from the Indigenous Authorities Movement to the minister of government dated March 10, 1988, and titled "Carta del Movimiento de Autoridades Indígenas del Sur-Occidente al Ministro de Gobierno, Presidente de la Comisión de Reajuste Institutional," in Bonilla 1988: 34–38.

43. Various ethnically differentiated communities and solidarity members have always converged, both in CRIC and in the Indigenous Authorities Movement.

44. Many and unprecedented were the results obtained by indigenous peoples from the National Constituent Assembly, particularly the creation of a new national territorial entity, which may or may not abide by established administrative territorial divisions and which entails full recognition of the resguardos, granting them possibilities for expansion. Within these territories, indigenous authorities have full autonomy over the systems of government and justice and the implementation of education, health, and "development" programs. Indigenous languages are also declared official within the autonomous territories, and education must be bilingual. In addition, two slots were permanently assigned to indigenous representatives in the senate of the republic; in the chamber of representatives, five slots were separated to be distributed (through appropriate electoral mechanisms) among indigenous peoples, ethnic minorities, and Colombians living abroad. These are some of the most important achievements, out of a complex package obtained mostly through the efforts of the Indigenous Authorities Movement. [Editors' note]

8

Power, Gender, and Development: Popular Women's Organizations and the Politics of Needs in Ecuador

Amy Conger Lind

Introduction

Popular women's organizations throughout Latin America in the past decade have become a focal point of discussion among scholars and activists because, like other grass-roots organizations, they represent a struggle for ideological autonomy from political parties, the state, and the development apparatus. For a variety of reasons, poor women have been at the forefront of struggles to gain increased access to infrastructural services, such as water, electricity, housing, and social services. Through collective struggle, women have revealed and challenged unequal power relations as they are manifested in the everyday sphere—that is, as they are embodied in reproductive activities of men and women on both a daily and a generational basis. Because activities like preparing the food, minding the children, and taking care of the home are "women's work," it has been women who have collectively organized to protest poor living conditions for they are the ones who have to put the food on the table, whether or not they contribute to the family income. And due to the inability of traditional political mechanisms (that is, class-based and/or male-based political interests and institutions) to address gender-specific needs, many women have opted to organize autonomously from men, further revealing that a dominant gender ideology persists in male-based political organizations and strategies.

The emergence of such organizations is also a result of the inability of the development apparatus (including international development agencies, the state, and other political institutions) to address adequately the needs of the poor and to change inequalities in the system. The emergence and increased visibility of popular women's organizations in Ecuador during the 1980s is at once particular to Ecuadorean history and representative of larger resistance struggles emerging throughout Latin America. The comparatively "late" emergence of gender-based struggles in Ecuador must be understood within a broader conceptualization of social movements in the country and among other Latin American countries: Though there have been various forms of resistance to manifestations of colonialist and postcolonialist processes of "development" (for example, indigenous, environmental, community, and traditional class struggles), Ecuadorean struggles have not been as widespread nor as visible as those in Peru, Bolivia, and other Latin American countries. Furthermore, there has been relatively less violence than in Peru and Bolivia. This is due in part to the history of authoritarianism and "democracy" in the respective countries, the role of the state in the international economy, the impact of colonialist discourse on indigenous cultures, and the subsequent development of intellectual thought and practice in each country. In Ecuador, women's resistance struggles initially emerged during the military dictatorship in the 1970s. It was not until the 1980s, however, when the economic infrastructure developed during the military years was eroded by a series of economic crises, that women began to organize in numbers unprecedented in the history of that nation. And, despite the fact that there was a return to democracy in Ecuador, the struggle of women demonstrates the ways in which relations within the household and social relations between men and women in general have not yet been democratized.

The fact that there are over eighty popular women's organizations throughout Ecuador today points us to these questions: Why have Ecuadorean women chosen to organize in the sphere of everyday life? And how has their particular history informed their political strategies? Possible answers to such questions require analyzing the breakdown of traditional political mechanisms, the discourse of development (especially as it is represented in the current economic crisis), and the shaping of a collective identity that is based on gender as a principal organizing strategy.

Popular women's organizations, then, represent a struggle operating at many levels, crossing many false divisions set up in the Western philosophical tradition between "private" and "public." They represent a struggle against engendered forms of power, as embodied in male and female subjects in the everyday sphere, as well as a struggle against institutionalized forms of power inherent in traditional class-based political institutions and in the dominant Western practice of development. This is not to say, however, that all of these questions are addressed by women in the act of collectively organizing. Rather, as I will show, relations of power inherent to dominant conceptualizations of gender, politics, and, in this case, "development," are recognized in varying and indirect ways: Challenges to power relations give meaning to and stem from the making of a collective identity. Based on this framework, I will show how power relations are manifested in the everyday sphere and how women have chosen to organize around their reproductive activities in collective neighborhood-based organizations. It is through the collectivization of reproductive work, at the neighborhood level, that women have become further politicized on issues pertaining to gender identity and subjectivity. This, in turn, has informed and influenced their political strategies and shaped their visions of a more just society. My analysis is based on fieldwork in Quito, Ecuador, as a researcher and participant in popular women's organizations in January 1989 and June through August 1989.

Power and Gender Relations in the Everyday Sphere:
Women's Reproductive Work

The emergence of grass-roots women's organizations in Latin America has been analyzed in various terms, stemming from several points of departure. In the development literature, given the underlying assumption that economic development is necessary and desirable in one form or another, the mobilization of poor women has been largely attributed to women's inferior role in the economy (Elson 1992; Benería and Roldán 1987; Benería 1989; Antrobus 1988). Based on the idea that women's reproductive work remains unaccounted for in economic and social terms and that it is women who are responsible for the maintenance of the household and the family on a daily and generational basis, the work of these authors suggests that poor women have chosen to organize collectively to combat increasing economic pressures felt at the household and community levels. Drawing on Marxist notions of what is "productive," "unproductive," and "reproductive," feminist social scientists have analyzed poor women's organizations as a type of "survival strategy," in which women collectivize their work at the community level in order to relieve themselves of part of their burden as working mothers (Barrig 1989b; Moser 1989a, 1989b; Benería and Feldman, eds., 1992). In other words, these social scientists have addressed the question of gender, politics, and development in terms of the intersections of class and gender and the role of women's work in the economy.

In this type of analysis, women are seen as crucial to the social reproduction of their communities. This is so because women are responsible for childbearing, child-rearing, and maintaining the household, and they also typically work to bring in primary or secondary incomes to sustain the households at their current standards of living. In addition, women's (unpaid) reproductive labor sustains the household so that men are able to work in the labor market. The position of poor women, then, is considered inferior to the position of their male counterparts because most women are forced to work both within and outside the household. And, with the economic crisis reaching unprecedented levels throughout Latin America, poor women have been forced to increase both their domestic labor (as they can no longer afford to pay for services) and their paid labor (as their husbands' wages no longer suffice to support their families). Furthermore, with increasing economic crisis, poor women are the ones who have to cope with the devastating effects of price increases and lack of basic resources on a daily basis.

Using this analysis, feminist social scientists have explained why it is typically women who choose to organize collectively, in popular women's organizations and other such informal networks, around reproductive activities such as day-care and increased access to basic resources such as housing, food, and water. The strength of this approach, as suggested by the researchers themselves, is that it reveals the ways in which women's (unpaid, invisible) work is essential to the maintenance and growth of the economy. Within economic development frameworks, this reveals major gaps in traditional economic analyses in which women's work remains unacknowledged, thereby allowing researchers to make false conclusions and misrepresentations about the impacts of economic crisis on households. Most importantly, such analyses overlook the fact that women's work is *increasing* rather than decreasing as a result of male-biased development strategies that exclude gender as a variable.[1] All of these factors, then, contribute to the reasons why women have chosen to organize informal networks and grass-roots women's organizations.

The emphasis on gender and class is not exclusive to the literature on household survival strategies: Quite often, social scientists have emphasized economic motivations for the mobilization of the poor (Eckstein, ed., 1989). In the literature on women's movements in Latin America, for example, distinctions have been made between "practical gender interests" and "strategic gender interests," implying or, in some cases, explicitly stating that poor women's movements are often based on "practical interests" (that is, based on their practical needs such as income and access to food, water, housing, and health care) and that feminist (typically middle-class) movements are more often based on "strategic interests" (that is, redefining gender roles and meanings) (Molyneux 1986; Barrig 1989b). Caroline Moser distinguished between "women's interests" (what she also referred to as "prioritized concerns") and "women's needs" (the means by which women's concerns may be satisfied) (see Moser 1989b: 1802–1804). She then distinguished between "practical gender needs" and "strategic gender interests" and claimed that development planners could better assess the needs and interests of women by basing their policies on these categories. Implicit in this approach is the assumption that women's "basic needs" are different from their "strategic needs" and that a "practical" or a "survival strategy" cannot simultaneously be a political strategy that challenges the social order. In this scenario, which forms the basis for many development policies and projects implemented throughout Latin America today, it is too often assumed that most poor women are only concerned with their daily survival and therefore do not have a strategic agenda beyond their economic welfare. Hence, such women are not *really* challenging the sexual division of labor.[2] Again, the plight of organized poor women is based on a notion of gender/class struggle, in which women fight on behalf of their households because of their particular reproductive roles. This type of analysis overlooks the critical contributions and challenges that organized poor women conceivably represent to the social order. Rarely, if ever, is discussion focused, for example, on how poor women negotiate power, construct collective identities, and develop critical perspectives on the world in which they live—all factors that challenge dominant gender representations.

Furthermore, this type of analysis does not go far enough in explaining the emergence of a politics based on identity. Studies of women's work and collective organizing are typically based on fixed categories of gender and class. But both empirical reality and other forms of theorizing point in new directions, which I will discuss only partially. Although there are infinite variations of group structure, purpose, and motivations for organizing, one principal organizing strategy among most, if not all, women's organizations is based on a reconceptualization and politicization of gender identity. The question, then, of why women organize specifically as women is based fundamentally on the idea that men and women are socialized differently and perhaps have different "identities."[3] This difference in socialization is believed to be based on the ways in which gender is produced and represented in society and how individuals interpret and embody these roles at a subjective level. Based on this notion, men and women are seen to have distinct needs, desires, expectations, and responsibilities, all of which shape the individual's identity and consciousness and ultimately contribute to his or her understanding of the world. In turn, these needs, desires, expectations, and responsibilities are represented in quotidian practices and in larger social, economic, and political structures that exist in the present and that are reproduced over time. In this sense, the production of identity is an ongoing process, in which identity (in this case gender) can change over time, according to the ways in which gender is represented at a societal level and embodied in the subject.[4] By virtue of understanding "gender" as produced through representations, then, I consider "gender" a socially constructed category and not one based on essentialist notions of being. Furthermore, gender as a produced category is not fixed: Identity is constantly in fluctuation in accordance with subjective interpretations of dominant representations of gender, race, culture, age, and so on.

In accordance with this approach, we need to further problematize the historical division made between "production" and "reproduction" inherent in most theories of women's collective organizing in Latin America. Within this type of framework, women are viewed only as reproductive and/or productive units, and causal relationships are made between women's economic activities and women's collective action. Ivan Illich (1982), in his anthropological study on gender, differentiated between "sex" and "gender" and claimed that only in the realm of "economic sex," in which beings are viewed primarily as economic units (primarily in modern industrial society) does the split between production and reproduction become possible and powerful. T. Minh-ha Trinh elaborated on this theme as it relates to the production of identities of Third World women and demonstrated the ways in which dominant Western conceptualizations of these women have reinforced stereotypes of poor women's struggles as being linked primarily to their economic roles (Trinh 1989: 105–116). One could extend this analysis to the realm of "development sex," in which poor women are positioned as "clients" by the state and the development apparatus, and their "needs" are interpreted as being solely "economic" or "domestic." Nancy Fraser addressed this aspect of the "politics of needs interpretation," suggesting that one has to see "needs" not only as a contested domain but as one in which expert/professional discourses, dominant/state processes, and social movements converge. People are positioned as "clients" by the state in ways mediated and made possible by expert knowledges, yet social movements politicize these interpretations; that is, they refuse to see "needs" as just "economic" or "domestic" (A. Escobar in press a; Fraser 1989: chapter 8). Adele Mueller analyzed the relationship between First World feminist researchers in the development apparatus (for example, international organizations, academic institutions, and state programs) and groups of Third World women being researched or "targeted" in development projects (Mueller 1991). She contended that First World feminist researchers and activists need to scrutinize women's roles more in terms of how they are implicated in the power structures of the development apparatus, particularly as research is conducted on other women who are extremely different than those in the First World *within* the development apparatus. Furthermore, differences among women need to be acknowledged both within the First World ruling development apparatus, among Third World women, and between First World and Third World women.

As much of the literature on women's organizing suggests, poor women in urban areas often base their politics on a certain set of "needs" derived from their perceived reproductive roles. As women discover inequalities in their living situations, they choose to organize with other women to (1) alleviate their burdens as women, mothers, and providers for families, and (2) gain strength in numbers, thereby becoming a form of counterresistance and further enabling themselves to perceive identity as something that can be utilized in struggle and, in some cases, consciously changed through politicization. In this way, the collectivization of women's reproductive activities and the combined effort to combat gender inequalities in society lead to the formation of new collective identities and new definitions of "needs." Such new collective identities, in turn, present the politicized subjects and society at large with new representations of gender—ones that challenge existing frameworks and possibly pose threats to established belief systems. Although these challenges are micro forms of resistance, they nevertheless demand our attention, as they clearly have changed the lives of women activists and those around them—this, too, holds true for popular women's organizations in Quito. Furthermore, such forms of resistance ultimately challenge the making of theory and policy at macroinstitutional levels. I will demonstrate how this is occurring in Ecuador in the remainder of this chapter.

The Rise of a Visible Women's Struggle

Popular women's organizations were not considered part of a cohesive movement until recent years in Ecuador. In fact, a visible struggle of women at *any* level of society is a relatively new phenomenon. As in many Latin American countries, women originally became mobilized during periods of military authoritarianism—in the case of Ecuador, during the 1970s. Between 1975 and 1978, there was widespread discontent with the military regime that led to increased mass mobilization against it. Throughout this process, which led to free elections on the basis of a new constitution and the election of a democratic government in 1979, women became noticeable participants in various protests. At this time, women's fronts were set up within trade unions, peasant federations, neighborhood organizations, and some political parties.

In general, popular organizations proliferated during the process of redemocratization, due, in part, to people's lack of trust in the formal political system—especially in resolving the growing economic crisis. It was during this time that social actors in the grass roots forged collective, pluralist strongholds to combat the crisis while simultaneously maintaining their autonomy from the state and other traditional political institutions. Such organizations provided a space for historically marginalized subjects, traditionally viewed as "outside" the realm of formal politics, to organize.

Despite women's participation in national struggles for democracy, there was little discussion specifically about women's demands. Rather, the "woman question," as is typical in the history of most women's movements throughout the region, was considered "unimportant" or "secondary" to the "real" questions being discussed in the struggle for human rights and national identity.[5] It was not until international influences, particularly those placed on the Ecuadorean state as a result of demands made during the United Nations Decade for the Advancement of Women, coupled with Ecuadorean women activists' experiences and frustrations working in patriarchal-based organizations, that an autonomous women's movement began to develop.

Popular women's organizations became particularly visible in the late 1970s and 1980s, as poor and working-class women helped to organize other women in neighboring communities and as feminists conducted workshops and formed networks among already existing and newly forming grass-roots organizations. My work and participation in eight popular women's organizations in Quito suggests most women have just recently become political activists around issues pertaining to their class and gender roles. Furthermore, most have not previously been politicized around traditional "class issues" as they have been addressed historically in working-class movements and organizations. Rather, the newly formed political consciousness of the participants is typically shaped by confrontations they have had with political authorities in their district municipalities and by the subsequent gender antagonisms that arise as women are denied voices in decisionmaking despite their key roles in the community. They have been exposed to political parties primarily during elections, when candidates try to gain stronger constituencies by making offers of social change in their neighborhoods. Again, this creates further antagonisms rather than forms of solidarity as politicians tend to dismiss the interests of women and rarely if ever fulfill their campaign promises.

Knowledge About Women and Women's Interests: Ecuadorean State Policy

The Ecuadorean state did not focus on "women's issues" until the late 1970s, after the initiation of the United Nations Decade for the Advancement of Women. Lack of pressure exerted on the state by interest groups, lack of informed opinions, and the paucity of research and publications on the subject have all contributed to the state's inattention to the "woman question."[6] In this sense, the Ecuadorean state is no different than most: Women's issues are introduced under pressure from below or from outside.

As early as 1970, the Interamerican Women's Commission of the Organization of American States (OAS) requested that the Ecuadorean government create a bureau or department within the state's administrative structure, "which would define and implement policies and strategies directed towards women, taking due account of Ecuador's social, political, economic, and cultural characteristics" (CEIS 1986: 62). In response to this formal request, the government created the *Departamento Nacional de la Mujer* (DNM) in February 1970, subordinated to what was then known as the Ministry of Labor and Social Welfare. The department had "no life beyond its formal existence, but was the direct antecedent of the National Office of Women (*Oficina Nacional de la Mujer*—OFNAMU)"

(CEIS 1986: 63). Under the León Febres-Cordero administration (1984–1988), the Oficina Nacional de la Mujer was changed to the *Dirección Nacional de la Mujer,* or DINAMU.

Among the programs the state has implemented, many have been directed toward poor women in rural and urban areas. Examples are the distribution of basic staples to poor sectors, such as the mother and infant food supplement program of the Ministry of Public Health; school breakfasts; and the organization of training courses for women to acquire skills such as dressmaking, beauty care and hairdressing, secretarial skills, accounting, and toymaking. These programs have been highly criticized by feminists in the women's movement as being "ineffectual" because they tend to reinforce traditional female roles or even create new stereotypes of female roles and do not offer alternative visions of a more just society. Rather, these feminists argue, through these programs women become dependent on the state for the acquisition of knowledge and resources, and there is little if any questioning of identity that typically comes about with grass-roots politicization. As welfarist ideological practices permeate state and development policy in general, so, too, do they permeate the everyday sphere, contributing to the constant production of hierarchical gender inequalities manifested in reproductive activities. In this case, though apparently nonpolitical, state programs legitimize existing inequalities and deter women from conceptualizing alternatives to their present living situations and organizing autonomously for social change.

By the late 1970s, partially as a result of feminists' direct experiences working at DNM and their subsequent exit from state agencies to work autonomously in research organizations and activist groups, the women's movement became significantly more cohesive and visible.

At the state level, the National Development Plan of 1980–1984, adopted by the democratically elected government of Jaime Roldós/Osvaldo Hurtado, was the first to define a national policy for the "integration of women into the development process."[7] One of its objectives was aimed at guaranteeing the popular classes' active participation in social and economic development. It is as part of this policy that new forms of social policy targeting women and popular sectors came about. The Program of Popular Promotion and, within it, the Subprogram for Women and the Young, were the first women's projects to be designed and implemented within a development context. These policies differed from the more obvious welfarist policies in that their attention was directed at popular organizations. Thus, state policies conceivably could contribute to social mobilization, increase poor people's access to knowledge and resources, and ultimately transform social relations. The policy (rhetorically coined the "popular promotion" of poor people) generated heated discussions about the question of women's subordination, both within state agencies and in independent women's organizations. However, the plan still fit within a liberal, reformist development framework, and ultimately it failed to challenge existing inequalities sufficiently. Furthermore, the plan was not carried out in the same fashion as it was originally presented. In reality, many obstacles kept the state agencies from accomplishing their original agenda. The Hurtado administration, which implemented the first stabilization program under a standby arrangement with the IMF in 1982, was accused of giving priority to debt repayment at the cost of tackling pressing social and economic problems in the country. In the end, few, if any, of the original goals were achieved.

The next official Comisión Nacional de Desarrollo (CONADE) document was the 1984 Outline of a Strategy for Development, drawn up after the inauguration of the new conservative government led by León Febres-Cordero in 1984. Like the 1980–1984 plan, it suggested that a policy oriented toward women be located within the more general policy framework of "social participation." Although there is a subtle difference between the concepts of popular promotion and social participation, the basic proposal is the same in both instances: namely, that women's productive work had been underutilized and that until women "participated" more in the development of the country (that is, until women's productive capacity was utilized more efficiently), the system would be unjust and women would be in a subordinate position vis-à-vis men.

The Dirección Nacional de la Mujer is currently the body charged with the responsibility of putting into practice state policies oriented toward women. Although what was then called the Oficina Nacional de la Mujer was officially created in the early 1970s during the military dictatorship, it was with the newly elected democratic president Jaime Roldós that it gained real political significance.[8] The initial tasks faced by OFNAMU were its institutional consolidation and the design of a plan of action. Regarding its institutional consolidation, the main problems facing the office were its lack of autonomy, the scarcity of qualified personnel, and the inadequacy of its budget. Even now, under the Rodrigo Borja Social Democratic administration (1988–present), the office is increasingly faced with very similar problems.

The most recent development plan, presented in February of 1989, did not originally have a section that discussed women's issues. Rather, after pressure was placed on CONADE by DINAMU, as well as by autonomous women's organizations, the commission that designed the 1988–1992 plan agreed to include an appendix specifically addressing the need to further integrate women into the development process. The absence of feminist researchers and policymakers in the government is reflected in the National Development Plan: Women's issues were essentially tacked onto the document at the last minute. Even in the appendix, which was officially presented in August 1989, the conceptual framework is not significantly different from the liberal, reformist framework used in the 1984–1988 plan. As a result of this and earlier decisions made within state agencies, middle-class feminists who had participated in the making of state policy recognized the need to organize autonomously from the state and other male-based political institutions. Consequently, a shift took place in the 1980s as feminists created their own autonomous base by institutionalizing independent women's organizations and networking throughout the country.

Autonomy and the Politics of Needs

The move toward autonomy has been key in shaping feminist frameworks and political strategies. Rocío Rosero (coordinator of the Women's Network of the

Consejo de Educación de Adultos de América Latina, or CEAAL, and previous director of Centro María Quilla), Lilia Rodriguez (director of the Centro Ecuatoriano para la Promoción y Acción de la Mujer, or CEPAM), and Dolores Padilla (director of the Centro de Información y Apoyo de la Mujer, or CIAM), all current leaders in the feminist movement, have worked in state agencies. They, along with many other women, have chosen to create their own organizations: The result has been a proliferation of independent women's research centers, legal services, communications services, activist organizations, support groups, a women's café, and popular women's organizations. Published materials on gender issues have become more accessible, women's studies are being promoted at the university level, and younger women have begun to become increasingly active in feminist organizations.

The strength in the movement is also partially a result of the support Ecuadorean organizations receive from other feminist groups throughout Latin America. Influences from the Peruvian women's movement, which began during the late 1970s, have been a key mobilizing factor for the Ecuadorean movement. Equally as important, in the past fifteen years Ecuadorean women have been able to gain momentum in their mobilization efforts as a result of the increased channeling of economic and ideological support from international development organizations and feminist movements throughout the world. This is due primarily to the initiation of the United Nations Decade for the Advancement of Women (1975–1985) and the subsequent development of international and Third World women's networks.[9]

In 1987, a number of feminists who had participated in the protest against the repressive government of Febres-Cordero initiated a new umbrella organization, *Acción por el Movimiento de Mujeres*. This group has since organized several marches and protests in Quito and Guayaquil, including the annual March 8 International Women's Day March and a series of protests outside Citibank and other donor banks to the Ecuadorean state.[10] Although women from the state sector and from political parties play a role in the organization, it has come to represent the interests of the autonomous women's movement rather than male-centric interests of traditional political parties or the state.

There have been three feminist *encuentros* (*Taller Encuentro Nacional de Teoría Feminista*) in 1986, 1987, and 1989, in which women from various sectors participated in what has been the first conference space designated solely for the purpose of giving meaning to and reflecting on the state of the current women's movement in the country. These conferences have come to represent the beginnings of a cohesive movement, in which Ecuadorean feminists have begun to build stronger coalitions among middle-class and working-class women's organizations, political parties, indigenous groups, and labor unions.[11] They have also served as one of the few collective spaces in which poor and middle-class women could establish a dialogue and discuss similarities among themselves, as well as recognize forms of power in their daily lives. What has been discovered is that though issues are articulated very differently by poor and middle-class women and though strategies among women's organizations across classes tend to differ, their concerns quite often coincide. It has been widely recognized, for example, that women are in inferior positions vis-à-vis men and that macro-level political and economic issues such as the debt crisis and political repression affect most, if not all, people in the everyday sphere. It has also been recognized by women— regardless of their economic class, race, and ethnicity—that they have particular "needs" as women, needs derived from their gender identity.

The politicization of "basic needs" demonstrates the ways in which such "needs" are actually much more than just the desire for bread and water. As poor women base their politics on their reproductive roles, they challenge the meaning of ascribed gender roles as well as the implications these roles have in the reproduction of society. They are not only struggling for access to resources, they are also challenging dominant representations of gender and incorporating this into their politics. State policy, then, cannot easily fulfill poor women's "needs" simply by providing them with economic resources. This also calls into question the theoretical division between "practical gender needs" and "strategic gender needs" as popular women's organizing strategies politicize so-called basic needs and challenge the boundaries within which their needs as women are perceived.

Gender, Power, and the Politicization
of the Everyday Sphere

Centro Femenino 8 de Marzo, located in the district of Chillogallo, is one of dozens of popular women's organizations in Quito. The center was established in 1985 by a group of local women who felt the threefold need to (1) gain a collective stronghold, as women, in the already existing community organizational structure, where issues such as the need for better infrastructural services were being discussed; (2) learn practical skills and collectivize costs; and (3) form a group in which they could talk among themselves and discuss themes relating to their lives as women.[12] This final need is perhaps the most important in terms of understanding the transformation and politicization of gender identity that occurs through collective participation. The creation of Centro Femenino has given the women a collective voice in the neighborhood and has forced the traditional community organization (*organización barrial*) to address the needs of women.[13] In fact, this organization has responded quite positively, lending the women a house in which to run their meetings and workshops and keep their documents. Occasionally, workshops have been held at the center by feminists who come on request; issues discussed include sexuality, state and domestic violence, and employment skills. Political tactics are also discussed and agreed on, and the organization has placed various demands on the city of Quito to improve living conditions in their neighborhood.[14] The women buy food collectively and then divide it among themselves for their families in an effort to reduce costs. And they are currently trying to gain legal representation by registering their organization with the city.

Presently, Centro Femenino has over forty members, and approximately twenty participate on a regular basis. By far the majority of women I interviewed (twenty-two) had just recently become political activists. One of the original organizers, Silvia Vega, is an exception: She completed her college education, has worked in a political party, and has served as a link between Centro Femenino and middle-class feminist organizations in Quito. She is also a member of *Acción por el Movimiento de Mujeres.* Ten other women have participated in neighborhood organizations that do not specifically address women's issues. In these organizations, the women rarely entered into positions of power, nor did they feel they were allowed equal opportunities to participate in decisions affecting the entire community. There, they discovered that their needs were not being met even at the level at which they had the most direct control over their lives. Centro Femenino provided a space that the traditional organization did not. The building of a women's organization, then, had required creative and alternative forms of strategizing by women with little political experience and few ties to traditional parties and other male-based groups.

Much attention has been focused on the question of why poor women struggle, an issue that especially interests middle-class Latin American feminists and feminists from the United States and Europe. Maruja Barrig, in her study on popular women's organizations in Lima, pointed out that such organizations do not necessarily challenge the existing sexual division of labor: Rather, popular women's organizations are often designed so that they reinforce gender stereotypes and consequently exclude women from participating more in the public, political sphere (Barrig 1989a, 1989b). Whether they be organized by the women themselves or by development institutions, popular women's organizations emphasize women's voluntary role in community development. Consequently, many women in Lima have actually had to work more both within the household and in the community. Despite the fact that some women have come in contact with state officials and despite their increased presence in resistance movements, Barrig asserted that women have not necessarily created a new public, political space for themselves but rather have expanded their private, domestic space into a wider sphere. In this sense, Barrig continued, women have not broken down gender barriers but instead have contributed to the reinforcement of the existing sexual division of labor.

Barrig's analysis was based on the assumption that poor women are struggling primarily for practical—not strategic—gender interests. Although it is true that poor and middle-class women have distinct political agendas based on perceived needs for themselves and their communities, poor women nevertheless have agendas. And though their ideas are articulated differently, they often coincide with those of middle-class feminists. In this sense, the division between "practical gender interests" and "strategic gender interests" misrepresents struggles of poor women who do, in fact, question or attempt to change the social (gender) order. Such categories maintain a false barrier in our thinking about political and economic strategies of survival and resistance. It would be more useful to understand change as it occurs at the site of identity production, as well as at the societal level, as new conceptualizations of gender are re-presented. Organizing strategies of popular organizations are based on the needs of the women participants (and they include material needs, as well as identity-based needs such as increased respect and rights for women in society), and they inherently represent a challenge to authority as it is manifested in the everyday sphere. It is not just for "survival" that they choose to organize: They are receiving something in return, and it is more than food on the table. Whether or not women directly challenge the sexual division of labor, transformations of identity that occur at the level of the subject and the subsequent ways these transformations are incorporated into organizing strategies are at least as significant, if not more so. In other words, the transcendence of the existing sexual division of labor, which, in the past, has referred primarily to the productive and reproductive work of men and women, is but one aspect of women's organizing strategies.

A fundamental strategy employed in all the organizations in my sample is consciousness-raising: Every group met weekly to discuss issues pertaining to their lives as women. Consciousness-raising was originally used by feminists as a form of support, as well as a tool to politicize other women. As one woman in Centro Femenino 8 de Marzo said:

> I joined Centro Femenino 8 de Marzo because I wanted to leave the routine of the household. . . . Also, I want to make new friendships, learn new things that will help me as a woman and as a mother. My biggest dream is to prepare myself more so that I can help other women like myself that need moral support so they can continue in their struggle to make others respect our rights, and to make others value us as women who think and have dreams, faith, and hope. We can enjoy good times with our compañeras by sharing new and productive ideas that will serve us in obtaining a better future for our organization and for society. For this reason I'm asking all women . . . to continue fighting for better ideals in the future. . . . For this reason we will shout, "Enough humiliations and discrimination against women! Long live organized women!"[15]

Consciousness-raising is recognized by feminists across economic classes as essential to the growth of the women's movement. Indeed, these groups "are the most important and rich creation of the feminist movement because it is the only space which has allowed us to recognize ourselves as different subjects" (CAM-CIAM 1988: 95). Furthermore, it is recognized by participants that though consciousness-raising meetings are necessary spaces for women, it is equally as important to be able to struggle as groups of women, so that women's political and ideological visions will impact society at large.

Centro Femenino 8 de Marzo and other popular women's organizations have consistently increased their participation in events, rallies, and marches organized and orchestrated by middle-class feminists. Although leadership in the movement consists of middle-class feminists, popular organizations that affiliate themselves with the movement have gained a voice, and their concerns have been given priority in the past decade.

Furthermore, poor and working-class women have created their own networks of neighborhood-based women's organizations. Centro Femenino 8 de Marzo has helped organize three other local groups: *Organización Buenaventura*, *Organización Ciudadela Ibarra*, and *Organización Martha Bucaram*, all of which are small groups (four to ten women) that hold discussions and sometimes arts and crafts workshops once a week, conducted primarily by women of Centro Femenino 8 de Marzo. Such efforts to create autonomous networks are critical to the struggle, and within the popular movement it is especially clear why: As women have become disillusioned with male-based neighborhood organizations and because middle-class women from the state sector have focused primarily on reforming the law,[16] women in the popular movement have recognized the need for a space within the community in which they can define and struggle around their own needs. Several women in Chillogallo, for example, joined Centro Femenino 8 de Marzo because they wanted more decisionmaking power in the community. They recognized, then, that their autonomy as working-class and poor women was needed in the everyday sphere, that is, directly in Chillogallo. Just as most women recognize forms of power manifested in their daily lives, they also recognize their own lack of power. The making of a collective identity through political organization is a way to reappropriate their own sense of power and identity.

Conclusion: The Making of a Collective Identity

It is through the making of a collective identity that women have come to take a stance against several forms of power represented in their daily lives: Lack of state support, despite the institutionalization of DINAMU and other national development projects targeting women, has prompted women to place demands directly on the city and community political structure. The current National Development Plan prioritizes the needs of poor women as primarily economic, and, though this may benefit some sectors of women to some extent, such policies fail to address many of the concerns organized poor women have made visible in their struggles— concerns that go far beyond economic causes and remedies. This, in conjunction with the increasing weakness of traditional political mechanisms such as local political parties, trade unions, and male-based neighborhood organizations, has forced women to create their own space. The heightening economic crisis, in which women's domestic work has increased and been coupled with a growing necessity for women to complement (male) household wages, further reveals the need for women to organize *on their own time,* as mothers, wives, and (sometimes) wage earners.

The struggle of women, then, is not only a struggle to address their reproductive work and gender/class relations. It is also a struggle to overcome their lack of power, primarily through the transformation and politicization of identity. Women in Centro Femenino 8 de Marzo recognize that power is inherent in people's daily actions, speech, language, and movements. They have recognized forms of power in their interpersonal and familial relationships and have made this politically visible by emphasizing "democracy within the household." They recognize that "democracy" exists only when social relations within the household are democratized as well—hence, the famous Chilean feminists' slogan that is also shouted throughout Ecuador: "Democracy in the country and in the home" (*Democracia en el país y en la casa*).

Furthermore, their politicization as poor women—the making of a collective identity based on gender—suggests that basic needs are not tied solely to survival but rather to constructions of identity and relations of power. This challenges, as well, the framework in which basic needs are interpreted and brings into question the theoretical division typically made between practical gender needs and strategic gender needs.

The localized nature of the women's movement—that is, the microsources of resistance that have sprung up throughout the country, constituting what we now call a social movement—has manifested itself in both positive and negative ways. The fact that women are the ones who have mobilized at the neighborhood level around such issues as food, housing, and water supply has also allowed the state and development apparatus to place on them a larger share of the reproductive burden via "self-help" projects and projects targeting women's work (Elson, forthcoming). The formation of autonomous women's organizations throughout the region demonstrates the inability of traditional political institutions to create a space in which the grass-roots movement can participate with some sort of bargaining power. Popular women's organizing strategies represent a challenge to the ways in which dominant representations of gender have been reproduced in social relations in the home and in society at large. And, though such organizations acknowledge that their communities need better infrastructures and social services, they are nevertheless critical of Western, male biases reproduced in the conceptual frameworks of development policies implemented by state agencies, nongovernmental organizations, and other development institutions. Ultimately, they challenge the social organization of society.

Notes

I would like to thank Silvia Vega and others at Centro de Planificación y Estudios Sociales (CEPLAES) in Quito, Ecuador, for their institutional support in conducting this research. I would also like to thank Lourdes Benería, Kim Berry, and Susana Wappenstein for their insightful comments and inspiring conversations, all of which contributed greatly to this chapter.

1. For a discussion on how male-biased development policies targeting women can actually increase women's reproductive work, see Elson, forthcoming.

2. For further discussion on the difference between "interests" and "needs" and how "practical gender needs" and "strategic gender needs" have been incorporated into Women in International Development (WID) policy, see Moser 1989b. Throughout the remainder of this chapter, I will refer to "practical and strategic gender needs." For a general history of WID policy, see Anderson and Chen 1988; Goetz 1988; Rathberger 1990.

3. For a classic discussion on gender and the making of identity, see Chodorow 1974, 1990. Chodorow's theory, however, has been refuted on grounds that it essentialized gender identity. By tying gender socialization to women's biological reproductive role and by focusing the analysis on males' and females' relationship to their mothers, she posited an essential difference in the formation of male and female identity. Furthermore, Chodorow's theory only spoke of the experience of white, middle-class Western women.

4. For discussion on gender, identity, and representation, see de Lauretis, ed., 1986, 1987. See also Butler 1990. For a discussion on the production of identity and feminist politics, see Lugones and Spelman 1983; Alarcón 1990.

5. See Saporta Sternbach et al., Chapter 12 of this volume. See also Chinchilla, Chapter 3.

6. For a complete history of women and development policy in Ecuador, see CEIS 1986.

7. In 1979, after almost ten years of military dictatorship, the populist Jaime Roldós was elected democratically. After his death in an unexplained airplane accident in 1981, Christian Democrat Vice President Osvaldo Hurtado took over Roldós's office.

8. In this section, I draw largely on CEIS 1986.

9. Development Alternatives with Women for a New Era (DAWN) is one strong example of a Third World women's network that has created a platform to specifically address the ways in which national and international development policies could more effectively address the needs of Third World women. See Sen and Grown 1987.

10. In particular, *Acción por el Movimiento de Mujeres* staged a protest outside Citibank in May 1989, after Citibank appropriated $80 million from the Ecuadorean state's account. Citibank informed the Central Bank of Ecuador on May 4, 1989, that it would no longer accept any transactions made by the Ecuadorean Bank because that bank had failed to make payments on one of its loans. The situation was considered very grave by Ecuadoreans for the economy was already extremely shaky. Furthermore, such an action by a donor bank could set a precedent for other structural adjustment arrangements in Latin America. The situation was finally resolved when Citibank agreed to give another, separate loan to Ecuador with better terms than usual.

11. Whether women's struggles in Ecuador constitute a movement continues to be the subject of much debate among activists and researchers. For example, Verdesoto (1986) contended that the political representation of women in Ecuador is characterized more by the multiplication and growth of women's organizations than by any form of centralized movement. Moreover, he argued that women specifically have chosen *not* to form a centralized, hierarchical movement and that the actual stage is characterized by the constitution of a pluralist identity as women, rather than the institutionalization of a centralized social movement.

12. The women collectively chose the name *Centro Femenino 8 de Marzo* ("March 8th Feminine Center") because of its tie to International Women's Day.

13. The already existing neighborhood organization in Chillogallo, though not officially part of the political structure of Quito, is the organization that represents the interests of Chillogallo vis-à-vis the city. In this sense, it is the only organization in the district that has had traditional ties with political parties and the state.

14. There is a relatively strong physical infrastructure in Chillogallo, although it is not adequate and remains costly. In my sample, more than half of the households have electricity and sewage.

15. Testimony of Beatriz Ortega, which appeared in the Centro Femenino 8 de Marzo newspaper, *Nuestra Voz*, March 1989.

16. Although the struggle for law reform is essential, it is not necessarily viewed as such by popular women. Laws are rarely adhered to, and widespread ideological beliefs uphold myths about violence against women, women's rights in the workplace, women's political participation, and so on. Poor sectors in particular have little access to knowledge about the law, further isolating them from that political arena. For these reasons, among others, popular women do not emphasize law reform about women's rights per se in their politics, except as it pertains to community infrastructure, social services, and drastic changes in the economy that affect standards of living and household budgets. For a strong analysis of law reform and women's rights in Ecuador, see CAM 1989.

9

The Venezuelan Ecology Movement: Symbolic Effectiveness, Social Practices, and Political Strategies

María Pilar García

Introduction and Objectives

In April 1987, it became known that the organizers of the Paris-Dakar Automobile Rally were busy promoting the Trans-Amazon Rally, which would start in Venezuela, cross the Amazon, and end in Brazil. Immediately, the Association of Friends for the Defense of the Great Savannah (*Asociación de Amigos en Defensa de la Gran Sabana*, AMIGRANSA) got mobilized, gathered extensive information about the situation, and complained to the appropriate authorities about the negative environmental impact that the rally would have on one of the most fragile ecological regions of the world. Simultaneously, AMIGRANSA secured the support and solidarity of national and international environmental organizations and launched a far-reaching campaign that was to enjoy wide acceptance in the mass media. As a result of these actions, the government suspended the permit already granted for the rally. In turn, the rally organizers opted to change their strategy. This time, they requested permission for a trans-Andean rally, still to start in Venezuela. And once again, the government rejected the new proposal, based on the environmentalists' arguments against the rally and because of the strong pressure exerted by the environmentalists via the print media.

Similar mobilizations occurred throughout the 1980s against, for instance, shipments of toxic waste from Europe, large-scale shrimp industries, assaults on environmentally important areas, and the destruction of the Amazon rain forest by gold miners. In these mobilizations, grass-roots groups, neighborhood organizations, and environmentalists have come together, sometimes with the support of opposition leaders and prominent national figures. These are a few of the ways in which the Venezuelan environmental movement, structured in a kind of informal or "submerged" network and using the mechanisms of symbolic effectiveness described by Alberto Melucci (1985, 1988a) and by Gabriela Uribe and Edgardo Lander (1990), has constructed "the environmental" into a new political fact. In this process of transformation, the movement, often through the media, has played a decisive role in the generation of the new political culture.

This chapter analyzes the formation and mobilization of environmental actors in Venezuela, following the two theoretical perspectives of identity and strategy, which have been most significant in the literature on social movements (Cohen 1985; Alvarez 1989b; A. Scott 1990). Part one succinctly describes the Venezuelan sociopolitical model in which the environmental organizations are inscribed and discusses the effects of the current economic crisis on the restructuring of the sociopolitical and environmental actors. Part two presents and analyzes a typology of the Venezuelan environmental organizations in order to assess their contribution to the creation of the new political culture and the generation of new political facts through mechanisms of symbolic effectiveness. It also discusses the role each environmental organization plays in the configuration of an informal network that serves as the space in which the state, political parties, the media, and other organizations of civil society articulate with each other.[1]

The third part presents a theoretical interpretation of the Venezuelan environmental movement and its political perspectives. Although no formal interorganizational framework exists, in practice the environmental movement behaves as a submerged network in which each organization performs a different function. The focus in this part is on the relation of the environmental network with other sociopolitical actors (such as the government, the parties, and other organizations or social networks) and on the form in which this environmental network has become a new actor and acquired its own identity in the changing sociopolitical context of Venezuela during the past thirty years. Also discussed are the democratizing effects of the environmental organizations; their perception of alternative models of development; and, lastly, the impact that the acute economic crisis, the loss of legitimacy of the political system, and the appearance of new actors and the restructuring of the old ones have had on the environmentalist network and on the mechanisms of symbolic effectiveness.

Crisis and the Sociopolitical Model

Venezuela is perhaps the first country in Latin America to institutionalize, since the 1970s, the environmental question through legislation, including the 1976 Organic Law on the Environment (*Ley Orgánica del Ambiente*, LOA). Additionally, the Ministry of the Environment and Renewable Natural Resources (*Ministerio del Ambiente y de los Recursos Naturales Renovables*, MARNR) was created to oversee compliance with the LOA; within the legislative branch, the Congress Committee on the Environment was established with representatives from the various political parties.

Thanks to the significant revenues generated by oil exports, during the 1960–1980 period Venezuela was one of the few Latin American countries to maintain relatively high rates of economic growth. The economic bonanza, together with external loans, helped to finance the government's modernization and industrialization policies, based on the strategy of establishing industrial and mining poles of development (Friedmann 1961; García 1986 and 1987). Venezuela is also one of the few Latin American countries that has maintained a "formal" democratic system during the last thirty years. The establishment of democracy in 1958, however, failed to open up a political space for civil society because the democratic value of participation was sacrificed in the 1961 constitution in favor of the stability of the political system (García 1988). The representative democracy institutionalized in 1961 had strong centralist, paternalist, populist, and clientelist features (Rey, ed. 1987).

Nevertheless, the political and economic models introduced in Venezuela since the end of the 1950s have created a great heterogeneity of social sectors with divergent interests (García 1986, 1987, 1990b). The autonomous growth of civil society, however, has been impeded by the co-option and institutionalization of social conflicts through sociopolitical pacts among the main actors—the armed forces, the church, the parties, the private sector, and the unions (García 1987; Gomez, ed., 1987). This has resulted in the structural weakness of all those social organizations excluded from such pacts (De la Cruz 1988; García 1990a; Gomez 1991).[2]

The deepening of the economic crisis in recent years—which began at the end of the 1970s with the sharp decline in the price of oil—caused the Venezuelan government, at the request of the International Monetary Fund, to adopt drastic measures of macroeconomic adjustment in 1989, which greatly deteriorated the people's quality of life. As a consequence of these measures and the lack of political institutional channels to express popular discontent and frustration, strong social protests erupted in the same year (García 1990a and 1991a), placing the Venezuelan political system at a crossroad between democracy and authoritarianism.

One of the most important consequences of the economic and political crisis is the restructuring of social actors and the redefinition of power relations. The following tendencies emerged as part of this process: (1) fissures in the previous sociopolitical pacts; (2) an increasing mistrust of the political parties on the part of civil society and the ensuing loss of the parties' ability to mobilize;[3] (3) the emergence of new actors calling for the transformation of representative democracy into a participatory democracy, emphasizing the local spheres of participation; (4) a new, increasingly complex political scenario due to the heterogeneity of interests, making consensus and negotiation among social actors difficult; (5) the appearance of new forms of mobilization and protest, including the violent social outbreaks of February 27, 1989, through which popular actors discovered a new potential for mobilization; and (6) the environmental and political nature of these actors' demands, related to the damaging effects of the crisis on the quality of life and on the satisfaction of basic needs—precisely the most significant environmental and political themes in the Third World (Slater 1985).

To achieve these political-environmental demands, new forms of articulation have emerged among popular organizations, neighborhood associations, grassroots Christian groups, women, and environmentalists. The mistrust of the sociopolitical model, the rejection of the political parties, and the deepening of the economic crisis have gradually delegitimized the "political" space as a privileged place to address the national problems. These very factors have displaced the party-state system as the only realm in which to create shared meanings about a desirable society. And in response to these challenges, the government created the Commission for the Reform of the State (*Comisión para la Reforma del Estado*, COPRE) in 1984.[4] In sum, it can be said that, as a result of all these processes, collective actors have restructured themselves, and the new spaces that have opened for the resignification of "the political" have been appropriated by the new collective actors, among whom the environmentalists are prominent.

Environmental Organizations, 1960–1990

Just as in other Latin American countries, the origin and characteristics of the Venezuelan environmental movement are related to economic, political, and social factors. In Venezuela, the following factors stand out: the economic strategy of development poles based on government-sponsored, large-scale industrial mining projects; the environmental impact of this strategy; the incipient level of democratization achieved by the political system; the low degree of complexity of civil society vis-à-vis the high level of institutional and juridical development concerning environmental issues; and the growing degree of popular awareness about the environmental question (García 1991a).[5]

Venezuela's environmental organizations can be classified in the following six types: (1) scientific-conservationist societies; (2) ecological communities; (3) environmental defense organizations or juntas (*Juntas de Defensa Ambiental*); (4) neighborhood organizations; (5) political-ideological organizations; and (6) symbolic-cultural organizations.[6] The above typology encompasses groups ranging from pioneering scientific-conservationist societies, which reached their zenith toward the end of the 1960s, to more recent symbolic-cultural organizations, which are reconstituting the environmental as new political facts via symbolic effectiveness (Melucci 1985; Uribe and Lander 1990).

As in Brazil and Mexico (Viola 1987; Quadri 1990; Puig 1990; Gerez-Fernandez 1990), the environmental organizations of Venezuela are highly heterogeneous, both intra- and interorganizationally, from the socioeconomic, ideological, and cultural points of view (García 1991b, 1991c). Interorganizational heterogeneity facilitates access to sources of information, to the agencies of political decision-making, and to the mass media. Another positive aspect emerging from this heterogeneity is that the environmental organizations must articulate with each other in order to deal with the great diversity of interpretations on environmental problems. In contrast, intraorganizational heterogeneity weakens the organization due to the ideological differences that surface during the process of transforming abstract objectives into concrete strategies and actions. By hindering internal consensus, internal heterogeneity can thus negatively affect the interorganizational articulation.

The formal structure of Venezuelan environmental groups varies according to the organizational and "participatory" opportunities offered by the political system, the organization's ideological background, and the gender composition of its leadership. Gender composition seems to be correlated with the adoption of strategies of negotiation. The symbolic-cultural organizations, where women predominate, tend to adopt negotiating strategies, propose alternatives, and use institutional channels more frequently than those organizations where men predominate. The latter organizations are oriented mainly toward confrontation, and they maintain a more defensive character.

Organizational structure also has implications for the group's relation to the state. The traditional vertical structures, like those of the scientific-conservationists, allow for greater efficiency and ease the relationship with the government, but they hinder the articulation with horizontally or semihorizontally structured environmental organizations. On the other hand, horizontally structured organizations, like the Federation of Organizations of Environmental Juntas (*Federación de Organizaciones de Juntas Ambientales*, FORJA), tend to sacrifice efficiency and run the risk of organizational collapse. In FORJA's case, the lack of an organizational structure encumbered the relations with the government and caused the links among its various groups to depend on interpersonal relationships.

In general, the Venezuelan environmental organizations are characterized by a paucity of members. The smaller groups tend to be more efficient than the larger ones due to a greater degree of internal homogeneity and the predominance of primary relationships among their members, characteristics that help to build consensus and organizational flexibility.

Economic, scientific, and political resources are crucial to the success of environmental groups. In Venezuela, obtaining these resources seems to be a function of the structural and strategic characteristics of each organization. And because success is a function of a given organization's capacity to reach public opinion, transform value codes, and generate new political facts, access to the mass media becomes a key factor for this success.

Throughout the three decades examined in this chapter, Venezuelan environmental organizations have evolved in their strategies, practices, and even identities in an effort to adapt to changing sociopolitical and economic conditions. Though born in different periods, the environmental organizations must be seen as part of a network in which each organization fulfills a specific, mutually complementary role, rather than as separate, disconnected entities. It is through this informal network that meanings are constructed and the environmental movement finds its expression as a social movement.

Scientific-Conservationist Societies

In this type of environmental organization, two tendencies can be found that were difficult to differentiate in the beginning: scientific societies and conservationists. The first of these date back to the 1930s and were formed by scientists who had an affinity for ecology and whose objective was the investigation of national ecological problems. Conservationist societies, mostly staffed by natural scientists and students, were founded toward the end of the 1960s, with the goal of denouncing the deterioration of the environment and cooperating in its protection and conservation.[7]

The most salient feature of the scientific societies is their mediating role through the Committee on the Environment, a congressional committee designed to settle conflicts between environmental movements and the government. Studies prepared by scientific societies have provided environmental organizations with a scientific basis. They have also contributed to the legitimation of the organizations' demands before public opinion, political parties, and the government.[8]

In contrast to the scientific societies, which work at the national level, the domain of action for the conservationists lies at the regional level. One example of this type of society is the *Sociedad Conservacionista Aragua* (Aragua Conservationist Society, SCA), founded in 1973 "to study and safeguard not only the physical-biological, but also the socio-cultural environment" of the state of Aragua. The simultaneous participation of many members of the conservationist societies in environmental coalitions like FORJA has facilitated their mobilization.

Ecological Communities

These environmental organizations emerged at the end of the 1960s and have a local (rural or suburban) domain of action. They profess ideas of solidarity, cooperativism, and "small is beautiful." In contrast to the rural environmental movements that have flourished in Colombia, Bolivia, Peru, Mexico, and Brazil, those in Venezuela have been scarcely significant. This is due to the limited emphasis placed on the countryside under an economic model based on oil exploitation, modernization, and industrialization. On the other hand, the environmental impact and the urbanizing effect of the oil economy caused many of the environmental organizations, including some with a rural domain of action, to spring up in the cities of Venezuela, just as they did in Mexico (Quadri 1990; Puig 1990; Gerez-Fernandez 1990).

The Venezuelan ecological communities can be classified into three groups:

(1) Alternative rural communities. This type of organization is a product of the counterculture of the 1960s and the post-hippie era of the early 1970s. Its members pursue an alternative life-style based on subsistence living standards, inner renewal, and primary relationships.[9] They primarily come from the middle classes and were disenchanted with the armed struggle of the 1960s, or from the upper class and have no political experience; as a group, they have been of little significance in the formation of the environmental movement.

(2) Peasant communities. Begun in the 1970s, peasant communities are connected with the consciousness-raising work developed mostly by grass-roots Christian organizations. Their strength lies in their cooperative organization. In the past, their demands were related to land ownership, the conditions of production-reproduction, and the cooperative distribution of their products. These demands were supported by other environmental organizations, particularly the politico-ideological, that transformed the local problems of the rural communities into political-environmental realities of national scope, through mobilizations and the use of the mass media.[10]

The support now received by peasant communities from the other environmental organizations could subside as a result the economic crisis. Additionally, the strong urban and middle-class composition of most environmental organizations could drive them away from rural concerns and lead them to identify primarily with the urban and/or national concerns of the middle class. On the positive side, the recent approval of COPRE's proposals for democratization has opened channels of participation at the local level. These channels could allow environmental groups to focus as much on the local urban level as on the local rural level. Issues of survival and basic needs forced by the economic crisis could also foster articulations between environmental organizations and peasant communities.

Rural communities have recently achieved a greater degree of autonomy and political significance as social actors. Through a large-scale government cooperatives program intended to promote food self-sufficiency, rural communities now act as direct interlocutors with the government.

(3) Suburban communities. Organizations of this sort have taken root in the cities' peripheries. They consist of middle-class religious groups that champion ecological practices as part of a more general inner moral renewal. These organizations have been repressed by the government and rejected by public opinion for allegedly being "sectarian." In general, suburban communities have exerted little or no influence on the environmental movement, which at no point has identified with them.

Environmental Defense Juntas (EDJs)

These organizations emerged in 1976 as a direct result of the LOA, and they are ascribed to the Ministry of the Environment, MARNR. Due to their local nature, they have gained the most acceptance in popular neighborhoods or in large, lower-class residential complexes built by the government during the 1960s. The legal constitution of the EDJs has facilitated the dialogue and negotiations with government agencies such as the MARNR, but it has also contributed to their co-optation. The EDJs have been most visible within FORJA, where they articulate themselves to mobilize for supralocal environmental causes.

One of the organizations within this category is El Samán Group, constituted as an EDJ in 1977 in Caricuao, one of the most densely populated neighborhoods in the Caracas metropolitan area. In contrast to other environmental groups, the members of El Samán belong to low-income, popular classes. The group's objectives are "to rescue the history and culture of Caricuao, identify the problems of the neighborhood, create awareness about such problems among the citizens and the bodies of government, and search for solutions."[11]

The strengthening of the neighborhood associations resulting from the 1989 New Organic Law of Municipal Government (Nueva Ley Orgánica del Régimen Municipal, NLORM) may contribute to the disappearance of the EDJs or to their being absorbed by neighborhood associations. According to the NLORM, all local problems and issues, including popular participation, must be formally channeled through neighborhood associations. Implementing the NLORM will require government action to legally redefine the participation of civil society in local environmental matters for the EDJs are now the only juridically institutionalized agencies.

Neighborhood Associations

Neighborhood associations in Venezuela, which proliferated during the 1970s and 1980s, are identified primarily with the urban middle class. According to both the former law and the new NLORM, neighborhood associations are the repositories of ecological concerns in the broad sense of the quality of life. As in Mexico, a characteristic feature of the Venezuelan urban environmental movement is that it was born within the neighbors' movement as part of the movement *de cuadro de vida* ("quality of life") (Ovalles 1987). One of the first of such movements, the Movement for Community Integration (*Movimiento de Integración de la Comunidad*, MIC), had among its objectives alternative proposals of a clearly ecological nature, including alternative energy sources, recycling, and the control of pollution at the community level through community organizing.

Since the late 1970s, neighborhood associations have become the articulating axis of social mobilizations for sociopolitical and economic democratization and decentralization. The neighbors movement succeeded in integrating cooperative, popular, environmental, and even feminist organizations around the question of democratization—the one issue that had the most symbolic effectiveness and mobilizing potential during the 1980s. As a result of this integration, the 1980s witnessed numerous joint actions by neighbors and environmentalists aimed at addressing not only participatory and social democracy but also environmental and/or urban issues at the local, regional, and even national levels.

Political-Ideological Organizations

Members of this type of organization, among which the groups Habitat and GIDA stand out, come from university backgrounds; most support leftist ideologies.[12] The emergence of political-ideological organizations in the late 1970s is related to national political events: for example, the failure of guerrilla struggles in the 1960s and the ensuing ideological crisis; the introduction of the strategy of development poles and the concomitant environmental costs; the solidarity with international mobilizations against pollution and with the large antinuclear rallies of the 1970s; and, finally, the influence of other mobilizations, such as the hippie movement and student protests.

Political-ideological organizations share an eco-Socialist view that criticizes the style of capitalist development in Venezuela as the cause of the gradual worsening of living conditions, the marginalization and impoverishment of large sectors of the population, and the growing deterioration of the physical and natural environment. In contrast with scientific-conservationists, EDJs, and neighborhood associations, political-ideological organizations shift the blame for environmental problems away from the physiconatural toward the social and political. The solutions they suggest are thus aimed at transforming the economic and sociopolitical model into a more socially egalitarian and technologically rational one, as embodied in the notion of "eco-development" (AMIGRANSA-ECOXXI-GRIDIA 1990; García 1991b, 1991c), although seemingly without awareness of the apparent contradiction that exists between eco-development and the structural transformation of dominant development models (Leff 1986).

Toward the end of the 1970s, political-ideological organizations tended to form federations, among which FORJA, established in 1978, is the most prominent. FORJA, formed by more than one hundred groups distributed across all of the country's regions, incorporates both rural and urban demands and acts at local, regional, and national levels. Its great internal heterogeneity forced FORJA to draft general and organizational objectives around the motto "creating, growing, and changing" and around the organizational strategy "in union there is strength," as stated in a 1981 FORJA document. Such objectives are textually expressed as the striving

> toward the formulation of a model of a Venezuela governed by the basic needs of the population, environmental conservation and improvement, self-sustained development, scientific and technological self-determination, and genuine intercultural cooperation within the sovereign national society, where an integral nationalization will serve as the foundation and point of reference, and community participation will be the model of self-government par excellence (FORJA 1981a, 1981b).

FORJA's style of organizing was, in general, horizontal and democratic, and its actions dealt with a variety of regional problems seen as representative of the environmental situation in the country.[13] An evaluation of FORJA's actions indicates that its general and abstract goals—such as "transforming the style of development"—though difficult to translate into concrete actions, were nevertheless maintained for they aided in the integration of heterogeneous organizations.[14] In fact, FORJA's greatest triumphs are evident in ecological demands for the physical and natural environment (for example, pressing for the establishment of national parks and natural landmarks), which are scarcely different from the demands of either scientific-conservationist or symbolic-cultural organizations.

Among the federation's achievements were the establishment of a wide capacity for national mobilization and the channeling of its demands through several spaces: first, a juridically legitimated space, such as the EDJs, which allowed for communication with the government; second, a space connected to political parties on the Left, which permitted confrontation with the government and facilitated political negotiation through the Committee on the Environment; and finally, a space, autonomous from the government and the parties, that allowed for the transformation of the environmental problematic into a new political fact, with the aid of the media. As a federation, FORJA proposed new, more democratic, and more decentralized forms of organization than those of its component organizations, and it brought attention to a systemic, global, interdisciplinary, and less elitist view of the environment by highlighting the nature-society relation.

Even though no consensus of opinion exists regarding the mistakes that led to FORJA's debilitation (García 1988), some factors can be identified from the organization's own self-evaluation: (1) the general scope of the federation's goals, which rendered them scarcely pragmatic; (2) the "inorganic growth of groups lacking an organizational structure" or with vertical structures quite different from the federation's horizontal model; (3) the lack of experience with the style of organizing and the difficulties in bringing together more than one hundred organizations that differed in size, structure, composition, and conceptions of reality; (4) the abandonment of the grass-roots groups from which FORJA's membership came and, thus, of the "support from below"; (5) difficulties in making the local, regional, and national levels of action compatible; (6) problems with leadership and individualism existing within each component organization; and (7) the great degree of internal disorganization caused by, among other factors, a mistrust of anything sounding like a "coordination" reminiscent of the political parties from which many FORJA members came.

During the second half of the 1980s, the worsening economic crisis forced environmentalists to redirect their objectives toward problems concerning survival, the quality of life, and the standards of living. They began to mobilize side by side with grass-roots, popular, and cooperative movements against the macro-economic measures the government had adopted in response to the crisis. Other organizations, such as ECOXXI, broke away from FORJA and initiated their own transition toward the symbolic-cultural position. Their response represented one way to adapt to the context of the economic crisis, to the democratizing possibilities arising from COPRE's and civil society's proposals, and to the approval of new laws that democratized the political system and opened new local spaces for such organizations.

Symbolic-Cultural Organizations

The emergence of this type of organization coincided with the lack of answers to the national environmental problems, the loss of credibility of political parties and the government, and the weakening of FORJA. In the second half of the 1980s, new organizations emerged that reconstituted environmental concerns into political facts via symbolic effectiveness.

These organizations are referred to as "symbolic-cultural" because they alert society to the existence of problems whose solution requires decoding dominant models and searching for alternative meanings and orientations for social action in the cultural sphere (Melucci 1985: 797). Further, these organizations fall within what Uribe and Lander (1990) called "new domains of the political," evident in the emergence of forms of social action that are independent from both the political parties and the state and that revolve around new themes. As in the case of the environment, these forms address problems "that can be acted upon and influenced upon, and around which a collective will can be created without going through parties or without their mediation, and without the need to validate proposals against the backdrop of a larger societal project or its corresponding strategy line" (Uribe and Lander 1990: 77).

The political significance of these groups does not rest in their size (they are not large), their degree of social homogeneity (they are heterogenous, albeit less so than the political-ideological groups), their permanence (they are unstable), their degree of organizational structuration or their representation (relatively low), nor even in their clarity about who the adversary is (at certain times, they confront the state; at others, they ally with it, depending on the problem). Rather, the significance of these groups stems from the fact that their themes and values generate new political facts that are nationally or internationally relevant, independent from traditional actors.

This type of organization is perhaps best exemplified by AMIGRANSA, a nonprofit civil association founded in 1985 with only five members, all of them women, who form the executive committee and design the group's strategies. AMIGRANSA's goal is to defend the natural environment by opposing destructive activities and by drafting alternative proposals. Most of AMIGRANSA's actions have focused on the defense of Canaima Great Savannah National Park, the world's fifth largest, and they have been quite successful. The success of AMIGRANSA's actions is due to its ability to access and use information and symbolic systems (particularly the media) as the main mechanisms through which the environmental is constructed, produced, and consumed as a new cultural and political fact. AMIGRANSA's composition by class and perhaps gender and occupation (middle- and upper-middle-class professional women), its greater economic and time resources, its access to sources of financing and to high-level government officials, and its connections with the mass media have all contributed to the widening of this group's communicative space.

The nature of AMIGRANSA's development from primary interpersonal relationships based on friendship has contributed to the organization's stability, and it has facilitated consensus in decisionmaking. The geographic area for the direct actions of AMIGRANSA, Canaima National Park, comprises about three million hectares, although indirectly its actions involve the entire state of Bolívar and part of the federal territory of Amazonas, which together represent nearly half of Venezuela's land mass. The fact that this is a highly sensitive and ecologically crucial area has fostered the mobilization of various national and international environmental groups and scientific-conservationist societies. And the links that AMIGRANSA has made with international organizations have created forms of external support that further pressure the state to adopt the alternative proposals presented by this and similar groups. Finally, the juridical legitimation of AMIGRANSA as a nonprofit organization reduces the risks of its being co-opted and gives it greater autonomy and flexibility in its relationships with the MARNR and other government agencies.

The category of symbolic-cultural organizations also includes those political-ideological groups, such as ECOXXI, that have evolved in order to adapt to the political, legal, and economic changes of Venezuela in the last five years. Toward the end of the 1980s, the Movement for Life (Movimiento por la Vida) arose, also with a symbolic-cultural orientation. This movement represents a new attempt to reconstruct the links and articulations between the various environmental organizations, which had been weakened by the economic, political, social, and ideological crisis.

The Movement for Life was advanced by some of FORJA's conservationist and political-ideological organizations. Its objectives were to bring together all those organizations concerned with the environment and with the defense of peoples' right "to life, and to a dignified life." The movement crystallized with the First Gathering for Life, held in the city of Valencia in February 1988, and attended by more than fifty organizations. The Movement for Life defines itself as a "spontaneous, dynamic, articulated, horizontal, democratic, and pluralistic" movement, whose role is to constantly renew itself as a space for the integration of movement groups, including a renewal of forms of communication and relations among its organizations. Supporters of this movement hope that values such as the defense of life, innovation, creativity, and transformation that characterize this new type of environmentalism will permeate political culture, chiefly through the actions of mass media and other mechanisms of symbolic effectiveness.

As with any other pluralistic process that rejects organizational form, it is not easy to evaluate this most recent expression of the environmental movement. Although the content of its proposal for mobilization was shared by all organizations participating in the First Gathering for Life, discrepancies over how this proposal should be realized surfaced. Symbolic-cultural organizations feared that the movement would be co-opted by the political-ideological camp in order to revitalize a frail and declining FORJA. With the 1988 publication of the environmental bulletin *Boletín de los Grupos Ambientalistas* as the "medium for the collective denunciation, reflection, and alternative proposals of environmental groups," the Movement for Life seems to be meeting its communicative objectives. The bulletin has included contributions by both environmental organizations and neighborhood and indigenous associations. Nonetheless, differences among the members of some political-ideological and symbolic-cultural organizations have gradually deepened, and they have affected the degree to which the bulletin reflects the opinion of the latter groups. FORJA, for its part, publishes annual "environmental balances" in which the federation's positions and strategies are delineated.

Building on the Movement for Life, AMIGRANSA, GRIDIA, and ECOXXI started a collaborative experience on a project-by-project basis. One such project was the analysis of the impact of the Canaima National Park Development and Management Plan on its indigenous communities and on the area's ecological diversity (AMIGRANSA-ECOXXI-GRIDIA 1990). Beside collecting scientific information, these studies politicized the environmental question (particularly through the use of the media) and actively involved the various groups affected in the drafting of politically viable alternative proposals.

The Environmental Movement and Its Political Perspectives

The Submerged Network as an Expression of the Environmental Movement

One of the most relevant features of the Venezuelan experience is the great flexibility each organization enjoys in adopting strategies and in developing actions to correspond with differing organizational forms. The dynamic of praxis surpasses the static categories of theory because it is, precisely, in collective mobilization—as expressed in the network, not in the objectives of each organization—that the movement's characterization as a social phenomenon eventually lies. Organizations such as the conservationist SCA, the institutional El Samán, or the political-ideological GIDA, among others, mobilize collectively as part of a "submerged" network, which itself becomes the environmental actor par excellence (Melucci 1988a, 1988b, 1989; see also A. Escobar, Chapter 5).

The submerged network, as Melucci would have it, underlies the more visible forms of collective action of environmental groups and can be said to include all of those actions that challenge destructive environmental practices and also the innovation, with new practices and new meanings, of the groups and the population at large. This innovation takes place largely in the process of involvement with concrete struggles,[15] although it can be detected as well at the level of daily life. The media—particularly environmental publications, documentary cinema, and, occasionally, television—operate as the unifying element through which the submerged network becomes visible. The submerged network (that is, the "latent" part of the movement) becomes manifest in localized and ephemeral ways in periods of mobilization. But it must be emphasized that the network itself is constructed day by day, through solidarity and new social practices that attempt to open up spaces for cultural innovation and the creation of new ecological understandings.

The high degree of differentiation and plurality of the Venezuelan environmental organizations hinders their strict classification. Preestablished categories do not seem to capture the specificity of their geographic, political, and socioeconomic contexts or of the organizations' praxis. Theoretical discussions about the status of Latin American environmental organizations as constituting either a social movement or a new social movement (Melucci 1988a, 1988b; Castells 1983; Touraine 1987, 1988a; Jelin, ed., 1987b; Scott 1990) cannot overlook the evidence that most organizations are actually of a mixed type. Be it harmoniously or conflictively, diverse types of social movements coexist in the creation and recreation of political facts that are a consequence of the actions of the environmental network and cannot be attributed to only one type of organization.

As a network—a "group of individuals sharing a conflictive culture and a collective identity" (Melucci 1985: 788–789)—the Venezuelan environmental movement displays a great capacity to affect the cultural production of the system. Social identities are created as collective actors assert themselves in the network. These identities emerge as a response to socioenvironmental conflicts—caused by the prevailing style of development—to which neither the state nor the political parties offer an answer.

The Venezuelan environmental network constitutes a system of information and resource exchange, within which each organization plays a specialized role. Scientific organizations provide technical information to the state, the environmental movement, and the media and function as intermediaries with government agencies; conservationist organizations have an educational role and mobilize support for specific causes within FORJA; institutional organizations act as interlocutors between low-income neighborhoods and the state (MARNR), and they also address quality-of-life issues as environmental problems and mobilize through FORJA; neighborhood associations, the local environmental organizations par excellence in middle-class neighborhoods and in low-income areas where no EDJs exist, receive support for some of their local demands from environmental groups and, in turn, tend to support the latter's regional and national demands.

Political-ideological organizations, on the other hand, emphasize structural causes and take environmental issues into political discourse. Because of their function and mode of operation, they bring about a "greening" of political parties and the different branches of the state; the environment has been infused with a social and political content because of their actions. Through FORJA, political-ideological organizations have built a space of convergence for environmental organizations and other groups, such as cooperative, indigenous, and women's organizations, in their search for the broader objectives of democratization and an improved quality of life.

Symbolic-cultural organizations helped to develop new social relations among the various environmental organizations—relations that have enabled these groups to more effectively articulate their positions within the context of the crisis. Given their access to the mass media, they have incorporated new environmental meanings into popular and political culture. Symbolic-cultural organizations facilitate communication between state agencies and the environmental movement, thanks to their informal relations with high government officials. Their knowledge and use of environmental legislation has also helped to "institutionalize" the environmental debate. Former political-ideological organizations recently transformed into symbolic-cultural ones, such as ECOXXI, provide a link between old and new environmental groups and between the latter and the political parties.

Needless to say, the environmental network also participates in broader networks that hope to achieve participatory democracy. These networks, such as the neighborhood organizations, provide a point of convergence for cultural, popular, women's, indigenous, and environmental groups.

Symbolic Effectiveness and Cultural Innovation

In the cultural field, a number of actors and practices converge to give life to the new political domains. The symbolic-cultural field provides an axis of signification around which the environmental movement articulates itself and projects its contents onto society at large. As a substitute for alternative education, these mechanisms have not only been effective in increasing awareness about the environment among the public but have also served to put pressure on political parties and the state on behalf of environmental causes.

Nevertheless, the environmental network lacks the economic resources to build the support infrastructure that is necessary for the type of alternative education it proposes. Therefore, no permanent mechanisms exist for this sort of alternative education, although the Neighbors' School (*Escuela de Vecinos*) has sporadically assumed an educational role. The true substitute for nonformal education and environmental consciousness-raising has been the media; it is through the media that the environmental object has been constituted (and disseminated) as a new political-cultural subject. This communicative space has been a more important tool for *concientización*, or critical consciousness-raising, and social pressure than other mechanisms, such as rallies and demonstrations, seminars, or magazines and bulletins. In other words, even though mobilizations and protests have an effect on journalistic campaigns, the definition of a given problem as environmental and its emergence as a political fact must inevitably be passed through the mass media.

The environmental network, invested with symbolic effectiveness, has exerted an innovative effect on the cultural codes that confer signification on collective action. However, if we analyze the habits and social practices of each organization's members, we can observe that the process of cultural innovation is primarily restricted to small middle-class groups—mainly the symbolic-cultural ones—that have access to "ecological" consumption habits, behaviors, and life-styles denied to large segments of the population and pejoratively labeled by political-ideological members as "eco-capitalist."

Environmental Actors:
The State and the Political Parties

In contrast to Brazil or Mexico, where Green parties have been formed, Venezuelan environmental groups do not aspire to political power through traditional party politics. Instead, the network seeks to create alternative meanings through the "greening" of political culture, state institutions, parties, and public opinion. The progressive ecologization of social and political life takes place through several mechanisms, including the following: (1) the juridical-institutional system, in the form of environmental laws, regulations, and institutions—an area in which Venezuela is perhaps the most advanced of all Latin American countries; (2) the utilization of gaps and contradictions within the state apparatus; (3) the forum offered by the Commission for the Reform of the State, itself a reflection of the demands for the democratization of the state from within; and (4) interpersonal relationships with government officials in high-level decisionmaking positions, which help to reinforce the mechanisms mentioned earlier.

In the relations with political parties, the Congress Committee on the Environment plays a major role; as part of the legislative body, the committee acts as a pressure mechanism against the executive. The "double militancy" of some network members who also work as technical advisers for the parties represented in the committee maximizes the effectiveness of such a relation. In general, network members take advantage of the mediation of political parties and the competition among them to appropriate new meanings because the old slogans no longer mobilize the population. Despite the reluctance on the part of most network organizations to relate directly with the parties, the quasi-dialectic relationship of rejection-rapprochement and mediation-cooperation developed through the Committee on the Environment has proven to be effective and successful.

Conceptions of Development

Within the praxis of the environmental network as a political subject, various contradictory explanations of the environmental question coexist. Scientific-conservationist organizations give priority to physiconatural aspects by proposing conservationist solutions. For political-ideological groups, environmental problems are the results of an imported economic rationality and style of development, which they seek to transform. For these groups, the cause of the problem is structural, and therefore their demands and solutions, although expressed through mobilizations by environmental groups, find their main institutional expression through political parties on the Left. What is needed, in their view, is a transformation of the nature-society relation and a new ecopolitical rationality. Ecological peasant communities share some of these views. In contrast to those of the political-ideological groups, however, the proposed solutions are channeled collectively inside each organization by searching for "alternatives to development" that might as well be inscribed within the ecotechnological rationality advocated by Enrique Leff (1986).

Symbolic-cultural organizations can be further classified into two groups. First, there are the mixed or transitional organizations such as ECOXXI, which, like the political-ideological groups, favor structural explanations. However, like the strictly symbolic-cultural organizations, their praxis is aimed at the creation of a new political-environmental identity and culture sustained by the practice of cultural and political innovation. Second, there are the symbolic-cultural organizations proper, such as AMIGRANSA, that give priority to physiconatural and cultural aspects in the belief that the current style of development can be made compatible with the environment and that this should be the joint task of the state and civil society. They advocate alternative life-styles (based on inner renewal and habits such as vegetarianism and transcendental meditation) and promote cultural innovations as part of the new environmental identity and culture. In contrast to the political-ideological proposals, the symbolic-cultural view involves a sort of moral utopianism. In line with the 1987 World Commission Report on Environment and Development, they do not call for the transformation of the nature-society relation as a condition for solving the environmental problem. Such a perspective most resembles, both in form and content, those of the environmental movements in developed countries, placing more demands on the transformation of the sociocultural system than on the economic system.

Much of the Latin American literature on social movements suggests that the majority of them focus on survival or on the satisfaction of basic needs, while in "developed" societies the focus is placed on postindustrial contradictions. In Venezuela (as in Mexico), however, we find a combination of both interpretations, actually calling into question the nature of these divisions. As a result of the oil boom during the 1970s, Venezuela's economy grew at the same time that social inequality and the income distribution gap widened. Each environmental organization, according to its ideology, aims at a different objective: either satisfying the basic needs of the population (peasant ecological communities, EDJs, political-ideological groups), confronting the environmental impact of the current model of development (scientific-conservationist and symbolic-cultural organizations), or confronting social inequality (political-ideological organizations). In the past, ideological differences would not affect the articulation of the various actors in their mobilizations for any of these objectives. The crisis, however, has led to a greater differentiation and specialization of the mobilizing demands, a fact that might affect future articulations.

Crisis, Symbolic Effectiveness, and Mobilization

Before the economic crisis, the factors of "identity-symbolic effectiveness" contributed to the environmental movement's success to a larger extent than did the so-called strategy factors. But the crisis has deepened the existing ideological differences among environmental organizations regarding the "desirable and possible" type of development. Now, ideological differences might limit the efficiency of the mechanisms of symbolic effectiveness because of the ambiguity and diversity of the message to be transmitted. With the economic crisis, the manifest dimension of the network could even collapse in the process of restructuring. Strategies take on a new signification under these circumstances as they may determine access to the media and to the mechanisms of symbolic effectiveness instrumental for the creation of political facts. The more structurally flexible organizations, those with more economic resources or easier access to the state and the media, and those whose environmental discourse and messages may be more compatible with the official model of development will prove the most efficient in the use of mechanisms of symbolic effectiveness. Conversely, those organizations lacking such resources will tend to disappear, to be co-opted by the political parties, or to change by adapting their discourse and structure to the context of the crisis.

With the economic crisis, the themes of participatory democracy and quality of life that now facilitate articulations between environmental and other organizations may undergo a process of resignification. The so-called economic democracy of neoliberalism is backed by neighborhood associations, but it is rejected by grass-roots popular organizations and some environmental groups who demand that the content of political democracy be enriched with the principles of equity and social justice (García 1991a). The macroeconomic measures of structural adjustment adopted by the government at the request of the IMF magnify the population's poverty and generate among the diverse actors competition for the distribution of the state's scarce resources. Consequently, the problematic of the quality of life is permeated by class contents, with popular grass-roots and middle-class neighborhood associations increasingly coming into conflict with each other.

Crisis, Democracy, and Articulations

In contrast to other Latin American countries (Evers 1985; Slater 1985), the emergence of Venezuelan social movements in general and the environmental movement in particular are not responses to the existence of authoritarian regimes or the suppression of the political Left. On the contrary, these movements appear within the system of formal democracy established since 1958. As in Western Europe and North America, some of the environmental organizations (for example, the political-ideological) acquired relevance in periods in which the New Left parties, such as the Movement Toward Socialism (*Movimiento Hacia el Socialismo*, MAS) gained political influence. In contrast to countries like Chile and perhaps Brazil, the Venezuelan environmental movements intend to fill a gap not in "representation" but in "participation," which had been sacrificed for the sake of democratic stability. They do not, however, aspire to compete with popular participation in political parties (García 1988, 1990a).

Because of the mistrust and discredit of political parties, the quest for participatory democracy in Venezuela has been channeled through social movements. The existence of a formal democratic substratum has favored the diversification of social movements and the specialization of their demands: Environmentalists orient themselves toward the environmental problematic; peasant organizations address rural problems; popular organizations emphasize survival; feminists focus on equal opportunities for women; and urban movements strive for the improvement of basic services and social infrastructure. Thus, in Venezuela, the issue is not to achieve democracy per se but to deepen it by mobilizing collectively for greater social pluralism and the modernization of the political system. This collective orientation was very strong in the 1980s, when it had a modernizing effect on political culture.

The establishment in 1989 of markedly neoliberal economic policies of structural adjustment, however, could widen the ideological differences among environmental groups and between environmentalists and the state. Along with the political and economic crisis, the environmental network system has been weakened by ideological conflicts over the objectives to be raised. Within the environmental network, the dilemma lies in the prioritization of either strictly ecological or sociopolitical objectives, favored by the symbolic-cultural and the political-ideological respectively. Within the mostly middle-class neighborhood network, the primary demand is the defense of the environment and of the "living conditions already achieved," to the exclusion of the lower class and in competition with it for underfunded basic and social services. Finally, interrelations through the broader social network are now more infrequent both because the groups that used to mobilize have been differentially affected by the crisis and because they must now compete among themselves for scarce public resources.

In the past, most articulations within the environmental network were built around physiconatural environmental problems. With the deepening of the economic crisis, however, political-ideological groups are less inclined to organize around such demands; in recent years, these have been directed by symbolic-cultural groups, with their focus on middle-class intellectual and technocratic sectors. Political-ideological groups remain closer to the grass-roots movements and tend to organize around socioeconomic demands related to survival and the quality of life.

The prospect of growth for the environmental network is further limited by the tendency of some of the component organizations to adopt an attitude of competition for spaces of power and interlocution with the state, the political parties, and the rest of civil society. The strategic and ideological gap between politico-ideological and symbolic-cultural organizations has widened as a result of the pact among political parties to take the issue of democracy in their own hands, the availability of new spaces in light of the adoption of some of COPRE's proposals,[16] and the widening of their differences regarding the options for development.

The disarticulating effect of the crisis extends to the other social organizations, as well. In the past, demands for participatory democracy and decentralization of the state were channeled through the broad network of the neighborhood movement, while those for the transformation of the economic development model were channeled through the political parties on the Left, where such demands originated. Neither the demands for democratization nor the search for alternatives to development constituted genuine demands of the environmental movement, even though they benefited from the social differentiation, political modernization, and democratic pluralism that were attained. Those processes constituted the substratum for the growing complexity and autonomy of social actors. The fact that the ideological interpretation of the democratization process and its spread to the economic domain has been imbued with a class content will result in a restructuring of the broader social network, that is, of the future alliances and articulations between the various organizations and social movements. In the future, it might be harder to find articulatory themes with as great a potential for mobilization as the question of democracy had during the 1970s and 1980s.

Despite these contradictions, there are still enough spaces for action within the environmental field in Venezuela to generate new ecological-political facts capable of altering dominant cultural, political, and economic models and rationalities. These spaces for action are primarily associated with what is called "Third World ecologism," which views the environment in terms of the possibility for an alternative strategy of development that may build on and recover the productive potential of cultural, ecological, and political processes as a group, rather than any one process in isolation (Leff 1986). Within this formulation, collective actions by the new environmental actors will play a crucial role as they will provide the necessary framework for cultural, political, technological, economic, and social innovation.

Notes

1. The methodological techniques used to gather information and develop this typology of organizations were mainly qualitative and included groups' self-evaluations, situational-strategic planning, actor analysis, and situational diagnostics. Direct sources of information were: participant observation, semistructured in-depth interviews, self-evaluation sessions where each actor and organization developed its own diagnosis according to shared parameters, and workshops of evaluation-negotiation between the state and civil society. Additionally, numerous works prepared for presentation at national and international seminars and workshops were reviewed. My own observations as an active member of the environmental movement during the last five years and as an organizer of self-evaluation workshops have also been incorporated.

2. The clientelism prevalent in the political system, along with the electoral system established by the 1961 constitution (which privileged voting by "a party" and not by individuals) contributed to the strengthening of the parties. These parties agreed on sociopolitical pacts in order to share power among themselves and the rest of the social forces, thus avoiding conflicts that could destabilize the political system.

3. The mistrust and rejection of political parties has entailed a questioning of the near-monopoly on power that parties retain but not of the basic rules of democracy or the political regime. In fact, one of COPRE's proposals for reform was the internal democratization of the political parties. Despite the initial resistance to self-democratization expressed by the parties, the high rate of electoral abstentionism (reaching 70 percent) in the regional and local elections of 1989 forced them to accept the proposed reforms.

4. COPRE's objectives were "to adopt measures to assure the establishment of a modern, essentially democratic, and efficient state, in which the postulates of the Constitution may enjoy full observance, and the citizens' participation may constitute an effective element in decision-making processes of public authority" (President Jaime Lusinchi's speech at the founding ceremony of COPRE, Caracas, 1984). This commission was responsible for achieving political, economic, and administrative decentralization, considered the most suitable means of democratizing and modernizing the Venezuelan state. Even though the commission's objectives incorporated civil society's aspirations, political pressures slowed its achievements.

5. In Mexico as in Venezuela, both the economic strategy of poles of development and the large-scale industrial mining projects—characteristic of the 1970s and backed by the oil bonanza—triggered important mobilizations against their environmental impacts. In Mexico, some ecological movements were formed to fight the impacts of oil drilling and nuclear energy. And even though no nuclear energy projects exist in Venezuela, contesting the exploitation of the Orinoco Oil Belt in the late 1970s and early 1980s was FORJA's most ambitious revindication.

6. According to the Environmental Directory of Venezuela, there are more than one hundred environmental organizations (García 1988). The present typology is only a summary of the most representative organizations; for a more exhaustive analysis of each type of organization, see García 1991b.

7. The following are among the most prominent of the scientific-conservationist societies: The National Association for the Defense of Nature (*Asociación Nacional para la Defensa de la Naturaleza*), founded in 1959; the Foundation for the Development of Marine Sciences (*Fundación Pro-Desarrollo de las Ciencias Marinas*), created in the state of Sucre in 1972; and the Foundation for the Defense of Nature (*Fundación para la Defensa de la Naturaleza*), which emerged in 1975 as an affiliate of the World Wildlife Fund.

8. The most recent and important case of mediation centered around the filming of *Arachnophobia* by U.S. movie producer Steven Spielberg, in the Venezuelan Tepuyes. As a result of this mediation, legal protective measures were adopted for these areas, which were classified as natural landmarks and/or integral protection zones; all types of activity are now prohibited in the Tepuyes. For more on this conflict, see Ramirez 1990.

9. Similar alternative rural communities also emerged in Brazil (Viola 1987), Bolivia, Peru, Mexico, and other Latin American countries in the late 1960s and early 1970s.

10. In Mexico, the transformation of ecological problems of the peasant communities into national problems was achieved through the Ribereño Pact and the Pact of the Ecology Groups, among others. See Pacto de Grupos Ecologistas 1987.

11. Despite their popular background, the group's members and leaders belong to the most privileged or educated sector of this segment of the population (Scott 1990).

12. The ideological provenance from the political Left and/or from the progressive intelligentsia is a characteristic shared by Mexican and Brazilian environmental groups (Viola 1987; Slater, ed., 1985; Quadri 1990).

13. Among such actions are: (1) defending Mount La Cruz in the state of Miranda, Mount Galicia in the state of Falcon, and the Sierra de San Luis, given its ecological importance; Mount La Cruz was eventually developed, and the other two sites were declared national parks; (2) rejecting the construction of a bridge to Margarita Island because of its demographic and environmental impact; the project was halted due to the economic crisis, not to FORJA's actions; (3) rejecting the construction of a club in the Tacarigua lagoon because it would alter the lagoon's rich ecological diversity; the club was redesigned and finally built; (4) opposing the touristic project of La Puerta in the state of Trujillo; and (5) opposing the exploration of heavy-grade crude oil in the Orinoco belt because of its strong environmental repercussions on the affected areas, which comprise nearly half of Venezuela's regions; the project was halted due to the dramatic decline in the price of oil. Finally, one of FORJA's most important projects was the proposed establishment of the Popular University of the Environment (*Universidad Popular Ambiental*, UPA), which never materialized due to the lack of economic resources.

14. To guarantee a greater degree of objectivity within the subjectivity of self-evaluation, FORJA's self-diagnosis was carried out by five of its most prominent members, each of whom belonged to a different organization.

15. The following are the most noteworthy areas of conflict fueling the environmental network over the past five years: the Trans-Amazon Rally (García 1990a); the import of toxic wastes from Italy (Uribe and Lander 1990); the filming of *Arachnophobia* by Steven Spielberg in the Venezuelan Tepuyes (García 1990a); the import of European meat and milk contaminated by

radiation after the Chernobyl accident; the environmental impact of the construction of the Great Savannah Freeway connecting Venezuela with Brazil; the ecological impact of shrimp farming industries in the rivers; the irrational exploitation of the rain forest; mercury poisoning and the deterioration of the Yanomamo habitat and culture caused by gold mining in Guayana; the hauling of fishing nets; the government's nonobservance of environmental regulations; industries' transgressions on the environmental laws in force and the government's failure to impose sanctions; the appropriation of green zones by private parties; the government's resistance to transforming ecologically valuable zones into national parks and the declaration of natural landmarks and protected areas; the environmental, cultural, and social impact of carbon mining in Guasare; the spoiling of indigenous lands and the relocation of their communities due to gold mining or large-scale construction projects such as dams; the environmental impact of large-scale irrigation and industrial projects; the construction of private clubs in ecologically rich and sensitive areas; and, more recently, the application of macroeconomic adjustment measures and the deterioration of the quality of life that resulted.

16. COPRE's neoliberal economic proposals were strongly criticized by the political-ideological organizations but were supported by the symbolic-cultural groups, which viewed them as the counterpart to the democratizing political process. For politico-ideological organizations, the issue is how to combine the ideals of participatory democracy, equity, and social justice with the possibility of a type of development based on ecotechnological rationality (Leff 1986, 1990), while simultaneously imagining more radical alternatives to development (A. Escobar, in press a).

10

Rethinking the Study of Social Movements: The Case of Christian Base Communities in Urban Brazil

John Burdick

The Problem

For over two decades, in what a few have called the most revolutionary Catholic movement since the Reformation and perhaps since the foundation of Christianity itself (Houtart 1979a, 1979b), priests throughout Latin America have preached the Gospel as a call for social justice and the democratization of religious authority (Gutierrez 1973, 1980; L. Boff 1981). Congregations where this effort is under way are known generally as "Christian base communities," or "CEBs." The CEB phenomenon in Brazil has come under special scrutiny because of the Brazilian episcopal hierarchy's support for pastoral plans shaped by liberation theology (De Kadt 1970; Alves 1979; Bruneau 1974; Mainwaring 1986a, 1986b). This literature—like the theology (A. Guimaraes 1978; L. Boff 1986; Teixeira 1988) on which it sometimes appears to be modeled—reveals considerable confidence about the progress of CEBs in Brazil. These groups, we are told, are sweeping through the Brazilian masses like wildfire (Romano 1979: 191; Paiva 1985a, 1985b; Souza Lima 1980; Oliveira 1986; Salem, ed., 1981; Hoornaert 1978). Ralph Della Cava expressed the sentiments of many when he declared that "the receptivity of ordinary and long-suffering believers to this 'revolution within the church' [is] itself extraordinary" (Della Cava 1986: 21; also see Della Cava 1976). Such writings assure us, further, that Brazil's CEBs are raising the consciousness of the masses and motivating them to enter into social movements (Nobrega 1988; Doimo 1984, 1986; Duarte 1983; Bruneau 1980).

There is no reason to doubt the accuracy of this portrayal—at least for some times and in some places. Accounts of CEB members involved in land occupations and neighborhood organizing are, after all, familiar enough to anyone acquainted with the current political situation in Brazil. Yet, the cumulative pastoral experience of the past twenty years and a growing number of analytic reports have begun to complicate the picture. Alberto Antoniazzi, in a recent assessment of the numerical strength of Brazilian CEBs, pointed out that "even calculating optimistically the number to be a hundred thousand CEBs, each one including fifty to a hundred people, the numbers are not even 5 percent of the Catholic population" (1986: 5). In contrast, at least 8 percent of the entire Brazilian population in 1980 identified themselves to census-takers as Protestant, the majority of whom are Pentecostal (Mariz 1989: 57; for similar figures at the local level, see Brandão 1988a, 1988b, 1988c). The image of the CEB as mighty political mobilizer may also have been overdrawn. It remains a notoriously common complaint among clergy working with CEBs that, as one told me, "it is we who do all the political work, while the people are just praying. It should be the other way around" (compare with Hewitt 1986, 1990; Oliveira 1986).

Although observations such as these have forced at least some Catholic progressives to step back and reconsider their once unlimited optimism (for example, Comblin 1987), numerous theologians still remain content with labeling as a victim of false consciousness anyone not swept up in the CEB movement (such as Dom Angelico in *Jornal do Brasil*, May 18, 1988). Brazilian sociologists, too, have been slow to describe and account for the gap between the millennial expectations swirling around the CEBs and their more mundane reality. This slowness is partly political choice and partly the result of analytic focus. Sociologists almost always focus on the most active CEB members, especially those who articulate most fluently the idea of the Gospel as a struggle for social justice (for example, Petrini 1984; Macedo 1986; Gaiger 1987; Passo Castro 1987). This focus is guaranteed to place anyone who is not an active and articulate "message carrier" into a blurry background. And it is precisely this blurring that interferes with our ability to understand the weak demographic and political state of the CEBs.

We need to add new lenses to our toolkit. In particular, we must realize that the progressive message of the CEBs is *but one contender in a contested arena of religious and ideological alternatives*. In any given locale—from town to city, from neighborhood to region—the Gospel as a call for social justice *exists alongside other messages and projects*, including (for starters) charity-centered and other-worldly Catholicism, Pentecostalism, spiritism, and Afro-Brazilian *umbanda*. To understand the fortunes of a CEB, we must therefore see how successfully it competes for energy, loyalty, and time in comparison to other options. To do this, we must define our analytic point of departure not as the CEB but as clusters of people that share either a constructed identity or some other existential commonality. By examining how people in such clusters encounter, interact with, and choose between the options of a given religio-ideological arena, we may, I believe, begin to grasp the reasons for the rise or fall of a particular CEB.

I will try to illustrate the fruitfulness of this approach through a limited comparison of a CEB and a Pentecostal church.[1] My discussion is based on fieldwork in São Jorge, a working-class town of 8,000 people located on the periphery of Rio de Janeiro. In 1982, a progressive priest arrived in the parish to which São Jorge belongs and replaced the chapels in the parish's towns with what he and laypeople close to him called "CEBs." Among other things, this meant the establishment of an elective directorate, the introduction of liturgical innovations, and the creation of new neighborhood-based groups, including small reflection circles. Above all, the priest has tried to infuse a progressive political consciousness into these groups, by means of sermons, pamphlets, study guides, and special courses for leaders.

São Jorge's CEB is typical in that it has been less successful than the local Assembly of God, the largest Pentecostal church in town, in attracting participants: Though there are currently about 90 active participants in the CEB, the Assembly of God boasts nearly 300 (compare with the figures in Brandão 1988c; Gomes 1985; Stoll 1986). Furthermore, in CEBs throughout the region, most participants have kept their distances from social movements, and the few who have not have slipped or are slipping away from them.

My starting point for shedding some light on these patterns is not the CEB itself but clusters of people encountering São Jorge's contested religious arena. Beginning with a perspective "external" to the CEB, I will suggest that illiterates, people with heavy and inflexible labor schedules, married women facing domestic conflict, and people who identify themselves as *negros*[2] find the CEB less effective than Pentecostalism in helping them cope with their respective predicaments. Then, in an effort to provide a partial explanation for the apparent political fragility of the CEBs, I will turn to an "internal" perspective, suggesting that within a given CEB, we must grasp the different understandings its own participants have of its purpose and message. I will conclude by suggesting how the approach I adopt here may illuminate the study of social movements in general.

People Who Have Difficulty Reading
or Speaking Articulately

In the decades before the arrival of the CEB model, illiterates rarely had roles of leadership in the Catholic church. At the same time, priests had never demanded from nonleaders either literacy or special articulateness but had simply expected them to learn prayer litanies and hymns and to recite them dutifully during masses and novenas. But with the CEB, the new priest de-emphasized preset prayers and instead began to send to the CEB a weekly flood of circulars, pamphlets, discussion guides, handbooks, newsletters, and songsheets, all filled with specialized vocabulary. Now, rote memorization could no long serve common church members: Indeed, those who read and spoke haltingly began to be assigned second-rate status.

The most striking evidence of this is that literate Catholics have begun, as never before, to take on airs. One literate man, for example, gleefully recounted how a participant in his Bible group had tried to interpret Jesus' summons that Peter build his church on a rock. "He thought it meant a real rock!" he remembered, a chuckle in his voice. "But anyone who knows how to read can see that Jesus meant by the rock the people of God." Similarly, I noticed that during Bible-circle meetings, group leaders did not hesitate to remark that so-and-so could not read from the guidesheet because he or she did not know how. Thus, it came as no surprise that such people consistently refrained from commenting in group meetings. As one woman said, "I won't say anything there, I just listen and pray. I don't want to look stupid." Another illiterate woman said,

"They make me feel dumb; the readers understand it all." This sentiment can have serious consequences. A less than literate woman, for example, who used to participate distanced herself from the church once reading became a central activity. "There in the groups," she said, "they only like people who can respond prettily, according to what's written there in their books. They no longer value faith, just reading."

In contrast, literacy as a value figures several notches lower in Pentecostalism than in the CEB. Though *crentes* (literally meaning "believers," the self-identifying term for Pentecostals) naturally value knowing the words of the Bible, they regard such knowledge as less essential to their identity than devotion to prayer and the experience of the Holy Spirit. "The Spirit revives," goes one oft-repeated quotation from the Apostle Paul, "but the letter kills." One prayer-healer remarked that if the crente grows too preoccupied with the written word, "he forgets about the Spirit, closes himself off to it. The Bible is fine, but someone can get too loaded with such wisdom, thinking they know a lot about the Bible, and then the spiritual part dies."

It should thus not surprise us that less educated people are better represented in São Jorge's Assembly of God than in its CEB.[3] Fewer than a quarter of the crente men, for instance, had attended school for four or more years, but nearly a third of active Catholics had this much schooling. Considered from a different angle, although four-fifths of the participating Catholic men had attended school for more than two years, only two-thirds of the crente men had done so. Or, though about a tenth of local active male Catholics had attended school beyond eighth grade, none of the crentes had gone this far.

The heightened emphasis on literacy in the CEB may, in fact, have contributed to the growth of the Assembly of God. I met several individuals with inferior reading skills who spoke of literacy as figuring prominently in their conversions from the CEB to the Assembly of God. One woman reported that "I have been a Catholic all my life. All my life. But they started getting very snobby. . . . In the crente church, they don't make someone like me, who doesn't know how to read, feel ashamed. You can go up and testify, you don't have to read anything!"

People with Little Time on Their Hands

Before the CEB model arrived in São Jorge, the right to call oneself "Catholic" had been limited only by the simple criteria of having been baptized and "having faith in God." The CEB placed these criteria into doubt, however, by demanding a level of church participation formerly confined only to lay leaders. As one progressive nun sermonized, "Our Church . . . demands work, effort; it's not easy. Things used to be easier in the church. Today, to pray also means to commit oneself." To be a good Catholic today means attending numerous pastoral, catechism, and Bible-circle meetings each week. Simple Mass-goers have, in fact, begun to find themselves the targets of criticism and gossip. "It used to be," said one woman, "if you missed Mass, the Church didn't concern itself with that. But not now: A person misses even a little, others start saying you're no longer a Catholic."

Not everyone in São Jorge can fulfill these criteria. Women who work outside the home, for example, are hard-pressed to participate at the level expected by the ideology of participation[4] and are thus underrepresented in the CEB: Though some 35 percent of all local women worked outside their homes, only a quarter of participating Catholic women did so. Meanwhile, younger women with small children tend to have less discretionary time than do older women with grown children. It is perhaps no accident, then, that even though only a third of the women in town were over forty years old, more than half of those who participated actively in the CEB were in that age group.

The CEB's demands for participation also make membership difficult for men who have to take on heavy or inflexible labor schedules. Only about a tenth of the active male participants in the CEB had to work overtime, second jobs, nighttime shifts, or Sundays, compared to a third of all local men. In addition, skilled factory workers were represented in the CEB twice as often and manual operatives only half as often as in the town at large, probably because, with slightly higher incomes, skilled workers can decline overtime, weekend, and nighttime shifts. Furthermore, one-third of male participants in the CEB were retired or on social security, as opposed to only a fifth of all local men: Such men clearly have more time available for church work.

But perhaps most intriguingly, over 40 percent of the male participants in the CEB worked in the self-employed construction trades, compared with only a third of all local males. A clue to why this is so can be found by considering the labor rhythms of construction work. Construction offers a maximum of scheduling flexibility: Labor stops at dusk, leaving evenings free; changes in weather and the availability of materials create greater intermittence than that in factory or service-sector work; small projects rarely have strict deadlines, allowing for control of work rhythms; and work sites in the vicinity permit workers to return home on short notice. One CEB participant, for example, was at work plastering the walls of a neighbor's house one Saturday when he was told that a major church meeting had been called that afternoon. "I could plaster any day," he said, "but the meeting was right then." No assembly-line worker could have said that.

Now, let me turn to the Assembly of God. In this church, the power of the Holy Spirit erodes the distinction between "leisure" and "spiritual" time: For crentes, all time is spiritual. This motivates many of them to replace what they used to regard as leisure time—at home or in the street—with time in church. But for many others, the main source of their identity has become not presence at a collective ritual but an inner transformation carried about wherever they go, expressed in constant daily prayers and efforts to evangelize others. Thus, though valuing church attendance, the Assembly of God recognizes as good crentes even those unable to maintain an intense level of participation in official church functions.

The contrast between the Catholics' and the crentes' expectations is well illustrated by comparing Oswaldo, a Catholic, with Antonio, a crente. Oswaldo had been a participating member of the CEB, until he took a job that made it impossible for him to attend church except on Sundays. His authority in the CEB plummeted immediately: Belittling talk began behind his back, his wife felt obliged to attend meetings and apologize profusely for his absence, and though he had once served on several CEB committees, his name was not even proposed at election time. Antonio, too, worked at a job that only allowed him to attend church on Sundays. Yet, he dutifully fulfilled his role as deacon and received the Holy Spirit during services; never did I hear an uncomplimentary word spoken of him.

In general, then, being a crente in São Jorge is compatible with a broader range of labor processes and time availability than is CEB membership. Consequently, it should not surprise us that the Assembly attracts, with greater frequency than the CEB, people with minimal discretionary time on their hands. The percentage of men who work overtime or second jobs in the Assembly of God is about twice that of such men in the CEB, and crentes are underrepresented in the construction industry. It is also interesting that the Assembly includes a large contingent of women with young children: Though only one-fifth of active Catholic women were in their twenties, nearly a third of the crente women were.

Women Facing Domestic Conflict

Though the proportions of women to men in the CEB and the Assembly of God are similar, in absolute numbers a woman is just about three times more likely to be a crente than an active CEB member. Among the 90 active members of São Jorge's CEB, 60 were women, compared to 180 of the Assembly of God's 270 crentes. Why might this be the case? I would suggest that a major contributing factor is the difference between how the two religions address the problem of domestic conflict.

It would seem at first glance that the CEB is ideally suited to helping women articulate and cope with domestic conflict. After all, theologians such as Leonardo Boff have long defined the CEB's Bible circle as a place where people are supposed to connect "faith with life" (L. Boff 1981; Mesters 1986). In my weekly visits to Bible circles, however, I never heard women discuss their own domestic problems. The commonest type of talk in the circles remained abstract moral exhortation to follow Christ's example—to be loving, charitable, faithful, committed, and so forth. Indeed, participants explicitly claimed that the circles should not be used to articulate personal problems. "If you talk about that," one group coordinator explained, "you're not connecting life with the Bible. Because the connection between life and the Bible doesn't mean things about husbands and wives, about children, or the problems that we have."

As I have argued elsewhere (Burdick 1990), this reluctance to speak of domestic problems in the reflection groups is due, in part, to the fear of gossip promoted by the circles' small-group and neighborhood-based dynamics. I want to supplement that argument here by suggesting that this reluctance is also due to the very ideological priorities of the progressive church. Progressive Catholic discourse presents domestic problems as secondary to the "really important" issues of the world beyond the household. As one pastoral agent explained, "If there's something wrong at home, it's because the husband is unemployed. But why is he unemployed? That's the question we want people to think about." "Consciousness" in this view means an understanding not of inequality in the household but rather of the extradomestic realm of "politics and production" (Alvarez 1990: 65). As the progressive priest justifying his discouragement of private confessions explained: "Women just talked about emotional stuff at home, there was very little space to raise their consciousness there."

It is therefore not surprising that Bible-group guidesheets consistently skirt domestic issues. On the rare occasion when a guidesheet *does* touch on domestic conflict, it lays the "macro" perspective on with a trowel. One guidesheet, for example, called for reflection on the following story:

> Dona Marta's husband lost his job, and he started taking it out on his family. Then Marta learned in her group that it was not just her husband who was unemployed but that unemployment was sweeping through the poor workers in Brazil. She learned that the minimum wage has fallen in value by 150 percent in the last two years. She started joining her *comunidade* when it went to the authorities to demand stability of employment and higher wages for all workers.

It is possible, of course, that some women may be able to overcome their domestic problems by learning wage statistics and throwing themselves into political work. But idealizing such women stigmatizes others who fail to respond in the same way (not to mention that it shifts responsibility from men to women). Many women resent being criticized for limiting themselves to the domestic struggle. For example, in response to the guidesheet's question, How are we, today, at the service of life? one woman replied, "By washing, making food, cleaning, sewing." She was met with the haughty retort that "no, the question is about helping people outside your home." Though she said nothing at the time, she later confided to me, "How am I supposed to help all these people outside my home! It's hard enough to take care of things at home!" And another former member complained, "They say 'struggle, struggle, struggle!' But they mean unions, and neighborhood associations, and political parties, things like that. But I struggle here in my own home every day. They don't speak about that."

It may seem surprising to claim that women in the Assembly of God find their religion a richer resource than the CEB for increasing their control over the social relations within their households. After all, Pentecostalism is well known for constantly resorting to that old patriarch the Apostle Paul and for its consequent sanctification of female submissiveness to men. On closer inspection, however, one may discover that female crentes exchange submission to men for otherwise unavailable sources of power over male behavior. One of Pentecostalism's many paradoxes is that women's strict observance of a subordinate role actually increases their authority to speak their minds at home. That is, by receiving the Spirit and observing divine law, the woman gains both the legitimacy and confidence to quietly but firmly challenge her husband's conduct. "I say that I could speak," one woman remembered, "and I did. . . . I would speak, speak gently, and he would have to listen." This authority is forged, in part, by acquaintance with Biblical pronouncements on marriage and family. One woman, before converting to the Assembly, was always fighting with her husband because of his drinking, but the more she tried to correct him, the more he drank. "After becoming a crente," she reported, "I didn't fight anymore, because I had more strength to speak about things, without having to fight. You feel there is always someone praying for you. . . . I'd talk with him [after conversion] with authority, and he would cry. I would talk, quietly, that it wasn't right for us to waste the small salary we had on things that weren't bread, because that's Biblical. . . . Being a member of the church gave me more authority to talk like this at home."

By converting to Pentecostalism, many women hope to influence their husbands' behavior, to turn them into more reliable spouses. This can happen without the man himself actually becoming a crente: In numerous cases, simple moral pressure from crente wives is enough to moderate men's drinking, smoking, adultery, and so forth. Once a man converts, however, his wife enjoys even stronger safeguards over his behavior. Pentecostalism rejects the male prestige complex as the work of the Devil, subjecting men to discipline should they indulge in any of its elements. A crucial source of this control is the presence of the Holy Spirit within the church: This gives members gifts of prophecy and vision that keep a constant vigil over the behavior of crentes. A man will think twice about partaking in an illicit affair or sneaking a drink when he imagines a prophet denouncing him during a church service. (This, indeed, has happened several times.) This sanction may also come in the form of dreams. One man had been flirting with the idea of seeing an old flame on the sly. While he was considering it, he was approached by a female prayer specialist who told him she had had a dream in which she saw him about to do something against God's will. Naturally, he dropped the idea of the tryst at once.

Thus it is that many women consciously regard their conversions as God's way of permitting them to regain control over their domestic affairs. As one woman put it: "I thought, on the day that I decided to be baptized, 'This is a decision that I have to take, in order to have more strength to control my house.' Because being baptized, you feel the Holy Spirit, you feel more energy to converse better at home."

People Who Call Themselves Negros

According to progressive Catholic discourse, racial equality is forged in the CEB. "We are all equal," declared a light-skinned minister of the Eucharist, "There's no racism, that's against the will of God." Deeper probing, however, reveals a more complicated situation. After some trust has been established, negro informants have reported that they feel treated like second-class citizens in the CEB. Many of them point out, for example, that only white and light *mulato* children are allowed to coronate the image of Our Lady during her May festivities. Others claim they are often passed over whenever people are needed to read from the Bible in front of the congregation. And all feel obstructed in their efforts to gain and hold positions of leadership. "People with less capacity than me," one negro complained, "get positions in the Church because they're lighter." Negros in positions of authority do, indeed, tend to be placed there by the priest, not elected, and white leaders seem bent on sabotaging them. When, for example, the priest appointed a *negra* to the directorate, a light-skinned leader approached him and claimed—dishonestly—that the negra did not want the post. Negro appointees say they are rarely consulted, are kept in the dark about meetings, and are never called on to represent the CEB to outsiders. Many feel they are compared unfavorably to lighter-skinned leaders. As one sighed, "No matter what we do, light people always find something wrong." One negra reported that if her husband, a Bible-group coordinator, takes a drink, "they say, 'Oh, that negro!' But when Mauricio [a white leader] drinks, no one comments." A negro who was appointed by the priest to be minister of the sick reported that "you always feel like you're not accepted. . . . Once, a lady even refused to let me give her the host, she wanted Dona Margarita [a white minister of the Eucharist]."

Part of the reason for the CEB's failure to erode racism is that its discourse, like the larger Catholic discourse of which it is a variant, does not admit of dramatic changes in personhood. Catholic identity does not represent a rupture with either a former or a current self. As one longtime Catholic explained, "That fire, that flash, that's ridiculous. No one converts in a day. It's a process, it's a path." In this view, one's self within the church is continuous with, not a transformation of, one's self outside of it. Who one is—or, at any rate, is perceived to be—in the "world" tends in the Catholic imagination to be transferred largely intact to the church's various sacred contexts. "I am a sinful creature," an old Catholic woman proclaimed, "and I am sinful in Church too! . . . If you have been a murderer, all you have to do is say 'I accept Jesus' and all that is gone forever? No! People don't change overnight!" This vision is reinforced by liberation theology's insistence on the unity of "church" and "world," on the importance of bringing people's worldly identity as "the poor" into the church itself, and on the lifetime commitment to struggle on a long, continuous "path" (*caminhada*).

This lack of transformative discourse feeds racist practice in at least two ways. Those who enjoy nonreligious leadership, long-term residence, or high status in the locale tend to become the leaders of the church. Over the course of the past thirty years, a group of light-skinned, literate, and skilled longtime residents became the core leadership of the local chapel. In addition, the absence of a strong Catholic discourse of transformation allows racist stereotypes of "how negros are in the 'world'" to be transferred largely intact to the church. Though these stereotypes include images of negros as lazy and dull, perhaps the most damning is the belief that "all *negros* are *macumbeiros*" ("practitioners of the Afro-Brazilian religion of *umbanda*") for this implies that negros continue to practice this "Devil-worship" within the church itself. "Look," one white said, "I don't think *pretos* ['coloreds'] are close to God. How could they be, they're always in *macumba*? [literally meaning 'black magic,' typically used as a pejorative misnomer for umbanda]."

If the CEB's discourse has made it difficult to develop a counterdiscourse to racism, the presence of a progressive bishop in the diocese since 1981 made space for a systematic attempt to create one. The church's Fraternity Campaign of 1988 aimed to empower negros and enlighten light-skinned Catholics through reworking conventional racial discourse. Yet, the campaign failed to attract negros. This was due largely to the fact that the campaign's guide booklet was designed, as in previous years, for preexisting Bible circles, thus ensuring that the core group of participants would be light-skinned. As one negro observed: "Most of the people who usually participate are white. So most of the people in the Campaign were white, too." This simple fact had far-reaching consequences for the ability of the campaign to attract negros, who could hear light-skinned members' double-talk loud and clear. One negra attended two meetings, then stopped. "There they preach brotherhood, all that," she reported, "but it's only in there. Outside, these things are not lived."

In stark contrast to the CEB, the Assembly of God has attracted negros in great numbers. Among the CEB's 40 most active participants, only 5 called themselves preto or negro, and among the other 50 regular participants, no more than 10 did. In contrast, among the 270 active members of São Jorge's Assembly of God, between a third and a half were negros. Among its 8 presbyters, half were negro, and numerous negro deacons and auxiliaries filled positions of visible authority. An important reason for this contrast is that Pentecostalism's vision of transformation forges the possibility for negros to be treated as equals—even better than equals—with light-skinned crentes. Pentecostal doctrine proclaims that the Holy Spirit is no respecter of persons: In fact, crentes commonly claim that the lower and humbler one is in the world, the more open one is likely to be to the power of the Spirit. Based on this principle, which Victor Turner (1974) once called the religious empowerment of "social-structural inferiors," negros discover that Pentecostalism allows them to develop a degree of authority impossible in any other social arena.

I first realized this when a white woman invited me to accompany her to the house of a negra prayer-healer. When I told her I could not go with her, she said, "No matter. There's another who prays for the sick on Thursdays. She's light, but her prayers are a blessing too." That little "but" spoke very loudly. There is, it turns out, a widely accepted opinion among all crentes that negros are able to come "closer to God" than anyone else in church, that they have "greater fervor," speak in tongues, prophesy, have visions, cure, and expel demons far more frequently than do lighter-skinned crentes. Light-skinned crentes attribute these special spiritual qualities to the fact that negros know better than others how to "humiliate themselves." "We whites," one white crente explained, "we're lazier in front of God, there are days when we miss church. But not them, they're always there. So you can see, God has more opportunity to work in people of color." In contrast, the notion of negro spiritual specialness remains foreign to the progressive Catholic imagination. I asked over 20 participants in the CEB whether they believed negros to be "closer to God" than whites. Their responses ranged from puzzlement to amusement to outright hostility to the idea.

Though CEBs may, for some of the reasons I have outlined here, be demographically weaker than crentes, this cannot alter the fact that throughout Brazil they have been an important historical force, supplying a political umbrella for popular struggles, inspiring and encouraging popular leadership, and providing a space for leaders to develop political networks (Krischke and Mainwaring, eds., 1986; Caccia Bava 1981). As I mentioned earlier, however, a growing amount of evidence suggests that CEB politics may be rather less radical than most liberation theologians have heretofore been willing to admit. In the progressive diocese of Vitória, for instance, the majority of CEB members have recently been found to be neither involved in social movements nor very concerned with matters of political consciousness (Oliveira 1986: 51); another researcher reported that among the most "mature" CEBs in São Paulo, interest in "charity" has "won out" over political reflection (Hewitt 1990: 2; compare with Hewitt 1986, 1987).

That this was the pattern in the region around São Jorge as well became apparent as soon as I stopped interviewing only the small militant minority and began instead to listen to the full range of interpretations of the progressive message among CEB participants. The CEB of São Jorge is typical of many other *comunidades* in the region in that the majority of its participants are men and women who have been active in the church *long before the arrival of the new* CEB *discourse.* These people tend to interpret "liberation" not as this-worldly emancipation but as the practice of charity and the seeking of one's own and others' otherworldly salvation. One woman who had grown up the child of observant Catholics in the 1940s gave voice to this older orthodoxy because, exercising no position of church authority, she did not need to articulate the new one. "Struggling means helping others," she explained. "We in the Church have always done this. I understand the new Church this way: helping others out more, helping a hungry person, giving to the person who needs medicine, or a friendly word, sometimes there's a sad person, depressed: you smile at them, give them a word." Her otherworldly concerns emerged when I asked her what "liberation" meant. "That's salvation," she said. "We pray for the poor, misguided people, those living in sin, for them to see a little bit of the light. We must struggle a lot for that too. And when a person dies, we pray for their soul, so it can be liberated."

A few old-time Catholics did articulate bits and pieces of progressive reading, but these individuals tended, significantly, to occupy positions of authority in the church. For them, it seemed, using the new lexicon was very much a part of their effort to retain authority amid changing discursive winds. A minister of the Eucharist who had been a leader of the local Apostolate of Prayer (a traditional Catholic lay association) for over thirty years found that, in order to continue receiving the priest's support, she had to adapt to him. If, in particular, the priest's support required her to incorporate phrases such as "struggle" and "the oppressed" into her speech, incorporate them she would. The tactical dimension of her new discourse was suggested to me when I pressed her on the question of social movements. "I am pretty disconnected from that stuff," she remarked and went on to insist that "the church was created to preach religion, the things of God. Politics has other sectors; it shouldn't be mixed with religion."

For Catholics such as these, participating in the CEB has far less to do with political reflection than with prayer. When such people call each other to attend the Bible-reflection groups, for example, they do not say "Let's go reflect" but rather "Let's go pray." One woman, in fact, used to nap through the "reflection" part of the meetings, bestirring herself only at moments of prayer, when she would stand and feverishly move her lips. Many participants go so far as to say they attend the groups only because they have heard similar groups meet simultaneously throughout Brazil. "That means," one said, "that the Church is uniting all our prayers together. So prayer there is strong."

When such Catholics participate in a social movement—say, in a neighborhood association—this is generally rooted less in a self-conscious effort to realize the liberationist project than in a simple desire to extend the traditional Catholic project of charity. One nonleading Catholic in her late forties said the neighborhood association was "not a social movement" but rather was "the same thing as our charity work." She thus conceived of her own involvement in neighborhood improvement as simply one more church activity: When I asked her why she participated in the association, she replied, "It's the Church that's doing it. I go because they announce it in Church. I am a member of the Church."

Though charity and church sponsorship are, of course, adequate reasons to become involved in social movements, clarifying these motives helps explain why the CEB members' activist commitment often proves so fragile. In at least three towns, I discovered that where CEB members had become involved in such organizations, they did so only as long as other CEB members remained in the organization's leadership, drifting away as soon as leadership passed to non-CEB hands. It seems likely that as long as CEB members view neighborhood organizations as primarily "church activities," they have little reason to remain in them as soon as they are no longer under the control of the church.

Meanwhile, those CEB participants who have been socialized into the church since the arrival of progressive discourse produce, not surprisingly, the most consistent version of the new liberationist message of human rights and material betterment. Even among these, however—partly because small neighborhood-based groups inhibit open debate, partly because of the strangeness of the new progressive vocabulary—there is no guarantee that discourse will be connected to practice. Still, a few locals have embraced the new discourse and translated it into action. This synthesis is commonest among younger people who early in their lives came to nurture aspirations for leaving their social class, usually through education, but found their hopes for social ascension frustrated by unjust, insurmountable social barriers. For such people, CEB activism in social movements is a way of bringing together their institutional Catholicism, education, aspirations for social and material improvement, and resentment of the wounds of class. Even among such militants, however, there is a high attrition rate,[5] as they become caught between being "too radical" for the CEBs from which they have come and "not radical enough" for the real-life political world into which they have been thrust. As one militant explained,

> I find the Church, and there they are all just talking about loving your brother, but they aren't doing anything, so I feel restless there. Then I go to a meeting of the PT [radical Workers' Party], and there they are all screaming at the top of their lungs. So I don't know where to turn any more. . . . Some days I think I'm just going to give up everything and go back to taking care of my family.

I have tried in this chapter to provide the beginnings of an explanation of the relative demographic and political fragility of CEBs in Brazil—first through an "external" focus on the CEB as one option in Brazil's religious arena, then through an "internal" focus on the CEB as an organization to bring together diverse points of view conditioned by different chronological, institutional, and class circumstances. There is no reason to suppose, however, that this approach must be confined to CEBs. It should, rather, be developed to raise questions about social movements in general. After all, as the foregoing analysis of Pentecostalism should have made clear, with this approach, one can portray movements across the spectrum of relative strength and success.

There are, I believe, two main blind spots in the literature on social movements that the approach suggested here may help to remedy. First, most studies of social movements, like those of CEBs, tend to focus on only one group of people— those who carry the "message," those who participate actively in the movement (see, for example, Eckstein, ed., 1989; for Brazil, see Cardoso 1983). The drawback of this focus becomes clear when we consider that social movements typically aggregate, in any given locale, something less than—often far less than—all those members of the local population whom the movement's leadership would like to mobilize. To take just one example (and it could be multiplied), in Brazilian *bairros* of 10,000 people, one is lucky to get 50 to come to a meeting of the neighborhood association (for example, Zaluar 1985; Diniz 1982).

This disproportion between participants and nonparticipants is quite obvious, both to people at the local level and to anyone who has been in the field. Yet, its empirical and theoretical implications have not been explored systematically. In social scientific writings, movements tend to become, as if by magic, "the people," the "town," or the "locale," as though there were not enormous differences—and enormously complex relations—between participants and nonparticipants. We are thus sidetracked from examining a whole universe of social processes (at which I have only hinted) that include processes of: connecting, relating, and distancing people from movements; insidership and outsidership; boundary-marking; access, socialization, and recruitment; rites of initiation; and the way in which all these processes articulate with local social differentiation along lines of gender, race, class, age, literacy, and so forth.[6]

In order to understand these processes, we must begin to look at social movements as existing not just within a given place but within complex fields of competing and overlapping practices and discourses—including households, families, television, churches, the male prestige sphere—all of which call for the investment of time and loyalty, as well as psychic, ideological, and practical energy. Looked at this way, a person's participation in a given social movement often carries with it an implied nonparticipation in a host of alternatives. We are thus impelled to inquire into the range of conscious and less-than-conscious choices and social pressures that condition our subject's behavior.

In shifting our focus from movements to the arenas in which they exist, it therefore becomes crucial to also shift our focus to clusters of people, whose identity and significance should emerge from an ethnographic grasp of local social relations. Thus, we should begin not by examining a particular social movement but by considering how, for example, women, youth, the unemployed, blacks, or the formal proletariat (the list can be as long and varied as are social relations) encounter a field of ideological, discursive, and practical options. Only then, I suggest, can we identify the processes through which people become involved in some options and not others, as well as the circumstances under which they desist and distance themselves from a given movement—a process that is perhaps just as common as participation itself.

The focus on the "message carriers" has led to a second blind spot: a striking skittishness about dealing with discursive, ideological, and practical variation within social movements. By this I mean not only the most obvious matter of internal stratification of authority, in which literacy, availability, flexibility of time, articulateness, mastery of discourse, access to intercalary figures, and so forth all come into play. A subtler matter has to do with the differences among movement participants in understanding and interpreting the very objectives of the movement itself. Such differences, of course, exist at various discursive levels—some semiconscious, some mired in habitus (Bourdieu 1977). Yet, at whatever level they are apprehended, grasping some of the different understandings of a movement's "message" by its participants, as well as how they are embedded in different historical circumstances, is essential to making sense of the movement's fortunes— why and when it succeeds, fails, or achieves mixed results.

Notes

1. Because of limitations of space—and to simplify the argument—I have not, for the purposes of this chapter, expanded the comparison to include non-Pentecostal Protestant churches, smaller Pentecostal congregations, or African-Brazilian mediumship religion. I have discussed these other options in my doctoral dissertation, "Looking for God in Brazil," Graduate Center of City University of New York, 1990.

2. I have retained the Brazilian term *negro* in preference to the North American term *black* because North Americans apply the latter term to many people Brazilians would call *mulato* or *moreno*.

3. These figures, like all those to follow, are derived from a census I undertook of some 300 households in 1987–1988.

4. Mariz (1989: 87) also found that in Recife, "most of the CEB leaders and members were women without jobs. They worked at home and could control their own time."

5. A growing number of observers have expressed concern about the difficulty even militant CEB members have in reconciling their church and political activities (C. Boff et al. 1987).

6. I would urge the reader to consider that studying a social movement by focusing on active members alone is akin to studying rural-urban migration by looking only at the migrants who have already made the trip. The limitations of this perspective in migration studies are by now commonplace: Without looking at people both in places of origin and in the process of moving, we miss the complex processes of step-migration, return migration, *non*-migration, and so on. So it is, I would argue, with social movements—religio-political and otherwise.

11

Homosexual Identities in Transitional Brazilian Politics

Edward MacRae

The Cultural Struggle Against the Regime and the Democratic Opening

At the end of the 1970s, Brazilians began to breathe a more optimistic air. For many, the nation was at the threshold of a new era, more just and more humane. The resurgence of civil society, coupled with the military regime's decision to curb the coercive apparatus, heralded great transformations. Workers, entrepreneurs, intellectuals, and students rose in protest.

In May of 1978, metalworkers staged a massive strike in the greater São Paulo region. This vigorous demonstration of the power of the labor movement immediately expanded to numerous other categories. As the sociologists Sebastião C.V. Cruz and Carlos E. Martins said of that period, "With the strike in the ABC [the location of the automobile industry in Santo André, São Bernardo, and São Caetano], and with the movement that it precipitated, an enormous space was opened in the field of ideas and in the political imaginary. Suddenly, the realm of the possible was expanded, the new began to sprout" (Cruz and Martins 1983: 59). Wage policy and antistrike legislation, master pillars of the military regime after 1964, fell into disarray. The government seemed disposed to abdicate its tutelage over the relationship between business and labor. Shortly thereafter, the idea of a workers' party emerged.

In June of 1978, President Ernesto Geisel announced new reforms that eliminated the most distinctly arbitrary instruments of the draconian authoritarian legislation in effect. He was careful, however, not to significantly weaken the security and intelligence forces who had defeated militant movements and guerrilla groups in the late 1960s and early 1970s.

The manner of contesting the status quo, nevertheless, began to change. Old discourses on "the people" and "their struggle" were left aside. Youth, students, and intellectuals began to emphasize questions relating to the subversion of values and the behavior of the challengers themselves. Matters like sexuality, the use of drugs, the underground press, and psychoanalysis were now discussed. The traditional values and practices of the Left began to be viewed as conservative. Opting in favor of marginality came to be seen as the main form of attack on "the system." As Heloisa Buarque de Holanda put it, "The use of drugs, bisexuality, the decolonialized behavior were 'lived' and felt as dangerous, illegal gestures and, as a result, were taken as a challenge of a political nature" (1980: 68).

When the student movement began to reorganize in the late 1970s, its meetings became important forums for the discussion of new positions. Students questioned old ideals of opposition unity, challenging the Left's notion that unity was essential to the "general struggle" and arguing that differences on "specific matters" should no longer be relegated to a secondary plane. Many of the themes raised would subsequently be taken up again by new movements, such as the feminist and homosexual movements. Power, understood in a generic sense, was rejected and condemned wherever it appeared, be it in the institutional form of government agencies, in the structure of the political parties, or in the day-to-day relationships between individuals—such as those between parents and children, teachers and students, owners and employees, married couples, and lovers.

Against the dictates of power, the pleasure of the individual was deemed the greater good. Wherever pleasure was absent, the effects of authoritarianism (also called fascism, racism, or machismo, almost indiscriminantly) were detected. As a result, one of the most serious accusations that could be leveled against any political assembly, such as those of the student movement, was that it had become bureaucratic and tedious.

The moralism of the orthodox Left became one of the principal targets of this new criticism. The Left had not yet begun to assimilate the new postures of the Brazilian youth, especially those stemming from the sexual liberty made possible by the advent of the birth control pill and other factors. Sexual relations outside marriage, along with homosexuality and drug use, were severely repressed within orthodox Left organizations. Indeed, militants who engaged in such activities faced expulsion from their organizations. Even a preference for foreign music, such as soul, funk, and rock, was attacked, considered "alien" or "suspect" by the leftists of the old guard.

As the regime's political liberalization made more open activities possible for the various clandestine leftist organizations and as the end of press censorship spurred more open debate, the ideal of unity among opposition forces proved ever less viable. Classical divisions among Marxists resurfaced, and new groups with specific claims began to appear as well. Particularly outstanding were the black and feminist movements. The problems of blacks and women and their methods of collective action went far beyond the questions classically considered political. Both movements were also concerned with issues previously considered cultural or related to the day-to-day experiences of political militants—hierarchal relationships between the races, between men and women, and even between the political leaders and the rank and file within leftist organizations themselves.

Blacks as well as women had a long history of struggle, formerly aimed at achieving the full rights of citizenship that had been systematically denied them. However, in the postwar years and especially after 1964, these campaigns dissipated and the black and feminist struggles were ignored, not only by the elite in power but by opposition groups as well. The transformations that occurred in society beginning in the 1970s led blacks and women to take up some of their old demands and raise new claims. Finding little support from most existing political groups (including some on the Left who deemed such struggles "secondary"), blacks and women elaborated new theories and new autonomous strategies for action. Due to shared political grievances and organizational dynamics, they would become the interlocutors and privileged allies of militant homosexual groups, who, like them, did not see any basis for downgrading their specific demands regarding their own immediate problems because they held minority status.

A new societal tendency began to manifest itself with particular intensity within the Left. It consisted of the revalorization of problems specific to certain sectors whose difficulties had been, until then, relegated to secondary positions within a Left that had focused exclusively on the "class struggle." The black movement, by emphasizing the additional oppression suffered by workers of African origin, shattered the idea of a great working class united by the same capitalist exploitation. The feminist movement, for its part, called attention to forms of sexist discrimination present in the methods of leftist militancy and other types of oppression beyond the purely economic. It can be said that feminists perhaps legitimatized values that were formerly disdained by groups of the Marxist-Leninist persuasion.

The Homosexual Movement

With the relative easing of censorship in 1979, Brazil's first homosexual newspaper, *Lampião*—edited in Rio de Janeiro by homosexual journalists, intellectuals, and artists—appeared in the nation's newsstands. *Lampião* originally intended to deal frankly with homosexuality and attempted to forge alliances with other "minorities," that is, blacks, feminists, Indians, and those in the ecological movement. Although this proposed alliance did not fully materialize, the newspaper certainly was of great significance to the extent that it systematically grappled with the homosexual question in its political, existential, and cultural aspects in a positive, not pejorative, manner.

In 1979, despite the relaxation of censorship and the fact that homosexuality was not even mentioned in the Brazilian Penal Code, Rio police launched an inquiry against the editors of *Lampião*. They were accused of violating press legislation by going against "morality and good customs." Despite the fact that these police and juridical acts were shelved after complicated legal procedures, the *Lampião* editors endured months of intimidation and humiliation. They were saved partly because of support received from the Journalists Union, whose lawyers defended them. Such support was a clear sign that homosexuality had ceased to be an object of scorn and that the legitimacy of homosexual demands had begun to be recognized.

The year 1978 also saw the birth of the so-called Unified Black Movement, the full blossoming of the feminist movement, and the rapid growth of the first nuclei of the homosexual movement in Brazil. Soon after the launching of *Lampião*, a group of artists, intellectuals, and liberal professionals, unhappy with a social life restricted to bars in homosexual "ghettos," began to meet weekly in São Paulo. Initially planning to discuss the social and personal implications of their sexual orientation, these individuals made their first public demonstration in an open letter to the Journalists Union, protesting the defamatory form with which "the yellow press" presented homosexuality.

In February 1979, the members of this group, already calling itself SOMOS–Grupo de Afirmação Homosexual ("We Are–Homosexual Affirmation Group"), appeared in public during a debate on minorities sponsored at the University of São Paulo. There, they established contact with other groups that had begun to discuss the question of homosexuality, and the idea of a future Brazilian homosexual movement was implanted. This debate also established the importance of the homosexual movement as a legitimate interlocutor in the discussion of national issues. In addition, it was a cathartic experience that increased the confidence of the participants and gave impulse to the formation of similar groups in São Paulo and other cities.

The example of the São Paulo group SOMOS and the influence of Lampião produced results. During the summer of 1980, a meeting of several homosexual groups that had formed in different states to promote homosexual militancy was held in São Paulo. Among the topics discussed, the following stood out: the question of homosexual identity, relations within the homosexual movement, political parties, procedures, and organization. Although there were plenty of polemics and expressions of different points of view, a generalized antipathy toward any form of authoritarianism became evident, be it within political parties (of the Right and of the Left), in relationships between men and women, or between people of the same sex. The proposed solutions emphasized, then, the autonomy of the homosexual movement in relation to political parties and support for feminism in the struggle against machismo. In a similar vein, the reproduction of machismo in homosexual relationships was criticized. Against the "active/passive," "dominator/dominated" dichotomy, participants proposed a new homosexual identity premised on essentially egalitarian sexual/affective relationships.

Though until now I have spoken of homosexual movements as such, I cannot fail to speak of the so-called homosexual ghetto, which has also been called the homosexual movimentação and which serves as background to the movement and directly affects a much greater number of people. The ghetto typically consists of a downtown area where certain bars, saunas, nightclubs, public baths, and parks act as contact points for homosexuals. In addition to this central area, there are other areas of homosexual conglomeration and cruising, smaller and spread out in upper-class neighborhoods as well as in working-class areas.

In fact, it was not the homosexual movement that initiated the reformulation of the old view of homosexuals as effeminate young men and masculine women. In the ghetto areas, new terms emerged in the 1960s to name increasingly common and accepted social figures—o entendido and a entendida, Brazilian equivalents to "gay." Entendido and gay came to basically designate people who have sexual relations with people of the same sex, without necessarily adopting the attributes often associated with the demeaning terms faggot or dyke. This new terminology was not pejorative.

This new model of homosexual relationships developed in São Paulo (as well as in other large urban centers) toward the end of the 1960s, when certain downtown areas became locales frequented not only by homosexuals but also by groups of politicized bohemians. The bohemians, artists, intellectuals, and students, all opposed to the military dictatorship, frequently engaged in diverse modalities of cultural resistance and tried to subvert the regime by questioning the conservative and authoritarian values that reigned in society.

A process of mutual influence resulted from the encounter of these two outsider populations. The cultural resisters found a new field in which to act, perceiving the importance of dissolving the rigidity of the norms that governed the roles of men and women in their society. And among homosexuals, a more democratizing influence was exercised in sexual and affective relationships. Two important results of this encounter were the consolidation of the figure of the entendido, the homosexual who looked for egalitarian sexual relationships, and the valorization of the androgynous with regard to political positions. The strength of the latter was due in large part to the rigors of censorship in effect at that time, which predisposed the public to look for ciphered messages in the ambiguities of scripts and shows.

In terms of the entendido (or gay, as he is frequently known today), the former emphasis on roles determined by sexual behavior (who penetrates whom) was displaced by a more complex view of relationships. People were no longer defined as active or passive but rather as heterosexual or homosexual, thus questioning the validity of preestablished sexual roles. Very often, entendidos would even feel extremely ill at ease if forced to play such roles. In comparison to the old hierarchy captured by the expressions "active/passive" (*bofe/bicha*), where only the latter was stigmatized for having to serve his "macho," the new sexual categorization was essentially egalitarian (Fry 1982: 87). Both partners were considered equally "men" and deserving of all the respect and rights of masculine citizenship.

Despite the diffusion of this gay model, the active/passive dichotomy continues to be important even today, and it is widely used by the mass media. And even in homosexual environments, the *bicha pintosa* ("screaming queen") and the transvestite are discriminated against, and gay members of the middle class frequently try to highlight characteristics traditionally considered masculine, such as weight lifter's muscles, mustaches, and so on.

In addition to the homosexuals who frequent the ghetto, there are many individuals who are given to sexual practices with partners of the same sex but who pursue them in a more discreet—and often furtive—manner. Many of these adhere to the traditional and hierarchical categorization of homosexuality and even consider themselves heterosexuals. This occurs frequently, for example, among the male prostitutes who repudiate a homosexual identity, in part, due to their clientele's demands, who desire to see in the prostitutes the incarnation of a traditional ideal of "virility." Like transvestites, these exponents of the hierarchical model of sexual categorization also suffer the contempt of other homosexuals, including their clients, as much for the fact that they are "closeted" as for their social marginalization—they frequently rob or attack their clients. In many cases, the risk they represent is itself a source of the attraction they exert (Perlongher 1987).

Currently, as a result of widespread information with respect to the homosexual world, "closet" homosexuals can maintain long-distance contact with the new developments and the new values of the ghetto. Nevertheless, the ghetto continues to be a most important center for questioning, for devising innovative sexual practices, and for developing diverse ways of thinking about them.

One of the peculiarities of the new groups that formed the homosexual movement was the rejection of the terms *entendido* and *gay*; they opted instead to designate themselves as *bichas* ("faggots"). By proposing a newly militant and aware bicha, the idea was to try to drain the word, as well as the concept, of its negative connotations. To call oneself bicha became a way to assume a homosexuality considered more "conscious" than that of the gays and the entendidos and a way of obliging public opinion to reconsider its attitudes toward homosexuality in general. Later, other groups would adopt other strategies, as in the case of the Grupo Gay of Bahia, which adopted the North American term.

Lesbians showed a special interest in the reproduction of machista relationships between homosexuals. This question touched women closely for two reasons. First, within the so-called lesbian ghetto, the "active/passive" (*franchona/lady*) dichotomy was extremely accentuated; roles have always been the target of criticism and attempts at transformation by the women militants of organized homosexual groups. Second, the oppression exercised over women by men was very real. Feminism had been criticizing gender roles since the mid-1970s, and lesbians now started approaching feminist groups, despite initial rejection. As a result, lesbians struggled on two fronts: against dominator/dominated relationships between the sexes and against the reproduction of such roles in the homosexual environment.

Since the February 1979 debates at the University of São Paulo, a small segment of women had been attracted to the homosexual groups, although they remained in the minority. Lesbians did not initially plead for special treatment—after all, as I will show, an ideology of total equality prevailed within the homosexual movement. But they soon began to feel the need for at least a subgroup exclusively for women, where they could discuss their specific problems in greater depth. Issues specific to lesbians were difficult to address at meetings where gay men predominated. It was this perceived need that prompted lesbian activists to seek closer contact with the feminist groups active in São Paulo since the mid-1970s.

Among lesbian participants in the homosexual movement, a sharpened sensitivity to the subtleties of machismo resulted from this contact. Despite the ideology of equality, it became evident to lesbian activists that, even among homosexual militants, it was men who dominated group discussions and decision-making. Furthermore, women complained of the barely disguised misogyny in jokes and treatment by gay men. Especially irritating to them was the frequent use of the pejorative term *racha* ("slit") to designate any woman, as well as many men's habit of treating each other as if they themselves were women. Tensions increased, and shortly thereafter, lesbian participants took advantage of a quarrel among the men that threatened the cohesion of the SOMOS group and decided to opt for total autonomy. They founded the Lesbian-Feminist Action Group in May of 1980.

At about this time, the São Paulo police chief began a moralist crusade with the goal of "cleaning up" downtown by removing the prostitutes and homosexuals in that area. The methods were the same as always—lightning strikes at meeting sites, illegal imprisonment for the investigation of criminal or political antecedents, even in the case of people whose documents were in order, and the use of an extreme brutality, especially with prostitutes and transvestites. The homosexual movement reacted, and, activating its contacts with the feminist, black, and student movements, it promoted an unprecedented march through downtown São Paulo. Almost one thousand people heeded the call to protest—prostitutes, some members of the black movement, students, feminists, and, above all, a large contingent of homosexuals who set the tone for the event through the use of satirical and campy slogans.

Gibes and derision thus entered the political scenario, which was normally dominated by much more "serious" issues. And, against the criticism of more traditional sectors of the opposition, homosexual militants maintained that the use of camp reflected the profoundly subversive and anarchic nature of the homosexual experience, always disposed to question and ridicule the sacred values of the Left as much as those of the Right.

This march represented a kind of apotheosis of homosexual militancy in São Paulo, which thereafter had to deal with the serious problems of the extinction of the newspaper *Lampião*, the splintering of several groups, and the disappearance of others. Although *Lampião* had never claimed to be the mouthpiece of the movement and had always asserted the total autonomy of its editorial line, it served as a central reference point and spread news of the activities of groups throughout the country. A climate of discouragement and distrust seemed to set in as the movement's initial transformational project appeared less viable, and the movement found itself at a loss, with no idea of what course of action to follow next.

Due to the influence of its founders, who had strong anarchist leanings, SOMOS, from the beginning, placed itself against any hierarchical type of structure. It emphasized instead a utopian equality among its members, who even tried to negate the differences between the situation of the male homosexuals and that of the lesbians. As a result, a more informal power structure was formed, composed of those who could commit more time to the cause or those who had a better education, better speaking skills, greater beauty or popularity, and so on.

Because its very existence seemed to contradict the anarchist ideals professed by the group, this elite segment was often ignored or denied, although it exercised significant power. This informal power elite was originally composed of the founders of the group, who professed a vision of the world that could loosely be labeled "anarcho-individualist." But after some time, this elite began to see its influence challenged by subsequent arrivals. These individuals began to meet under the leadership of a militant from a Trotskyite group, Socialist Convergence, that, according to the members of the founding elite, sought to take over SOMOS and through it exercise influence over the homosexual population. This strategy would be executed, they said, through a sector of the party political organization called the Gay Faction of the Socialist Convergence, where the homosexual struggle was conceived of not as a priority but as subordinate to a more general class struggle.

These partisan interventions intensified the existing tensions among the members of SOMOS. Shortly after the first general meeting of Brazilian homosexual groups in 1980, when the women formalized their separation, a group of men also dissented. They allegedly wanted to reestablish the original principles of the group, which they claimed were being distorted by the excessive influence of Marxist militants.

In fact, a struggle for the control of SOMOS developed. The dissidents were those identified with the founding faction of the group, which had been losing its original position of control due to the rapid influx of new members. A series of accusations and quarrels ensued and were leaked to the press. This led to the departure of many militants in the two organizations and ultimately weakened homosexual militancy, robbing it of its capacity to excite and attract new followers.

These dissensions received much attention, and more emerged at the core of other homosexual groups. As a result, many of these groups were dissolved; the few that survived frequently promoted more specific demands within the wider context of the homosexual question.

Perhaps one of the most successful developments was the campaign to eliminate the code number 302.0 used by the Department of Social Welfare and Health, which classified homosexuality as a "mental deviation"—one of the only instances where homosexuality was officially discriminated against in Brazil. Homosexual groups mounted a petition drive throughout the country, marshaling the support not only of the homosexuals but also of many other people, including numerous outstanding personalities in the scientific, artistic, and political worlds.

Declarations of support were also obtained from scientific associations, such as the Brazilian Society of Anthropology. More than a simple bureaucratic measure, this move to abolish the code was an attempt to discuss and eliminate the pathological connotation frequently attributed to homosexuality. With the purpose of rethinking homosexual identity and fighting prejudice in all its aspects, the groups' general strategy was to make homosexuality much more visible to the population at large. This the militants achieved, clearly assisted by a climate of cultural challenge already in place at the time.

Movement, Community, and Identity

The 1970s witnessed, in various parts of the world, the growing importance of a "third way" for political activity. Abandoning dependence on traditional parties—of the Right as much as of the Left—new social movements emerged, with immediate purposes for the solution of specific problems. Such movements tend to have an expressive character, developing forms of experience and participation that are "lived" as positives in themselves.

Western Europe saw the development of the peace movement, movements for the defense of nature and the preservation of certain communities against the abuses of real estate speculation, and so on. In Latin America, labor organizations appeared, organized independently of (or even in opposition to) traditional unions and political parties. Urban and rural associations were organized with the support of radical Roman Catholic church groups, claiming the right to land for housing or for cultivation. Black and Indian movements were formed, determined to make themselves heard and to act at the political level alongside women's associations, feminist groups, human rights committees, and the like. This was the context within which the homosexual movement made its appearance.

Tilman Evers called attention to certain aspects common to all such political manifestations, arguing that they always experiment with new relationships in the spheres of life that are normally divided into "public" and "private." Such movements attempt to humanize public life in the sense of making it function according to norms and values more frequently found in private life. They seek to valorize the "private," to recognize its importance as a "political" topic to be discussed and thought of on an equal footing with the other, more "general" ones. As Evers himself said, all this constitutes much more of a "state of spirit" and a possible tendency than a real practice. Nevertheless, its effects on organizational practice are quite evident. The new movements attempted to form small groups based on interpersonal relationships and strove to make debates accessible and clear to all the members of the group. New forms of grass-roots democracy were experimented with, such as the imperative mandate, rotational representation, and a plebiscitary decisionmaking process. The new movements rejected any type of grandiose, anonymous, and bureaucratic structures, like the state, for example (Evers 1983: 34). The Brazilian homosexual and feminist groups exhibit several of these characteristics.

Similar values were manifested in the proposals of the newspaper *Lampião*, as much in the negation of commercial relationships intrinsic to consumerism as in the rejection of the "ready-made schemata" of the traditional Left. Instead, *Lampião* and the homosexual groups attempted to valorize perception and action at the individual level. Yet, despite *Lampião's* repudiation of the commercialization of human relations, it was disposed to defend prostitution, thereby discarding the sacredness of sexual activity—an apparent contradiction. *Lampião* preferred to investigate how, in fact, commercialized sexual relationships occurred, and it attempted to highlight their pleasurable aspects as well. This would constitute an attempt to favor individuals and not personifications, a characteristic also attributed to those movements by Evers.

The new forms of relationships and political participation that develop within contemporary social movements represent efforts to establish an egalitarian practice that is normally implicit in the notion of "community." As Ruth Cardoso showed, the construction of that egalitarian community does not come about because of the possession of common positive attributes but rather through a shared "lack" (*carência*) or oppression. In that way, a community can be perceived as an experience of equality. Differences that may exist among the participants, such as class differences, are de-emphasized (Cardoso 1983: 32).

Thus, SOMOS required that all its members exhibit the same identity of discrimination and, on various occasions, people who did not identify primarily as homosexuals were forced to leave SOMOS meetings. The equality promoted within the group was held as a fundamental value for all aspects of its members' lives. There was always an effort to neutralize any larger difference that emerged among them.

Although only partially successful, one of the central concerns of the group was to combat the consolidation of any type of hierarchy at its core. On several occasions, for example, even when confronted with the inefficiency of the system, the members of SOMOS reaffirmed the principle of rotating the coordinators of the subgroups, attempting to give everyone, even its less experienced members, a chance to assume positions of command. Nevertheless, this was not sufficient to prevent the crystallization of an informal leadership that, on certain occasions, used some of the supposedly libertarian aspects of the structure (such as the requirement of consensus) to avoid changes that would diminish the power of that elite.

One of the methods used to promote the feeling of community and of equality in need was the creation of consciousness-raising subgroups. Here, the life experiences of homosexuality were discussed publicly in great detail, with the declared goal of promoting a better understanding of their political significance. That process socialized individual experiences, helping to integrate what had been fragmented and enclosed in the limits of private life (see Durham 1984). As a result, participants established very intense and emotional relationships among themselves, and a strong identification among group members was created, frequently accompanied by feelings of euphoria and even of universal brother-hood, or *comunitas*.

Encountering difficulties in developing a sense of their own identity, due to the heterogeneity among homosexuals, movement participants had an easier time finding a counterpart to that identity, adopting for this the feminist concepts of "machista" or macho. Using machismo as their common enemy, homosexuals constructed for themselves a complementary identity: that of *bichas* ("faggots"). As the "macho" was also a counterpart to "feminists," these feminists, especially lesbian feminists, were also perceived to be very close to the homosexuals. The group's habit of agglomerating the men as well as the women of SOMOS in the category of bichas stemmed from this identification.

Nevertheless, certain differences could not be ignored for very long, and the absolute equality created by the homosexual condition was shattered by the notion of "double discrimination" (for example, that affecting individuals who were both homosexual *and* female or black), which served as a catalyst in the formation of new, more specific groups, such as GALF (Lesbian-Feminist Action) and the black gay group *Ade Dudu*. That segmentation was also cut across by affinity groups. These groups were connected by personal friendships, frequently based on joint participation in consciousness-raising groups or on other shared characteristics such as political orientation, level of education, preferred sexual practice, and so on.

Originally, gender differences within SOMOS were assigned little significance. That led to the initial dispersion of the few lesbian participants among the several subgroups "so that all could have the advantage of the feminist contributions." Not only were the women considered equal among themselves (they would all have contributions of the same value to make), they were also treated as if their needs were exactly the same as the men's and were given little opportunity to elaborate specifically lesbian demands. Racial differences were also glossed over. Although these were never discussed much in São Paulo, in Salvador, a largely black city, such racial differences later gave rise to the autonomous Ade Dudu group. This group intended to act within the homosexual movement as much as in the black movement, aiming to combat the racism manifested by the former and the endemic machismo of the latter.

As was already suggested, the members of SOMOS customarily designated themselves as bichas, under the pretext of emptying the word of its pejorative connotations. This form of treatment among equals, using a term that would normally be considered offensive if used by a heterosexual to refer to a homosexual, was already a commonplace practice in certain homosexual circles. Nevertheless, the attempt to generalize this practice to everyone encountered strong resistance from those who, despite defining themselves as homosexuals, refused the label *bicha*. For many, the term was synonymous with *bicha louca*, a type of homosexual who emphasized effeminate mannerisms and who was frequently scorned and discriminated against by those of a more masculine appearance. The women of the group became even more irritated when their female identity was submerged by the tendency of the men in SOMOS to refer to all members as bichas. After many protests against that practice, which was quite difficult to eradicate, the lesbians ended up leaving the group.

Another factor differentiating the group internally was the varying degree of public exposure that members were willing to face regarding their homosexuality. In contrast with the much more furtive posture of the traditional homosexual, who tried to hide his or her sexual orientation most of the time, modern homosexuals—inhabitants of large metropoles and protected by relative anonymity—can give themselves the luxury of being more open. Nevertheless, even these individuals feel the need to take certain precautions, especially in situations where anonymity is less possible: at work, at the place of study, or, at times, in the residential neighborhood. Carmen Guimarães gave us examples of that manipulation of sexual identity, contrasting the Brazilian situation to that in the United States, where it is more common for homosexuals to feel the need to be open about their homosexuality in all situations, twenty-four hours a day. Although SOMOS had never explicitly adopted a policy of being "out" at any cost, entering the group, in practice, implied one's homosexual identity. The possibility of being called on to act publicly, to appear at demonstrations carrying signs or giving interviews intimidated many who preferred to be more discreet. These individuals consequently did not enter the group, in order to avoid exposing themselves too much.

A group such as SOMOS, which placed great emphasis on the idea that the "private" was also the "political" and should be discussed in public, became especially vulnerable to disaggregation. And because one of the basic principles of this type of organization was the outright refusal of any type of hierarchy or democratic centralism, there was no formal power that could mediate between factions in dispute. This frequently led to a rupture in the feeling of equality and belonging to one community.

Once such a sentiment is broken, groups may break up and their members disperse or form new groupings. These new groups might then establish alliances with former enemies and quarrel with former allies. Thus, the exit of the lesbians from SOMOS may be understood not only as an affirmation of political differences but also as a realignment of groups with similar affinities. The importance of personal factors may be perceived there, reinforcing the affective aspect in the internal processes of differentiation and identification.

In any case, SOMOS found itself overtaken in 1980 by a series of cleavages that outlined different groups of political interests and personal affinities. The instability of the whole was increased by the fact that there was no objective or very precise antagonist to the militant homosexual in Brazil. In contrast to the situation in the United States, here there was no legislation to be fought, and police repression against homosexuals tended to be sporadic and asystematic.

In the absence of a great, clearly defined external enemy against whom to fight, the field of disputes among homosexual groups ended up being limited to the inter- and intragroup relationships. Perhaps the most perceptible external enemies for these groups were the institutionalized political parties and the Marxist-Leninist organizations. This is because the latter had different organizational practices and methods and acted in the same oppositional field, competing, in many cases, directly with the new alternative movements, as Evers suggested.

In the case under study, this conflict occurred sharply with the Socialist Convergence and especially with its Gay Faction, which sought to apply the most traditional Leninist schema to the mobilization of the homosexuals. For SOMOS, the emphasis that group gave to the construction of a workers' party was intolerable, with its constant reference to class struggle implicitly taken as a "greater" struggle, where sexual repression served to maintain the passivity of response to the political-economic structure. After all, for many members of SOMOS, the reverse was probably the more correct view, where the political parties themselves would be perceived to be the promoters of the repression of pleasure.

The departure of the lesbians from SOMOS, which simply formalized an already existing differentiation between men and women that was more or less accepted within the group, was legitimatized by the same arguments of "specificity of struggle" (especifidade) used by homosexual militants in general. Nevertheless, quarrels among the men, where differences were more difficult to delineate, were justified by the dissidents as stemming from the interference of the Socialist Convergence, which purportedly had brainwashed those who had remained in the group. This accusation and its corollary, the loss of autonomy that SOMOS would suffer, provoked a violent polemic that lasted many months and that, at the level of personal relationships, ended up destroying or rocking several old friendships. To differentiate such similar groups, it was necessary to resort to what was deemed the worst possible accusation—the identification with groups of the traditional Left.

The rigid adherence to a homosexual identity on the part of its militants served to delineate the boundaries of the so-called homosexual movement, establishing a differentiation in relation to other liberation groups interested in altering the traditional Brazilian way of dealing with sexuality. The community and the strong affective ties uniting the homosexual militants also had the effect of separating them from the rest of the population given to homosexual practices. This occurred despite the fact that the "conscious homosexual"—as the militant conceived himself—was little more than a politicized version of the entendido who is today one of the most common visitors to the ghetto. The latter, as I mentioned earlier, rejected the traditional hierarchical classification of homosexuals as "active" or "passive" (*bofes* or *bichas*), favoring a more egalitarian concept.

Homosexuals who insisted on the old stereotype of the bicha were sometimes criticized for their way of speaking, their extravagant clothes, their "sole preoccupation with sex," and their "passive" sexual behavior, although they could also be admired for facing society's prejudice head on. But among the entendidos, as well as among a large part of the founding members of SOMOS, the notion prevailed that, apart from their sexual preference, homosexuals did not differ from the other people who surrounded them. The practice of "passing," or the concealment of one's homosexuality, was common at work, in family relationships, or with less intimate acquaintances. Nevertheless, the need to adopt a strategy of passing in itself became a disagreeable burden that, in certain cases, led individuals not only to conceal their sexual preferences but to simulate a heterosexual life, inventing girl- or boyfriends and fiancé(e)s. Many in SOMOS felt that this was a dishonest strategy. Even among those who adopted passing as a frequent strategy, it was generally preferred to let others presume a nonexplicit heterosexuality than to lie directly about false heterosexual experiences.

In addition to passing, other strategies are available to help individuals deal with characteristics that make them stigmatizable. One of the most effective, in many cases, is voluntary revelation, frequently perceived as a more honest and more dignified approach. Although the element of choice is not always present (in some cases, dissimulation is impossible), this is the basis of many minority movements. In the case of homosexuals, this led to a curious ambivalence in the attitude toward those who were very blatant. Sometimes, they were criticized for "being too exaggerated," for "only being concerned with sex," or for "reproducing sexual roles," and so on; in other cases, they were praised for their "courage" and for "assuming" their homosexuality.

For a great number of people who identify themselves as homosexuals, the possibility of passing as heterosexual is a reality and may be a constant practice. This brings more difficulties for the organization of a homosexual community. In such circumstances, one might expect considerable emphasis to be placed on coming out or, better, that the homosexual identity be held as the main truth about the individual, which may be a general tendency of our culture, as pointed out by Michel Foucault. According to him, the question of sex became, from the eighteenth century on, the basis for the constitution of knowledge of the subject and the source of its "truth" (Foucault 1979: 68).

For that same reason, in addition to the concept of homosexuality as an option, there was still the predominant notion that the homosexual identity was anchored in some immutable "essence" that was of congenital origin or acquired very early in life. That view, which was theoretically elaborated in the nineteenth century, became more and more widespread; eventually, it constituted a type of "common sense," at least among the more cultured levels of Brazilian society, including the middle-class homosexual inhabitants of large metropoles.

In *Lampião* articles, an ambiguity clearly appeared regarding the nature of homosexuality. At one moment, *Lampião* defended its legitimacy, claiming full rights of citizenship for homosexuals; at another, it praised the challenging aspects of its marginality. To emphasize the virtue of this challenge, it became important to highlight its conscious aspect, thus promoting the rejection of the notion that individuals are in some way preprogrammed with regard to their sexual orientation. This, together with the consciousness of the problems already caused by medical determinism that presented homosexuality as pathological, also engendered a refusal to speculate on the supposed etiology of homosexuality. The individualism of homosexuals and their supposed autonomy in the face of great social pressure were considered their greatest gifts, making them "undigestible" to the system. Many articles advocated a sharpening of the differences between individuals and instituted normality in order to "turn the tables" and "invent Utopia," that is, to make a "revolution for pleasure."

Thus, on the one hand, the construction of a collective homosexual identity was made difficult by the emphasis on the irreducible individuality of each person. But, on the other hand, to emphasize that the homosexual was already endowed with a predefined sexual preference was important in establishing a field in which a collective identity could be constructed.

As a corollary to his or her social marginality, the homosexual was idealized as eminently antiauthoritarian. This view of the essentially democratic nature of homosexuality had been manifest in the first document produced by the São Paulo group in 1978—its letter of protest against the way in which the press portrayed homosexuals. Homosexuality, according to this document, threatened the power retained by certain groups in society by challenging "the ideology where one being (the male) dominates another (the female) for a sole end (reproduction)." One can see here, in exemplary form, the political elaboration of the emerging egalitarian vision of homosexuality, wherein the old hierarchical model of relationships based on the different expectations of the roles attributed to the "active" and "passive" partner was rejected once and for all. The group contributed to the construction of a new homosexual identity and, through its activism and access to the media, helped legitimatize it as "politically correct" and to broadcast it throughout society.

Uniting with feminists in their rejection of the inadequacies of Marxist theory to account for sexual questions, homosexual militants, although they still knew little of the details of feminist theory, adopted some of the feminists' antihierarchical organizational methods and certain concepts, such as machismo and patriarchy. Nevertheless, the most marked feature of the Brazilian homosexual movement's philosophical posture perhaps may be considered an exacerbated individualism.

As a result, within SOMOS, the rejection of any hierarchical or more restrictive organizational structure was considered essential to preserve the individuality of its members. This was reflected in the emphasis given to linking politics and pleasure and the tendency to reject any type of "taskism" that justified disagreeable jobs in the name of the common good. During the crisis that led to the schism of SOMOS, one of the most bruising accusations that could be made against the group was to say its meetings were becoming boring.

Another aspect of that hedonistic individualism of homosexuals is the valorization of their permanent sexual availability. This characteristic, found especially among male homosexuals but also present among lesbians, was reflected in the proclamations of Lampião and in the casual attitude with which sexual relationships were viewed within SOMOS. Questioning all types of authoritarianism or reproduction of roles, members rejected monogamy, and casual sex and one-night stands were encouraged because they were thought to exclude feelings of possessiveness or jealousy. This view of sex was, in fact, more accentuated within the group than in the ghetto, where fidelity was a requirement in many relationships that purported to be stable. These, though, were relatively few, and the organized homosexuals, as well as the nonorganized ones, generally understood the possibility of promiscuity to be one of the important aspects of sexual liberty. In that regard, homosexual men do not appear to be very different from heterosexuals in Brazil. Lesbians, on the other hand, frequently value monogamy more, but even so, those who participated in the homosexual movement also began to develop a less committed sexual behavior. This frequently led to their being considered "easy" by other lesbians who were not organized.

In fact, though this individualism was quite widespread in the homosexual population, SOMOS's attempt to give it political meaning and to accommodate it to the precepts of an organized militancy and a community ideal was incomprehensible to the vast majority of those who frequented the ghetto. The latter exhibited considerable distrust of any political activity and of the posture of superiority sometimes adopted by the militants. Although homosexual activists never formally declared themselves the vanguard of homosexuals, such a position was, nevertheless, frequently assumed in informal conversations. There were many complaints of alienated bichas who did not appreciate the efforts of the militants. A certain disdain for the nonorganized homosexuals also seeped into their designation as such and into their classification as being "ghettoized" or "closeted."

Though originally conceived as evidence of progress in sexual relations, the homosexual egalitarian identity itself (also called "gay" or "entendido" identity) began to be questioned in the second half of the eighties. Some alleged, for example, that this new identity would contribute to a new standardization and territorialization of deviant sexualities. As defenders of this identity, homosexual militants were now seen to be playing a conservative role. However, a more attentive study of the development of that new gay identity reveals that it is not static but rather is endowed with historicity and changes.

A study of the entendidos of Rio de Janeiro in the mid-1970s showed that those men still felt a need to assert their masculinity in a society that, by pushing homosexuals underground, kept itself almost entirely ignorant about them and was content to equate homosexuality with the desire to play the role appropriate to the opposite gender (Guimarães 1977). Some years later, as homosexuality became one of the main themes diffused by mass media, the public was familiarized with the tangle of the gay world. The entendidos of today feel free of the need to constantly reaffirm their masculinity and, on certain occasions, may give themselves the luxury of participating with the other "bofes," "bichas," "homosexual militants," "gays," "real men," "real women," *sapatonas* ("butches"), and so on in the "carnivalization" of gender roles so popular among Brazilians.

Even in the early days, when SOMOS was still intent on educating the public, spreading a "normal" image of homosexuals, there was much toying with the question of gender roles, and camping was constantly resorted to, both in the promotion of group solidarity and as political defiance. In fact, such was the ridicularization of the traditional rigidity of gender roles (reflected, for example, in the use of the term *bicha* with grammatical agreement in the feminine, as a form of self-designation by the men of the group) that it even led newly recruited militants to criticize what they considered a stereotypical representation of homosexuality. However, after attending meetings for some weeks and taking part in discussions of sexuality, those same individuals often adopted more tolerant attitudes toward the immense spectrum of possible variations in the homosexual role. This differentiated new militants from others who frequented the ghetto, where far more traditional patterns of behavior prevailed—in effeminate behavior as much as in circumspection and dignity.

SOMOS militants formed a fairly sui generis group, different from the frequenters of the ghetto and distinct from other political militants. Their libertarian manner of organizing also served to differentiate them from the other homosexuals with militant experiences in more traditional opposition groups. These individuals could not understand the anarchy of the SOMOS meetings, the disrespect with which concepts that were nearly sacred to the Left (such as class struggle) were treated, and the total lack of precision with respect to the objectives of the group and the ways in which these might be achieved. This is how the differences were established, for example, between members of SOMOS and the Gay Faction of the Socialist Convergence.

A large number of ghetto frequenters, accustomed to considering the opening of new commercial establishments to cater to the homosexual public as "victories for the cause," did not understand the reservations SOMOS militants had against the integration of homosexuals into consumer society. The militants perceived the homosexual question as a fuse for a more encompassing social revolution, but the nonorganized tended to think of it more in terms of civil rights to be conquered within the existing social structure.

Many studies of the new urban social movements have pointed out that though these movements declare the elimination of certain deprivations as their principal objective, they end up considering the simple maintenance of the group to be their main aim. In feminist and homosexual groups, for example, long meetings took place without preestablished goals and ended without arriving at any decision. And in many cases, "political" meetings acquired a purely affective and social function. Similarly, the interruption of theoretical discussions for deliberations on the private lives of the participants was frequent.

Another constant characteristic was the emphasis on the importance of the private aspects of the lives of the militants, for whom participation in these movements was perceived to be a form of personal enrichment or achievement, in contrast with the "massification" that occurred in the external world. It is common to hear reports about this type of participation in terms that recall the effects of religious conversions. In the case of groups concerned with homosexual militancy, which are greatly focused on the sexual and affective problems of their members, this dimension acquires an even greater importance. Many of their members declared that they were searching for a group with the main intention of finding new friends and maybe even a lover. As a result, despite its initial success, it was inevitable that SOMOS should lose much of its attraction, once the news got around of its internal quarrels and of the alleged takeover by the Socialist Convergence.

Still another frequently mentioned aspect of new social movements is that, through the definition of new needs, they make claims for new rights. SOMOS promoted the idea that everyone had the right to pleasure and to sexual gratification, regardless of whether the object of his or her desire was a member of the opposite sex. Thus, SOMOS demanded that the state recognize the Gay Group of Bahia and Rio de Janeiro's Pink Triangle Group as openly homosexual legal entities. The recognition of homosexuality as a legitimate sexual expression and the repeal of its classification as a "sexual deviation and disturbance" in the code of diseases of the state health department were also achieved. Even the portrayal of homosexuality in the press could change if the media's code of ethics were followed. In 1986, thanks to the initiative of SOMOS militants, that code was changed to include among the acts prohibited to journalists "that of being party to the practice of persecution or discrimination for reasons of a social, political, religious, or racial nature, sex or sexual orientation."

Less successful, yet reflecting a change of attitudes on the part of important segments of the population, was the ephemeral victory achieved by the Rio group Pink Triangle and its tireless vice president. Thanks to his efforts and persistence, in the first project of the new Brazilian constitution, elaborated by the Systematization Commission in July of 1987, sexual orientation was listed among the unacceptable reasons for prejudicial treatment. Nevertheless, in the constitution's final version, the term was again removed. Such a provision was, however, included in the municipal constitution of Salvador, Bahia, São Paulo, and two other cities, giving a legal basis for the actions of the homosexual militants of those urban centers.

It is sometimes said that though movements such as Christian base communities or residents' associations can exert influence due to their sheer numbers, others with a smaller number of supporters, like feminists (and homosexuals can also be included here), influence political and social life through elite resources, such as political parties, the media, and cultural institutions (Viola and Mainwaring 1987: 140). Today, the discussion of homosexuality is generalized in Brazil, based on a more informed and less prejudicial comprehension. But at a certain moment, the diffusion of new attitudes and practices was immensely facilitated by the existence of individuals or organizations prepared to express them. Without these interlocutors who served as catalysts for the new tendencies, the press, for example, would have had greater difficulty in dealing with the homosexual question in a positive way. Similarly, at the universities, where the subject has been attracting much interest, the new social approach was strongly legitimatized by the inclusion of the homosexual struggle under the topic of urban social movements and by the numerous lectures, debates, and events promoted by homosexual intellectuals and artists.

The effectiveness of homosexual groups is undeniable in several ways. Perhaps the principal one has been the construction of friendship networks uniting (and also promoting) a new type of homosexual, who is not dominated by feelings of guilt and who does not consider him- or herself ill or abnormal. Even after the openly militant activities ceased, those networks survived, and, in numerous cases, they have been crucial to the lives of many of their participants, influencing their choices of dwelling, work, leisure activities, and political options.

Currently, with the tragic outbreak of AIDS that has principally affected homosexuals, the importance of those networks and of the adoption of a homosexual identity has been underlined; both are essential for a better administration of the crisis.

In 1983, when AIDS began to manifest itself in Brazil and especially in São Paulo, some of the old militants met again to debate measures to be taken to combat the syndrome, which was then still considered "a gay plague." They contacted medical authorities of the recently installed democratic state administration. This mobilization revealed that: (1) increasingly sharp contours of a gay identity were being outlined among the sectors of the population involved in homosexual practices in São Paulo and (2) although homosexuals were willing to review their sexual habits, they refused to give up some of the conquests of the recent years, such as greater tolerance on the part of society and the space in which to live a more open and accepted sexuality (Silva 1986).

Thanks to these contacts, the first official program for the prevention and treatment of AIDS in the country was then established. It was directed by doctors who were generally committed to a respectful position and sympathetic to the population with homosexual practices. This greater acceptance was also facilitated by the past actions of the militants, who had made homosexuality more respectable and legitimate and thereby enabled political, medical, or academic authorities to declare their support without many constraints.

In an underdeveloped society like Brazil's, public health services are inevitably precarious, and thus the performance of government organizations becomes very important in supporting and supervising them. In recent years, there has been an upsurge of new groups—largely formed by homosexuals (and frequently the old militants of the gay movement)—that propose to unite family, friends, and AIDS victims, irrespective of their sexual orientation. In addition to the fact that they were structured on the friendship networks established during the days of militancy, these groups have frequently cited episodes of that militancy as instructive experiences or points of reference, even if only experiences to be avoided.

In sum, one can say that, despite the fact that it drew on a minority segment of the population whose aspirations and way of life have been severely stigmatized in almost all sectors of society, SOMOS was very similar in organization and development to numerous other social movement groups focused on promoting political change. Thus, like them, SOMOS also exhibited important deficiencies: a reduced number of militants and a general unpreparedness for political action, especially at a broader level, that was less related to its specific demands. The dictatorship favored a simplistic Manichaeism, where political forces could be divided between the existing regime and the opposition, but the gradual installation of a more pluralistic order brought new difficulties for all these movements. The reorganization of the party system was quite divisive, generating, for example, schisms at inter- and intragroup levels (see Cardoso, Chapter 16). The state itself has been refining its strategy vis-à-vis civil society, thus increasing its power to co-opt sectors that form the basis of these movements. Certainly, such movements are incapable of transforming Brazil into a democratic society by themselves, but their importance in the cultural realm should not be belittled, especially in promoting the renewal of the values at the base of their ideologies, discourses, and political practices.

For its part, SOMOS, like other manifestations of the Brazilian homosexual movement, encountered its greatest difficulties and challenges precisely because of its aspiration to build a more egalitarian society. The homosexual movement hoped to expand the limits of tolerance for diversity, and it examined generally accepted notions of sexuality and gender roles. Emphasizing the playful and the noncomformist, the movement questioned the "naturalness" of social relationships and celebrated the sovereignty of the individual, promoting libertarianism explicitly in its demands as well as implicitly in its ideals of nonhierarchical organization.

Part 3
Articulating Strategies and Democratizing Democracy

12

Feminisms in Latin America: From Bogotá to San Bernardo

Nancy Saporta Sternbach
Marysa Navarro-Aranguren
Patricia Chuchryk
Sonia E. Alvarez

Introduction

In the last decade, North American and Western European feminist scholars have become increasingly aware of Latin American women and their political activism. Yet this awareness has by no means dispelled the once prevalent notion in the United States that Latin American women do not consider themselves feminists, a notion that has been reinforced recently by texts that fall within the domain of "testimonial" literature and by research focusing on women's participation in grass-roots movements and in national liberation struggles, rather than on feminism.[1] Additionally, North American feminists are frequently heard to comment that "feminism is not appropriate for Latin America," a comment that in our view reflects unfamiliarity with the contemporary reality of Latin American women.[2] As recent research has shown and as we shall argue in this chapter, not only is feminism appropriate for Latin America but it also is the kind of thriving, broad-based social movement that many other feminist movements are still aspiring to become.

The assumption that Latin American women do not define themselves as feminists ironically mirrors the stance adopted by much of the Latin American Left in the mid-1970s when the first stirrings of second-wave feminist voices were heard. At that time, Latin American feminists were dismissed as upper-middle-class women who were concerned with issues that were irrelevant to the vast majority of women throughout the region. Some Latin Americans, both women and men, contended that the absence of a movement of continental proportions was not surprising because feminism was the product of contradictions existing in highly industrialized countries but not in underdeveloped societies. Others argued that a movement for women's liberation was unnecessary because liberation could be achieved only through socialism, and once firmly established, it would eliminate women's oppression. And all agreed with the widely held notion that Latin American feminists were small groups of misguided petites bourgeoises, disconnected from the reality of the continent; women who had thoughtlessly adopted a fashion, like others had done with jeans or the miniskirt, without realizing that in so doing *le hacían el juego al imperialismo yanqui* ("they were tools of Yankee imperialism"). In Chile, some sectors of the Left have even asserted that *El Poder Femenino*, a right-wing women's organization that partici-pated in the downfall of the democratic government of Salvador Allende, was a feminist movement.[3]

In the last decade, however, Latin American feminist movements or feminisms have grown steadily and undergone profound transformations, emerging today at the very center of international feminist debates. In some cases, their movements have continually challenged oppressive regimes (e.g., Chile); in others, they have achieved recognition from their governments (e.g., Nicaragua, Brazil). In still others, the concurrent battles of women's and people's liberation (e.g., Honduras, El Salvador, and Guatemala) give us new definitions of what it is to be a feminist.

In this chapter, we sketch a general picture of the political trajectory of Latin American feminisms during the 1970s and 1980s.[4] It is, of course, difficult, if not dangerous, to generalize across countries in a region as diverse as Latin America when discussing any sociopolitical phenomenon. But here, for heuristic and analytical purposes, we will view feminist development in Latin America and the Caribbean as a whole by examining the regionwide feminist *Encuentros* convened biannually since 1981.[5] Held in Bogotá, Colombia (1981), Lima, Peru (1983), Bertioga, Brazil (1985), Taxco, Mexico (1987), and San Bernardo, Argentina (1990), these meetings can serve as historical markers, highlighting the key strategic, organizational, and theoretical debates that have characterized the political trajec-tory of contemporary Latin American feminisms.

Attended by grass-roots and professional feminist activists alike from through-out Latin America and the Caribbean, the Encuentros have provided critical forums in which participants could share experiences as well as measure their respective countries' progress in relation to a continental movement. A close look at the principal issues and debates manifest during each of these Encuentros will enable us to view the landscape of contemporary feminisms in the Latin American region, albeit very broadly.

Latin American nations are plagued by chronic economic and political crises. In all countries, feminist groups must make heroic efforts to stay afloat organiza-tionally amid staggering national debts, painful austerity plans, and dramatic political changes. In this context, the Encuentros provide feminist activists with periodic forums wherein they can gain theoretical and strategic insights as well as sisterly support from feminists in other nations struggling to overcome analo-gous organizational and theoretical predicaments. Moreover, the core issues debated at each of the Encuentros have had significant repercussions within movement groups in individual countries, sometimes foregrounding and even defusing potential areas of ideological and organizational conflict before these have fully played themselves out in that particular national setting. The decision to center our analysis on the Encuentros, then, stems from the belief, shared by many feminists in Latin America, that these regional meetings have been crucial to the development of Latin American feminist theory and practice. Encuentro documents have been widely disseminated among feminists throughout the region. Although not all the issues raised and ideological struggles waged at the Encuentros have precise counterparts in every national context, the Encuentros nonetheless have served as springboards for the development of a common Latin American feminist political language and as staging grounds for often contentious political battles over what would constitute the most efficacious strategies for achieving gender equality in dependent, capitalist, and patriarchal states.

The analysis presented in this chapter also draws on our own experiences as Latin Americanists and feminists who have done research on women's movements in at least six Latin American countries. We have all been involved in at least two Latin American feminist Encuentros; two of us have participated in three, and one of us has attended all five. We are one U.S. woman, one Vasca/Española/ Latinoamericana, one Canadian woman, and one Latina/Cubana. Although each of us feels she has experienced the richness and diversity of Latin American feminism individually, the scope of our collective experience motivated us to write this chapter. In it, we also try to include some of the perspectives of the hundreds of Latin American women with whom we have talked and worked over these years—women who define themselves as feminists. Collectively, we represent the humanities and the social sciences, a collaboration that provides a uniquely interdisciplinary approach to our understanding and discussion of Latin American feminisms. Among us, we teach literature, history, sociology, political science, Latin American studies, and women's studies. All of us teach and write about Latin American women on a regular basis.

The purpose of this chapter is not only to trace the growth of Latin American feminisms in the last decade but also to dispel the myth that Latin American women do not define themselves as feminists. From our observation, not only is the Latin American model unique in its organization of women but it also has garnered a political base that could, and most certainly should, be the envy of feminists elsewhere.[6]

The questions we address are: What is distinctive about Latin American feminisms? And what can we learn from them? To contextualize our discussion of the Encuentros themselves, we begin with a brief overview of the emergence and early development of feminisms in Latin America. We then discuss the first four Encuentros, emphasizing their significance for the theory and practice of feminism in the region. We closely examine what transpired at the fourth Encuentro, in Taxco in October 1987, as a turning point in the movement, so as to delve more deeply into the contemporary political conjuncture—the principal organizational and strategic issues and dilemmas faced by Latin American feminisms in the late 1980s and early 1990s. Finally, we present a brief discussion of the most recent Encuentro, held in San Bernardo in November 1990 and end with our conclusions about feminisms in Latin America.

The Genesis of Late Twentieth-Century Feminisms
in Latin America

Paradoxically, feminism emerged during one of the most somber decades in Latin American history. During the 1970s (and, in some cases, the 1960s), military regimes and nominal democracies alike crushed progressive movements of all sorts, "disappeared" thousands of people, and unleashed the repressive apparatus of the state on civil society—all in the name of national security. Contemporary feminisms in Latin America were therefore born as intrinsically oppositional movements.

From the moment the first feminist groups appeared in the mid-1970s, many Latin American feminists therefore not only challenged patriarchy and its paradigm of male domination—the militaristic or counterinsurgency state—but also joined forces with other opposition currents in denouncing social, economic, and political oppression and exploitation. Thus, the realities of both state repression and class warfare were instrumental in shaping a Latin American feminist praxis distinct from that of feminist movements elsewhere. For example, from the beginning, feminists in countries ruled by military regimes unveiled the patriarchal foundations of state repression, militarism, and institutionalized violence, a stance that was gradually adopted more generally by Latin American feminists.

Whereas male analysts stressed the cultural or economic determinants of the militarization of civilian rule and the entrenchment of modern military dictatorships in the 1970s,[7] feminists argued that such politics are also rooted in the authoritarian foundations of patriarchal relations, in the so-called private sphere: the family, male-female relations, and the sexual oppression of women.[8] Authoritarianism, feminists proclaimed, represented the "highest form" of patriarchal oppression. As one Latin American feminist, referring to Chile, has declared: "The Junta, with a very clear sense of its interests, has understood that it must reinforce the traditional family, and the dependent role of women, which is reduced to that of mother. The dictatorship, which institutionalizes social inequality, is founded on inequality in the family."[9]

Under both civilian and military rule, traditional conceptions of women's roles and impassioned appeals to "Western Christian family values" were, indeed, at the core of national security ideology, counterinsurgency, and regressive social policies. But a wide gap separated the state's discourse on gender and the family from the reality of women's lives. While official discourse extolled the virtues of traditional womanhood, regressive economic policies thrust millions of women into the work force. Furthermore, female victims of state repression were brutalized, sexually violated and humiliated, and subjected to abuse that was hardly consonant with the military's ideological exaltation of femininity and its quintessential incarnation, motherhood.[10] By the late 1970s, in countries ruled by civilians and military men alike, reactionary social and political policies sparked widespread opposition movements; women of all social classes defied their historical exclusion from things political and joined the opposition in unprecedented numbers. In Peru in the early 1980s, for example, working-class women were in the vanguard of grass-roots survival struggles that increasingly challenged the social and economic policies of the conservative civilian Belaúnde Terry administration.[11] Similarly, during the 1970s in military-ruled Argentina, Chile, Uruguay, and Brazil, women enlisted massively in the opposition's struggle for democracy and became known internationally for their participation in human rights struggles.[12]

In the early part of the 1970s, at least, much of the opposition to oligarchical democracy and military authoritarianism came from the left of the political spectrum. As in North America (Canada and the United States) and Western Europe, then, second-wave Latin American feminism was born of the "New Left."[13] But, because the progressive opposition was male-dominated and its practice sexist, women and "their issues" were invariably relegated to a secondary position within Latin American progressive and revolutionary movements. Feminist consciousness was thus fueled by multiple contradictions experienced by women active in guerrilla movements or militant organizations, forced to go into exile, and involved in student movements, politicized academic organizations, and progressive political parties.[14] The prototypical early Latin American feminist activist in many countries was a former radical student militant or *guerrillera* and hardly a self-obsessed bourgeois "lady," as many of the Left would have us believe. However, unlike North American radical feminists, Latin American feminists retained a commitment to radical change in social relations of production—as well as reproduction—while continuing to struggle against sexism within the Left. That is, although feminism in many countries broke with the Left organizationally, it did not fully do so ideologically.

The alliance with progressive sectors of the opposition, though uneasy at best, was essential to the viability of the feminist project. In countries ruled by exclusionary and repressive regimes (hardly disposed to grant concessions to movements pursuing progressive change of any kind), feminists could find political space only within the larger opposition struggle. Many early feminist groups functioned clandestinely; some were formed as "front" groups for the left-wing opposition; others avoided the term *feminist*, forming "women's associations" and taking refuge in the age-old belief that anything women do is "by nature" apolitical and therefore less threatening to "national security." As economic crises and cuts in social welfare threatened the very survival of Latin America's "popular" classes,[15] many feminists joined the Left in seeking solutions to the absolute impoverishment of the vast majority of the region's people.

The legacy of the Left weighed heavily on Latin American feminism during the early years of the movement, an inheritance that led early feminists to privilege class over gender struggle and, in the Marxist tradition, to focus on women's work and on women's integration or incorporation into the public world of politics and production. The Guevarist/Leninist legacy also led early feminists to view themselves as the vanguard of what was to become a mass-based, cross-class, revolutionary women's movement.

The "rearguard," in this view, was to be made up of the hundreds of working-class women's groups then proliferating throughout much of Latin America.[16] Economic crises impelled working-class women to devise creative, collective survival strategies. Often under the tutelage of the Catholic church and the male Left, women's groups formed at the neighborhood level to provide the basic necessities of life, a responsibility consistent with women's traditionally defined roles. In keeping with their socially ascribed responsibilities as "wives, mothers, and nurturers" of family and community, women have taken the lead in the day-to-day resistance strategies of Latin America's popular classes. In every country in the region, women have participated disproportionately in movements to secure better urban services, to protest the rising cost of living, and to secure health care and education for their children. Torture, disappearances, and other forms of political repression also united women of all social classes to organize human rights movements.[17]

In Latin America, both these types of movements are commonly referred to as *movimientos de mujeres* ("women's movements") or *movimientos femeninos* ("feminine movements").[18] Contemporary Latin American feminists, then, form but one part of a larger, multifaceted, socially and politically heterogeneous women's movement. And in most Latin American countries, feminists initially prioritized working with poor and working-class women active in that larger movement, helping women organize community survival struggles while fostering consciousness of how gender roles shaped their political activism.

For fear of alienating this potential mass base, many early feminists shunned doing political work on, or even discussing, "classic" feminist issues such as sexuality, reproduction, violence against women, or power relations in the family. An additional deterrent was the fear of losing legitimacy in the eyes of their "macho-Leninist" comrades-in-struggle. In the view of these comrades, only two kinds of feminism existed: a good one, which privileged the class struggle and could therefore assume its "rightful" place within the ranks of the revolutionary opposition, and a bad one, which supposedly was "one more instance of ideological imperialism"—an imported, bourgeois, man-hating feminism that had no place in Latin America.[19]

Still today, in many popular women's organizations linked to the progressive Catholic church or the secular Left, women are continually admonished against adopting "bad" feminist beliefs, such as abortion rights and the right to sexual self-determination, as these are seen as intrinsically bourgeois and likely to "divide" the united struggle of the working class. It is significant, then, that many grass-roots women's groups are sponsored or controlled by the church or the Left as, together with the mainstream media, male religious and secular activists have tergiversated and misrepresented the meaning and character of feminism, often deliberately blocking the development of a critical gender consciousness among the participants of the *movimientos de mujeres*. This, in many cases, explains the reticence of women in "popular" organizations to embrace the feminist label even when they espouse feminist beliefs. That is, this reluctance is not a "natural" outcome of their class position.

Partly in response to their leftist interlocutors, feminists in the region were careful to emphasize the specifically Latin American dimension of their banners. The problem of women's health, for example, is not only a question of controlling one's body; feminists insist that it also includes an understanding of how international organizations and multinational corporations determine national health and population policies in their countries. As for the campaign against sexual violence, it must have a different dimension in Latin America because in many countries, women political prisoners have been systematically subjected to sexual torture.[20]

Moreover, many Latin American feminists see their movement as part of the continent's struggle against imperialism. As one feminist explained, imperialism controls "biological reproduction which favors [imperialism's] economic and political interests in Latin America through its need to retain domestic work for material reproduction and for the survival of the whole system."[21] Yet not all groups enthusiastically espouse the anti-imperialist stand, nor do they make a point of calling themselves Socialist-feminists.

Feminism, in Latin America as elsewhere, has taken a wide variety of organizational forms and has combatted women's oppression in the full range of political, economic, and cultural arenas in which patriarchal domination is embedded. But again, the distinctive Latin American context of economic dependence, exploitation, and political repression gave rise to feminist political projects centered at the intersection of gender oppression with other more local forms of exploitation and domination. In Brazil, for example, the first contemporary feminist organizations paid only minimal attention to the "inward-oriented" activities—such as consciousness-raising—so central to early feminists in the United States and Europe. During much of the 1970s, Brazilian feminists instead focused their energies on "outward-oriented" activities in an effort to spread the feminist message to women of the popular classes, to link feminism to other progressive forces, and to relate women's struggles to the society's struggle against military rule. Feminists published women's newspapers that were made available to working-class women's groups in the urban periphery; they collaborated closely with women in the human rights movement and in the community survival struggles; they organized women's congresses to recruit ever larger numbers of women to the feminist cause; and they actively promoted the organization of women of the popular classes.

Over time, feminists found at least two reasons to challenge the Left's notion of good and bad feminisms. First, in working with women of the popular classes, feminists learned that so-called taboo issues such as sexuality, reproduction, or violence against women *were* interesting and important to working-class women— as crucial to their survival as the bread-and-butter issues emphasized by the male opposition. In fact, as will become amply evident from our discussion of the Encuentros, many working-class, black, and Indian women in Latin America have reclaimed the feminist label, refusing to accept the male Left's tergiversation of its meaning as another form of colonialist oppression, many now insistent that feminism is neither inherently bourgeois or Western nor intrinsically divisive of the people's struggle. In so doing, they have expanded the parameters of feminist theory and practice.

As the ranks of feminism grew larger and the movement developed a political identity distinct from that of the male-dominated revolutionary Left, feminists undertook increasingly more focused or specialized activities, centered not only on working with the *movimiento de mujeres* but also on deepening a specifically gendered vision of politics, culture, and society. The number of feminist magazines, film and video collectives, centers for battered women and rape victims, feminist health collectives, lesbian rights groups, and other gendered feminist projects steadily expanded throughout the 1980s.

As parties attempted to manipulate women's organizations by imposing their political agenda on the movements and the male Left continued to insist that sexism would "wither away after the revolution," feminists in many countries found a second reason to contest the notion that gender struggle was inherently divisive. Arguing that male-dominated parties sought to instrumentalize and direct women's struggles, feminists' critique of the Left became ever more pointed.

Latin American feminists began redefining and expanding the prevailing notion of revolutionary struggle, calling for a revolution in daily life, asserting that a radical social transformation must encompass changes not only in class but in patriarchal power relations as well. Some feminists increasingly denounced hierarchical, Leninist, or Trotskyist styles of "doing politics," typical of male-dominated revolutionary groups in most countries, insisting on more participatory, democratic forms of pursuing radical social change.

In this context, the regional Encuentros have provided critical forums for movement debates about evolving feminist politics and the movements' relationship to the overall struggle for social justice in Latin America. But the feminists who attended the first Encuentro in Bogotá could hardly have known that would occur. Rather, it was the feeling of political isolation in their individual country, coupled with the desire to chart an autonomous political path, that led Colombian women to call a regionwide meeting of feminist activists.

The Latin American and Caribbean Feminist Encuentros

Bogotá

In July 1981, more than two hundred Latin American feminists, representing some fifty organizations, convened for four days in Bogotá, Colombia, in the first continental meeting of its kind since the early years of the century. Instantly, the Latin American feminist map was extended, both literally and metaphorically. By the end of the first day, walls were covered with poems, proclamations, information about organizations, announcements, posters describing women's conditions in various countries, and a large map of Latin America where participants wrote the names of feminist organizations in their countries.[22] According to the announcement Latin American feminists made at the United Nations Decade Conference in Copenhagen (July 1980), the purpose of the Bogotá Encuentro was to offer Latin American women, "engaged in feminist practice," the opportunity "to exchange experiences and opinions, identify problems and evaluate different practices, as well as plan tasks and projects for the future." Although such a definition has served to characterize all five Encuentros, the principal axis of discussions at the Bogotá meeting was the historical conflict with the male Left.

Word of the Bogotá Encuentro spread through established international feminist networks, primarily reaching white, middle-class, university-educated women. Women from the movimiento de mujeres were largely absent from the critical debates that ensued about the proper relationship of feminism to the revolutionary struggle, for the spheres of feminisms and the *movimientos* were yet to coalesce politically on a regional scale. The following countries were represented: Mexico, the Dominican Republic, Puerto Rico, Panamá, Curaçao, Venezuela, Ecuador, Peru, Chile, Brazil, Argentina, and, of course, Colombia. Some participants were young university students, others were older, working-class organizers. There were homemakers, medical doctors, professors, lawyers, government employees, agricultural workers, poets, and filmmakers. They came from centers for battered women, peasant organizations, research groups; some were women working in the slums of Latin America's large cities; others worked for movie collectives and feminist magazines. Some had been active in feminist movements since the early 1970s; one Colombian woman had even taken part in her country's 1954 campaign for women's suffrage; others had only recently encountered feminism and had never attended a feminist meeting before; many had been members of left-wing political parties but had abandoned them when they discovered feminism; and a substantial number, though not the majority, were feminists who were still active members of left-wing parties.

Except for the Colombians, who had representatives from Bogotá and several other cities, the largest delegation—sixteen women—came from the Dominican Republic. The registration fee, US$50 for Latin Americans and US$80 for all others, included expenses for the four days. Though the conference was conceived for Latin American women, a few "foreigners" were admitted: two from Canada, three from the United States, and a dozen from Europe (Spain, Italy, France, Switzerland, Holland, and Germany). A few women, forced into exile by repressive governments (Brazil, Uruguay, Argentina, and Chile) also attended.

This historic regionwide gathering was itself the outcome of a prolonged and conflicted organizing process, characterized by dissension and acrimonious debates among a politically heterogeneous, if socially relatively homogeneous, group of middle-class, educated, Colombian women.[23] These discussions and confrontations have been echoed in other countries and in planning subsequent regional meetings, so a detailed consideration of the organization of this first Encuentro will provide a broad map of the debates that have demarcated radically differing conceptions of gender struggle in Latin America and the Caribbean in the last decade.

In major Colombian cities where feminists were active, collectives were formed to undertake the planning of the Encuentro. In Bogotá, one such collective emerged, composed of *independientes* (women who did not belong to any particular group), members of feminist organizations (the *Círculo de Mujeres, Mujeres en la Lucha,* and *El Grupo*), as well as feminists who belonged to political parties—the *Partido Socialista de los Trabajadores* (PST, Socialist) and the *Partido Socialista Revolucionario* (PSR, Trotskyist). All the collectives met April 19–20, 1980, in Sopó, Cundinamarca, to coordinate their efforts, and they resolved that the Encuentro would take place in December 1980. In addition to being open to feminists, it would also be *amplio* ("broad-based"). The topics to be discussed would be feminism and political struggle; sexuality and daily life; women and work; and women, communication, and culture.[24]

Despite these agreements, the definition of the conference, which had already provoked long and heated discussions between *militantes* or *políticas* (left-wing party activists) and independent or "autonomous" feminists in the various collectives, was far from settled: The debate regarding who should attend the meeting persisted among the various constituencies. Should it be open to women belonging to all kinds of women's groups (*amplio*) or should it be restricted to self-proclaimed feminists? Should participants be asked to attend the meeting on an individual basis, or should they take part in it as representatives of organizations or political parties? These questions were vital ones given ongoing conflicts with nonfeminist women and men on the Left. "Independent" or nonpartisan feminists eschewed what they considered to be false representational stances, and women affiliated with traditional parties and unions preferred a more structured, formal "congress." Independent feminists also feared that "party women" would impose their sectarian agendas on the meeting, insist on discussing women's role in "the revolution," and divert participants from discussions of issues that a nonfeminist revolution would not encompass—issues central to feminist organizing such as reproductive rights or domestic violence. Because the disagreements were paralyzing the preparation of the Encuentro, the Cali *Coordinadora* ("coordinating committee"), made up mostly of *militantes* or *políticas*, called a national meeting to settle the issues, it was hoped, once and for all.

Before attending the national meeting, however, the Bogotá collective met on August 21, 1980, and decided to sponsor a conference for Latin American women engaged in feminist practice; moreover, they decided that participants would attend as individuals, representing themselves rather than organizations or parties. The agreement was even supported by the three PSR members of the collective who were also members of the *Coordinadora*.

In Cali, the assembly voted to open the meeting to all women "engaged in the struggle for their liberation" and to make representation of organizations and political parties the basis for participation. The votes taken in Cali broke down the precarious alliance between the *políticas* and *feministas*. The *Coordinadoras* from Medellín and Bogotá (with the exception of the three PSR members) refused to honor the decision. Accusations and recriminations ensued while the Encuentro, still to be held in December, remained unprepared. In October, the Cali *Coordinadora* called another meeting, attended by representatives of only four cities, and decided to cancel the conference. At that point, the Bogotá *Coordinadora* resolved to proceed and organize a feminist Encuentro to take place July 16–19, 1981.

The divisions between *militantes* and *feministas* were exacerbated when a group of *políticas* was denied entry to the actual Encuentro, a denial they refused to accept. Although the first morning was spent listening to both versions of the confrontation, sectarianism and recriminations were eventually set aside. An extraordinary spirit of conciliation prevailed throughout the four days: The fact that the Encuentro was finally taking place overshadowed everything else.

In the most widely attended session, "Feminism and Political Struggle," participants agreed to discuss the three topics considered to be most relevant for Latin American feminists: the autonomy (ideological and organizational political independence) of the feminist movement; *doble militancia* ("double militancy," or concurrent participation in, and dual commitment to, a political party and to feminism); and feminism and imperialism. Discussion questions ranged from how to widen, strengthen, and deepen the organized participation of women from the popular sectors to the actual shape an Encuentro should take and the specific conditions of feminist political practice in Latin America. The chaotic and frequently heated debate centered on two of the three points: autonomy and *doble militancia*. Though participants agreed on some basic principles, for example, the existence of gender inequality, they differed greatly as to the strategies feminists should adopt to end women's oppression.

All participants concurred that women suffer a specific oppression that becomes particularly acute in the most exploited classes. Women, therefore, need to articulate and struggle for their specific demands: the end of the double burden, equal pay for equal work, the right to work, the right to have an abortion, and "maternidad libre y voluntaria."[25] Furthermore, participants agreed that these demands had heretofore not been included in political party platforms.

Beyond these points of agreement, two recognizable positions emerged, which divided women's movement activists irrespective of their country of origin, class, or educational status. Each national "delegation" included women who adhered to one or the other position.

The first position held that neither capitalism nor socialism alone could eliminate women's oppression and that, consequently, women's specific demands must be articulated in a movement outside and independent of all existing political parties. For those who defended this position, feminism represented a new revolutionary project, the first real alternative for the total transformation of oppressive social relations in Latin America. As for the issue of *la doble militancia*, these feminists began by redefining the conventional dichotomy between feminism and *militancia política* ("political activism"). They rejected the use of the name *militantes* or *políticas* in opposition to *feministas* because they viewed feminism as a legitimate and comprehensive political praxis. Therefore, feminists should focus their political work primarily, if not exclusively, in their own feminist organizations: The sexist structures of political parties, as well as the conflicts that emerge within those structures when feminist issues are raised, make *doble militancia* extremely difficult in practice. These were women disenchanted with the manipulative strategies of the Left and who decried its androcentric conceptions of the privileged revolutionary agent, the (male) working class. Nevertheless, some did defend the possibility of establishing alliances with political parties in pursuit of specific goals.

Those who held the second position advanced at the Bogotá Encuentro insisted that feminism in and of itself could not be a revolutionary project. Because of their primary commitment to socialism, they argued that feminism should not be separated from the party but that it should have an organic autonomy within that structure. Feminists' objectives, in this view, could not be separated from those of the working class and its struggle to end class oppression. They saw *doble militancia* as a false problem, and while not denying that being a feminist within a political party presented practical difficulties, they believed that such difficulties were not insurmountable.

On the final day of the Encuentro, the plenary session heard reports from the various sessions and adopted numerous resolutions. These ranged from concrete expressions of solidarity with women in specific countries (including Chile, Colombia, Guatemala, and the *Madres de Plaza de Mayo* of Argentina) and with specific national struggles (Nicaragua and El Salvador) to more general issues such as equal pay for equal work, reproductive rights, day-care, improved education, and the right to work. In a resolution to end violence against women, participants declared November 25 as the International Day of Non-Violence Against Women, in memory of three Dominican women, the Miraval sisters, who were killed in 1960 by Rafael Leonidas Trujillo's henchmen. Following a resounding vote of thanks to the Encuentro's organizers, a final resolution to meet again in two years in Lima, Peru, was adopted amid tears and enthusiastic expressions of international feminist solidarity.

Indeed, despite the sometimes acrimonious debates, it was this joyful enthusiasm and spirit of solidarity that made the Bogotá Encuentro an unforgettable experience for most of the participants. For four days, there was a nonstop exchange and sharing of ideas and experiences. The dialogue followed the workshops into the central patio, surrounded by laughter, singing, poetry, and dancing. This, more than anything else, represented the sense of feminist collectivity that was to become Bogotá's legacy to future Encuentros.

One of the most important consequences of the Bogotá meeting was that it bore witness to the existence of a feminist movement of continental proportions, though still uneven in its composition, and revealed a broad process of mobilization among Latin American women. However, as subsequent Encuentros demonstrated, such mobilization was informed and guided by two distinct approaches to gender struggle. The dialogue and confrontation between the *feministas* and the *políticas* manifest at Bogotá were replete with all the conflict and contradictions that characterized most Latin American feminist practice in the 1970s and the 1980s.

Lima

No one was quite prepared for the growth that the Latin American feminist movement had experienced in the two years since Bogotá. Over six hundred women arrived in Lima in July 1983 to participate in the second Encuentro. Least prepared of all was the *Comisión Organizadora*, which had to find a new site for the Encuentro close to the meeting date because the one originally chosen was washed out by floods.

In an effort to further a specifically feminist, autonomous, or nonpartisan women's politics, the Lima *Comisión Organizadora* decided that the second Encuentro was to center on "patriarchy," a bold and ultimately controversial theme still associated with "bad," imperialist feminism by many nonfeminist women and men on the Left. Following the position adopted by the Bogotá *Coordinadora*, it also decided that participation in the Encuentro should be on an individual basis as opposed to consisting of delegated representatives of groups and organizations. Participants became aware politically and strategically that being a feminist and working with women were not necessarily the same thing.

The distinction that grew between the feminist movement and the *movimientos de mujeres* would prove to be acutely concretized and problematized at later Encuentros. Organizers were concerned that a *feministómetro*[26] ("feminist yard-stick") not be used to invalidate all the different kinds of work done by, for, and with women. At the same time, they wanted to preserve a uniquely feminist "space" for feminist activists. Indeed, many *veteranas* or *históricas* ("veteran" or "historic feminists," those present at Bogotá) lamented the absence of an intimate feminist space or *espacio feminista* with less theory and more *convivencia* ("sharing"). Those who were at Bogotá were especially nostalgic for what had occurred there, claiming that it was impossible to feel and live closeness and solidarity with six hundred women. In spite of this discontent, one of the most important consequences of the Lima Encuentro was the involvement in feminism of large numbers of women who would become identified with the feminist movement as a result of their participation in the Encuentro, thus establishing a pattern that would be repeated in subsequent meetings.

Women from all over Latin America came to *El Bosque* (an enclosed vacation spot for middle-class families approximately 40 kilometers outside of Lima) to share their experiences as feminists, researchers, grass-roots activists, health workers, university students, union organizers, political exiles, party militants, filmmakers, and writers. Although throughout Latin America, and Peru in particular, the grass-roots *movimientos de mujeres* had grown massively in the late 1970s and early 1980s, noticeably underrepresented were Indian women, working-class activists, or women from Central American countries, a reflection of either the prohibitive registration fee (US$50) or the state of the feminist movement in their countries. A large proportion of those who attended were, like the organizing commission, nonpartisan, academic, and professional *feministas;* their presence was reflected in the organization and atmosphere of the entire four-day Encuentro.

A wide range of workshops (*talleres*), nineteen in all, had been organized, all of which were prefaced with "Patriarchy and . . ."; among these were patriarchy and health, church, power, sexuality, violence against women, and feminist research. All of these workshops had an expert facilitator or *encargada de taller,* usually an academic, who was responsible for coordinating the discussion and, in many cases, for the "papers" that would be presented.[27] Predictably, this structure smacked of hierarchy and elitism to many participants and yet again raised issues regarding the form and expression of Latin American feminisms. Where was the "space" for less-structured discussion and for spontaneity? Where was the "space" for nonintellectuals who came to share their experiences in the *poblaciones, barriadas,* and *favelas* ("shantytowns")? Where were all of the women from the *sectores populares* ("poor and working class sectors")? Questions were asked and heated debates ensued about whether the second Encuentro's focus on patriarchy was indeed too academic or too theoretical and whether or not the workshop format prevented a *verdadera convivencia* ("true coming together").

In spite of some resistance to so much emphasis on patriarchy, Lima did represent an advance over the central political debates that had been formulated and articulated in Bogotá. Most importantly, the discussions in Lima, informed by a need to establish a theoretical understanding of Latin American patriarchy in all of its material, ideological, cultural, linguistic, institutional, and sexual expressions, deepened and advanced the movement's analysis of gender power relations and how these intersect with other relations of power in Latin American societies. The debates in Bogotá that centered on *doble militancia* as a political strategy and on the role of the (male-dominant) political party in feminism were reformulated in an analysis of the political party as an example of a patriarchal institution. For some Latin American feminists, then, an analysis of the role of the party moved from a debate about strategy to a debate about structure. Moreover, the focus on patriarchy allowed some Latin American feminists to further distinguish their Socialist feminism from the way in which the Left had traditionally defined the "woman question." That is, by the second Encuentro, many feminists, from a wide range of countries, had begun to insist that sexism was not the "outcome" of capitalism and imperialism but rather was shaped by a relatively autonomous, patriarchal sex-gender system.

There were several workshops, not part of the original program, that represented a significant departure from conventional Marxist understandings of the woman question and signaled the growing complexity and diversity of struggles considered "feminist." For example, "miniworkshops" on lesbianism and racism were held, neither of which had an expert facilitator. With an estimated three hundred women in attendance, the "miniworkshop" on lesbianism had to be moved from a small room to one of the larger halls. For the first time, there was a public response to the demands of lesbians that their presence within Latin American feminism be recognized. Historically, this workshop signaled the emergence of lesbian visibility within the movement and challenged heterosexual feminists to confront their homophobia. For many, this was one of the most significant accomplishments of the Lima meeting.

Similarly, the mini-*taller* on racism, although not as massively attended or as publicly visible, provided a forum in which to criticize the lack of "space" in the Encuentro to confront the problematic of feminism and racism. This workshop, in which primarily black and Indian women participated, challenged the Lima and subsequent Encuentros to address the issue of racism, not only in the context of the lived experiences of women in their various social, cultural, and national contexts but also within the feminist movement itself.

At Lima, *feministas* and *militantes* also continued to do battle over who represented the "true" interests of women of the popular classes. Both women from the *movimiento de mujeres* and women who considered themselves feminists, though active in parties of the Left, were among the participants. As in Bogotá, class and ideological differences were expressed in discussions about the structure, content, and cost of the Encuentro. Many of the participants insisted that conference organizers had not done enough outreach to women from Peru's *movimiento de mujeres*, that the issues that were central to those women's lives were not being discussed. Still others pointed out that the organizers had assumed all feminists were middle class and would be able to afford the registration fee.

Although the Lima Encuentro represented important advances in the articulation of Latin American feminisms, at the same time it established a framework within which some issues could later resurface. An analysis of patriarchy and gender power relations, for example, gave a new context to the dialogue between *feministas* and *militantes* as well as to the discussion of feminist strategy. The participation of those who worked with women but did not necessarily define themselves as feminists set the stage for the future conceptualization, within the feminist movement, of the *movimientos de mujeres*. The final plenary produced an often tearful and emotional dialogue regarding the relationship between *feministas* and *militantes*, which in some women evoked a nostalgic longing for the solidarity with which the Bogotá Encuentro concluded. Essentially, participants at Lima felt that the issue was not to repeat Bogotá but rather to question why the *históricas* felt it so necessary to reproduce what had occurred there. In retrospect, the discontent with and critique of the structure of the Lima Encuentro was a fitting precursor to the next Encuentro, at Bertioga, which, although well organized, was based not on structure but rather on *auto-gestión*.[28]

Bertioga

The third time Latin American feminists met (in July 1985, just as the UN Decade was winding down in Nairobi), there was a special air of anticipation as women arrived. Nearly nine hundred women came to the Encuentro in Bertioga, at a little-known, union-owned *colonia de vacaciones* ("vacation resort club") on the Brazilian coast. The number of participants once again surprised and delighted all those involved. The Brazilian organizers had procured a physical space that most participants had only visited in dreams—with palm trees, open breezeways, and a beach—and that had many places for spontaneous, unstructured meetings. It seemed as if nothing could go wrong. And as participants looked at themselves and at each other, they saw among Latin American feminists an extraordinary cultural, ethnic, and political diversity that they had, until then, only imagined.

Indeed, by the time of the Brazil Encuentro, Latin American feminism had truly come into its own, politically and culturally. Feminists were pursuing their goals in a wide variety of institutional and extrainstitutional arenas, from government ministries to trade unions to alternative health centers to lesbian-feminist collectives.

The nearly four hundred Brazilians present embodied the broad range of ideologies and activities among self-proclaimed feminists in the mid-1980s. The Brazilians had created what was perhaps the largest, most radical, most diverse, and most politically influential of Latin America's feminist movements. Their national and regional Encuentros, their experience with elections and political parties, and their visibility in national politics had made the Brazilian movement both the envy of and, to some extent, the model to emulate for Latin American feminist movements.[29] Perhaps for this reason what ensued at the Brazil meeting not only left many participants perplexed but, more importantly, also exacerbated existing tensions between *militantes* and *feministas* and between feminisms and the *movimiento de mujeres*.

On the first day, a busload of women from the shantytowns of Rio de Janeiro arrived at the Bertioga conference site, their bus compliments of the Rio Lion's Club (known for its ties to the state's dominant political party); the women asked to be admitted to the Encuentro although they lacked the money to pay the registration fees. Consistent with the previous Encuentro, the US$60 registration fee was prohibitive for the vast majority of Latin American women.[30] Most of the women on the bus were black, all were poor, and Brazilian participants suspected them all of being manipulated by political leaders in Rio who had undermined the feminist movement on previous occasions. Yet another hypothesis declared that the Lion's Club was attempting to garner the *favela* vote by providing the bus. Some *feministas* insisted that sectarian parties of the Left had orchestrated the arrival of the *favela* women in an attempt to discredit the feminist movement as elitist, bourgeois, and hence divisive to the working-class struggle.[31]

Participants' opinions about admitting the *faveladas* became greatly polarized. The organizing committee (Brazilians) took the position that everyone would play by the same rules; that is, nobody could enter without paying the registration fee. They tried to assure the participants from other countries that their position was formulated in relation to suspected party manipulation rather than as a response to the women on the bus, with whom they empathized.

The organizers insisted that anyone who was not Brazilian would have difficulty understanding the complexities of Brazilian politics. Sectarian political parties had repeatedly disrupted national and regional feminist meetings in Brazil during the early 1980s. This incident, many Brazilians present maintained, was but another manifestation of the relentless and insidious partisan efforts to manipulate, discredit, and distort feminist politics. They pointed out that the Encuentro organizers had secured one hundred scholarships for Brazilian women unable to pay the registration fee and that the group now clamoring at the gate had received five of those scholarships. Many among the hundreds of poor and working-class participants from Brazil's *movimiento de mujeres* argued that their groups had raised funds to attend and had applied for scholarships. Most agreed that it was improper and politically manipulative for the women on the bus to insist on being admitted at that late date. Yet here were twenty-three women, camped outside the gates of the Encuentro, refusing to leave when not admitted as a group, and thereby creating a separate and distinct space for those who wished to talk to them. Many participants did.

Immediately, it seemed as if the battle lines were drawn: those who supported the organizers' decision and those who opposed it. The first position held that allowing the women to participate would constitute a capitulation to partisan manipulation, tantamount to admitting that feminism was indeed an elitist movement and that the organizers had made no effort to include working-class women in the Encuentro—even though poor and working-class women were present in far greater numbers than at either Bogotá or Lima, and many among them were proudly proclaiming themselves *feministas*. Those who did not support the organizers' decision were a politically heterogeneous group. Some were *militantes* who saw the bus incident as an opportunity to fan the flames of the decade-long debate about whether gender or class was most important for Latin American women. Others were members of Brazil's recently created black feminist collectives who argued that barring the *favela* women from the Encuentro was emblematic of the racism that pervaded Brazilian feminism. Still others, black, white, and *mestizas*, working class and middle class, insisted that the women on the bus should be allowed to participate in the Encuentro, if only to counteract the negative press coverage that it immediately generated and to get on with the meeting as planned.

The implications of these political divisions among participants informed much of the discussion for the next days. While some argued that the organizers "showed great courage in their decision," others questioned whether or not it was really courage; still others thought that it constituted feminist political suicide and would cause a great scandal with the media, most particularly the press, always looking to malign feminism and thereby discredit the movement. Some women swore they would never participate in another Encuentro; others spent sleepless nights drafting documents or press releases in solidarity either with the *faveladas* or the organizing committee. Aside from the fact that the *faveladas* were denied entry, the most unfortunate aspect of the incident was that discussions centered on the bus (who had sent it for what reasons?) and admitting the women, rather than on the race and class implications for the movement raised by its presence. By the end of the Encuentro, the issue was still not resolved. It was a situation that would not go away.

Nevertheless, the Encuentro continued. For one thing, not all participants were equally disturbed by the bus issue. They had come for an Encuentro, and an Encuentro was what they planned to get. The physical space itself allowed and fostered a spontaneity that permitted enough privacy to divulge untold secrets, yet enough openness to welcome wanderers. Everyone present was injected with the Brazilian style of feminism that seemed to infuse a certain flair and panache into everything. In retrospect, many Latin American feminists, especially if they had not attended Bogotá, recall Bertioga as the most imaginative and creative Encuentro, the most relaxed, and the one with the perfect number of participants and the most ideal setting. Here, the two Nicaraguans in attendance helped to focus attention on the political significance of the intersection of feminism and revolutionary struggles. Significant as well was that lesbians, made visible at the Lima Encuentro, now chose to meet on their own in closed session, when only two years earlier discussing lesbianism had been practically taboo. Instead of having to explain their existence to heterosexual women, lesbians were now able to politicize a lesbian identity. Women met not only by sexual preference but also by country, by profession, by years of involvement in the movement, by class, by race, by age, by religion, and any other characteristic that seemed to identify a group. Repeatedly, feminists discovered that they had counterparts in other countries. The Bertioga Encuentro made participants keenly aware of the growth of the movement and the concomitant diversity that it had created; few suspected that Bertioga was the prelude to the next Encuentro, in Mexico.

Taxco

To this day, nobody is quite sure to what one could attribute the presence of over fifteen hundred women at the fourth Encuentro held in Taxco, Guerrero, Mexico, in October of 1987: the perfection of the region's feminist network; Mexico's strategic geographical location; unprecedented advertising in the feminist press; finely developed organizational skills of women from more distant countries; or, more simply, the geometric expansion of feminist activism throughout the region since the mid-1980s. For the first time, women from all the countries of Central and South America and the Spanish-speaking Caribbean were present. Despite the enormous distances and the disastrous economies of their nations, it was surprising that over one hundred fifty women came from the Southern Cone alone (Argentina, Chile, Paraguay, and Uruguay). Although the significant presence of women from countries with the longest histories of feminist struggle (Peru and Brazil) was expected, the unprecedented participation of hundreds of Central Americans, mostly from the *movimientos de mujeres,* was remarkable.[32] And the enthusiastic participation of over fifty Nicaraguan women truly caused a stir. Unprecedented, as well, was the presence of four representatives from the Federation of Cuban Women, an organization that had been reluctant to identify ideologically with the feminist cause. The very interest of the Cubans in participating signals their recognition of feminism as a force in Latin America that can no longer be ignored by progressive and/or revolutionary forces.

Participants were engaged in every conceivable type of political, cultural, and educational feminist activity. There were women who worked for the state, in recently established commissions or ministries on the status of women, "party women" who may or may not have considered themselves feminists, union women (both urban and rural), and, of course, women from the *movimientos de mujeres.*[33] Also present were "cultural workers"—women who work in the arts, film, and video and writers and poets. Other participants included those who work with specifically feminist projects—battered women's support groups, women's health centers, and feminist documentation centers—and, for the first time, a significant number of Catholic feminist activists. This time, lesbian feminists not only participated in the Encuentro but also held their own Encuentro immediately prior to Taxco, attended by over two hundred and fifty women.

Following the Brazilian example of securing funding from outside sources, the Mexican organizing commission provided scholarships for dozens of low-income women, enabling poor and working-class women from Mexico and other nations to participate in the Encuentro in great numbers. Nevertheless, fewer black and Indian women attended than in Brazil, not to mention the invisibility of Latin American Jewish women and Latin American Asian women. The cost of attending the fourth Encuentro—US$100—remained prohibitive by Latin American standards, making it extremely difficult even for middle-class women to participate. Though economic issues did not erupt into overt conflict as they had at Bertioga, questions of outreach and economic accessibility were once again a central focus of discussions and pointed to the need to devise alternative organizational schemes. In this respect, the financing of the Encuentros has remained a point of contention.

How the Latin American feminist revolution is to be financed is a problem confronted by feminist organizations in every country and at every Encuentro; women systematically raised questions about appropriate funding sources. Some have always protested the reliance on outside funds (such as those provided by the Ford Foundation). Yet other potential sources of financial assistance have been problematical. For example, the long-standing insistence on absolute autonomy among some sectors of the movement has thus far discouraged organizers from accepting subsidies from national governments and/or political parties. Alternatively, as suggested by some in Bertioga, the infrastructure work of the Encuentro has not been modified in ways that might reduce the overall cost (i.e., sliding scales, work exchange, use of public or government facilities). As participation in the Encuentros has increased dramatically over the years, the financial and organizational burdens are still shouldered exclusively, and perhaps unfairly, by a small group of organizers in the host country.

At Bertioga, many Latinas—and others sympathetic to their position—had hoped that the Mexico Encuentro would provide the ideal forum for a long-overdue dialogue between Latinas in the United States (some of whom had been consistent Encuentro participants) and their feminist counterparts in Latin America. However, there were few U.S. Latinas among the participants. The small numbers are, in part, attributable to the fact that the Mexican organizing commission only reluctantly and belatedly accepted that such a dialogue was necessary or even desirable. In setting a quota of one hundred "foreign" participants, in which they included Latinas,[34] organizers effectively discouraged many Chicanas and those Latin Americans living abroad from attending the Encuentro. Despite the steady participation of Latinas at Encuentros since Lima and their repeated efforts to bring Latina issues to the attention of Latin American feminists, vital links between the two movements have yet to be consolidated.

On a more positive note, Taxco provided ample evidence that Latin American feminism was confronting a new political conjuncture. The absolute increase in numbers, in spite of economic inaccessibility and distance, signaled the quantitative expansion of feminist movements in the region. More importantly, Taxco demonstrated that there had been qualitative improvements as well. We witnessed the increased diversity of spheres of feminist activism and a movement that had grown and been enriched by that diversity. Feminists now seemed to pervade all walks of life and were no longer the fringe, marginal group that had once given definition to the term.

At Taxco, it seemed that Latin American feminism had finally accomplished what it originally set out to do: foster a mass movement of women. But it did so almost in spite of itself and not without complaints from veteran feminists (*las históricas*), who saw their own feminist space being usurped by women from the *movimientos de mujeres*. Yet feminist discourse and practice clearly have had a critical and significant impact on a wide variety of social and political movements—from unions to peasant organizations to urban squatters to traditional and progressive political parties to the state. Today, all kinds of movements have absorbed some of the basics of feminist politics.

The *movimientos de mujeres* are now themselves quite diverse. Included within this vast category, for example, are women's groups that explicitly identify with feminism, whose work in communities centers not only on gender-related issues—such as urban services that would facilitate women's domestic work and thus are crucial to poor and working-class women—but also on gender-specific issues such as women's health, reproductive rights, and violence against women. In many working-class communities, women have organized consciousness-raising groups that deal with unequal power relations in their marriages and families and with contraception, abortion, and sexuality. In others, women's health centers and battered women's support groups have been established. In the process of organizing around "survival issues," many women participants in the *movimientos de mujeres* are empowered both as citizens and women and consequently often begin to articulate demands for sexual equality in their homes and communities. Since the Catholic church, the Left, and conventional political parties have deliberately blocked this process of women's empowerment, the spread of feminist ideas among women of the popular classes has been in no small measure due to the persistent grass-roots organizing efforts of feminists in many countries.[35] What was confirmed at Taxco was that feminist ideas and projects are not the exclusive preserve of women of the bourgeoisie.

The massive presence of poor and working-class women at Taxco, then, was not merely the consequence of the availability of scholarships. Rather, many were there because they had been politicized through their participation in community struggles and were beginning to grapple with the status of women in those communities. Some, among the hundreds of working-class women present, still rejected the label *feminist*, sometimes because they formed part of groups controlled by the church or antifeminist political parties. But many others had been exposed to feminism through direct contact with feminist organizations or indirectly through feminist electoral campaigns or the media. In countries such as Brazil, Peru, and Mexico, feminists have succeeded in deploying an alternative discourse on gender and the family that has influenced everything from the evening soap opera to government policy pronouncements.

These quantitative and qualitative changes in Latin American feminisms, however, also increased the complexity of feminist politics and presented new challenges for feminists in the region. "Just who is a feminist?" became a key axis of discussion at Taxco. "Just what is a feminist politics?" participants asked; "if all of the types of political work represented here are feminist, then what does that mean?" Some sarcastically reinvoked the *feministómetro*, as the "measure" that gauges a woman's "degree" of feminist commitment and consciousness.

Some of the organizers of the Encuentro and other veteran feminists insisted they knew the answers to these difficult questions. They mistrusted women who "still" engaged in what they perceived to be ill-informed and ultimately ill-fated double militancy, their version of false consciousness. The same *históricas* emphasized that the movement needed to advance on specifically feminist political projects, to delve more deeply into the many long-standing problems that plague feminist organizations and confound feminist political practice. Yet at the final plenary, Central American women, women from unions, parties, and popular movements were all chanting "TODAS SOMOS FEMINISTAS" ("We are all feminists"), demanding that veteran feminists acknowledge the growth and diversification of the feminist cause.

These divergent positions obscure the fact that there were at least two new political developments manifest at Taxco. Whereas feminism was a dirty word even as late as 1981 in Bogotá, feminism definitely had become much more acceptable in public discourse by 1987. Perhaps this can be attributed to the UN's Decade for Women that validated portions of the feminist agenda and/or feminism's newfound legitimacy in leftist circles via the Nicaraguan revolution.

Because in some countries the feminist movement has had a political impact and garnered a significant mass base (e.g., Brazil, Chile, and Nicaragua), male-dominated parties, unions, and governments have jumped on the "pro-woman" bandwagon—at least rhetorically—as never before in an attempt to reap the benefits of feminism's new political respectability. Partisan antifeminist manipulators unquestionably had sent "their women" to Taxco to foment debate and discord about the priority of class versus gender struggle. The manipulation, co-optation, and tergiversation of feminism clearly continued—not only by that "unacceptable" Left but now also by the political Center and Center-Right (representatives from the new "democratic" governments). Feminism, indeed, now provided liberal-democratic legitimacy for new civilian regimes and a fertile recruitment ground and new slogans for political parties.

But that fact need not overshadow the second and much more encouraging phenomenon evidenced at Taxco: the growth, expansion, and diversification of women's struggles, imbued with and informed by the region's feminisms. Some of the party or rural women who had never before participated in a feminist event of any sort appeared nevertheless to have been reached by feminist ideas and influenced by feminist actions. They were not all mere "dupes" of the manipulative Left, as some *históricas* claimed, and seemed sincere in proclaiming themselves to be legitimate advocates of feminist goals, even as they insisted on the need to broaden and redefine those goals.

Taxco as a Reflection of Latin American Feminists Today: New Issues, Old Debates

Despite—or perhaps even because of—some of the problematic issues that (re)emerged at the fourth Encuentro, most Taxco participants recognized that something different, indeed unique, was happening: that, in fact, Taxco represented a transition from the small group of dedicated feminists to a large, broad-based, politically heterogeneous, multiracial movement. Yet not all Taxco participants (especially the *históricas*) were necessarily pleased with this transition. For within the rubric of a large-scale, continental, multiclass movement also existed the less pluralistic reaction to it: that diversity was composed of women at differing stages of feminist thought, a frustration for those who wanted to pick up where they had left off at the last Encuentro.

Encuentro participants met in Mexico City and piled up in a caravan of rented buses that stopped en route to Taxco for a surprise ceremony planned by the organizing committee to be held in a cave, La Gruta. The confused and dramatically differing reactions to this opening ritual, a mystical celebration of women's (magical) power and culture, seemed not to bode well of things to come. Advocates of "cultural feminism," which invokes the Great Mother and celebrates the caves of the Earth as her womb, were enthralled by this event. Cultural feminism had only recently gained currency in some Latin American nations. "Socialist" and "professional" feminists as well as *militantes*, anxious to get down to the work of the Encuentro, expressed their consternation at the unannounced detour. Finally at the Taxco town site, participants were dispersed in five hotels, the two largest of which were hosts to the major events. Because the event sites were located at different ends of the city, two separate or parallel Encuentros appeared to be taking place. Furthermore, it was perceived by some participants that the lodging arrangements reflected an altogether not inadvertent segregation along national and class lines, with many of *las históricas* concentrated in one hotel, while activists in the *movimientos de mujeres* and the *centroamericanas* were lodged in the others.

These space and structural difficulties, in addition to effectively inhibiting dialogue, complicated the organizers' intention to facilitate an Encuentro based on a strategy of *auto-gestión*. An often confusing array of hastily composed posters announcing workshops was plastered over the walls of hotel lobbies (if one could find, beg, or borrow appropriately sized paper and the necessary markers). A recurring comment was that some of the workshops were wonderful—if one could only find them. Clear to most of the participants was that *auto-gestión* does not work well with fifteen hundred people and that the space limitations could neither accommodate nor facilitate the spontaneity *auto-gestión* required.

Tensions surfaced between feminists and women active in the *movimientos de mujeres*. Many veteran feminists thought the presence of "neophyte" feminists (or of women who did not yet call themselves feminists) rendered the "level" of discourse "too elementary." They expressed fatigue at having to explain basic feminist stances and, particularly, at having to teach women how to speak without using sexist language. Hundreds of feminists had been doing this work on a daily basis among working-class women for years and, as one woman put it, "we need the Encuentro to recharge our batteries." They attend Encuentros to nourish themselves, to get sustenance for the feminist battles of the next few years, and to find others who share their point of view. Tired of having to "reinvent the wheel" each time a new woman became interested in feminism, veteran feminists wanted their own Encuentro. What they got, in the sentiments of some, was an "invasion," especially from Central America.

Few women from Central America had attended previous Encuentros because of distance, the state of their economies, and the omnipresent life/death struggles in most Central American countries. The massive presence in Taxco of women from all over Central America—including combatants, Indian women, and campesinas—altered the complexion of the entire Encuentro and not just because—unlike other Encuentro events—the workshops on women in Central America were meticulously planned and publicized.[36] For the Central American women, issues that were considered key for feminists elsewhere appeared less important. Rather, those very circumstances that had prevented Central American women from attending previous Encuentros now seemed to have politicized them. Women made positive associations between their political situation in the state with their private situation at home, evidenced by one woman's remark: "I was as sick of my husband's regime as I was of Somoza's." At the same time, statements such as "It's hard to argue about who's going to do the dishes when your compañero is going into battle" imply a distrust of feminism. Likewise, it highlights one of the most critical issues facing Latin American feminists today: how to promote and advance a more ideological, theoretical, and cultural critique of dependent capitalist patriarchy while maintaining vital links either with poor and working-class women organizing around survival struggles or with revolutionary women organized around national liberation struggles. Yet *veteranas* and *históricas* responded to the Central American women and those from other *movimientos de mujeres* with some impatience, as this *veterana's* remark reveals:

> We have to find a way to organize ourselves and be self-financed. I think we need much smaller Encuentros. There's a history behind these Encuentros and we can't deny it, nor can we start from zero every time. In Latin America the *movimientos de mujeres* is growing. We're calling this a feminist Encuentro and it turns out to be an *Encuentro de mujeres*. The feminist movement can't remain stagnated. We have to move forward. Our Encuentros helped to revitalize us and now they're not doing that anymore. We're tired of being the "compañeras agitadoras, activistas" who have to explain why we're feminists, why lesbians have to explain why they're lesbians. I'm tired of feeling guilty. In Latin America we need two spaces, one for feminists and one for the *movimientos*. We can't mix those two spaces. Bertioga showed us that they could be mixed, but that we also need to have some order. There are two spaces here and each one needs to be respected. The problem with this Encuentro is that they wanted to do it all, to have one big beautiful event with *the participation of every country and, therefore, of every problem*. But we can't resolve it all here. We can't sit down and talk about countries, I want to talk as María, not Ecuador. It's not that I don't think there's a need to talk about Ecuador, but this Encuentro was created to talk about María, Cecilia, María Rosa, etc. Each Encuentro gives us one of these injections. So it's time to rethink the Encuentros. If we don't have money, we need smaller spaces. And of course we must still keep meeting, but [the organization] shouldn't depend on the efforts of just one country, but various countries.[37]

The tension that emerged in Taxco reflected the contradiction—emerging since Lima—between Latin American feminists' commitment to a movement that is broad-based, multiracial, and multiclass and both their tacit assumption that the Central American reality is not quite "feminist" enough and their frustration with the *movimientos de mujeres's* lack of feminist discourse. This tension was exacerbated by the absence of a "space" at the Encuentro to discuss country- or region-specific problems.

For many *históricas* and *mujeres* alike, Taxco represented a new conjuncture in feminist politics, calling for new feminist political strategies. Some *históricas* argued that the *feministas* should pull out of the women's movement (*movimientos de mujeres*), create something "new," and leave this watered-down version of feminism to the parties, the unions, the governments, the manipulators, and the "mujeres." Other participants maintained that in the future two Encuentros should be held—one for the feminist movement, another for the *movimientos de mujeres*.

Critics of these proposals argued that the male manipulators might absorb or preempt feminist mobilizations entirely if the *feministas* retreat and that it would be impossible to establish an objective criterion to determine who is and who is not a "true" feminist.

Perhaps the most extreme example of all the attempts at Taxco to impose a restricted proprietary stance over the "true" definition of feminism was the small group of feminists who spent the entire Encuentro, divorced from the entire event, in a closed room drafting a statement on the state of "the movement" that was delivered at the final plenary session. The fact that they had not really participated in the Encuentro but offered critiques of it flared some tempers. In other instances, some *históricas* argued that merely organizing other women irrespective of issue content did not constitute feminist practice. They insisted that the movement's energies should not be consumed by the *mujeres'* efforts to secure running water or adequate sewage for working-class women, for instance. Instead, feminism must promote an alternative "women's culture" and concern itself with those issues that community groups and progressive parties are never going to address—such as abortion, domestic violence, and sexual and reproductive freedom. Only women prioritizing these gender-specific issues and concerns could be considered "true" feminists in this view.

Many feminists, both middle and working class, stressed that gender oppression takes different forms among women of different classes and racial/ethnic groups. In this view, organizing for running water can be seen as a feminist undertaking given that women are held socially responsible for the care and nurture of their families and that, in poor communities, the lack of basic services imposes further burdens on women's work. A feminist-inspired community organizing effort, unlike those led by nonfeminist or antifeminist forces, would promote a critical consciousness among local women, emphasizing how and why gender shapes their particular organizing efforts. Black and Indian feminists in Latin America argue that race, like class, is constitutive of gender consciousness and oppression, that their interests as women are not identical to those of white or mestiza Latin American women, that is, one's *lived* experience of gender encompasses class-and/or race-specific dimensions. For instance, in pointing to the representation of the *muluta*, marketed to tourists and the ultimate symbol of Brazilian sensuality, black feminists in Brazil stress the ways in which racism shapes black women's gendered oppression.

Most women insisted that the diversification of arenas of feminist struggle represented an advance for the movement. They seemed to be developing a revised conception of double militancy: Instead of carrying her party line into a feminist organization, a woman would carry her feminist line into her party, her union, her neighborhood organization, or her job. This reformulation of feminist practice, they argued, would be more appropriate in an era of democratizing regimes and extensive popular political mobilization. A grass-roots feminist movement responding to new democracies would develop new critiques, new ideas, and newer ways of "doing politics," thus ensuring that feminists working in parties and in government remain honest and accountable to a movement constituency. A suggested strategy entailed questioning, criticizing, and watching the "manipulators" carefully and relentlessly. At the same time, they would continue to promote feminist consciousness among women from all social sectors, thus preempting co-optation by male movements, parties, and institutions, such as the alleged mobilization of the women on the bus in Bertioga.

The San Bernardo Encuentro

After meeting for almost two years, the organizing committee of the fifth Encuentro issued a bulletin in March 1990 announcing that the next Encuentro would take place in San Bernardo, Argentina, a newly developed resort town on the Atlantic coast, 400 kilometers south of Buenos Aires. It would begin on November 18 and would conclude with a march in downtown Buenos Aires on November 25, the day feminists throughout Latin America take to the streets to denounce violence against women, in accordance with the declaration adopted at the Bogotá Encuentro. The fifth Encuentro theme, "Feminism as a Transformational Movement: Evaluation and Perspectives in Latin America," was chosen purposely to celebrate "almost a decade of historic Encuentros which have allowed us to follow step by step the development and growth of feminism in our countries." The organizers also set aside a time slot for collective reflection on the obstacles, achievements, or discoveries of Latin American and Caribbean feminisms during the last decade. They invited participants to write papers or otherwise to prepare to discuss topics such as feminism and the *movimientos de mujeres*, feminism and the state, public policy and political parties, sexuality, and violence against women. As the Encuentro approached, the organizers received enough responses from potential participants to propose morning discussion sessions and afternoon *talleres* centered on four subthemes: "The Construction of Collective Identities and Conflicting Values"; "Organizational Variants and Development Spaces"; "Relations Between Feminism and Other Social Areas"; and "Political Proposals, Perspectives, and Strategies." Each of these would take one day, and the conclusions would be read in a plenary.

Despite the uneasy political situation and disastrous economic crisis in Argentina, a group of thirty-two women from five different Argentine cities and Uruguay's capital, Montevideo, organized the fifth Encuentro and had obtained unprecedented financial support—a total of $280,000.[38] They chose San Bernardo because it had a big hotel with 800 rooms, numerous meeting areas, and eating facilities for 1,600 people. Unfortunately, in the month of July, as the organizers were ready to sign a contract with the Peronist union that owns the hotel, they were told that inflation had resulted in a $10 increase per person. Unable to meet the new price and having already prepaid several other hotels, the organizers decided to remain in San Bernardo and, if necessary, put the overflow in the next town—a decision that ultimately compromised space for meetings and workshops.

Coordination began to go astray on the very first day when the computer system broke down and between 2,500 and 3,000 women, most of whom had not preregistered, had to be processed by hand. In an operation that required much goodwill on the part of the travelers and tireless efforts on the part of the organizers, participants were finally placed in twenty-one hotels situated in San Bernardo and Mar de Ajó, an area covering roughly forty blocks. They came from thirty-eight countries, including Haiti, Ethiopia, Turkey, and, once again, Cuba. The largest single foreign group was composed of 650 Brazilians, many of whom had traveled by bus. Although the Mexicans were also numerous, some

300, Central American representation was comparatively small this time; in contrast, there was an unusually large number of Spaniards.

On the first evening, participants found themselves celebrating the inauguration of the Encuentro in the middle of a central plaza, divided by countries, as if they were delegations to a political congress. They were surrounded by astonished San Bernardinos who, as they would for the rest of the week, stared at the renowned exuberance of the Brazilians, the uninhibited expressions of affection among many women, and the performances on the makeshift stage.

All the problems attendant with crowd control seemed to emerge at once. For the next four days, including one very stormy one, participants stood in line, waiting for their shift to eat in a cavernous and loud gymnasium, wandering in search of friends, seeking a solution for the lack of day-care, acquiring information about the supposedly free buses that ran between the two towns, but most often looking for the commercial galleries, coffee shops, restaurants, movie houses, and even sidewalks where the workshops were scheduled to take place. Despite the apologies of the organizers, their willingness to provide these spaces, and their efforts to improve the situation—they even published a daily schedule of events—they could not overcome everyone's frustration. By the second day, the fifth Encuentro had become El Encuentro del Des/Encuentro[39] or El Encuentro de la Búsqueda ("the Encuentro of the Search").

However, after complaining bitterly about the prevailing chaos, participants decided to make the best of it, and undeterred by distances, electricity blackouts caused by the storm, closed workshops, or lack of available meeting rooms, they attended massively scheduled and spontaneous video sessions, movies, and performances (including a repeat performance of the feminist Mass created, composed, and performed by a group of feminists from Rio de Janeiro) and celebrations on the beach in honor of the earth mother. They managed to find the space to listen to formal papers and to hold new workshops and discussion sessions on topics such as: "The Anniversary of the Five Hunded Years," "Feminism and Socialism," "Women and AIDS," "Feminist Theology," "Pornography," "The Environment," and many others. On two consecutive days, the number of scheduled workshops surpassed eighty.

At one such gathering, Indian women meeting separately to discuss the celebration of the so-called 1492 "discovery" expressed their repudiation of the anniversary and proposed that October 11 be declared Indigenous Women Day. Thirty-eight journalists from mainstream or alternative publications attended a workshop where they discussed their profession and their own relationships with the movimientos de mujeres and feminism. Lesbian issues were the subject of at least four very well-attended sessions, whose topics included homophobia among feminists and the planning of an Encuentro of Latin American and Caribbean lesbians in the near future. Two human rights organizations—Familiares de Desaparecidos y Prisioneros por Razones Políticas (Relatives of Disappeared and Imprisoned for Political Reasons) and Madres de Plaza de Mayo–Línea Fundadora (Mothers of the Plaza de Mayo–Founding Group)—sponsored video presentations and discussions of human rights abuses in Argentina. They also sought support from participants for their campaign against granting pardon to the military for atrocities committed in the 1970s and 1980s.

In several instances, the *talleres* resulted in the creation of new organizations. A group of black women met separately, formed a network they called *Red de Mujeres Negras de Latinoamérica y el Caribe* (The Latin American and Caribbean Black Women Network), and agreed to meet again in order to prepare an Encuentro in Uruguay sometime in 1992. Some forty mental health organizations founded a mental health network whose activities will be publicized by ISIS International. After holding several meetings, a large group of women—some feminists and others belonging to the *movimientos de mujeres*—organized the Latin American and Caribbean Coordinating Committee for Mobilization in Support of the Right to Have an Abortion. They drafted a document stating that the right to have a "legal abortion, and the right to access to safe and efficient contraceptives are human rights, regardless of our social and economic conditions, our ethnic origin, our religion or the country to which we belong. The states must guarantee these rights." It also called for the creation of national commissions on abortion and the participation of women throughout the region in the campaign to legalize abortion, and it declared September 28 the day to celebrate the cause of abortion rights in Latin American and Caribbean countries (a date chosen in memory of the 1871 Brazilian law that declared free all children born of slave mothers).

The presence in San Bernardo of legislators from Uruguay, Argentina, and as far north as Venezuela underscored the importance that Latin American and Caribbean feminism has assumed; it also demonstrated that women engaged in establishment politics now also view an Encuentro as a place to meet. Though many had never been in contact with feminists prior to their trip to San Bernardo—and several only remained for a few hours—their participation in a *taller* became a significant event. One of the outcomes of their discussions was the creation of a network that will sponsor a meeting in Brazil before the end of 1991 for women in politics.

Established networks used the Encuentro to meet for the first time—except of course for the writers of mujer/fempress, the feminist alternative press founded in 1981, who have met at every Encuentro since Lima. *Católicas por el Derecho a Decidir* (Catholics for Free Choice), a recent Latin American offshoot of the group of the same name, held an open meeting to explain its activities and publicize its book on abortion in Latin America, a collective endeavor analyzing abortion from the perspective of Latin American Catholics.[40] The Southern Cone Domestic Violence Network also held four meetings and decided to widen its structure and scope to become the Latin American and Caribbean Network Against Sexual and Domestic Violence, which will be coordinated by ISIS International. Latin American members of DAWN (Development Alternatives for Women in the New Dawn) sponsored a three-day workshop attended by some 100 women on *El Feminismo de los 90: Desafíos y Propuestas* (Feminism in the '90s: Challenges and Proposals). The discussion was based on topics agreed on at two previous DAWN meetings and resulted in a document that was probably the only real attempt to evaluate Latin American and Caribbean feminism during the fifth Encuentro.

The DAWN document began by acknowledging the rapid and visible growth of feminism over the past ten years, although it has not always found smooth outlets for its expression, which has been more quantitative than qualitative; which has, at times, diluted our subversive character by being diverted into other movements and challenges; which is presently raising problems of internal democracy, of leadership, of structures within the movement, of creating new knowledge, of better channels of communication, of projection into the future; and which challenges us to rethink our movement in order to transform quantitative richness into political vitality and quality. Accordingly, as we enter the 1990s, the movement needs to recapture some of its original spark and develop actions that will allow us to shape our proposals in the face of the new demands and the needs of the women of our countries and our continent; directions that will help us to consolidate a democratic, effective, efficient, nurturing, and daring feminist movement in which we all feel expressed.[41]

The Encuentro ended with passionate declarations of feminist faith, and some 5,000 women marched along the streets of Buenos Aires on the final day. However, organizationally, from the perspective of an histórica—of whom there were noticeably fewer—the fifth Encuentro was a disaster.[42] For one thing, there was no respect for or commitment to the long-standing promise to meet in Chile as soon as the Pinochet dictatorship ended. At previous Encuentros, the históricas' widespread admiration for the courageous actions of Chilean women in general and the Chilean feminists in particular had led them to favor Chile as the site of a future Encuentro. Yet in San Bernardo, when Chile was proposed as the next site and explicitly discarded in favor of Cuba, many históricas experienced a painful moment for their commitment of 1981 held little currency with the thrust of a movement that now appeared dominated by the movimientos de mujeres. Nevertheless, Cuba, too, was discarded after a Cuban participant said it would be impossible to hold the Encuentro there, and the final selection was "somewhere in Central America."

It was ironic that the selection of Central America, where feminism has only recently reemerged, should be felt as a disappointment by many feministas históricas, when in fact it is also a measure of the movement's growth and vitality. Additionally, holding the Encuentro in Central America will surely strengthen the movement, as has been the case elsewhere. It was also ironic that insofar as San Bernardo demonstrated the existence of numerous networks in the region and their need to hold specialized gatherings, the feministas found themselves as one more constituency of groups free to meet separately. Therefore, although feministas históricas will undoubtedly attend the sixth Encuentro, like the other networks, they will also undoubtedly now meet alone as well—probably in Chile— to discuss the challenges and elaborate proposals for El Feminismo de los 90.

San Bernardo was unmistakably the culmination of a process that had begun in Bogotá and that is no longer viable in the conditions of the 1990s. Nobody would deny that today's movement differs radically from the relatively small group of women who met in Bogotá ten years ago. Now, it is the task of Latin American and Caribbean feminists to elaborate the appropriate structures for the articulation of an ever larger and ever more diverse movement of true continental proportions.

Conclusion

The ideological and strategic debates characteristic of contemporary Latin American feminisms have revolved around two central axes: the relationship between feminism and the revolutionary struggle for justice and the relationship between what was a predominantly middle-class feminist movement and the growing popular-based *movimientos de mujeres*. As the five Encuentros demonstrated, these debates have been repeatedly recast and are far from resolved.

But political and ideological polarization has not stunted the growth of Latin American feminisms. Instead, Latin American feminism today is a politically and socially heterogeneous movement composed of women who identify with feminism but who retain an unwavering commitment to socioeconomic justice and popular empowerment. In a supposedly "postfeminist" era, Latin American feminism is clearly a powerful, vibrant, energetic, creative, and exuberant political force, if still fraught with tensions. Women from all social sectors and with wide-ranging personal and political trajectories now call the movement their own. The movement's new visibility and legitimacy have enabled feminists in many countries to proudly proclaim a distinctive political identity. That identity has in turn empowered women to have an impact on public policies, political and social organizations, and revolutionary theory in ways that were unthinkable when feminists first met in Bogotá. Even Chilean feminists, in the face of one of the continent's most nefarious military dictatorships, remained undaunted, and they were strengthened by a flourishing women's movement that has become increasingly feminist.

Although some old debates have not been resolved, many of them are currently being reformulated. Such is the case with the never-ending, strategic conflict over *doble militancia*. In Bogotá, the debate revolved around participation in political parties versus feminist organizations, but today many feminists find that their energies are split between their activism in feminist groups and in the growing *movimientos de mujeres*. The feminist movement and the *movimientos de mujeres*, though too often perceived as diametrically opposed, have, in Chile and elsewhere, reinforced, strengthened, and supported each another. In Central America, this interaction has led the Central American Women's Permanent Assembly for Peace "to begin to articulate and aggressively push for an explicitly feminist perspective."[43] In Argentina, since 1990, the campaign to legalize abortion has been led by a committee composed of feminists and women belonging to the *movimientos de mujeres*. Also in Argentina, members of the human rights group Madres de Plaza de Mayo–Línea Fundadora, participate in national Encuentros and often coordinate specific actions with one feminist group in particular, ATEM 25 de Noviembre (Asociación de Trabajo y Estudios de la Mujer, 25 de Noviembre, or Work and Study Association on Women, November 25).

However, as women learned in the case of Taxco, mutual support between *veteranas* and *movimientos de mujeres* will only be solidified if the feminist agenda can be expanded to include the specific concerns of women of the popular classes. Incorporating the demands of an increasingly feminist *movimiento de mujeres* for the construction of a more inclusive, racially aware, and class-conscious feminist transformational project is the biggest challenge facing Latin American and Caribbean feminisms in the 1990s.

Though the tensions between *militantes* and *feministas* remain in evidence, they are mostly in the background. Many women of both groups now insist that they must organize around issues of class and race insofar as these shape the way gender oppression is manifest in the lives of women of varied classes and racial/ethnic groups. And it is now recognized by many that participation in male-dominated institutions, parties, and unions is not intrinsically antithetical to feminist political practice—that feminist activists committed to radical change must struggle for gender equality in a wide variety of contexts.

Contrary to the belief of many North American feminists, Latin American and Caribbean feminism is thriving. Not only that, Latin American feminisms hold lessons for feminists in industrialized countries. We North American and Western European feminists could revitalize our own movements if we tapped the enormous creative energies embodied in our own *movimientos de mujeres*. The present vitality of Third World feminisms *within* the industrialized world is indicative of this potential. Regressive economic policies and right-wing governments in the First World have also created conditions ripe for the mobilization of poor and working-class women and women of color; witness, for example, the recent expansion of organizing efforts concerning welfare rights and publicly funded day-care. Just as North American or European feminism once provided crucial insights for the second wave of feminism in Latin America, perhaps now Latin American feminisms can enrich and inspire our own movements.

Notes

We have listed our names in reverse alphabetical order. This order in no way reflects the magnitude of individual contributions.

We acknowledge the assistance of the following: Tinker Foundation, Kirkland Endowment and Picker Fellowship (Sternbach); Darmouth Faculty Research Fund and the John Sloan Dickey Endowment for International Understanding (Navarro); University of Lethbridge Faculty Research Fund and the Social Sciences and Humanities Research Council of Canada Isolation Fund (Chuchryk); and the UC-MEXUS Travel Fund (Alvarez). Alvarez and Navarro would like to thank Pat Sanders and Gail Vernazza, respectively, for their assistance in the preparation of the manuscript. Alvarez would also like to thank Judit Moschkovich for her helpful suggestions. In addition, the authors are most grateful to the anonymous *Signs* readers for their comments.

1. For examples of testimonial literature, see Barrios de Chungara (with Moerna Viezzer) 1978; Burgos-Debray, ed., 1984; and Randall and Yanz, eds., 1981.

2. Bloch 1985: 18.

3. See, for example, the arguments suggested in Mattelart 1980 and Crummett 1977.

4. We use the word *feminisms*—as do Latin American feminists themselves—because Latin America and the Caribbean are composed of many discrete nations, races, and classes and therefore many interpretations of reality. Within the Latin American and Caribbean context, feminism varies from country to country. When we speak of those diverse interpretations of feminism, we shall refer to them as *feminisms*.

5. "*Encuentro* (from the Spanish encontrar)—to meet or to find, oneself or another, to confront oneself or another. Also used in the reflexive, encontrarse—to find oneself, or to meet

each other, as in coming together, to share. A meeting place where one exchanges ideas, expresses feelings, thoughts and emotions; listens and is listened to, agrees and disagrees, affirms and contradicts." Cited in Ortega and Sternbach 1986: 1.

Throughout this article, we have maintained the original Spanish in terminology that would either get lost or confused in translation. In addition to Encuentro, readers will also find terms such as *movimientos de mujeres* (women's grass-roots organizations), *históricas* and *veteranas* (veterans of the feminist movement), and *militantes* or *políticas* (left-wing political activists).

6. The very uniqueness of Latin American feminisms as social phenomena may further be evidenced by the coinage of a terminology appropriate to the region's circumstances. Although we have given English equivalents to all these terms, we prefer to refer to them in their original Spanish in order to maintain their integrity.

7. For a comprehensive discussion of the mainstream theoretical debates surrounding the origins and the dynamics of military authoritarian regimes in Latin America during the 1960s and 1970s, see Collier, ed., 1979.

8. The most sophisticated theoretical treament of this aspect of military rule can be found in the work of Julieta Kirkwood. See especially Kirkwood 1980, 1981, 1983, 1986, 1987 and Crispi 1987. See also Neto 1980. For an analysis of gender ideology and policies of militaristic states in different national contexts, see Tornaría 1986; Bunster-Burotto 1988; M. Valenzuela 1987; and Chuchryk 1984, especially chapters 3 and 4.

9. Cited in Chuchryk 1984: 320. See also M. Valenzuela 1986. In this paper, Valenzuela argued that the Chilean military state is the quintessential expression of patriarchy. She drew similarities between the military's control over civil society and male domination over women.

10. See especially Bunster-Burotto 1985.

11. On Peruvian women's movements, see Barrig 1989a; Vargas 1985, 1987; Anderson Velasco 1985; Bourque 1985; and Andreas 1985.

12. On Uruguay, see Perelli 1989; Villamil Rodríguez and Sapriza 1987; Tornaría 1986. On Argentina, see Feijóo 1985, 1989 and Chester 1986. On Chilean women's movements, see Chuchryk 1989a and Kirkwood 1986, 1987. On Brazil, see the discussion of the Bertioga Encuentro later in this chapter.

13. The Argentine case stands as the exception that proves the rule. There, feminism emerged primarily from professional women and not necessarily from women who had been involved with the Left.

14. For a comparative discussion of the emergence and development of women's movements in Peru, Chile, Argentina, Uruguay, and Brazil, see Jaquette, ed., 1989. See also Flora 1984. On the contradictions experienced by women active in militant organizations, see Brito 1986.

15. We take the word *popular* in English from the Spanish *popular*, which means "of the people," and use it accordingly. Throughout this chapter, we shall use it in this context to refer to everyone who is not of a professional or owning class: the workers, campesinos, shopkeepers, working class, lower middle class, and so forth.

16. For the most comprehensive comparative treatment of the "movimiento de mujeres," see Jelin, ed., 1990.

17. On the important role of human rights organizations in the Argentine transition from authoritarian rule, see Sonderéguer 1985; Navarro 1989. On Chile, see Chuchryk 1989b.

18. A distinction between "feminine" and "feminist" women's movement organizations is commonly made by both movement participants and social scientists in Latin America. Paul Singer clarified the usage of these concepts: "The struggles against the rising cost of living or for schools, day care centers, etc., as well as specific measures to protect women who work interest women closely and it is possible then to consider them *feminine* revindications. But they are not *feminist* to the extent that they do not question the way in which women are inserted into the social context." Singer and Brant 1980: 116–117. On feminine movements or the *movimientos de mujeres*, see Andreas 1985; Schmink 1981; and Jelin, ed., 1987a.

19. This distinction between "good" and "bad" feminisms is elaborated in Goldberg 1982a: 10–11. Portions of the ensuing discussion draw on Alvarez 1990a, especially chapters 3, 4, and 5.

20. See Partnoy 1986; Argentina's National Commission of Disappeared People 1986; and Bunster-Burotto 1985.

21. The textual quotations in this article are based on interviews conducted by all four coauthors. When no citation appears, readers should assume that these remarks are from one of the Encuentros.

22. Navarro 1982a, 1982b.

23. Actually, it was a group of Venezuelan feminists, La Conjura, who first thought about organizing an Encuentro in August 1979. Only after it was clear that they could not do it did the Colombian feminists take up the challenge.

24. See Navarro 1982b.

25. In Spanish, maternidad libre y voluntaria essentially means "every child a wanted child."

26. This term was first encountered in the report on the Lima Encuentro. See "II Encuentro Feminista Latinamericano y del Caribe" 1984.

27. A document published about the Lima Encuentro listed sixty-three papers that had been presented. See "El Encuentro Feminista Latinoamericano y del Caribe" 1984: 140–144. Until San Bernardo, the formal presentation of papers tended to be minimized. Rather, each taller becomes a working group that comes together to address a single issue.

28. Auto-gestión literally means self-gestating, that is, a free form, a spontaneous structure that would permit participants to organize and create their own talleres on the spur of the moment. It should be pointed out that in spite of its emphasis on auto-gestión, the Bertioga Encuentro was structured and organized.

29. On the Brazilian feminist movement and the issues it has politicized, see Alvarez 1990a. See also Sarti 1989; Moraes 1985; Goldberg 1982a, 1982b; Pinheiro 1981; and Alves and Pitanguy 1981.

30. For a more detailed account of this polarizing series of events, see Ortega and Sternbach 1986 and Moschkovich, Cora, and Alvarez 1986.

31. For a background to the long-standing conflicts between the Brazilian feminist movement and the sectarian Left, see Alvarez 1989a.

32. On the development of revolutionary feminism in Sandinista Nicaragua, see Chinchilla 1990 and Molyneux 1986, 1988.

33. For example, some of the groups represented included mothers' clubs, housewives' associations, ollas comunes, comedores populares, Mexico City's damnificadas, and rural women's organizations. (Ollas comunes and comedores populares are economic survival strategies designed by shantytown women to provide basic necessities of life; the damnificadas are also shantytown women's organizations to assist the victims of natural disasters, such as floods or earthquakes.)

34. A Latina is defined as "a woman of Latin American heritage or descent permanently residing in the U.S." Ortega and Sternbach 1989. This definition is adapted from Juan Bruce-Novoa's definition of Chicano, in Bruce-Novoa 1980.

35. See Alvarez 1990b.

36. For a discussion of the interface of revolutionary struggles and gender struggles in contemporary Central and South America, see Chinchilla, Chapter 3.

37. Speech by a veterana at a workshop entitled "Visions for the Future," Taxco, October 1987.

38. The problem of financing the Encuentro at a time of deep economic crisis, including the questions of alternative financing and use of public facilities, has been central to all organizing committees. After a heated debate, members of the Argentine group decided to forsake government support (though they received it from a Dutch government agency) and seek foreign funding. They received funds from several foundations, including the Global Fund for Women, the Ford Foundation, the World Council of Churches, Match and CIDA–Canada and Aktions-

gemeinschaft Solidarische. The funds allowed the organizers to cover 60 percent of the costs of the Encuentro and subsidize attendance. Argentines and Uruguayans paid 25 percent of the real cost, and women from other Latin American and Caribbean countries paid 50 percent. First World women paid US$100.

39. The name in Spanish is deeply ironic. It conveys the idea that although an Encuentro is a place to meet people and come together, San Bernardo was actually an Encuentro where people missed each other.

40. See Portugal, ed., 1987.

41. "El Feminismo de los 90: Desafíos y Propuestas" 1991. The authors defined the feminist movement as a social movement that needs to transform itself into a political movement, committed to democracy and diversity. Although they did not elaborate how this would be accomplished, they discussed two important issues for the movement: the reluctance of feminists to deal with leadership and the funding some women receive from research centers.

42. At this point, it is impossible to draw conclusions from the small number of *históricas* in attendance at the fifth Encuentro: We would be reluctant to conclude at this date whether their absence was significant or coincidental.

43. Personal correspondence from Norma Stoltz Chinchilla to Sonia Alvarez, August 21, 1990.

13

The Evolution of Urban
Popular Movements in Mexico
Between 1968 and 1988

Vivienne Bennett

Introduction

From 1940 to 1970, Mexico experienced sustained, high economic growth as government policies focused on providing incentives and infrastructure for diversified industrialization and for commercial agriculture. Throughout this period, widely known as the "Mexican Miracle," Mexico's cities grew at unprecedented and unexpected rates. Yet, living conditions in urban areas deteriorated as the government was unable or unwilling to extend public services to burgeoning outlying neighborhoods, many of which did not have legal land tenure. Job opportunities in the cities did not keep pace with the high rate of rural-to-urban migration or with the growing number of high school and university graduates seeking professional employment.

In 1968, urban dissatisfactions exploded as the urban poor, including housewives, joined students in protesting government repression, the lack of jobs, and inadequate living conditions. The 1968 protests ended with violent repression as government troops fired on a peaceful rally in Mexico City, killing an estimated 200 people (Stevens 1974: 237).

During the period between 1968 and 1988, which is the setting for this chapter, distortions in Mexico's development model were evident in the nation's economy. Although the latter half of the 1970s was known as a boom due to the discovery of Mexico's enormous petroleum reserves, warning signals for the oncoming economic crisis were already visible in the first half of that decade during President Luís Echeverría's term in office. His attempts at economic reform not only failed but brought on a serious split between Mexico's business community and the government. After his election in 1976, President José López Portillo sought to regain the confidence of the business community by investing heavily in the so-called modern sectors of Mexico's economy. His presidency was marked by a heavy reliance on external loans using Mexico's petroleum reserves as a guarantee. In 1982, after world prices for oil plummeted, President López Portillo was forced to halt payments on Mexico's foreign debt, and he nationalized Mexican banks.

When President Miguel de la Madrid took office in late 1982, he inherited a virtually bankrupt economy, a distrustful private sector, and a newly cautious international banking community. Capital flight grew through the 1970s and 1980s, inflation escalated, and the national currency was progressively devalued.

Mexico's economic woes coincided with conflicts within its political system. President Echeverría's "democratic opening" of the early 1970s was followed in 1977 by President López Portillo's electoral reform law, which facilitated the registration of opposition parties. Yet, by 1986, the ruling party (the *Partido Revolucionario Institucional*, PRI) was still sufficiently rigid and nondemocratic in its internal organization that a "Democratic Current" was formed within the party itself, urging democratic reforms. The appeals of the Democratic Current created schisms within the PRI between groups who supported the continuation of Mexico's "old-style" politics and those who favored liberalization. Those schisms reached a peak in 1987 when the Democratic Current split from the PRI, formed a new party (the *Frente Democrático Nacional*, FDN), and nominated its own candidate, Cuauhtémoc Cárdenas, for the 1988 presidential elections. In the 1988 elections, the PRI won the presidency with 50.7 percent of the votes, its lowest percentage ever. However, the vote count showed that the PRI had suffered a spectacular loss of the urban vote throughout much of Mexico and had lost resoundingly to Cárdenas in Mexico City itself.

What happened in Mexico during the two decades between the violently repressed student movements of 1968 and the near victory of opposition presidential candidate Cuauhtémoc Cárdenas in 1988? How was the opposition movement in Mexico able to evolve from one that experienced tremendous repression in 1968 to one that achieved partial victory at the polls during the presidential elections twenty years later? The vote in 1988 indicates a significant shift in the political behavior of the poor, yet it is a change that has to do not only with electoral politics but also with widespread grass-roots movements that traditionally had rejected the electoral process.

Until the 1980s, with the exception of a handful of seminal studies exploring the politics of urban poverty,[1] scholars were more concerned with electoral politics and decisionmaking at the top than with the seemingly secondary activities of the urban masses. Recently, however, scholars have increasingly turned their attention to a multitude of diverse activities originating primarily in low-income neighborhoods throughout Latin America that voice the discontent and the needs of the poor: land invasions, Christian base communities, protests over inadequate and expensive public services, soup kitchens, rallies against the high cost of living and political persecution, and more.[2] In reviewing the case studies emerging over the last decade, two observations can be made readily. First, a broad array of actions is taking place in urban areas. And second, their characteristics vary across regions and over time.

Touraine (1984b) suggested three categories for collective action. The first consists of defensive collective actions that he termed conflictual actions. The second, social struggle, consists of actions that "modify decisions or whole systems of decision-making" (cited in Slater 1985b: 19). The third, social movement, consists of collective actions that are explicitly intended to change social relations of power in key areas of society. Castells (1982) distinguished between urban movements and social movements. Like Touraine, he suggested that collective actions may be properly termed social movements only if they seek social transformation. Calderón (1986) identified four types of collective action: small groups that independently create their own forms of organization; collective actions that imply or demand the decentralization of urban politics and the right to neighborhood democracy; actions that imply the transformation of sociocultural relations; and urban movements that create the possibility of communication between different groups, either through class alliances or national associations (Calderón 1986: 354–355).

Although there seems to be a sense that the collective actions of the urban poor in Latin America should not be called social movements unless they explicitly aim to transform society, it is not clear at what point collective actions without such an explicit goal become transformative by their proliferation. Is it possible that one neighborhood action alone would fall into Touraine's first category (conflictual action) but one hundred conflictual actions occurring in one major city simultaneously, even if independently, could cause social transformation?

In Mexico, in particular, there has been a wide array of grass-roots-based, "popular" activities over the last twenty years. And today, there is a fast-growing stock of case studies and histories of urban popular movements for cities throughout Mexico that offer rich details about participants, strategies, decisionmaking, state response, successes, and failures.

The results of the 1988 presidential election constitute an obvious change in the relationship between civil society and the political system in Mexico. Observers of contemporary Mexico have linked the turn of the urban vote away from the PRI to the increase of urban dissatisfactions and of popular organizing since 1982 and particularly since the earthquake in 1985. Yet, urban popular organizing in Mexico did not start in the years preceding the 1988 elections; rather, by that time, it already had a long and serious history in many Mexican cities. Incidents of the urban poor organizing around issues of housing and public services occurred even in the 1950s and 1960s but rapidly grew in number after 1968, the year that is commonly recognized as the cutoff between past and present in terms of popular response to weaknesses in Mexico's development model.

Urban popular movements have occurred in three principal waves, the first in the early 1970s, the second from 1979 through 1983, and the third between 1985 and 1988. This chapter explores in detail the first two waves and provides an overview of the third, suggesting that urban popular movements have had a transformative effect on Mexico's social and political system.

Urban Popular Movements in Mexico: Antecedents

Urban popular movements are a direct response to the inability of Mexico's development model to provide a decent standard of living for the majority of the population. Between 1930 and 1980, there was a radical shift of the population from rural to urban areas: In 1930, two-thirds of Mexico's population lived in the countryside; by 1980, two-thirds lived in urban areas. And from 1940 to 1970,

TABLE 13.1   Population: Mexico City, Guadalajara, and Monterrey Metropolitan Areas, 1940–1980

Year	Mexico City	Guadalajara	Monterrey
1940	1,802,679	274,733	206,152
1950	3,137,599	440,528	375,040
1960	5,251,755	851,155	708,300
1970	8,799,937	1,491,085	1,246,181
1980	13,354,271	2,192,557	1,913,075

Source: Instituto Nacional de Estadística, Geografía e Informática, *Estadísticas Históricas de México* (México: Secretaría de Programación y Presupuesto, Dirección General de Estadística, 1985), 24–28.

the population of Mexico City more than quadrupled, and the populations of Monterrey and Guadalajara more than quintupled.[3] (See Table 13.1.) Yet until the mid-1970s, the Mexican government paid little attention to urban planning (Herzog 1990: 215).

It was not until 1976, with the Law of Human Settlements and the creation of a new Ministry of Settlements and Public Works (*Secretaría de Asentamientos Humanos y de Obras Públicas*, SAHOP), that recognition was given to the need for systematic regulation and planning of urban areas. However, even then, urban planning was oriented to meeting the needs of the dominant economic sectors, and SAHOP itself was never given adequate funding to implement its plans (Herzog 1990: 215–216). In fact, the SAHOP ministry barely lasted the six years of President López Portillo's administration before being replaced with an even less effective ministry in 1983 after President de la Madrid came to power (the *Secretaría de Desarrollo Urbano y de Ecología*, SEDUE).

Sustained high urbanization rates in Mexico with inadequate government attention to social welfare meant that an urban crisis was already latent in the 1960s. Government investment in social infrastructure in the 1970s was too late and too little, and in the 1980s, it was severely constrained by the economic crisis. By 1980, the secretary of planning and budget estimated a countrywide housing deficit of 4 million homes, affecting 30 percent of the population (Schteingart 1985–1986: 170). In that same year, it was estimated that in Monterrey, Mexico's third largest city, 21 percent of homes had only one room (Villarreal and Castañeda 1986: 188). Approximately half the homes nationwide did not have running water and sewage service.[4] Meanwhile, the economic crisis that exploded in 1982 exacerbated the deteriorating living conditions of the urban majority. Real minimum wages fell by 41.9 percent from 1982 to 1987 (Middlebrook 1989: 292), while inflation surged from 28 percent in 1981 to 101.9 percent in 1983, 132 percent in 1987, and 114 percent in 1988.[5]

The First Wave of Urban Popular Movements: Early 1970s

The first wave of urban popular movements (UPMs) in Mexico occurred in the early 1970s in response to the general inadequacy of urban life: lack of jobs, lack of mobility, inadequate urban services, and housing shortages, as well as government indifference, inability, or violence in dealing with these problems.[6] These UPMs arose in the northern states of Chihuahua, Nuevo León, and Durango and in the southern state of Oaxaca.

In Durango, student activists who had emerged during the 1968 student movement began trying to organize in urban areas. After focusing on what they thought were the most urgent issues—land and housing—the students noticed that the urban poor they had contact with were more concerned with high water rates than with anything else. The students' strategy was to work on issues that addressed the people's immediate needs, and once they began to organize around the issue of water rates, there was a solid response. In 1972, 1,500 poor people attended two rallies at the *Junta Federal de Agua Potable* and participated in a sit-in at the Municipal Palace that received widespread popular support. Within three months, the government granted the rate reductions demanded by the protesters. At the end of the year, the neighborhoods that had won the battle over water rates united over a new goal: the acquisition of land. After nine months of varied tactics—including a rejected petition to the governor requesting land, two severely repressed land invasions, and harassment and imprisonment of members—the group achieved a negotiated settlement with the federal government's housing agency, INDECO, that gave them twenty hectares of land at very low cost. The September 1973 creation of the *Colonia División del Norte* on that land allowed the consolidation of the group, the organization of several further land invasions that were successful, the support of various labor and peasant struggles, and the eventual formation in 1979 of the *Comité de Defensa Popular-Durango*, (CDP-Durango) (Cruz, Yañez, Villaseñor, and Moguel, eds., 1986).

In Chihuahua, the killing of five urban guerrillas during a triple bank assault in 1972 served as the catalyst for the formation of the *Comité de Defensa Popular-Chihuahua* (CDP-Chihuahua). The *Colonia Francisco Villa*, a squatter settlement, organized protests against government violence and repression, which received substantial support and led to the establishment of the CDP-Chihuahua, a coalition consisting of the villa, seven independent labor organizations, and a student organization (Orozco 1976).

In Monterrey, land invasions began occurring with regularity in 1971 as the city's population, swollen from heavy migration to the city in the 1950s and 1960s, confronted massive housing shortages. Some of the invasions were directed by student activists who, after 1968, decided that the next course of action was to work with the people on what they needed most. Though most land invasions were met with state repression, eventually many succeeded in establishing themselves, primarily because the state could offer no alternative until the mid-1970s.[7] Many of the new squatter settlements were very well organized and had highly politicized leaders who sought to place the appropriation of land within a larger context of class struggle. One in particular, the *Colonia Tierra y Libertad*, was led by militant students who taught the community to address its practical needs of shelter, electricity, water, schools, and so forth through a Maoist approach of community organization, including block leaders, neighborhood assemblies, and community-labor Sundays. This neighborhood was successful in achieving a high degree of solidarity and sustaining internal morale in the face of state repression. Its ability to construct an internal organization and at the same time support other land invasions, renters' struggles, and workers' strikes led to the formation of the umbrella organization *Frente Popular Tierra y Libertad* (FPTyL) in 1976. The FPTyL was directed from the Colonia Tierra y Libertad by the original student leaders of the invasion. The group initially consisted of 31 *colonias populares* (poor urban neighborhoods), 16 tenant groups, 3 *ejido* (collective farm) associations, and various working-class subgroups (including bus drivers, street vendors, and street photographers) (Pérez Güemes and Garza del Toro 1984: 42), comprising 50,000 to 350,000 people (according to different sources).[8]

In Oaxaca, the urban popular movement was centered in the city of Juchitán. Once again, it was students who became the leaders, forming the *Coalición de Obreros, Campesinos, y Estudiantes del Istmo* (COCEI) in 1973.[9] The COCEI used strikes, marches, the occupation of government buildings, and negotiations to pressure the government for improvements in living and working conditions. It rapidly gained widespread support among both peasants and low-income city residents because it worked on behalf of both groups. In the agricultural sector, the COCEI successfully fought for enforcement of land ownership limitations, for land distribution to peasants, and against tax increases; it also improved peasants' access to local power structures. In the city, the COCEI supported and organized strikes that led to wage and benefit improvements, protested transportation rate increases, and generally tried to make the city administration more responsible to the citizenry.

Of the organizations that formed the first wave of urban popular movements, the COCEI was the only one to participate in elections. The other UPMs rejected electoral participation as reformist and as an ineffective way to meet the real needs of the people, but the COCEI considered it a useful and valid strategy. Thus, in addition to its direct organizing tactics, the COCEI fielded independent candidates in municipal elections starting in the early 1970s. Given the PRI's control of election outcomes and the fact that, until 1977, there were no legally registered leftist parties, the COCEI stood no chance of winning during the 1970s. However, it successfully used its participation in elections as a concrete goal around which to organize and as a forum from which to denounce electoral fraud and expose nondemocratic practices. And despite violent repression by the government and right-wing paramilitary groups, the COCEI continued to organize with significant popular support.

What stands out about the movements that composed the first wave of UPMs in Mexico? First, each of them entailed the construction of new channels to express the needs of poor urban residents. It was the explicit intent of these movements to bypass the traditional channels, which were seen as incapable of resolving the growing urban crisis. Since the late 1930s, the Mexican government had tried to channel the needs of the people—peasants, workers, and popular sectors—through the mass organizations of the ruling party, the PRI.[10] The ostensible purposes of these mass organizations were to serve as the voice of a defined sector of the population, to reflect and channel that sector's needs to decisionmakers in Mexico City, and to mediate the government's response.

However, as Mexico's development model led the country to higher unemployment and underemployment and as the government's economic policy explicitly favored large-scale industrialization and the commercialization of agriculture, the mass organizations acted less and less as representatives of the people and more as representatives of the capital-state alliance. This meant that basic needs were met primarily when doing so would provide political capital for the PRI and only insofar as it meshed with government policies and budgets.

Starting in the 1970s, two of the mass organizations of the PRI, the *Confederación de Trabajadores Mexicanos* (CTM) and the *Confederación Nacional de Organizaciones Populares* (CNOP), themselves began organizing land invasions in Mexico's cities. Actually, given the huge gap between the need for and the provision of low-income housing, there had been an increase in illegal land invasions throughout urban Mexico. The government considered it safer to have its own mass organizations lead new invasions, where they could continue to have an administrative presence and impede the formation of autonomous urban popular groups. Thus, allowing its mass organizations to set up land invasions was one way to keep the urban poor linked to the PRI and under its control. Yet, neither the CTM nor the CNOP could keep up with the demand for shelter, and neither truly represented the people. The UPMs, therefore, were vying for the same constituency as the official mass organizations, and their success in terms of popular support is an indication that they were, indeed, filling a gap left by the dominant system.[11]

The second noteworthy characteristic of the UPMs is that they were more responsive to the needs of the people. A new relationship was created between the masses who formed the base of the popular sector and the activists who were their leaders. This was accomplished by creating organizational structures that allowed communication between the masses and their leaders—block meetings, open assemblies, and so on. The base of the UPMs was represented in a way that was absent with the official mass organizations. At the same time, the leaders of many of the new UPMs were strongly influenced by political ideologies rooted in Maoism and Marxist-Leninism that served as guidelines for their militant activity. And to an extent that varied at different moments and within different UPMs, these political ideologies created a filter through which the leaders interpreted the needs of the masses, thereby diminishing the democratic nature of the movements. In addition, in some UPMs, the same leaders have held power—formally or informally—since the movement's beginning. However, though their internal structures may have been less than truly democratic, most of the new UPMs successfully met the minimum needs of their constituencies for shelter and services and represented an alternative to the official mass organizations that the poor had long understood to be co-optative. And it is evident that when particular UPMs faltered, it was because the leadership had lost the ability to remain in touch with the needs of the base.[12]

Finally, the third aspect that stands out about the first wave of UPMs is their timing: All four emerged in 1972 (Chihuahua and Durango) or 1973 (Monterrey and Juchitán). This first wave clearly responded to two characteristics of political culture in Mexico in the early to mid-1970s—the existence of a cohort of militant students who responded to the violent repression of 1968 and 1971 by looking for direct links with the masses and the "democratic opening" offered by President Luís Echeverría after 1972. The democratic opening created a space for autonomous organizations, and Echeverría's administration even supported some of the new movements. An organization like the COCEI, for example, might have been eliminated under previous administrations, might have been forced to take a different form (such as guerrilla activity), or simply might not have emerged at all. However, in 1973, the COCEI was formed "with the tacit support of the president and several government ministries" (Rubin 1987b: 135). This is not to say that all UPMs received government support at that time or that repression was not used—as it was against the COCEI itself in the mid-1970s. Rather, the democratic opening created new spaces for organizing while retaining for the government the prerogative of applying any of its usual methods of control when necessary.

The influence of radical students on the first wave of UPMs should not be underestimated for they provided leadership, ideology, and structure to the movements in Monterrey, Durango, and Juchitán. After the repression of the student movements of 1968 and 1971, a large number of student leaders were either dead, in prison, or in exile, and militant student organizations were in disarray. The early 1970s was a time of political reconstruction for progressive students throughout Mexico. As they evaluated the failures and successes of 1968 and 1971, it was apparent that the deep dissatisfaction they themselves had voiced had been echoed by the lower classes and that the student movement had received support from the lower classes for that reason. It is not surprising, therefore, that at a time when high school– and university-based militancy had been severely repressed, the students would search for new forms of organizing and emerge as leaders of the most significant new urban popular movements.

The Repression and Ebb of Urban Popular Movements: 1976 to 1978

From 1976 to 1978, there was an ebb in the development of urban popular movements, primarily in response to an increase in repression.[13] President Echeverría had given up his attempts at social reform by 1976 in the face of widespread protest by the high bourgeoisie (expressed in capital flight, a moratorium on new investments, and a slowdown in production of agricultural export commodities). Mexico entered a period of inflationary recession, and both Echeverría and his successor, López Portillo, responded by cutting the government budget for social welfare. The more tolerant climate for UPMs fostered by Echeverría during his democratic opening gave way to a policy of repressing the movements and co-opting their leaders. The eradication of squatter settlements, isolation of popular movements, repression of movement leaders, uncontrolled speculation with rental housing rates, and the assassination of two residents of a land invasion settlement in Mexico City and six in Monterrey characterized this period. The mayor of the Federal District mandated a halt to land invasions, and mayors throughout Mexico followed his lead (Ramírez Saiz 1986: 59–60).

In 1977, President López Portillo approved a new electoral law that made sweeping changes in Mexico's electoral system, opening the possibility for a range of opposition parties to participate in elections for the first time in 1979. The president fostered an opening in electoral politics while maintaining a repressive stance toward UPMs for two reasons. First, officially, he had run unopposed in the 1976 presidential elections, therefore garnering 100 percent of the vote.[14] However, at least 38 percent of registered voters did not cast ballots that year (Middlebrook 1986: 129), which was an embarrassment and made it very difficult to sustain the myth that Mexico was a democracy with multiparty elections. Second, the new law allowed opposition parties to participate in elections under rules defined by the dominant party, the PRI. A key difference between opposition political parties and the UPMs was that, after the 1977 electoral reform, the former operated in an arena controlled by the dominant party, while the latter continued to seek autonomy. For a regime dedicated to finding ways to absorb, manipulate, subvert, or control all challenges, the continued existence of UPMs was unacceptable. Repression and co-optation were the only responses seen as possible by the government during the late 1970s.

Under these conditions, though a handful of new land invasions took place and a few new organizations were set up, most UPMs primarily worked to sustain levels of organization achieved earlier. *Frentes de Acción Popular* were set up in Saltillo, Puebla, and Guadalajara to confront the rising cost of urban services, but they rapidly disintegrated because they were leadership-heavy and had virtually no organic support (Ramírez Saiz 1986: 54–57). (A notable exception was in Monterrey, where the Frente Popular Tierra y Libertad was formed in 1976.) Furthermore, during the late 1970s, movements in Monterrey, Durango, and Torreón struggled with internal dissension created by ideological differences on such topics as the relationship between leadership and the mass base of the movements (Ramírez Saiz 1986: 57–59). But a strong resurgence of popular activity would begin in 1979.

The Second Wave of Urban Popular Movements: 1979 to 1983

From 1979 to 1983, there was a steady increase throughout Mexico in the formation of independent popular urban neighborhoods, in the creation of neighborhood-based organizations, and in the structuring of regional and even national coalitions of urban popular movements. Although the five-year period is consistent with regard to the renaissance of UPMs, it divides into two distinct stages with respect to economic and political context. The first two years, 1979 and 1980, correspond to the end of the petroleum boom, a period in which Mexico was awash with international loans and optimistic that its immense petroleum reserves would pay for the future. The last three years, 1981 through 1983, mark the onset of Mexico's economic crisis, with sudden devaluations, inflation, recession, massive budget cuts, layoffs, and the accelerated deterioration of standards of living for the majority. In 1981, lame duck President López Portillo presided over the rapid disintegration of the Mexican economy. In 1982, new

President de la Madrid faced an economy in crisis and a government without the resources it had habitually counted on to fund the social service programs that attempt to meet basic needs and contain national frustration.

From 1979 to 1983, new neighborhoods and organizations were formed in Baja California Norte, Guerrero, Jalisco, the Valley of Mexico, Durango, and Sinaloa. Two high points of the period came in 1981 with the creation of a national-level federation of urban popular movements and a regional coordinating body for the UPMs in the Valley of Mexico.

The urban popular movement in Acapulco, Guerrero, illustrates the maturity, level of organization, and support achieved by the most successful UPMs during this period. In 1980, massive plans for continued tourism development of the Acapulco Bay led the government to attempt the forced removal of 125,000 low-income residents, alleging that their presence along the port had polluted the bay.[15] The *Consejo General de Colonias Populares de Acapulco* (CGCPA) was formed by the residents to prevent relocation from settled neighborhoods in the convenient and central port area to an unserviced zone on the outskirts of the city.

The platform of the CGCPA centered on four demands: (1) no eviction and relocation, (2) improved urbanization of the threatened neighborhoods, (3) a halt to repression within those neighborhoods, and (4) the regularization of land tenancy. The CGCPA acted on four fronts simultaneously. First, it researched the causes of Acapulco Bay's contamination and widely publicized the results, which wholly absolved the neighborhoods in question. Second, it held rallies and marches not only in Acapulco but also in Chilpancingo, the state capital, and in Mexico City. Thirty thousand attended the rally in Chilpancingo, even though it meant traveling to another city. Third, it negotiated with the state government, reaching one agreement in July 1980, whereby the state agreed to stop repression and to improve public services to the port neighborhoods, and a second agreement in July 1981, whereby only residents living beyond 225 meters above sea level would be relocated. Lastly, the CGCPA worked within the movement to educate and inform the population. The group had broad contacts with leftist political parties, and it was articulated locally with the student movement and nationally, after 1981, with the National Coordinator of Urban Popular Movements (CONAMUP). The government responded by using all the resources at its disposal and achieved the relocation of a good many residents. In the end, however, despite the government's failure to keep its side of the negotiated agreements and its continuous use of intimidation tactics, the CGCPA maintained the support of twenty-eight of the port neighborhoods.

The Valley of Mexico, which contains almost one-quarter of Mexico's population, was the site of many land invasions and independently organized squatter settlements in the 1970s, but coalitions among neighborhood organizations were scarce.[16] Two groups attempted to create coordinating organizations, the *Frente Popular Independiente* (FPI) and, later, the *Bloque Urbano de Colonias Populares* (BUCP). Both groups were constrained by limited mass support, and until 1979, the urban popular movement in the Valley of Mexico was mainly of a spontaneous nature, directed at issues of immediate concern on the individual neighborhood level (Moctezuma 1986: 203).

Between 1979 and 1981, three important coalitions of popular neighborhoods were constituted in the Valley of Mexico. The first was the *Unión de Colonias Populares* (UCP), formally constituted in July 1979 with 300 members from 7 colonias (although it has its roots in a previous UPM, the Frente Popular Independiente).[17] By the time of its first anniversary in 1980, the UCP had 1,100 members in 9 colonias. The organization worked to forge links with other groups, first with the Left through the Mexican Communist Party (PCM) and later with other popular organizations. The UCP was one of four groups that coordinated the first nationwide meeting of urban popular movements, held in Monterrey in 1980, and it has remained active in creating new political organizations.[18]

The second coalition of neighborhoods in the Valley of Mexico was the *Movimiento Popular de Pueblos y Colonias del Sur* (MPPCS), created in 1980. The MPPCS consists of rural ejidos that had been transformed into urban neighborhoods as Mexico City expanded. A series of expropriations of ejidal land on the southern outskirts of Mexico City in 1949, 1952, 1972, and 1974 first led to the formation of *Campesinos Unidos* in 1974. Two years later, the organization was renamed *Lucha Popular*, in keeping with the social recomposition of the area over time. The group was once again renamed in 1980 and became the MPPCS, reflecting the part-urban and part-rural nature of the member neighborhoods. The MPPCS has supported numerous workers' strikes, peasant marches, and Central American liberation groups (Arau Chavarría 1987a, 1987b).

The year 1980 was a watershed for the evolution of urban popular movements in Mexico because, for the first time, individual UPMs transcended their local nature and participated in a dialogue on the national level. In May of that year, Monterrey was the site of the first national congress of urban popular movements, organized by three of the strongest UPMs in Mexico: the UCP, the FPTyL in Monterrey, and the CDP in Durango, along with the *Frente Popular de Zacatecas* (FPZ). Some 15 organizations and 700 delegates attended the congress, which was designed to give the leaders and participants of the UPMs a chance to discuss strategies, conditions, and political ideology. The meetings concluded with a pact of solidarity, a decision to hold a second congress in 1981, and the creation of a national coordinating body (*Coordinadora Nacional Provisional del Movimiento Popular*) that proceeded to meet monthly until the next national congress (Moctezuma 1984: 71-73).

The second national congress of UPMs was held in Durango in April of 1981. This time, 2,000 delegates from 60 organizations in 14 states attended. The biggest achievement of the second congress was the creation of a formal, national-level coordinating body for the UPMs across Mexico—the *Confederación Nacional del Movimiento Urbano Popular*. CONAMUP is a peak organization whose purpose is to support the evolution of UPMs throughout Mexico in several ways. It provides an umbrella structure that organizes yearly meetings that permit the exchange of information and strategies. It mediates between the government and local or regional UPMs. And it synthesizes and disseminates information on the current status of the urban popular movement in Mexico through its publications. CONAMUP's plan of action is concentrated on two areas: improving living conditions for the impoverished majority and working toward a more democratic society with full respect for human rights. CONAMUP holds the state and the private sector responsible for the widespread poverty of urban Mexico and calls on the state to cease evictions of squatters and renters, to freeze rents, to provide adequate public services, to eliminate the value-added tax (IVA—a regressive sales tax), to sustain consumer price subsidies, to release political prisoners, and to respect the democratic freedom of the population. CONAMUP recognizes that its members and their struggles are part of a larger context of an unequal society, and it has promoted links and solidarity with coalitions representing other sectors, such as peasants, workers, and teachers.[19]

CONAMUP is not a political party, and no political parties are allowed to join it. In fact, one of the fiercest causes of dissent within CONAMUP has been whether to participate in elections. Those who favor electoral participation argue that it is a valid tactic that allows UPMs to reach a wider population with their message; those who are against fielding candidates—and even against voting—argue that elections in Mexico are a means for the government to legitimate its system of hegemonic control. From its inception, CONAMUP's members have agreed that individual UPMs would retain their autonomy on this matter, each deciding for itself the extent of its participation in electoral politics, and that CONAMUP as an organization would not participate.[20]

The third coalition of popular movements in the Valley of Mexico, the *Coordinadora Regional del Valle de México* (CRMUP),[21] was created after the second national congress in 1981, as mandated by the formal structure of CONAMUP. The CRMUP was formed to coordinate the UPMs in the Valley of Mexico; in 1981, there were approximately twenty-five. CRMUP targeted six areas of concern: (1) land tenure, (2) public services, especially water, transportation, and education, (3) neighborhood pollution, (4) excessively high property taxes, (5) stopping the mass evictions and forced relocation of the urban poor to make way for profitable urban redevelopment, and (6) the right of independent popular organizations to exist and the exercise of democratic freedom. But though CRMUP worked hard to organize itself both within different zones of the valley and across zones on a regional level, it was unable to develop a consistent membership because each participating organization gave priority to its own local needs. The willingness of each organization to participate in CRMUP actions was, to a great extent, determined by the results achieved through prior participations.

As new UPMs were formed during the second wave, popular movements created in the first wave continued to evolve. In Durango, for example, new land invasions were successfully carried out throughout the 1970s. In 1979, 600 residents from 22 neighborhoods (not all of them land invasions) created an umbrella organization, the CDP–Durango.[22] The CDP was formed explicitly as a popular organization, independent of political party affiliation. In 1980, it led three new land invasions and was one of the four movements that organized the first national congress of UPMs.

In Monterrey, Nuevo León, the years between 1976 and 1980 were a period of consolidation for the Frente Popular Tierra y Libertad. New invasion settlements were formed, the FPTyL supported numerous workers' strikes in Monterrey, and a bus drivers' union for FPTyL drivers was established. However, profound disagreements within the leadership of the group were beginning to develop. Key issues included decisionmaking procedure, the role of the mass base, and the objectives of the organization with respect to settlement of land tenure problems. The inauguration of a new governor for the state of Nuevo León deepened the conflict for Alfonso Martínez Domínguez, who became governor in 1979, was determined to eliminate squatter settlements from the face of the capital city, Monterrey, by force or by co-optation. His methods included the temporary jailing of FPTyL leaders, mediating the squatters' purchases of land from owners in the private sector, and expropriating the land invaded by the original Tierra y Libertad neighborhood and then giving it to the squatters so they could no longer base their movement on the direct appropriation of their land. In 1983, the FPTyL split into two groups, the old FPTyL and the new *Movimiento Popular Tierra y Libertad* (MPTyL). Two of the original leaders of the frente, who believed in allowing squatters to obtain legal title to their land even if through government mediation, left with their followers to form the MPTyL. The remaining leader, who rejected the need for legal title to land the squatters had long ago achieved control over, remained at the head of the FPTyL. These leadership fights, together with the splintering and realignment of member neighborhoods into two factions, limited the effectiveness of the urban popular movement in Monterrey for much of the 1980s.

In Oaxaca, the COCEI spent the 1970s engaged in mass mobilizing, to pressure the government for concessions on numerous peasant and worker issues. Although many of the COCEI's struggles were successful, this was not without a cost. Government repression was high during these years: Between 1974 and 1977, more than 20 COCEI supporters were killed. In 1980, the COCEI made an alliance with the Communist Party of Mexico (because it was a registered political party and the COCEI was not) allowing the COCEI to field candidates for municipal office in Juchitán. Ultimately, after committing widespread electoral fraud, the PRI declared its candidates the winners. The COCEI, however, responded with outraged denunciations, forced the annulment of election results, and won new special elections, which were held in 1981. In the new elections, the COCEI candidates were victorious, and from 1981 to 1983, Juchitán was the first city in Mexico ever governed by a leftist coalition.[23]

In summary, the five years from 1979 through 1983 constituted a new phase in the evolution of urban popular movements in Mexico. Problems of daily life in Mexican households were no longer articulated within the neighborhood; now they were also debated on the regional and national level. UPMs moved beyond the neighborhood to form coalitions within cities and across the nation. And despite the fact that the first two years of this period overlap with the last years of Mexico's petroleum boom and the last three years witnessed the beginning of Mexico's economic crisis, there was a remarkable consistency to the period for the urban poor. Macroeconomic measures of Mexico's situation in these years paint a picture of boom and bust, but these large swings in national economic health have a much more limited impact on the urban poor. Lack of housing, inadequate services, and speculation with land prices and rents characterized Mexico's cities in 1968, and they characterized Mexico's cities in 1983.

National economic crisis has two main impacts on the urban poor: It aggravates and extends existing poverty, and it narrows windows of economic opportunity.

During the boom, President López Portillo chose to decrease public spending for social welfare. Then, during the crisis, the IMF mandated further cuts in social spending to the de la Madrid government, and a low rate of social spending thus decreased even further. The main difference between the boom and the bust periods was in the possibilities that were available. During the boom years, the possibility of gaining a daily income existed even for the unskilled; during the crisis, the competition for the unskilled, bottom-line jobs only increased as unemployment rose. Furthermore, during the boom, the government could respond to UPMs with concessions; during the crisis, the possibility of concessions was reduced. Indeed, in the crisis years, the potential for social transformation actually may have increased as the budget for concessions shrank and standards of living deteriorated.

The urban poor in Mexico were living a life of daily struggle well before 1982. The economic crisis therefore had a greater impact on the life-styles of the middle-income population because the low-income groups had already developed survival strategies to cope with poverty (for example, see Lomnitz 1975). One of those strategies was the creation of UPMs. The expansion of UPMs from 1979 through 1983—equally through a period of boom and a period of bust—is thus not paradoxical because it is not a response to national economic cycles but a response to persistent poverty.

The Third Wave of Urban Popular Movements: 1985 to 1988

The outstanding characteristic of the third wave of urban popular movements in Mexico is that almost all new UPMs arose in the nation's capital city. The earthquake of 1985 acted as a catalyst for the formation of UPMs. After tens of thousands found themselves homeless and unemployed as their homes and places of work were destroyed, the government's relief efforts were slow, insensitive, and poorly managed. And when the government did not provide leadership, moral support, or guidance, the people turned to each other. From the immediate activities of searching through the rubble and providing shelter and food for the homeless came a new empowerment, a new awareness of what could be accomplished outside government channels.

A formal sign of this was the creation of a coordinating committee to represent the needs of those affected by the earthquake. The *Coordinadora Unica de Damnificados* (CUD) was constituted one month after the quake by a group of 20 neighborhoods. Although the first CUD petition was delivered to President de la Madrid by a crowd of 30,000, the government refused to recognize the CUD as the representative of the quake victims until the group organized a sit-in in the main plaza of the city. And in meetings and assemblies that continued throughout the fall, the CUD designated its priority areas: housing and work (Massolo 1986).

Less than two years after the earthquake, another significant UPM was formed in Mexico City, also initially in response to housing problems exacerbated by the quake. In early 1987, two committees representing renters in central Mexico City started a list of families still seeking housing who had not been accommodated by the government's postearthquake housing program. As word of mouth spread that such a list was being made, thousands came to register. In April 1987, at the First General Assembly of Neighborhoods of Mexico City (*Primera Asamblea General de los Barrios de la Ciudad de México*), the *Asamblea de Barrios* was formally constituted. It was based on the understanding that the housing problems of renters in the central city were far too large to be addressed on a case-by-case basis and that collective action was likely to be more successful. By December 1988, 55,000 renters with inadequate housing had registered. One feature of the Asamblea de Barrios gained the organization citywide, national, and even international recognition: *Superbarrio*, a masked representative dressed in a Superman-like costume whose identity was never revealed. Superbarrio showed up at neighborhood rallies, meetings of the asamblea, and at meetings with the government. The symbolism was obvious: The barrio was in constant crisis in Mexico, so a superhero emerged who could step in to guarantee that lawmakers heard the needs of the people. Yet, because contemporary Mexican history is not material for a comic book, it is most important to recognize that the people themselves had engendered an invincible representative.[24]

An unprecedented number of new urban popular movements and coalitions of UPMs were formed in Mexico City after 1985.[25] Even the university students began a new series of protests. In 1986, students at the National Autonomous University in Mexico City (UNAM) organized protests against far-reaching university reforms that had been decreed while they were on vacation. For example, one repercussion of the reforms would have been to make higher education difficult or impossible for lower-income students. The student protests led to a university strike in early 1987, and the eventual repeal of most of the reforms.

While the new UPMs created during the third wave arose in Mexico City, those formed before 1985 evolved further. In Monterrey, the Frente Popular Tierra y Libertad faced continued attempts at co-optation from the state governor, as well as the aftereffects of the movement's split in 1982. The FPTyL reversed its policy of not participating in elections in 1988, and its candidate won a seat in the National Congress. In Oaxaca, despite severe government repression in 1983 and 1984, the COCEI maintained its constituency and, after fraudulent elections in 1986, achieved another first for a city in Mexico: the formation of a COCEI-PRI coalition government in Juchitán, in which the COCEI held half the city offices and maintained its platform for social change. In Durango, the CDP continued to grow and strengthen, even in the face of government repression: In 1985 and 1986, for example, two CDP members were killed. In 1986, the group reversed its adamant opposition to electoral politics and decided to participate in state elections, doing so again in 1988 and gaining a seat in the National Congress.

Conclusions

By the mid-1980s, the urban popular movement had spread to most Mexican cities. There was great diversity among the movements in terms of history, longevity, strategies, and government response. In some cities, UPMs were facing repression; in others, they were achieving dialogue with the government. Mexico City saw a surge and flourishing of UPMs, while the CDP in Durango was facing repression and the frente in Monterrey was worn down and realigning itself. The explanation for this diversity lies with the histories of the individual movements, with their changing relationships to local, state, and federal governments, and with their particular regional contexts.

One way of assessing the long-term impact of UPMs is by comparing the two moments that present themselves as turning points in the political history of Mexican civil society, 1968 and 1988. In 1988, Cuauhtémoc Cárdenas provided a serious challenge to the PRI candidate for president of the Republic of Mexico, the first in decades. The PRI claimed overall victory at the polls but admitted that Cárdenas and his party, the FDN, had won in Mexico City.[26] Although current debate asks whether it was Cárdenas, the man, or the FDN, as an opposition party, that won the vote in the 1988 elections, there is no question that those elections *both changed and reflected a change* in Mexican politics. Contributing to Cárdenas's victory in Mexico City was the decision by many among the poor not to abstain and by those who voted to switch their vote away from the PRI.

In 1968, students and the urban poor, who had paid the cost of the Mexican miracle, joined together in mass protests. The rallies and marches of that year were an attempt to get the government to respond to their demands. An inherent weakness of the 1968 movement was that, although it started within an identifiable sector of the population—students—it quickly escalated to include other sectors, especially from the urban poor. The rallies and marches were organized primarily by students and attended by anyone who sympathized, which turned out to be many more than either the students or the government had expected. The 1968 movement was a movement about negatives: what was wrong (the distribution of benefits from Mexican development) and what was lacking (jobs, housing, services).

But by 1988, the urban poor, along with peasants, teachers, and some sectors of the working class, had almost two decades of experience organizing autonomous or dissident movements. Formal organizations that were independent of the PRI, with leaders, bylaws, meetings, ideologies, goals, and strategies, existed with varying degrees of success in most Mexican cities. Marches and rallies were focused on specific demands and were usually part of more diversified and longer-term strategies. The collective memory of the urban poor now included organizing as an expected feature of city life. This is not to say that all of these people participated in urban popular movements but rather that most of the poor now accept UPMs as part of the new urban landscape. They are involved themselves or know someone who is or hear about UPM organizing through word of mouth, from the mass media, from the political parties, and from the PRI itself. A significant difference between 1968 and 1988, therefore, is that after twenty years, the urban poor had their own movements, and new channels for expressing the daily problems of poverty existed. Two decades of popular organizing had changed the face of civil society in Mexico.

No sector of the population has been more affected by the evolution of urban popular movements than women. UPMs address issues such as housing, services, and the high cost of living, which are traditionally the domain of the mother-wife-housewife: the organizer of the family's social reproduction. Over the last twenty years, women in Mexico have also moved into the workplace—either in the formal or the informal economy—yet, they remain responsible for the social reproduction of their families, giving rise to the infamous double day. And the double day is especially arduous under conditions of poverty as all of the women's household tasks are made more complicated. Not surprisingly, therefore, poor urban women have been the first to protest living conditions in Mexico's cities. In fact, women constitute the majority of participants of almost every UPM described in this chapter.[27]

In a society where women traditionally have been expected to be submissive and accepting, women have learned to be vociferous and demanding. Because, on the whole, they have been shut out from the traditional channels of political communication in Mexico—unions and political parties—these women had to develop new avenues and new strategies to ensure that their needs were expressed and met. Consequently, the Mexican government's neglect of the social welfare of the majority of the population has led, in the last twenty years, not only to the greater exploitation of women (the double day) but also to the empowerment of women through their mass participation in UPMs.

The 1988 vote was a demand for change. The confidence to vote at all came from the previous two decades of organizing and from the real alternative seemingly presented by the FDN. Despite the fact that the FDN was a coalition of parties that did not have a detailed platform, the vote suggests that its appeal may have been that it was perceived as a vision of the future instead of a link to the recent past.[28] Ultimately, the 1988 elections were the result of the convergence of two key elements: the popular classes' willingness to use their votes as another strategy to demand change and the emergence of a candidate who symbolized a more just Mexico.

The vote in 1988 was significant enough that the government responded with new strategies toward the urban poor. President Carlos Salinas mandated the creation of a new government program, *Programa Nacional de Solidaridad*, (PRONASOL), funded to improve the living conditions of these people. A new mechanism was developed whereby resources were channeled to specific UPMs that signed agreements (*convenios de concertación*) with the government. And finally, the president scheduled well-publicized overnight stays in the shacks of residents of Mexico City's poorest neighborhoods to signal that he had heard their voices and that his government would not ignore them.[29] To be sure, the Salinas administration's efforts to address the urban poor are a response to increased urban poverty and to a rise in urban popular organizing, but they are also prompted by the PRI's diminished control over the urban population. They are an attempt to regain lost ground: the political allegiance of the urban masses.

The evolution of UPMs in Mexico raises interesting questions about urban movements in other Latin American countries. Mexico, along with most nations in the region, has a highly centralized government headquartered in a capital city that is many times larger than the next most important city in the country. As a result, these capital cities often house as much as one-quarter of their countries' populations and all the decisionmaking agencies of their governments. What, then, is the impact when UPMs are concentrated in these capital cities? In Mexico, the oldest UPMs are located in secondary cities; do such UPMs therefore have more space to develop because they are not under the nose of the central government? Can the concentration of UPMs in the capital city have as strong an impact if there is no network of UPMs in secondary cities? Or is the potential for social change *only* realized once UPMs emerge in the capital, where they can communicate directly with the federal government? In Mexico, the government developed new strategies after both of these conditions existed: There was a network of UPMs in secondary cities and a concentration of UPMs in the capital.

Developments in Mexico after 1968 illustrate the urban poor's gradual discovery of the neighborhood as a political vehicle and of the potential of that vehicle for forging social change.[30] Apart from revolution, the process of social transformation is often one of serial changes. This is certainly the case in Mexico, where, during the early 1970s, the poor developed an autonomous response to the impoverishment created by the Mexican miracle. The government responded at first with a democratic opening that allowed emerging popular organizations to strengthen. Next, during the late 1970s, the government responded with the violent repression and co-optation of UPMs and with a political opening that would not benefit UPMs directly. The UPMs ebbed, then developed new strategies, including the formation of national and regional networks during the early 1980s. Finally, after 1988, the government responded with new programs addressing the basic needs voiced by the UPMs.

The social programs and funding of the Salinas administration are reminiscent of populist policies to embrace the urban poor. Yet, the Salinas policies occur within a substantially different political landscape, one that calls into question the PRI's hegemony and politics-as-usual, one in which democratization is a central issue. This new political landscape has been at least partially shaped by the continuous autonomous organizing of the urban poor over the last two decades, presenting evidence for the hypothesis that many small conflictual actions can have the cumulative impact of creating social transformation.

Notes

Lawrence Herzog, Sonia Alvarez, Arturo Escobar, Jeff Rubin, Judy Adler Hellman, and Maria Lorena Cook provided thoughtful and helpful comments on various drafts of this chapter. Roderick Michener was invaluable in helping to collect data. Of course, I am solely responsible for the presentation and interpretation of the information contained herein.

1. Collier 1976; Cornelius 1975; Eckstein 1977; Lomnitz 1975; Perlman 1976.

2. Alonso 1984, 1986, ed., 1988; Bennett 1989; Borja 1981; Castells 1983; Cook 1990; Eckstein, ed., 1989; Fals Borda 1980; Foweraker 1990; Foweraker and Craig, eds., 1990; Haber 1990; Jacobi 1988a; Jelin 1986; Laclau 1985; Laclau and Mouffe 1985; Cardoso 1987; Mainwaring 1987; Mainwaring and Viola 1984; Moctezuma 1984; Mouffe 1984; Perló and Schteingart 1985–1986; Rubin 1990; Slater 1985a; Touraine 1981; Zolezzi and Calderón 1985.

3. Preliminary data from the 1990 census give population totals for Mexico City, Guadalajara, and Monterrey that are far below what common sense and common consensus dictate. Total population for the Mexico City metropolitan area is given as 14,028,639; for the Guadalajara metropolitan area as 2,884,052; and for the Monterrey metropolitan area as 2,562,547. (Instituto

Nacional de Estadística, Geografía e Informática 1990.) In contrast, for example, the Mexico City metropolitan area is commonly thought to have a population of between 18 and 20 million.

4. Instituto Nacional de Estadística 1985: 127.

5. *La Economía Mexicana en Cifras, 1986;* Inter-American Development Bank, 1990.

6. Most discussions of urban popular movements in Mexico do not define UPMs directly but make a deducted definition possible from their case studies. According to the many case studies, UPMs can consist of a single movement organization, a confederation of several movement organizations, a loosely allied group of popular neighborhoods, or even a single popular neighborhood. Most of the UPMs referred to in this chapter fall into the first three categories.

7. In the mid-1970s, the state government created a low-income housing program.

8. A government document claimed in 1982 that there were approximately 34,000 families living in 190 "irregular" settlements in Monterrey. This works out to an average of 179 families per settlement—a ridiculously low figure. Of the 34,000 families, the document assigned 25 percent (8,500 families or 51,000 people) to the FPTyL. On the other hand, Pérez Güemes and Garza del Toro (1984, Appendix) cited the 1976 membership of the FPTyL at 350,000 squatters, for an average of 11,290 people per settlement (or 1,881 families). For anyone who knows the popular neighborhoods of Monterrey, the official estimate of 179 families per settlement is clearly far too low, although Pérez Güemes and Garza del Toro's estimate may be too high. The real membership of the FPTyL probably lies somewhere in the middle.

9. Rubin 1987b. Also see Rubin 1987a, 1990; Bennett and Rubin 1988.

10. The mass organizations are the *Confederación de Trabajadores Mexicanos,* the workers federation; the *Confederación Nacional Campesina* (CNC), the peasants federation; and the *Confederación Nacional de Organizaciones Populares,* the federation of popular organizations.

11. I am grateful to Paul Haber for his insights on how UPMs challenge the mass organizations of the PRI.

12. This was the case, for example, with the FPTyL in Monterrey during the late 1970s and early 1980s (Pozas Garza 1989: 72).

13. Moctezuma (1984) set the period of ebb at 1977–1979, while Ramírez Saiz (1986) set the ebb at 1976–1978. Between 1976 and 1979, the word from the executive branch of the government to the state governors was that they should take the steps necessary to prevent any further progress of the UPMs (Meza Ponce 1984: 90).

14. Valentín Campa ran as the presidential candidate of the *Partido Comunista Mexicano* (PCM) in the 1976 elections. The PCM, however, did not have electoral registration, so Campa did not appear on the official ballots. The *Partido de Acción Nacional* (PAN), which did have electoral registration, did not field a candidate in 1976, partly as a statement of disagreement with the PRI's hegemony and partly as a result of internal dissent within the party (Middlebrook 1986: 124).

15. The government cited an ecological study that claimed that the proximity of poor neighborhoods to the bay was resulting in contamination. This study was later shown to have been falsified, and existing contamination was discovered to be caused by tourism-related development and not by the neighborhoods in question (Ramírez Saiz 1985–1986).

16. One issue that needs further exploration is whether the repression of the 1968 and 1971 student movements in Mexico City had repercussions on the formation of coalitions among neighborhood organizations there during the 1970s. Were coalitions perceived of as too dangerous by their potential members, or were the potential leaders needed to create such coalitions eliminated by the repression?

17. All the information presented here on the *Unión de Colonias Populares* comes from Enzástiga Santiago 1986.

18. The UCP participated in the organizing commissions for the *Movimiento Revolucionario del Pueblo* (MRP) and for the *Unidad Obrero Campesino Popular* (UOCP).

19. Information on CONAMUP presented here comes from Ramírez Saiz (1986: 172–195).

20. In the mid- to late 1980s, some UPMs that had been vehemently against electoral participation made tactical decisions to participate by fielding candidates of their own. Examples are the *Comité de Defensa Popular* of Durango, in 1986 and 1988, and the *Frente Popular Tierra y Libertad* of Monterrey, in 1988.

21. The information on the CRMUP comes from Moctezuma (1986).

22. Many other UPMs also have antecedents in land invasions and prior attempts to organize popular fronts. However, the level of prior organizing, the continuity of it, and the mass support are much stronger for the CDP than for any other UPM that I know of that formed after 1979. The CDP rightfully belongs with the FPTyL and the COCEI as the first generation of UPMs, despite the fact that it was constituted formally only in 1979.

23. In 1981, a Communist Party candidate also won the municipal elections for mayor of Alcozauca, a small town with a population of 2,200 in the state of Guerrero.

24. Hernández 1988 and Tirado Jiménez 1990. Also, Mexico's lower-income groups are big readers of comic-strip novels, featuring superheros like Kaliman. Superbarrio functions, then, on many levels—as the voice of the people, as an intermediary, and as a media device.

25. For example, the *Unión Popular Nuevo Tenochtitlán* in 1986, the *Unión Popular Revolucionario Emiliano Zapata* in 1987, the *Frente Metropolitana* in 1987, the *Coordinadora de Colonias y Pueblos del Sur*, and the *Coordinadora de Lucha Urbana*, among others.

26. The FDN garnered most of its votes in urban zones in central, southern, and Gulf Coast states, and the PRI won in the countryside and in some northern cities (including Monterrey and Chihuahua). The PAN carried some districts in the Valley of Mexico and won in Mérida, Ciudad Juárez, San Luis Potosí, and León (Aziz 1989: 105).

27. For analysis of the change in women's roles and women's participation in social movements throughout Latin America, see Nash and Safa, eds. (1980); Nash and Safa, eds. (1985); Leacock and Safa, eds. (1986); Schmink, Bruce, and Kohn, eds. (1986); Jaquette, ed. (1989); and Alvarez (1990a). See also Lind, Chapter 8.

28. Cárdenas was probably also perceived as a link to the *far* past: the past of his father, President Lázaro Cárdenas, who is often remembered as Mexico's most socially just president of the postrevolutionary period. Nevertheless, Cárdenas represented an alternative to the *recent* past: the PRI politics of the twenty-year period discussed here.

29. Needless to say, the government's new strategies have evoked debate among the UPMs. Some refuse to participate on the grounds that the new programs are merely new methods of co-optation. Others have chosen to participate, believing that they can retain sufficient control, vis-à-vis the government, that co-optation will not occur.

30. The residents of poor urban neighborhoods were not the only ones to discover the politics of neighborhood organizing; so did groups of progressive activists and parties of the Left.

14

Radical Opposition Parties and Squatters Movements in Pinochet's Chile

Cathy Schneider

On September 11, 1973, the Chilean armed forces attacked the presidential palace of democratically elected Marxist President Salvador Allende. Within hours, the palace was in flames, the president dead, and leading members of the government imprisoned or in hiding. Before the flames were extinguished, tanks and helicopters assaulted Santiago's impoverished *poblaciones* ("urban slums and shantytowns"), forcing tens of thousands of Chileans from their homes.

In the months following the coup, over 100,000 civilians were detained, and most of them were brutally tortured. Thousands were summarily executed or simply "disappeared." Every traditional feature of Chilean society came under attack—congress, political parties, labor unions, neighborhood organizations, even local parishes.

For ten years, the only national institution capable of defying the regime was the Catholic church, which through its gradual absorption into the struggle for human rights, moved into direct confrontation with the regime. At the local level, the church acted as a safety umbrella, protecting activists and victims alike. In the shantytowns, small human rights and economic subsistence organizations began to appear. In factories, underground political networks were reestablished, and in universities, students defied regulations prohibiting political discussion and organized demonstrations in opposition to the regime. Yet, these struggles all shared a common denominator—they were localized, ephemeral, and easily repressed. As Alfred Stepan noted, "In Chile, eight years of authoritarian rule passed without significant movement out of the initial authoritarian situation: civil society remained debilitated in the face of state strength" (Stepan 1985: 322). The military appeared invincible. In May 1980, Augusto Pinochet held a plebiscite on a new constitution institutionalizing his rule and won overwhelmingly.

A previous version of this chapter appeared in *Latin American Perspectives* 18, no. 68 (Winter 1991): 92–112. Copyright © 1991 by Cathy Schneider. Reprinted by permission of Sage Publications, Inc.

Suddenly, on May 11, 1983, a storm of protest swept through Santiago's streets. The 1982 economic crisis had created a widening fissure between the military and its supporters, opening the doors to a growing movement of opposition. And, as if a spell had been broken, unarmed students, workers, and shantytown residents flooded the streets, demanding an immediate end to military rule. At its helm were the same poblaciones that had been the target of military repression for almost a decade.

In the western zone of Santiago, residents erected burning barricades, drummed pots and pans, and organized marches. In Santiago's southern zone—poblaciones La Victoria, La Legua, El Piñar, Guanaco, Germán Riesco, and Villa Sur in the *comuna* ("district") San Miguel, and the poblaciones San Gregorio, Nuevo San Gregorio, Joáo Goulat, Yungay, and La Bandera in the comuna La Granja (CETRA/CEAL 1983)—residents sprayed shantytown walls with political slogans, led mass marches, and cut electricity to large portions of the city by throwing metal objects at electric cables. When the armed forces attacked these seemingly defenseless communities, residents responded by digging trenches, erecting burning barricades, and pelting military tanks with rocks. The deluge of protests in the same shantytowns that had experienced severe military repression between 1973 and 1983 challenged the military's claim to have reshaped political loyalties in Chile. "In 1983, with the protests," Genaro Arriagada would later reflect, "Chile rediscovered the part of its reality that, in the delirium of the economic miracle, it had forgotten. From the start of those mass demonstrations, names like La Pincoya, La José María Caro, La Victoria regained their Chilean citizenship and a place among the concerns of Chileans" (cited in Timerman 1987: 70).

For three years, the protests raged. On July 2 and 3, 1986, they reached their peak with a massive nationwide strike. The military responded with a new wave of repression. Ten people were killed, raising the number of protest-related deaths to over 400. In the población Los Nogales, two teenagers (one a U.S. resident who had been in Chile less than a month) were arrested by a military patrol, doused with gasoline, and set on fire. In the población La Victoria, a thirteen-year-old girl was shot dead on her way to buy bread.

By August 1986, exhaustion had set in, and shantytown residents returned to the safety of their homes. Those who continued to resist the dictatorship through direct confrontation had become isolated. By 1987, only a small minority of *pobladores* ("residents of poblaciones") were either organized or active. As one organizer noted, "In 1984 I went underground. I wanted to fight the dictatorship directly. I was not alone in this. By 1987 there was not a single public Communist working in my población."

The Christian Democratic and "renovated" sectors of the Socialist party abandoned the protests. In 1987, they formed a coalition for "free elections," and in the following year, the coalition became the basis for the "*Concertación* [Coalition] for the No," a broad front aimed at defeating Pinochet in the upcoming, constitutionally mandated plebiscite. Pinochet lost the October 11, 1988, plebiscite on his presidency, and in the democratic elections held in December 1989, his hand-selected candidate was soundly defeated. On March 11, 1990, a democratically elected civilian government took office.

This story of protest and repression raises critical questions about the nature of political life in authoritarian Chile. Why did impoverished and almost defenseless shantytown residents risk arrest, torture, and even death to fight a regime that they seemed to have so little chance of defeating? Why did protests center in some shantytowns but not others? Why did they suddenly decline in 1986? And lastly, to what extent and in what way did the shantytown struggle contribute to the return to democratic rule in 1990?

Most of the literature on the Chilean protest movement fails to address these questions. Writers either treat protests as a spontaneous response to economic grievance, real or imagined, or they see them as the manipulation of a skilled political elite. Such approaches focus on protests only as they appear from outside or above. They omit history and historical continuities, leave aside the political context that determines how individuals organize around grievances, blur the distinctions between successful and unsuccessful centers of protest, and, most broadly, fail to flesh out the nexus between political and civil society.

Political scientists and sociologists such as Genaro Arriagada (1988) and Eduardo Valenzuela (1984), for example, focused on the deprivation, social dissolution, and anger produced by the 1982 economic crisis to explain the eruption of protest violence in Santiago's shantytowns. "During the protest years the poblaciones were comprised of a mass of unorganized individuals and a few isolated, weak and unfinanced organizations of several thousand residents" (Arriagada 1988: 61). Yet, this explanation runs counter to a major set of facts. In 1983, there was no association between the level of economic depression and the intensity and scope of protest action. Those poblaciones hit hardest by the crisis, in relative or absolute terms, responded weakly to the call for protests. And when protests did emerge in these areas, they were short-lived for the protesters were unable to withstand the repression.

Other sociologists, including Tilman Evers (1985), Fernando Ignacio Leiva and James Petras (1986), and Teresa Valdés (1987), focused on the construction of autonomous neighborhood organizations and the formation of a new social actor, the poblador movement, to explain the eruption of protests. But the new social movement interpretation fails to explain the peculiar configuration of protest in authoritarian Chile. Had the 1983 protests been the consequence of a new social movement in the shantytowns, the distribution of such protests would have been evenly spread, rather than concentrated in those poblaciones that had previously been the center of left-wing political activity. As sociologists such as Alain Touraine and Eugenio Tironi observed, those who joined soup kitchens or economic cooperatives did not necessarily participate in the protest or so-called poblador movement. As Tironi observed:

The network of social organizations that they [the pobladores] managed to construct . . . resulted in the reactivation of the political militants within the poblaciones. . . . The so-called *poblador* movement has been completely confused with the political militants that we have identified above (1988: 74).

However, the 1983–1986 Chilean protest movement, if not the harbinger of a new social actor or a spontaneous response to the 1982 economic crisis, was more than the product of isolated political militants operating out of shantytowns. The capacity of these urban neighborhoods to mobilize mass political resistance, despite ten years of severe military repression, lay in the political heritage of decades of work in the popular culture and in the formation of a skilled generation of grass-roots militants. As Roger Burbach noted,

> Grassroots militants who had been active years before the coup played key leadership roles in all of these organizing activities. As one party leader noted "we as parties were able to do little, but the political militants at the local level rebuilt the social movement during the darkest moments of the regime." The ideological and political consciousness that broad sectors of the population had acquired over the years prepared them for political work at the community level and for organizing around local needs, even when their ties to the political leadership had been broken (1988: 5).

The Chilean protest movement was like its Spanish equivalent in the 1940s and 1970s, "dependent on the underground survival of the parties of the Left. Those parties provided the strategies and the leaders, and it was the capacity of these parties to survive that kept the . . . resistance alive in the long and difficult period . . . and that later rekindled the struggle" (Maravall 1978: 166). And it was in the same left-wing neighborhood that had been most active in the decades before the coup that resistance struggles began and were strongest.

The high degree of politicization, organization, and solidarity in such neighborhoods was a direct consequence of the historical connection between these areas and the Chilean Communist party, as well as the party's consistent emphasis on the creation of solidarity communities with skilled grass-roots leaders. Much like the left-wing enclaves of the U.S. civil rights movement described by Gitlin, "these enclaves of elders and subterranean channels, rivulets, deep-running springs [nurtured] unconventional wisdom, moods and mystiques. With left wing politics in a state of collapse most of these opposition spaces were cultural—ways of living, thinking, and fighting oneself free of the . . . consensus" (1987: 28).

Those who became politicized as a result of contact with the Communist party or Communist neighborhoods—even those who became militants of other political parties or never joined a political party at all—shared a political conception: They identified their problems in structural terms and sought solutions through collective action. Contact with the Communist party and life in traditional Communist neighborhoods overcame "the fundamental attribution error—the tendency of people to explain their situation as a function of individual rather than situational factors" (McAdam 1982: 50). As one Christian Democrat living in a Communist población explained, "I used to be ashamed of my poverty, I saw it as personal failure. A communist neighborhood organizer explained to me that I needn't be ashamed. That we all shared the same problems."

Residents of Communist-influenced neighborhoods absorbed the lesson that individuals can make a difference, that they can, in collective organization with others, take control over their lives. Those who lived in such communities continued to resist military rule despite the high personal cost because they believed that (1) their particular organizational skills were critical to movement success, (2) collective solidarity action was capable of defeating even the most powerful military regime, and (3) their own intense collective identity was such that passive acceptance of the regime was incompatible with the personal and individual sense of self.

These communities were critical in reestablishing political activity after the coup and the destruction of the traditional political parties. Christian Democratic poblaciones were weakened by the ambivalence of their party toward the military government, and the traditional Socialist party was paralyzed by internal division and infighting. The traditional right-wing parties had dissolved themselves in support of the military regime, and the Communist party as a formal institution was also decimated, with most of its leadership either dead or in exile. Yet, that party's traditional emphasis on the creation of coherent grass-roots communities and skilled grass-roots leaders had left a legacy that was not so easily destroyed.

After the coup, grass-roots activists in poblaciones that had traditionally depended on elite support or state resources found it impossible to maintain a defense against military repression. They either ceased political work or attempted to keep a semblance of political organization by working under the protective auspices of the Catholic church. Others moved to the traditional left-wing, Communist-influenced poblaciones, where a history of grass-roots political activity had created a supportive environment and set apart potential informants.

In these traditional communities, resistance activity often began within weeks of the coup. In Granadilla, for instance, the first political act of resistance was the building of a collective farm or *huerta*. This farm became the basis for a communal kitchen, which, in turn, inspired a series of women's workshops (producing clothes and toys) and youth groups (mainly cultural). In 1977, the leaders of the popularly elected neighborhood council convinced the mayor to fund the entire gamut of popular organizations through the Minimum Employment Program (PEM) and the Public Works Program for Heads of Household (POJH). Thus, in 1978, a Communist neighborhood council was administering the minimum employment program for the Pinochet government.

By 1979, political activity in the poblaciones accelerated. Activists began to branch out to develop organizations in the less traditional activist poblaciones, but they avoided working in the poblaciones they lived in for fear of informants. They also avoided the larger mass organizations set up by Pinochet—such as sports clubs or mothers' centers—for the same reason. Instead, they began to create parallel organizations, such as cultural centers and human rights groups. These groups developed a reputation in the area as a front for political activists and further isolated the activists from the nonpolitical members of the community.

When the 1982 economic crisis sparked a political crisis, alienating former supporters of the military regime, the poblaciones exploded. As the protests reached their peak, the less organized neighborhoods and political parties were swept into activity. The Christian Democratic party and the Renovated Socialists became critical to the movement and forged a powerful Democratic Alliance coalition. But those poblaciones without a tradition of political activity remained dependent on the political skills of their national leadership and found it increasingly difficult to withstand the escalating military repression.

The traditional Communist-influenced poblaciones, on the other hand, maintained high levels of resistance throughout the protest cycle. These neighborhoods had been "the small motor that later turned the larger motor of the mass movement" (Gitlin 1987: 26). Even after the protests had ceased and the majority of Chileans had returned to their homes, the traditional Communist poblaciones maintained a high level of political mobilization, their continued activity and increasing militancy eventually isolating them from the population at large. When the military was finally defeated in 1988, these poblaciones, along with the Communist party, found themselves at the margins of political life. The following interviews stress the differences that existed, during the 1983–1986 cycle of protest, between traditional Communist poblaciones and those with less of an activist history.

Interviews

Low-Mobilization Poblaciones

Villa Wolf. Villa Wolf is typical of poblaciones that failed to mount significant protest after 1983. It is both very poor and very small (it has barely 1,000 inhabitants, and the unemployment rate exceeds 65 percent). Despite its size, however, Villa Wolf is poorly organized. The only neighborhood organizations it has been able to sustain are the soup kitchens, and these are maintained with great difficulty. "The problem here," explained the head of the soup kitchen who is a member of the Christian Left,

> is lack of resources. . . . The community rejects the soup kitchens, they don't help with the construction. The other villas within La Pincoya receive more help from the community. *In comparison with other villas, Villa Wolf has very little sense of community, little solidarity and almost no social mobilization or protests.* The soup kitchens have tried to function as a source of information for women and as a primary health organization, but it is the same women who act in several capacities.

"Villa Wolf was originally established by the Christian Democrats," observed another resident. "And since the Christian Democrats supported the coup, many of the leaders of the población are still with Pinochet." According to the residents, the community lacks a collective identity, and the political parties that try to organize here are bitterly divided among themselves. The lack of community networks leaves Villa Wolf vulnerable to infiltration by government-linked groups, such as the *Unión Democrática Independiente* (UDI). The government then uses the information provided by such groups to persecute and arrest community activists and to frighten the other residents into passivity. "The majority of protests," argued the Left Christian organizer in Villa Wolf, "have taken place in those sectors such as Pablo Neruda, which resulted from land occupations organized by the Communists."

Sporadically Combative Poblaciones

The success of any day of national protest depended in large part on the level of protest activity in the sporadically combative poblaciones. Because these poblaciones were characterized by political infighting and factionalism, they were unable to maintain a constant level of resistance. They were pulled into the fray of battle, however, when changes in the external opportunity structure made protests costly.

Sara Gajardo. Located in the western comuna Cerro Navia, Sara Gajardo was originally founded as a land grant under *Operación Sitio.* In 1967, residents from a nearby land occupation were relocated to Sara Gajardo, but none of the political parties established deep roots in the community. There is a great deal of delinquency and drug addiction in Sara Gajardo, especially among the youth. On national protest days, many of these young people explode in rage, throwing stones and epithets at soldiers who are often backed up by tanks and helicopters. But the older members of this community are largely passive, even those who participated in the Popular Unity.

"The depth of participation within the población is of extreme importance," insisted the twenty-one-year-old director of an art workshop. "If there is a history of struggle and organization the regime can decapitate the organizations but the organizations rise again." But another community leader explained that "while the young people here have managed to recreate the neighborhood associations eliminated by the military, there is very little participation from the adults in the community. Consequently we have to learn everything on our own. We are given little direction." The local priest concurred:

> There is a basic problem at the grass roots with the political parties. There is a tendency for the political parties to try to take control. The Communist Party is always trying to get in and control things. They get orders from outside and don't always consider the real needs of pobladores. There is a lot of disillusionment. People want to create their own future, not just leave things in the hands of a central committee. . . . The parties are not always honest and the people see them as utilitarian. They want socialism to transform the society radically but the parties don't seem suitable for that task.

The problem is not simply lack of direction: The lack of political solidarity raises the cost of political participation. "It's more costly to organize here than in La Herminda," contended a young activist, "because the population is afraid of participating." "Disunity is the major problem," a twenty-year-old political organizer suggested. "People are afraid to get involved. There are many *soplones* [informants]." Another political organizer (a non-Communist) stated:

> The risk is not only in the streets, they attack us from helicopters. Although the repression is focused against La Herminda, Sara Gajardo has a higher rate of fatalities. La Herminda is better defended since it receives more back up from the community. There are more political militants in La Herminda, more Communist activists.

Villa O'Higgens. Villa O'Higgens is an extremely poor población with sporadic levels of protest activity. On the day I conducted this interview, the military had occupied Villa O'Higgens in anticipation of the September 4 general strike. Armed soldiers patrolled the streets, making it impossible to cross from one house to the next without help from neighborhood sentries.

In one of the homes, I was greeted by a five-year-old boy with a toy gun. "This is to stop the soldiers from breaking in," he told me. But there were no protests in Villa O'Higgens on September 4. The high rate of fatalities on July 2 and 3 and the confusion surrounding the strike plans for September had convinced the vast majority that the risk was simply too great.

Villa O'Higgens, like many of the other sporadically mobilized poblaciones, is divided between land-grant sectors set up under Operación Sitio in 1968 and land-occupation sectors led by the Movimiento Izquierda Revolucionaria (MIR) in 1969. But the popular organizations died shortly after housing needs were settled.

Villa O'Higgens is still poorly organized, and the political parties are weak and divided. "The people lack political consciousness," complained a human rights worker. "They are seduced by whatever organization provides economic assistance."

"Even the church," explained another human rights worker, "while predisposed to help is not active, because there are not political parties demanding help as there are in La Victoria." (The priest in Villa O'Higgens and the priest in La Victoria, for example, arrived from France together and shared political convictions. Their level of activism since their arrival in Chile, however, has reflected the level of activism in their respective communities.)

The weakness of the political parties means that protests in the población are tentative and easily discouraged. As a member of a cultural group explained:

> There were many protests here in 1983, but they were mostly spontaneous and lacked the organization to maintain themselves or defend the community. This was in marked contrast with those poblaciones where the defense was greater due to the strength of the political parties.

The level of political mobilization in Villa O'Higgens is, as in other sporadically mobilized poblaciones, dependent on changes external to the población itself. For instance, a human rights worker explained that the protests in Villa O'Higgens in 1985 reached a low due to lack of confidence, but in 1986,

> confidence increased due to what appeared to be the organization of the political parties, and the clarity of their new strategy. The July 2 general strike was especially strong because of a commando unit for the general strike made up of leaders of all political parties within the población. The organization and publicity began early, and there was support from many other sectors such as the mobilization of doctors and other professionals. But the costs were high. In Villa O'Higgens alone we sustained 14 bullet injuries, 5 injuries from bird shot, 34 arrests and one death."

"There is a lot of repression here now," she continued, "because this community is of strategic importance and there is little organization here to defend it." (As we were talking the military arrived and began shooting at the homes and church even though no protests were taking place. The shooting continued without interruption for four hours.)

The Focus of Resistance: The Combative Poblaciones

The poblaciones that emerged as the central core of the resistance movement in 1983 were those formed by the Communist party. Political activity was not new to these areas. In fact, the character of these poblaciones had been forged by earlier waves of political activity. In such neighborhoods, political activists lived and organized in the same población and maintained an organic relationship with the residents. And they did more than organize protest. They held public events to strengthen community ties and revive cultural traditions, and they created new forms of grass-roots democracy.

La Victoria. La Victoria is a small población, no larger than three square kilometers in area and populated by 32,000 inhabitants. It was one of the earliest illegal land occupations in Chile. "Most of us were *allegados* [homeless or living in the homes of other people]," explained one of the original participants of the *toma* ("illegal land seizure"). "The government had no program to provide for the homeless," argued María, a representative to the neighborhood council from 1960 to 1964.

> We began organizing for the land occupation six months early. We met clandestinely in different houses. . . . On the day of the land occupation we were surrounded by police. There were 15 deaths from cold and disease. We faced fear by organizing. The solidarity was incredible. . . . We just stayed on the land until the government agreed to sell us the rights. We formed a *Comando de Población* [Community Defense Organization] with committees on every block. Only after three years of struggle and organization did we win water rights in 1963. The Communists led the struggle. We created a school of adobe for the children with 14 rooms. Everyone in the población contributed something. Later we began to organize and fight for a health care clinic. . . . It was only through struggle that we won the eight-hour working day. Everything we have, we won through struggle.

"Even the solidarity and activism of our local priests was won through struggle," contended María. "The first priest in the población was not progressive." It was the community that demanded a different kind of church. "The first church in this area was only interested in the rich. The priest tried to 'buy' and divide the community, like a salesman offering bread. We chased him out in 1963. There was bread for all or there was bread for none. . . . We always worked for the good of all." From then on, she explained, La Victoria always had priests who worked with the community, "fighting with us, never against us." "We held elections with secret ballots," contended another original participant. "The Communist party won. The first president of the community was a Communist, and he remained president until 1968 when he died. We always held elections by block, and the Communists always won," María insisted.

In 1973, the military attacked the población. La Victoria, along with four or five other poblaciones, constituted the main force of the resistance movement. Despite a lack of preparation or central leadership, residents confronted tanks alone. A journalist who lived in La Victoria during the coup explained that "there were no armaments, no medical equipment for the injured, anyone who helped a resister was also killed." La Victoria defended itself with pure commitment and solidarity through weeks of military assault, long after the Popular Unity government was destroyed. "At the leadership level the political parties were in disarray," explained the journalist, "but at the base, in La Victoria, there were no divisions, we all worked together."

By 1974, most of the leaders were in concentration camps or dead. Those who were still alive withdrew from politics or fled the población to organize clandestinely. It took ten years to rebuild community organization: "We began with nothing," they explained. In 1977, they reestablished the first cultural and human rights groups, and within two years, they had functioning popular economic subsistence organizations, *bolsas de cesantes* ("organizations of the unemployed"), *talleres laboral y cultural* ("technical and cultural workshops"), and so forth. These organizations allowed the pobladores to regroup, to share grievances, and to express dissatisfaction. Furthermore, it was difficult for the government to repress these groups because they served a function: They allowed people to survive during the implementation of the economic model. But they also allowed the atomized residents of the población to reorganize.

"We are more organized now," one of the members of the senior citizens' club told me, "than in 1983, in spite of the repression. We have an organization for every block, like Nicaragua." La Victoria boasts 30 social organizations in addition to the block organizations. Each block elects its own delegates, and the block delegates and social organizations together elect the president of the *Comando Nacional* of La Victoria.

La Herminda de Victoria. Like many of the combative poblaciones, La Herminda de Victoria arose from an illegal land occupation organized by the Communist party's Committee of the Homeless, and it has the distinction of being the first land occupation in Pudahuel (what was the Barrantas and is now Cerro Navia). It was also the first población under authoritarian rule to gain the official recognition of a democratically elected neighborhood council.

Like the occupation of La Victoria, the occupation of this neighborhood in 1967 was met with extreme police repression. The población was roped in by police forces and virtually under siege for nine months. During the siege, a young girl named Herminda took ill and, unable to reach the hospital, died: The población was named in her honor. Finally, an agreement was reached with the government. The occupants were transported to a vacant area, to be named La Herminda de Victoria, and were sold rights to the land. The residents were given 45 hectares for 1,464 families and asked to sign a contract requiring that they pay on a sliding scale. In three years, the new occupants would be provided with the deeds to their homes. Corporación de Vivienda (CORVI), the government housing authority, would provide water and sanitary services.

But in 1973, the población was hit very hard; most of the political leaders were killed and all the organizations were decapitated. In addition, the government simply ignored the contract that gave residents of La Herminda de Victoria deeds to their homes. In 1979, Juan Araya, the ex-president of the Committee of the Homeless, and the *Metropolitana de Pobladores* (the población coordinating organization linked to the Communist party) began a series of meetings in La Herminda. The Church-linked *Agrupación Vecinal* (Organization of Neighbors, AVEC) also participated. The idea was to reclaim not only housing rights but also rights in general and to learn the provisions of the law.

These meetings became the basis of the Committee of Pobladores, which led the struggle to recover the rights granted in the original housing contract. "We pointed to a clause in the contract that guaranteed that all pre-1976 agreements be honored," asserted a member of the committee:

> The government responded with threats. The residents of the población began to gather to defend us. They held meetings with lawyers. The first week 40 attended, the second week 200 attended, the third week 500 attended. Then there were no more meetings. We gathered in front of the official neighborhood council to denounce them. They responded with extreme repression, attempting to eliminate the Committee of Pobladores. The secret police threatened the leaders of the committee with arrest or even death.
>
> We had, however, our ideas very clear, and we simply continued. The official press launched a campaign against us. The secret police began an investigation and followed up with threats. The carabineros surrounded the church and the Christian community. But the residents of the community responded en masse and continued to meet every Sunday. If the police or secret police tried to single out one of us for punishment, the rest of the población responded, and made it impossible for the police to arrest or "disappear" only one.

Finally, in April 1980, the government gave in, and 95 percent of La Herminda de Victoria's residents were given deeds to their homes. After the official neighborhood council resigned in embarrassment, the municipality was obliged to call for free elections. "Ninety-five percent of the población voted for us," exclaimed Pablo, an ex-member of the democratic council. Through community participation and solidarity, the población was able to resist the regime's repression and reclaim its housing rights.

The community did not cease political activity once housing claims had been satisfied. They demanded recognition of their democratically chosen neighborhood council, as well, and became the first community in Santiago to reestablish democratic self-government. As Pablo explained:

> Pedro was voted president. He and I were the only two in the junta [neighborhood council] that were not Communists. We were elected in June 1980. On December 25, 1980, we held a Christmas festival to celebrate our victory. 2,500 children participated. All of the pobladores contributed something.
>
> On the 16th of March we celebrated our anniversary. Everyone participated. We invited people to dance in the streets, to join in parades.

But the political leaders were unable to maintain the relationship with the community that had made their victory possible. The government took advantage of this weakness, pitting the council against political militants by giving the former the responsibility of keeping order on protest days. The willingness of the council members to assume this role and act against sectors of their own community permitted the military to recapture control of the población. As the former council member explained:

> Our problems began because we were obligated to use the office of the official neighborhood council. In this way we became dependent on the municipality. We lost contact with the pobladores. We were required to be in charge of the workers on the minimum employment program. We were put in charge of maintaining order during the protests, criticizing acts of vandalism. This badly split the población. Finally, a group of former directors of the Communist party argued that we had completed our mission, that it was time to call elections for a new neighborhood council.

"The new council," explained a young political leader, "lacked knowledge of the laws, and a clear project or analysis of future consequences." Pablo contended that "they began to divide among themselves." He stated:

> Finally they had to resign and the government appointed its own neighborhood council, and all that we had done was lost. Other communities learned from our mistakes. In such communities the democratic councils are functioning well because they are clear on what they want to accomplish. Here the Communists simply wanted to dominate the council.

Yungay. Yungay, originally Villa Lenin, is a small población of 14,000 inhabitants, but it is one of the most combative. Unlike the residents of La Victoria and Herminda, the people of Yungay never partook in an illegal land occupation. Rather, their strong sense of solidarity, belief in the power of collective action, and confidence in themselves grew out of their relationship with the Communist party. Although Yungay was settled legally during the government of Allende, it was the Communist party that organized the población and led the struggle for housing, water, schools, and electricity. More importantly, Communists in Yungay lived in Yungay and stressed the needs of the población over the needs of the national party.

The maturity of the political parties and their deep roots in the población allowed them to work with the church toward a common goal. In poblaciones without a long tradition of organization, the local priest observed, both the political parties and the church tend to direct the población from the outside, resulting in dogmatism and rigidity on both sides. But in Yungay, "there is more maturity in both the political parties and in the Christian community, there is more participation from the base in both. Thus, there is more cross membership, more linkages between members, and more people that participate in both organizations."

It was this responsiveness to the community that allowed grass-roots activists to reconstruct democracy at the local level. These individuals began reorganizing in the población in 1974, when they established the *Central Juvenil Latina* (Center for Latin American Youth). Later, they created a sports club and, later still, a soup kitchen under the auspices of the local parish. By 1978, they had re-created two cells of the Communist Party, and in 1980, they created a Committee on Human Rights and a neighborhood cooperative (*comprando juntos*). They also created a women's center and a health center and began the process of democratizing the neighborhood council.

They began meeting with lawyers in 1979 to seek legal authorization for a neighborhood council, and by 1984, they had grouped representatives of every block in the población. The block representatives then chose twelve delegates to form the new democratic neighborhood council. The president of the neighborhood council explained:

> The entire población participated in the selection. We then challenged the legitimacy of the government's neighborhood council. We embarked on a plan of action. As we began to produce ideas, we awakened the población. We began a momentum, a rhythm. Demanded that the municipality provide a building and a telephone. We told them that we would take them to court if they didn't comply. They submitted. We made a public declaration and a contract requiring them to install a telephone in our building. We now have a telephone, which is open to the community from 8:00 A.M. to 12:00 midnight.

The democratic neighborhood council used the money collected from telephone calls to buy the community an ambulance (they charged 20 pesos a call, the normal price for a telephone call in Chile). In March, Yungay was the only población in the area with a telephone and in December, it became the only población with its own ambulance.

"The neighbors began to have more confidence in us," the president of the neighborhood council observed. "They became more involved in the process, they worked more. With unity and democracy, all of the sectors in the población got involved." Next, the neighborhood council opened a library, the first library in the area. They called it Pablo Neruda Library, after the famous Communist poet. "All of this was done on our own," the president proudly acknowledged.

> We received no help from anyone outside the población, neither economic nor material. Next we began to create sidewalks. We never had sidewalks. We constructed 5,000 meters of sidewalks. The neighbors laid the cement. The municipality provided the materials. They say they gave them to us, but in reality they robbed us. The materials were bought with the money they took from the community. They have to provide these things.

But the achievements of Yungay were not simply material. With each successful struggle, the residents grew bolder: They developed more confidence in themselves and a broader conception of their rights as citizens. As the president of the new democratic neighborhood council observed, "We used to think that we had to give something to receive something from the municipality. Now we demand that which we deserve, what corresponds to us as citizens of this country. We demand what is legally ours. We demand our rights."

Community solidarity enabled the neighborhood council to challenge the legitimacy of the government's appointed representatives. And it allowed the community to reassert its democratic will. The president of the neighborhood council explained:

When we demand these things the other neighborhood council does not say anything, for fear that the mayor will simply fire them. We, on the other hand, have the población on our side. He can't fire us, he didn't hire us. When he tries to throw us out, the entire población says NO. Unity rises from democratic foundations.

Sometimes the neighborhood council members use the law to apply pressure, but usually they rely on the people themselves—the community—to do this. Every week they call a meeting in every sector. "We are always in meetings," insisted the president of the council, adding, "we work through grass-roots democracy." Another member of the neighborhood council emphatically concurred:

Here the political parties work from the base, not like the United States where the parties run things from the top. Here we have the capacity to organize and resist. They can repress and kill us as individuals, but the organizations survive and the resistance rises again. Here we have a history of combativeness, dating from the struggles in the nitrate mines at the turn of the century.

"The people support the neighborhood council with their own funds, every one contributes something even when they don't have enough to eat," a member of the high school support group told me. "The mayor has created his own neighborhood council, with all the government money, but we ignore it."

Thus, in Yungay, a history of radical militancy and political solidarity, along with the continued presence and integration of grass-roots political militants, has allowed the población not only to maintain a high level of militant resistance to the regime but also to reestablish democracy at the local level.

Conclusions

In all of the less combative poblaciones, the political parties and party militants were viewed with suspicion. Residents sought individual solutions to their problems or accepted their fate. They distrusted political activists, whom they saw as outsiders and opportunists callously exploiting the suffering of the pobladores. The political organizers, lacking support, responded, in turn, with a rigidity and dogmatism uncharacteristic of those in the more combative poblaciones. This tension between the political activists and the pobladores paralyzed the población. Residents in these communities often expressed deep frustration and anger but lacked the direction and organization to act on these frustrations. Even the more radical residents found themselves restricted by the weakness of political organizations. And residents of Sara Gajardo complained that the repression aimed against La Herminda de La Victoria resulted in more fatalities in their own población. Only when a nonpartisan coalition from the center, such as the

Asamblea de Civilidad, led the call for protests were the pobladores in these communities mobilized.

The only poblaciones that were highly mobilized throughout the protest cycle were those that had originally been created by the Chilean Communist party. The Communist party and resistance movements survived in such shantytowns because the party's work in the popular culture before 1973 had created a skilled generation of grass-roots militants, capable of maintaining community support. But individual militants did not determine the extent or success of protest action. They were often killed or arrested and thus replaced by other youths who found themselves heirs to the same tradition. What was important was the extent to which community solidarity and a shared political vision had made all the residents potential militants. Even the priests in such shantytowns took a more active role because residents demanded political commitment from their clergy.

By 1986, the protest cycle was drawing to a close. The Christian Democratic and Socialist parties moved to a negotiating stance, concentrating their efforts on the 1988 plebiscite. The Communist party became less crucial to the movement, especially after the *Frente Patriótico Manuel Rodriguez* (a guerrilla group linked to the party) attempted to assassinate General Pinochet on September 7, 1986. Indeed, the Communist party's national strategy from 1983 onward weakened grass-roots organizing efforts in several respects. Although the party's focus prior to 1983 was on rebuilding social organizations and bringing together people who shared grievances, after 1983, it stressed an explicitly insurrectional strategy. In trying to control the grass-roots organizations, the party alienated the non-Communist members. Furthermore, the party also began to pull its leaders out of mass organizations to employ them in clandestine military operations, thus isolating itself from its mass base. Finally, the Communist party's armed strategy and unwillingness to consider alternative strategies (most notably its reluctance to participate in the 1988 plebiscite) cost it support even in some of the traditional Communist strongholds.

The Communist party's isolation coincided with the final phase of the protest cycle—the government's concession to the moderates, which led to the plebiscite in 1988 and the government's defeat. As a consequence, the more radical movement activists were relegated to the margins of political life, and the more moderate activists were reabsorbed into normal political channels.

The Chilean protests followed a pattern similar to successful cycles of protest in Western democracies (Tarrow 1989a). They began in traditionally active grass-roots communities, and as the protest movement gathered momentum, it absorbed new adherents, often people with no previous political experience. A political crisis provided a new political opportunity, energizing the movement and extending its scope. And as the protest cycle reached its peak, organizers found themselves engaged in increasingly costly and violent confrontations with the state. In response, the more moderate political leaders and activists moved to a negotiating stance, and the state was able to defuse the movement by granting significant concessions to the more moderate movement organizers. Thus, the políticos were reabsorbed into normal political channels, having won their most essential demand, while the more committed organizers were stripped of their mass support.

What becomes, then, of the grass-roots activists and popular organizations now that political parties have returned to the forefront? Will they be rendered obsolete by the return to "politics as usual"? The answer appears to be yes. Although the democratic opening created by the 1988 plebiscite and election campaigns originally encouraged a flourishing of grass-roots political activity, this activity lasted only as long as the campaigns themselves. Since the inauguration of the democratic government in March 1990, many grass-roots militants have returned to their homes, and participation in social organizations has dramatically declined.

Still, the vitality of the new democracy will continue to depend on the ability of the parties to channel the energies of grass-roots militants into a deepening of the democratic process. If grass-roots organizations are demobilized and their militants excluded from political participation, the consequential alienation of this sector will weaken the democratic forces. To some extent, this process has already begun, leaving bitterness and disillusionment in its wake.

If, on the other hand, the decentralization of political power and the redemocratization of local and municipal governments guarantee a political space for popular participation, the new democracy may be fortified by its grass-roots support. The same militants that allowed political parties and resistance to survive authoritarian rule will then ensure the commitment of political parties to the needs of pobladores.

15

Democratization and the Decline of Urban Social Movements in Uruguay: A Political-Institutional Account

Eduardo Canel

November 1984 was an important time in Uruguay's political history. At last, this small South American nation regained its precious democracy, after eleven years of military dictatorship. As Uruguayans celebrated the beginnings of a new era, a contagious sense of optimism could be felt throughout the country. The nation's jails—filled with hundreds of political prisoners—began to open their doors, and political refugees were returning to the homeland, bringing with them new ideas and renewed energies. In looking to the future with optimism, the "Switzerland of America"—as the country was known in better times because of its stable democratic system of government—was trying to put behind the darkest chapter in its entire history, when torture, fear, and intimidation replaced the relatively calm and free life-style of the past.

If the country's future looked bright, the future of grass-roots movements—the new actors that had emerged in the neighborhoods during the military period—looked even better, at least in the eyes of many social scientists and enthusiastic nongovernmental organizations (NGOs). These movements had sought to solve the problems of the urban poor through collective action and self-reliance. Although they were weak and in their formative stages, it was proposed that they could play a central role in the process of constructing a more democratic Uruguay. The movements were said to represent embryos of new, more democratic social practices, with the potential to transform power relations in daily life. Their democratic-participatory nature and the solidarity and cooperative values on which they were based could help promote a qualitatively more democratic society. In the hopeful mood of the times, the movements themselves experienced important growth following the return to democracy.

But the optimism was short-lived. Soon after the elections, Uruguayans realized that the return to democracy would not bring back the prosperity and the welfare policies of the past. Furthermore, the newly established democracy began to look very much like the old one, which, incidentally, had led to the military takeover and the economic downturn. The winds of renewal that many had hoped would blow through Uruguay had little impact, if any, and restoration of old habits and political practices triumphed over renewal. It was as if the country's political process had simply been frozen during the eleven years of military rule, preserving old political traditions intact—traditions that returned with renewed strength once the political process opened up. In this context, grass-roots activities declined, and many of the new organizations disappeared or were assimilated into more traditional ones. The hope of establishing a new way of doing politics did not materialize, and the country missed a good opportunity to develop a more open and democratic political system.

This chapter will explain the decline of social movement (SM) activity in Uruguay in reference to political variables. I will argue that the nature of the country's political institutions and traditions, the dynamics of negotiated redemocratization processes, and the policies of Montevideo's municipal government were the central factors that inhibited the emergence of effective SMs and narrowed the "structure of opportunities" for collective action.[1] The approach adopted here seeks to bring institutional politics back into the analysis of social movements, which in recent studies has been displaced by a growing emphasis on identity, cultural production, and civil society.[2] Although the new social movement approach has correctly highlighted the "hidden side" of the new movements, it has tended to neglect political factors. This is partly the result of the manner in which social movements have been conceptualized as alternatives to parties and state, thus making a clear demarcation between traditional and nontraditional actors, civil society and state, politics and culture, institutional and noninstitutional action.[3]

It is important to explore the relationship between social movements and other political actors, without losing sight of questions of collective identity and the politics of everyday life. Social movements do not operate in a passive, nonpolitical environment, and the outcomes of their actions are partially determined by political processes.[4] Therefore, instead of conceiving of the constitution of new identities as endogenous processes, researchers must recognize the relational character of identity formation and must seek to explain the manner in which political parties and state agencies intervene in this process. For instance, the state affects how groups perceive their interests, how they organize collectively, and what tactics and strategies they adopt by including or excluding certain issues from the political agenda, by encouraging or discouraging local participation, and by legitimizing certain forms of collective action. Likewise, political parties do not merely represent preconstituted interests because they actively intervene in the definition of these interests and the constitution of local identities through their mode of intervention in national and local affairs.[5]

The redemocratization processes under way in Brazil and the Southern Cone countries have encouraged researchers to explore some of these issues and have led to more realistic forecasts regarding the transformative potential of SMs.[6] With the return of democracy, the relationship between state and civil society has been redefined. In some countries, especially in those with well-established party systems like Chile and Uruguay, political parties have regained their central role in interest articulation and displaced the emerging SMs. In other cases, the movements themselves have begun processes of negotiations with the state, seeking to institutionalize some of the demands for which they have been fighting. The ensemble of these changes has underscored the inadequacy of theories stressing a radical opposition between civil society and the state and the autonomy of SMs from political actors. This is not to suggest that questions of identity and autonomy are no longer relevant for social movement analysis. Rather, I would suggest that a more comprehensive analysis of SMs can be obtained by also exploring the institutional aspects of social movements.

Urban Social Movements in Uruguay: Late Emergence, Sudden Decline

In the last years of the authoritarian period (which lasted from 1973–1984), Uruguay witnessed the emergence of a number of new collective experiences that researchers identified as embryonic social movements. These collective practices sought to meet the immediate basic needs of urban low-income people. Although they relied on traditional practices and organizational forms, they also gave rise to new forms of action and new social relations emphasizing solidarity, cooperation, and self-reliance at the local level. These incipient social movements included a variety of grass-roots experiences, the most important being *soup kitchens* and *food-purchasing clubs*, engaged in the collective production, distribution, and consumption of food; *local health-care centers*, seeking to improve accessibility and quality of health-care service; and a variety of *neighborhood associations*, dealing primarily with collective consumption issues but also with cultural and political concerns.[7]

Food-purchasing clubs (*clubes de compra*) organized the purchase and distribution of food at the local level. Neighbors reduced the cost of food by pooling the community's resources and buying wholesale, thus eliminating intermediaries in food marketing and distribution. Researchers identified 15 such clubs in 1982, all of them in Montevideo. Four years later, the number had risen to 60.[8] Through soup kitchens (*ollas populares*), the country's poor organized the collective preparation and consumption of food. These collective efforts required the participation of local residents—especially women—in activities such as organizing, cooking, purchasing, and fund-raising. The community supported these activities through food and cash donations and by lending space in community centers, sports clubs, or trade union locals for the group's activities. Several types of soup kitchens have been identified: first, those that united families from the same community; second, those where the families came from different neighborhoods but shared a common problem, such as being unemployed; third, soup kitchens organized by other institutions, like trade unions or churches; and fourth, *merenderos* ("programs") providing after-school snacks for children.[9] The first reported ollas date back to 1982 and were organized by trade unions. By 1985, there were 43 soup kitchens in the country, providing food for an estimated 10,000 people.[10]

Nonprofit health-care clinics (*servicios de salud populares privados*) sought to improve accessibility and quality of health-care services in low-income communities, to make the relationship between the user and the provider of health services more open and democratic, and to encourage neighbor participation. Most of their activities were funded through contributions by foreign NGOs and local resources. These clinics counted on the support of many professionals and technicians, such as newly graduated doctors, nurses, dentists, and social workers who contributed their services at a very low cost. In 1985, there were 55 such health clinics in Montevideo, representing 20 percent of the city's total number of health-care units.[11]

Many neighborhood commissions (*comisiones barriales*) emerged in Montevideo—especially among the urban poor—to fight for "collective consumption" needs (like access to basic urban services) or against the city government's forced relocation plans for shantytown dwellers. These commissions brought together local residents and provided an organizational framework wherein neighbors could begin to discuss issues and seek collective solutions to their problems. Some of these commissions were rooted in the more traditional *comisiones de fomento* ("local development commissions"), which had existed in Montevideo prior to the 1973 military coup and had established a clientelistic relationship with the state. The majority, however, were formed after 1980, and some of them sought to redefine their relationship with the state. In 1985, a total of 740 neighborhood commissions were registered with Montevideo's city government, and, according to city officials, 80 percent of these were active.[12]

In their initial stages, these grass-root organizations tended to be reactive and localized experiences, and their concerns focused on immediate local problems. In subsequent stages, they began to broaden their understanding of the causal factors determining their communities' problems and to realize that these problems were also experienced by other neighborhoods. They also began to build coordinating organizational structures at the city or national levels. For example, representatives from 12 clubs in the capital city set up the Coordinating Committee of Food-Purchasing Clubs (*Mesa Coordinadora de Clubes de Compra*) in 1982. The Soup Kitchens Coordinating Committee (*Coordinadora de Ollas Populares*) was established in 1984, bringing together 43 soup kitchens across the country.[13] The Coordinating Committee of Neighborhood Health-care Clinics (*Coordinadora de Policlinicas Barriales*) was founded in December 1983, and in the same year, a group of neighborhood commissions formed the Neighborhood Movement of Montevideo (*Movimiento de Vecinos de Montevideo*, MOVEMO). MOVEMO held a congress in December 1985, attracting 250 people representing close to 100 neighborhood commissions from Montevideo. Residents of the shantytowns also created citywide organizations. In December 1982, for example, representatives of 9 neighborhood commissions from marginal areas established the Movement for Decent Housing (MOVIDE, *Movimiento Pro-Vivienda Decorosa*), and by 1986, its membership had grown to include 22 commissions.

The building of new organizational structures was accompanied by a significant process of goal transformation. As the movements began to challenge the broader social order, engage in alternative social practices, and propose their own solutions to their problems, their defensive and reactive nature became more offensive and proactive. And at the same time, these collective experiences helped foster a new, more confident sense of identity among the urban poor. This was due to the growing awareness of their potential strength, not only in the sense of negotiating with the state but also—and most significantly—in terms of having the power to solve their problems using their own resources, through self-help collective solutions based on links of solidarity and cooperation. These changes—which were by no means generalized—illustrate the beginnings of a process of reconstituting identity at the local level.

External agents—such as religious organizations and NGOs—played a decisive role in promoting goal transformation and citywide organizational structures. For example, a study of 15 food-purchasing clubs found that more than half were linked to religious organizations and that the rest had connections with trade unions or production co-ops.[14] Similarly, in 1988, 70 percent of the existing soup kitchens in the country were run by religious groups, and financial support for *Coordinadora de Ollas Populares* (COP) came primarily from these groups and trade unions.[15] The Catholic church was also instrumental in initiating and supporting local health-care clinics; in 1985, 63 percent of Montevideo's centers had direct links with religious institutions.[16] In the case of MOVEMO, support came primarily from NGOs working with low-income neighborhoods but also from religious organizations. Several NGOs, for instance, were active in promoting MOVEMO's first congress and offered technical advice and support. Moreover, the initiative to establish MOVEMO and to call for the congress came from individuals who had political experience and who were affiliated with left-wing parties. In the case of MOVIDE, more support came from NGOs than from religious groups, although one of its central activists is a Catholic priest.

These embryonic SMs experienced a rapid decline following the return to democracy in 1985; in fact, many disappeared as organizations or were assimilated into traditional political institutions. The Coordinating Committee of Food-Purchasing Clubs, which had the support of 60 local clubs in 1986, had only 35 groups registered as members in 1988, and less than 25 percent of these were actively involved in the organization. The decline was even more evident among the city's soup kitchens. In the period before the elections, there were 40 soup kitchens in the country, but two years later, in 1986, only half of these remained in existence. By 1988, the number of soup kitchens remained the same, but this stability in numbers hid a more important reality: The nature of these kitchens had changed. The original soup kitchens were primarily collective, cooperative experiences, through which local residents (or trade unionists) addressed the needs of their communities. By 1988, however, the remaining soup kitchens had become church-run assistance programs for the communities. Moreover, they had been transformed into merenderos, which provided snacks—especially for children, who represented 70 percent of those benefiting from these assistance programs.[17]

Following the 1985 congress, MOVEMO began to "go downhill," to use the expression of one of its leaders. Participation declined as many neighborhood commissions were dissolved or as their members saw no need to invest their energies in MOVEMO. By 1988, MOVEMO had the support of 8 local commissions and 2 umbrella organizations representing local groups from 2 other neighborhoods. Its regular meetings were attended by 10 or 12 individuals.

The movements that managed to secure better levels of organizational maintenance were the Coordinating Committee of Health-care Centers and MOVIDE,
the organization of shantytown dwellers. Paradoxically, the former was the least
participatory group and more dependent on technical-professional support.
MOVIDE was also dependent on NGO support, which provided it with invaluable
advice, but its success may be attributed as well to the small size of shantytown
communities and the achievement of partial victories, which provided the basis
for the emergence of the self-confident identity described above. In fact, by 1988,
shantytown residents had the highest rate of community participation in all of
Montevideo.[18] And in that year, MOVIDE still had the support of close to 30
neighborhood commissions, 60 percent of which had joined since the 1984
elections.[19]

Explaining the Sudden Decline

Before assessing the reasons for the decline of these movements, it is important
to stress the following points regarding their history, extension, and degree of
autonomy: First, they had a relatively short history because most of them emerged
in the early 1980s, although their origins can be traced to earlier periods. Uruguay,
unlike other Latin American countries, did not have a strong tradition of
autonomous grass-roots activity; second, quantitative data on these organizations
show that they were not a widespread phenomenon as suggested by some, although
their significance should not be underestimated; third, many of these movements
were dependent on external agents in their day-to-day operation and did not
always represent participatory experiences; fourth, most of them had a dual
orientation toward assistentialism and self-management, although the former was
predominant in most cases.

In addition, the decline of SMs cannot be understood in isolation from the
overall sociopsychological and political context in the country following the
return to democracy. After experiencing a 50 percent reduction of real income
during the eleven years of military rule, Uruguayans had hoped that the return
to democracy would bring back the "old" Uruguay, with all its prosperity and
welfare politics. The country, therefore, experienced an "explosion of expectations" following the establishment of the civilian government in March 1985. But
soon afterward, it became clear to everyone that these expectations were not
going to be fulfilled, at least in the time and degree expected. Uruguayans
experienced "aspirational deprivation,"[20] which, rather than leading to collective
violence (as relative deprivation theory would suggest), ultimately brought on an
overall process of demobilization, based on a generalized belief that collective
action was ineffective. This demobilization affected the whole of Uruguayan
society, not just the social movements described above.[21]

In addition to the relative weakness of existing social movements and the
conjunctural sociopsychological and political context in the country, two additional sets of factors converged to inhibit the development of these incipient
social movements into alternative political and social actors: (1) factors at the local
level, such as a low degree of local organization and participation in community

affairs, limited material resources, the siphoning-off of local leaders toward political party and trade union activity, and so forth, and (2) political factors, including a highly centralized state that dominated civil society, a tight political system (wherein parties have virtually monopolized the process of demand transmission), a particular type of political culture, the dynamics of the process of redemocratization, and the policies of Montevideo's city government from 1985 to 1989. These political factors were the most important determinants in the decline of social movements described above, and, in fact, they also caused the lack of resources at the local level. The remainder of this chapter will document this assertion.

Strong State, Weak Civil Society

A central characteristic of Uruguayan society has been the dominance of the state over civil society. Traditionally, societal projects have been implemented from the top down, as a political class (rather than a social class) shaped the socioeconomic and cultural life of the country through its control of the state. The prominence of the state can be explained, in part, by the fact that the emergence of the modern state—at the beginning of the twentieth century—preceded the consolidation of a rigid class structure.[22] Indeed, the modern state was built within the context of "social stalemate," wherein none of the existing social groups was strong enough, on its own, to impose its societal projects on society. This gave the state relative autonomy from existing social classes and civil society and thereby allowed a political class to gain access to state power and develop its own program of social reform.[23]

Luis Batlle y Ordoñez (known as Batllismo) carried out a reformist project,[24] seeking to create a meritocratic society where political democracy was not an end in itself but a means to achieve social justice.[25] This notion of "social citizenship"—which stressed the need to protect the poor through welfare policies—meant that resources were redistributed through the state with the mediation of the political elite.[26] The state, therefore, became a central factor in social integration—by anticipating and preventing the emergence of social conflicts—and a mediator between various social groups and interests.[27]

The Uruguayan state enjoyed a degree of legitimacy and stability unusual within the Latin American context, which was partly the result of the effectiveness of its redistribution policies. Legitimacy and stability were also obtained by the early institutionalization of the "principles and procedures of negotiated solutions to social conflicts,"[28] like the early consolidation of representative democracy, the integration of all citizens into the political system,[29] and the institutionalization of consensus and compromise between the two traditional Blanco and Colorado parties through the establishment of (proportional) coparticipation in the state administration and a collegiate executive system.[30]

The combination of a strong and activist welfare state with a weak civil society and a type of representative democracy that emphasized consensus and compromise as the legitimate means to solve social conflicts produced a political culture in which democratic values were an integral component. The state was perceived as the guarantor of meritocratic principles and provider of goods and services, rather than as the agent of class rule. The task of solving the problems of the subordinated groups was delegated to the political class, whose access to the state gave it the means to meet this challenge. Thus, most actors addressed the state and channeled their demands through existing political parties. In this political culture, forms of action that operated outside institutional channels and/or sought corporativist representation were delegitimized: Political parties acquired a virtual monopoly in demand articulation and assumed a central role in Uruguayan political and cultural life.

Political Parties: The Central Actors

Political parties became the key link between the state and civil society and performed important socializing functions. Thus, political party traditions and symbols became central elements in the definition of social identities. This primacy of political identity over social identity meant that political loyalties were even more important than membership in a certain class or occupational group in the constitution of identity.[31] The convergence of several factors led to the centrality of politics in social life: the existence of long-lasting political traditions, the flexibility and adaptability of traditional political parties, their control of the state, their multiclass and "catchall" nature, and a complicated set of electoral laws.

The symbolic weight of political parties in national culture is also related to the strong continuity that characterizes Uruguayan political life. Uruguay and Colombia are the only Latin American nations where traditional parties dating from the early nineteenth century have continued to exist and to govern the country.[32] Because the emergence of national parties preceded the consolidation of the modern state, it can be argued that this modern state was, to a significant degree, the creation of political parties. Parties and state became indistinguishable from each other in most Latin American countries, but Uruguay was characterized by the dominance of the former over the latter. Traditional political parties managed to survive, in part, by successfully adapting to changing circumstances while retaining their symbols and traditions. Thus, continuity does not refer to absence of change but to stability "with change and through change."[33] For instance, the development of a welfare system and the politics of compromise and coparticipation were unique and creative initiatives (in the Latin American context) of the political class.

Luís González explained that the Blanco and Colorado parties are nonideological, "catchall" parties—with heterogeneous ideological tendencies ranging from extreme right to moderate left of center—that display no significant ideological or social base differences between them.[34] The country's electoral laws allow divergent tendencies within each party to have their own organizational structures and to run their own presidential candidates without undermining party unity. These features strengthened the internal heterogeneity of traditional parties, allowing them to appeal to multiple social groups and to incorporate diverse interests into the political process. This, in turn, inhibited the rise of alternative political parties and enhanced the role of traditional parties as central actors in interest articulation and in the constitution of social identities.[35]

Redemocratization: Restoring the Old Order

These political arrangements began to show signs of exhaustion in the late 1950s and early 1960s due to economic and political factors that cannot be analyzed in this chapter. The political impasse that followed led to a crisis in the "politics of compromise" and to the introduction of new political actors and new forms of collective action that challenged both the two-party system and existing legal-institutional arrangements. Prominent among these are the Tupamaro urban guerrilla organization, a radical student movement, and the Frente Amplio, a broad-based, left-wing coalition formed in 1971.

Yet another new actor—the military—was to break the political impasse through a military coup in 1973.[36] The military sought to redefine the relationship between the state, civil society, and political parties. A peculiarity of the Uruguayan case is that the military rulers—while attempting to delegitimize the political class—always retained the rules of the traditional political system as reference points. They never challenged the centrality of parties in a democratic system, and they made the Blanco and Colorado parties the central axis in the process of redemocratization; they also retained in office a civilian president (appointed by the military and possessing limited powers) during eight of the eleven years of military rule.[37] Unlike other military regimes in Latin America, the Uruguayan military high command adopted a collegiate structure—where decisionmaking was achieved through consensus and compromise—and thereby prevented the emergence of a strongman.[38]

Not surprisingly, in the transition to democracy, the logic of restoration was imposed over the logic of renewal.[39] The political elites negotiated with the military on the conditions for a redemocratization that restored old political loyalties and organizational forms, with parties as central actors in the political system.[40] Civil society—which had shown unusual vitality and initiative toward the end of the dictatorship—quickly became dominated, as in the past, by political structures. Given this outcome, many analysts argue that Uruguayan political life appears to have been "frozen" during the military period, allowing old traditions to be restored with the return to democracy. One example of this is the fact that the percentages of votes obtained by the three main contenders in the 1984 elections were strikingly similar to those obtained in the previous elections thirteen years earlier.[41]

The persistence of traditional political values and institutions was reinforced by the dynamics of negotiated transitions from authoritarian rule to democracy— where the military institution remains strong—that commit political and social actors to strengthen democratic institutions and minimize conflict and to contain alternative, noninstitutional practices. In addition, the logic of the consolidation of democratic institutions—which required the active participation of political parties—made party-building a central priority, contributing further to the tendency toward the assimilation or displacement of nontraditional collective actors. And with redemocratization, the Frente Amplio made a historic break-through by gaining access to the polity and effectively weakening the traditional two-party system. But this inclusion also placed constraints on this force for it could no longer as effectively pressure a system of which it was now an integral part.

In addition to the pressures of redemocratization, the attitudes of the main left-wing parties, where restoration also triumphed over renewal, helped to bring about the decline of the SMs. At a time when civil society had experienced a sense of empowerment and when new actors were beginning to emerge, the attitudes of the Left contributed to the movements' isolation and decline. And party organizational needs were placed ahead of the needs of the new movements. For example, many of the leaders of SMs that emerged during the military period—who had prior political affiliation and experience with left-wing parties—were pulled out of urban social movement (USM) organizations and reassigned to party functions. This "decapitated" the incipient social movements and accelerated their decline. Meanwhile, those party militants who remained in movement organizations began to make their party affiliation more visible. This created problems of double loyalties, where loyalty to the party was more important than loyalty to the movement. The high visibility of party affiliation among movement members brought internal conflict and dissent—along party lines—into urban social movements and contributed to their decline.[42] Finally, the Left's traditional emphasis on mobilization—by which a given leadership shows its capacity to mobilize masses of people in order to increase its bargaining power with other elites—helped to discourage new forms of participation, with actors involved in the conception and execution of certain forms of action.[43]

Municipal Policies: Clientelism and the Fragmentation of Local Actors

The policies of Montevideo's city government reinforced the factors outlined earlier by limiting resources at the local level and further reducing opportunities for collective action outside institutional channels.[44] The municipal government created *Unidad Asesora de Proyectos Especiales* (UAPE) in 1985 to coordinate city policies and provide advice and support to local development and social assistance programs at the community level. The target group consisted of low-income people—those marginalized from power and wealth—whose interests were not articulated by the existing organizations of civil society.[45]

Soon after coming to power, the city government announced a plan to establish direct links with grass-roots community groups. One of the aims of this plan was to bypass those organizations that presented themselves as representatives of local actors or as intermediaries between local actors and the authorities. Umbrella community organizations—of the type built by SMs—were excluded from receiving aid, in the form of advice or material resources, from UAPE. This limitation affected not only citywide coordinating organizations but also a multiplicity of organizations linking voluntary associations within neighborhoods. City officials were suspicious of grass-roots organizations because they believed that many of them, especially the most organized, were controlled by left-wing parties. They questioned the legitimacy of their leadership by arguing that there was a gap between the leaders' political beliefs and those of the members (the former leaning further left than the latter). In addition, they argued that NGOs working with the urban poor also had a hidden (left-wing) political agenda and/or tended to place their organizational needs before those of the urban poor. Regardless of the accuracy of this assessment, what is important about it is how the political-ideological logic was perceived to overdetermine the dynamics of grass-roots movements.[46]

The implementation of these policies discriminated against organizations that had begun to break with the isolation of their small communities by joining umbrella organizations linking immediate local demands with broader issues. By only helping more traditional grass-roots organizations—those with no horizontal linkages within the community or vertical integration with other social sectors—municipal social assistance programs weakened those groups that had just begun the long and difficult process of becoming social movements. Their organizations and forms of action were delegitimized because they failed to attain basic goals as a result of being excluded from the resources of city assistance programs. One direct effect of this was to promote a more traditional local identity and forms of action isolated from other conflicts and circumscribed within a clientelistic orientation. Thus, the establishment of direct links between the city government and grass-roots organizations (in isolation from each other) helped to atomize local actors and to inhibit collective actions at the community level.[47] Emerging urban movements were weakened and prevented from completing the passage from "reactive" to "proactive" forms of collective action.

Conclusions

This chapter has examined the factors that inhibited the development of social movements in Uruguay following the return to democracy in 1985. Some scholars have suggested that the decline in social movement activity can be attributed to the convergence of a variety of factors: the nature of the country's political traditions and institutions (the relative weakness of civil society vis-à-vis the state, the centrality of political parties in the country's social and political life, a specific type of political culture, and so forth), political processes and state policies (the dynamics of the democratic transition and the policies of Montevideo's city government), social-psychological factors (aspirational deprivation, causing generalized demobilization), the realities of local communities (such as the lack of resources and the low degree of organization and participation in community affairs), and the embryonic nature of the movements (their brief existence, the relative low incidence of these experiences, and so on).

My argument, however, is that political factors intervened as the central constraints that truncated the incipient development of the new social practices that were emerging at the local level. Paradoxically, the country's return to formal democratic rule—which eliminated the repressive measures instituted by the dictatorship and opened up the political opportunity structure in the country—

had the short-term effect of narrowing the structure of opportunities for SMs. The set of political constraints unleashed by the democratic opening proved too strong for the new movements. Thus, the optimistic forecasts about the potential democratizing force of SMs proved inaccurate, and the new collective actors were either assimilated into traditional groups or disappeared as organizations.

The success or failure of collective actors, however, cannot be determined by exclusive reference to organizational maintenance. For instance, many movements tend to disappear after their goals have been achieved. In addition, measures of success cannot rely exclusively on the movement's goal achievement record; they must also take into account the indirect or unintended outcomes of social movement activity. For example, even in cases when a movement does not achieve its stated goals, its activities might bring other positive outcomes, like the constitution of new identities or the development of a sense of empowerment among social movement participants. These outcomes might leave their imprint on the collective memory of local actors, and even if the movement disappears (organizationally), these experiences can be inserted into other fields and organizations. Hence, in assessing the success or failure of collective actors, one must look beyond the maintenance of organizational forms or the achievement of goals. Social movements represent more than whatever their organizational forms and limited demands may express: They are fluid processes of constituting new actors and are constantly undergoing transformations, in both form and content.

In the case of Uruguayan social movements, whether one examines organizational maintenance, goal achievement, or the direct or indirect outcomes of collective action, the overall assessment must be that they had few successes. I have already described the disappearance of many grass-roots organizations, and goal achievement was also low, especially among neighborhood commissions seeking improved access to urban services and other collective consumption questions. Trying to measure success, however, in terms of cultural change and/ or the indirect outcomes of SMs is more difficult. Nevertheless, it appears doubtful that great accomplishments were made at either level. For instance, while the "local question" began to be considered as a legitimate issue for discussion (judging from the parameters of the debates within political parties, including those of the Left, and other traditional institutions like trade unions), it appears that no significant transformations were accomplished. The absence of renewal, especially within the Left, seems to suggest that even in those cases where SM activists entered political parties and trade unions, they had little short-term impact in transforming traditional ways of doing politics. Yet, cultural change and new practices are slow to develop, and changes at this level may not be felt at the same speed or with the same intensity as political-structural changes. Thus, it is too early to say whether these movements will have a long-term impact on the political culture of the country.

A good test for this is the experience of the present city government of Montevideo. In 1990, for the first time in the city's history, the left-wing coalition Frente Amplio formed the municipal government. It would be wrong to assume that this important electoral victory could be attributed to the social movement experiences described in this chapter. The Frente Amplio coalition, in fact, obtained almost the same proportion of votes in Montevideo that it did in the 1984 elections. Nonetheless, the policies of new government may open new opportunities for collective action. A plan seeking to establish a more decentralized structure of government, for instance, is already being implemented, and having more sympathetic city officials and more accessibility to public government may ultimately encourage local initiatives and participation in community affairs. If this is the case, the previous experiences of grass-roots organizing may prove to be very useful indeed, and local actors may be able to establish a new relationship with the municipal administration. However, it must be pointed out that decentralization does not necessarily lead to democratization and increased levels of participation, although it is a precondition for these. The Frente Amplio government may also reproduce more traditional left-wing methods that encourage mobilization and supportive activities at the expense of full participation. If this occurs, the fate of social movements will be sealed for a long time to come, once again, by political factors.

Notes

This article is based on my fieldwork in Uruguay in 1987–1988 as part of my doctoral dissertation work. I wish to thank the International Development Research Center (IDRC) for providing the funds that made the project possible.

1. Tilly 1978.
2. See Evers 1985; Fals Borda 1986; Jelin 1987b, 1990; Karner 1983.
3. This argument is made by Ruth Cardoso in Chapter 16.
4. For Brazil and Peru, for example, Cardoso (Chapter 16) and Arnillas (1986) have shown how municipal administrators' positive perceptions of SMs led to significant changes in terms of the movements' growth and impact, respectively.
5. See González Bombal and Palermo 1987.
6. See Alvarez 1989b; Cardoso 1983, 1988; Coraggio 1985; Jacobi 1989; Palermo 1987.
7. For an analysis of these collective experiences, see Marsiglia, Piedra Cueva, and Rodé 1985a and 1985b; Filgueira, ed. 1985.
8. From my interview with Ana María Rodríguez, leader of the Soup Kitchens Coordinating Committee, June 6, 1988.
9. Marsiglia, Piedra Cueva, and Rodé 1985.
10. "Historia de las Ollas Populares," document produced by the Soup Kitchens Coordinating Committee, mimeo, 1985.
11. Marsiglia, Piedra Cueva, and Rodé 1985.
12. The number of neighborhood commissions registered with the city government increased more than tenfold in 1985, from 70 in March to 740 at the end of the year. It is difficult to estimate exactly how many of these commissions were actually active. In addition, not all of them were formed in 1985; many of them had been set up in previous years but had not been registered with the city government due to fear of reprisals by the military. Figures obtained in my interview with Luis Muslera, operations assistant, Unidad Asesora de Proyectos Especiales, Montevideo municipal government, April 1988.
13. *Nuestra Gente* 11, no. 3 (n.d.).
14. Ibid., 65.
15. Interview with Ana María Rodríguez, leader of the Soup Kitchens Coordinating Committee, June 6, 1988.

16. Filgueira 1985. Also, health-care units display a great degree of dependency on outside institutions (which provide medical personnel, financing, training, administrative skills, and so forth), and, in consequence, local participation tends to be low. See Marsiglia, Piedra Cueva, and Rodé 1985.

17. Interview with Ana María Rodríguez, leader of the Soup Kitchens Coordinating Committee, June 6, 1988.

18. A survey conducted by CLAEH found very low levels of local participation in Montevideo. For instance, figures for all of Montevideo show that only 6.7 percent of all female interviewees and 8.5 percent of male interviewees participated in a local organization. In contrast, the level of local participation among residents of shantytowns was 16.5 percent for females and 19.2 percent for males. Study conducted by CLAEH for UNICEF, directed by Pablo Terra.

19. From an interview with father Cacho Alonso, MOVIDE activist and Catholic priest, June 1, 1988.

20. According to relative deprivation theory, aspirational deprivation occurs when expectations increase but the capability of society to meet these rising expectations remains unchanged.

21. Many Uruguayans began to seek individual solutions to their problems. For example, in 1987, the number of applications to emigrate to the United States was greater than in any year of the military regime.

22. See Rial 1989.

23. On the question of the relative autonomy of the state, see Barrán and Nahum 1982.

24. Batlle y Ordoñez was a central figure in the building of the country's welfare system and democratic institutions. Batllismo introduced important social and political reforms: the restriction of the president's powers through the creation of a council of government (which later gave rise to the collegiate system of government), the transformation of the state into an active entrepreneur, the separation of church and state, the introduction of free universal education, the granting of trade union rights and an eight-hour workday, the introduction of the right to divorce, the granting of the right to vote to women, and so on. See Rama 1972; Lindahl 1962.

25. See Cocchi and Klaczko 1985; Perelli and Rial 1983.

26. Perelli and Rial (1983: 151) argued that the Batllista reformist project, though progressive and egalitarian, rested on the premise that "the state was the central engine of a civil society that was mobilized but not consulted."

27. Cocchi and Klaczko (1985: 30–39).

28. Riz 1985.

29. Between 1905 and 1931, the electorate grew by 668 percent. In the 1930 national elections, 80 percent of those eligible to vote turned out (which constituted 91 percent of all persons who had citizen rights). See Caetano, Rilla, and Pérez 1987.

30. The collegiate executive system replaced the president with a council of nine elected members—three of them from the opposition party—who took turns serving as president of the council. In 1931, the Blanco and Colorado parties agreed to divide executive positions in state enterprises and ministries among members of these two parties, on a three-to-two basis in favor of the winning party. This encouraged clientelism and the artificial growth of state employment, but it also provided stability because losing an election did not mean—as it did in many Latin American countries—being thrown completely out of power.

31. Beisso and Castagnola (1987: 9–18) defined Uruguayan society as "politico-centric" and argued that political loyalties constitute the dominant axis in the process of identity constitution.

32. See Mainwaring 1988: 8; Gillespie 1985: 21–22.

33. Caetano, Rilla, and Pérez 1987: 54.

34. Luís González 1985.

35. Aguiar (1985) argued that the Uruguayan political system worked as a "fragmented two-party system" until the 1970s. The Blanco and Colorado parties obtained the support of 90 percent of the electorate until 1971, when they received 81 percent support. In the 1984 elections,

support for the Blanco and Colorado parties dropped to 76 percent, and it continued to decline in 1989, when they received 70 percent of the votes.

36. The military dictatorship lasted until the end of 1984, when the Colorado party was put back in office in the national elections.

37. In 1976, the military removed President Juan María Bordaberry for proposing the abolition of political parties and the restructuring of the political system along corporatist lines. The military attributed the country's problems to the attitudes of the political elite, not to the political institutions themselves. See Gillespie 1984: 132.

38. Luís González 1985b: 108–110; Riz 1985: 130–133.

39. Rial 1985.

40. Filgueira 1984.

41. In the 1971 elections, the Colorado and Blanco parties and the Frente Amplio left-wing coalition obtained, respectively, 41 percent, 40 percent, and 21 percent of the votes. In 1984, they received almost the same percentage of votes: 41 percent, 35 percent, and 21 percent. Although the overall distribution by party remained almost constant, there was a tendency to vote for centrist positions within each party/coalition.

42. Local residents observed that the return of democracy brought division within the ranks of USMs because activists placed party loyalty ahead of the need for united local action. During the military period, in contrast, participants in grass-roots activities concealed their political loyalties—for security reasons—and worked together with other neighbors regardless of party affiliation.

43. For a discussion of the distinction between mobilization and participation in the Uruguayan case, see Martorelli 1986.

44. Under the Uruguayan electoral system, municipal elections are held on the same day as national presidential and parliamentary elections, although voters can cast separate ballots. In the November 1984 elections, the Colorado party won the presidency and control over Montevideo's municipal government.

45. City government policies were outlined in two working papers produced by UAPE in 1985. See "Informe Anual de Actividades de la UAPE" and "Proyecto Promoción Social y Asistencia Comunitaria (Pomotores Sociales)," Documentos de Trabajo, Unidad Asesora de Proyectos Especiales, Intendencia Municipal de Montevideo.

46. The position of the city government was outlined by Horacio Martorelli, a well-known Uruguayan sociologist who headed the local development projects of the city government, in my interview with him in May 1988. See also Martorelli 1986.

47. One example of this was the implementation of an Emergency Food Relief Program through which the city government distributed food door to door—or through "ghost" neighborhood committees—instead of working with existing soup kitchens. These measures helped to disarticulate existing grass-roots cooperative efforts.

16

Popular Movements in the Context of the Consolidation of Democracy in Brazil

Ruth Corrêa Leite Cardoso

Introduction

Discussions about how to consolidate democracy in Brazil have always tacitly assumed the need to change the country's political culture in order to incorporate full citizenship rights, free from traditional clientelistic controls. Conservative analysts have argued that electoral mishaps are usually the result of the general population's lack of information (that is, "the people don't know how to vote"), and they have therefore stressed the need for civic education. Those who seek to change political practice itself agree that the general population's level of information should be improved, but progressive analysts and activists advocate, instead, a political pedagogy aimed at furthering the popular sectors' autonomy. From the latter perspective, social movements and popular organizations are vigorous indicators of a society beginning to express its interests spontaneously.

Since the early 1970s, groups seeking radical changes in political practices have been the supporting nuclei of the popular sectors' struggles for their urban demands. Moreover, they have formed the bases from which previously excluded sectors, such as women, blacks, and homosexuals, engaged in their own battles to broaden political participation. Popular movements created new political arenas, voicing demands for schools, day-care centers, public transportation, and other services previously unavailable on the outskirts of the large urban centers. Through their aggressive discourse, movement groups showed that they were aware of their exclusion from the benefits they expected from a modern state with a growing economy. And, though movement discourse defined the state as the movements' enemy, it also recognized it as their interlocutor at the negotiating table.

Given this scenario, it is not surprising that academic studies of popular movements emphasized the process through which social identities were being created and used to establish new relations between excluded citizens and the state apparatus. The movements' challenging stance was often interpreted as a particular, although vague, type of "class consciousness," now reemerging in a new form. Nevertheless, when more specifically class-based explanations of these groups were attempted, they often ended up clashing with the heterogeneous nature of the grass-roots movements and the local character of their mobilization. The movements' weakness became their strength for their very local nature was interpreted as indicating a participatory process that stemmed from the society's grass roots. Building autonomous associations and endowed with a new role, local neighborhood groups made their demands in ways that revealed their ability to bypass traditional mechanisms of political co-optation. They were thus devising a new practice that dismissed the mediation of professional politicians and created a new scenario whereby previously excluded sectors demanded recognition of their presence. It is not by chance that analyses before the 1980s emphasized the spontaneity of the groups, as both an indicator of their authenticity and as proof of the broadening of a democratic vision, which until then had been considered absent in the daily lives of the disadvantaged sectors.

Insofar as the organized groups have challenged the state to expand its role to meet previously neglected demands, these interpretations tended to reinforce the belief that both a more democratic ideology and the continued pressure to build a social democracy can be furthered solely by the growth of the popular movements.

Today, there are numerous studies on the efforts, achievements, and failures of the social movements. They cover a relatively lengthy period and point to the diverse types of activity covered by the label "popular movement." The hope that popular groups would unite and expand throughout urban areas can no longer be sustained. Hence, the assumption that these organizations act as a single agent capable of renewing the entire political system has also become untenable.

In fact, the growth of the social movements was actually not as extensive as initially envisioned. Moreover, the continuity of the military regime's *abertura* or political liberalization, launched in the mid-1970s and gradually, if erratically, expanded thereafter, created new and unexpected conditions for the actions of popular groups. In the first place, the state apparatus gradually became more receptive to popular participation. Consequently, whenever social policies were to be implemented, local organized groups became recognized as significant interlocutors. Secondly, the multiparty system splintered the opposition block, which had previously been united against both state repression and the economic policies detrimental to the popular sectors.[1] Many of the militants already involved in grass-roots organizations also began to identify with particular political parties and sought to establish some link between these two forms of participation.

As a result of this new political scenario, latent conflicts, which had long permeated the local demand-oriented groups' relations both with the social agencies and with the political parties, began to surface. I will discuss both of these relations in the following two sections of this chapter. My aim is to discuss the process of negotiation among the movements, the parties, and the state apparatus, in order to better understand the way new sociopolitical identities are forged. These identities stem from the popular movements' continuous interaction with various collaborators. The process can thus basically be seen as a play of mirrors, through which the grass-roots groups construct their self-image so that it reflects their dialogue with different interlocutors.

Although it is true that these struggling nuclei emerged out of a common experience of exclusion and lack of access to collective consumer goods, this does not adequately explain either the diversity of the movements' negotiating strategies or the way each group defines its boundaries in the context of the neighborhood within which it acts. At the end of the chapter, I will return to the popular movements' contribution to Brazilian society's democratization process.

Policies Promoting Participation

In the final years of the military regime, some public agencies began to encourage contact between public officials and the population targeted by social service policies. Some state and municipal agencies supported initiatives to foster participation among users of the social services, although with varying results.

State employees who were in tune with popular interests guaranteed the space for community demonstrations within their respective social agencies. Some state agencies began to take the first steps toward recognizing that popular pressure was actually a healthy sign and should no longer necessarily be considered dangerous. But most of these attempts were haphazard and irregular and elicited a combination of tolerance and repression.

The 1982 election in São Paulo both sanctioned and broadened this trend for the discourse of the winning *Partido do Movimento Democrático Brasileiro* (Party of the Brazilian Democratic Movement, PMDB), which was the direct political heir of the electorally successful *Movimento Democrático Brasileiro* (Brazilian Democratic Movement, MDB), focused on the decentralization-participation binomial. Other opposition parties such as the *Partido dos Trabalhadores* (Workers' Party, PT) and the *Partido Comunista do Brasil* (Communist Party of Brazil, PC do B) also supported this approach as a means of building a more democratic decisionmaking process. The chorus of support in the dialogue between civil society and the state, in turn, further reinforced the demand-based groups.

Nevertheless, the lack of a clear political project under the PMDB led each government agency to promote popular participation in its own way. Several formulas were attempted, ranging from visits to popular-sector neighborhoods by officials from state or municipal agencies to the creation of local neighborhood councils. Many of the new "opposition" public agency directors in the popular neighborhoods championed participation, offered meeting-hall space (as the church already had), sponsored community get-togethers, and even prioritized demands submitted collectively.

Because there were no general guidelines, however, this process differed in each neighborhood and in each public sector. Nonetheless, in every case, a broadening range of associations became recognized as legitimate interlocutors within each specific government area. These groups created direct channels through which to negotiate their demands and, in so doing, eliminated the previous common practices based on politicians' mediation and endless bureaucratic procedures.

As an example, recall the changes in some of the regional administrations of the municipality of São Paulo, where the power of one of the sectors in this agency—the Núcleos de Atendimento ao Público (Public Assistance Nuclei, NAPs), which had once been fully in charge of recording application submissions and petition-based demands—now declined significantly. During the PMDB's entire municipal term, leaders of several local associations were constantly on the local government premises, which led the administration to designate specific employees to assist them. Only individual or very routine requests were passed on to the NAPs. In other government areas, pressure was applied through either neighborhood "caravans" or the intervention of the authorities. Some public agencies focused on the question of how to further popular organization, turning it into a subject of endless discussion. Others began to encourage action by already recognized associations, such as the Sociedades Amigos do Bairro (Neighborhood Friends Societies, SABs), the favelas, health movements, and others. Sometimes, new entities were created, such as the community councils or the plenary assemblies of various associations. The civil servants hired to replace employees appointed by the military governments valued direct negotiation with social service users, seeing this approach as a means of increasing the politicization of the popular sectors.

It is important to note that I am not evaluating the adequacy or efficacy of these participation models. My aim here is solely to point to a trend that reinforced the popular determination to address public authorities directly and to try to influence decisions that affected their interests.

The local public administrations' regional branches became both the main targets of users' pressures for participation and the most inclined to foster it. Because public employees were so immersed in the local political contexts, they had to establish a dialogue with the popular associations. But they also had to maintain some contact with the local political bosses, with parties, and with the church. Moreover, their agenda had to follow the guidelines put forth by the central agencies of their respective sectors. The result of the interaction of these different interests was that each case was resolved individually.

Some agencies, such as the municipality's regional administrations, defined themselves as open spaces for local politics; others, such as the schools or the community health clinics, rendered specialized services, and their professional staffs were more removed from local interests. Because dialogue with these various public sectors necessarily calls for different strategies, the popular groups ended up specializing in particular sectors and being recognized as their main interlocutors. The SABs were in their element in the regional administrations. The favela population and the pro-day-care movements used to be served by the now dismantled *Secretaria da Família e do Bem-Estar Social* (Greater São Paulo's Family and Social Services Departments, FABES). The popular health councils, when they existed, or the various health movements discussed their demands at the health clinics.

This need to "specialize" led local-level groups to diversify so that they would either complement or compete with one another, depending on the particular situation. Because some of the leaders participated in more than one association, they sometimes reached a peaceful coexistence whereby each group respected the others' turf. But their relations with the local party and religious leaders could also be strained. This created a political game, which was never made explicit, in which each group claimed to represent the "true will" of the entire neighborhood within its particular sphere of action.

The situation is thus paradoxical because, although the strength of local groups depended on their ability to appear as delegates for their entire population, existing circumstances ultimately forced these groups to specialize. This, in turn, made each more viable as community delegates and hence actually intensified competition.

I have dealt in previous work with the nature of these delegations or so-called community mobilizations, which in theory do not allow internal differences or leadership hierarchies to emerge because all neighbors supposedly have the same needs and have experienced the same forms of discrimination (R. Cardoso 1982, 1983). The feeling of community, which church action always strove to reinforce, created an illusory unity of purpose. Each association presented itself as the true representative of the neighborhood "community," and the public agencies did not question that representation. It only became a problem for competing groups and agency administrators alike when actual conflicts did surface. The public agencies' directors and employees, for their part, found it difficult to deal with political divisions and tended to negotiate with the associations as if each expressed the general will. The result was that when administrators were actually confronted with conflicts between groups or party sectors, they reacted with surprise and disappointment.

These newfound tensions were most apparent in areas where community councils were created.[2] Because these councils are not spontaneous organizations, they have to be created through meetings or elections. The leadership selection process, however, is almost always directed by a few individuals who organize their own campaign tickets and mobilize local voters; this procedure most often results in the creation of homogeneous councils that frequently end up isolated from the other local groups. When the selection process includes various types of leaders, different party or religious identities surface, and the result is a more heterogeneous council. Hence, health councils using the first type of election may ensure their monopoly of community representation at the health clinics but consequently do not manage to broaden participation. Those using the second procedure often become embroiled in controversy, despite rhetorical efforts to maintain unity. Some of the leaders accuse others of failing to sever their ties with outside interests (parties, churches, clientelist politicians) or of manipulating their less militant colleagues. In either case, the dispute is over a dubious hegemony for no one association actually has the legitimacy to represent everyone, and, at the same time, as mentioned above, each group negotiates with different public agencies: Mothers' clubs fight for day-care centers, the neighborhood committees or the SABs crusade for urban improvement, the favela movements struggle for housing, and the health groups demand that clinics be built and managed.

Each time a "community" carved out an opening in a public agency, the number of actors participating in the institutional game increased. The various roles civil servants have begun to play have led them to adopt attitudes toward popular participation that can range from mistrust to enthusiasm. Each agency is also fraught with internal conflicts, often forcing employees to position themselves within their own agencies. This can often spill over into the movement's own actions, as employees either make alliances with the movement's leadership or effectively damage the agency's capacity to render services by adopting an oppositional stance.

Associations experience the least conflict when their representativity is not questioned. This often happens when they direct their pressure for neighborhood improvements toward nonlocal government agencies and the agencies' employees become their allies. Indeed, given the new value placed on popular participation, the directors of local agencies do not have much space to maneuver unless they make alliances with some of the movements' leaders to demand the expansion or maintenance of the services they render. Thus, because the neighborhood has to seem united to achieve its aims, its internal divisions can be concealed more easily.

When different local interests (those of government employees, users, parties, or groups) are at stake, it is more difficult to control the confrontation among the various groups, which tends to emerge as each questions the legitimacy of its opponent's claims to representation. This continuous interaction has begun to impose its own rules, effectively qualifying and disqualifying specific interlocutors. For example, even though the political parties are present, their presence in this game cannot be made explicit. All the associations know that they must maintain apolitical semblances and discourses, even when their practices themselves deny this. They cannot take sides precisely because they represent everyone, and the public administration, too, has to maintain its neutrality and avoid privileging any given party.

Parties and Local Politics

The problems that arise in efforts to integrate parties and social movements are not only apparent in local struggles. As studies made in a number of countries and under different regimes have shown, this coexistence has been difficult, in spite of the hopes of the various political currents involved.

Much of what has been written on social movements and demand-based groups has emphasized their innovative role and stressed their positive impact on political systems considered to be rigid. Because parties are hierarchically organized, they have been accused of keeping the decisionmaking centers (the parties' helm) distant from their rank-and-file members. Compared to community forms of mobilization, parties seem lifeless and unable to hear the spontaneous demonstrations stemming from a newly mobilizing society.

The sudden vigor with which feminism, antiracism, pacifism, and other movements exploded in the 1960s reinforced interpretations that expressed this disillusionment (for example, compare with Rowbotham et al. 1982). Some writers believed we were undergoing a period of transition in which these two forms of political practice could influence one another to their mutual benefit: The parties would become less elitist and the movements would be able to go beyond the specificity of their struggles. Still, despite some positive consequences of this coexistence, the tension between these two forms of political participation persists.

One of the sources of this tension is the way community groups operate: They always assume that a consensus will be achieved. Because they focus on satisfying immediate demands, these groups are united by what has to be, necessarily, a nonpartisan and universal discourse.

Leftist parties support the demand-based movements, seeing them as healthy indicators of the popular sectors' strength. And perhaps this explains why they try to enlist the most militant popular leaders, creating a double militancy for them. Still, as members of local associations, these leaders have to continually reaffirm the nonpartisan nature of their interventions. Their need to appear neutral in the eyes of the public administration is not their only motivation: The internal operation of their associations also depends on unanimity. This is why the associations' internal conflicts were less apparent when the opposition was under the one-party (MDB) umbrella.

Since the creation of the multiparty system, the popular groups have come to perceive discord as a threat to their survival, which has led them either to inertia or to splintering. For this reason, the presence of certain parties in particular neighborhoods is always disguised, even when their influence there is quite well known (as is often the case with the PT or the PC do B). Their influence nevertheless appears, for example, in the groups' support of specific congress members, who can help them channel particular demands. The groups are more likely to choose those politicians who encourage greater popular participation and are willing to subordinate themselves to the movements' guidelines, where-upon they serve as intermediaries to set up appointments with mayors or state authorities. These congress members also stress their own positions as participating members of local groups and support the latter's criticism of "electoral clientelism." The criterion for distinguishing so-called popular congress members from those identified as populists is thus based on the former's ideological ties to popular demonstrations; the latter's actions merely reflect their own electoral concerns.

Nevertheless, the movements sometimes need to have access to politicians who are well accepted by the executive but cannot really be classified as representatives of the popular groups. They achieve their aim by enlisting the assistance of campaign canvassers and the local leaders of the various parties. Some associations consider this to be deceitful and clientelistic, but other popular leaders openly resort to it, justifying their action as a pragmatic and necessary step toward ensuring their victory. Even so, success is never credited to the parties themselves but is, instead, invariably presented as an achievement of collective action.

Insofar as the public agencies opened their doors to popular pressures, the belief in the strength of the organized population was reinforced. This also reinforced an instrumental view of contacts with the parties. Hence, to speak of clientelism today is to apply an old concept to new situations: At least for the active popular groups, congress members are perceived as representatives of the people and must work on their behalf, without allowing their support of the movements' struggles to necessarily become tied to electoral adherence.

This dissociation between the vote and the conquest of rights is quite explicit in the discourse of the popular leadership. Nevertheless, in practice, the distance is not as great as they claim because, ultimately, when campaign time arrives, everyone has to choose a candidate. Personal contact with candidates who collaborate with popular associations then tends to influence voters' decisions. But insofar as the public agencies today tend to prioritize their services to organized groups, the old mechanisms to control electoral clienteles are no longer as effective.

Still, it is important not to simplify or generalize this process. Not every neighborhood has popular associations, but, as seen above, in those that do, the associations' range of actions often spills over into the local politicians' spheres of influence. The administrative machine has an important role in this because it is under pressure to meet the interests dictated by the alliances supporting the governing party. In certain situations, state agency employees are forced to recognize local politicians, accepting them as the popular sectors' mediators. Even though they fight against it, the community associations ultimately have to turn to political pragmatism for they need to enlist the support of those local congress and assembly members who do have access to the authorities.

For their part, politicians who have local support and hope to maintain it need to ensure their effectiveness in helping to meet the demands of popular associations. As a result, they try to establish links between the movements and those who will serve as their advisers in the public agencies. However, once again, though they qualify as useful mediators, in the process they also lose their direct control over the voters. They themselves no longer convey the people's needs to the state agencies; at most, they can continue to pressure state officials to expedite the demands that the now-recognized associations always present collectively to particular sectors of the state apparatus.

The opposition's election to São Paulo state government in 1982 and later to the federal government did not generate the administrative reforms necessary to ensure political autonomy of state offices from the parties. The mechanisms of political influence on the state persisted in several areas of government, and politicians unofficially continued to control public resources through politically endorsed nominations. This practice of politically partitioning the state apparatus limited the influence of popular mobilization per se over state appointments. Still, in some cases, popular groups in the city of São Paulo's more mobilized neighborhoods did influence the hiring of directors at public agencies because one of the ways candidates could qualify for these positions was to be endorsed by the popular movements' most significant leaders.

Thus, survival in this web of local politics has prompted demand-oriented community groups to act pragmatically and make use of their most effective contacts, on the one hand, and, on the other, to adopt an ideological stance that constantly reaffirms the popular sectors' autonomy from both the parties and the state. The movements' strategies of action are defined in the context of the tension created by these two opposing guidelines and stem from their evaluation of the resources at their disposal in any given situation. Moreover, their tactics are constantly redefined in an effort to balance their practical conquests with their display of autonomy.

This process becomes particularly apparent during periods of change of government, when the movements have to establish new alliances with parties to ensure their access to the new nuclei of power. This is not an easy process, and many groups are forced to withdraw. These periods are, therefore, particularly interesting for analyzing the relations between the popular movements and the parties because they show the movements once again forging paths to the various public administration agencies.

At the same time, this renegotiation of space for popular participation does not begin from scratch. For one thing, the legitimacy of popular associations is no longer questioned, and though some may experience more difficulties than others, on the whole the local administration does not close its agencies' doors to them.

The movements realign themselves and come closer to the politicians and administrators without establishing permanent relations. They defend themselves from the party system by reasserting their community-based identity, which ultimately ensures their continued partnership in the political game.

Popular Movements and the Building of Democracy

When we ask ourselves about these demand-oriented movements' contribution to Brazil's democratization, we have to answer the two questions I raised initially: (1) To what extent did these movements actually force the creation of a space in which neighborhood communities could express their collective will? (2) To what extent did participation lead to a change in the popular sectors' worldview? In terms of the first question, we have already shown that during the 1970s, popular organizations emerged as demand-based movements and marked the political scenario with their presence for the first time. During the 1980s, some sectors of the state apparatus began to see direct dialogue with their public in a positive light and to use popular pressure as an added criterion when allocating the scarce resources destined for social policies.

Nevertheless, this interaction only took place at local-level public agencies and did not include a redefinition of priorities for existing resources. Discussions about how to implement programs defined by the upper echelons of the public administrations were few and far between. For example, in several neighborhoods in São Paulo, the need for hospitals in the outskirts is undisputed, but there are few political channels to influence the relevant bureaucracy in charge. Mass mobilizations and meetings are most effective when they put pressure on those responsible for distributing already existing services. Such demands are left unanswered when they try to define new priorities because they do not have access to the information needed to make decisions.

Within the rules defined by government policies, small communities fight among themselves over the available resources. This is why popular action is successful when communities make alliances with local government employees and pressure central agencies. In such cases, support from politicians and parties and even the sponsorship of religious leaders act as important influences on the bureaucracy.

This strategy does not work when there are conflicts of interest between state employees and users of a given service. In these situations, the inspection role that the community should play to improve the rendering of services becomes difficult. Participation is always greater when it has civil servants' support. And, for the most part, the movements do have it because many of the professionals who become directors in the new democratic governments agree that greater popular participation is essential to making the state apparatus more democratic.

Nevertheless, demands are not always supported, and when the alliance breaks down, mutual accusations surface. State employees who do not meet the movements' expectations are denounced as authoritarian, and popular leaders are disqualified as not being truly representative, as self-serving, or as mere pawns of parties opposed to the government.

These situations occur because the limits and objectives of popular participation have not been formally defined, even when the public administration itself promotes it. The rules defining the rights of the communities are obscure, having been created ad hoc to meet the particularities of each context. It is thus very difficult to evaluate the results of the various regional and local experiences.

The discontinuities of participation can only be understood when we remember that neither the state nor the parties were prepared for an institutional dialogue with popular associations. Neither the limits of legitimate pressure nor the rules for resisting illegitimate pressure were clear. The neighborhood communities' victories and defeats suggest that some innovative steps were taken under civilian, democratic administrations. Popular associations established direct dialogue with sectors of the public administration. The process was part and parcel of the struggles for democratization. Although in one sense this broadened their scope, in another it created specific problems because political democratization and the democratizing of the state apparatus did not necessarily evolve at the same pace.

Although the contribution of popular movements toward institutionalizing participation depends on their interlocution with other actors, their role in inducing change in popular political culture (the second question) is conditioned by the extent of their autonomy. New practices and new ideas about the social and political rights of every citizen are generated within each group. And this, in turn, shapes their collective identity, which is only validated to the extent that it can clearly mark the movements' differences from the parties and the state. Hence, the process described earlier of defining the boundaries of the movements' own political sphere of action takes place concomitantly with the building of a group spirit based on self-determination.

These groups' forms of action rely on a unity of purpose that goes beyond the act of raising their immediate demands. They are not solely pressure groups. They define their existence through their very struggle against both the defects of traditional politics and the popular sectors' lack of interest in their own future. In this context, their rejection of clientelism leads them to affirm both the independent display of each citizen's will and respect for the rights of the poor communities.

This ideological discourse is supported by demand-oriented practices. The collective life nurtured by these practices, in turn, leads the groups to reformulate their conceptions about daily life beyond the political sphere. It provides them with the opportunity to discuss their expectations about the future, women's lives, the neighborhood's situation, and so forth. Thus, they articulate a common view whereby solidarity and self-determination play an essential role, and they are able to define both their allies and their enemies.

This definition is important because, as I said earlier, popular associations have to further their contacts both with politicians and with the public agencies, although the groups only call on them as resources in specific circumstances. For this very reason, the groups' recourse to politicians or public agencies does not jeopardize the critical worldviews that underlie and ensure the groups' internal cohesion. In other words, insofar as popular associations strive to maintain an identity cemented by a strong participatory ideology, movements can even give themselves the luxury of taking part in a game that they disdainfully refer to as "clientelistic" for they know how to resist it. Is this an indication of the irresistible power of clientelism, or is it an example of the hypocrisy of the popular movements' democratic discourse?

In his various analyses of cooperativism in Latin America, Albert Hirschman (1984) provided an interesting clue to the relations between these groups and electoral clientelism. Describing the richness of the Colombian fishermen's collective experience, he emphasized their desire for self-determination. This does not prevent them from using a sophisticated fishing net donated by a very well-known politician. And not only did they use the net, they also had the politician's name inscribed on it as a constant reminder of his donation. Hirschman commented that this sort of contact with a politician is merely one of many examples of the increasing influence that the poor exert when they organize themselves in societies where politicians are accountable to voters (1984: 100). The Colombian fishermen can name their fishing net after a politician because, as a collective, they are not tied to unilateral political commitments and can thus negotiate with different interlocutors.

Although the process of building collective identities is fluid and discontinuous, it only reaches a small part of the poor population and depends, to a large extent, on the political conjuncture. Thus, this process cannot be seen as a broad reaction to clientelism. The latter *does* have strong roots in the power structures and cannot be defeated merely by the presence of a relatively small number of popular groups. On the contrary, these groups must coexist with clientelism and, in order to do so, develop some defenses of their own.

If we want to know what the chances are of expanding the popular groups' relative independence, we have to turn our attention once again to the actions of both parties and the state. The focus on the popular movements has shown that their dynamic depends on this interaction and that, when space for participation opens, changes in the balance of power do occur, allowing for greater, although still restricted, popular autonomy. Nonetheless, without institutional changes, this process will remain chaotic and reversible. It is thus unpredictable.

Notes

An earlier version of this chapter was previously published as "Popular Movements in the Context of the Consolidation of Democracy," Ruth Corrêa Leite Cardoso, Kellogg Institute, Working Paper #120, March 1989.

1. In 1979, the military authoritarian regime issued legislation that forced the only opposition party, the *Movimento Democrático Brasileiro* (Brazilian Democratic Movement, MDB), to dissolve and regroup into five new parties, each representing a different strategy for defeating military rule and restoring democracy. [Editors' note to this edition]

2. Several PMDB opposition state and municipal governments experimented with various forms of popular political participation after coming to power in 1983. Among these experiments were community councils, established to advise government agencies on matters pertaining to specific urban services and general neighborhood welfare. More recently, municipalities governed by the leftist Workers' Party or PT have established such participatory mechanisms. [Editors' note to this edition]

17

Social Movements and Political Power in Latin America

Orlando Fals Borda

More than two decades have passed since a new surge of social and popular movements began to arise in the Third World. Today, these movements are no longer "new, " and they have been taking on other modalities.

In Latin America, they have involved an extraordinary cycle of action and discussion, which was particularly intensive around 1964 when João Goulart, the president of Brazil, was overthrown. Some of the first signs, though, had appeared even earlier (Germani 1962). The European phenomenon, however, which also had its antecedents, came to prominence some four years later—and for different motives and reasons relating to angst and culture. We Latin Americans responded—and continue to respond—to military authoritarianism, to foreign intervention, to the indigence of the masses, and to the ill-conceived approach of the so-called "economic and social development" policies imposed by the rich countries, abetted by local oligarchies.

Most observers of contemporary movements have regarded them with favor and wished them luck. They believe these movements have undertaken the necessary historical function of articulating protest. The movements themselves still cherish the hope of real progress being achieved by the communities, and they see a chance of building a new social order in which they can help to resolve the contradictions of capitalism and correct the ethical inconsistencies of bourgeois democracy. Discussions on all these aspects abound in the literature on the subject.[1]

To interpret what has been going on in Latin American social movements and to place these in a broader perspective, I will present two aspects of them in this chapter: first, an analytical aspect derived from my own observations and direct experience with social movements in the last twenty years and then, stemming from this, a projective or interpretive aspect in which I express my personal concern as a social scientist who is unable to stand by silently watching events develop.

Redefining Political Action:
From the Micro to the Macro Level and Vice Versa

Two practical aspects of social and popular movements that have aroused great curiosity—and expectations—among scholars are: (1) their duration in time and (2) their expansion in territorial or sociogeographic space. Both aspects are important because each is an indication of the strength or weakness of the movements, because they have repercussions on the political component, and because they create "political culture." This is a very significant point for politics has been an activity that the movements never felt ready to undertake, especially in their earlier years. And, in fact, they or those leading and guiding them have always been distrustful—and justifiably so—of anything resembling traditional politicking.

Sufficient explanations have already been given, at least in Latin America, for this initial negative reaction. As will be recalled, these movements arose almost spontaneously from the base and periphery of society, in specific places and for concrete needs. Their leaders were people concerned about economic stagnation and militarism and frustrated by the verticality and sectarianism of revolutionary vanguard groups. Some were academics and schoolteachers who abandoned the universities and schools because these institutions were unable to meet the challenges of the times. There were also men and women of vision, critical of religiosity, who wanted to build a New Jerusalem. In those days, they dwelt in the realm of the micro and the quotidian; they took short, careful steps. Virtually all the early activities of social movements were carried on outside party structures or established organisms.

On the basis of historical experience, especially that of the nineteenth-century cycle of movements, analysts expected that the movements of our time would last no longer than the circumstances that produced them or that their leaders would yield as easily to co-optation by politicians or fall victim to official repression, as had occurred in a great number of painful cases from Tlatelolco to the Mapuche. In this case, however, a concatenation of conflicts made it necessary to link one protest or struggle for rights or services to another, to look for steadfast allies of different social backgrounds, and to form networks of mutual support and coordination at several levels. Forums, gatherings, or festivals on specific topics proved to be flexible and effective tools. These networks gradually expanded the space of confrontation and raised the level of self-recognition, thereby prolonging the life of a good number of the movements and making them more effective. Some became articulated for political, social, and cultural action in larger arenas, especially "regions," as defined sociogeographically. In this way, the foundations were laid for a different civic political culture.

In many places, this first schematic, functional coordination broke down any initial resistance that existed internally against formalization, and, paradoxically enough, it led to the institutionalization of those same movements. Nevertheless, this did not involve establishing any hierarchies or central commands, nor was there any predominance by bureaucracies. The governing principles of social movements at this stage were internal democracy, participation by the grass roots, open meetings, collectivization and rotation of leadership, and absolute administrative transparency. In this way, a hitherto unthought of continuity of action was achieved, and the boundaries of work were extended beyond the local community.

It seemed as though the original raison d'être of the movements was being contradicted. But, because of the depth and seriousness of the socioeconomic crisis, social movements began to visualize new courses of practical action—other than specific protest. The focal point of some movements gradually shifted toward the monopolistic, authoritarian, technocratic, developmentalist state, as well as the social contracts that gave it life and legitimacy. Consequently, efforts at change had to be aimed at the state, with as much—or even greater—intensity as in the earlier struggles, by articulating a new "countervailing power." Many local movements and their leaders were thus obliged to broaden their original outlook, discard the remains of their restricting sectarianism, branch out in various directions, and join forces in united-action fronts. Therefore, the movements shifted from the micro to the macro level and from protest to proposal. In doing so, they shed the two original characteristics described above: that of arising from a conjuncture limited in time and that of being localized in space. They also established two-way channels, from the grass roots upward and from above down to the grass roots, in new and more symmetrical forms of interchange. This new stage of expansion and equilibrium has been in progress in several countries for about five years. That is not a long time, but the fact that this stage has been reached at all is of far-reaching significance to the people concerned.

On the whole, the survival of the social and popular movements against all odds during these twenty years of serious conflicts and multiple violence is nothing short of extraordinary. They live on while a number of political parties and groups founded during this same period according to time-honored rules of organization disappeared very quickly. Despite inevitable internal fissures, strains, and inconsistencies and despite assassination, imprisonment, and torture, the movements have carried on and have expanded to embrace sociogeographic regions by means of the networks and coordination mechanisms referred to earlier (among them, associations of community boards and voluntary communal-labor groups, cooperatives of low-cost housing and shantytown residents, and people's education campaigns). Thus united, they continue to resist the temptations of radical leftist instrumentation, as well as the assaults of co-optation and repression against them and their leaders launched by existing parties and governments. It is true that there have been desertions from the movements and that some old political habits have filtered into them. But many dominant institutions, such as the traditional parties, have lost their legitimacy in the eyes of movement participants, partly because they are no longer able to mediate for or uphold the interests of defenseless or persecuted groups and because they have allowed the social fabric to fray.

In many areas, the loss of legitimacy by parties and governments has created a power gap, which the movements, in their expansive evolution, have been filling locally and regionally in their own way. Today, through networks and other mechanisms of regional and national coordination, many of the movements are beginning to propose or demand programmatic or structural changes for society at large. These particular movements are at the forefront of action and commitment, while others are carrying on the task of asserting claims and making demands that were characteristic of the early years.

By making the leap from the micro to the macro and by entering onto the plane of general proposals and objectives without losing their identity, integrity, leadership, and autonomy as movements, the most advanced of these are becoming (or, in several places, have already become) major political alternatives. Unlike movements of former times, many of the important ones of today have neither lent strength to existing parties nor given birth to new ones (of the Right or the Left) as we conceive them for these parties are regarded as obsolete formulas of political organization or, worse still, as instigators of violence, corruption, and abuse of power. Many of the advanced movements have begun to assume the role of the traditional parties more directly and efficiently, marking out a greater area of democratic participation.

This critical attitude toward parties is serving the important purpose of demystifying them. Many activists are discovering, as Marx did in his time, that parties are not the only possible forms of organization for political action; that they came into being in Europe in a specific historical and cultural context in the eighteenth century; that they have not been indispensable for acceding to power (witness the cases of Cuba and Nicaragua); and that they become a dead weight impeding change when they take hierarchization and verticality to extremes, are reduced to defending the vested interests of certain groups or social classes, make an ideal of and practice violence (as they often do), or allow manipulation and debasement to fester (which they also often do).

It is more than a question of being called a party or a movement. The more advanced movements present a far-reaching challenge in regard to the conceptions, structures, and procedures of parties;[2] indeed, the parties will have to change if they want to survive. Moreover, the movements *as such* can continue to be political alternatives and to lead the way in the necessary search for new ways of doing politics. Because experience continues to be a good teacher, I will analyze some actual cases that are relevant here.

There is the Workers' Party of Brazil (*Partido dos Trabalhadores*, PT), which, despite its name, is not, for any practical purposes, a party (at least not like the others are), a fact that its founders and directors admit (Weffort 1989). It is the outcome of an all-embracing process of organization involving sectors of workers, community and religious leaders, and organic intellectuals (including Paulo Freire, the educator) who drew up a common program of political, economic, social, and cultural action that went beyond the limits of associational or local concerns and now covers the whole of Brazilian society.[3]

The persistence and extensive impact (both open and underground) of social, educational, and trade union movements in Chile were decisive factors in the no vote given to Pinochet. In the reconstruction of Mexico City after the earthquake of 1985, local social and civic movements revealed how solid their invisible infrastructure was by being able to fill in for the state; this set the basis for the eventual creation of the "Cardenista" alliance that made the hitherto unbeatable

Institutional Revolutionary Party totter. And new political forces in Peru (Fujimori's *Cambio '90, Izquierda Unida* ["United Left"]), in Bolivia (regional action), in Venezuela (*Causa-R*), and in other countries would not have made any headway without the support of coordinated social movements or the help of grass-roots organizations. The Nicaragua of the Sandinistas has a good deal to teach us in this respect.

The Growth of Movements in Colombia

In Colombia, social movements underwent a process of growth that, in ten years, took them from micro activities to macro concerns—from protest to proposal—therefore evolving toward organized politics.[4] The 1960s had seen the faltering of development projects like "community action," which were co-opted and deformed by regional bosses. Nevertheless, the seeds of change were planted in many rural and urban neighborhoods where a different breed of local leaders, inspired by traditional mutual-aid values and supported by some formal education, took partial command of civic ventures. Encouraged by agrarian reform policies, peasant leaders of this important type were then able to construct a most formidable movement for "recuperating land" from latifundists; thousands of hectares were taken by the organized peasantry during the early 1970s. But the growth and impact of this social movement were blunted by two forces: official repression from the National Front government and the two main parties (Liberal and Conservative) and internal divisions fostered by immature exigencies of vanguard revolutionary organizations.

Left somewhat orphaned for a while, many survivors of the civic and peasant movements were able to keep functioning on a local, limited scale by returning to a renovated community-action scheme that incorporated popular cultural elements that were previously neglected or despised. In fact, the cultural input became a distinct characteristic of social movements in which sentiment counted as much as intellect.

Such movements focused on concrete projects, mainly economic and educational (roads, schools), for which they were able to wrest resources from the state. Their example spread to towns and cities where activists were encouraged by disillusioned intellectuals who were quitting schools and universities. Inspired by Maoist teachings of personal commitment, these barefoot professionals learned more than they taught, yet they were able to sow the seeds of discontent and nurture hope in many townships. Marxism was then supplemented by *concientización* campaigns, often blessed by church authorities inspired by Vatican II and the Medellín Episcopal Declaration.

The 1980s witnessed the reappearance of the social movements, now with more vision and sophistication. Previous experiences, including a massive and bloody 1977 national labor strike against the government, started to pay off. One of the first of such movements, significantly called *Inconformes* ("Nonconformists"), was started in 1981 in the peripheral region of Nariño by teachers, trade unionists, and civic leaders. Since then, this movement has put people's culture to very good use, promoted campaigns (such as one for low-cost housing), and applied participatory-action research techniques. And by 1990, it was the second largest political force in Nariño, having succeeded in electing mayors, council members, and representatives to the national congress (J. Rodriguez 1988).

A dozen similar movements sprouted soon afterward in other regions, with similar results: *Fuerza Popular José M. Obando, Movimiento Amplio Democrático del Tolima, Frente Amplio del Magdalena Medio, Movimiento Cívico Popular Causa Común, Movimiento Participación Ciudadana* (in several cities), *Movimiento Firmes de Fusagasugá, Movimiento Manos Limpias de Tunja, Movimiento Popular Democrático de Sucre,* and others inspired by social, economic, and cultural needs. Many of their leaders came from leftist and guerrilla groups that had lost their original political justification (Chaparro 1989). Important black and indigenous movements also emerged during this period (see Findji, Chapter 7).

But the first attempts at coordinating these new forces nationally, in 1983, did not succeed. The weight of habits derived from previous authoritarian, dogmatic, and/or selfish partisan endeavors impeded the formation of the needed political umbrella for all. In January 1987, however, during a meeting attended by fourteen regional movements, a more permanent network was adopted that paid heed to a variety of ecological, cultural, youth, feminist, and ethnic initiatives, among others. Henceforth, political events such as "marches for the defense of life and environment," people's forums, workshops, and concerts, as well as communal strikes, were more easily coordinated.

To almost everyone's surprise, such incipient and national organizations, coming in a wave from the peripheries and the grass roots, did well as political alternatives in the March 1988 elections, the first to allow direct voting for mayors. It turned out that more than 10 percent of all elected mayors belonged to social and civic movements, independent of the two major parties. (Detailed analysis did show nuances that should be taken into account in this regard.) Thus encouraged, a national convention in June 1989 gave birth to the *Movimiento Democrático Colombia Unida* with an initial coalition of 37 groups, which elected a former attorney general as their director. By September, the number had grown to 120. Becoming more and more political without losing their autonomy, leadership, and names, the network components of Colombia Unida received the input of leftist organizations like the former guerrilla M-19 (which joined after it had turned over its weapons to the Socialist International), perestroika circles seceded from the Communist Party, and former Socialists; this group eventually became *Alianza Democrática M-19.* Subsequent elections (in March and May 1990), in spite of the consecutive assassinations of the two presidential candidates supported by the movements, established Alianza Democrática as the largest opposition force in Colombia, with 14 percent of the votes.

How can this unexpected and rapid sociopolitical development in Colombia be explained? For one thing, it represents the filling of a void produced by the failure of established parties to function as legitimate intermediaries between the people and the state. The parties have been involved in violence and corruption on such a massive scale that the majority of Colombians have deserted them (there is a consistent 50–60 percent voting abstention rate). This crisis, heightened by ill-conceived policies regarding the production and export of cocaine, reached a climax during 1989 with a mounting number of violent deaths by interconnected causes. The only political organizations free of violence and corruption that could morally lead the struggle for national reconstruction turned out to be the social movements of the Alliance. This trend still continues.

Colombia Unida, as well as the new Alliance, has proposed to function on the basis of two general rules: (1) to ban violence as a political expedient and (2) to apply internally a nonhegemonic, pluralist philosophy of tolerance and accommodation of divergent views. As for a political vision for the nation and the state, these movements have proposed to construct an authentic "participatory democracy," inspired by autochthonous values in which grass-roots organizations can control their representatives and impose policies for greater economic justice and equitable opportunities for all, especially in favor of exploited and/or marginalized groups like women, youth, and ethnic minorities. This is called "people's power." For these groups, "development" as practiced thus far is no longer acceptable.

Therefore, thanks to the breakup of the old caudillo tradition and the search for alternative solutions to a very critical situation produced in Colombia by the two old parties and their leaders, the new social movements have turned political in the best sense of the term. Today, they are re-creating politics and moving away from current European and North American models imposed on them by elites.

Even in Colombia, then, despite—or perhaps because of—its violent terrorism, many movements during these years have been redefining politics, creating a new political culture on their own terms, and casting doubt on the legitimacy of the present authoritarian, developmentalist state (Lechner 1982). They have done so with a certain spontaneity (and maybe even unwittingly) by offering constructive solutions to the violence and the structural problems afflicting many regions.

But today, the more advanced movements, with their accumulated experience on this hazardous course and with their coordinated networks, find themselves on the threshold of another change, one involving a serious dilemma that was referred to above: whether to carry on with the broad and creative political action they are already engaged in (without giving up their status as movements or feeling apprehensive or reluctant about putting forward shared political views) or whether to become new parties or join forces with any of the existing ones in or outside governments, after inducing their necessary regeneration. This is, of course, the age-old co-optation dilemma.

The strong sociopolitical movements of the 1920s in Colombia were co-opted and otherwise neutralized by the rising Liberal party that acceded to power in 1930. Peasant leagues and Socialist parties slowly disappeared, and their former leaders joined the Liberals or their splinter groups. The Communist Party, the sole organization to survive co-optation, never grew.

But contemporary events in Colombia are pointing to a different type of process. The Democratic Alliance M–19 (with Colombia Unida as a component), through its recent electoral success, earned the right to go into the new government inaugurated on August 7, 1990. In fact, in a gesture that, amazingly, did not produce an outcry from the powerful reactionary groups, incoming President César Gaviria appointed the Alliance's leader (former guerrilla Antonio Navarro) as minister of public health.

Even though this may appear as the beginning of a new co-optation process (this ever-present danger should not be overlooked), the negative effect for the new forces of such an appointment, as well as that of the Alliance's participation in the National Constituent Assembly, is not so clear or definite.[5] On the contrary, there is a noticeable adaptive stance in circles of government caused by the impact of the Alliance as an independent force. Is this Lampedusa's principle of changing so that everything remains the same? In any case, this permeability seems to be a consequence of the moral fund accumulated by the Alliance as described earlier, and thus far, the Alliance has not lost its impetus.

Instead of co-optation, we could interpret the present process as a sort of "Trojanism," as it reflects efforts to foster significant change inside the dominant system without relinquishing original radical mandates. This also could be put in terms of a "beachhead technique" as exemplified by Allied armies in Normandy in 1945. The invitation to participate in the government was accepted by the Alliance's movements without internal dissent, except for criticism due to the resurrection of vanguardism in some ranks of the M–19 movement. Accustomed to perennial opposition, such positive response from the Alliance's components was unexpected. Of course, the extreme Left started to attack the Alliance for apparently bowing to traditional enemies. On the inside, however, the hope was that long- and medium-range goals would not be compromised. This point of view has been strongly expressed by the grass roots, and such pressure from below may make this experience different from the 1930 co-optation. Today, the leadership of the Alliance appears to be apt to resist co-optation because the leaders have become more aware of such temptations. Pertinent historical research on this topic has not been in vain. If this critical attitude is maintained in both aspects—historical and ideological awareness, as well as participatory control by base groups—the future of the Alliance may be assured.

Such political developments in Colombia contrast with recent events in Brazil and Mexico, where popular movements and parties such as the PT and Cuauhtémoc Cárdenas's Democratic Revolutionary Party adopted tactics of frontal resistance to the governments of Fernando Collor and Carlos Salinas. The PT has organized a "parallel government" reminiscent of the British "shadow cabinet." Instead, Colombian contemporary experiences in Trojanism may teach new lessons on how to conduct well-balanced political affairs without capitulating, by combining inside beachhead action with external confrontation to the system.

Civilianism-Autonomy-Pluralism

The most prominent characteristics that could allow the more advanced, democratic, sociopolitical movements to continue to exist and grow in strength are: their civic and pacific nature, their commitment to decentralization and autonomy, and their pluralistic tolerance founded on cultural and human diversity. These characteristics have become fundamental concerns for developing their structure, shaping their ideology, and giving them a coherent and dynamic outlook to bring them closer to a new type of democracy that is participatory and direct in character (Fals Borda 1989).

In the first place, the civilianism of these advanced movements is expressed as a reaction against the use of violent means to accede to state power, whether by the revolutionary Socialist methods of the 1920s or by the guerrilla methods of the 1960s, which still persist in several countries. In this respect, these movements have learned an important lesson: that the seizure of power in itself is not the whole answer; that if this act is not fully prepared, it runs the risk of continuing the violence that preceded it or of indefinitely reproducing the warlike tendencies that were rife during the process of struggle. The model of the Jacobinic seizure of the Winter Palace of Petrograd as a requisite for successful revolution has been largely dispelled.

Hence, there is an insistence on putting democratic forms of authentic participation into practice right away, together with the experiential philosophy of otherness, among people of different standing, in the daily round and in the relations between the sexes. It is another way of seeing, understanding, and coping with life. Basically, what is involved is an ethical approach with profound implications: The Machiavellianism of force and maneuvering, the Hegelian excuse of abuses by great men, and the thesis of the means justifying the end, including power itself, are called into question.

Likewise, the strong delegitimizing reaction against technocratic, developmentalist institutions and governments is directed especially against the most centralist and authoritarian of them all, that is, those that monopolize decisionmaking. This seems natural given the local origins of the movements, which continue to be very jealous of their identity and autonomy as forms of physical survival. One interesting aspect of the current efforts to redefine politics is the insistence on fragmenting existing power and amending the prevailing rules to leave the field open to various novel approaches: (1) promoting ways in which ordinary citizens may have a say in and control the acts of those governing them ("people's power," open council meetings, referendums); (2) favoring different forms of territorial government or regime (such as the region-state); and (3) creating more efficient and decentralized forms of administrative organization (such as autonomous provinces and districts) to establish an ecological-cultural regionalization that reflects the actual dynamics of community life. These tendencies toward splitting up the present territorial arrangement have shown the inadequacy of existing power-unit structures, such as the electoral constituencies of local party bosses, that are now seen to be obsolete or unsuitable. The territories are the sites of conflict and appropriation where the state is made or unmade.

Lastly, the emphasis on pluralism and tolerance is one of the most important lessons learned by social and popular movements during the last twenty years. In fact, the movements owe their survival to the ethical rules of opening up to "the Other," respecting his or her right to be different, valuing ideological, artistic, cultural, and social diversity, and recognizing the relativity of history. These are the moral secrets of their resistance. A large part has been played in this by two oppressed, marginal groups that in one way or another defend and proclaim their particular cultural roots: young people and women. Both groups are bringing about a new ethos, a better kind of society and social relations in which unity may coexist with diversity. In doing so, they have given valuable lessons to the male-dominated, patriarchal, ethnocentric tradition characterizing underdevelopment; they have also shown how mistaken those dogmatic parties and groupings of the old Left were that prided themselves on being the vanguards or custodians of revolutionary truth—a belief that only destroyed the vigor of their ideals.

Generally speaking, the more advanced social and popular movements favor negotiation, dialogue, and reasonable solutions for existing conflicts (whether armed or unarmed); they reject unbridled or ritual violence and rely on elections. Some have revived Mahatma Gandhi and Martin Luther King as suitable models of civil resistance. Others recall Camilo Torres, whose *Frente Unido* insisted on pluralism as a political ideology and on the church's transformation through participation to play a liberating role. The recent upsurge of interest in salvaging oral regional history and popular culture and art, together with a growing respect for Indian and black legacies, are other outcomes of this positive political attitude.

Projections

Reinventing Power and the State

These emphases on civilianism stemming from respect for human life, on decentralized autonomy with regional fragmentation of state power through new pacts, and on being open to pluralism and ethical values, together with other elements of participatory democracy that also deserve mention, may serve to reorganize society using democratic models that will put a stop to the disastrous onrush of violence and exploitative underdevelopment. And they have led some observers to think that certain of today's sociopolitical movements, including the most advanced ones, may be coming close to a particular kind of anarchism. This has been suggested by A. G. Frank and Marta Fuentes (1987) and R. Falk (1987), among others, and I, too, have made this point (Fals Borda 1986a).

Of course, I am not referring to the "red" brand of anarchism of Mikhael Bakunin's disciples or to the unconvincing, radically antistate position of "doing away with all government." Neither do I proclaim unconditional adherence to the convergent Marxist doctrine of the withering of the state. More than anything, my position involves a different way of conceiving of and understanding power, as is suggested by some movements, albeit still rather timidly. I describe a humanist neoanarchism, whose followers are in the process of articulating their positions more precisely. They may derive further inspiration from the reading of some hermeneutic texts, such as those of Michel Foucault (1980), Pierre Clastres (1987), and other contemporary critics who tend to rescue from oblivion the function that civil society has performed and continues to perform as ideological cement in the structuring of contemporary nation-states.

It has been stated that an analytical distinction must be made between the state as an apparatus of coercion and power as a cultural category made up of nodes of social relations. Foucault explained it in a way that approaches what many participants in movements have sensed in their practical experience. The latter maintain that all power "emanates" from the people, while Foucault wrote that "power should be analyzed as something that circulates or operates like a chain. . . . It is used and exercised through a network-like organization" (1980: 98). Obviously, power does not rest only in the state, and one must look beyond this for its sources because the state, "with all the omnipotence of its apparatuses, is unable to occupy all the actual fields of power relationships, and because the State can only function on the basis of other previously existing power relationships . . . [the resultant metapower], with its prohibitions, can only take hold where there is a whole series of multiple, indefinite power relationships to provide it with the necessary force for exercising negative forms of power" (Foucault 1980: 122). Clastres (1987) distinguished between coercion and power and maintained that "the coercive power [of the state] is not the only form of power" but is one among many, the one adopted by the West and regarded today as the dominant standard or model.[6]

These ideas do more than explain the paradoxical situations faced by many sociopolitical movements in their efforts to promote "people's power" and combat violence and injustice; they also shed light on the concrete effects states have on society by worsening situations or intensifying conflicts. A case in point is that of the eastern plains of Colombia, where the state was once the main source of violence, spreading it wherever the state appeared for the first time. As a result, guerrilla groups emerged immediately in the region, and there was a tendency toward autonomous legislation by the communities themselves, as well as a regional movement for social reconstruction (Barbosa 1989; Molano 1989). The same negative effect of the state can be seen in ethnic regions that have been arbitrarily divided by political frontiers, such as those of the Guaraní of Paraguay and Argentina, the Guajiro of Colombia and Venezuela, or the Maya of Yucatán, Guatemala, and El Salvador.

It is not surprising, therefore, that many members of present-day movements, whether described as neoanarchist, postmodernist, or ethnocultural, are beginning to talk about hitherto taboo subjects, such as "reinventing power" and "demolishing myths." This, of course, does not rule out the struggle for exercising control over the state as it exists today, delegitimized though it may be. And use can still be made of some mechanisms of liberal or representative democracy and of formally established civic rights as well. Thus, many members of the advanced movements, driven to despair by the state's inefficiency, have taken the convergent step from the micro to the macro level and are being articulated today as alternative political forces.

It would be foolish to ignore the moral challenge presented to all by the sight of the resources of the state remaining in the hands of individuals who are so often inept, corrupt, and cruel. The essential question, however, lies in the philosophical conception of the new popular power that would feed this other state in the stages of society's reconstruction. The ideas of Foucault and Clastres and other authors can be of service here. They are discussed and studied for there is a need to sow, from this very moment throughout civil society, the ideological seed of respect for life, the environment, and cultural diversity—to obtain life's fruits, in the form of better social bases and more consistent leaders of movements, without waiting for these movements "to seize power."

It goes without saying that it is equally important for all the political forces of this unequal civil society—from the progressives and leftists to the rightists and paramilitary—that power and the state be reconceptualized, demystified, and considered under a less authoritarian, less menacing, and more ethical light than the Hobbesian idea bequeathed to us by Simón Bolívar, the creator of our nationalities. This will be particularly helpful in limiting the deleterious or violent effects of social Darwinism and fascism, which are resurfacing among us.

An Intellectual and Professional Challenge

Will it be possible to articulate these nodes of collective power in new social pacts and thereby prevent force from being hierarchically concentrated and decision-making monopolized by a few? Can formal power be exercised openly, without the principles of secrets or reasons of state, with full glasnost? Will it be possible to form borderless states that will be democratic expressions of real participation and direct civic interchange—the two forms of authentic popular power? Would it not be better to move away from Karl Marx and V. I. Lenin, with their theses of social class monopolies over states, and closer to Antonio Gramsci to define the multiclass orientation of new, more generous political hegemonies? How applicable are the philosophical recommendations formulated on the subject of state violence by scholars such as Paul Ricoeur (effects of reconciliation among people, 1957), or Walter Benjamin (creation of a new body of laws for the new forces, 1965)?

These are some of the "scientific" questions being asked today in collectives of the more advanced movements that seek peace together with social justice, that want to make democracy more participatory and direct, and that hope to build alternative forms of state, such as region-states, by revealing, reconstructing, and reinforcing the diffuse power of the citizenry. Efficient organization of these nodes of power to lead them toward autonomous forms of nonviolent conception and action, different from nation-states and parties as we have conceived them, is the order of the day.

This is why the analytical and cognitive functions of intellectuals and professionals committed to these political possibilities, the so-called "agents of change," are so important. To develop new pacts, it is necessary to balance the present arrogant reductionist tendencies of Cartesian science and technology, which lead to the deformation of essential values, the enthroning of violence as the principal historical explanation, the debasement of man to the condition of an object, and the destruction of the environment, as I have explained in detail elsewhere (Fals Borda 1988b). This balancing can be effected by using alternative ways of producing knowledge that was formerly rejected as unscientific, such as popular knowledge and daily, common-sense knowledge, which tend to be culturally richer and more respectful of life and nature. Intellectuals and agents of change could synthesize these different types of knowledge experientially, as proposed by participatory action-research (PAR), and apply the resulting enriched body of knowledge toward demolishing existing structures of unsanctioned force and inadmissible domination and exploitation, as well as toward furthering social and economic reconstruction. They would become teachers of peaceful change by helping the subordinated and oppressed classes to gain a better understanding of what they already know from experience, as well as to broaden their knowledge and take part in the creative task of producing a new society (Fals Borda 1987; Fals Borda and Rahman, eds., 1991).

The possibility is provided for pursuing the intrinsic question of a new democratic power to be built by the movements for the achievements of collective peace and progress and the satisfaction of basic needs. It is neither advisable nor necessary, for this purpose, to translate French, English, or German constitutions or political science treatises that correspond to other cultural traditions and are only republican in letter. Instead, we must continue to reinvent power in our own terms, in more humane, less cruel, and less violent forms that are more accountable to the people.

This is a theoretical and practical challenge that must be taken up if the independent social and political movements of today are not to waste away or to become absorbed by parties, as has been happening, but are, instead, to continue their vigorous, fruitful existence as leading actors in historical developments in the future. For they are the soundest part of our otherwise tattered social fabric. Our future as nations and as peoples depends in good measure upon them.

Notes

A shorter version of this chapter appeared in *International Sociology* 5, no. 2 (June 1990): 115–127.

1. This is not the place for a complete review of the relevant publications, so I will only mention those that have given me the greatest guidance—the first dramatic descriptions of Bhoomi Sena of India in 1979; Tilman Evers's useful delving into the "hidden identity" of the movements (1985); the dynamic analyses by D. L. Sheth (1987), Rajni Kothari (1984), and Luis Alberto Restrepo (1987, 1988); the tactical possibilities offered by the movements, according to André Gunder Frank and Marta Fuentes (1987); their relationship to socialism and democracy, according to David Slater (1989) and Ernesto Laclau and Chantal Mouffe (1987); and their "global promise," postulated by Richard Falk (1987). European analysts have, on the whole (as is their wont), ignored the different nature of Third World phenomena and tended to globalize or universalize things on the basis of their own limited experience (Hegedus 1989). But a reasonably positive, duly critical balance has been drawn up, with some suitable doses of skepticism, romanticism, and utopianism, by Ruth Cardoso (1987).

2. The same thing happened in previous cycles of movement upsurge, when politics were redefined by their action. Recall, for example, the case of Chartism in England (1838–1848), which became the springboard for the Labor party, or the case of peasant, Indian, labor union, and student movements in Colombia, Peru, and other countries during the 1920s, which gave new strength and orientation to liberalism. Older movements—such as the feminist, universal suffrage, Indian Gandhian, and even the workers' movements—had the same challenging and renovating effect on the parties of their time.

3. A similar course was run by Poland's Solidarity Movement, which today is governing the country, and the People's Power movements of the Philippines and Haiti in their early postdictatorship period. Other movements, such as those for the defense of human rights and the environment (the Greens) and the antinuclear movements, have spread out from Europe and acquired international dimensions. Symptoms of this nonpartyism can also be observed in India, as well as in the Soviet Union and other Socialist countries.

4. For a general treatment of social movements in Colombia, see Gallón 1989; Escobar y de Roux 1989; Santana 1989.

5. I and two participants of the indigeneous movement were elected to the National Constituent Assembly. Over 20 percent of the members of that body belonged to the Democratic Alliance-M-19. The new Constitution of Colombia was promulgated on July 5, 1991. It recognizes as its foremost mandate the building of a participatory democracy, and the new nation describes itself as a united, pluralist republic with autonomy for its territorial divisions (Article 1). Many of the ideas proposed by the Alliance, as described in this chapter, were adopted by the assembly. "Beachhead tactics" appear to be paying off well in Colombia for social movements thus far.

6. It is a formula for historical societies; other societies, such as the archaic ones (for example, that of the Maya) developed quite different, collective forms of power, many of which still prevail among various segments of the earth's population—for example, the tribal groups of India or Native Americans with their councils of elders. Modern political links, in contrast, are created by hierarchy or formal authority. Consequently, the ultimate and most complete form of violence is found in the domineering, homogenizing, monopolistic central state.

18

Conclusion:
Theoretical and Political Horizons
of Change in Contemporary
Latin American Social Movements

Sonia E. Alvarez
Arturo Escobar

Progressive and conservative analysts alike regard the 1980s as a "lost decade" for Latin America. Apocalyptic prognoses about the grim fate awaiting the region abound in both the media and the academy. Latin America's persistent economic crisis and fragile democracies, coupled with the restructuring of capital on a world scale and the collapse of "real, existing socialism," lead many to the premature conclusion that the continent is doomed. Structure would appear to have overwhelmed human agency once and for all.

But this volume attests to the tenacity of human innovation even in the face of seemingly insurmountable structural obstacles. It testifies not only to the endurance of microresistances but also to the ability of some collective actors to translate such resistances into protests, proposals, and even power alternatives. This chapter reflects on what we have learned from the preceding essays and considers how those lessons might inform our analyses of resistance, social change, and political practice in Latin America in the 1990s.

Conceptualizing Latin American Social Movements

This collection was inspired by our interest in bringing the two prevailing paradigmatic approaches to the study of social movements into creative conversation with one another. In their critical review of European and North American approaches to the study of social movements, Bert Klandermans and Sidney Tarrow identified the theoretical and methodological limitations of an exclusive reliance on either approach:

> Resource mobilization theory has been criticized for focusing too much on organization, politics, and resources while neglecting the structural precondition of move-

ments—that is, for focusing too much on the "how" of social movements and not enough on the "why." . . . The new social movement approach has stimulated the opposite criticisms. Some contend that it focuses in a reductionist way on the structural origins of strain and does not pay enough attention to the "how" of mobilization (Klandermans and Tarrow 1988: 9).

The resulting theoretical gap, they argued, stands in the way of a better understanding of "how structural change is transformed into collective action" (1988: 10). We shared these authors' concerns and therefore urged our contributors to explore both the "why" and the "how" of social movements, to consider the interaction of structure and agency, identity and strategy in shaping the dynamics of collective struggles in Latin America today.

In exploring the "why" of contemporary social movements, several of our contributors show that conjunctural forces and systemic changes at work since at least the late 1960s—such as the exhaustion of "development," the crisis of the developmentalist/populist state, and the weakening of party systems and populist and corporatist mechanisms of representation—gave rise to new contradictions and created new potential fields of action for social movements in the region. We must, however, refine the prevalent notion that these structural contradictions in themselves are responsible for the emergence of "new" social movements throughout the region. The principal problem with this formulation, as we have seen, is that structural changes alone cannot account for the rise of organizational and ideological resources and the production of cultural meanings that are critical to movement emergence and development.

Several ideological, organizational, and institutional developments facilitated the rise of particular forms of social movement in the 1970s and 1980s. The following factors are highlighted in the preceding chapters: (1) the progressive church's liberation discourse and pastoral activism (Burdick); (2) the Left's self-criticism and reevaluation of strategies of social change pursued in the 1960s and 1970s (Chinchilla; Fals Borda); (3) the generation of new interactional networks among urban and rural residents of different social sectors (Starn; Bennett; Schneider); (4) the massive expansion of the developmentalist state itself and the role of state agents in encouraging their clients to demand social services (Cardoso); and (5) the targeting of new groups, particularly women and indigenous peoples, by national and international development establishments (Lind; Findji).

Essays by Canel, Schneider, García, and Bennett detail the ways in which national and local political settings shape movement dynamics—placing constraints on or providing opportunities for movement emergence and expansion. These authors demonstrate that some of the factors identified by resource mobilization theorists help us better understand the diverse dynamics and trajectories of social movements in different national or regional settings. Political variables such as the strength of political parties (Canel; Schneider), the prominence of the state over civil society (Canel), the existence of formal democratic (García) or corporativist (Bennett) channels for interest representation, and the pervasiveness of clientelism (Cardoso) have been shown to condition the emergence, development, and political or policy effectiveness of particular types of social movement organizations.

The neglect of these factors in much of the early literature on social movements in contemporary Latin America resulted, in part, from a rejection of resource mobilization or political process approaches to social movements that, despite their neglect of the structural, discursive, and cultural dimensions of movement dynamics, do call our attention to these more discrete systemic variables. Most studies of social movements in Latin America heretofore have ignored the contributions of such frameworks for understanding contemporary social struggles.

The case studies assembled in this volume focus on how structural forces are translated into new or reconstituted identities, contestatory discourses and strategies, and articulatory practices. However, as the essays by Escobar, Lind, Starn, and Findji reveal, the "how" of social movements does not solely depend on the availability of organizational and ideological resources, opportunity spaces, and other factors privileged by resource mobilization theory; the emergence and development of movements also entail the production of meanings and the construction of collective identities. Culture mediates the movement from structural conditions to social and political action.

An examination of the cultural dimensions of movements is therefore an essential component of social movement research. Escobar entreats us to see social movements "equally and inseparably as struggles over meanings and material conditions, that is, as cultural struggles." That the production of oppositional and alternative meanings is a political fact is a realization that has to be brought to bear on social movement theory and methodology. He advocates the development of ethnographic approaches that allow researchers to investigate the production of meanings by movement participants and the role of these meanings in identity construction and political practices. Like Escobar, Starn stresses the importance of focusing on the "semiotics" of rural protest in order to understand how collective actors such as peasants construct their identities and produce fresh political visions—not on the basis of prefabricated schemas but through a creative process of engagement with their everyday life conditions.

In analyzing complex, multilayered processes through which collective identities are constructed, contested, and continually negotiated, our contributors suggest a way out of the reductionistic trap that sees social movements and other forms of collective action as emerging either from a structurally predetermined "class consciousness" (in a Marxist framework) or as an expression of rational or knowable political "interests" (in functionalist parlance). The alternative view of social movements and collective action emerging from our collected essays thus poses an important challenge to earlier theories, especially modernization and dependency, within which human agency and multiple subjectivities receded in the face of overarching and formidable "forces of modernization" or "structures of dependency."

In sum, this volume reveals that a more disaggregated and nuanced view of contemporary Latin American social movements and social change depends on a careful blending of the two prevailing theoretical and methodological approaches we have been discussing. Such a view requires us to explore the nexus of the institutional and the extrainstitutional, the "old" and the "new," the cultural and the political, the local and the global, the modern, the premodern, and the postmodern. We emphatically concur with Starn's assessment that, in theorizing social movements, we must "share the postmodern skepticism about model-building and master narratives without jettisoning modernist concerns for how and why . . . [movement] studies need to be more sensitive to the contours of meaning. But this should accompany, not replace, the study of tactics, interests, and organization."

Constructing Collective Identities

Several contributors enjoin us to view social movements not only as "survival struggles" or struggles over "basic needs" but also as cultural struggles over the production of meaning and as collective forms of cultural production. As Lind's essay reminds us, poor women, though seemingly organizing around their families' needs, are also negotiating and sometimes challenging power relations in their daily lives and thus are chipping away at hegemonic discourses about gender, development, and politics and developing critical perspectives on the world in which they live. The chapters by Sternbach, Navarro, Chuchryk, and Alvarez and by Chinchilla echo Lind's admonition (see also Caldeira 1990; Blondet 1990). This alternative understanding of gender identity and consciousness is a welcome corrective to the notion, still advanced by many scholars working within the developmentalist paradigm, that poor women's (and, indeed, poor peoples') needs are exclusively or even predominantly material and are structurally given or predetermined.

Scott Mainwaring critiqued this reductionistic view of poor peoples' needs:

> Material needs have traditionally (and not only by Marxists) been conceptualized as in some sense more "real" or fundamental than other kinds of needs, and in the case of poor people this tendency is even more accentuated. But poor people, like others, do not define their needs strictly along material lines. . . . To dismiss these affective and religious priorities as "alienation," and then to question why the poor are alienated and analyze what must be done to change this alienation, is simplistic social science; it denies to the poor dimensions of human life that we recognize as important for people whose material needs are less pressing (Mainwaring 1987: 141).

The "politics of needs" must be retheorized if we are to apprehend the rich and varied texture of social struggles and the diversity of subject positions and discursive interventions these manifest (Lind, Chapter 8; see also Fraser 1989). The struggle of popular women's groups forces a reinterpretation of the politics of needs. That is, we must pay attention to how the definition of poor women's needs is a contested process in which the state, the development establishment, "experts" of various kinds, feminists, and poor women themselves all have a stake.

The very notion of what constitutes a "survival struggle" must also be expanded and reconceptualized to include noneconomic dimensions. Latin American feminists proclaim, for example, that, for women of all social sectors, struggling for survival necessarily encompasses the elimination of life-threatening violence against women (see Sternbach et al., Chapter 12). The study of Latin American social movements, as several of our authors suggest, provides useful analytical guideposts for such reconceptualizations.

By drawing selectively from each of the prevailing approaches to the study of social movements, several of our chapters also lay a theoretical foundation for a more nuanced understanding of the process of collective identity formation itself. Collective identities shape movement strategies and are, in turn, reconstituted at various points in the course of a movement's struggle. Cardoso argues that the process of identity formation must be understood "as a play of mirrors, through which the grass-roots groups construct their self-image so that it reflects their dialogue with different interlocutors." Echoing Cardoso, Canel stresses that we must "bring institutional politics back into the analysis of social movements" as these not only mediate the constitution of identities but also partly determine the outcomes of movement actions. Political regime structures, representational systems, and state policies and practices "facilitate the expression of some identities and may help to shape the formation of others" (Craig 1990: 283).

Identity formation, then, is hardly an endogenous process. Communities themselves are not "given" by place of residence or kinship but must also be actively constructed. Several contributors to this collection stress that collective identities and oppositional consciousness are relational, that is, shaped by a movement's interactions with other social forces and with the movement's interlocutors, principally institutions, political parties, the Catholic church and other religious institutions, and the state itself. Canel shows, moreover, that existing institutional and political structures and traditions often inhibit the effectiveness and continuity of social movements.

MacRae and Burdick further caution us against the uncritical celebration of "identity" and "community." Indeed, identity politics can lead to rather undemocratic political and discursive practices, as most graphically revealed in MacRae's analysis of the Brazilian homosexual movement. Identities are sometimes rigidly constructed, thus alienating potential movement participants or obstructing a movement's articulation with other social forces (see Sternbach et al., Chapter 12; Kauffman 1990; Epstein 1990). The construction of "community" also sometimes contains exclusionary dimensions, such as those documented by Burdick, MacRae, and Cardoso.

Articulating Strategies

At the heart of the articulation of strategies is the question of autonomy. All our contributors concur that today most Latin American social movements furiously defend their political, ideological, and organizational autonomy, even if Hellman is skeptical about the strong claims about autonomy put forth by some authors.

To be sure, analytical skepticism about proclamations of absolute autonomy by movement participants is certainly warranted. Food riots, mob actions, or other forms of unorganized or sporadic resistance may well arise spontaneously from the societal strains induced by structural change. But social movements—organized collective actors who engage in sustained political or cultural contestation through recourse to institutional and extrainstitutional forms of action—seldom emerge spontaneously, nor do they develop in isolation from other social and political actors. Our case studies reveal that forces exogenous to the movements play a critical role in movement emergence and development.

Extracommunity actors, as Schneider, Bennett, and Cardoso show, often intervene in crucial ways to shape the political trajectories and discursive content of social struggles. Bennett documents the pervasive presence and catalytic influence of student movement militants and leftist parties in Mexico's urban movements. Schneider demonstrates that there is a strong correlation between previous left-wing activism and the resurgence of protest in Chile in 1983. Because of earlier experience with political mobilization and contact with activists, previously politicized neighborhoods (especially those where the Communist party had an active presence) shared a series of features that were critical in reestablishing political activity after the 1973 coup. Her analysis thus points to the centrality of parties and party militants in fostering political activity among the poor.

Students of social movements, in an effort to portray movements as genuine expressions of the "real" interests of the economically exploited, culturally marginalized, and politically disenfranchised, have too often glossed over these external interventions in their analyses of movement dynamics. But to recognize and document such external interventions is not to deny that autonomy, as the preceding essays reveal, is at once a core movement value and a shrewd political strategy. Participants view movement autonomy as essential to forging and preserving identity and community. Autonomy is also considered a strategic imperative necessitated by the persistence of very "old" societal ills, such as instrumentalism on the Left, clientelism on the Right, patronage politics, political corruption, and electoral fraud.

The insistence on autonomy also stems from the movements' reaction to the pervasive presence and intervention of an expansive but politically and financially bankrupt state—the movements' principal referent in most of the cases examined in this volume. In this regard, Escobar reminds us, however, that "if it is true that the state is a key interlocutor for the movements, the latter cannot be reduced to the logic of the former." Because movements are "spread thin throughout a vast social domain," he contends, they retain a position of exteriority in relation to the state and can thus often resist state efforts to co-opt or repress them.

Cardoso's chapter further suggests that movements' emphasis on autonomy does not necessarily lead to ideological rigidity or political intransigence. Instead, the Brazilian urban movements she examines have constantly, creatively, and pragmatically tempered their ideological insistence on autonomy when appealing to the state for urban services or community improvements. Particularly at the local level, the line between "new" and "old" ways of doing politics appears to be more fluid and less rigid than envisioned in much of the early literature on contemporary social movements.

And that fluidity in movement practices, shaped by the interface of ideological and pragmatic considerations, is characteristic of local movement organizations that succeed in obtaining concrete goals or securing social rights. To be sure, such fluid practices do not fully supersede clientelism, but, as Cardoso suggests, they do undermine it and thus help forge a new relationship between institutional politics and civil society. Resorting to politicians and public agencies in specific circumstances, she maintains, does not necessarily erode the internal cohesion and critical worldviews of the movements. To the extent that they are able to maintain an identity anchored in a strong participatory ideology, "movements can even give themselves the luxury of taking part in a game they disdainfully refer to as 'clientelistic,' for they know how to resist it."

In Colombia, as Fals Borda argues, social movement coalitions have so far avoided both co-optation by parties and the state and open confrontation with these forces, adopting instead a politics of "Trojanism," that is, of utilizing the opening of spaces within existing institutions to pursue movement goals without excessively compromising values of autonomy, civilianism, and pluralism. Without disregarding the importance of the state, Fals Borda sees the future of these options in terms of a type of "neoanarchism" that allows movements to maintain a degree of autonomy while at the same time reorienting the state's actions.

Hellman further cautions us against adopting an undifferentiated view of co-optation when assessing movement strategies or the relationship of movements to political parties and the state. Not all forms of movement-party-state articulation, she insists, are equally detrimental to social movements' autonomy or subversive of movement goals. Analysts must resist the temptation to label the "partial or total fulfillment of the demands of the movement" as necessarily co-optative. We must develop more precise conceptual distinctions between genuine concession and manipulative co-optation.

Cardoso's essay, like those by Starn and Findji, details the complex interplay of ideological autonomy and political pragmatism, resistance and accommodation, protest and negotiation that typically inform movement strategies. It is this intricate interweaving of ideological and strategic considerations, several contributors insist, that enables some movements to survive—and sometimes even succeed—in the labyrinthine web of local and national politics.

This labyrinth compels most movements to struggle simultaneously on a wide variety of fronts, carving out diverse cultural and political spaces for collective action. This common movement practice challenges what we might call the "unitary action paradigm," until recently upheld by most sectors of the Left in Latin America and elsewhere. That is, a "united front," commonly thought to require the formation of some sort of peak organization (such as a national or regional confederation), was assumed to be the most efficient means of promoting popular interests and pursuing social change.

Yet, the dispersion of a social movement's political energies and the fragmentation of movement groups can sometimes have constructive consequences. Seen more positively, this so-called fragmentation can prove highly effective from a strategic point of view, even when it runs contrary to the movement's stated goals. For example, when no single organization can claim to represent a movement, it is more difficult for politicians or policymakers to manipulate or distort the goals of the movement as a whole. Moreover, the existence of numerous groups or organizations, pursuing similar overall goals through different strategies and tactics, may simply mean that a given movement's sociocultural and political agenda is being articulated simultaneously in a wide range of institutional and extrainstitutional arenas—and this can have potentially salutary effects (Sternbach et al., Chapter 12; Bennett, Chapter 13; García, Chapter 9; see also Alvarez 1990a).

Several chapters highlight the effectiveness of loosely articulated movement networks, of acting in the manifold arenas where power is exercised and reproduced. Calderón, Piscitelli, and Reyna make perhaps the strongest claim in this regard, arguing that there is hidden strength in the "fragmentation of collective action." Essays by García, Sternbach et al., and Bennett suggest, moreover, that the political isolation and inefficacy that would seem to result from such fragmentation are often counterbalanced by the formation of formal and informal coordinating bodies or networks. García contends, for example, that Venezuelan environmental organizations "must be seen as part of a network in which each organization fulfills a specific, mutually complementary role." This network serves as "an articulating space" through which the movement structures its relationship to the state, political parties, the media, and other organizations of civil society.

Other authors, however, insist that the contemporary explosion of localized struggles and identity-centered politics will prove to be an ephemeral phenomenon unless social movements—arising from what Calderón, Piscitelli, and Reyna call the "mosaic of Latin American diversity"—find common political ground and advance an alternative societal project (see Hellman, Chapter 4; Fals Borda, Chapter 17; Chinchilla, Chapter 3). The preceding chapters indeed make clear that movement heterogeneity, fragmentation, and competition make unified strategies difficult to implement, much less institutionalize.

Today, the search for a common political ground, however, is often informed by a logic that differs substantially from the one that typified Latin American social struggles two decades ago. In Central America, the role of vanguard forces, for example, has undergone significant reconceptualization and restructuring, and this new understanding is shared by proponents of the "new Marxism" and many social movements alike. Chinchilla argues that important sectors of both the Central and South American Left today have revalued "culture, ideology, democratic practice, and daily life in the struggle against capitalism and the construction of socialism." In countries like Brazil, Colombia, and Mexico, movements are inventing new modalities for forging unity out of diversity, forming or backing the Workers' Party, the M-19/Democratic Alliance, and the Partido Democrático Revolucionario, respectively.

In assessing the strategies and trajectories of contemporary movements, we must also resist the teleological temptation whereby movements are valued only if they progress ineluctably from daily resistance to protest actions to political projects, finally transforming themselves into veritable power alternatives. The wide range of movement trajectories and outcomes discussed in this volume should alert us to the fact that there is not necessarily a linear progression in the movement from quotidian resistance to transformational projects.

We must, instead, view movements' changing strategies as contingent "moments" in a cycle. Even the most combative or militant of protest actions surely can disappear or revert to everyday resistance if the larger political environment severely sanctions protest, for example. But that quotidian resistance can just as surely explode again into protest when the environment shifts again, perhaps moving gradually and erratically toward demandmaking or goal expansion, in articulation with emergent societal or party forces. Exploring the "movement of movements" between these various strategic moments would enhance our understanding of contemporary social struggles in the Latin American region.

Democratizing Democracy and Demystifying Development

Political scientists critical of economic or cultural reductionism should be sensitized by the preceding essays to the pitfalls of what Melucci has called "political reductionism":

> Such reductionism can have a negative version, but it can also represent a conscious methodological choice. If the concept of protest is explicitly limited to the political level, that is, to the forms of collective action which implicate a direct confrontation with authority, then, necessarily other levels of the collective action are not included in that concept. If, however, reductionism is applied implicitly, it tends to eliminate or to deny all those dimensions of the collective action which are not reducible to the political (they are dismissed, as the case may be, as uninteresting, unmeasurable, expressive, folkloristic, and so on) (1988: 337).

Our contributors make clear that, for Latin American social movements today, "politics" and "the political" encompass a broad array of power relations embedded in the cultural, social, economic, and quotidian as well as the "conventionally" political spheres. Politics, in short, permeates all social relations.

In defining the practices of social movements as those that extend or redefine the parameters of "the political," however, analysts working within the identity-centered paradigm too often neglect the fact that the conventionally political also remains in place. As several essays in this volume demonstrate, existing political institutions significantly constrain, mediate, and impact the alternative political spheres in which social movements are said to operate. That is, contemporary social movements may well be charting new political terrain, but that domain is contiguous to and sometimes overlapped by the more traditional political terrain of trade unions, parties, and the state.

Adopting a nonreductionistic and more expansive conception of politics nevertheless has important implications for our assessment of social movements' contributions to the much celebrated processes of democratization under way in many countries in the region. During the late 1970s and early 1980s, in Brazil and other military authoritarian regimes in transition, many observers heralded social movements as portenders of a new, transformed democracy—the "last, best hope" for "real" democratization. We now know that social movements are unlikely to radically transform large structures of domination or dramatically expand elite democracies, certainly not in the short run. We must be wary, as Starn insists, of perceiving contemporary social movements as a "step in the inevitable rumble of history toward human emancipation." Yet, we must also acquire a new appreciation of the "politics of the possible." Smaller transformations in power relations of daily life and in the practice of institutional politics, promoted by social movements, *are* in evidence today.

At the most basic level, social movements must be seen as crucial forces in the democratization of authoritarian social relations. This influence is most evident, of course, in the cases of feminist, gay, and racial/ethnic movements. Several of the studies collected in this volume document the spread of issues and ideas first articulated by social movements into a multiplicity of political and social spaces. The feminist movement, for instance, has garnered sufficient political clout and increased its social reach in some countries, so much so that trade unions, political parties, and policymakers have incorporated (however begrudgingly) some of its political banners. Feminism has, in some cases, also impacted the media and popular culture—even the evening novelas now portray women in more "liberated" roles (see Sternbach et al., Chapter 12; Chinchilla, Chapter 3; see also Jaquette, ed., 1990; Jelin 1990).

Social movements also play a crucial mediating role between communities and party systems, one that potentially strengthens the connection between civil society and institutional politics. Political parties, especially those on the Left, not only transform or intervene in social movements but, as Hellman shows, are also sometimes transformed themselves by the movements. The crisis of party politics in Latin America, Hellman contends, has forced parties to reassess their relationship to organized civil society, and some parties have opened up to movements in the hope of reaching the dynamic and growing sectors of the population that these movements sometimes have the capacity to mobilize.

Our case studies also document the important role of social movements in "democratizing" both authoritarian and nominally democratic regimes. In assessing the contributions of urban movements to democratization in Brazil, Mainwaring echoed the findings of several of the contributors to this volume:

> Although I am critical of those who foresaw a unilinear growth of social movements, I am equally skeptical about the view that politics in democratic societies consists almost exclusively of institutional channels (parties, interest groups, the state). In the Brazilian context, the dawning of democracy has created new dilemmas for urban popular movements, but these movements continue to struggle for important rights and material improvements. Although the stability of democracy does not depend on being responsive to popular movements, the quality of democracy does. Furthermore, these movements help define some of the parameters of political life: They call attention to new issues, establish some of the symbolic content of politics, and prompt changes in the discourse and actions of other political actors (1987: 132-133).

Social movements, the preceding essays reveal, have enhanced the quality of the region's restricted democracies in several important ways. They have, for example, placed previously suppressed or marginalized demands on the political agenda—claiming rights to better urban services and land, as well as to increased popular participation and more meaningful democratic citizenship. They thus sometimes create what Uribe and Lander (1990) referred to as "new political facts" (see García, Chapter 9). Findji and Starn demonstrate that, in the process of reasserting "traditional" rights and reclaiming their collective history, social movements sometimes appropriate and reconfigure the state's democratic discourses on rights, citizenship, and "nation."

Cardoso stresses that though Brazilian movements did not live up to the overly optimistic expectations of early movement analysts, they nevertheless made several important contributions to Brazilian democracy. Movements brought popular demands to the attention of public authorities, even in the final stages of military rule; state agencies and political parties gradually came to recognize social movements as legitimate interlocutors; and grass-roots organizations, though involving only an infinitesimal proportion of the Brazilian citizenry, served as important conduits for the direct expression of popular demands.

Movement researchers must apprehend the multiple possibilities and tensions arising from the movements' multifaceted negotiating strategies, the wide range of state policies that encourage or discourage popular participation, and the varied efforts undertaken by both parties and social movements to integrate their politics. Such a multilayered view might shed a different light on social movements' actual contributions to democratization, highlighting how they affect existing institutions and, conversely, how the latter also alter the popular sectors' worldviews and organizing strategies.

Bennett and Hellman show that popular movements have helped shape Mexico's new political landscape. "The continuous autonomous organizing of the urban poor over the last two decades," Bennett contends, supports "the hypothesis that many small conflictual actions can have the cumulative impact of creating social transformation." Her overall assessment is that contemporary urban movements have called into question the role and practices of the Mexican state and the dominant party. Autonomous organizing of this type, through its articulation, becomes a significant national force in its own right.

Certainly, all social movements in the region are not equally radical or potentially transformative. Many forms of collective resistance, as Schneider points out, remain "localized, ephemeral, and easily repressed." This fact should not, however, distract us from the significance of "small resistances," however short-lived. If power is manifest and reproduced in a vast array of cultural, economic, and political domains, including the domain of everyday life, then seemingly small changes can have revolutionary implications for how people lead their daily lives and construct and reconfigure their worlds.

We must also pay closer attention to the democratizing impact of the symbolic challenge to dominant discourses on politics and development posed by some contemporary movements. As they evolved from purely scientific-conservationist perspectives in the 1960s to more politically and symbolically oriented positions in the 1980s, Venezuelan ecology movements, for example, have increasingly relied on their challenge to conventional cultural and economic models of development to advance their politics. The creation of political facts by the environmental movement, García argues, takes place through the generation of spaces wherein new meanings are forged. These new meanings, she insists, not only announce to society that a fundamental problem exists with its cultural models and forms of behavior but also provide elements for the construction of alternative development models and democratic practices. That symbolic challenges can also contribute to democratization and the redefinition of development is corroborated by the struggle of indigenous peoples in Colombia and elsewhere. Indigenous peoples present perhaps the most striking challenge to the dominant cultural and socioeconomic models of *Latin* American societies.

These cases suggest that movements can have a significant symbolic impact even when they involve a relatively small number of participants. The symbolic reach of movements, in other words, often exceeds their social reach or measurable policy impact. The symbolic challenge posed by social movements has sometimes pushed other political and social actors, especially institutional actors such as parties, to reformulate their political programs and recast their discourses about seemingly consensual concepts such as democracy and citizenship. The symbolic politics of social movements, in short, merits much closer social scientific scrutiny than it has heretofore received.

Several essays in this volume identify another pressing issue to be further investigated by students of Latin American social movements in the 1990s: the impact of democratic politics on movement strategies and dynamics. Cardoso warns that democratization poses many thorny new problems for the region's social movements. We learn from Schneider and Canel that, in countries with historically strong states and effective party systems (such as Chile and Uruguay), the return to civilian rule has propelled parties onto center stage, displacing movements and diminishing their vital role in forging a more autonomous and vibrant civil society.

Yet, though parties in Uruguay and Chile today appear to be absorbing much of the dynamism that characterized autonomous collective action under military authoritarian rule, social movements are challenging the parties' monopoly of representation and participation in two of the region's longest-standing democracies, Colombia and Venezuela. Movements in the latter countries are working to revitalize and expand democratic institutions forged through the intraelite pacts of the 1950s and to fashion more meaningful, inclusive representational mechanisms. In Venezuela and Colombia, as García puts it, the issue is not "how to achieve democracy per se as much as to deepen it."

As García points out, Venezuela's pacted democracy structurally weakened organizations and social sectors excluded from the pact. But Venezuelan movements have successfully pressured the regime to expand institutionalized participatory arenas and to promote administrative reforms that decentralize policymaking and thus make citizen participation potentially more effective. As the essays by Findji and Fals Borda show, similar reforms have been placed on the political agenda by Colombian social movements. Perhaps, then, the ebbing of social movement activities in Chile's and Uruguay's pacted democracies is only temporary and movements there may experience a resurgence as collective actors begin to unveil the exclusionary and undemocratic character of pacted, elite democracy.

This is not to suggest that the advent of formal political democracy and the increased centrality of party and electoral politics in much of the region do not have positive consequences for social movements. On the contrary, as García demonstrates, in Venezuela, the "existence of a formal democratic substratum has favored the diversification of social movements and the specialization of their demands." And Cardoso shows that, as the democratization process unfolds, a similar dynamic is under way in Brazil today.

As students of social movements, we must direct more of our attention to the terrain of formal democratic institutions because it now intersects the terrain of quotidian politics so crucially expanded by social movements during the 1980s. Analyses of democratic consolidation would similarly be enhanced if we shifted our theoretical gaze to examine the nexus of institutional and extrainstitutional democratic practices at both the local and national levels.

We are not suggesting that political scientists should not be concerned with crafting viable and effective democratic political institutions. Rather, we are arguing that we need to explore how more inclusive and meaningful democratic institutions might be designed, that we must concern ourselves with the quality as well as the stability of Latin America's new democracies. In particular, we need to pay closer attention to routes to or strategies for ensuring nonelite access to policymaking and implementation. And in the context of highly stratified Latin American societies, we must also think about the design of democratic institutions so that the basic interests of the bourgeoisie are not "virtually guaranteed" (Przeworski 1986: 60) and those of the popular classes are not "virtually excluded."

The history of democracy and development in the post–World War II period has been precisely a history of exclusion for the majority of Latin Americans. The redefinition or dismantling of development will therefore certainly not be the product of government action or the efforts of international organizations such as the IMF or the World Bank. As several of our essays imply, collective actors, who find expression in the region's social movements, represent a tangible hope for imagining and bringing about different means of organizing societies in ways more conducive to genuine improvements in living conditions—both cultural *and* material. Social movements theorists and activists can contribute to the realization of that hope by elucidating the multiple struggles in which people are already engaged, as they attempt to forge alternatives to development and to regenerate ways of living individually and collectively that have been under attack for many decades and most significantly damaged in the 1980s.

Acronyms

AIDS	autoimmune deficiency syndrome
AMIGRANSA	Asociación de Amigos en Defensa de la Gran Sabana (Association of Friends for the Defense of the Great Savannah)
ANUC	National Association of Peasant Producers (Asociación Nacional de Usuarios Campesinos)
APRA	American Popular Revolutionary Alliance
ASCOIN	Asociación Colombiana Indigenista (Indigenist Association)
ATEM 25 de Noviembre	Asociación de Trabajo y Estudios de la Mujer, 25 de Noviembre (Work and Study Association on Women, November 25)
AVEC	Agrupación Vecinal (Organization of Neighbors)
AVM	strategies (Anomie/Volitional-emotional/Mutating)
BUCP	Bloque Urbano de Colonias Populares
CDP–Chihuahua	Comité de Defensa Popular–Chihuahua
CDP–Durango	Comité de Defensa Popular–Durango
CEAAL	Consejo de Educación de Adultos de América Latina
CEB	Christian base community
CELAM	Latin American Bishops' Conference
CEPAM	Centro Ecuatoriano para la Promoción y Acción de la Mujer
CEPLAES	Centro de Planificación y Estudios Sociales
CGCPA	Consejo General de Colonias Populares de Acapulco
CIAM	Centro de Información y Apoyo de la Mujer
CLACSO	Consejo Latinoamericano de Ciencias Sociales (Latin American Social Science Council)
CLAEH	Centro Latinoamericano de Economía Humana
CNC	Confederación Nacional Campesina
CNOP	Confederación Nacional de Organizaciones Populares
CNPA	Plan de Ayala National Coordinating Committee
COCEI	Coalición de Obreros, Campesinos, y Estudiantes del Istmo
CONADE	Comisión Nacional de Desarrollo
CONAMUP	National Coordinator of Urban Popular Movements
COP	Coordinadora de Ollas Populares
COPRE	Comisión para la Reforma del Estado
CORVI	Corporación de Vivienda
CRIC	Consejo Regional Indígena del Cauca (Indigenous Council of the Cauca Region)
CRMUP	Coordinadora Regional del Valle de México
CTM	Confederación de Trabajadores Mexicanos
CUD	Coordinadora Unica de Damnificados
DAWN	Development Alternatives with Women for a New Era
DINAMU	Dirección Nacional de la Mujer

DNM	Departamento Nacional de la Mujer (National Department of Women)
ECOXXI	environmental group
EDJ	Environmental Defense Juntas
ELN	Ejército de Liberación Nacional (National Liberation Army)
FABES	Secretaria da Familia e do Bem-Estar Social (Greater São Paulo's Family and Social Services)
FARC	Fuerzas Armadas Revolucionarias de Colombia (Revolutionary Armed Forces of Colombia)
FDN	Frente Democrático Nacional, the Cardenista Front
FENOC	National Federation of Peasant and Indigenous Peoples
FIAT	Fabbrica Italiana Automobili Torino
FORJA	Federación de Organizaciones de Juntas Ambientales
FPI	Frente Popular Independiente
FPTyL	Frente Popular Tierra y Libertad
FPZ	Frente Popular de Zacatecas
GALF	Lesbian-Feminist Action
GIDA	Grupo de Ingenieriá y Arborización
GRIDIA	environmental group
IDRC	International Development Research Center
IMF	International Monetary Fund
INCORA	Instituto Colombiano de Reforma Agraria (Land Reform Institute)
INDECO	Mexican government's housing agency
IU	Izquierda Unida (United Left)
IVA	value-added tax
LASA	Latin American Studies Association
LOA	Ley Orgánica del Ambiente (Organic Law on the Environment)
M–19	Movimiento 19 de Abril
MAIC	Movimiento de Autoridades Indígenas de Colombia (Indigenous Authorities Movement of Colombia)
MARNR	Ministerio del Ambiente y de los Recursos Naturales Renovables (Ministry of the Environment)
MAS	Movimiento Hacia el Socialismo (Movement Toward Socialism)
MDB	Movimento Democrático Brasileiro (Brazilian Democratic Movement)
MEMCH	Movement for the Liberation of Chilean Women
MIC	Movimiento de Integración de la Comunidad (Movement for Community Integration)
MIR	Movimiento Izquierda Revolucionaria
MNR	Movimiento Nacional Revolucionario
MOVEMO	Movimiento de Vecinos de Montevideo (Neighborhood Movement of Montevideo)
MOVIDE	Movimiento Pro-Vivienda Decorosa
MPPCS	Movimiento Popular de Pueblos y Colonias del Sur
MPTyL	Movimiento Popular Tierra y Libertad
MRP	Movimiento Revolucionario del Pueblo
NAP	Núcleos de Atendimento ao Público (Public Assistance Nuclei)
NGO	nongovernmental organization
NLORM	Nueva Ley Orgánica del Régimen Municipal (New Organic Law of Municipal Government)
NSM	new social movement
OAS	Organization of American States

OFNAMU	Oficina Nacional de la Mujer (National Office of Women)
ONIC	Nueva Ley Orgánica del Régimen Municipal (National Indigenous Organization of Colombia)
PAN	Partido de Acción Nacional
PAR	participatory action-research
PC do B	Partido Comunista do Brasil (Communist Party of Brazil)
PCI	Italian Communist Party
PCM	Partido Comunista Mexicano (Mexican Communist Party)
PDS	Partito Democratico della Sinistra (Italian Communist Party)
PEM	Minimum Employment Program
PIP	Policía de Investigación de Perú
PMDB	Partido do Movimento Democratico Brasileiro (Party of the Brazilian Democratic Movement)
PMT	Mexican Workers' Party
POJH	Public Works Program for Heads of Household
PRI	Partido Revolucionario Institucional (Institutional Revolutionary Party)
PRONASOL	Programa Nacional de Soldaridad
PRT	Revolutionary Workers' Party
PSR	Partido Socialista Revolucionario
PST	Partido Socialista de los Trabajadores
PSUM	Unified Socialist Party of Mexico
PT	Partido dos Trabalhadores or Brazilian Workers' Party
PUM	Partido Unificado Mariateguista
SAB	Sociedade Amigos do Bairro (Neighborhood Friends Society)
SAHOP	Secretaría de Asentamientos Humanos y de Obras Publicas (Ministry of Settlements and Public Works)
SCA	Sociedad Conservacionista Aragua (Aragua Conservationist Society)
SEDUE	Secretaría de Desarrollo Urbano y de Ecología
SM	social movement
SOMOS	Grupo de Afirmação Homosexual (We Are–Homosexual Affirmation Group)
UAPE	Unidad Asesora de Proyectos Especiales
UCP	Unión de Colonias Populares
UDI	Unión Democrática Independiente
UNIR	(National Union of the Revolutionary Left)
UOCP	Unidad Obrero Campesino Popular
UPA	Universidad Popular Ambiental (Popular University of the Environment)
UPM	urban popular movement
USM	urban social movement
WID	Women in Development

Bibliography

Abramo, Lais. 1987. "Se as Rocas do Fiandeiros Fiassem Por Si Sós os Robots Poderiam Chamar a Greve." *David y Goliath*, no. 52.

Agosín, Marjorie. 1987. "Metaphors of Female Political Ideology: The Cases of Chile and Argentina." *Women's International Studies Forum*, no. 10: 571–577.

Aguiar, C. 1985. "Perspectivas de Democratización en el Uruguay Actual." In *Apertura y Concertación*, edited by D. Sarachaga, J. P. Terra, I. Wonsewer, and C. Aguiar. Montevideo: Ediciones de la Banda Oriental.

Alarcón, Norma. 1990. "The Theoretical Subject(s) in 'This Bridge Called My Back' and Anglo-American Feminism." In *Making Face, Making Soul/Haciendo Caras*, edited by Gloria Anzaldúa. San Francisco, Calif.: Aunt Lute Foundation.

Alonso, Jorge. 1984. "Notas Acerca de la Situación de los Pobladores Depauperados y su Relación con el Movimiento Urbano Popular." *Nueva Antropología* 6, no. 24: 35–50.

————. 1988. "El Papel de las Convergencias de los Movimientos Sociales en los Cambios del Sistema Político Mexicano." Manuscript.

————, ed. 1986. *Los Movimientos Sociales en el Valle de México*. México: Centro de Investigaciones y Estudios Superiores en Antropología Social.

Alvarado, Arturo, ed. 1987. *Electoral Patterns and Perspectives in Mexico*. La Jolla: University of California, San Diego, Center for U.S.-Mexican Studies.

Alvarez, Sonia E. 1986. "The Politics of Gender in Latin America: Comparative Perspectives on Women in the Brazilian Transition to Democracy." Ph.D diss., Yale University.

————. 1988. "Women's Participation in the 'People's Church': A Critical Appraisal." Paper presented at the Fourteenth International Congress of the Latin American Studies Association, New Orleans, La., March 17–19.

————. 1989a. "Women's Movements and Gender Politics in the Brazilian Transition." In *The Women's Movement in Latin America: Feminism and the Transition to Democracy*, edited by Jane Jaquette. Boston, Mass.: Unwin Hyman.

————. 1989b. "Theoretical Problems and Methodological Impasses in the Study of Contemporary Social Movements in Brazil and the Southern Cone: An Agenda for Future Research." Paper presented at Fifteenth International Conference of the Latin American Studies Association, Miami, Fla., December 4–6.

————. 1990a. *Engendering Democracy in Brazil: Women's Movements in Transition Politics*. Princeton, N.J.: Princeton University Press.

————. 1990b. "Women's Participation in the Brazilian 'People's Church': A Critical Appraisal." *Feminist Studies* 16, no. 2: 381–408.

————. 1992. "'Deepening Democracy': Social Movement Networks, Constitutional Reform and Radical Urban Regimes in Contemporary Brazil." In *Mobilizing the Community: Local Politics in a Global Era*, edited by Robert Fischer and Joseph Kling. Newbury Park, Calif.: Sage Publications.

Alves, Branca Moreira, and Jaqueline Pitanguy. 1981. *O Que é o Feminismo*. São Paulo: Brasiliense.

Alves, Márcio Moreira. 1979. *Igreja e a Política no Brasil*. São Paulo: Brasiliense.

AMIGRANSA-ECOXXI-GRIDIA. 1990. "Evaluación del Plan de Ordenación del Sector Oriental del Parque Nacional Canaima." Manuscript.

Amin, Samir. 1990. *Maldevelopment*. London: Zed Books.

Anderson, J. Velasco. 1985. "The UN Decade for Women in Peru." *Women's Studies International Forum* 8, no. 2: 107–109.

Anderson, Mary B., and Marty A. Chen. 1988. *Integrating WID or Restructuring Development?* Washington, D.C.: Association for Women in Development (AWID) Occasional Papers.

Andreas, Carol. 1985. *When Women Rebel: The Rise of Popular Feminism in Peru*. Westport, Conn.: Lawrence Hill.

Angus, Ian. 1989. "Media Beyond Representation." In *Popular Culture in Contemporary America*, edited by Ian Angus and Sut Jhally. London: Routledge.

Angus, Ian, and Sut Jhally, eds. 1989. *Cultural Politics in Contemporary America*. New York: Routledge.

Antoniazzi, Alberto. 1986. "O Catolicismo no Brazil." Paper presented at Meeting on Religious Diversity of ISER.

Antrobus, Peggy. 1988. "Consequences and Responses to Social Deterioration: The Experience of the English-speaking Caribbean." Paper presented at the Program on International Development and Women, Cornell University, Ithaca, N.Y., September.

ANUC. 1974. "Hacia la Unidad Indígena." Bogotá: Secretariado Indígena de la ANUC.

Anzaldúa, Gloria, ed. 1990. *Making Face, Making Soul/Haciendo Caras*. San Francisco, Calif.: Aunt Lute Foundation.

Apffel Marglin, Frédérique, and Stephen Marglin, eds. 1990. *Dominating Knowledge: Development, Culture and Resistance*. Oxford: Clarendon Press.

Arau Chavarría, Rosalinda. 1987a. "Organización de los Pueblos y Colonias del Sur." *Revista Mexicana de Sociología* 19, no. 4: 9–35.

——. 1987b. *Historia de una Organización Urbano-popular en el Valle de México*. Mexico: Centro de Investigaciones y Estudios Superiores en Antropología Social.

Archetti, E., ed. 1987. *Sociology of "Developing" Societies: Latin America*. New York: Monthly Press Review.

Argentina's National Commission of Disappeared People. 1986. *Nunca Más: A Report by Argentina's National Commission of Disappeared People*. London: Faber and Faber.

Aricó, José. 1980. *Marx y America Latina*. Lima: CEDEP.

Arizpe, Lourdes. 1990. "Democracy for a Small Two-gender Planet." In *Women and Social Change in Latin America*, edited by Elizabeth Jelin. London: United Nations Research Institute for Social Development and Zed Books.

Arnillas, F. 1986. "El Movimiento Popular Urbano. Algunos Puntos para el Debate." *Nuevos Cuadernos Celats*, no. 9.

Arriagada, Genaro. 1988. *Pinochet: The Politics of Power*. Boston, Mass.: Unwin Hyman.

Aziz Nassif, Alberto. 1989. "Regional Dimensions of Democratization." In *Mexico's Alternative Political Futures*, monograph series, edited by Wayne Cornelius, Judith Gentleman, and Peter Smith. La Jolla: University of California, San Diego, Center for U.S.-Mexican Studies.

Ballón, Eduardo. 1986. *Movimientos Sociales y Democracia: La Fundación de un Nuevo Orden*. Lima: DESCO.

——, ed. 1986. *Movimientos Soiciales y Crisis: El Caso Peruano*. Lima: DESCO.

Barbieri, Teresita de, and Orlandina de Oliveira. 1986. "Nuevos Sujetos Sociales: La Presencia Politica de las Mujeres en América Latina." *Nueva Antropología* 8, no. 30: 5–29.

Barbosa, R. 1989. *Centauros de Guadalupe o la Insurrección Llanera, 1946–1966*. Bogotá: National University, History Department.

Barrán, José, and Benjamin Nahum. 1982. *Batlle, los Estancieros y el Imperio Británico*. Montevideo: Ediciones de la Banda Oriental.

Barrig, Maruja. 1989a. "The Difficult Equilibrium Between Bread and Roses: Women's Organizations and the Transition from Dictatorship to Democracy in Peru." In *The Women's Movement in Latin America and the Transition to Democracy*, edited by Jane S. Jaquette. Boston, Mass.: Unwin Hyman.

———. 1989b. "Women and Development in Peru: Old Models, New Actors." Paper presented at the Association for Women in Development conference, Washington, D.C., November.

Barrios de Chungara, Domitila, with Moema Viezzer. 1978. *Let Me Speak! Testimony of Domitila, a Woman of the Bolivian Mines.* New York: Monthly Review Press.

Barros, Robert. 1986. "The Left and Democracy: Recent Debates in Latin America." *Telos*, no. 68: 49–70.

Bateson, Gregory. 1974. *Steps Towards an Ecology of Mind.* New York: Bantam Books.

Baudrillard, Jean. 1975. *The Mirror of Production.* St. Louis, Mo.: Telos Press.

Behar, Ruth. 1990. "Rage and Redemption: Reading the Life Story of a Mexican Marketing Woman." *Feminist Studies* 16, no. 2: 223–258.

Beisso, R., and J. L. Castagnola. 1987. "Identidades Sociales y Cultura Política." *Cuadernos del Claeh*, no. 4.

Benería, Lourdes. 1989. "The Mexican Debt Crisis: Restructuring the Economy and the Household." Paper presented at the Workshop on Labor Market Policies and Structural Adjustment, International Labor Organization, Geneva, November.

Benería, Lourdes, and Marta Roldán. 1987. *The Crossroads of Class and Gender: Industrial Homework, Subcontracting, and Household Dynamics in Mexico D.F.* Chicago, Ill.: University of Chicago Press.

Benería, Lourdes, and Shelley Feldman, eds. 1992. *Unequal Burden: Economic Crises, Persistent Poverty and Women's Work.* Boulder, Colo.: Westview Press.

Benjamin, W. 1965. *Angelus Novus.* Buenos Aires: EUDEBA.

Bennett, Vivienne. 1989. "Urban Public Services and Social Conflict: Water in Monterrey." In *Housing and Land in Urban Mexico*, monograph series, edited by Alan Gilbert. La Jolla: University of California, San Diego, Center for U.S.-Mexican Studies.

Bennett, Vivienne, and Jeffrey W. Rubin. 1988. "How Popular Movements Shape the State: Radical Oppositions in Juchitán and Monterey, Mexico, 1973–1987." Paper presented at the Latin American Studies Association International Congress, New Orleans, La., March.

Bloch, Jayne. 1985. "The Women Outside the Gate." *The Progressive* 49, no. 12: 18.

Blondet, Cecilia. 1990. "Establishing an Identity: Women Settlers in a Poor Lima Neighborhood." In *Women and Social Change in Latin America*, edited by Elizabeth Jelin. London: United Nations Research Institute for Social Development and Zed Books.

Bobbio, Luigi. 1979. *Lutta Continua: Storia di una Organizzazione Rivoluzionaria.* Milan: Savelli.

Bobbio, Norberto. 1989. *Democracy and Dictatorship.* Minneapolis: University of Minnesota Press.

Boege, Eckart, and Giberto López Rivas. 1985. "Los Miskitos y la Cuestión Nacional en Nicaragua." In *Movimientos Populares en Centroamérica*, edited by Daniel Camacho and Rafael Menjívar. San José, Costa Rica: UNU-CLACSO-IISUNAM.

Boff, Clodovis, et al. 1987. *Cristãos: Como Fazer Política.* Petrópolis, Brazil: Vozes.

Boff, Leonardo. 1981. *Igreja: Carisma e Poder.* Petrópolis, Brazil: Vozes.

———. 1986. *E a Igreja se Fez Povo.* Petrópolis, Brazil: Vozes.

Bonder, Gloria. 1989. "Women's Organizations in Argentina's Transition to Democracy." In *Women and Counter-power*, edited by Yolande Cohen. Montreal: Black Rose Books.

Bonilla, Víctor Daniel. N.d. *Carta al CRIC No. 4.* Mimeographed.

———. 1968. *Siervos de Dios y Amos de Indios.* Bogotá: Author's Edition.

———. 1976. "Política de Unidad Indígena." *Carta al CRIC No. 1.* Mimeographed.

———. 1977. *Carta al CRIC No. 2.* Mimeographed.

———. 1977. *Carta al CRIC No. 4.* Mimeographed.

_____. 1978. "El Pensamiento Político del Indio Hoy." *Semanario Cultural de El Pueblo* (Sunday magazine of the daily newspaper *El Pueblo*, Cali, Colombia).

_____. 1988. *Derechos Humanos y Pueblos Indígenas*. Cali, Colombia: Colombia Nuestra.

_____. 1989. "Los Indígenas Frente al País Nacional: Todos Tenemos Derechos, Pero no Todo es Igual." In *Derechos Humanos y Modernidad*, edited by Carlos Martínez and Edgar Verela. Cali, Colombia: Personería Municipal.

Borja, Jordi. 1981. "Movimientos Urbanos y Cambio Político." *Revista Mexicana de Sociología* 43, no. 3: 1341–1369.

Borja, Jordi, Teresa Valdés, Hernan Pozo, and Eduardo Morales, eds. 1987. *Decentralización del Estado: Movimiento Social y Gestion Local*. Santiago: FLACSO.

Boschi, Renato, ed. 1982. *Movimentos Coletivos no Brasil Urbano*. Rio de Janeiro: Zahar.

_____. 1987. *A Arte de Associação: Política de Base e Democracia no Brasil*. São Paulo: Vêrtice.

Boschi, Renato, and Lícia do Prado Valladares. 1983. "Problemas Teóricos na Análise de Movimentos Sociais: Comunidade, Ação Coletiva e o Papel do Estado." *Espaço e Debates*, no. 8.

Bourdieu, Pierre. 1977. *Outline of a Theory of Practice*. Cambridge: Cambridge University Press.

Bourque, Susan C. 1985. "Urban Activists: Paths to Political Consciousness in Peru." In *Women Living Change*, edited by Susan C. Borque and Donna C. Divine. Philadelphia, Pa.: Temple University Press.

_____. 1989. "Gender and the State: Perspectives from Latin America." In *Women, the State, and Development*, edited by Sue Ellen M. Charleton, Jana Everett, and Kathleen Staudt. Albany: University of New York Press.

Bourque, Susan C., and Donna C. Divine, eds. 1985. *Women Living Change*. Philadelphia, Pa.: Temple University Press.

Brandão, Carlos Rodrigues. 1988a. *Condições de Vida e Situação de Trabalho do Povo de Goiás: As Pessoas e as Famílias*. Goiás, Brazil.

_____. 1988b. "Catolicismo Popular: Etica, Ethos e Sentido de Vida." Mimeograph for the Encyclopedia of Liberation Theology.

_____. 1988c. *Crença e Identidade: Campo Religioso e Mudança Cultural*. Manuscript.

Brito, Angela Neves-Xavier de. 1986. "Brazilian Women in Exile: The Quest for an Identity." *Latin American Perspectives* 13, no. 2: 58–80.

Brown, Doug. 1990. "Sandinismo and the Problem of Democratic Hegemony." *Latin American Perspectives* 17, no. 2: 39–61.

Bruce-Novoa, Juan. 1980. *Chicano Authors: Inquiry by Interview*. Austin: University of Texas Press.

Bruneau, Thomas C. 1974. *The Political Transformation of the Brazilian Catholic Church*. New York: Cambridge University Press.

_____. 1980. "The Catholic Church and Development in Latin America: The Role of the Basic Christian Communities." *World Development* 8 (July/August): 535–544.

Bunster-Burotto, Ximena. 1985. "Surviving Beyond Fear: Women and Torture in Latin America." In *Women and Change in Latin America*, edited by June Nash and Helen Safa. South Hadley, Mass.: Bergin and Garvey.

_____. 1988. "Watch Out for the Little Nazi Man That All of Us Have Inside: The Mobilization and Demobilization of Women in Militarized Chile." *Women's Studies International Forum* 2, no. 5: 485–491.

Burbach, Roger. 1989. *Chile: A Requiem for the Left?* Berkeley, Calif.: Strategic Perspectives, Center for South American Studies.

Burbach, Roger, and Orlando Nuñez. 1987. *Fire in the Americas: Forging a Revolutionary Agenda*. New York: Verso.

Burdick, John. 1990. "Gossip and Secrecy: Women's Articulation of Domestic Conflict in Three Religions of Urban Brazil." *Sociological Analysis* 50, no. 2: 153–170.

Burgos-Debray, Elizabeth, ed. 1984. *I, Rigoberta Menchú: An Indian Woman in Guatemala.* London: Verso.

Burke, Edmund, ed. 1988. *Global Crisis and Social Movements.* Boulder, Colo.: Westview Press.

Butler Flora, Cornelia. 1984. "Socialist Feminism in Latin America." *Women and Politics* 4, no. 1: 69–93.

Butler, Judith. 1990. "Gender Trouble, Feminist Theory, and Psychoanalytic Discourse." In *Feminism and Postmodernism,* edited by Linda Nicholson. London: Routledge.

Caccia Bava, Silvio. 1981. "O Movimento de Onibus: A Articulação de um Movimento Reivindicatório de Periferia." *Espacos e Debates,* no. 1.

Caetano, G. J. Rilla, and R. Pérez. 1987. "La Partidocracia Uruguaya." *Cuadernos del Claeh,* no. 4: 42–43.

Caldeira, Teresa Pires do Rio. 1986–1987. "Electoral Struggles in a Neighborhood in the Periphery of São Paulo." *Politics and Society* 15, no. 1: 43–66.

———. 1990. "Women, Daily Life and Politics." In *Women and Social Change in Latin America,* edited by Elizabeth Jelin. London: United Nations Research Institute for Social Development and Zed Books.

Calderón, Fernando. 1989. "La Importancia de Llamarse Ernesto." *Utopia,* no. 19.

———. In press. *El Gato que Ladra.* Mexico.

———, ed. 1986. *Los Movimientos Sociales ante la Crisis.* Buenos Aires: CLACSO/UNO.

———, ed. 1988. *La Modernidad en la Encrucijada Postmoderna.* Buenos Aires: CLACSO.

Calderón, Fernando, and Alejandro Piscitelli. 1990. "Paradigm Crisis and Social Movements: A Latin American Perspective." In *Comparative Methodology: Theory and Practice in International Social Research,* edited by E. Oyen. Beverly Hills, Calif.: Sage/ISA.

Calderón, Fernando, and Joel Rufino dos Santos, eds. 1991. *Modernización y Democratización en América Latina.* Buenos Aires: CLACSO.

Calderón, Fernando, and Mario dos Santos, eds. 1987. *Latinoamérica: Lo Político y lo Social en la Crisis.* Buenos Aires: CLACSO.

CAM (Centro Acción de la Mujer). 1989. *Guía Legal de los Derechos de la Mujer.* Quito: CAM/Fundación Friedrich Naumann.

Camacho, Daniel, and Rafael Menjívar, eds. 1985. *Movimientos Populares en Centroamérica.* San José, Costa Rica: UNU-CLACSO-IISUNAM.

———, eds. 1989. *Los Movimientos Populares en América Latina.* Mexico: Siglo XXI.

CAM-CIAM. 1988. *Tomando Fuerzas para Volar con Fibra.* Ecuador: Ediciones CAM-CIAM.

Campero, Guillermo. 1984. *Los Gremios Empresariales en el Período 1970–1983: Comportamiento Socio-Político y Orientaciones Ideológicas.* Santiago: ILET.

———, ed. 1986. *Los Movimientos Sociales y la Lucha Democrática en Chile.* Santiago: CLACSO-ILET.

Cardoso, Fernando Henrique, and Enzo Faletto. 1979. *Dependency and Development in Latin America.* Berkeley: University of California Press.

Cardoso, Ruth. 1982. "Duas Faces de Uma Experiência." *Novos Estudios CEBRAP* 1, no. 2.

———. 1983. "Movimentos Sociais Urbanos: Balanço Crítico." In *Sociedade e Política no Brasil Pós-64,* edited by B. Sorj and M. H. Tavares de Almeida. São Paulo: Brasiliense.

———. 1987. "Movimentos Sociais na América Latina." *Revista Brasileira das Ciências Sociais* 3, no. 1: 27–37.

———. 1988. "Os Movimentos Populares no Contexto da Consolidação da Democracia." In *A Democracia no Brasil: Dilemas e Perspectivas,* edited by F. Reis Wanderley and G. O'Donnell. São Paulo: Vértice.

Carlson, Marifran. 1988. *Feminismo! The Women's Movement in Argentina from Its Beginnings to Eva Perón.* Chicago, Ill.: Academy Chicago.

Carr, Betsy, and Ricardo Anzaldúa Montoya. 1986. *The Mexican Left, the Popular Movements, and the Politics of Austerity.* La Jolla: University of California, San Diego, Center for U.S.-Mexican Studies.

Castañeda, Victor. 1986. "La Acción del Estado Frente a las Demandas de Suelo y Vivienda de los Sectores Populares en Monterrey." *Estudios Políticos*, no. 4/5: 73–84.

Castells, Manuel. 1982. "Squatters and Politics in Latin America: A Comparative Analysis of Urban Social Movements in Chile, Peru and Mexico." In *Towards a Political Economy of Urbanization in Third World Countries*, edited by Helen Safa. Delhi: Oxford University Press.

———. 1983. *The City and the Grassroots.* Berkeley: University of California Press.

———. 1986. "High Technology, World Development, and Structural Transformation: The Trends and the Debate." *Alternatives* 11, no. 3: 297–344.

Castells, Manuel, and Roberto Laserna. 1989. "La Nueva Dependencia: Cambio Tecnológico y Reestructuración Socioeconómica en Latinoamérica." *David y Goliath*, no. 55: 2–16.

Castillo, Manuel. 1986. "La Identidad Confundida: El Movimiento Empresarial Frente a la Crisis Reciente." In *Movimientos Sociales y Crisis: El Caso Peruano*, edited by E. Ballón. Lima: DESCO.

Castro Pozo, Hildebrando. 1979. *Nuestra Comunidad Indígena.* Lima: Editorial Castro Pozo.

Cattaneo, Angela, and Marina D'Amato. 1990. *La Politica Della Differenza: Dati e Análisi per uno Studio del Rapporto Donne/Partiti.* Milan: Franco Angeli Libri.

Cavarozzi, M., and M. A. Garretón, eds. 1989. *Muerte y Resurreción: Los Partidos Políticos en el Autoritarismo y las Transiciones del Cono Sur.* Santiago: FLASCO.

CEIS (Centro Ecuatoriano de Investigaciones Sociales). 1986. "Problems That Concern Women and Their Incorporation in Development: The Case of Ecuador." In *Women's Concerns and Planning: A Methodological Approach for Their Integration into Local, Regional and National Planning*, edited by UNESCO. Belgium: UNESCO.

Centro Femenino 8 de Marzo. 1989. *Nuestra Voz*, no. 3.

Centro María Quilla. 1990. *Mujeres, Educación, y Conciencia de Género en Ecuador.* Quito: Centro María Quilla/CEAAL.

Centro María Quilla, CEAAL Red de Mujeres, CIM-CECIM. 1990. *Trabajando con Mujeres en el Ecuador.* Quito: Directorio Feminista.

CETRA/CEAL. 1983. "Tercera y Cuarta Protestas." *Páginas Sindicales* 6, no. 57.

CGM (Cartilla de los Gobernadores en Marcha). 1981. "Cómo Recuperamos Nuestro Camino de Lucha." *Cartilla de los Gobernadores en Marcha* (CGM), no. 2 (June).

———. 1985a. "Reconocimiento de los Cabildos de Munchique-Tigres, la Paila, Jebalá, Novirao." *Cartilla de los Gobernadores en Marcha* (CGM), no. 6 (June).

———. 1985b. "Nuestra Idea y los Problemas de Hoy." *Cartilla de los Gobernadores en Marcha* (CGM), no. 7 (June): 40.

———. 1985c. "Por Qué Hoy Nosotros Luchamos Distinto." *Cartilla de los Gobernadores en Marcha* (CGM), no. 8.

Chaparro, J. 1989. "Los Movimientos Políticos Regionales: Un Aporte para la Unidad Nacional." In *Entre Movimientos y Caudillos*, edited by G. Gallón. Bogotá: CINEP-CEREC.

Charleton, Sue Ellen M., Jane Everett, and Kathleen Staudt, eds. 1989. *Women, the State, and Development.* Albany: University of New York Press.

Chester, Silvia. 1986. "The Women's Movement in Argentina: Balance and Strategies." In *The Latin American Women's Movement: Reflections and Action*, edited by ISIS International. Santiago: ISIS International.

Chinchilla, Norma Stoltz. 1977. "Mobilizing Women: Revolution in the Revolution." *Latin American Perspectives*, no. 4: 83–102.

———. 1985–1986. "Women in the Nicaraguan Revolution." *Nicaraguan Perspectives*, no. 11: 18–26.

———. 1990. "Revolutionary Popular Feminism in Nicaragua: Articulating Class, Gender, and National Sovereignty." *Gender & Society* 4 (September): 370–397.

Chinchilla, Norma Stoltz, and James Lowell Dietz. 1982. "Towards a New Understanding of Development and Underdevelopment." In *Dependency and Marxism: Toward a Resolution of the Debate*, edited by Ronald Chilcote. Boulder, Colo.: Westview Press.

Chiriboga Vega, Manuel. 1986. "Movimiento Campesino e Indígena y Participación Política en Ecuador: La Construcción de Identidades en una Sociedad Heterogéna." In *Movimientos Sociales en el Ecuador*, edited by Manuel Chiriboga et al. Quito: CLACSO, ILDIS, CAAP, CEDIME, IEE, CEPLAES, CIUDAD.

Chiriboga Vega, Manuel, et al., eds. 1986. *Movimientos Sociales en el Ecuador.* Quito: CLACSO, ILDIS, CAAP, CEDIME, IEE, CEPLAES, CIUDAD.

Chodorow, Nancy. 1974. "Family Structure and Feminine Personality." In *Woman, Culture and Society*, edited by M. Rosaldo and L. Lamphere. Stanford, Calif.: Stanford University Press.

————. 1990. "What Is the Relation Between Psychoanalytic Feminism and the Psychoanalytic Psychology of Women?" In *Theoretical Perspectives on Sexual Difference*, edited by D. Rhode. New Haven, Conn.: Yale University Press.

Chuchryk, Patricia M. 1984. "Protest, Politics and Personal Life: The Emergence of Feminism in a Military Dictatorship, Chile 1973-1983." Ph.D. diss., York University, Toronto.

————. 1989a. "Feminist Anti-Authoritarian Politics: The Role of Women's Organizations in the Chilean Transition to Democracy." In *The Women's Movement in Latin America: Feminism and the Transition to Democracy*, edited by Jane Jaquette. Boston, Mass.: Unwin Hyman.

————. 1989b. "Subversive Mothers: The Women's Opposition to the Military Regime in Chile." In *Women, the State, and Development*, edited by Sue Ellen M. Charlton, Jane Everett, and Kathleen Staudt. Albany: State University of New York Press.

Clastres, P. 1987. *Society Against the State.* New York: Zone Books.

Clifford, James. 1988. *The Predicament of Culture.* Cambridge, Mass.: Harvard University Press.

————. 1989. "Notes on Travel and Theory." *Inscriptions*, no. 5: 177–185.

Clifford, J., and G. Marcus, eds. 1986. *Writing Culture: The Poetics and Politics of Ethnography.* Berkeley: University of California Press.

Cocchi, A., and J. Klaczko. 1985. "Notas Sobre Democracia Política e Idelogía en el Uruguay." In *Uruguay y la Democracia*, edited by C. Gillespie, L. Goodman., J. Rial, and P. Winn. Montevideo: Ediciones de la Banda Oriental.

Codina, V. 1986. *Qué es la Teología de la Liberación?* Oruro: CICEP.

Cohen, Jean. 1985. "Strategy or Identity: New Theoretical Paradigms and Contemporary Social Movements." *Social Research* 52, no. 4: 663–716.

Collier, David. 1976. *Squatters and Oligarchs: Authoritarian Rule and Policy Change in Peru.* Baltimore, Md.: Johns Hopkins University Press.

————, ed. 1979. *The New Authoritarianism in Latin America.* Princeton, N.J.: Princeton University Press.

Colón, Hector Manuel. 1986. "Las Calles que los Marxistas Nunca Entendieron." *David y Goliath*, no. 49.

Comaroff, Jean. 1985. *Body of Power, Spirit of Resistance.* Chicago, Ill.: University of Chicago Press.

Comblin, José. 1987. "Os Leigos." *Comunicações do ISER*, no. 26: 26–37.

"Compañeras, Solidarity, Movement: Women Talk About the Encuentro." 1988. *Off Our Backs* 18, no. 3 (March).

Congress Committee on the Environment. 1990. "Subcommission on the Tepuyes." Minutes. Caracas.

Cook, Maria Lorena. 1990. "Organizing Opposition in the Teachers' Movement in Oaxaca." In *Popular Movements and Political Change in Mexico*, edited by Joe Foweraker and Ann L. Craig. Boulder, Colo.: Lynne Rienner.

Coordinación de Grupos Organizadores de las Jornadas Feministas. 1987. "Uruguay." In *Jornadas Feministas: Feminismo y Sectores Populares en América Latina*, edited by Coordinación de Grupos Organizadores de las Jornadas Feministas. Mexico: Ed. Electrocomp.

————, ed. 1987. *Jornadas Feministas: Feminismo y Sectores Populares en América Latina*, Mexico: Ed. Electrocomp.

Coraggio, J. L. 1985. "Social Movements and 'Revolution': The Case of Nicaragua." In *New Social Movements and the State in Latin America*, edited by David Slater. Amsterdam: CEDLA.

Cordero, Margarita. 1986. "Latin American and Caribbean Feminism: A Multiple Challenge (an interview with Magaly Piñeda)." In *The Latin American Women's Movement*, edited by ISIS International. Santiago: ISIS International.

Corkill, David, and David Cubitt. 1988. *Ecuador: Fragile Democracy*. London: Latin American Bureau.

Cornelius, Wayne. 1975. *Politics and the Migrant Poor in Mexico City*. Stanford, Calif.: Stanford University Press.

Cornelius, Wayne, Judith Gentleman, and Peter Smith, eds. 1989. *Mexico's Alternative Political Futures*, monograph series. La Jolla: University of California, San Diego, Center for U.S.-Mexican Studies.

Cornia, Giovanni Andrea. 1987. "Adjustment at the Household Level: Potentials and Limitations of Household Strategies." In *Adjustment with a Human Face*, edited by Giovanni Andrea Cornia. Oxford: Clarendon Press.

———, ed. 1987. *Adjustment with a Human Face*, Oxford: Clarendon Press.

Correa, Guillermo. 1984. "La Marcha Rechazó Oportunismos." *Processo*, no. 389 (April 16): 29–31.

Craig, Ann L. 1990. "Institutional Context and Popular Strategies." In *Popular Movements and Political Change in Mexico*, edited by Joe Foweraker and Ann L. Craig. Boulder, Colo.: Lynne Rienner.

CRIC (Consejo Regional Indigena del Cauca). 1973. "Nuestras Luchas de Ayer y de Hoy." *Cartilla del CRIC*, no. 1.

———. 1974. "Como nos Organizamos?" *Cartilla del CRIC*, no. 2.

———. 1980. "Comunidades en Lucha y Comité Ejucutivo." Bogotá: Gobernadores Indígenas en Marcha.

———. 1984. *Realidad y Fantasía Sobre las Contradiciones del Movimiento Indígena del Cauca*. Bogotá: Gobernadores Indígenas en Marcha.

Criquillón, Ana. 1988. "Acabamos con el Mito del Sexo Debil." *Terra Nuova Forum*, no. 13: 31–35.

Criquillón, Ana, and Olga Espinoza. 1987. "Mujeres en Transición: De lo Específico a lo Integral." In *Mujeres, Crisis y Movimiento en América Latina*, edited by ISIS International. Santiago: ISIS International.

Crispi, Patricia. 1987. *Tejiendo Rebeldías: Escritos Feministas de Julieta Kirkwood*. Santiago: Centro Estudios de la Mujer and La Morada.

Crouch, Colin, and Alessandro Pissorno, eds. 1978. *The Resurgence of Class Conflict in Western Europe Since 1968*. London: Macmillan.

Crummett, Maria. 1977. "El Poder Femenino: The Mobilization of Women Against Socialism in Chile." *Latin American Perspectives* 4, no. 4: 103–113.

Cruz, Marcos, Gonzalo Yañez, Elio Villaseñor, and Julio Moguel, eds. 1986. *Llegó la Hora de Ser Gobierno: Durango, Testimonios de la Lucha del Comité de Defensa Popular General Francisco Villa*. Mexico D.F.: Equipo Pueblo.

Cruz, Sebastiõ C. V., and Carlos E. Martins. 1983. "De Castello à Figueiredo: Uma Incursão na Pré-História da 'Abertura.'" In *Sociedade e Política no Brasil Pós-64*, edited by B. Sorj and M. H. Tavares de Almeida. São Paulo: Brasiliense.

Cueva, Augustín. 1987. *La Teoría Marxista: Categorías de Base y Problemas Actuales*. Mexico D.F.: Planeta.

Custred, Glynn, and B. Orlove, eds. 1980. *Land and Power in Latin America*. New York: Free Press.

de Certeau, Michel. 1984. *The Practice of Everyday Life*. Berkeley: University of California Press.

De Kadt, Emanuel. 1970. *Catholic Radicals in Brazil*. London: Oxford University Press.

de la Cruz, Rafael. 1988. *Venezuela en Busca de un Nuevo Pacto Social*. Caracas: Alfadil/Tropicos.

de Lauretis, Teresa, ed. 1986. *Feminist Studies/Critical Studies*. Bloomington: Indiana University Press.

————, ed. 1987. *Technologies of Gender*. Bloomington: Indiana University Press.

Deane, John, ed. 1988. *Civil Society and the State: New European Perspectives*. London: Verso.

Degregori, Carlos Iván. 1986. "Sendero Luminoso: Los Hondos Immortales Desencuentros." In *Movimientos Sociales y Crisis. El Caso Peruano*, edited by Eduardo Ballón. Lima: DESCO.

————. 1990. *El Surgimiento de Sendero Luminoso*. Lima: Instituto de Estudios Peruanos.

Deleuze, Gilles, and Félix Guattari. 1987. *A Thousand Plateaus. Capitalism and Schizophrenia*. Minneapolis: University of Minnesota Press.

Della Cava, Ralph. 1976. "Catholicism and Society in Twentieth-Century Brazil." *Latin American Research Review* 11, no. 2: 7–50.

————. 1986. "A Igreja e a Abertura, 1974–1985." In *A Igreja nas Bases em Tempo de Transição (1974–1985)*, edited by Paulo Krischke and Scott Mainwaring. Porto Alegre, Brazil: LPM.

Deutsch, Sandra McGee. 1989. "Feminism." In *Latinas of the Americas: A Source Book*, edited by K. Lynn Stoner. New York: Garland.

Diamond, Irene, and Lee Quinby. 1988. *Feminisms and Foucault: Reflections on Resistance*. Boston, Mass.: Northeastern University.

Diaz, M., G. Foster, and J. Potter, eds. 1967. *Peasant Society*. Boston, Mass.: Little, Brown.

Díaz-Barriga, Miguel. 1990. "Urban Politics in the Valley of Mexico: A Case Study of Urban Movements in the Ajusco Region of Mexico D.F., 1970–1987." Ph.D. diss., Stanford University.

Dietz, James, and Dilmus James, eds. 1990. *Progress Toward Development in Latin America*. Boulder, Colo.: Lynne Rienner.

Diniz, Eli. 1982. *Voto e Máquina Política*. Rio de Janeiro: Paz e Terra.

DNP (Departamento Nacional de Planeación de Colombia). 1989. *Los Pueblos Indígenas de Colombia (Población y Territorio)*. Bogotá: Departamento Nacional de Planeación de Colombia.

Doimo, Ana Maria. 1984. *Movimento Social Urbano: Igreja e Participação Popular*. Petrópolis, Brazil: Vozes.

————. 1986. "Os Rumos dos Movimentos Sociais nos Caminhos da Religiosidade." In *A Igreja nas Bases*, edited by Paulo Krischke and Scott Mainwaring. Porto Alegre, Brazil: LPM.

dos Santos, Joel Rufino. 1985. "O Movimento Negro e a Crise Brasileira." *Política e Administração* 1, no. 2.

Duarte, Laura Maria. 1983. *Isto não se Aprende na Escola*. Petrópolis, Brazil: Vozes.

DuBois, Marc. 1991. "The Governance of the Third World: A Foucauldian Perspective of Power Relations in Development." *Alternatives* 16, no. 1: 1–30.

Durham, Eunice. 1984. "Movimentos Sociais e a Construção da Cidadania." *Novos Estudos CEBRAP*, no. 10 (October): 24–30.

Ebert, F., ed. 1990. *Consecuencias Regionales de la Restructuración de los Mercados Mundiales: Políticas Alternativas Relativas a la Escala Regional y Local*. Buenos Aires: CEUR.

Eckstein, Susan. 1977. *The Poverty of Revolution: The State and the Urban Poor in Mexico*. Princeton, N.J.: Princeton University Press.

————, ed. 1989. *Power and Popular Protest: Latin American Social Movements*. Berkeley: University of California Press.

La Economía Mexicana en Cifras, Edición 1986. 1986. Mexico D.F.: Nacional Financiera.

Elias, Norbert. 1978. *The History of Manners*. New York: Pantheon Books.

Ellman, Steve. 1989. "The Latin American Left Since Allende: Perspectives and New Directions." *Latin American Research Review* 24, no. 2.

Elson, Diane. 1991. "The Male Bias in Macro-Economics: The Case of Structural Adjustment." In *The Male Bias in the Development Process*, edited by Diane Elson. Manchester: Manchester University Press.

_____. 1992. "From Survival Strategies to Transformation Strategies: Women's Needs and Structural Adjustment." In *Unequal Burden: Economic Crises, Persistent Poverty and Women's Work*, edited by Lourdes Benería and Shelley Feldman. Boulder, Colo.: Westview Press.

_____, ed. 1991. *The Male Bias in the Development Process*. Manchester: Manchester University Press.

EMAS (Equipo de Acción Sindical) et al. 1987. *Feminismo y Sectores Populares en América Latina*. Mexico D.F.: Editorial Electrocomp.

"II Encuentro Feminista Latinoamericano y del Caribe." 1984. *Revista de las Mujeres* 1 (June): 140–144.

Enloe, Cynthia H. 1983. "Women Textile Workers in the Militarization of Southeast Asia." In *Women, Men and the International Division of Labour*, edited by June Nash and María P. Fernandez-Kelly. Albany: State University of New York Press.

Enzástiga Santiago, Mario. 1986. "La Unión de Colonias Populares de Cara al Movimiento Urbano Popular: Recapitulación Histórica." In *Los Movimientos Sociales en el Valle de México*, edited by Jorge Alonso. Mexico D.F.: Centro de Investigaciones y Estudios Superiores en Antropología Social, Ediciones de la Casa Chata.

Epstein, Barbara. 1990. "Rethinking Social Movement Theory." *Socialist Review* 20, no. 1 (January–March): 35–66.

Escobar, Arturo. 1984. "Discourse and Power in Development: Michel Foucault and the Relevance of His Work to the Third World." *Alternatives* 10, no. 3: 377–400.

_____. 1988. "Power and Visibility: The Invention and Management of Development in the Third World." *Cultural Anthropology* 3, no. 4: 428–443.

_____. In press a. "Imagining a Post-Development Era: Critical Thought, Development, and Social Movements." *Social Text*.

_____. In press b. "Culture, Practice and Politics: Anthropology and the Study of Social Movements." *Critique of Anthropology*.

Escobar, Cristina, and Francisco de Roux. 1989. "Movimientos Populares en Colombia (1970–1983)." In *Los Movimientos Populares en América Latina*, edited by Daniel Camacho and Rafael Menjívar. Mexico D.F.: Siglo XXI.

Escobar, Saul. 1988. "The Possibility for Democracy." *The Other Side of Mexico*, no. 6 (August 15).

Espinoza, Carlos. N.d. *Froilán Alama el Bandolero*. Piura, Peru: Imprenta Ubillus.

Esteva, Gustavo. 1987. "Regenerating People's Space." *Alternatives* 12, no. 1: 125–152.

Evers, Tilman. 1983. "De Costas para o Estado, Longe do Parlamento." *Novos Estudos CEBRAP* 2, no. 1: 25–39.

_____. 1985. "Identity: The Hidden Side of New Social Movements in Latin America." In *New Social Movements and the State in Latin America*, edited by David Slater. Dordrecht, the Netherlands: Foris Publications/CEDLA.

Fagen, Richard R., Carmen Diana Deere, and José Luis Coraggio, eds. 1986. *Transition and Development: Problems of Third World Socialism*. New York: Monthly Review Press.

Falk, R. 1987. "The Global Promise of Social Movements: Explorations at the Edge of Time." *Alternatives* 12, no 2: 173–196.

Fals Borda, Orlando. 1980. *Historia Doble de la Costa: Mompox y Loba*. Vol. 1. Bogotá: Carlos Valencia Editores.

_____. 1984. *Resistencia en el San Jorge*. Bogotá: Carlos Valencia Editores.

_____. 1986a. "El Nuevo Despertar de los Movimientos Sociales." *Revista Foro*, no. 1: 76–83.

_____. 1986b. *Retorno a la Tierra*. Bogotá: Carlos Valencia Editores.

_____. 1987. "The Application of Participatory Action-Research in Latin America." *International Sociology*, no. 4: 329–347.

_____. 1988a. *Ciencia Propia y Colonialismo Intelectual: Los Nuevos Rumbos*. Bogotá: Carlos Valencia Editores.

————. 1988b. *Knowledge and People's Power*. Delhi: Indian Social Science Institute.

————. 1989. "Ocho Tesis para una Opción Democrática Participativa." *Vía democrática*, no. 1.

Fals Borda, Orlando, and Anisur Rahman, eds. 1991. *Action and Knowledge: Breaking the Monopoly with Participatory Action-Research*. New York and London: Apex Press and Technical Publications.

Feder, Ernesto. 1971. *The Rape of the Peasantry*. Garden City, N.Y.: Anchor Books.

Feijoó, María del Carmen. 1985. "El Movimiento de Mujeres." In *Los Nuevos Movimientos Sociales*, edited by Elizabeth Jelin. Buenos Aires: Centro Editor de América Latina.

————. 1989. "The Challenge of Constructing Civilian Peace: Women and Democracy in Argentina." In *The Women's Movement in Latin America: Feminism and the Transition to Democracy*, edited by Jane S. Jaquette. Boston, Mass.: Unwin Hyman.

Ferguson, James. 1990. *The Anti-Politics Machine: "Development," Depoliticization and Bureaucratic Power in Lesotho*. Cambridge: Cambridge University Press.

Ferguson, Russell, et al. 1990. *Out There: Marginalization and Contemporary Cultures*. Cambridge, Mass.: MIT Press.

Filgueira, C. 1984. *El Dilema de la Democratización en Uruguay*. Montevideo: CIESU/Ediciones de la Banda Oriental.

————. 1985. "Movimientos Sociales en la Restauración del Orden Democrático: Uruguay, 1985." In *Movimientos Sociales en el Uruguay de Hoy*, edited by C. Filgueira. Montevideo: CLACSO/CIESU/Ediciones de la Banda Oriental.

————, ed. 1985. *Movimientos Sociales en el Uruguay de Hoy*, Montevideo: CLACSO/CIESU/Ediciones de la Banda Oriental.

Findji, María Teresa. 1983. "Las Relaciones de la Sociedad Colombiana con las Sociedades Indígenas." *Boletín de Antropología* (Universidad de Antioquia, Medellín) 5, nos. 17–19.

————. 1987. "En el Cauca Cordillerano: Comunidades Haciendo y Otros Deshaciendo . . ." Paper presented at the Sexto Congreso de Sociología, Bucaramanga, September 1987. Manuscript, Universidad del Valle, Cali, Colombia.

————. 1990a. "Indígena-Bewegung und 'Wiedererlangung' der Geschichte." In *Latein Amerika Geschichtslehrbücher, Geschichtsbewusstsein, Studien zur Internationale Schulbuchforschung Schriftenreihe*, edited by M. Rickenberg. Frankfurt: G. Eckert Institut.

————. 1990b. "Movimiento Indígena y Poderes Locales." *Intercambio*, no. 2 (March).

Findji, María Teresa, and J. M. Rojas. 1985. *Territorio, Economía y Sociedad Páez*. Cali, Colombia: Universidad del Valle, CIDSE.

Firth, Raymond. 1950. "The Peasantry of South East Asia." *International Affairs*, no. 26: 503–512.

Fiske, John. 1989a. *Understanding Popular Culture*. Boston, Mass.: Unwin Hyman.

————. 1989b. *Reading the Popular*. Boston, Mass.: Unwin Hyman.

————. 1990. "Ethnosemiotics: Some Personal and Theoretical Reflections." *Cultural Studies* 4, no. 1: 85–99.

Flores, Gonzalo. 1985. "Movimiento Regional Cruceño: Aproximación e Hipótesis." In *Crisis, Democracia y Conflicto Social*, edited by Roberto Laserna. La Paz: CERES.

Foguel, Ramón. 1986. "Las Invasiones de Tierra: Una Respuesta Campesina a la Crisis." In *Los Movimientos Sociales en Paraguay*, edited by Domingo Rivarola. Asunción, Paraguay: Centro Paraguayo de Estudios Sociológicos.

Foster, George. 1967. "What Is a Peasant?" In *Peasant Society*, edited by M. Diaz, G. Foster, and J. Potter. Boston, Mass.: Little, Brown.

Foucault, Michel. 1972. *The Archeology of Knowledge*. London: Harper Colophon.

————. 1977. *Discipline and Punish*. New York: Vintage Books.

————. 1979. *História da Sexualidade: A Vontade de Saber*. Vol. 1. Rio de Janeiro: Graal.

————. 1980. *Power/Knowledge*. New York: Pantheon Books.

Foweraker, Joe. 1990. "Popular Movements and Political Change in Mexico." In *Popular Movements and Political Change in Mexico*, edited by Joe Foweraker and Ann L. Craig. Boulder, Colo.: Lynne Rienner.

Foweraker, Joe, and Ann L. Craig, eds. 1990. *Popular Movements and Political Change in Mexico*. Boulder: Lynne Rienner.

Fraser, Arvonne. 1987. *The UN Decade for Women: Documents and Dialogue*. Boulder, Colo.: Westview Press.

Fraser, Nancy. 1989. *Unruly Practices: Power, Discourse and Gender in Contemporary Social Theory*. Minneapolis: University of Minnesota Press.

Friedmann, John. 1961. *Regional Development Policy: A Case Study of Venezuela*. Boston, Mass.: MIT Press.

Froebel, Folker. 1980. *The New International Division of Labor: Structural Unemployment in Industrialised Countries and in Industrialisation in Developing Countries*. Paris: Editions de la Maison des Sciences de l'Homme.

Fry, Peter. 1982a. "Da Hierarquia à Igualdade: A Construção da Homossexualidade no Brasil." In *Para o Inglês Ver*, by Peter Fry. Rio de Janeiro: Zahar.

———. 1982b. *Para o Inglês Ver*. Rio de Janeiro: Zahar.

Fuentes, Annette, and Barbara Ehrenreich. 1983. *Women in the Global Factory*. Boston, Mass.: South End Press.

Gaiger, Luís Inácio. 1987. *Agentes Religiosos e Camponeses Sem Terra no Sul do Brasil*. Petrópolis, Brazil: Vozes.

Gallón Giraldo, Gustavo, ed. 1989. *Entre Movimientos y Caudillos*. Bogotá: CINEP/CEREC.

García, María del Pilar. 1986. "La Experiencia Venezolana como un Polo de Desarrollo: ¿Un Fracaso del Modelo Teórico, de la Institución Planificadora o del Estilo de Planificación?" *Revista de la Sociedad Venezolana de Planificación*, no. 162.

———. 1987. "Impactos Socio-Económicos, Políticos y Espaciales de los Grandes Inversiones Mineroindustriales en América Latina: Aproximación Teórico-metodológica." *Revista Interamericana de Planificación* 21, no. 81.

———. 1988. *Viabilidad Política de las Demandas y Propuestas Ambientalistas del Estado y la Sociedad Civil en Venezuela*. Caracas: ILDIS.

———. 1990a. "Actores y Movimientos Sociales en los Grandes Proyectos de Inversión Minero-Industriales en América Latina: Hipótesis para la Estructuración de la Organización Social." *Revista Interaméricana de Planificación* 23, no. 89.

———. 1990b. "Crisis y Conflictos Socioeconómicos en la Venezuela Post-Saudita: Hacia una Redefinición de los Actores, los Roles y las Demandas Sociales." In *Consecuencias Regionales de la Restructuración de los Mercados Mundiales: Políticas Alternativas Relativas a la Escala Regional y Local*, edited by F. Ebert. Buenos Aires: CEUR.

———. 1991a. "Crisis, Estado y Sociedad Civil: Conflictos Socio-ambientales en Venezuela." In *Estado, Ambiente, y Sociedad Civil*, edited by María del Pilar García. Caracas: USB/CENDES.

———. 1991b. "La Estructuración del Movimiento Ambientales en Venezuela." In *Estado, Ambientes, y Sociedad Civil*, edited by M. P. García. Caracas: USB/CENDES.

———. 1991c. *Efectividad Simbolica, Identidad y Estrategia: Treinta Años del Movimiento Ambientalista en Venezuela*. Caracas: USB.

———, ed. 1991. *Estado, Ambiente, y Sociedad Civil*. Caracas: USB/CENDES.

García Canclini, Néstor. 1990. *Culturas Híbridas. Estrategias para Entrar y Salir de la Modernidad*. Mexico D.F.: Grijalbo.

Gargallo, Francesca. 1987. "La Relación Entre Participación Política y Conciencia Feminista en las Militantes Salvadoreñas." *Cuadernos Americanos* Nueva Epoca 2 (April–May): 58–76.

Gargani, A. 1983. *Crisis Della Ragioni*. Turin: Einaudi.

Garretón, Manuel Antonio. 1989. "Popular Mobilization and the Military Regime in Chile: The Complexities of the Invisible Transition." In *Power and Popular Protest*, edited by Susan Eckstein. Berkeley: University of California Press.

Geertz, Clifford. 1983. *Local Knowledge*. New York: Basic Books.

Gentleman, Judith, Peter Smith, and Wayne Cornelius, eds. 1989. *Mexico's Alternative Political Futures*. Monograph series. La Jolla: University of California, San Diego, Center for U.S.-Mexican Studies.

Gerez-Fernandez, Patricia. 1990. "Movimientos y Luchas Ecologistas en México." Manuscript.

Germani, Gino. 1962. *Política y Sociedad en una Epoca de Transición*. Buenos Aires: Paidós.

Gilbert, Alan, ed. 1989. *Housing and Land in Urban Mexico*. Monograph series. La Jolla: University of California, San Diego, Center for U.S.-Mexican Studies.

Gillespie, C. 1984. "Electoral Stability, Party System Transformation and Redemocratization: The Uruguayan Case in Comparative Perspective." Paper presented at the conference on "Recent Electoral Changes in the Americas," February 21-22.

Gillespie, Charles. 1985. "Desentrañando la Crisis de la Democracia Uruguaya." In *Uruguay y la Democracia*, edited by C. Gillespie et al. Montevideo: Ediciones de la Banda Oriental.

Gillespie, C., L. Goodman, J. Rial, and P. Winn, eds. 1985. *Uruguay y la Democracia*. Montevideo: Ediciones de la Banda Oriental.

Gilroy, Paul. 1987. *There Ain't No Black in the Union Jack*. London: Hutchison.

Giraldo, Javier, ed. *Movimientos Sociales ante la Crisis en Sudamérica*. Bogotá: CINEP.

Giraldo, Javier, and Santiago Camargo. 1986. "El Movimiento Cívico en Colombia." In *Movimientos Sociales ante la Crisis en Sudamérica*, edited by Javier Giraldo. Bogotá: CINEP.

Gitlin, Todd. 1987. *The Sixties: Years of Hope, Days of Rage*. New York: Bantam Books.

Gitlitz, John. 1985. "Twenty Years of Pastoral Experimentation: The Option for the Poor in Bambamarca, Peru." Columbia-NYU Latin American, Caribbean, and Iberian Occasional Papers, New York.

Gitlitz, John, and Telmo Rojas. 1983. "Peasant Vigilante Committees in Northern Peru." *Journal of Latin American Studies* 15, no. 1: 163-167.

Goetz, Anne Marie. 1988. "Feminism and the Limits of the Claim to Know: Contradictions in the Feminist Approach to Women in Development." *Millenium* 17, no. 3: 477-496.

Gohn, M.G.M. 1985. *A Força da Periferia*. Petrópolis, Brazil: Vozes.

Goldberg, Anette. 1982a. "Feminismo em Regime Autoritário: A Experiência do Movimento de Mulheres no Rio de Janeiro." Paper presented at the twelfth Congresso Mundial da Associação Internacional de Ciência Política, Rio de Janeiro, August 9-14.

————. 1982b. "Os Movimentos de Liberação de Mulher na França e na Italia (1970-1980): Primeiros Elementos para Um Estudo Comparativo do Novo Femenismo na Europa e no Brasil." In *O Lugar de Mulher*, edited by M. T. Luz. Rio de Janeiro: Graal.

Goldrich, Daniel. 1970. "Political Organization and the Politicization of the Poblador." *Comparative Political Studies* 3, no. 2 (July): 176-202.

Gomes, José. 1985. "Religião e Política: Os Pentecostais no Recife." Ph.D. diss., Federal University of Pernambuco.

Gomez, Luis. 1991. "Estado, Ambiente, y Sociedad Civil en Venezuela: Convergencias y Divergencias." In *Estado, Ambiente, y Sociedad Civil*, edited by M. P. García. Caracas: USB/CENDES.

————, ed. 1987. *Crisis y Movimientos Sociales en Venzuela*. Caracas: Tropycos.

González, L. E. 1982. "O Movimento Negro na Ultima Década." In *O Lugar do Negro*, edited by L. E. González and C. H. Hasenbalg. Rio de Janeiro: Marco Zero.

González, L. E., and C. H. Hasenbalg, eds. 1982. *O Lugar do Negro*. Rio de Janeiro: Marco Zero.

González, Luis. 1985a. "El Sistema de Partidos y las Perspectives de la Democracia Uruguya." Documento de Trabajo #90.

————. 1985b. "Transición y Restauración Democratica." In *Uruguay y la Democracia*, edited by C. Gillespie et al. Montevideo: Ediciones de la Banda Oriental.

González, Maruja, S. Cecilia Loria, and Itziar Lozano. 1988. *Utopía y Lucha Feminista en América Latina y El Caribe*. Mexico D.F.: Comunicación Intercambio y Desarrollo Humano en

América Latina (CIDHAL), Equipo de Mujeres en Acción Solidaria (EMAS), and Grupo de Educación Popular con Mujeres (GEM).

González Bombal, M. I. 1987. "Madres de Plaza de Mayo: Un Signo en la Historia?" *David y Goliath*, no. 52.

González Bombal, M. I., and V. Palermo. 1987. "La Política Local." In *Movimientos Sociales y Democracia Emergente*, edited by E. Jelin. Buenos Aires: Centro Editor de América Latina.

González Casanova, Pablo. 1986. *La Hegemonía del Pueblo y la Lucha Centroaméricana*. Managua, Nicaragua: Editorial Nueva.

Gorriti, Gustavo. 1990. *Sendero*. Lima: Apoyo.

GSI (Grupos de Solidaridad con los Indígenas). 1982. "Pueblo Colombiano, Pueblos Indígenas: Exterminio o Convivencia?" *Carta a la Comisión de Paz*. Grupos de Solidaridad con los Indígenas (GSI).

———. 1986. "Antecedentes Sobre el Movimiento Indígena y la Oposición Armada en el Cauca." In *Más Allá de la Denuncia: A Dónde Va la Violencia Revolucionaria en el Cauca*. Grupos de Solidaridad con los Indígenas (GSI).

GSP (Grupo de Solidaridad de Pasto). 1982. *Tercer Encuentro de Autoridades Indígenas y Primer Encuentro de Autoridades Indígenas y Autoridad Blanca*. Pasto, Colombia: Grupo de Solidaridad de Pasto (GSP).

GSPC (Grupos de Solidaridad de Pasto y Cali). 1984. *¿Temor o Solidaridad? La Masacre de Caloto y la Nueva Violencia en el Cauca (a propósito de López Adentro)*. Grupos de Solidaridad de Pasto y Cali (GSPC).

———. 1986. *Más Allá de la Denuncia, a Dónde Va la Violencia Revolucionaria en el Cauca*. Cali, Colombia: Grupos de Solidaridad con los Indígenas (GSI).

Gudeman, Stephen, and Alberto Rivera. 1990. *Conversations in Colombia. The Domestic Economy in Life and Text*. Cambridge: Cambridge University Press.

Guha, Ranajit. 1983. *Elementary Aspects of Peasant Insurgency in Colonial India*. Delhi: Oxford University Press.

———. 1988a. "On Some Aspects of the Historiography of Colonial India." In *Selected Subaltern Studies*, edited by R. Guha and G. Spivak. Delhi: Oxford University Press.

———. 1988b. "The Prose of Counter-Insurgency." In *Selected Subaltern Studies*, edited by R. Guha and G. Spivak. Delhi: Oxford University Press.

Guha, Ranajit, and Gayatri Spivak, eds. 1988. *Selected Subaltern Studies*. Delhi: Oxford University Press.

Guimarães, Almir. 1978. *Comunidade Eclesial de Base no Brasil: Uma Nova Maneira de Ser Igreja*. Petrópolis, Brazil: Vozes.

Guimarães, C. D. 1977. "O Homosexual Visto por Entendidos." Master's thesis, Museo Nacional, Rio de Janeiro.

Gunder Frank, Andre, and Marta Fuentes. 1987a. "Nine Theses on Social Movements Internationally." *Newsletter of International Labour Studies*, no. 34 (July).

———. 1987b. "Para una Nueva Lectura de los Movimientos Sociales." *Nueva Sociedad*, no. 93.

Gutierrez, Gustavo. 1973. *A Theology of Liberation*. Maryknoll, N.Y.: Orbis.

———. 1980. "A Irrupção do Pobre na América Latína e as Comunidades Cristãs Populares." In *A Igreja que Surge da Base: Eclesiologia das Comunidades Cristãs de Base*, edited by Sérgio Torres. São Paulo: Paulinas.

Guzman, Virginia, María Gabriela Vega, and Nora Galer, eds. 1985. *Mujer y Desarollo*. Lima: Centro de la Mujer Flora Tristán.

Haber, Paul L. 1990. "Cárdenas, Salinas and Urban Movements in Mexico: The Case of El Comité de Defensa Popular General Francisco Villa, de Durango." Manuscript.

Habermas, J. 1981. "New Social Movements." *Telos*, no. 49: 33–37.

Hall, Stuart. 1991. "Brave New World." *Socialist Review* 21, no. 1: 57–64.

Hänninen, S., and L. Paldán, eds. 1984. *Rethinking Marx*. Berlin: Argument-Sonderband AS 109.

Haraway, Donna. 1985. "A Manifesto for Cyborgs: Science, Technology and Socialist Feminism in the 1980s." *Socialist Review*, no. 80: 65–107.

Harding, Sandra. 1987. *Feminism and Methodology*. Bloomington: Indiana University Press.

Hardy, Clarisa, and L. Raseto. 1984. "Nuevos Actores y Prácticas Populares: Derrotas a la Concentración." Manuscript, Santiago.

Hartmann, Heidi. 1981. "The Unhappy Marriage of Marxism and Feminism: Towards a More Progressive Union." In *Women and Revolution: A Discussion of the Unhappy Marriage of Marxism and Feminism*, edited by Lydia Sargent. Boston, Mass.: South End Press.

———. 1987. "The Family as the Locus of Gender, Class and Political Struggle: The Example of Housework." In *Feminism and Methodology*, edited by Sandra Harding. Bloomington: Indiana University Press.

Harvey, David. 1989. *The Condition of Postmodernity*. Oxford: Basil Blackwell.

———. 1991. "Flexibility: Threat or Opportunity?" *Socialist Review* 21, no. 1: 57–64.

Hebdige, Dick. 1986. "Postmodernism of 'the Other Side.'" *Journal of Communication* 12, no. 2: 78–98.

Hegedus, Z. 1989. "Social Movements and Social Change in Self-Creative Society." *International Sociology* 4, no. 1: 19–36.

Hellman, Judith Adler. 1983a. *Mexico in Crisis*. New York: Holmes and Meier.

———. 1983b. "The Role of Ideology in Peasant Politics." *Journal of Interamerican Studies and World Affairs* 25, no. 1: 3–29.

———. 1987. *Journeys Among Women: Feminism in Five Italian Cities*. New York: Oxford University Press.

———. 1988. "Women's Organizations and Politics in the Italian Republic: Continuity and Change in the Nature of Women's Collective Action." Paper presented at the Conference on Culture and Politics in the Italian Republic, 1948–1988, Bellagio, Italy, July 4–8.

Hellman, Stephen. 1987. "Feminism and the Model of Militancy in an Italian Communist Federation: Challenges to the Old Style Politics." In *The Women's Movements of the United States and Western Europe: Consciousness, Political Opportunity, and Public Policy*, edited by Mary Fainsod Katzenstein and Carol McClurg Mueller. Philadelphia, Pa.: Temple University Press.

Hernandez, Luis. 1981. *Las Luchas Magisteriales, 1979–1981*. Mexico, D.F.: Editorial Machehual.

———. 1986. "The SNTE and the Teachers' Movement, 1982–1984." In *The Mexican Left, the Popular Movements, and the Politics of Austerity*, edited by Barry Carr and Ricardo Anzaldúa Montoya. La Jolla: University of California, San Diego, Center for U.S.-Mexican Studies.

Hernández S., Ricardo. 1988. *Asamblea de Barrios*. Mexico D.F.: Información Obrera y Equipo Pueblo.

Herzog, Lawrence A. 1990. *Where North Meets South*. Austin: University of Texas Press.

Hewitt, Ted. 1986. "Strategies for Social Change Employed by the Comunidades Eclesiais de Base (CEBs) in the Archdiocese of São Paulo." *Journal for the Scientific Study of Religion*, no. 25: 16–30.

———. 1987a. "The Influence of Social Class Activity on Preferences of Comunidades Eclesiais de Base (CEBs) in the Archdiocese of São Paulo." *Journal of Latin American Studies*, no. 19: 141–156.

———. 1987b. "Strategies for Social Change Employed by the Comunidades Eclesiais de Base (CEBs) in the Archdiocese of São Paulo." *Journal for the Scientific Study of Religion*, no. 25: 16–30.

———. 1990. "Religion and the Consolidation of Democracy in Brazil: The Role of the Comunidades Eclesiais de Base." *Sociological Analysis* 51, no. 2: 139–153.

Hirschman, A. 1984. *Getting Ahead Collectively: Grassroots Experiences in Latin America*. New York: Pergamon Press.

Hodges, Donald C. 1974. *The Latin American Revolution*. New York: William Morris.

Holanda, H. B. 1980. *Impressões da Viagem*. São Paulo: Brasiliense.

Hoornaert, Eduardo. 1978. "Comunidades Eclesiais de Base: Dez Anos de Experiência." *Revista Eclesiástica Brasileira*, no. 38: 474–502.

Houtart, François. 1979a. "Religion et Lutte des Classes en Amérique Latine." *Social Compass*, no. 26: 195–236.

——— . 1979b. "Religion et Champs Politique: Cadre Théorique pour l'Etude des Sociétés Capitalistes Péripheriques." *Social Compass*, no. 26: 265–272.

Huber, Ludwig, and Karin Apel. 1990. "Comunidades y Rondas Campesinas en Piura." *Bulletine Institute Frances d'Etudes Andines* 19, no. 1: 165–182.

Hunt, Lynn. 1984. *Politics, Culture, and Class in the French Revolution*. Berkeley: University of California Press.

Illich, Ivan. 1977. *Toward a History of Needs*. Berkeley, Calif.: Heyday Books.

——— . 1982. *Gender*. Berkeley, Calif.: Heyday Books.

Instituto Nacional de Estadística, Geografía e Informática. 1985. *Estadísticas Históricas de México*. Mexico, D.F.: Secretaría de Programación y Presupuesto, Dirección General de Estadística.

——— . 1990. *XI Censo General de Población y Vivienda: Resultados Preliminares*. Mexico D.F.: Secretaría de Programación y Presupuesto, Dirección General de Estadística.

Inter-American Development Bank. 1990. *Economic and Social Progress in Latin America*. Washington, D.C.: Inter-American Development Bank.

ISIS International. 1988. *Mujeres, Crisis y Movimiento: América Latina y el Caribe*. Santiago: ISIS International.

——— , ed. 1986. *The Latin American Women's Movement: Reflections and Action*. Santiago: ISIS International.

Jacobi, Pedro. 1980. "Movimentos Sociais Urbanos no Brasil." *BIB—Boletim Informativo Bibliográfico*, no. 9.

——— . 1985. "Políticas Públicas de Saneamento Básico e Saúde e Reivindicações Sociais no Município de São Paulo." Ph.D diss., Universidade de São Paulo.

——— . 1988a. "Movimentos Sociais e Estado: Efeitos Político-Instituciones de Ação Coletiva." *Ciências Sociais Hoje*, pp. 290–310.

——— . 1988b. "Movimentos Reinvindicatorios Urbanos, Estado e Cultura Política: Inflexão em Torno da Ação Coletiva e Dos Seus Efeitos Político—Institucionais no Brasil." Paper presented at Universidade Federal de Santa Catarina, Porto Alegre, Brazil.

——— . 1989. "Atores Sociais e Estado." *Espaço e Debates*, no. 26: 10–21.

Jaquette, Jane S., ed. 1989. *The Women's Movement in Latin America: Feminism and the Transition to Democracy*. Boston, Mass.: Unwin Hyman.

Jelin, Elizabeth, 1986. "Otros Silencios, Otras Voces: El Tiempo de la Democratización en Argentina." In *Los Movimientos Sociales ante la Crisis*, edited by Fernando Calderón. Buenos Aires: Universidad de las Naciones Unidas.

——— . 1987. "Movimientos Sociales y Consolidación Democrática en la Argentina Actual." In *Movimientos Sociales y Democracia Emergente*, edited by E. Jelin. Buenos Aires: Centro Editor de América Latina.

——— . 1990. "Citizenship and Identity: Final Reflections." In *Women and Social Change in Latin America*, edited by E. Jelin. London: United Nations Research Institute for Social Development and Zed Books.

——— , ed. 1985. *Los Nuevos Movimientos Sociales*. Buenos Aires: Centro Editor de América Latina.

——— , ed. 1987a. *Cuidadanía e Identidad: Las Mujeres en los Movimientos Sociales Latino-Americanos*. Geneva: UNRISD.

——— , ed. 1987b. *Movimientos Sociales y Democracia Emergente*. Buenos Aires: Centro Editor de América Latina.

———— , ed. 1990. *Women and Social Change in Latin America.* London: United Nations Research Institute for Social Development and Zed Books.

Jelin, Elizabeth, and Pablo Vila. 1987. *Podría Ser Yo: Los Sectores Populares Urbanos en Imagen y Palabra.* Buenos Aires: CEDES/Ediciones de la Flor.

Jenkins, J. C. 1983. "Resource Moblization Theory and the Study of Social Movements." *Annual Review of Sociology,* no. 9: 527–553.

Jimeno, M. 1985. "Cauca: Las Armas de lo Sagrado." In *Estado y Minorías Etnicas en Colombia,* edited by M. Jimeno and A. Triana. Bogotá: Cuadernos del Jaguar/FUNCOL.

Jimeno, M., and A. Triana, eds. 1985. *Estado y Minorías Etnicas en Colombia.* Bogotá: Cuadernos del Jaguar/FUNCOL.

Karner, Hartmut. 1983. "Los Movimientos Sociales: Revolución de lo Cotidiano." *Nueva Sociedad,* no. 64 (January/February): 30–31.

Katzenstein, Mary Fainsod, and Carol McClurg, eds. 1987. *The Women's Movements of the United States and Western Europe: Consciousness, Political Opportunity, and Public Policy.* Philadelphia, Pa.: Temple University Press.

Kauffman, L. A. 1990. "The Anti-Politics of Identity." *Socialist Review* 20, no. 1: 67–80.

Kirkwood, Julieta. 1980. *La Formación de la Conciencia Feminista y los Partidos.* Santiago: FLACSO.

———— . 1981. *Chile: La Mujer en la Formulación Política,* Documento de Trabajo no. 109, FLACSO.

———— . 1983. *El Feminismo como Negación del Autoritarismo.* Santiago: Programa FLACSO, Materia de discusión, no. 52.

———— . 1986. *Ser Política en Chile: Las Feministas y los Partidos.* Santiago: Facultad Latinoaméricana de Ciencias Sociales.

———— . 1987. *Feminarios.* Santiago: Ediciones Documentas.

Klandermans, Bert, and Sidney Tarrow. 1988. "Mobilization into Social Movements: Synthesizing European and American Approaches." In *International Social Movements Research,* edited by Hanspeter Kriesi, Sidney Tarrow, and Bert Klandermans. London: JAI Press.

Kothari, R. 1984. "The Non-Party Political Process." *Economic and Political Weekly* 19, no. 5: 216–223.

Kowarick, Lucio. 1985. "The Pathways to Encounter: Reflections on the Social Struggle in São Paulo." In *New Social Movements and the State in Latin America,* edited by David Slater. Amsterdam: CEDLA.

———— . 1987. "Movimentos Urbanos no Brasil Contemporâneo: Uma Análise da Literatura." *Revista Brasileira de Ciências Sociais* 1, no. 3.

Kriesi, Hanspeter, Sidney Tarrow, and Bert Klandermans, eds. 1988. *International Social Movements Research.* London: JAI Press.

Krischke, Paulo, and Scott Mainwaring, eds. 1986. *A Igreja nas Bases em Tempo de Transição (1974–1985).* Porto Alegre, Brazil: LPM.

Laclau, Ernesto. 1985. "New Social Movements and the Plurality of the Social." In *New Social Movements and the State in Latin America,* edited by David Slater. Amsterdam: CEDLA.

———— . 1988. "Politics and the Limits of Modernity." In *Universal Abandon: The Politics of Postmodernism,* edited by Andrew Ross. Minneapolis: University of Minnesota Press.

Laclau, Ernesto, and Chantal Mouffe. 1985. *Hegemony and Socialist Strategy: Towards a Radical Democratic Politics.* London: Verso.

———— . 1987. "Post-Marxism Without Apologies." *New Left Review,* no. 166 (November/December): 79–106.

Lamas, Marta, ed. 1990. *Debate Feminista.* Vol. 1. Mexico D.F.: n.p.

Lampe Romero, Armando. 1987. "Los Nuevos Movimientos Religiosos en el Caribe." In *Movimientos Sociales y Crisis en el Caribe,* edited by A. Lampe Romero. Santo Domingo: Instituto Tecnológico de Santo Domingo.

——, ed. 1987. *Movimientos Sociales y Crisis en el Caribe,* Santo Domingo: Instituto Tecnológico de Santo Domingo.

Laserna, Roberto, ed. 1985. *Crisis, Democracia y Conflicto Social.* La Paz: CERES.

Lau, Ana Javier. 1987. *La Nueva Ola del Feminismo en México.* Mexico D.F.: Planeta.

Leacock, Eleanor, and Helen I. Safa, eds. 1986. *Women's Work.* South Hadley, Mass.: Bergin and Garvey.

Lechner, Norbert. 1982. *¿Qué Significa Hacer Política?* Lima: DESCO.

——. 1988. *Los Patios Interiores de la Democracia: Subjetividad y Política.* Santiago: FLACSO.

——. 1990. "De la Revolución a la Democracia." In *Debate Feminista,* vol. 1, edited by Marta Lamas. Mexico D.F.: n.p., pp. 29–46.

Leff, Enrique. 1986. *Ecología Política y Capital: Hacia una Perspectiva Ambiental del Desarrollo.* Mexico D.F.: UNAM.

——. 1991. "El Movimiento Ecologista-Ambientalista en México." In *Estado, Ambiente, y Sociedad Civil,* edited by M. P. García. Caracas: USB/CENDES.

Leiva, Fernando Ignacio, and James Petras. 1986. "Chile's Poor in the Struggle for Democracy." *Latin American Perspectives* 13, no. 4: 5–25.

León, Magdalena, ed. 1982. *Sociedad, Subordinación y Feminismo,* Bogotá: ACEP.

Lindahl, G. 1962. *Uruguay's New Path.* Stockholm: Institute of Ibero-American Studies.

LNR (Libro Negro de la Represión). 1980. *Libro Negro de la Represión, 1958–1980.* Bogotá: FICA.

Lomnitz, Larissa. 1975. *Como Sobreviven los Marginados.* Mexico D.F.: Siglo XXI.

Lowy, Michael. 1982. *El Marxismo en América Latina (de 1909 a Nuestros Días).* Mexico D.F.: Era.

——. 1986. "Mass Organization, Party and State: Democracy in the Transition to Socialism." In *Transition and Development: Problems of Third World Socialism,* edited by Richard R. Fagen, Carmen Diana Deere, and José Luis Coraggio. New York: Monthly Review Press.

Lozano, Itziar, and Maruja Gonzales. 1986. *Feminismo y Movimiento Popular: ¿Desencuentro or Relación Histórica?* Mexico D.F.: Equipo de Mujeres Solidarieas: Equipo de Mujeres Solidarias.

Lugones, María, and Vicky Spelman. 1983. "Have We Got a Theory for You!" *Women's Studies International Forum* 6, no. 6: 573–581.

Luz, M. T., ed. 1982. *O Lugar de Mulher.* Rio de Janeiro: Graal.

Macedo, Carmen Cinira. 1986. *Tempo de Gênesis: O Povo das Comunidades Eclesiais de Base.* São Paulo: Brasiliense.

Machado da Silva, L. A., et al. 1983. *Movimentos Sociais Urbanos, Minorias Étnicas e Outros Estudos.* Brasília: ANPOCS.

MacRae, Edward. 1990. *A Construção da Igualdade.* Campinas: Unicamp.

Mainwaring, Scott. 1986a. *The Catholic Church and Politics in Brazil, 1916–1985.* Stanford, Calif.: Stanford University Press.

——. 1986b. "A Igreja Católica e o Movimento Popular: Nova Iguaçu, 1974–1985." In *A Igreja nas Bases em Tempo de Transição,* edited by Paulo Krischke and Scott Mainwaring. Porto Alegre, Brazil: LPM.

——. 1987. "Urban Popular Movements, Identity and Democratization in Brazil." *Comparative Political Studies* 20, no. 2: 131–159.

——. 1988. "Political Parties and Democratization in Brazil and the Southern Cone." *Comparative Politics* 21, no. 1: 97–117.

Mainwaring, Scott, and Eduardo Viola. 1984. "New Social Movements, Political Culture, and Democracy: Brazil and Argentina in the 1980's." *Telos,* no. 61: 17–52.

Mancina, Claudia, et al. 1990. "Il PCI e le Differenze fra le Donne." *Reti,* no. 1 (February): 5–40.

Mani, Lata. 1989. "Multiple Mediations: Feminist Scholarship in the Age of Multinational Reception." *Inscriptions,* no. 5: 1–24.

Maravall, Jose. 1978. *Dictatorship and Political Dissent.* London: Tavistock.

Marglin, Stephen. 1990. "Toward the Decolonization of the Mind." In *Dominating Knowledge*, edited by Frédérique and Stephen Marglin. Oxford: Clarendon Press.

Mariátegui, José Carlos. 1968. *Siete Ensayos de Interpretación de la Realidad Peruana*. Lima: Amauta.

Mariz, Cecilia. 1989. "Religion and Coping with Poverty in Brazil." Ph.D. diss., Boston University.

Marley, Bob. 1980. "Redemption Song." In *Survival*. Island Records.

Marsiglia, J., J. Piedra Cueva, and P. Rodé. 1985a. "Experiencias Recientes de Movilización Urbana en las Areas de la Salud, Nutrición y Organización Barrial." In *Movimientos Sociales en el Uruguay de Hoy*, edited by C. Filgueira. Montevideo: CLACSO/CIESU/Ediciones de la Banda Oriental.

―――. 1985b. "Movimientos Sociales Urbanos en Montevideo." *Cuadernos del Claeh*, no. 33: 37–57.

Martin, Biddy. 1988. "Feminism, Criticism, and Foucault." In *Feminisms and Foucault: Reflections on Resistance*, edited by Irene Diamond and Lee Quinby. Boston, Mass.: Northeastern University.

Martínez, Carlos, and Edgar Verela, eds. 1989. *Derechos Humanos y Modernidad*. Cali, Colombia: Personería Municipal.

Martorelli, H. 1986. "Políticas Sociales, Participación Ciudadana, y Acción Municipal." Documento de Trabajo #34. Montevideo: CIEDUR.

Massolo, Alejandra. 1986. "'Que el Gobierno Entienda, lo Primero es la Vivienda!' La Organización de los Damnificados." *Revista Mexicana de Sociología* 48, no. 2: 195–238.

Mattelart, Michele. 1980. "Chile: The Feminine Version of the Coup d'Etat." In *Sex and Class in Latin America*, edited by June Nash and Helen Safa. Brooklyn, N.Y.: J. F. Bergin.

Mayer, Margit. 1991. "Politics in the Post-Fordist City." *Socialist Review* 21, no. 1: 105–124.

McAdam, Doug. 1982. *Political Process and the Development of Black Insurgency, 1930–1970*. Chicago, Ill.: University of Chicago Press.

McCarthy, J. D., and M. N. Zald, eds. 1987. *Social Movements in an Organizational Society: Collected Essays*. New Brunswick, N.J.: Transaction Books.

―――. 1988. "Social Movements." In *Handbook of Sociology*, edited by Neil Smelser. Beverly Hills, Calif.: Sage Publications.

Medellín Solidarity Group. 1981. "The Struggle of the Guambiano People." Slide show.

Melucci, Alberto. 1977. *Sistema Político, Partiti e Movimenti Sociali*. Milan: Feltrinelli.

―――. 1981. "Ten Hypotheses for the Analysis of New Social Movements." In *Contemporary Italian Sociology*, edited by D. Pinto. Cambridge: Cambridge University Press.

―――. 1984. "An End to Social Movements?" *Social Science Information* 23, no. 4/5: 819–835.

―――. 1985. "The Symbolic Challenge of Contemporary Social Movements." *Social Research* 52, no. 4: 789–816.

―――. 1988a. "Getting Involved: Identity and Mobilization in Social Movements." In *International Social Movement Research: From Structure to Action–Comparing Social Movements Research Across Cultures*, vol. 1, edited by Hansperter Kriesi, Sidney Tarrow, and Bert Klandermans. London: JAI Press.

―――. 1988b. "Social Movements and the Democratization of Everyday Life." In *Civil Society and the State: New European Perspectives*, edited by John Deane. London: Verso.

―――. 1989. *Nomads of the Present: Social Movements and Individual Needs in Contemporary Society*. Philadelphia, Pa.: Temple University Press.

Mesters, Carlos. 1986. *Círculos Bíblicos: Guia do Dirigente*. Petrópolis, Brazil: Vozes.

Meza Ponce, Armando. 1984. "El Movimiento Urbano Popular de Durango." *Nueva Antropología* 6, no. 24: 89–98.

Michels, Roberto. 1959. *Political Parties*. New York: Dover.

Middlebrook, Kevin. 1986. "Political Liberalization in an Authoritarian Regime: The Case of Mexico." In *Transitions from Authoritarian Rule: Latin America*, edited by Philippe Schmitter,

Laurence Whitehead, and Guillermo O'Donnell. Baltimore, Md.: Johns Hopkins University Press.

————. 1989. "The CTM and the Future of Government-Labor Relations." In *Mexico's Alternative Political Futures*, edited by Judith Gentleman, Peter Smith, and Wayne Cornelius. La Jolla: University of California, San Diego, Center for U.S.-Mexican Studies.

Mies, Maria. 1986. *Patriarchy and Accumulation on a World Scale*. London: Zed Books.

Mires, Francisco. 1987. "Continuidad y Ruptura en el Discurso Político." *Nueva Sociedad*, no. 91: 129–140.

Misztal, Bronislaw. 1991. "One Movement, Two Interpretations. The Orange Alternative Movement in Poland." *British Journal of Sociology*, no. 2.

————, ed. 1985. *Poland After Solidarity. Social Movements Versus the State*. New Brunswick, N.J.: Transaction Books.

————, ed. 1988. *Social Movements as a Factor for Change in the Contemporary World*. Greenwich, Conn.: JAI Press.

Moctezuma, Pedro. 1984. "El Movimiento Urbano Popular en México." *Nueva Antropología* 6, no. 24: 61–87.

————. 1986. "La Coordinadora Nacional del Movimiento Urbano Popular en el Valle de México." In *Los Movimientos Sociales en el Valle de México*, edited by Jorge Alonso. Mexico D.F.: Centro de Investigaciones y Estudios Superiores en Antropología Social—Ediciones de la Casa Chata.

————. 1988. "Apuntes Sobre la Autogestión y el Movimiento Urbano Popular." Paper presented to the Foro Sobre Movimientos Sociales y Autogestión, Oaxtepec, Morelos, September.

Moises, J. A., et al. 1982. *Cidade, Povo e Poder*. Rio de Janeiro: Coleção CEDEC/Paz e Terra.

Molano, Alfredo. 1989. *Siguiendo el Corte. Relatos de Guerras y de Tierras*. Bogotá: El Ancora Editores.

————. 1989. *Yo le Digo una de las Cosas. . . .* Bogotá: FEN y Araracuara.

Molina, Natacha. N.d. "Movimiento de Mujeres en Chile, 1983–1986." Manuscript.

————. 1986. *Lo Feminino y lo Democrático en el Chile de Hoy*. Santiago: Vector, Centro de Estudios Económicos y Sociales.

Molyneux, Maxine. 1982. "Socialist Societies Old and New: Progress Toward Emancipation?" *Monthly Review* 34, no. 3: 56–100.

————. 1986. "Mobilization Without Emancipation?: Women's Interests, State and Revolution." In *Transition and Development: Problems of Third World Socialism*, edited by Richard R. Fagen, Carmen Diana Deere, and José Luis Coraggio. New York: Monthly Review Press.

————. 1988. "The Politics of Abortion in Nicaragua." *Feminist Review*, no. 29 (Spring): 114–132.

Monroy Limón, Lilia. 1987. *Memorias del Taller: Mujer, Centroamericana, Violencia y Guerra*. Taxco, Guerrero, Mexico: Fourth Encuentro Feminista Latinoamericano y del Caribe.

Montaldo, Graciela. 1991. "Estrategias del Fin de Siglo." *Nueva Sociedad*, no. 116: 75–87.

Moraes, Maria Lygia Quartim de. 1985. *Mulheres em Movimento*. São Paulo: Nobel and CECF.

Morin, Edgar. 1980. *La Méthode*. Paris: Seuil.

Morris, Aldon, and Cedric Herring. 1987. "Theory and Research in Social Movements: A Critical Review." *Annual Review of Political Science*, no. 2: 137–198.

Moschkovich, Judit N., María Cora, and Sonia E. Alvarez. 1986. "Our Feminisms." *Connexions*, no. 19 (Winter).

Moser, Caroline. 1987. "The Experience of Poor Women in Guayaquil." In *Sociology of "Developing" Societies: Latin America*, edited by E. Archetti. New York: Monthly Review Press.

————. 1989a. "The Impact of Recession and Structural Adjustment Policies at the Micro-Level: Low-Income Women and Their Households in Guayaquil, Ecuador." Paper prepared for UNICEF-Ecuador, January.

————. 1989b. "Gender Planning in the Third World: Meeting Practical and Strategic Gender Needs." *World Development* 17, no. 11: 1799–1825.

————. 1989c. "Changing Policy Approaches to Low-Income Third World Women for Gender Planning." Paper presented at the Association of Women in Development conference on "Development Challenge for the 1990's: The Global Empowerment of Women," Washington, D.C., November 17–19.

Mouffe, Chantal. 1984. "Towards a Theoretical Interpretation of New Social Movements." In *Rethinking Marx*, edited by S. Hänninen and L. Paldán. Berlin: Argument-Sonderband AS 109.

————. 1988a. "Hegemony and New Political Subjects: Towards a New Concept of Democracy." In *Marxism and the Interpretation of Culture*, edited by C. Nelson and L. Grossberg. Urbana: University of Illinois Press.

————. 1988b. "Radical Democracy: Modern or Postmodern." In *Universal Abandon? The Politics of Postmodernism*, edited by Andrew Ross. Minneapolis: University of Minnesota Press.

Moulián, Tomas. 1982. "Evolución de la Izquierda Chilena: La Influencia del Marxismo." In *Qué Significa Hacer Política*, edited by Norbert Lechner. Lima: DESCO.

Movimiento de Autoridades Indígenas and Comisión Andina de Juristas. 1988. *Justicia y Hermandad: Debate CRIC-Movimiento de Autoridades Indígenas del Suroccidente.* Lima: Comisión 5 del Congreso de Toez.

Mueller, Adele. 1986. "The Bureaucratization of Feminist Knowledge: The Case of Women in Development." *Resources for Feminist Research* 15, no. 1: 3–6.

————. 1991. "In and Against Development: Feminists Confront Development on Its Own Ground." Manuscript.

Munck, Gerardo. 1990. "Identity and Ambiguity in Democratic Struggles." In *Popular Movements and Political Change in Mexico*, edited by Joe Foweraker and Ann Craig. Boulder, Colo.: Lynne Rienner.

Munck, Ronaldo. 1990. "Farewell to Socialism? A Comment on Recent Debates." *Latin American Perspectives* 17 (2): 113–121.

Murguialday, Clara. 1989. "Una Brecha en el Muro del Machismo: Diez Anos de Lucha de las Mujeres Nicaraguenses." *Terra Nuova Forum*, no. 13: 9–65.

————. 1990. *Nicaragua, Revolución y Feminismo, 1977–1989.* Madrid: Editorial Revolución.

Nandy, Ashis. 1983. *The Intimate Enemy: Loss and Recovery of Self Under Colonialism.* Delhi: Oxford University Press.

————. 1989. "Shamans, Savages and the Wilderness: On the Audibility of Dissent and the Future of Civilizations." *Alternatives* 14, no. 3: 263–278.

Nash, June. 1990. "Women in the World Capitalist Crisis." *Gender and Society*, no. 4 (September): 338–353.

Nash, June, and María P. Fernandez-Kelly, eds. 1983. *Women, Men and International Division of Labor.* Albany: State University of New York Press.

Nash, June, and Helen I. Safa, eds. 1980. *Sex and Class in Latin America.* Brooklyn, N.Y.: J. F. Bergin.

————. 1985. *Women and Change in Latin America.* South Hadley, Mass.: Bergin and Garvey.

Navarro, Marysa. 1982a. "El Primer Enceuntro de Latinoamérica y el Caribe." In *Sociedad, Subordinación y Feminismo*, edited by Magdalena Léon. Bogotá: ACEP.

————. 1982b. "First Feminist Meeting of Latin America and the Caribbean." *Signs* 8, no. 1: 154–157.

————. 1989. "The Personal Is Political: Las Madres de Plaza de Mayo." In *Power and Popular Protest: Latin American Social Movements*, edited by Susan Eckstein. Berkeley: University of California Press.

Nelson, C., and L. Grossberg, eds. 1988. *Marxism and the Interpretation of Culture*. Urbana: University of Illinois Press.

Neto, María Inacia d'Avila. 1980. *Autoritarismo e A Mulher: O Jogo da Dominação Macho-Fêmea no Brasil*. Rio de Janeiro: Achiamê.

Nicholson, Linda J., ed. 1990. *Feminism/Postmodernism*. New York: Routledge.

Nobrega, Lígia. 1988. *CEBs e Educação Popular*. Petrópolis, Brazil: Vozes.

Noonan, Norma C. 1988. "Marxism and Feminism in the USSR: Irreconcilable Differences." *Women and Politics* 8, no. 1: 31–48.

"Nuevas Formas de Hacer Política." 1983. *Nueva Sociedad*, special edition, no. 64.

Nun, José. 1989. *La Rebelión del Coro: Estudios Sobre la Racionalidad Política y el Sentido Común*. Buenos Aires: Editorial Nueva Visión.

O'Connor, James. 1988. "Theoretical Introduction." *Capitalism, Nature, Socialism* 1, no. 1: 11–38.

Offe, C. 1985. "New Social Movements: Challenging the Boundaries of Institutional Politics." *Social Research* 52, no. 4: 817–868.

Oliveira, Pedro A. Ribeiro. 1986. "Comunidade, Igreja e Poder: Em Busca de um Conceito Sociológico de Igreja." *Religião e Sociedade* 13, no. 3: 43–60.

Ong, Aihwa. 1987. *Spirits of Resistance and Capitalist Discipline*. Albany: State University of New York Press.

Orlove, Benjamin. 1980. "The Position of Rustlers in Regional Society: Social Banditry in the Andes." In *Land and Power in Latin America*, edited by Glynn Custred and B. Orlove. New York: Free Press.

Orozco, Víctor. 1976. "Las Luchas Populares en Chihuahua." *Cuadernos Políticos*, no. 9: 49–66.

Ortega, Eliana, Nina M. Scott, Nancy Saporta Sternbach, and Asunción Horno-Delgado, eds. 1989. *Breaking Boundaries: Latina Writing and Critical Readings*. Amherst: University of Massachusetts Press.

Ortega, Eliana, and Nancy Saporta Sternbach. 1986. "Gracias a la Vida: Recounting the Third Latin American Feminist Meeting in Bertioga, Brazil, July 31–August 4, 1985." *Off Our Backs* 26, no. 1: 1.

———. 1989. "At the Threshold of the Unnamed: Latina Literary Discourse in the Eighties." In *Breaking Boundaries: Latina Writing and Critical Readings*, edited by Eliana Ortega, Nina M. Scott, Nancy Saporta Sternbach, and Asunción Horno-Delgado. Amherst: University of Massachusetts Press.

Ovalles, Omar. 1987. "Movimientos de Cuadro de Vida en la Venezuela Actual." In *Crisis y Movimientos Sociales en Venezuela*, edited by L. Gomez. Caracas: Tropycos.

Oyen, E., ed. 1990. *Comparative Methodology: Theory and Practice in International Social Research*. Beverly Hills: Sage/ISA.

Pacto de Grupos Ecologistas. 1987. "El Movimiento Ecologista-Ambientalista en México." Working paper of the Organization Committee.

Paige, Jeffrey. 1975. *Agrarian Revolution: Social Movements and Export Agriculture in the Underdeveloped World*. New York: Free Press.

Paiva, Vanilda. 1985a. "A Igreja Moderna no Brasil." In *Igreja e Questão Agrária*, edited by Vanilda Paiva. São Paulo: Loyola.

———. 1985b. *Igreja e Questão Agrária*. São Paulo: Loyola.

Palermo, V. 1987. "Movimientos Sociales y Partidos Politicos: Aspectos de la Cuestión en la Democracia Emergente en La Argentina." In *Movimientos Sociales y Democracia Emergente*, edited by E. Jelin. Buenos Aires: Centro Editor de América Latina.

Partnoy, Alicia. 1986. *The Little School: Tales of Disappearance and Survival in Argentina*. San Francisco, Calif.: Cleis Press.

Pasquinelli, Carla. 1988. "Emancipation or Liberation Theorizing on Feminism and the Left in Italy." In *Women's Struggles and Strategies*, edited by Saskia Wieringa. Brookfield, Vt.: Gower.

Passoe Castro, Gustavo do. 1987. *As Comunidades do Dom: Um Estudo de CEBs no Recife*. Recife, Brazil: Fundação Joaquim Nabuco.

Perelli, Carina. 1989. "Putting Conservatism to Good Use: Women and Unorthodox Politics in Uruguay, from Breakdown to Transition." In *The Women's Movement in Latin America: Feminism and the Transition to Democracy*, edited by Jane S. Jaquette. Boston, Mass.: Unwin Hyman.

Perelli, C., and J. Rial. 1983. "El Discreto Encanto de la Socialdemocracia." *Nueva Sociedad*, no. 64 (January-February).

Perez Acre, Francisco. 1990. "The Enduring Union Struggle for Legality and Democracy." In *Popular Movements and Political Change in Mexico*, edited by Joe Foweraker and Ann L. Craig. Boulder, Colo.: Lynne Rienner.

Pérez Güemes, Efraín, and Alma Rosa Garza del Toro. 1984. "El Movimiento de Posesionarios en Monterrey, 1970-1983." Paper presented at the conference on "Perspectivas para América Latina: Seminario Sobre Movimientos Sociales en México—Región Noreste," Monterrey, Nueva León, Mexico, January.

Perlman, Janice. 1976. *The Myth of Marginality: Urban Poverty and Politics in Rio de Janeiro*. Berkeley: University of California Press.

Perló, Manuel, and Martha Schteingart. 1985-1986. "Movimientos Sociales Urbanos en México: Algunas Reflexiones en Torno a la Relación: Procesos Sociales Urbanos—Respuesta de los Sectores Populares." *Revista Mexicana de Sociología* 46, no. 4: 105-125.

Perlongher, N. 1987. *O Negócio do Michê*. São Paulo: Brasiliense.

Petchesky, Rosalind. 1979. "Dissolving the Hyphen: A Report on Marxist-Feminist Groups." In *Capitalist Patriarchy and the Case for Socialist Feminism*, edited by Zillah R. Eisenstein. New York: Monthly Review Press.

Petras, James. 1981. *Class, State, and Power in the Third World with Case Studies on Class Conflict in Latin America*. London: Zed Press.

Petrini, João Carlos. 1984. *CEB's: Um Novo Sujeito Popular*. Rio de Janeiro: Paz e Terra.

Pinheiro, Ann Alice Costa. 1981. "Avances y Definiciones del Movimiento Feminista en el Brazil." Master's thesis, El Colegio de México.

Pinto, D., ed. 1981. *Contemporary Italian Sociology*. Cambridge: Cambridge University Press.

Piscitelli, Alejandro. 1988. "Sur, Postmodernidad y Después." In *La Modernidad en la Encrucijada Postmoderna*, edited by Fernando Calderón. Buenos Aires: CLACSO.

Pizzorno, Alessandro. 1978. "Political Exchange and Collective Identity in Industrial Conflict." In *The Resurgence of Class Conflict in Western Europe Since 1968*, edited by Colin Crouch and Alessandro Pizzorno. London: Macmillan.

Platt, Tristán. 1982. *Estado Boliviano y Ayllu Andino*. Lima: IEP.

Poma de Ayala, Guamán. 1978. *Letter to a King*. Translated and edited by Christopher Dilke. New York: E. P. Dutton.

Pontes, H. A. 1986. "Do Palco aos Bastidores: O SOS Mulher (São Paulo)." Master's thesis, State University of Campinas, São Paulo.

Portantiero, Juan Carlos. 1982. "Socialismos y Política en América Latina: Notas para una Revisión." In *Qué Significa Hacer Política?* edited by Norbert Lechner. Lima: DESCO.

Portes, Alejandro. 1969. *Cuatro Poblaciones: Informe Preliminar Sobre Situación y Aspiraciones de Grupos Marginados en el Gran Santiago*. Programa de Sociología del Desarrollo de La Universidad de Wisconsin, Estudio en Areas Marginadas de Santiago de Chile, 1968-1969, Santiago.

———. 1976. *Urban Latin America*. Austin: University of Texas Press.

———. 1985. "Latin American Class Structures: Their Composition and Change During the Last Decades." *Latin American Research Review*, no. 20: 7-40.

Portes, Alejandro, and Douglas Kincaid. 1989. "Sociology and Development in the 1990's: Critical Challenges and Empirical Trends." *Sociological Forum* 4, no. 4: 479-503.

Portes, Alejandro, Manuel Castells, and Lauren Benton, eds. 1989. *The Informal Economy. Studies in Advanced and Less Developed Countries.* Baltimore, Md.: Johns Hopkins University Press.

Portugal, Ana María. 1986. *On Being a Feminist in Latin America.* Santiago: ISIS International Women's Information and Communication Service.

———. 1989. "Feminismo y Movimiento Popular Revisados en Jornadas de Quito." *Mujer/Fempress*, no. 97 (November).

———, ed. 1987. *Mujer e Iglesia. Sexualidad y Aborto en América Latina.* Washington, D.C.: Catholics for Free Choice.

Pozas Garza, María de los Angeles. 1989. "Land Settlement by the Poor in Monterrey." In *Housing and Land in Urban Mexico*, edited by Alan Gilbert. Monograph series no. 31. La Jolla: University of California, San Diego, Center for U.S.-Mexican Studies.

Prates, Susana, and Silvia Rodríguez. 1985. "Los Movimientos Sociales de Mujeres en la Transición a la Democracia." In *Movimientos Sociales y Crisis en el Uruguay*, edited by Carlos Filgueira. Montevideo: CLACSO-CIESU-Ediciones de la Banda Oriental.

Price, Richard. 1983. *First Time: The Historical Vision of an Afro-American People.* Baltimore, Md.: Johns Hopkins University Press.

———. 1990. *Alabi's World.* Baltimore, Md.: Johns Hopkins University Press.

Przeworski, Adam. 1986. "Some Problems in the Study of the Transition to Democracy." In *Transitions from Authoritarian Rule: Comparative Perspectives*, edited by P. Schmitter, L. Whitehead, and G. O'Donnell. Baltimore, Md.: Johns Hopkins University Press.

Puig, Juan. 1990. "Larga Marcha por la Vida." *Revista Nuestro Ambiente* 15, no. 3.

Quadri, Gabriel. 1990. "Una Breve Crónica del Ecologismo en México." *Revista Ciencias/UNAM*, no. 4.

Quijano, Aníbal. 1988. *Modernidad, Identidad y Utopia en América Latina.* Lima: Sociedad y Política Ediciones.

Quintero Rivera, Angel. 1985. "La Cimarronería como Herencia y Utopía." *David y Goliath*, no. 48.

Rabinow, Paul. 1986. "Representations Are Social Facts: Modernity and Post-Modernity in Anthropology." In *Writing Culture. The Poetics and Politics of Ethnography*, edited by J. Clifford and G. Marcus. Berkeley: University of California Press.

———. 1988. "Beyond Ethnography: Anthropology as Nominalism." *Cultural Antropology* 3, no. 4: 355–364.

Rabinow, Paul, and William Sullivan. 1987. *Interpretive Social Science: A Second Look.* Berkeley: University of California Press.

Rahnema, Majid. 1988a. "A New Variety of AIDS and Its Pathogens: Homo Economicus, Development and Aid." *Alternatives* 13, no. 1: 117–136.

———. 1988b. "Power and Regenerative Processes in Micro-Spaces." *International Social Sciences Journal*, no. 117: 361–375.

Rama, C. 1962. *Uruguay's New Path.* Stockholm: Institute of Ibero-American Studies.

———. 1972. *Historia Social del Pueblo Uruguayo.* Montevideo: Editorial Comunidad de Sur.

Ramirez, Ana-María. 1990. "Spielberg en La Gran Sabana: ¿Conflicto de Intereses?" Manuscript.

Ramírez Saiz, Juan Manuel. 1985-1986. "El Consejo General de Colonias Populares de Acapulco (CGCPA), 1980-1982." *Estudios Políticos* 4, no. 5: 24–29.

———. 1986. *El Movimiento Urbano Popular en México.* Mexico D.F.: Siglo XXI.

———. 1990. "Urban Struggles and Their Political Consequences." In *Popular Movements and Political Change in Mexico*, edited by Joe Foweraker and Ann L. Craig. Boulder, Colo.: Lynne Rienner.

Randall, Margaret. 1981. *Sandino's Daughters: Testimonies of Nicaraguan Women in Struggle.* Seattle, Wash.: Left Bank.

Rascón, Maria Antonietta. 1975. "La Mujer y la Lucha Social." In *Imagen y Realidad de la Mujer*, edited by Elena Urrutia. Mexico D.F.: Sep Setentas.

Rathberger, Eva M. 1990. "WID, WAD, GAD: Trends in Research and Practice." *The Journal of Developing Areas,* no. 24 (July): 489–502.

Redfield, Robert. 1956. *Peasant Society and Culture.* Chicago, Ill.: University of Chicago Press.

Restrepo, L. A. 1987. "El Protagonismo Político de los Movimientos Sociales." *Revista Foro.*

———. 1988. "Los Movimientos Sociales, la Democracia y el Socialismo." *Análisis Político,* no. 5: 56–67.

Rey, Juan Carlos. 1987. "El Futuro de la Democracia en Venezuela." In *Venezuela Hacia el Año 2000: Desafíos y Opciones,* edited by Juan Carlos Rey. Caracas: Editorial Nueva Sociedad.

———, ed. 1987. *Venezuela Hacia el Año 2000: Desafíos y Opciones.* Caracas: Editorial Nueva Sociedad.

Rhode, Debra, ed. 1990. *Theoretical Perspectives on Sexual Differences.* New Haven, Conn.: Yale University Press.

Rial, J. 1985. "Los Partidos Tradicionales: Restauración Democratica." In *Uruguay y la Democracia,* edited by C. Gillespie et al. Montevideo: Ediciones de la Banda Oriental.

———. 1989. "Continuidad y Cambio en las Organizaciones Partidarias en el Uruguay: 1973–1984." In *Muerte y Resurreción. Los Partidos Políticos en el Autoritarismo y las Transiciones del Cono Sur,* edited by M. Cavarozzi and M. A. Garretón. Santiago: FLASCO.

Rickenberg, M., ed. 1990. *Latein Amerika Geschichtslehrbücher, Geschichtsbewusstsein, Studien zur Internationale Schulbuchforschung Schriftenreihe.* Frankfurt: G. Eckert Institut.

Ricoeur, P. 1957. *The State and Coercion.* Geneva: John Knox House.

Rivarola, Domingo. 1986. *Los Movimientos Sociales en Paraguay.* Asunción: Centro Paraguayo de Estudios Sociológicos.

Rivera, Silvia. 1985. "El Movimiento Sindical Campesino en la Coyuntura Democrática." In *Crisis, Democracia y Conflicto Social,* edited by Roberto Laserna. La Paz: CERES.

Riz, Liliana de. 1985. "Uruguay: La Transición Desde una Perspectiva Comparada." In *Uruguay y la Democracia,* edited by C. Gillespie et al. Montevideo: Ediciones de la Banda Oriental.

Rodriguez, Jaime. 1988. "En Nariño: La Lucha Cívica, una Respuesta para la no Violencia." *Revista Foro,* no. 6: 69–74.

Rodriguez, O., ed. N.d. *Estado y Economía en la Constitución de 1886.* Bogotá: Contraloría General de la República.

Rofel, Lisa. N.d. "Rethinking Modernity: Space and Factory Discipline in China." Mimeograph.

Rojas, Telmo. 1989. *Rondas, Poder Campesino, y el Terror.* Cajamarca, Peru: Universidad Nacional de Cajamarca.

Roldán, Roque, ed. 1990. *COLOMBIA, Presidencia de la República, PNR. Fuero Indígena Colombiano,* compiled and edited by Roque Roldán. Bogotá: n.p.

Romano, Roberto. 1979. *Brasil: Igreja Contra Estado.* São Paulo: Kairos.

Rosaldo, Michelle, and Louise Lamphere, eds. 1974. *Woman, Culture and Society.* Stanford, Calif.: Stanford University Press.

Rosaldo, Renato. 1980. *Ilongot Headhunting–1974.* Stanford, Calif.: Stanford University Press.

Rosero, Rocío. 1988. "Balance y Perspectivas del Movimiento de Mujeres." In *Mujeres, Crisis y Movimiento: América Latina y el Caribe,* edited by ISIS International. Santiago: ISIS International.

Rosero, Rocío, and Susana Wappenstein. 1989. "Impacto de la Crisis en Mujeres del Sector Urbano Marginal." Paper prepared for UNICEF-Ecuador conference, Centro Maria Quilla, Quito, May.

Ross, Andrew, ed. 1988. *Universal Abandon? The Politics of Postmodernism.* Minneapolis: University of Minnesota Press.

Rowbotham, Sheila. 1974. *Women, Resistance, and Revolution: A History of Women and Revolution in the Modern World.* New York: Vintage Books.

Rowbotham, Sheila, et al. 1982. *Além Dos Fragmentos.* São Paulo: Brasiliense.

Rubin, Jeffrey W. 1987a. "Elections, Repression and Limited Reform: Update on Southern Mexico." *LASA Forum* 18, no. 2: 1-5.

――――. 1987b. "State Policies, Leftist Oppositions, and Municipal Elections: The Case of the COCEI in Juchitan." In *Electoral Patterns and Perspectives in Mexico*, edited by Arturo Alvarado Mendoza. La Jolla: University of California, San Diego, Center for U.S.-Mexican Studies.

――――. 1990. "Popular Mobilization and the Myth of State Corporatism." In *Popular Movements and Political Change in Mexico*, edited by Joe Foweraker and Ann L. Craig. Boulder, Colo.: Lynne Rienner.

Rueschemeyer, Dietrich, Theda Skocpol, and Peter Evans, eds. 1985. *Bringing the State Back In.* Cambridge: Cambridge University Press.

Sachs, Wolfgang, ed. 1992. *The Development Dictionary.* London: Zed Books.

Safa, Helen, ed. 1982. *Towards a Political Economy of Urbanization in Third World Countries.* Delhi: Oxford University Press.

――――. 1990. "Women's Social Movements in Latin America." *Gender & Society* 4, no. 3 (September): 354-369.

Sahlins, Marshall. 1985. *Islands of History.* Chicago, Ill.: University of Chicago Press.

Said, Edward. 1979. *Orientalism.* New York: Vintage Books.

――――. 1983. *The World, the Text, the Critic.* Cambridge, Mass.: Harvard University Press.

Salem, Helena, ed. 1981. *A Igreja dos Oprimidos.* São Paulo: Editora Debates.

Santana, Elias, and Luis Perroni. 1991. "La Vision Ambiental Desde el Movimiento Vecinal: Relación Estado-Sociedad Civil." In *Estado, Ambiente, y Sociedad Civil*, edited by M. P. García. Caracas: USB/CENDES.

Santana, Pedro. 1989. *Los Movimientos Sociales en Colombia.* Bogotá: Ediciones Foro.

Santos, C. N. Ferreira dos. 1981. *Movimentos Urbanos no Rio de Janeiro.* Rio de Janeiro: Zahar.

Sarachaga, D., J. P. Terra, I. Wonsewer, and C. Aguiar, eds. 1985. *Apertura y Concertación.* Montevideo: Ediciones de la Banda Oriental.

Sarlo, Beatriz. 1991. "Un Debate Sobre Cultura." *Nueva Sociedad*, no. 116: 88-93.

Sarti, Cynthia. 1989. "The Panorama of Brazilian Feminism." *New Left Review*, no. 173 (January/ February): 75-90.

Scherer-Warren, Ilse. 1987. "O Carater dos Novos Movimentos Sociais." In *Uma Revolução no Cotidiano? Os Novos Movimentos Sociais na América do Sul*, edited by Ilse Scherer-Warren and Paulo J. Krischke. São Paulo: Editora Brasiliense.

Scherer-Warren, Ilse, and Paulo J. Krischke, eds. 1987. *Uma Revolução no Cotidiano? Os Novos Movimentos Sociais na América do Sul.* São Paulo: Editora Brasiliense.

Schmink, Marianne. 1981. "Women in Brazilian Abertura Politics." *Signs* 11, no. 7: 115-134.

Schmink, Marianne, Judith Bruce, and Marilyn Kohn, eds. 1986. *Learning About Women and Urban Services in Latin America and the Caribbean.* New York: Population Council.

Schmitter, Philippe, Laurence Whitehead, and Guillermo O'Donnell, eds. 1986. *Transitions from Authoritarian Rule: Latin America.* Baltimore, Md.: Johns Hopkins University Press.

Schmukler, Beatriz. 1990. "The Democratization of the Family and Social Relations in Argentina." Speech presented at Cornell University, Ithaca, N.Y., April 19.

Schneider, Cathy. 1989. "The Mobilization at the Grassroots: Shantytowns and Resistance in Authoritarian Chile." Ph.D. diss., Cornell University.

Schteingart, Martha. 1985-1986. "Movimientos Urbano-Ecológicos en la Ciudad de México: El Caso del Ajusco." *Estudios Politicos* 4, no. 5: 17-23.

Scott, Alan. 1990. *Ideology and the New Social Movements.* London: Unwin Hyman.

Scott, James. 1976. *The Moral Economy of the Peasant: Rebellion and Subsistence in Southeast Asia.* New Haven, Conn.: Yale University Press.

――――. 1985. *Weapons of the Weak: Everyday Forms of Peasant Resistance.* New Haven, Conn.: Yale University Press.

Sen, Gita, and Caren Grown. 1987. *Development, Crises and Alternative Visions: Third World Women's Perspectives.* New York: Monthly Review Press.

Sheth, D. L. 1987. "Alternative Development as Political Practice." *Alternatives* 12, no. 2: 155–171.

Shiva, Vandana. 1989. *Staying Alive: Women, Ecology and Development.* London: Zed Books.

Shorter, Edward, and Charles Tilly. 1989. *Strikes in France, 1830–1968.* New York: Cambridge University Press.

Silva, L. L. 1986. "AIDS e a Homossexualidade em São Paulo." Master's thesis, Pontífica Universidade Católica de São Paulo.

Singer, P., and V. C. Brant. 1980. "O Feminino e O Feminismo." In *São Paulo: O Povo em Movimento,* edited by P. Singer and V. C. Brant. Petrópolis, Brazil: Vozes.

———, eds. 1980. *São Paulo: O Povo em Movimento.* Petrópolis, Brazil: Vozes.

Skocpol, Theda. 1982. "What Makes Peasants Revolutionary?" *Comparative Politics* 14, no. 3: 351–375.

Slater, David. 1985. "Social Movements and a Recasting of the Political." In *New Social Movements and the State in Latin America,* edited by David Slater. Amsterdam: CEDLA.

———. 1988. "New Social Movements and Old Political Questions: Some Problems of Socialist Theory with Relation to Latin America." Paper presented at the International Congress of Americanists, Amsterdam, July 4–8.

———. 1989. "Nuevos Movimientos Sociales y Viejas Políticas." *Revista Foro,* no. 8: 4–19.

———. 1990. "Social Movements Across the Center Periphery Divide—Latin America and the First World." Speech presented at Cornell University, Ithaca, N.Y., April 24.

———, ed. 1985. *New Social Movements and the State in Latin America.* Amsterdam: CEDLA.

Smelser, Neil, ed. 1988. *Handbook of Sociology.* Beverly Hills, Calif.: Sage Publications.

Sojo, Ana. 1985. *Mujer y Política.* San José, Costa Rica: DEI.

Somarriba, M.M.G., M. G. Valadares, and M. R. Afonso. 1984. *Lutas Urbanas em Belo Horizonte.* Petrópolis, Brazil: Vozes.

Sonderéguer, Maria. 1985. "El Movimiento de los Derechos Humanos en la Argentina." In *Los Nuevos Movimientos Sociales,* edited by Elizabeth Jelin. Buenos Aires: Centro Editor de América Latina.

Sorj, B., and M. H. Tavares de Almeida, eds. 1983. *Sociedade e Política no Brasil Pós—64.* São Paulo: Brasiliense.

Souza Lima, Luiz Gonzaga de. 1980. "Comunidades Eclesiais de Base." *Revista de Cultura Vozes* 74, no. 5: 61–82.

Starn, Orin. 1989. "Rondas Campesinas: Peasant Justice in a Peruvian Village." Ph.D. diss., Stanford University, on file at the Department of Anthropology.

———. 1991. "Missing the Revolution: Anthropologists and the War in Peru." *Cultural Anthropology* 6, no. 1: 63–91.

Stavenhagen, Rodolfo, ed. 1970. *Agrarian Problems and Peasant Movements in Latin America.* New York: Anchor Books.

Stein, William. 1962. *Hualcan: Life in the Highlands of Peru.* Ithaca, N.Y.: Cornell University Press.

Stepan, Alfred. 1985. "State Power and the Strength of Civil Society in the Southern Cone of Latin America." In *Bringing the State Back In,* edited by Dietrich Rueschemeyer, Theda Skocpol, and Peter Evans. Cambridge: Cambridge University Press.

———. 1988. "Chile and the Plebiscite." Speech presented at Columbia University, N.Y., October 19.

Stephen, Lynn. 1990. "Women in Mexican Popular Movements: A Critical Discussion of the New Social Movements Theory." Paper presented at the 89th Annual Meeting of the American Anthropological Association, New Orleans, November 28–December 2.

Stern, Steve, ed. 1987. *Resistance, Rebellion, and Consciousness in the Andean Peasant World, 18th–20th Century.* Madison: University of Wisconsin Press.

Stevens, Evelyn P. 1974. *Protest and Response in Mexico.* Cambridge, Mass.: MIT Press.

Stoll, Sandra. 1986. "Púlpito e Palanque: Religião e Política nas Eleições de 1982 num Município da Grande São Paulo." Ph.D. diss., Unversidade Estadual de Campinas.

Stoner, K. Lynn, ed. 1989. *Latinas of the Americas: A Source Book.* New York: Garland.

Street, Susan. 1989. "The Role of Social Movements in the Analysis of Sociopolitical Change." Paper presented at the Fifteenth International Conference of the Latin American Studies Association, Miami, Florida, December 4–6.

Tamayo, Jaime. 1990. "Neoliberalism Encounters Neocardenismo." In *Popular Movements and Political Change in Mexico,* edited by Joe Foweraker and Ann L. Craig. Boulder, Colo.: Lynne Rienner.

Tarrow, Sidney. 1985. "Struggling to Reform: Social Movements and Policy Change During Cycles of Protest." Western Societies Program Occasional Paper no. 15, Center for International Studies, Cornell University, Ithaca, N.Y.

———. 1988. "National Politics and Collective Action: Recent Theory and Research in Western Europe and United States." *Annual Review of Sociology* 14: 421–440.

———. 1989a. "Struggle, Politics, and Reform: Collective Action, Social Movements, and Cycles of Protest." Western Societies Program Occasional Paper no. 15, Center for International Studies, Cornell University, Ithaca, N.Y.

———. 1989b. *Democracy and Disorder.* New York: Oxford University Press.

Tatafiore, Roberta, ed. 1990. *A Prova di Donna: Interviste Sulla Svolta del PCI.* Rome: Cooperative Libera Stampa.

Taussig, Michael. 1980. *The Devil and Commodity Fetishism in South America.* Chapel Hill: University of North Carolina Press.

Taylor, Charles. 1985. *Philosophy and the Human Sciences.* Cambridge: Cambridge University Press.

Teixeira, Faustino Luiz Couto. 1988. *Comunidades Eclesias de Base: Bases Teológicas.* Petrópolis, Brazil: Vozes.

Tilly, C. 1978. *From Mobilization to Revolution.* Reading, Mass.: Addison-Wesley.

———. 1985. "Models and Realities of Popular Collective Action." *Social Research* 52, no. 4: 717–748.

Timerman, Jacobo. 1987. *Chile: Death in the South.* New York: Alfred Knopf.

Tirado Jiménez, Ramón. 1990. *Asamblea de Barrios: Nuestra Batalla.* México City: Editorial Nuestro Tiempo, SA.

Tironi, Eugenio. 1983. *La Clase Obrera en el Nuevo Estilo de Desarrollo: Un Enfoque Estructural.* Santiago: FLACSO.

———. 1988. "Pobladores e Integración Social." In *Proposiciones: Marginalidad, Movimientos Sociales y Democracia,* edited by E. Tironi. Santiago: SUR.

Tobar, Teresa. 1986. "Barrio, Ciudad, Democracia y Política." In *Movimientos Sociales y Crisis: El Caso Peruano,* edited by Eduardo Ballón. Lima: DESCO.

Todorov, Tzvetan. 1984. *The Conquest of America.* New York: Harper and Row.

Tornaría, Carmen. 1986. "Women's Involvement in the Democratic Process in Uruguay." In *The Latin American Women's Movements: Reflections and Action,* edited by ISIS International. Santiago: ISIS International.

Torres, Santiago, and Federico Arenas. 1986. "Medio Ambiente y Región, Ambitos Claves para la Participación en las Gestión Democrática de un Desarrollo Nacional Sostenible." *Revista Interamericana de Planificación* 20: 77.

Torres, Sérgio. 1980. *A Igreja que Surge da Base: Eclesiologia das Comunidades Cristãs de Base.* São Paulo: Paulinas.

Torres Rivas, E. 1986. *Industrialización en América Latina: Crisis y Perspectivas*. San José: FLACSO/CEDAC.

Touraine, Alain. 1975. "Les Nouveaux Conflits Sociaux." *Sociologie du Travail* 1.

—————. 1977. *The Self-Production of Society*. Chicago, Ill.: University of Chicago Press.

—————. 1981. *The Voice and the Eye: An Analysis of Social Movements*. Cambridge: Cambridge University Press.

—————. 1984a. "Les Mouvements Sociaux: Object Particulier ou Problème Central de l'Analyse Sociologique." *Revue Française de Sociologie*, no. 25: 3–19.

—————. 1984b. "Social Movements: Special Area or Central Problem in Sociological Analysis." *Thesis Eleven*, no. 9: 5–15.

—————. 1987. *Actores Sociales y Sistemas Políticos en América Latina*. Santiago: PREALC/OIT.

—————. 1988a. *The Return of the Actor*. Minneapolis: University of Minnesota Press.

—————. 1988b. *La Parole et le Sang. Politique e Société en Amérique Latine*. Paris: Editions Odile Jacob.

Trinh, T. Minh-ha. 1989. *Women Native Other*. Bloomington: Indiana University Press.

Tsugawa, Tracey. 1991. "Cartographies of Struggle, Cartographies of Resistance." Manuscript.

Turner, Victor. 1974. *Dramas, Fields and Metaphors*. Ithaca, N.Y.: Cornell University Press.

United Nations International Childrens' Emergency Fund, ed. 1986. *Women's Concerns and Planning: A Methodological Approach for their Integration into Local, Regional and National Planning*. Belgium: UNESCO.

—————. 1987. *The Invisible Adjustment: Poor Women and the Economic Crisis*. Santiago: The Americas and the Caribbean Regional Office of UNICEF.

Universidad de Chile. 1986. *Encuestas de Empleo y Desempleo (1970–1985)*. Santiago: Universidad de Chile, Departmento de Economía.

Uribe, Gabriela, and Edgardo Lander. 1988. "Acción Social y Efectividad Simbólica y Nuevos Ambitos de lo Político en Venezuela." In *La Modernidad en la Encrucijada Postmoderna*, edited by Fernando Calderón. Buenos Aires: CLACSO.

—————. 1991. "Acción Social, Efectividad Simbólica y Nuevos Ambitos de lo Político en Venezuela." In *Estado, Ambiente, y Sociedad Civil*, edited by M. P. García. Caracas: USB/CENDES.

Urla, Jackeline. 1990. "Statistics and the Construction of Basque Identity." Manuscript.

Urrutia, Elena, ed. 1975. *Imagen y Realidad de la Mujer*, Mexico D.F.: Sep Setentas.

Valdés, Teresa. 1987. "El Movimiento de Pobladores: 1973–1985: La Recomposición de Las Solidaridades Sociales." In *Decentralización del Estado: Movimiento Social y Gestion Local*, edited by Jordi Borja, Teresa Valdés, Hernan Pozo, and Eduardo Morales. Santiago: FLACSO.

Valenzuela, Eduardo. 1984. *La Rebelión de Los Jovenes*. Santiago: Ediciones SUR.

—————. 1986. "Estudiantes y Democracia." In *Los Movimientos Sociales y la Lucha Democrática en Chile*, edited by Guillermo Campero. Santiago: CLACSO-ILET.

Valenzuela, María Elena. 1986. "El Fundamento Militar de la Dominación Patriarcal en Chile." Paper presented at Second Chilean Sociology Conference.

—————. 1987. *Todas Ibamos a Ser Reinas: La Mujer en Chile Militar*. Santiago: Ediciones Chile y América.

Vargas, Virginia. 1985. "Movimiento Feminista en el Perú: Balance y Perpectivas." In *Década de la Mujer: Conversatorio Sobre Nairobi*, edited by Virginia Vargas. Lima: Centro Flora Tristán.

—————. 1987. "El Aporte a al Rebeldía de las Mujeres." In *Jornadas Feministas: Feminismo y Sectores Populares en América*, edited by Coordinación de Grupos de las Jornadas Feministas. Mexico D.F: Ed. Electrocomp.

—————. 1988a. "The Feminist Movement in Peru: Inventory and Perspectives." In *Women's Struggles and Strategies*, edited by Saskia Wieringa. Brookfield, Vt.: Gower.

—————. 1988b. "Movimiento de Mujeres en América Latina: Un Reto para el Analisis y para la Acción." In *Mujeres, Crisis y Movimiento: América Latina y el Caribe*, edited by DAWN Collective. Santiago: ISIS International.

_____. 1989. *El Aporte de la Rebeldía de las Mujeres*. Lima: Ediciones Flora Tristán.

_____, ed. 1985. *Década de la Mujer: Conversatorio Sobre Nairobi*. Lima: Centro Flora Tristán.

Vasconi, Tomas A. 1990. "Democracy and Socialism in South America." *Latin American Perspectives* 17, no. 2: 25–38.

Vega, María Gabriela. 1985. "Participación Laboral de las Mujeres en un Contexto de Crisis." In *Mujer y Desarrollo*, edited by Virginia Guzman, María Gabriela Vega, and Nora Galer. Lima: Centro de la Mujer Flora Tristán.

Velez, H. 1986. "La Regeneración y el Gran Cauca: De la Autonomía Relativa a la Desintegración Territorial, 1860-1910." In *Estado y Economía en la Constitución de 1886*, edited by O. Rodriguez. Bogotá: Contraloría General de la República.

Verdesoto Custode, Luis. 1986. "Los Movimientos Sociales, la Crisis y la Democracia en el Ecuador." In *Los Movimientos Sociales ante la Crisis*, edited by UNU/CLACSO/IISUNAM. Buenos Aires: UNU/CLACSO/IISUNAM.

Viale, Guido. 1978. *Il Sessantotto fra Rivoluzione e Ristorazione*. Milan: Gabriele Mazzotta.

Vila, Pablo. 1985. "Rock Nacional: Crónicas de la Resistencia Juvenil." In *Los Nuevos Movimientos Sociales*, edited by Elizabeth Jelin. Buenos Aires: CEAL.

Vilas, Carlos. 1985. "El Sujeto Social de la Insurreción Popular: La Revolución Sandinista." *Latin American Research Review* 20, no. 1: 119–148.

_____. 1986. *The Sandinista Revolution: National Liberation and Social Transformation in Central America*. New York: Monthly Review Press.

Villamil Rodríquez, Silvia, and Graciela Sapriza. 1987. "Mulher e Estado no Uruguay en Seculo XX." *Revista das Ciências Sociais* 1, no. 2: 209–219.

Villarreal, Diana, and Victor Castañeda. 1986. *Urbanización y Autoconstrucción de Vivienda en Monterrey*. Mexico D.F.: Centro de Ecodesarrollo, Editorial Claves Latinoamericas.

Vink, N. 1985. "Base Communities and Urban Social Movements—A Case Study of the Metalworkers' Strike 1980: São Bernardo Brazil." In *New Social Movements and the State in Latin America*, edited by David Slater. Amsterdam: CEDLA.

Viola, Eduardo. 1987. "O Movimento Ecológico no Brasil (1974-1986)." *Revista Brasileira de Ciências Sociais* 1, no. 3.

Viola, Eduardo, and Scott Mainwaring. 1987. "Novos Movimentos Sociais: Cultura Política e Democracia no Brasil e Argentina." In *Uma Revolução no Cotidiano? Os Novos Movimentos Sociais na América do Sul*, edited by Ilse Scherer-Warren and Paulo J. Krischke. São Paulo: Brasiliense.

Wanderly, F. Reis, and G. O'Donnell, eds. 1988. *A Democracia no Brasil: Dilemas e Perspectivas*. São Paulo: Vêrtice.

Watts, Michael. 1988. "On Peasant Diffidence: Non-Revolt, Resistance, and Hidden Forms of Political Consciousness in Northern Nigeria, 1900-1945." In *Global Crisis and Social Movements*, edited by Edmund Burke. Boulder, Colo.: Westview Press.

Weffort, F. G. 1989. "Democracia y Revolución." *Cuadernos Políticos* 5: 5–18.

Weinbaum, Batya. 1978. *The Curious Courtship of Women's Liberation and Socialism*. Boston, Mass.: South End Press.

Weiringa, Saskia, ed. 1988. *Women's Struggles and Strategies*. Brookfield, Vt.: Gower.

Williams, Patricia. 1991. *The Alchemy of Race and Rights*. Cambridge, Mass.: Harvard University Press.

Williams, Raymond. 1980. "Base and Superstructure in Marxist Cultural Theory." In *Problems in Materialism and Culture*, edited by Raymond Willams. London: NLB.

Willis, Paul. 1990. *Common Culture*. London: Verso.

Winn, Peter. 1989. "Socialism Fades Out of Fashion." *The Nation* (June 26): 882–886.

Wiwiorka, M. 1988. *Societé et Terrorisme*. Paris: Fayart.

Wolf, Eric. 1969. *Peasant Wars of the Twentieth Century*. New York: Harper and Row.

World Commission on Environment and Development. 1987. *Our Common Future*. Oxford: Oxford University Press.

Yang, Mayfair Mei-hui. 1988. "The Modernity of Power in the Chinese Socialist Order." *Cultural Anthropology* 3, no. 4: 408–427.

Young, Kate, ed. 1988. *Women and Economic Development: Local, Regional and National Planning Strategies.* Oxford: Berg Publishers Ltd./UNESCO.

Zaluar, Alba. 1985. *A Maquina e a Revolta.* São Paulo: Brasiliense.

Zapata, Antonio. 1990. "Los Hijos de la Guerra: Jóvenes Ladinos y Criollos ante la Violencia Política." In *Tiempo de Ira y Amor: Nuevos Actores para Viejos Problemas,* edited by Carlos Iván Degregori et al. Lima: DESCO.

Zarzar, Alonso. 1991. "Las Rondas Campesinas de Cajamarca: De la Autodefensa al Autogobierno?" In *La Otra Cara de la Luna: Nuevos Actores Sociales en el Peru,* edited by Luis Pasara. Lima: CEDYS.

Zermeño, Sergio. 1978. *México: Una Democracia Utópica, el Movimiento Estudiantil del 68.* Mexico D.F.: Siglo XXI.

———. 1990. "El Regreso del Líder." *David y Goliath,* no. 56.

Zimmerman, Matilde. 1987. "1500 Women Attend Latin American Feminist Conference in Mexico." *The Militant* (November 20).

Zolezzi, Mario, and Julio Calderón. 1985. *Vivienda Popular: Autoconstrucción y Lucha por el Agua.* Lima: DESCO, Centro de Estudios y Promoción del Desarrollo.

About the Book

During the last decade, Latin American social movements have brought about a profound transformation in the nature and practice of protest and collective action. This book surveys the full spectrum of movements in Latin America today—from peasant and squatter movements to women's and gay movements, as well as environmental and civic movements—examining how this diverse mosaic of emergent social actors has prompted social scientists to rethink the dynamics of Latin American social and political change.

Whereas the prevailing theories of social movements have largely drawn on Western cases, this volume includes the work of prominent Latin American scholars and incorporates analytical perspectives originating in the region. Contributors discuss the three dimensions of change most commonly attributed to Latin American social movements in the 1980s: their role in forging collective identities; their innovative social practices and political strategies; and their actual or potential contributions to alternative visions of development and to the democratization of political institutions and social relations.

This interdisciplinary text provides both specialists and students of social movements with a unique, comprehensive, and accessible collection of essays that is unprecedented in theoretical and empirical scope. It will be useful in a wide range of graduate and advanced undergraduate courses in Latin American studies, comparative politics, sociology and anthropology, development studies, political economy, and contemporary political and cultural theory.

Series in Political Economy
and Economic Development in Latin America

Series Editor

Andrew Zimbalist
Smith College

Through country case studies and regional analyses this series will contribute to a deeper understanding of development issues in Latin America. Shifting political environments, increasing economic interdependence, and the difficulties with regard to debt, foreign investment, and trade policy demand novel conceptualizations of development strategies and potentials for the region. Individual volumes in this series will explore the deficiencies in conventional formulations of the Latin American development experience by examining new evidence and material. Topics will include, among others, women and development in Latin America; the impact of IMF interventions; the effects of redemocratization on development; Cubanology and Cuban political economy; Nicaraguan political economy; and individual case studies on development and debt policy in various countries in the region.

Index

Abortion, 233, 235
Acapulco, Mexico, 249, 258(n15)
Acción por el Movimiento de Mujeres, 143, 149(n10)
Action
 defining, 4
 environmental organizations and alternative social, 159
 and protest in Chile, 263-264. *See also* Protest
 and social movements, 7, 13-14, 70-71, 72, 305-306
 and urban poor, 241-242
 See also Social movements
Ade Dudu, 194, 195
Afro-Latin American movements. *See* Black movement
Agreement on Missions, 114
Agrupación Vecinal (AVEC) (Chile), 270
AIDS. *See* Autoimmune deficiency syndrome
Alcozauca, Mexico, 259(n23)
Alianza Democrática M-19 (Colombia), 5, 13, 308-310, 316(n5), 324
Allende, Salvador, 260
Alternativa (weekly), 132(n20)
Alternative communities, 155, 169(n9). *See also* Christian base communities; Community
Alvarez, Sonia, 58
Amador, Carlos Fonseca, 42
Amaru, Tupác, 97
American Indians
 Colombian indigenous, 113, 115-116, 117-118, 122, 131(n5)
 and feminist movement, 219, 232
 Venezuelan indigenous, 169-170(n15)
 See also Identity, indigenous; Indigenous movements
American Popular Revolutionary Alliance (APRA) (Peru), 103-104, 109
AMIGRANSA. *See* Asociación de Amigos en Defensa de la Gran Sabana
Andean region, 21, 33, 113, 124
Annales School, 84(n9)

Anti-imperialism, 213, 217
Antisocial movements, 36(n1)
Antoniazzi, Alberto, 171-172
ANUC. *See* National Association of Peasant Producers
Appadurai, Arjun, 109
APRA. *See* American Popular Revolutionary Alliance
Arachnophobia, 169(n8), 169-170(n15)
Aragua Conservationist Society. *See* Sociedad Conservacionista Aragua
Araya, Juan, 270
Argentina
 feminism in, 39, 41, 50(n1), 211, 233, 235, 237(n13)
 human rights abuses in, 232
 and Madres de Plaza de Mayo, 20. *See also* Madres de Plaza de Mayo
Arhuacos, 122, 132(n24)
Arriagada, Genaro, 261, 262
Art, 23, 68
Articulation, 78-82, 85(n15)
Asamblea de Barrios, 254
Asamblea de Civilidad, 274
ASCOIN. *See* Indigenist Association
Asociación Colombiana Indigenista. *See* Indigenist Association
Asociación de Amigos en Defensa de la Gran Sabana (AMIGRANSA), 150, 159-160, 165
Asociación de Trabajo y Estudios de la Mujer, 25 de Noviembre (ATEM 25 de Noviembre), 235
Asociación Nacional de Usuarios Campesinos. *See* National Association of Peasant Producers
Association of Friends for the Defense of the Great Savannah. *See* Asociación de Amigos en Defensa de la Gran Sabana
ATEM 25 de Noviembre. *See* Asociación de Trabajo y Estudios de la Mujer, 25 de Noviembre

Authoritarianism
  and Chile, 260
  and growth of social movements, 43, 52, 303,
    311
  patriarchy as, 210
  and women, 46, 139
  See also Repression; State
Autoimmune deficiency syndrome (AIDS), 11,
    202
Autonomy
  versus co-optation, 54–60, 309–310, 321–325
  development and social, 26
  and feminist movement, 216–217, 224–225
  and homosexual movement, 188
  indigenous, 124, 130, 133(n44)
  national, and liberation movements, 22
  of peasantry, 94, 105
  of social movements, 10, 39, 47–48, 278, 298,
    300, 301
  and urban movements, 248, 251
  and women's organizations, 134, 142–143
  See also Identity
Autoridades Indígenas de Colombia. See
    Indigenous Authorities Movement of
    Colombia
AVEC. See Agrupación Vecinal

Bahia, Brazil, 201
Bailey, Mary, 37
Ballón, Eduardo, 80
Bambamarca, Peru, 98, 104
Barrig, Maruja, 145
Batlle y Ordoñez, Luis, 282, 289(n24)
Behar, Ruth, 77
Belaúnde, Fernando, 105
Bellido, José Dammert, 98
Benjamin, Walter, 314
Bertioga, Brazil, 221–223
Betancur, Belisario, 124, 126–127
Bichas, 194, 195
Black movement
  and feminists, 233
  formation of, x, 193, 308
  and fragmentation of the Left, 186–187
Blanco party (Uruguay), 283, 284, 289(n30), 289–
    290(n35), 290(n41)
Bloque Urbano de Colonias Populares (BUCP)
    (Mexico), 249
Bobbio, Norberto, 42
Boff, Leonardo, 176
Bogotá, Colombia, 214–218
Boletín de los Grupos Ambientalistas, 161
Bolivia, 96, 135
  Katarista movement, 21, 26–27, 36(n2)

Bordaberry, Juan María, 290(n37)
Borja, Rodrigo, 142
Bourdieu, Pierre, 96
Brazil
  Christian base communities in, 171–182
  democratization in, 277, 326, 329
  ecology movement in, 22, 169(n12)
  feminism in, 38, 39, 211, 213, 221, 224, 226,
    227, 231
  homosexual movement in, 11, 185–203
  labor movement in, 21–22, 31
  politics and social movements in, 13, 57, 58–59,
    288(n4), 291–299, 306, 310, 322, 324, 325,
    327
Brazilian Democratic Movement. See Movimento
    Democrático Brasileiro
Brazilian Workers' Party. See Partido dos
    Trabalhadores
Bridges, Ann B., 37
BUCP. See Bloque Urbano de Colonias Populares
Burbach, Roger, 45, 46, 48, 263
Bureaucratization, 56

Cabildos (Colombian), 116, 117, 124, 133(n35)
  combative, 119, 120, 122, 123, 126, 128, 129
Cajamarca, Peru, 97–98, 104–105, 105–106
Calderón, Felix, 109
Calderón, Fernando, 242
Cali, Colombia, 115, 216
California, 93
Campa, Valentín, 258(n14)
Campesinos, 96, 122. See also Peasant
    movements; Rondas campesinas
Canada, 60(n5)
Canaima Great Savannah National Park, 160, 161
Capitalism, 28, 38, 44–45
Caracas, Venezuela, 156
Cárdenas, Cuauhtémoc, 57–58, 241, 255,
    259(n28)
Cárdenas, Lázaro, 259(n28)
Cardenista Front. See Frente Democrático
    Nacional
Cardoso, Fernando Henrique, 35, 36(n6)
Cardoso, Ruth, 6, 193
Caribbean, 20, 21
Carr, Barry, 53
Castells, Manuel, 81, 105, 242
Castro Pozo, Hildebrando, 94
Catastrophic analysis, 28
Catholic church
  and Christian base communities, 171–182
  and Colombian government, 131(n8)
  and feminism, 40, 211–212, 224, 226
  and indigenous movement, 114, 119, 126

liberal transformation of, 33, 36(n5)
and protest in Chile, 260, 264, 267, 268, 271
and rondas, 98
and social movements, 193, 307, 318
and social movements in Brazil, 294–295
and Uruguayan urban movement, 280
Católicas por el Derecho a Decidir, 233
Cauca departamento, Colombia, 113, 115–122
militarization of, 122, 128
Caudillismo, 105–106
CDP-Chihuahua. *See* Comité de Defensa
Popular-Chihuahua
CDP-Durango. *See* Comité de Defensa Popular–
Durango
CEAAL. *See* Consejo de Educación de Adultos
de América Latina
CEBs. *See* Christian base communities
CELAM. *See* Latin American Bishops
Conference
Censorship, 189
Central America
and class analysis, 33
feminism in, 219, 224, 228–229, 232, 234, 235
and liberation movements, 2, 324
Central American Women's Permanent Assembly
for Peace, 235
Central Juvenil Latina, 271–272
Centro de Información y Apoyo de la Mujer
(CIAM), 143
Centro Ecuatoriano para la Promoción y Acción
de la Mujer (CEPAM), 143
Centro Femenino 8 de Marzo, 144–145, 146, 147,
149(n12)
CEPAM. *See* Centro Ecuatoriano para la
Promoción y Acción de la Mujer
CGCPA. *See* Consejo General de Colonias
Populares de Acapulco
Change
global sociotechnological, 27–28, 31–32, 35–36
Latin America and sociocultural, 24–26, 30
and social movements, x, 2, 9, 287, 299–301,
305
structural, and social movements, 318
and urban movements, 241, 242, 257
See also Action; Social movements,
effectiveness of
Chihuahua, Mexico, 244
Chile
feminism in, 20, 38, 41, 211, 227, 234, 235
patriarchy in, 210, 237(n9)
political parties in, 208, 277, 328
social movements in, 260–275, 306, 322
and urban movements, 12

Chilean Communist party, 263, 264, 265, 266,
268, 271, 274
Chodorow, Nancy, 148(n3)
Chota, Peru, 89, 98, 99, 103, 104–105, 109, 110
Christian base communities (CEBs), 33, 171–182
and participation, 11, 174–176
and women, 41
Christian Democratic party (Chile), 261, 264,
265, 274
CIAM. *See* Centro de Información y Apoyo de la
Mujer
Class
analysis, 33
as base of social movements, 54, 55
and ecology movement, 167, 168
and feminist movement, 222–223, 230, 236
and indigenous movement, 117–118, 121
struggle and gender, 45–47, 136–137, 211, 212,
217, 227
Uruguay's political, 282, 283
See also Left; Marxism
Clastres, Pierre, 312, 313
Clientelism, 297–298, 300, 301, 318, 322–323
Clifford, James, 93
CNOP. *See* Confederación Nacional de
Organizaciones Populares
CNPA. *See* National *Plan de Ayala* Coordinating
Committee
Coalición de Obreros, Campesinos, y
Estudiantes del Istmo (COCEI) (Mexico),
245, 247, 252, 254, 259(n22)
COCEI. *See* Coalición de Obreros, Campesinos,
y Estudiantes del Istmo
Cohen, Jean, 5, 93
Collective action. *See* Social movements
Colombia
feminism in, 215–218
indigenous movement in, 10, 112–131, 328
political parties in, 283
social movements and culture in, 80
social movements and politics in, 27, 307–310,
316(n5), 323, 324, 328
state and violence in, 313
Colonia División del Norte, 244
Colonia Francisco Villa, 244
Colonia Tierra y Libertad, 244–245
Colorado party (Uruguay), 283, 284, 289(n30),
289–290(n35), 290(nn 36, 41, 44)
Comisión Nacional de Desarrollo (CONADE)
(Ecuador), 142
Comisión para la Reforma del Estado (COPRE)
(Venezuela), 153, 155, 159, 164, 167, 168(nn
3, 4), 170(n16)

Comité de Defensa Popular-Chihuahua (CDP-Chihuahua), 244
Comité de Defensa Popular-Durango (CDP-Durango), 244, 250, 251, 254, 255, 259(nn 20, 22)
Commission for the Reform of the State. *See* Comisión para la Reforma del Estado
Committee of Pobladores (Chile), 270
Communist Party of Brazil. *See* Partido Comunista do Brasil
Communitarianism, 28, 33
Community
  and Chilean protest movement, 264–274
  constructing, 321
  councils in Brazil, 294, 295, 302(n2)
  ecological, 155–156
  egalitarian, 193–195
  indigenous, of Colombia, 115–131, 132(n16)
  See also Alternative communities; Christian base communities; Neighborhood(s)
CONADE. *See* Comisión Nacional de Desarrollo
CONAMUP. *See* Confederación Nacional del Movimiento Urbano Popular
"Concertación (Coalition) for the No," 261
Confederación de Trabajadores Mexicanos (CTM) (Mexico), 246
Confederación Nacional del Movimiento Urbano Popular (CONAMUP) (Mexico), 249, 250–251
Confederación Nacional de Organizaciones Populares (CNOP) (Mexico), 246
Consciousness-raising
  and Christian base communities, 171, 173
  and ecology movement, 155, 163
  and feminism, 146, 213, 230
  and homosexual movement, 194
Consejo de Educación de Adultos de América Latina (CEAAL), Women's Network, 142–143
Consejo General de Colonias Populares de Acapulco (CGCPA), 249
Consejo Regional Indígena del Cauca. *See* Indigenous Council of the Cauca Region
Conventions. *See* Encuentros
Cooperativism, 120
Coordinadora de Ollas Populares (COP) (Uruguay), 280
Coordinadora Nacional Provisional del Movimiento Popular, 250
Coordinadora Regional del Valle de México (CRMUP), 251
Coordinadora Unica de Damnificados (CUD) (Mexico), 253

Coordinating Committee of Food-Purchasing Clubs, 279, 280
Coordinating Committee of Neighborhood Health-care Clinics, 279, 281
COP. *See* Coordinadora de Ollas Populares
COPRE. *See* Comisión para la Reforma del Estado
Corporación de Vivienda (CORVI) (Chile), 269
Corruption, 97–98, 99
CORVI. *See* Corporación de Vivienda
Craig, Ann L., 6
CRIC. *See* Indigenous Council of the Cauca Region
Crime, 97–98, 99, 108
CRMUP. *See* Coordinadora Regional del Valle de México
Cruz, Sebastião C. V., 185
CTM. *See* Confederación de Trabajadores Mexicanos
Cuba, 224, 234
CUD. *See* Coordinadora Unica de Damnificados
Cultural feminism, 227
Cultural movements, 20
Culture
  Brazilian political, 291
  changing political, 7, 300, 304
  and development strategies, 66. *See also* Modernity
  ecology movement and political, 150, 151, 163–164, 165, 167
  effect on social movements of, 10, 307, 319, 320
  Mexican political, 246–247
  peasant, 94, 95–96, 98, 100, 109–110
  and political action in Chile, 263–264
  and politics, 20
  social movements as manifestations of, 63–83
  Uruguayan political, 282–283, 287
Cutervo, Peru, 109
Cuyumalca, Peru, 101

DAWN. *See* Development Alternatives with Women for a New Era
Debt
  and global economic change, 4, 27, 64
  Mexican, 240–241
  repayment and social costs, 1, 141–142, 149(n10)
  See also Economy
Decentralization
  and Brazilian politics, 293
  and social movements, 311
  and Uruguay, 288
  See also Democracy
de Certeau, Michel, 74

Della Cava, Ralph, 171
Democracy
  in Brazil, 291
  and Colombian politics, 129-130
  within households, 135, 147
  and Latin American Marxists, 42-44. *See also*
    Left
  local Chilean, 270-273, 275
  in Mexico, 247
  and organizational autonomy, 48. *See also*
    Autonomy
  and pluralism, 39, 309, 310-312, 314. *See also*
    Pluralism
  and rondas, 101-102
  and social movements, x, 4, 193, 292, 299-301,
    304-305
  and sociopolitical restructuring, 1, 25, 29, 67,
    68, 325-329
  and Uruguay, 12-13, 276-277, 280, 281-288,
    289(n26), 290(n42)
  and Venezuela, 151-152, 157, 159, 163, 166-
    168, 168(nn 2, 3, 4)
Democratic Alliance (Chile), 264
Democratic Current. *See* Frente Democrático
  Nacional
Demographics, 114, 243, 257-258(n3)
Departamento Nacional de la Mujer (DNM)
  (Ecuador), 140
Developed countries
  and articulatory politics, 79
  conservative politics in, 27
  environmental movements in, 165
  feminism in, 49, 138-139, 236
  sociotechnological transformations in, 31
Development
  crisis in, 1, 4
  and ecology movement, 157, 164-165, 168,
    170(n16)
  gender and class in, 11, 136-137, 138, 148,
    149(n9)
  and identities, 80
  Mexican, 240, 246
  programs and women, 141-142
  redefining, 68, 327-328, 329
  resistance to, x, 82, 84(nn 5, 6), 135
  social movements and crisis of, 63-69, 134, 303
  Venezuelan, 151
Development Alternatives with Women for a
  New Era (DAWN), 149(n9), 233-234,
  239(n41)
DINAMU. *See* Dirección Nacional de la Mujer
Dirección Nacional de la Mujer (DINAMU)
  (Ecuador), 141, 142
DNM. *See* Departamento Nacional de la Mujer

Domestic conflict, 176-178
Dominican Republic, 38, 215
Drugs, 185-186
Durango, Mexico, 244, 247, 248, 251, 254

Echeverría, Luís, 240, 241, 247
Eckstein, Susan, 14(n6)
Ecology movements
  in Brazil, 22
  and historicity, 80
  symbolic challenge of, 11, 327-328
  Venezuelan, 150-151, 153-168, 169(n13), 169-
    170(n15), 324
Economic adjustment policies, 31, 38
  Ecuadorian, 141-142
  and Venezuela, 152, 166, 167
Economy
  Chilean protest movement and crisis in, 261,
    262, 264
  crime and crisis in, 97
  as cultural construct, 69
  ecology movement and crisis in, 151-153, 155-
    156, 159, 165-166
  Mexican, 240-241
  political instability and, 38
  urban movements and crisis in, 243, 248-249,
    252-253
  and women, 136-137, 138-139
  world-wide restructuring of, 1, 4, 14(n3), 22,
    27-28, 31-32, 64-65, 68, 77-78, 85(n13). *See
    also* Economic adjustment policies
ECOXXI, 159, 160, 161, 163, 165
Ecuador
  rural movements in, 93
  social movements and culture in, 80-81
  women and state policy of, 140-142
  women's organizations in, 134-135, 139-140,
    149(n11)
EDJs. *See* Environmental Defense Juntas
Education
  and Christian base communities, 173-174
  civic, 291
  and environmental organizations, 162, 163
  and Mexico, 254
  and societal change, 24
  and urbanization, 26
Egalitarianism
  and homosexual movement, 193-195, 198, 203
Ejército de Liberación Nacional. *See* National
  Liberation Army
Elections
  Chilean, 261
  Colombian, 112, 129, 308

Mexican, 241, 242, 245, 248, 251, 252, 254, 255, 256, 258(n14), 259(n26)
Uruguayan, 284, 289(n29), 290(nn 41, 44)
Elias, Norbert, 84(n9)
ELN. *See* National Liberation Army
El Poder Femenino (Chile), 208
El Salvador, 38, 42
El Samán Group, 156, 161, 169(n11)
Emigration, 289(n21)
Employment, 240, 253
Encuentros, 208–209, 236–237(n5)
    Bertioga, 221–223, 238(n28)
    Bogotá, 214–218, 238(n23)
    Lima, 218–221, 238(n27)
    San Bernardo, 231–234, 239(nn 39, 42)
    Taxco, 223–230, 238(n33)
Entendidos, 188, 189, 190, 197, 199–200
Environment. *See* Ecology movements
Environmental Defense Juntas (EDJs), 156, 158
Ethics
    movements concerned with, 20
    of power and social movements, 311–315
    See also Values
Ethnic movements. *See* Black movement; Indigenous movements
Ethnosemiotics, 76–77. *See also* Meaning
Europe
    development of social movements in, 52–53, 54, 192, 303
    social movements and politics in, 59–60
    social movement theory from, 3, 5, 34, 63
Evers, Tilman, 56, 81, 193, 262
Exclusion
    and development era, 68, 329
    and global integration, 28
    and indigenous movements, 21
    and state-societal tension, 25

FABES. *See* Secretaria da Familia e do Bem-Estar Social
Faletto, Enzo, 35, 36(n6)
Falk, R., 312
Fals Borda, Orlando, 79–80
Familiares de Desaparecidos y Prisioneros por Razones Políticas, 232
FARC. *See* Revolutionary Armed Forces of Colombia
Farmers' Union of Eastern Cauca, 117
FDN. *See* Frente Democrático Nacional
Febres-Cordero, León, 142
Federación de Organizaciones de Juntas Ambientales (FORJA) (Venezuela), 154, 155, 156, 157–159, 161, 162, 169(nn 5, 13, 14)
Federation of Cuban Women, 224

Feminist movements
    in developed countries, 49
    and fragmentation of the Left, 186–187
    homosexual support for, 188, 198
    in Latin America, 12, 38–42, 50(nn 1, 7), 207–236, 326
    and lesbians, 190
    and Marxism, 9, 37–39, 44–50
    versus women's organizations, 237(n18). *See also* Women's organizations
FENOC. *See* National Federation of Peasant and Indigenous Peoples
Fiesta del Gran Poder, 21
First General Assembly of Neighborhoods of Mexico City, 254
Fiske, John, 76
Food-purchasing clubs, 278, 280
FORJA. *See* Federación de Organizaciones de Juntas Ambientales
Foucault, Michel, 84(n9), 92, 197, 312–313
Foweraker, Joe, 6
FPI. *See* Frente Popular Independiente
FPTyL. *See* Frente Popular Tierra y Libertad
FPZ. *See* Frente Popular de Zacatecas
Fragmentation
    and Chilean protest movement, 71
    of the Left, 185–187
    social, 28, 68
    of social movements, 323–324
    of urban movements, 252, 285–286
    See also Pluralism
Frank, A. G., 312
Fraser, Nancy, 138
Freire, Paulo, 306
Frente Amplio, 284, 285, 287–288, 290(n41)
Frente Democrático Nacional (FDN) (Mexico), 57–59, 241, 255, 256, 259(n26), 306–307, 310
Frente Patriótico Manuel Rodriguez (Chile), 274
Frente Popular de Zacatecas (FPZ) (Mexico), 250
Frente Popular Independiente (FPI) (Mexico), 249
Frente Popular Tierra y Libertad (FPTyL) (Mexico), 245, 248, 250, 251–252, 254, 255, 258(nn 8, 12), 259(nn 20, 22)
Frente Unico Pro Derecho de la Mujer, 40
Frente Unido, 312
Fuentes, Marta, 54, 312
Fuerzas Armadas Revolucionarias de Colombia. *See* Revolutionary Armed Forces of Colombia
Fujimori, Alberto, 104
Functionalism, 2, 30
Funding
    and feminist movement, 224–225, 231, 238–239(n38), 239(n41)

GALF. *See* Lesbian-Feminist Action Group
Gandhi, Mahatma, 312
Gang of Four Maoists, 108
García, Alan, 103, 105
Gaviria, César, 309
Gay Group of Bahia, 201
Gay movement. *See* Homosexual movement
Geisel, Ernesto, 185
Gender
    and class struggle, 45–47, 136–137, 211, 212,
        217, 227
    and environmental strategies, 153–154
    and identity, 11, 137–139
    movements in Chile, 20
    roles and homosexuality, 199–200
    specific needs and women's organizations, 134,
        135, 144, 145–146, 148, 320
    See also Feminist movements; Women
Germani, Gino, 28, 35, 36(n6)
Ghetto, homosexual, 188–190, 199
GIDA. *See* Grupo de Ingeniería y Arborización
Gitlitz, John, 98
González, Luís, 283
Gonzalez, Maruja, 47
Goulart, João, 303
Government
    environmental organizations and Venezuelan,
        154, 158, 162, 163, 164
    Peruvian, 98
    urban movements and Mexican, 243, 245–246,
        247–248, 252–253, 256–257, 258(n13)
    See also State
Gramsci, Antonio, 28, 42, 44, 314
Great Britain, 38
Greater São Paulo's Family and Social Services
        Departments. *See* Secretaria da Familia e do
        Bem-Estar Social
GRIDIA, 161
Grupo de Afirmação Homosexual (SOMOS)
        (Brazil), 188, 190, 191–192, 193–203
Grupo de Ingeniería y Arborización (GIDA), 157,
        161
Grupo Gay of Bahia, 190
Grupo Wara, 21
Guadalajara, Mexico, 243, 248, 257–258(n3)
Guajiro, 313
Guambianos, 10, 117, 122–124, 129, 132(n28)
Guaraní, 313
Guatemala, 38, 42
Guejía, Bautista, 133(n38)
Guha, Ranajit, 94
Guimarães, Carmen, 195
Gunder Frank, Andre, 54
Guzmán, Abimael, 21

Habitat, 157
Hacienda system, 98, 99, 100, 116, 117, 131(n1)
    and indigenous movement, 118–120, 123–124
Hall, Stuart, 82
Haraway, Donna, 95
Hartmann, Heidi, 37
Health
    and AIDS, 202
    -care clinics, 278–279, 280, 289(n16)
    and women, 212
Hebdige, Dick, 93
Hirschman, Albert, 301
Historical processes
    Colombian historiography, 121, 131(n3)
    historicity, 71–72, 80, 82, 84(n11)
    and social movements, 23
Holanda, Heloisa Buarque de, 186
Homosexual movement
    in Brazil, 187–203
    evolution of, 11
    and historicity, 80
    See also Lesbians
Housing
    and Chilean protest movement, 270
    and Mexican urban movements, 243, 244, 246,
        253–254, 258(n7)
Hualgayoc, Peru, 98, 104, 109
Huanuco, Peru, 109
Human rights
    abuses, 38, 107, 260
    and authoritarianism, 43
    and internationalization process, 31
    and urban movements, 250
    and women, 41, 211, 212, 232, 235
    See also Rights
Hunt, Lynn, 92
Hurtado, Osvaldo, 141–142, 148(n7)

Identity
    and autonomy, 322. *See also* Autonomy
    constructing, x, 4, 5, 11, 72–73, 78–81, 85(n14),
        92–96
    development and cultural, 26
    and ecology network, 162
    fragmentation of, 65–66, 82
    and gender, 11, 46, 135, 137–139, 145–146, 147–
        148, 148(n3), 235
    homosexual, 188, 193, 194, 197–198, 199, 202
    indigenous, 21, 113, 117–118, 122, 130–131,
        132(n24), 133(nn 30, 31)
    and political institutions, 277
    and rondas campesinos, 100, 109–110
    and rural protest, 90, 95–96

social movements and political, 179, 291–292, 300–301
and social movement theory, 33, 319, 320–321
and urban poor, 280
Uruguayan social, 283, 289(n31)
Ideology
and environmental organizations, 153–154, 164–168. *See also* Political-ideological environmental organizations
and feminist movement, 208–209, 216–218, 218–221, 225–226, 228–230, 235–236
religious, 172
social movements and participatory, 301, 310–315
versus strategy, 322–325
and theory, 23
and urban movements, 246
and Uruguayan political parties, 283
See also Democracy
Idrogo, Daniel, 103
Illich, Ivan, 138
IMF. *See* International Monetary Fund
Inconformes, 307–308
INCORA. *See* Land Reform Institute
India, 94
Indigenismo, 94
Indigenist Association (ASCOIN), 114
Indigenous Authorities Movement of Colombia (MAIC), 112, 121, 122, 125, 126–129, 130–131, 133(nn 40, 43, 44)
Indigenous Authorities of the Southwest. *See* Indigenous Authorities Movement of Colombia
Indigenous Council of the Cauca Region (CRIC), 113, 117, 121, 122, 125–126, 127, 132(n24), 133(n43)
and guerrilla groups, 128, 133(n37)
Indigenous movements
Colombian, 112–131, 132(nn 19, 22), 133(nn 34, 43, 44), 308, 328
growth of, 10, 21, 193
and internationalization process, 31
support for, 132(n20)
and women, 41
See also American Indians
Individualism, 198–199, 203
Information, 162
Infrastructure, 134, 149(n14)
Mexican, 240, 243
Innovation
and ecology movement, 161–162, 163–164, 165
and rural protest, 92
Institutional Revolutionary Party (PRI) (Mexico), 57, 307

Instituto Colombiano de Reforma Agraria. *See* Land Reform Institute
International Monetary Fund (IMF), 31, 38, 152, 166, 253, 329
International organizations
and social movements, 318
and women's issues, 212
See also Nongovernmental organizations
ISIS International, 233
Italian Communist Party (PCI), 54, 58, 59
Italy, 54, 59–60
IU. *See* United Left

Jelin, Elizabeth, 5, 6, 15(n7), 70, 80
Journalists Union (Brazil), 187
Juchitán, Mexico, 245, 247, 252
Justice system
disenchantment with, 97–98, 99
rondas as alternative, 90, 99–100, 101–102, 104–105, 108
See also Legislation

Karner, Hartmut, 60(n8)
Katari, Tupaj, 36(n2)
Katarista movement, 21, 26–27, 36(n2)
King, Martin Luther, 312
Kirkwood, Julieta, 46
Klandermans, Bert, 317–318
Kowarick, Lucio, 56–57

Labio, Luciano, 133(n38)
Labor
new international division of, 77
women and reproductive, 43, 136–139
Labor movements
Brazilian, 21–22, 31, 185
in Latin America, 192–193
and urban popular movements, 244
Laclau, Ernesto, 7, 14(n5), 56, 64, 69, 78–80, 81
La Conjura, 238(n23)
La Herminda de Victoria, Chile, 269–271
Lampião (newspaper), 187, 191, 193, 198, 199
Land
invasion and urban movements, 244, 246, 247, 249, 251
occupation and Chilean protest, 268, 269
recovery and indigenous movement, 118–125, 133(n30)
recovery in Colombia, 114–115, 120, 307
rights and Catholic church, 193
Lander, Edgardo, 80, 326
Land Reform Institute (INCORA), 120, 121, 124
Latin America
cultural politics in, 75, 76, 80

and modernity, 67–69
politics and social movements in, 53–60, 71–72, 317
research and theory in, 5, 9, 14(n2), 34–35, 63, 81–82
and rural politics, 91, 95
social movements in, 52–53, 192–193, 303–307
sociocultural change in, 24–26, 30, 64–65
women's organizations in, 38–42, 139, 143, 207–236
See also specific countries; Third World
Latin American and Caribbean Coordinating Committee for Mobilization in Support of the Right to Have an Abortion, 233
Latin American and Caribbean Feminist Encounters, 50(n1), 51(n8)
Latin American and Caribbean Network Against Sexual and Domestic Violence, 233
Latin American Bishops Conference (CELAM), 36(n5)
Latin American Studies Association, 52
Latinas, 225, 238(n34)
La Victoria, Chile, 268–269
Law. *See* Legislation
Leadership
church, 178–179
of Colombian social movements, 308
grass-roots militants and protest in Chile, 263, 264, 273, 274–275
within homosexual movement, 191–192, 194
indigenous, 117, 132(n10)
and rondas, 105–106
within social movements, 304, 307
of social movements in Brazil, 295, 297
of urban movements, 246, 247, 251
Lechner, Norbert, 44
Leff, Enrique, 165
Left
and autonomy issues, 56
and Chilean protest movement, 12, 263
and ecology movement, 158, 164, 169(n12)
and feminism, 207–208, 211–212, 213, 214, 220, 226, 227
and homosexual movement, 196. *See also* Socialist Convergence
and indigenous movements, 121, 123
marginality and fragmentation of the, 185–187
and social movements, 52, 53–54, 167, 297, 312, 318, 322
and urban movements, 249, 250, 259(n30)
and Uruguayan urban movement, 285, 287
See also Leadership; Political parties; Revolutionary movements

Legislation
Brazilian political, 302(n1)
environmental, 151, 156, 164, 169(n8)
and homosexuality, 201
indigenous, 114, 125–127, 132(n23)
law reform and women, 149(n16)
Mexican electoral reform, 248
See also Government; Justice system
Leguía, Augusto, 100
Leiva, Fernando Ignacio, 262
Lesbian-Feminist Action Group (GALF), 190, 194
Lesbians
and feminist movement, 220, 223, 224, 232
and homosexual movement, 194–195, 196
social relations and, 190, 199
Ley Orgánica del Ambiente (LOA) (Venezuela), 151, 156
Liberal party (Colombia), 114
Liberation movements. *See* Revolutionary movements
Liberation theology, 98, 171, 179, 318. *See also* Christian base communities
Lima, Peru, 22, 145
feminist encuentro in, 218–221
Literacy, 173–174
Lleras Restrepo, Carlos, 131(n6)
LOA. *See* Ley Orgánica del Ambiente
López Portillo, José, 240, 241, 247, 248, 253
Loria, S. Cecilia, 47
Lowy, Michel, 43–44
Lozano, Itziar, 47

Machismo, 188, 190, 194. *See also* Social relations
Madres de Plaza de Mayo, 20, 41, 218
   –Línea Fundadora, 232, 235
Madrid, Miguel de la, 241, 243, 249, 253
Magical realism, 68
MAIC. *See* Indigenous Authorities Movement of Colombia
Mainwaring, Scott, 320, 326
Maoism
and Colombian social movements, 307
and Peruvian rural movements, 98, 103, 109
and urban movements, 244–245, 246
"Marching Governors," 126
Mariátegui, José Carlos, 42, 92
MARNR. *See* Ministerio del Ambiente y de los Recursos Naturales Renovables
Martínez Domínguez, Alfonso, 252
Martins, Carlos E., 185
Marxism, 2, 28, 42–44, 50(n3)
and feminism, 9, 37–39, 40, 41, 44–50, 136
and homosexual movement, 191–192, 196, 198

post-, 56, 78
and social movements, 56–57
and urban movements, 246
See also Left; Maoism
MAS. *See* Movimiento Hacia el Socialismo
Maya, 313
MDB. *See* Movimento Democrático Brasileiro
Meaning, 74–83, 90, 319. *See also* Culture;
Identity
Medellín, Colombia, 113–114, 216
Medellín Episcopal Declaration, 307
Media
and environmental issues, 150, 154, 158, 160,
161, 162, 163
and feminism, 40, 223, 232, 326
and homosexuality, 189, 201
and market homogenization, 27, 34
Melucci, Alberto, 7, 8, 14(n5), 15(n8), 69, 72, 73,
161, 325
MEMCH. *See* Movement for the Liberation of
Chilean Women
Mental health, 233
Mestizo, 113, 132(n12)
Metropolitana de Pobladores, 270
Mexican Communist Party. *See* Partido
Comunista Mexicano
Mexican Workers' Party (PMT), 53
Mexico
crisis in, 1, 38
ecology movement in, 155, 169(nn 5, 10, 12)
feminism in, 38, 39, 226, 231–232
indigenous movements in, 21
social movements and political parties in, 53–
54, 310, 324, 327
social movements in, 306–307, 322
and urban movements, 12, 22, 240–257
Mexico City
and elections, 241
population of, 243, 257–258(n3)
protest and repression in, 240
urban movements in, 247, 253–254, 255, 256,
258(n16), 259(n25), 306
MIC. *See* Movimiento de Integración de la
Comunidad
Michels, Roberto, 56
Michoacán, Mexico, 21, 27
Militants. *See* Leadership
Military
dictatorships and repression, 43
rondas and Peruvian, 101, 108–109
Uruguayan, 284, 290(nn 36, 37)
Minimum Employment Program (PEM) (Chile),
264

Ministerio del Ambiente y de los Recursos
Naturales Renovables (MARNR)
(Venezuela), 151, 156, 160
Ministry of Settlements and Public Works. *See*
Secretaría de Asentamientos Humanos y de
Obras Públicas
Ministry of the Environment and Renewable
Natural Resources. *See* Ministerio del
Ambiente y de los Recursos Naturales
Renovables
Minorities, 85(n13). *See also* Race
MIR. *See* Movimiento Izquierda Revolucionaria
Mires, Francisco, 80
Miskitos, 26
M–19, 122, 128, 308
M–19/Democratic Alliance. *See* Alianza
Democrática M–19
MNR. *See* Movimiento Nacional Revolucionario
Modernity
alternative, 109–110
social movements and crisis of, 63–69, 82
and state-societal tension, 24
See also Development; Postmodernism
Monterrey, Mexico
population of, 243, 257–258(n3)
urban movement in, 244–245, 247, 248, 251–
252, 254, 258(n8)
Montevideo, Uruguay, 278–279, 282, 285–286,
287–288, 289(n18), 290(nn 44, 47)
Moser, Caroline, 137
Mosquera Chaux, Víctor, 119
Mothers of the Plaza de Mayo. *See* Madres de
Plaza de Mayo
Mouffe, Chantal, 7, 14(n5), 56, 64, 69, 78–80, 81
Movement for Community Integration. *See*
Movimiento de Integración de la
Comunidad
Movement for Decent Housing. *See* Movimiento
Pro-Vivienda Decorosa
Movement for Life, 160–161
Movement for the Liberation of Chilean Women
(MEMCH), 40
Movement Toward Socialism. *See* Movimiento
Hacia el Socialismo
MOVEMO. *See* Movimiento de Vecinos de
Montevideo
MOVIDE. *See* Movimiento Pro-Vivienda
Decorosa
Movimento Democrático Brasileiro (MDB), 293,
302(n1)
Movimiento de Autoridades Indígenas de
Colombia. *See* Indigenous Authorities
Movement of Colombia

Movimiento de Integración de la Comunidad (MIC) (Venezuela), 157
Movimiento Democrático Colombia Unida, 308–310
Movimientos de mujeres. *See* Women's organizations
Movimiento de Vecinos de Montevideo (MOVEMO), 279, 280
Movimiento Hacia el Socialismo (MAS), 166
Movimiento Izquierda Revolucionaria (MIR) (Chile), 267
Movimiento Nacional Revolucionario (MNR) (Bolivia), 96
Movimiento Popular de Pueblos y Colonias del Sur (MPPCS), 250
Movimiento Popular Tierra y Libertad (MPTyL) (Mexico), 252
Movimiento Pro-Vivienda Decorosa (MOVIDE) (Uruguay), 279, 280, 281
Movimiento Revolucionario del Pueblo (MRP) (Mexico), 258(n18)
MPPCS. *See* Movimiento Popular de Pueblos y Colonias del Sur
MPTyL. *See* Movimiento Popular Tierra y Libertad
MRP. *See* Movimiento Revolucionario del Pueblo
Muelas, Lorenzo, 124, 129
Mueller, Adele, 138
Munchique-Tigres, 124
Munck, Gerardo, 73
Murguialday, Clara, 47
Music, 21, 186

NAPs. *See* Núcleos de Atendimento ao Público
Nariño, Colombia, 121, 133(n30), 307–308
National Association of Peasant Producers (ANUC), 114, 115, 121, 131(n6)
National Autonomous University (UNAM), 254
National Coordinator of Urban Popular Movements. *See* Confederación Nacional del Movimiento Urbano Popular
National Federation of Peasant and Indigenous Peoples (FENOC) (Ecuador), 93
National Front (Colombia), 115, 131(n7)
National Indigenous Organization of Colombia (ONIC), 112, 125–126, 127, 128
Nationalism, 102
National Liberation Army (ELN) (Colombia), 115
National *Plan de Ayala* Coordinating Committee (CNPA) (Mexico), 53
National Union of the Revolutionary Left (UNIR) (Peru), 98
Natural disasters, 1, 99
    Mexican earthquake, 253

Navarro, Antonio, 309
Neighborhood Friends Societies. *See* Sociedades Amigos do Bairro
Neighborhood Movement of Montevideo. *See* Movimiento de Vecinos de Montevideo
Neighborhood(s)
    Christian base communities and social action in, 182
    commissions in Uruguay, 279, 287, 288(n12)
    and ecology movement, 156–157, 162, 163, 166, 167
    and protest in Chile, 262
    and women's organizations, 135
    See also Community; Urban movements
Neighbors' School, 163
Neoanarchism, 312, 323
Neoliberalism, 166, 170(n16)
Networks
    Christian base communities and political, 180–182
    Colombian social movement, 308
    and ecology movement, 150, 151, 154, 161–163, 168
    feminist, 233, 234
    homosexual, 202
    politics and social movement, 304, 305, 324
    and social movement theory, 73, 318
    urban, 257
New Organic Law of Municipal Government. *See* Nueva Ley Orgánica del Régimen Municipal
New social movements (NSMs), 2–3, 110–111(n2)
    theoretical approaches and, 5, 7–8, 15(n8)
    See also Social movements
NGOs. *See* Nongovernmental organizations
Nicaragua
    feminism in, 38, 42, 45–46, 224, 226, 227
    revolution in, 22, 44
    social movements in, 38, 307
Nicaraguan Agricultural Workers Union, 42
NLORM. *See* Nueva Ley Orgánica del Régimen Municipal
Nongovernmental organizations (NGOs)
    and Uruguay, 276, 280, 281, 286
    See also International organizations
North American social movement theory, 5
Núcleos de Atendimento ao Público (NAPs), 294
Nueva Ley Orgánica del Régimen Municipal (NLORM) (Venezuela), 156
Nuñez, Orlando, 45, 46, 48

OAS. *See* Organization of American States
Oaxaca, Mexico, 245, 252, 254
Oblitas, Régulo, 101, 103

Oficina Nacional de la Mujer (OFNAMU)
(Ecuador), 140–141, 142
OFNAMU. *See* Oficina Nacional de la Mujer
ONIC. *See* National Indigenous Organization of
Colombia
Operación Sitio, 167, 266
Opposition movements. *See* Revolutionary
movements
Organic Law on the Environment. *See* Ley
Orgánica del Ambiente
Organización Buenaventura, 146
Organización Ciudadela Ibarra, 146
Organización Martha Bucaram, 146
Organización Nacional Indígena de Colombia.
See National Indigenous Organization of
Colombia
Organization of American States (OAS)
Interamerican Women's Commission, 140

Padilla, Dolores, 143
Paéz, 10, 121, 122–123, 132(n13)
Paige, Jeffrey, 92
PAN. *See* Partido de Acción Nacional
Participation
and Christian base communities, 174–176
and democracy, 275, 310–311. *See also*
Democracy
in homosexual movement, 11, 183–184,
184(n6), 200–201
and protest in Chile, 265–273
of researcher, 33, 314–315
social movements and political, 20, 38, 71–72,
291, 292, 293–301, 302(n2)
and Uruguayan urban movement, 280–281,
288, 289(nn 16, 18)
and Venezuelan democracy, 152, 166
voter, 255, 256, 289(n29)
of women in social movements, 41, 54–55,
60(n4)
See also Politics; Social movements
Partido Comunista do Brasil (PC do B), 293, 297
Partido Comunista Mexicano (PCM), 250,
258(n14), 259(n23)
Partido de Acción Nacional (PAN) (Mexico),
258(n14), 259(n26)
Partido Democrático Revolucionario, 324
Partido do Movimento Democrático Brasileiro
(PMDB), 293–294, 302(n2)
Partido dos Trabalhadores (PT), 5, 55, 56, 293,
297, 302(n2), 306, 310, 324
Partido Revolucionario Institucional (PRI)
(Mexico), 241, 245–246, 248, 252, 255, 256,
259(n26)

Partido Unificado Mariateguista (PUM) (Peru),
103
Partito Democrático della Sinistra (PDS) (Italy),
59–60
Party of the Brazilian Democratic Movement. *See*
Partido do Movimento Democrático
Brasileiro
Patriarchy, 210
and feminism, 214, 218, 219–220, 237(n9)
and the ronda, 106
Patria Roja. See Red Homeland party
PC do B. *See* Partido Comunista do Brasil
PCI. *See* Italian Communist Party
PCM. *See* Partido Comunista Mexicano
PDS. *See* Partito Democrático della Sinistra
Peace movement, 192
Peasant movements
and communal practices, 33
and environmental issues, 155–156, 164–165
influence of, 10, 90–96, 307
rondas campesinas, 90, 97–110
types of, 21
and urban popular movements, 244, 245
and women, 41
Pentecostalism, 11, 173, 174, 175–176, 177–178,
180
Peru
development resistance in, 135
rondas campesinas of, 89–90, 96, 97–110
Sendero Luminoso, 21
social movements in, 80, 288(n4), 307
urban movements in, 2
women's organizations and feminism in, 38,
143, 210–211, 224, 226
Petras, James, 262
Pink Triangle Group, 201
Pinochet, Augusto, 260, 261, 274
Piura, Peru, 99, 104
Pluralism
and environmental groups, 153–154, 162, 164–
165, 167
within feminist movement, 216, 217, 218, 220–
221, 226, 227, 229–230, 235
within homosexual movement, 191–192, 194–
197
of identities and liberation movements, 22, 39,
44–45, 49
and issue specialization in Brazil, 203, 294–296
and social movement political philosophy, 33,
309, 310, 311–312
and Uruguayan political parties, 283–284
See also Democracy; Fragmentation
PMDB. *See* Partido do Movimento Democrático
Brasileiro

PMT. *See* Mexican Workers' Party
Poblador movement, 262
POJH. *See* Public Works Program for Heads of
    Household
Political-ideological environmental organizations,
    157–159, 160, 161, 162–163, 164, 167,
    170(n16)
Political parties
  and alienation, 60(n8)
  and Brazilian labor movement, 185
  and Chilean protest movement, 261, 263–275
  Colombian, 115, 129, 131(n7)
  and democratization, 49, 328
  and feminism, 48–49, 217, 220, 222, 226, 227
  and homosexual movement, 188, 191–192, 196
  loss of legitimacy of, 4, 305, 306, 308
  Mexican, 241, 248, 249, 258(n14), 259(n30)
  and rondas, 98, 103–104, 108–109
  and social movements, 5, 10, 12–13, 19, 53–54,
    55–60, 203, 277–278, 292, 294–295, 296–
    299, 300, 301, 318, 326
  Uruguayan, 283–284, 285
  and Venezuelan ecology movement, 158, 162,
    164, 167
  Venezuelan mistrust of, 152, 166, 168(n3)
  and women's organizations, 140, 214
  See also Elections; Left; Politics; *specific parties*
Political system
  Mexican, 241, 245–246, 258(n10)
  and social movements, 6, 166–167
  societal restructuring and redefining, 25, 29
  Uruguayan, 276–277, 282, 289(n30), 289–
    290(n35), 290(n37)
  See also Authoritarianism; Democracy;
    Political parties; Socialism
Politics
  and Christian base communities, 172, 180–182,
    184(n5)
  conservative, in developed countries, 27, 38
  cultural, 70–83. *See also* Culture
  and ecology movement, 150, 159, 162–163
  and feminism, 38, 41, 209, 214, 225, 226–227,
    235
  and homosexual movement, 202–203
  indigenous movement and Colombian, 114–
    115, 125–131
  and the ronda, 101–106
  rural, 91–96
  and social movements, 38–39, 53–60, 94–95,
    193, 304–315, 315(nn 2, 3), 322–329
  and society, 24–26, 325
  and urban movements, 241, 242, 245, 249, 251,
    252, 255, 259(nn 20, 30)

and Uruguayan social movements, 276–277,
    282–288
  and women, 210–211, 233
  and women's organizations, 135, 138–139, 140,
    144–145, 147, 149(n16)
  See also Elections; Political parties; State
Pollution, 251, 258(n15)
Poma de Ayala, Guamán, 97
Popkin, Samuel, 94
*Popular Movements and Political Change in
    Mexico*, 6
Postdevelopment, 33–34
Post-Fordism, 77–78, 85(n13)
Postmodernism, 5, 33–34, 50(n2), 63, 68–69,
    84(n8), 93
Poststructuralism, 93, 95
Poverty, 252–253, 256, 303
Power
  alternative forms of, 316(n6)
  and control in modern society, 67
  and gender relations, 134, 135, 138–139, 147,
    210, 214, 220, 320
  and homosexual movement, 186, 191–192
  relations and global sociotechnological change,
    27, 31
  relations and Venezuelan sociopolitics, 152–
    153, 167
  semiotic, 75
  and social movements, 19, 85(n15), 311, 312–
    315
  theory as, 62–64, 66
  and Third World peoples, 83
  and Uruguayan politics, 282–283
PRI. *See* Partido Revolucionario Institucional
Programa Nacional de Solidaridad
    (PRONASOL), 256
Program of Popular Promotion (Ecuador), 141
PRONASOL. *See* Programa Nacional de
    Solidaridad
Protest
  in Brazil, 185, 191
  and environmental issues, 163
  Mexican, 240, 244, 254, 255
  movement in authoritarian Chile, 261–275
  rural, 89–96
  social movements as articulating, 303, 325
  Venezuelan, 152
  and women, 43, 139, 149(n10)
  See also Social movements
PRT. *See* Revolutionary Workers' Party
PSUM. *See* Unified Socialist Party of Mexico
PT. *See* Partido dos Trabalhadores
Public Assistance Nuclei. *See* Núcleos de
    Atendimento ao Público

Public Works Program for Heads of Household (POJH) (Chile), 264
Puebla, Mexico, 248
PUM. See Partido Unificado Mariateguista
Punta del Este, 114

Quijano, Aníbal, 69
Quintín Lame group, 128, 131(n9), 133(n39)
Quito, Ecuador, 144–145, 146–147, 149(nn 13, 14)

Race, x, 123, 184(n2)
    and Christian base communities, 178–180
    and feminist movement, 37, 220, 222–223, 230, 236
    and homosexual movement, 195
    See also Black movement; Indigenous movements
Rastafarians, 20
Recife, Brazil, 184(n4)
Red de Mujeres Negras de Latinoamérica y el Caribe, 233
Redfield, Robert, 94
Red Homeland party (Peru), 98, 103–104, 109
Religious organizations, 280. See also Catholic church
Renovated Socialists party (Chile), 264
Representation. See Democracy; Participation
Repression
    and Chilean authoritarianism, 260, 261, 265, 266, 268, 269–270, 273
    and development of social movements, 52, 305, 307
    and feminism, 210–211
    of homosexual groups, 187, 191
    and indigenous peoples, 116, 119, 129
    and Mexican government, 240, 244, 245, 247–248, 252, 254, 255, 258(n16)
    and military dictatorships, 43
    See also Violence
Research
    ethnographic techniques in, 76–77, 319
    and issues of autonomy, 54–57, 60(n5)
    on Latin American social movements, 14(n2)
    and popular culture, 71
    and theory, 32, 33, 314–315. See also Theory
Resettlement, 251, 279. See also Settlements, squatter
Resistance
    to Brazilian regime, 189
    to development, 84(nn 5, 6), 135
    and indigenous peoples, 91–92, 117, 132(n12)
    and popular culture, 74–77
    and social change, 2, 327
    See also Protest; Social movements

Resource mobilization theories, 5, 14(n4), 72, 317–318, 319
Revolutionary Armed Forces of Colombia (FARC), 115, 128
Revolutionary movements
    and pluralism, 22, 45, 49
    and women, 41, 42, 47–48
    See also Left
Revolutionary Workers' Party (PRT) (Mexico), 53
Ricoeur, Paul, 314
Rights
    homosexual, 200, 201
    indigenous, 123–125, 126, 131(n4)
    and social movements, 327
    women's, 217, 218
    See also Human rights
Rio de Janeiro, Brazil, 199
Rio Lion's Club, 221–222
Risco, Pedro, 103
Rodriguez, Lilia, 143
Rojas, Telmo, 98
Roldós, Jaime, 141, 142, 148(n7)
Rondas campesinas, 90, 97–110. See also Peasant movements
Rosero, Rocío, 142–143
Rural movements. See Peasant movements

SABs. See Sociedades Amigos do Bairro
SAHOP. See Secretaría de Asentamientos Humanos y de Obras Públicas
Said, Edward, 65
Salinas, Carlos, 256
Saltillo, Mexico, 248
Salvador, Brazil, 195, 201
San Bernardo, Argentina, 231–234
Sandino, Agusto César, 42
Sanjines, Jorge, 21
Santiago, Chile, 12, 261
São Jorge, Brazil, 172–182
São Paulo, Brazil
    homosexual movement in, 188–192, 198, 201, 202
    labor movement in, 21–22, 27
    social movements in, 58, 293–294, 298
    and social services, 299
Sara Gajardo, Chile, 266, 273
Saucedo, Francisco, 59
SCA. See Sociedad Conservacionista Aragua
Science, 67
Scientific-conservationist environmental societies, 154–155, 162, 164, 169(n7)
Scott, James, 74, 91, 92, 94
Secretaria da Familia e do Bem-Estar Social (FABES), 294

Secretaría de Asentamientos Humanos y de
  Obras Públicas (SAHOP) (Mexico), 243
Secretaría de Desarrollo Urbano y de Ecología
  (SEDUE) (Mexico), 243
SEDUE. *See* Secretaría de Desarrollo Urbano y
  de Ecología
Self-understanding, 63, 76–77
Sendero Luminoso, 21, 90, 108–109
Settlements, squatter
  and Mexican urban movements, 244–245, 247,
  249, 251–252, 258(n8)
Shining Path. *See* Sendero Luminoso
Siervos de Dios y Amos de Indios, 114, 131(n8)
Slater, David, 5, 53, 81
Socialism
  and feminism, 38, 217
  and Latin American Marxists, 43–44, 48
  See also Left; Marxism
Socialist Convergence, 191–192, 196, 200
Socialist party (Chile), 261, 264, 274
Social movements
  assessing, 27–29, 85(n15), 95, 108, 287
  change in, 8, 9, 19
  and Christian base communities, 182. *See also*
    Christian base communities
  as cultural struggles, 69–83, 320–321
  defining, 6–7, 15(n7), 131(n2), 241–242
  development of, 1–5, 38, 52–53, 192–193, 304–
  305, 318–321
  and development discourses, 66
  development in Venezuela of, 151–153, 166–168
  effectiveness of, x, 133(n44), 158, 201–202, 226,
  257, 321–329. *See also* Strategy
  and internationalization process, 31
  participation in, 183–184, 184(n6), 200–201.
    See also Participation
  and peasant protest, 90–96. *See also* Peasant
    movements
  and political institutions, 277–278
  and political parties, 53–60, 296–299. *See also*
    Political parties
  and politics, 13–14, 25–26, 33, 38–39, 94–95,
  202–203, 291–301, 304, 305–315, 315(nn 2,
  3), 326. *See also* Politics
  types of, 20–23
  See also Ecology movements; Feminist
    movements; Homosexual movement;
    Indigenous movements; Urban movements;
    Women's organizations
Social relations
  and democratizing power, 193, 312–313, 325–
  329
  feminists on, 210, 214
  and homosexuality, 188–190, 199–200, 203

See also Machismo
Social services
  and Mexico, 240, 243, 249, 251, 253, 257,
  258(n7), 259(n29)
  and political pressure, 299
  public health, 202
  and rondas, 100
  urban movement and Uruguayan, 279, 282,
  283, 285–286, 290(n47)
  and user participation, 293
  and women, 141
Sociedad Conservacionista Aragua (SCA)
  (Venezuela), 155, 161
Sociedades Amigos do Bairro (SABs), 294
Society
  power relations and civil, 3, 312–315
  as a self-creating process, 71, 93
  sociocultural change in Latin America, 9, 19,
  24–26
  Uruguayan civil, versus the state, 282–284,
  289(n31)
  See also Culture; Social relations
SOMOS. *See* Grupo de Afirmação Homosexual
Soup kitchens, 278, 280
Soup Kitchens Coordinating Committee, 279
Southern Cone countries
  and class analysis, 33
  and feminist movement, 224
  redemocratization in, 277
Southern Cone Domestic Violence Network. *See*
  Latin American and Caribbean Network
  Against Sexual and Domestic Violence
Soviet Union, 38
Spanish, 97
State
  changing management of power by, 32, 203
  versus civil society in Uruguay, 282–283
  development of social movements and role of
  the, 53, 82–83, 210–211, 318
  and power, 312–315, 316(n6). *See also* Power
  and rondas, 104–105
  and social movements, 277–278, 291, 292, 293–
  301, 305, 322
  and societal tension, 24–26, 38
  See also Government; Politics
Stepan, Alfred, 260
Stern, Steve, 92
Strategy
  and autonomy issues, 321–325. *See also*
    Autonomy
  AVM, 23
  Chilean Communist party, 274
  and environmental organizations, 153–154,
  166–168

and feminist movement, 217, 220–221, 229–230, 236
homosexual, 197
and social movements, 4–5, 299–300. *See also* Social movements
and social movement theory, 5, 73, 74, 82, 93
and urban movements, 244, 253, 255
and women's organizations, 136–137, 145–146, 211–212
Structuralism, 23, 30
Student movement
and challenging the Left, 186, 311–312
and Chilean protest, 260
and protest in Mexico, 254, 322
and urban popular movements, 244–245, 247, 249, 255, 258(n16)
in Uruguay, 284
Subaltern Studies Group, 94
Superbarrio, 22, 254, 259(n24)
Symbolic-cultural environmental organizations, 159–161, 165, 167, 170(n16)
Symbolic effectiveness
and ecology movement, 150, 151, 157, 163–164, 165–166, 327–328
Syncretism, 35, 63

Tactics, 74, 82. *See also* Strategy
Tama, Juan, 121
Tamayo, Jorge, 59
Tarrow, Sidney, 317–318
Taxco, Mexico, 223–230
Taxes, 251
Technology, 27, 31, 32, 77
Terminology
feminist, 236(n4), 237(n6)
homosexual, 188, 190, 195
Terraje system, 116–118, 118–120, 131(n1), 132(n14)
Territory, 121, 132(n23). *See also* Land
Terrorism, 30, 36(n1). *See also* Repression; Violence
Terry, Belaúnde, 211
Theater, 21
Theory
approaches to social movement, x, 2–3, 5–8, 14(nn 4, 6), 30, 32–36, 78, 317–321
limitations of traditional, 23, 30
and new social movements, 7–8, 15(n8)
politics of, production, 81–82, 85(n16)
power of, 62–64, 66, 84(n1)
relative deprivation, 281, 289(n20)
and rural protest, 92–96
sociohistorical processes and social exclusion, 28

Third World
articulatory politics in, 79
development and modernity crisis in, 63
and development strategies, 65–67
ecologism, 168
power and collective action in, 83
and socioeconomic control by the north, 34
women in, 138–139
Tironi, Eugenio, 262
Torreón, Mexico, 248
Torres, Camilo, 312
Torture, 107. *See also* Human rights, abuses; Violence
Touraine, Alain, 6, 7, 14(n5), 15(n7), 32–33, 69, 71–72, 81, 84(n11), 92–93, 241–242, 262
Trade unions, 42, 53, 280. *See also* Labor movements
Trans-Amazon Rally, 150, 169–170(n15)
Trinh, T. Minh-ha, 138
Tunubala, Juan, 133(n38)
Tupamaro urban guerrilla organization, 284
Turbay Ayala, Julio César, 126
Turner, Victor, 180

UAPE. *See* Unidad Asesora de Proyectos Especiales
UCP. *See* Unión de Colonias Populares
UDI. *See* Unión Democrática Independiente
Ulcué, Father Alvaro, 133(n39)
Umbanda, 179
UNAM. *See* National Autonomous University
Unidad Asesora de Proyectos Especiales (UAPE) (Uruguay), 285
Unidad Obrero Campesino Popular (UOCP) (Mexico), 258(n18)
Unified Black Movement, 187
Unified Socialist Party of Mexico (PSUM), 53, 55, 56
Unión de Colonias Populares (UCP), 250, 258(n18)
Unión de los Comuneros "Emiliano Zapata," 21
Unión Democrática Independiente (UDI) (Chile), 265
UNIR. *See* National Union of the Revolutionary Left
United Left (IU) (Peru), 98, 108
United Nations, 65
Conference on Women, 39–40
Decade for the Advancement of Women, 140, 143, 226
United States
conservative politics in, 38
homosexuals in, 195
Latinas in, 225

UOCP. *See* Unidad Obrero Campesino Popular
Urbanization
  as activator of social movements, 26
  and ecology movement, 155
  Mexican, 240, 242–243, 243(table), 257–258(n3)
  and societal change, 9
Urban movements
  and cultural articulation, 80, 81
  defining, 242, 258(n6)
  development in Mexico of, 243–254
  and environmental issues, 156–157
  growth of, 12–13
  and Mexican politics, 241, 242, 245, 249, 250, 251, 252
  and microlocal democratization, 22
  national congresses of, 250
  in Uruguay, 276–277, 278–288
  and women, 41
Urban planning, 243
Uribe, Gabriela, 80, 326
Uruguay
  decline of grass-roots movements in, 12–13, 328
  feminism in, 211, 233
  social movements in, 276–288

Valdés, Teresa, 262
Valenzuela, Eduardo, 262
Valley of Mexico, 249–250
Values
  and homosexual movement, 185–187
  rural, 94
  and social movements, 193, 203, 314
  See also Ethics
Vargas, Virginia, 46–47, 47–48
Vega, Silvia, 144–145
Velasco Alvarado, Juan, 96, 98, 99
Venezuela
  Congress Committee on the Environment, 151, 154, 164
  ecology movement in, 150–151, 153–168, 169(nn 6, 13), 169–170(n15), 324
  feminism in, 233
  social movements and culture in, 80
  sociopolitics in, 151–153, 168(n2), 307, 327–328, 328–329

Verdesoto, Luis, 80–81
Villa O'Higgens, Chile, 267–268
Villa Wolf, Chile, 265
Violence
  and indigenous movement, 128, 133(n37)
  and political parties, 308–309
  and the ronda, 106–108
  sexual, 212–213, 218. *See also* Domestic conflict
  social movement rejection of, 311, 312, 314
  and the state, 313, 316(n6)
  See also Repression; Terrorism

Water rates, 244
Watts, Michael, 91
We Are–Homosexual Affirmation Group. *See* Grupo de Afirmação Homosexual
Welfare policies. *See* Social services
Williams, Patricia, 83
Women
  and Christian base communities, 175–178, 184(n4)
  and global restructuring, 85(n13)
  and participation in social movements, 8, 54–55, 60(n4), 265, 278, 320
  and politics, 210–211, 233, 311–312
  and the ronda, 106
  and urban movements, 255–256
  See also Feminist movements; Gender; Women's organizations
Women's organizations
  Chilean, 20
  in Ecuador, 139–140, 142–147
  and feminist movement, 212, 214–215, 219, 220–221, 224, 225–226, 228–230, 234, 235–236, 237(n18). *See also* Feminist movements
  and historicity, 80
  and social/political action, 11, 70, 134–139, 145–146, 147–148
Work and Study Association on Women, November 25. *See* Asociación de Trabajo y Estudios de la Mujer, 25 de Noviembre
World Bank, 65, 329
World Commission Report on Environment and Development (1987), 165

Youth. *See* Student movement
Yungay, Chile, 271–273